The Old-House Journal
CATALOG

The Old-House Journal

CATALOG

Bill Gay of Charlotte, North Carolina, photographed the elegant Victorian parlor shown on the cover. Bill and his wife Frances restored the house, a circa 1890 Queen Anne, which is now listed in the National Register of Historic Places.

The Old-House Journal
CATALOG

catalog editor
Eve M. Kahn

advertising coordinator
Tricia A. Martin

assistant
Elizabeth Mauceli

design & production
Cole Gagne

cover design
Bekka Lindstrom

Published by The Old-House Journal Corporation, 69A Seventh Avenue, Brooklyn, N.Y. 11217 Tel. (718) 636-4514. Executive Editor, Patricia Poore. Publisher, Clem Labine.

Library of Congress Catalog Card Number 81-641968
ISBN 0-942202-15-5

Contents

Preface: Good News For Restorers 7

How To Use This Book 10

Key To State Abbreviations 12

The Indexes

General Index to Products & Services 14

Advertisers' Index 22

Company Listing By State 24

Product & Service Directory 33

Exterior Building Materials 34

Masonry Supplies, Roofing Materials, etc.

Exterior Ornament & Architectural Details 41

Millwork, Porch Parts, Windows, etc.

Exterior Hardware 58

Cresting, Doorbells, Garden Ornament, etc.

Building Materials For Interiors 66

Built-Ins, Flooring, Wainscotting, etc.

Decorative Interior Materials & Supplies 75

Ceiling Medallions, Glass, Mantels, etc.

Furniture & Furnishings 83

Fabric, Rugs, Wallpaper, etc.

Interior Hardware, Plumbing, & House Fittings 92

Bathtubs, Carpet Rods, Kitchen Cabinets, etc.

Heating Systems 107

Chimney Linings, Stoves, Storm Windows, etc.

Lighting Fixtures & Parts 113

Antique & Reproduction Lamps, Gas Mantles, etc.

Paints, Finishes, Removers, & Supplies 123

Brass Lacquer, Gold Leaf, Waxes, etc.

Tools & Other Supplies 131

Adzes, House Plans, Stencilling Supplies, etc.

Antique & Recycled House Parts 136

Renovation & Restoration Supply Stores 140

Restoration & Decorating Services 141

Design, Landscaping, Plastering, etc.

Company Directory 151

Other OHJ Books 232

Compiled and Edited by the staff of The Old-House Journal

Good News For Restorers

IT'S AMAZING what's happened in the world of restoration products since we published the first *OHJ Buyer's Guide Catalog* back in 1976. Restoration was almost a cult activity back then; it took only 32 pages to contain all the information about the 205 companies listed.

Today, restoration of houses built before 1939 is a mainstream activity. In fact, it seems there aren't enough old houses to go around. So people are building new "old" houses in record numbers. And today many commercial buildings incorporate elements from historic architecture. The explosive market growth is apparent with this 1987 *OHJ Catalog*: It has more pages, more restoration items, and more companies — 1,423! — than ever before.

Whether you're restoring an 1820 Greek Revival, or looking for the right stuff for a neo-Victorian you plan to build next year, you'll find exactly what you need in this latest *Catalog.*

Most of the products listed in this book are high-quality reproductions. But equally exciting are the "revivals": items that had gone out of production but now, in response to market demand, are being manufactured again — on the original equipment or by the same company.

One dramatic example of product revival is the sheet-metal architectural ornament formerly produced by the Miller & Doing Co. of Brooklyn, N.Y. When Miller & Doing went out of business many years ago, their metal-forming dies were purchased by Kenneth Lynch & Sons of Wilton, Conn. There, the Miller & Doing dies lay dormant. . . until 1986, when they were purchased by the W. F. Norman Co. of Nevada, Missouri. Now this stamped metal ornament from the late-19th and early-20th centuries is commercially available again (see page 64).

a panel ornament from Kenneth Lynch / W.F. Norman

Another exciting product revival are the Lincrusta and Anaglypta wallcoverings from England's Crown Company. These high-quality embossed wallcoverings were extremely popular in the late Victorian period. As tastes changed in the 20th century, the Victorian patterns went out of production. Crown, fortunately, saved most of the embossing rollers. And now, due to the Victorian Revival on this side of the Atlantic, these wonderful wallcoverings are back (see page 89).

A product that's returning after an absence of 75 years is the Victorian encaustic tile that adorned late-19th-century hearths and hallways. These colorful tiles, which are extremely difficult to produce, are being manufactured again by H. & R. Johnson (see page 76). H. & R. Johnson, a direct corporate descendant of one of the original encaustic tile makers, re-developed processes that had been lost for decades.

In addition to product revivals, we've noticed a second trend: the developing interest in post-Victorian styles such as Craftsman, Mission, and Colonial Revival. In the past year, for example, several companies have introduced Craftsman-inspired lighting fixtures (see page 119). Furnishings that evoke everything from Mission oak to European Arts & Crafts — and even Art Deco — are being produced (see pages 86, 87). And a few wallpaper manufacturers have introduced Craftsman and Art Nouveau border papers and rugs (see pages 88, 90).

Reproduction, adaptation or revival, the products in this *Catalog* have three things in common: (1) They are based on traditional forms; (2) They are made with high-quality materials and good workmanship; (3) They've been screened for appropriateness by the editors of *The Old-House Journal*.

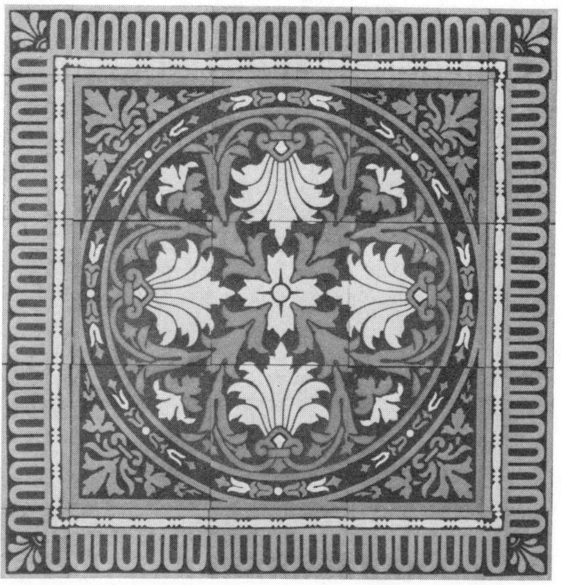

encaustic tile from H. & R. Johnson

Supaglypta from Crown Company

The items you find here are things that hardware clerks insist "aren't made anymore." Most mass-market products are made to sell at the lowest possible price. The manufacturer — and most buyers — don't mind that the item will break or wear out within months or a few years.

People working on buildings that are 100 years old, however, take a longer view. We want things that are as good or better than the originals, things that will last for generations, things that don't compromise a solid old place worthy of our care. This concern for quality and durability has also carried over into the new construction that's based on traditional architecture. There's undeniably a reawakened feeling that we should build it with pride and build it to last.

The hunger for tradition coupled with old-fashioned quality has spawned an entirely new market: what we've termed "the heritage market." Companies serving the heritage market are not mass marketers. Rather, they cater to people who combine historical sensibility with a desire for excellence.

You'll find the 1,423 leading suppliers to the heritage market listed in this *Catalog*. We hope you have as much fun browsing through these pages as we did assembling them.

Eve Kahn

Catalog Editor

Tips On Contacting Companies

Once you've used the Catalog to find the companies you wish to contact, consider these points of mail-order manners. Being aware of these hints will help avoid misunderstandings — and may make shopping by mail a bit more fun.

1. Before writing to a company and saying "Send catalog," check the write-up in the Company Directory to see if they have literature — and if there's a charge for it. It wastes their time and yours if the company has to write back to tell you there is a charge for literature.

2. Don't send out form-letter inquiries to dozens of companies. Many companies will ignore these. Choose a few companies most likely to suit your needs and write them each a personalized letter. You'll be surprised at the number of personalized responses you'll receive in return.

3. Write "Catalog Request," "Order," or a similar clarifying phrase on the outside of your envelope to aid in accurate handling.

4. If you're asking for more information than their catalog can provide, a telephone call is usually the fastest and most satisfactory way to get the answers to your questions. Many companies have toll-free numbers for customer service. Check the write-up in the Company Directory as well as the company's advertisement for these telephone numbers.

5. If you do write to a company asking a non-routine question, enclosing a self-addressed, stamped envelope (SASE) is a thoughtful gesture. It may mean the difference between getting an answer and not.

6. Be patient. With mail service what it is, it can take four weeks or longer for catalogs and merchandise to arrive.

7. Always mention The Old-House Journal Catalog when you write — it helps identify you as part of 'the family.'

If You Have A Problem

The Catalog Editors have made every effort to screen out companies we feel have shoddy products or shady business ethics. Of course, we can't guarantee the performance of every company listed in the Catalog. But we can follow up on any problems that you might have. If someone doesn't reply to your inquiry, or you aren't happy with the way your order was handled or the quality of the merchandise you've ordered, please let us know.

The Editors can do two things when you are not satisfied with a company's performance:

1. We will follow up on your behalf and attempt to bring about a satisfactory solution.

2. If the company does not make a good-faith effort to resolve the problem, and its bad performance seems to be part of a pattern, the firm will be barred from all future editions of the Catalog.

Happily, customer complaints have been few. And most of those that are brought to our attention are quickly resolved as soon as the company is made aware of the problem.

If you are dissatisfied with a company listed in this Catalog, please let us hear from you. Contact:

Catalog Editor
The Old-House Journal
69A Seventh Avenue
Brooklyn, NY 11217

Give us the specifics of your problem and tell what corrective action you've already taken. If it's an order and money has already changed hands, Xerox copies of your checks — plus any previous correspondence.

We also like to hear about companies you find exceptionally helpful as well as companies you know of that are not listed in the Catalog. We'll send them a questionnaire and give them the opportunity to be listed in the next edition.

How To Use This Book

The OHJ Buyer's Guide Catalog lists 1,423 companies. Most of them are cited several times, for each of the products they sell. We haven't repeated the detailed ordering information with each listing — that would make a very fat book. Instead, we separated this Buyer's Guide into two major Sections: a Product & Service Directory and a Company Directory. The Product & Service Directory tells you what companies offer which products. The Company Directory lists all the companies in alphabetical order; here's where you will find the complete address, phone number, and further information for each company.

The series of steps that follows shows you how to use this Buyer's Guide most efficiently. First, look up the product or service you require. Second, among the companies that offer that product, select the one that is closest to you and best serves your needs. Third, look up specific information on that company — its address, phone number, even the cost of its catalog or brochure (if it offers one).

The directions below also explain special features of this Buyer's Guide: the advertisements, a helpful listing of companies by city and state, and color coding of each major section.

1. Consult The General Index (p. 14)

Consult the General Index on page 14 to locate the product or service you need. The Index contains numerous cross-references that take into account common synonyms for the same item.

The General Index will refer you to the appropriate page in the Product & Service Directory.

Coal Grates 69
Coal Scuttles 69
Coat Hooks, ... 63
Coat Racks and Umbrella Stands. 56
Collars, Stove Pipe — *see Stove Pipe & Fittings*
Columns, Exterior. 22
Columns, Interior 45
Columns, Porch. 26
Commode Seats. 60
Composition Ornaments 51
Concrete Roofing Tiles 17
(under Other Roofing Materials)
Conductor Heads — *see Leaders & Leader Boxes*
Conservator's Tools. 89
Consolidants, Wood — *see Rot Patching Materials*
Consulting Services 103
Contour Gauges. 89

from the General Index to Product & Services

2. Go To The Product & Service Directory (p. 33)

In the Product & Service Directory beginning on page 33, you'll find the heading for the item you are after. Below that heading will be the names of all the companies whom the editors have validated as providing that product.

In addition to the listings, you'll also find useful advertisements from companies who supply that type of item.

Sub-categories

SHAKES & SHINGLES, WOOD

(1) Handsplit
(2) Machine Cut
Brewster's Lumberyard (CT) *2*
Crawford's Old House Store (WI) *2*
Essex Tree Service (WA) *1,2*
Hendricks Tile Mfg. Co., Inc. (VA)
Koppers Co. (PA) *2*
Mad River Wood Works (CA) *2*
Puget Sound Shake Brokers (WA)
Renovator's Supply (MA)
Shakertown Corporation (WA) *2*

More information is available in a product display

After each company name is a two-letter state abbreviation. This helps you find nearby suppliers when there are many companies in a category. If you have any difficulty deciphering these standard Post Office abbreviations, you will find the key on page 12.

The small numbers after the company name in some categories tell which of the sub-categories the firm sells.

A company's name in **boldface** means they have placed an ad that you can consult for additional details. If the ad isn't adjacent to the company's listing, refer to the Advertiser's Index on page 22.

3. Turn To The Company Directory (p. 151)

The basic information about each company is found in the grey-edged Company Directory that starts on page 151.

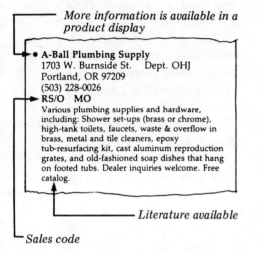

More information is available in a product display

● **A-Ball Plumbing Supply**
1703 W. Burnside St. Dept. OHJ
Portland, OR 97209
(503) 228-0026
RS/O MO
Various plumbing supplies and hardware, including: Shower set-ups (brass or chrome), high-tank toilets, faucets, waste & overflow in brass, metal and tile cleaners, epoxy tub-resurfacing kit, cast aluminum reproduction grates, and old-fashioned soap dishes that hang on footed tubs. Dealer inquiries welcome. Free catalog.

Literature available

Sales code

A boldface bullet (●) next to the company name means the company has placed an advertisement to provide you with more data.

KEY TO ABBREVIATIONS

MO	**sells by Mail Order**
RS/O	**sells through Retail Store or Office**
DIST	**sells through Distributors**
ID	**sells only through Interior Designers or Architects**

The Sales Code tells HOW the company sells its products. Some sell nationwide by mail order (**MO**). Others sell through their local distributors (**DIST**). Some companies will sell direct to consumers from a retail store or office (**RS/O**), while a few sell only to interior designers and architects (**ID**).

4. Locate Suppliers In The Company Listing By State (p. 24)

The Company Directory By State, which begins on page 24, lists companies according to their location. For each state, companies are listed alphabetically *by city*. You can tell at a glance who the restoration suppliers are in your area.

KENTUCKY

Berea — Berea College Student Craft Industries
Campbellsville — Campbellsville Industries
Covington — Stewart Manufacturing Company
Covington — Stripper, The
Lexington — Huskisson Masonry & Exterior Building Restoration Co.
Louisville — Bentley Brothers
Louisville — Devoe & Raynolds Co.
Louisville — Glass Designs
Louisville — Kentucky Wood Floors, Inc.
Louisville — Joe Ley Antiques, Inc.
Louisville — Louisville Art Glass Studio
Louisville — Morgan Woodworking Supplies
Louisville — Restore-A-Tub and Brass, Inc.
Murray — Jack Wallis' Doors
Sparta — Wallin Forge

from the Company Listing By State

You'll find a new feature in this edition of our Buyer's Guide. We've color coded the three major sections so you can quickly find what you need.

The Indexes are the "yellow pages" located at the beginning of the book. The Product & Service Directory, the largest section, is printed on white paper. The Company Directory is edged with gray.

5. Check The Advertisers' Index (p. 22)

When you've located a company that has the advertiser code (●), refer to the Advertiser's Index on page 22. These ads supplement the editorial listings, providing such things as product illustrations and additional ordering information.

C & H Roofing	116
Campbellsville Industries, Inc.	23
The Canal Co.	104
Cane & Basket Supply Co.	98
Carlisle Restoration Lumber	39
Cat Tales Press	115
Cathedral Stone	115
Charles Street Supply Co.	98
Chemical Products Co., Inc.	95
Chimney Relining International	78
Cirecast, Inc.	64E
City Barn	88
City Knickerbocker, Inc.	84
City Lights	82
Classic Accents	64E
Classic Architectural Specialties	26
Classic Castings	69
Coalbrookdale	79
Colonial Charm	33
Conant Custom Brass	72
Condon Studios	49
Copper House	37
Country Curtains	55
Country Iron Foundry	76
Country Stencilling	56
Craftsman Lumber	40
Craftsman's Corner	57

from the Advertisers' Index

When you contact a company, remember to tell them you found them in The Old-House Journal Buyer's Guide Catalog. And if you know about other good sources for old-house products and services, please let us know about them. We'll send them a questionnaire and give them the opportunity to be listed in the next edition of the Catalog.

A Note About State Abbreviations

Alabama	AL
Alaska	AK
Arizona	AZ
Arkansas	AR
California	CA
Canada	CAN
Colorado	CO
Connecticut	CT
Delaware	DE
District of Columbia	DC
Florida	FL
Georgia	GA
Hawaii	HI
Idaho	ID
Illinois	IL
Indiana	IN
Iowa	IA
Kansas	KS
Kentucky	KY
Louisiana	LA
Maine	ME
Maryland	MD
Massachusetts	MA
Michigan	MI
Minnesota	MN
Mississippi	MS
Missouri	MO
Montana	MT
Nebraska	NE
Nevada	NV
New Hampshire	NH
New Jersey	NJ
New Mexico	NM
New York	NY
North Carolina	NC
North Dakota	ND
Ohio	OH
Oklahoma	OK
Oregon	OR
Pennsylvania	PA
Puerto Rico	PR
Rhode Island	RI
South Carolina	SC
South Dakota	SD
Tennessee	TN
Texas	TX
United Kingdom (England)	UK
Utah	UT
Vermont	VT
Virginia	VA
Washington	WA
West Virginia	WV
Wisconsin	WI
Wyoming	WY

After each company name in the Product & Service Directory, you will find a two-letter state code. This indicates the state in which the company is located. The state code helps you find nearby suppliers when there is a long list of companies within a category.

The full name, address, and telephone number of every company can be found in the Company Directory starting on page 151.

The Indexes

This is where you start.

The General Index that follows will direct you to the right page for the product or service you require. The Index is carefully cross-referenced, so you'll rapidly find what you need.

The Advertisers' Index follows the General Index. Here you will find every company that has a display advertisement and the page upon which the ad appears.

You can quickly find companies located in your area by turning to the Company Listing By State that starts on page 24.

General Index

A

Accessories — *see Furniture & Furnishings*
Adzes 131
Alarm Systems, Fire & Burglar 136
Aluminum, Cast 59
Anaglypta — *see Wallcoverings other than Wallpaper (Embossed Paper)*
Anchors & Washers, Plaster 135
Andirons 110
Antique & Recycled House Parts .... 136 - 139
Antique (Old) Hardware 104
Antique Repairs 141
Antique Shops .... 136 - 139
Archeological Surveys 141
Architectural Design — Restoration 142, 143
Architectural Millwork 41
Architectural Salvage — *see Antique & Recycled House Parts*
Art Deco and Moderne Furniture 86
Art Glass — All Types 78, 79
Art, Original 88
Asbestos Tiles 39
Awning Hardware 61
Awnings 61

B

Balances, Window 54
Balconies, Iron 60
Balusters, Iron 59
Balusters, Porch 51
Balusters, Staircase 71
Balustrades, Roof 61
Bar Rails — *see Restaurant Fittings*
Barnboard 40
Barns, Recycled 138
Barometers, Antique 91
(under Other Decorative Accessories)
Baseboards 66
Basement Waterproofing Paints 34
Bathroom Accessories 92
Bathroom Faucets & Fittings 94
Bathroom Fixtures .... 96 - 99
Bathroom Tile 76
Bathtubs, Old-Fashioned 98
Beams, Hand-Hewn 66
Beams, Salvage 41
Bed Hangings 83
Bed Hardware — *see Furniture Hardware*
Beds, Brass 86
Beds, Murphy 86
Bellows 110
Benches, Promenade 65
Bevelled Glass 78, 79
Bird & Pest Control Products 34
Bisque Repair — *see Porcelain, Glass, & China Repair*
Bleach, Wood 123
Blinds & Shutters, Exterior Wood 51
Blinds, Shutters, & Shades, Interior 91, 105
Blinds, Wood Venetian 91
Bluestone 36
Boards, Salvage 41, 66
(see also Salvage Building Materials, Barnboard)
Bobeches, Ceramic 120
Bollards & Stanchions 65
Brackets 43, 75
Braided Rugs 88
Brass & Bronze, Custom Casting — *see Hardware, Interior*
Brass Beds 86
Brass Lacquer 123
Brass Polish 123
Brick Cleaners 34
Bricks, Handmade 35
Bricks, Salvage 35
(see also Salvage Building Materials)
Bronzing & Gilding Liquids 123
Brownstone 36
Brownstone (Sandstone) Repair 150
Brushes, Chimney 107
Brushes, Stencilling 135
Building Inspection 145
Building Maintenance Materials 34, 35
Building Materials, Interior .... 66 - 75
Built-Ins & Dumbwaiters 67
Bulbs, Carbon Filament 121
Bull's Eye Windows — *see Windows, Special Architectural Shapes*
Burglar Alarms 136
Busybodies 43
Buttresses 43

C

Cabinet Hardware 101
Cabinetmaking & Fine Woodworking 143
Cabinets, Kitchen 104
Cable, Armored Electrical 66
Calcimine Paint 129

C *continued*

Candelabra 83
Candles, Electric 121
Candlestands & Candlesticks 83
Caning, Chair — *see Furniture Restoration*
Caning Supplies 131
Canopies, Bed 83
Canvas for Floors 131
(see also Floorcloths)
Canvas For Walls 131
Capitals, Exterior 43, 44
Capitals, Interior 77
Carbon Filament Bulbs 121
Carpentry 145
Carpet Rods 101
Carpets 88
Carved & Cut Glass 79
Carving, Wood — Custom 150
Casein Paints 129
Casings, Door & Window 66
Cast Aluminum, Exterior Ornamental 59
Cast Iron, Custom 60
Cast Iron, Ornamental 60
Casting, Custom — Plaster, Fiberglass, Compo, Etc. . 145
Casting Kits 132
Casting Materials 132
Casting, Metal — Custom 147
Ceiling Anchors — *see Plaster Washers*
Ceiling Fan Restoration 141
Ceiling Fans 104
Ceiling Medallions 75
(see also Ornaments, Interior)
Ceiling Papers 90
Ceilings, Metal 72
Ceilings, Wood 66
Cements, Specialty 36
Centerpieces — *see Ceiling Medallions*
Ceramic Roofing Tiles 39
Ceramic Tile 76
Ceramic Tile Flooring 76
Chair Caning — *see Furniture Restoration*
Chair Rails 66
Chair Replacement Seats 131
Chair Tapes 131
Chairs 83, 84
(see also Furniture)
Chandeliers — *see Lighting Fixtures*
Channels, Window 54
Chimney Brushes 107
Chimney Collars — *see Stove Pipe & Fittings*
Chimney Linings 108
Chimney Lining Services — *see Fireplace & Chimney Restoration*
Chimney Pots 61
Chimney Restoration 144
China, Porcelain, & Glass Repair 141
Chinking — *see Specialty Mortars*
Christmas Decorations 84
Circular Staircases 70
Clapboards, Beaded Edge 40
(see also Salvage Building Materials)
Cleaners & Polishes, Metal 123
Cleaners, Marble 125
Cleaners, Masonry & Brick 34
Cleaners, Textile 129
Cleaners, Wallpaper 130
Clock Kits 84
Clock Repair & Parts 141
Clocks 84
Clocks, Street 65
Clothing, Period 84
Clothing, Period Patterns 84
Coal Grates 108
Coal Scuttles 110
Coat Hooks 101
Coat Racks & Umbrella Stands 90
Collars, Stove Pipe — *see Stove Pipe & Fittings*
Color Consulting 149
Columns, Exterior 43
Columns, Interior 77
Columns, Porch — *see Porch Parts*
Commode Seats 96
Composition Casting — *see Casting, Custom*
Composition Ornaments 82
Concrete Roofing Tiles 39
Conductor Heads — *see Leaders & Leader Boxes*
Conservator's Tools 131
Conservatories 62
Consolidants, Wood — *see Rot Patching Materials*
Consulting Services 142, 143
Contour Gages 131
Contracting Services — Restoration 144
Contractors, Decorating 148
Cookstoves 110
Copper Polish 123
Copper Roofing — *see Metal Roofing*
Corbels 43, 75
Corner Bead Moulding 77
Cornices, Exterior 45
Cornices, Interior Decorative 82
Costume, Period 84
Country Primitive Furniture 86
Coverlets & Quilts 83
Cranes 110
Cresting 60
Crewel 85
Cupolas 61
Curtain Patterns, Period 85
Curtain Rod Finials — *see Drapery Hardware* •
Curtain Rods 84
Curtains & Drapery 85
Curtains, Bed 83
Curtains, Shower — Extra Size 98

D

Damask 85
Dampers, Fireplace 108
Dating Old Houses — *see Historical Research*
Deck Canvas — *see Canvas*
Decorative & Painting Services 148
Decorating Contractors 148
Decorative Interior Materials & Supplies .... 75 - 82
Delft Tile — *see Tile, Ceramic*
Design & Consulting Services 142, 143
Doorbells 59
Door Framing Woodwork 53, 66
Door Hardware, Exterior 58
Door Hardware, Interior 102, 103
Door Knobs & Escutcheons 103
Door Knockers 58

D *continued*

Doors, Exterior Antique 52
Doors, Exterior Reproduction 52
Doors, Exterior Salvage 52
Doors, Exterior Steel 136
Doors, Interior 67
Doors, Screen 52
Doors, Security 136
Doors, Sliding — Tracks & Hardware 105
Doors, Steel 136
Downspout Fittings — *see Gutters & Leaders*
Drapery & Curtains 85
Drapery Hardware 84
Drapery Patterns, Period 85
Drapery Rod Finials — *see Drapery Hardware*
Drapery Trimmings 85
Drapes, Insulated — *see Window Coverings, Insulating*
Drawings, Original (House) — *see Prints & Original Art*
Dry Sinks & Liners 103
Dumbwaiters & Built-Ins 67
Dust Corners — *see Cabinet & Furniture Hardware, Period*
Dutch Tile 76

E

Early American Furniture 86, 87
Electric Candles 121
Electric Cable, Armored 66
Electric Switches, Push-Button 122
Embossed Wallcoverings 89
Encaustic Tile 76
Energy-Saving Devices .... 107 - 112
(see also Fireplace Devices)
Engraved Glass 79
Engraving, Brass — *see Plaques & Historic Markers*
Entryways 53
Epoxy Resins — *see Building Maintenance Materials; Casting Materials; Rot Patching Materials*
Escutcheons 103
Etched Glass 78
Etched Glass Kits 132
Exterior Building Materials .... 34 - 41
Exterior Ornament & Architectural Details .... 41 - 65

F

Fabric Cleaners — *see Textile Cleaners*
Fabric, Reproduction 85
Fabric Restoration — *see Antique Repair & Restoration*
Fabric, Traditional 85
Fancy Painting — Gilding, Glazing, etc. 148
Fanlights 58
Fans, Ceiling 104
Fans, Ceiling, Restoration 141
Faucets & Faucet Parts, Bathroom 94
Faucets & Faucet Parts, Kitchen 104
Fences & Gates 62
Fenders, Fireplace 110
Fiberglass Casting — *see Casting, Custom*
Fiberglass Mouldings, Exterior 51
Finials 45
Finish Revivers 123
Finish, Stove — *see Cleaners and Polishes*
Finishes, Interior — Specialty Paints 129
Finishes, Oil 125
Fire Alarms 136
Firebacks 110
Fireboards — *see Firescreens*
Firegrates 110
Fireplace Accessories 110
Fireplace & Chimney Restoration 144
Fireplace Dampers 108
Fireplace Devices 107
Fireplace Parts 108
Fireplace Surrounds 108
Fireplace Tools 110
Fireplaces, Manufactured 108
Firescreens 110
Flags & Poles, Period 62
Flatting Oils 123
Floor Coverings — *see Rugs & Carpets, Linoleum*
Floor Registers 70
Floorcloths 88
Flooring, Linoleum 67
Flooring, Parquet — Installation 149
Flooring, Stone & Ceramic 69
Flooring, Wood 69
Flue Liners — *see Chimney Linings*
Folk Rugs 88
Fountains 62
Frames, Door & Window 53, 54, 66
Frames, Picture 88
Franklin Stoves — *see Stoves*
Frescoes & Murals 148
Fretwork & Grilles, Wood 46, 77
Fringe, Lampshade 87
Froes 131
Furnace Parts 110
Furnaces, Coal-Fired 107
Furnaces, Wood-Burning 107
Furniture & Accessories 86, 87
Furniture & Furnishings .... 83 - 91
Furniture Hardware 101
Furniture Kits & Patterns 86, 87
Furniture, Lawn & Porch 63
Furniture — Period Styles 86, 87
(see also Chairs)
Furniture, Reproduction — Custom-Made 86
Furniture Restoration 141
Furniture Stripping 149

G

Galvanized Metal Roofing 37
Garden Ornament 62
Gas Lamp Mantles 120
Gas-Light Parts — *see Gas Mantles and Bobeches*
Gas Lighting Fixtures 120
Gas Logs 110
Gates & Fences 62
Gazebo Plans 131
Gazebos 62
Gilding & Bronzing Liquids 123
Gilding Services 148
Gingerbread Trim 46

G *continued*

Glass, Antique 78
Glass, Art — All Types 78, 79
Glass Bending 79
Glass Block 46
Glass, Curved — For China Cabinets 77
Glass, Curved — Window 57, 79
Glass, Etched 78
Glass, Etched — Kits 132
Glass, Leaded & Stained — New 79
Glass, Leaded & Stained — Repair 79
Glass, Leaded & Stained — Supplies 132
Glass Repair 141
Glass Shades 120
Glass, Window — Handmade 57
Glazing Services 148
Glazing Stains & Liquids 125
Globes, Glass 120
Glue Chip Glass 79
Gold Leaf 125
Gold Leafing — *see Gilding*
Graining Services 148
Graining Tools 131
Granite 36
Grates, Coal 108
Grates, Tree 65
Greenhouses 62
Grilles & Fretwork, Wood 46, 77
Grilles, Hot Air Register 70
Grilles, Iron 60
Gutters & Leaders 48

H

Hammocks 62
Handrails, Iron 59
Handrails, Staircase 71
Hangers, Picture 88
Hardware, Antique (Old) 104
Hardware, Awning 61
Hardware, Cabinet 101
Hardware, Drapery 84
Hardware, Exterior 58, 59
Hardware, Exterior — Custom 59
Hardware, Furniture 101
Hardware, Hoosier 104
Hardware, Ice Box 104
Hardware, Interior — Custom 104
Hardware, Plumbing & House Fittings .... 92 - 107
Hardware, Shutter 59, 105
Hardware, Transom 107
Hardware, Trunk 106
Hardware, Window 107
Hardwood Strip Flooring 69
Hardwoods, Suppliers 69
Heart Pine Flooring 69
Heat Guns — *see Heat Stripping Devices*
Heat Plates — *see Heat Stripping Devices*
Heat Shields 110
Heat Stripping Devices 133
Heating Systems, Fireplaces, & Stoves .... 107 - 111
Heating Systems, Central — Solid Fuel 107
Heating Systems, Solar 107
Hewing Tools 131
Hexagonal Ceramic Tile 76
High-Tank Toilets 96
Hinges, Door 58, 102
Hinges, Shutter 59
Historical Research 142, 143
Holdbacks 59
Hooked Rugs 88
Hooks, Coat 101
Hoosier Hardware 104
Horsehair Fabric 85
Hot-Air Guns — *see Heat Stripping Devices*
House Inspection Services 145
House Moving 146
House Parts, Salvage .... 136 - 139
House Plans 132
Houses, Recycled 138

I

Ice Box Hardware 104
Ice Guards For Roofs 38
Ingrain Carpets 88
Inlays & Veneers 74
Inspection Services 145
Integral Weatherstripping 112
Interior Hardware, Plumbing, & House Fittings . 92 - 107
Iron, Cast — Ornamental 60
Iron Furniture 63
Iron, Wrought — Ornamental 60
Ironing Boards, Built-In — *see Dumbwaiters & Built-Ins*
Ironwork, Exterior 59, 60
Isinglass for Stove Doors 111

K

Kerosene Lamps & Lanterns 120
Key Blanks 104
Kitchen Cabinets 104
Kitchen Faucets 104
Kitchen Sinks 104
Kits, Casting 132
Kits, Clock 84
Kits, Furniture 86, 87
Kits, Needlework 88
Kits, Quilts 88
Kits, Stained & Leaded Glass 132
Kits, Stencil 135
Knockers, Door 58

L

Lace 85
Lacquer, Brass 123
Lacquers, Clear & Colored 125
Ladders, Library 104
Lamp Posts & Standards 121
Lamp Repairs — *see Lighting Fixture Restoration*

L *continued*

Lamp Shade Kits, Glass ... 132
Lamp Shade Fringe ... 87
Lamp Shades ... 87
Lamp Shades, Glass ... 120
Lamp Wicks & Lamp Oil ... 121
Lamps, Antique ... 113
Lamps, Exterior ... 122
Lamps, Kerosene ... 120
Lamps, Reproduction ... 114 - 122
Lamps, Street ... 65, 122
Landscape Design ... 146
Lanterns ... 122
Lanterns & Lamps, Exterior ... 65, 122
Lanterns & Lamps, Kerosene ... 120
Latches ... 58, 102
Lathe, Long-Bed — *see Specialty Power Tools*
Lawn Furniture ... 63
Leaded & Stained Glass Supplies ... 132
Leaded Glass ... 78, 79
Leaded Glass Repair ... 79
Leaders & Leader Boxes ... 48
Leather Replacement Seats ... 131
Leather Wallcovering ... 89
Lectures & Seminars ... 142, 143
Letterdrops ... 58
Library Ladders ... 104
Light Bulbs, Carbon Filament ... 121
Lighting Fixture Parts ... 120
Lighting Fixture Restoration ... 146
Lighting Fixtures & Parts ... 113 - 122
Lighting Fixtures, Antique ... 113
Lighting Fixtures — Gas Burning ... 120
Lighting Fixtures, Reproduction ... 114 - 122
Lightning Rods ... 63
Limestone ... 36
Lincrusta-Walton — *see Wallcoverings Other Than Wallpaper*
Linen ... 85
Linings, Chimney ... 108
Linoleum ... 67
Locks, Door ... 58, 102
Locks, Security — *see Security Features*
Log Houses — *see Recycled Houses & Barns*
Lumber Suppliers ... 70

M

Magnifiers, Portable ... 131
Mail Boxes ... 63
Mail Slots ... 58
Maintenance Supplies, Exterior ... 34, 35
Mall Furniture & Equipment ... 65
Mantels ... 81
Mantles, Gas ... 120
Marble ... 36, 81
Marble Cleaners & Polishes ... 125
Marble Flooring ... 69
Marble, Replacement Pieces ... 81
Marbleizing Services ... 148
Markers, Historic ... 63
Masks & Respirators — *see Safety Equipment*
Masonry & Supplies ... 35, 36
Masonry Cleaners & Paint Strippers ... 34
Masonry Paint-Stripping Services — *see Masonry Repair & Cleaning*
Masonry Paints ... 34
Masonry Repair & Cleaning ... 147
Masonry Sealers ... 34
Masonry Tools ... 133
Materials Analysis ... 149
Mechanical Doorbells ... 59
Medallions, Ceiling ... 75
Medicine Cabinets ... 92
Metal Casting, Custom ... 147
Metal Ceilings ... 72
Metal Ornament (Sheet Metal) ... 64
Metal Polishes & Cleaners ... 123
(see also Rust Removers)
Metal Polishing ... 147
Metal Replating ... 147
Metal Roofing ... 37
Metal Shingles ... 38
Metal Window Frames and Sash ... 54
Metallic Paints ... 129
Metalwork Repairs ... 148
Mica For Stove Doors — see Isinglass
Microcrystalline Wax ... 130
Milk Paint ... 129
Millwork, Architectural — Exterior ... 41
Mirror Resilvering ... 148
Miscellaneous Decorative Ornament ... 91
Moderne Furniture ... 86
Moisture Meters ... 131
Morris Chairs ... 84
Mortar Analysis — *see Materials Analysis*
Mortars, Specialty ... 36
Mortise Locks ... 58, 102
Moulding & Casting Supplies ... 132
Moulding, Corner Bead ... 77
Moulding Planes ... 133
Mouldings, Exterior ... 50, 51
Mouldings, Exterior Wood ... 50
(see also Architectural Millwork)
Mouldings, Interior ... 82
Mouse Traps — *see Bird & Pest Control Products*
Moving Historic Structures ... 146
Murals & Frescoes ... 148
Murals, Wallpaper ... 90
Murphy Beds ... 86
Musical Instrument Repair ... 148

N

Nails, Handmade ... 133
National Register Applications — *see Consulting Services*
Needlework Kits ... 88
Needlework Rugs ... 88
Newel Posts, Staircase ... 71

O

Oil & Wicks, Lamp ... 121
Oil Finishes ... 125
(see also Tung Oil)
Oriental Rugs ... 88

O *continued*

Ornaments, Interior — Plaster, Wood, & Composition 82
Ornaments, Sheet Metal 64
Ornaments, Wrought Iron 60
Outbuilding Plans 131
Outbuildings, Prefabricated 62
Overdoor Treatments 70

P

Paint and Materials Analysis 149
Paint Brushes, Specialty 133
Paint Removers, Masonry 34
Paint Stripping Chemicals 126
Paint Stripping Gun — *see Heat Stripping Devices*
Paint Stripping Services 149
Paint Stripping Tools 133
Painting & Decorating Services 148
Paints, Exterior — Masonry 34
Paints, Finishes, Removers, & Supplies .... 123 - 130
Paints, Period Colors 126
Paints, Specialty 129
Paints, Waterproofing 34
Panelling, Wall — Wood 75
Parquet Flooring 69
Parquet Repair & Installation 149
Patching Materials & Fillers, Wood 128, 130
Patching Materials, Stucco 36
Patching Plaster 135
Patterns, Curtains & Drapery 85
Patterns, Period Clothing 84
Patterns, Quilt 88
Pedestals & Plant Stands 88
Pest Control Products 34
Photo Restoration 149
Picture Frame Repair — *see Moulding & Casting Supplies*
Picture Frames 88
Picture Hangers 88
Pierced Tin 106
Pigeon Control 34
Pigments & Tinting Colors 126
Planes, Wood — Moulding 133
Plans, Gazebo 131
Plans, House 132
Plant Stands & Pedestals 88
Planters 62
Plaques & Historic Markers 63
Plaster Analysis — *see Materials Analysis*
Plaster Casting, Custom — *see Casting, Custom*
Plaster Casting Materials 132
Plaster Mouldings 51, 82
Plaster Ornaments 82
Plaster Patching Materials 135
Plaster Washers & Anchors 135
Plastering, Ornamental 149
Plastering Tools 133
Plastics for Casting 132
Plating, Metal 147
Plumbing Fixtures .... 92 - 99
Pocket Door Hardware 105
Pokers 110
Poles, Drapery 84
Polishes 123
Polishing, Metal 147
Porcelain, Glass, & China Repair 141
Porcelain Knobs — *see Door Knobs; Cabinet Hardware*
Porcelain Refinishing Materials 125
Porcelain Refinishing Services 150
Porch Furniture 63
Porch Parts 51
Porch Swings 64
Porticoes — *see Overdoor Treatments*
Portraits, House — *see Prints & Original Art*
Post-and-Beam Houses — *see Recycled Houses & Barns*
Posts, Lamp 65, 121
Posts, Porch 51
Posts, Salvage — *see Salvage Building Materials*
Power Tools 135
Preservatives, Wood 35
Prints & Original Art 88
Prisms 120
Pull-Chain Toilets 96
Pully Seals For Windows — *see Other Exterior Hardware*
Putty, Colored 128

Q

Quarry Tile — *see Ceramic Tile; Flooring, Ceramic*
Quilt Patterns and Kits 88
Quilt Repair — *see Textile Restoration*
Quilts & Coverlets 83

R

Radiators 105
Railings, Balconies, & Window Grilles 60
Railings, Brass — *see Restaurant Fittings*
Railings, Iron 59
Recycled House Parts .... 136 - 139
Recycled Houses & Barns 138
Reed Organs, Harmoniums, & Melodeons — Repair — *see Musical Instrument Repair*
Refinishing Products .... 123 - 130
Registers & Grilles 70
Renovation & Restoration Supply Stores 140
Replating Services 147
Researching Buildings — *see Historical Research*
Respirators — *see Safety Equipment*
Restaurant Fittings, Period Styles 88
Restoration Consultants 142, 143
Restoration Services .... 141 - 150
Retinning, Copper — *see Metal Replating; Metalwork Repairs*
Rim Locks 58, 102
Risers & Treads, Staircase 71
Rocking Chairs 84
Rollers, Stencil — *see Wallpapering & Decorating Tools*
Roof Guards for Snow 38
Roofers, Specialty 150
Roofing Materials .... 37 - 39
Roofing Tools, Slate 135
Rosettes, Ceiling — *see Ceiling Medallions*
Rot Patching Materials 128
Rubber Stamps 91
(under Other Decorative Accessories)

R *continued*

Rug Kits ... 88
Rugs & Carpets ... 88
Rust & Corrosion Removers ... 128
Rustic Furniture ... 86

S

Safety Equipment ... 135
Salvage Building Materials ... 41
Salvage House Parts ... 136 - 139
Sandstone ... 36
Sandstone (Brownstone) Repair ... 150
Sash Weights — *see Window Balances*
Sash, Window ... 54
Schools, Restoration/Preservation — *see Training Courses & Workshops*
Sconces — *see Lighting Fixtures*
Scrapers, Paint ... 133
Screen Doors ... 52
Screens, Window ... 91
Sculpture, Garden ... 62
Scuttles, Coal ... 110
Sealers, Masonry ... 34
Sealers, Wood ... 128
Seats, Chair — Replacement ... 131
Security Alarms ... 136
Security Features ... 136
Seminars & Lectures ... 142, 143
Shades & Blinds ... 91
Shades, Glass ... 120
Shades, Insulating — *see Window Coverings, Insulating*
Shades, Lamp ... 87, 120
Shades, Window ... 91
Shakes, Wood ... 38, 40
Sheet Metal Ornaments ... 64
Shingles, Metal ... 38
Shingles, Special Architectural Shapes ... 40
Shingles, Wood ... 38, 40
Shower, Curtains — Special Sizes ... 98
Shower Rings ... 98
Shutter Hardware ... 59, 105
Shutters & Blinds, Exterior Wood ... 51
Shutters & Blinds, Interior ... 105
Sidelights ... 58
Siding, Barn ... 40
Siding Materials ... 40, 41
Siding, Salvage — *see Salvage Building Materials*
Signs, Old-Fashioned ... 64
Silk ... 85
Silver Plating ... 147
Silver Polish ... 123
Sink Bowls, Replacement ... 98
Sinks, Bathroom ... 98
Sinks, Dry ... 103
Sinks, Kitchen ... 104
Skylights ... 64
Slate ... 36
Slate Flooring ... 69
Slate Roofers — *see Roofers, Specialty*
Slate Roofing Tiles ... 39
Slater's Tools ... 135
Sliding Door Tracks ... 105
Slumping, Glass ... 79
Snow Guards ... 38
Soap Dishes, Period Styles ... 92
Solar Heating Systems ... 107
Specialty Mortars & Cements ... 36
Spindles, Porch ... 51
Spiral Staircases ... 70
Stained, Etched & Leaded Glass Kits ... 132
Stained Glass ... 78, 79
Stained Glass Repair ... 79
Stained Glass Supplies ... 132
Stains, Exterior ... 35
Stains For Glazing ... 125
Stains, Masonry — *see Paints, Exterior — Masonry*
Stains, Wood ... 35, 129
Stair Rods ... 101
Staircase Parts ... 71
Staircase Repair ... 150
Staircases ... 72
Staircases, Spiral ... 70
Stamped Metal Ornament ... 64
Stamps, Rubber ... 91
(under Other Decorative Accessories)
Stanchions & Bollards ... 65
Standards, Lamp ... 65, 121
Star Washers for Tie-Rods & Turnbuckles — *see Turnbuckle Stars*
Statuary, Garden ... 62
Steel Ceilings ... 72
Steeples — *see Cupolas*
Stencilling ... 148
Stencilling Supplies ... 135
Stone ... 36
Stone & Ceramic Flooring ... 69
Stores, Renovation & Restoration Supply ... 140
Storm Windows ... 112
Stove Heat Shields ... 110
Stove Parts ... 111
Stove Pipe & Fittings ... 111
Stove Polish & Finish ... 123
Stove Restoration ... 141
Stoves ... 110
Strap Hinges ... 58
Straw Matting ... 88
Street Lamps ... 65
Streetscape Equipment ... 65
Strippers, Masonry ... 34
Strippers, Wood ... 126
Stripping Paint — Services ... 149
Stripping Tools ... 133
Stucco Patching Materials ... 36
Stucco Restoration — *see Masonry Repair & Cleaning*
Sundials — *see Garden Ornament*
Supply Stores For Renovation Products ... 140
Swings, Porch ... 64
Switch Plates ... 106
Switches, Electric Push-Button ... 122

T

Table Bases — *see Pedestals & Plant Stands*
Tapestry ... 85
Telephone Repair & Parts ... 141
Terne-Metal Roofing ... 37

T *continued*

Terra-Cotta Mouldings 51
Terra Cotta Restoration & Casting 150
Terra-Cotta Roofing Tiles 39
(see also Concrete Roofing Tiles)
Textile Cleaners 129
Textile Reconstruction 141
Texture Paints 129
Tiebacks 84
Tie-Rod Washers — *see Turnbuckle Stars*
Tile, Asbestos-Cement 39
Tile, Ceramic 76
Tile, Concrete 39
Tile, Encaustic 76
Tile, Roofing — Terra-Cotta & Ceramic 39
Tile, Slate 39
Timber Frame Houses — *see Recycled Houses & Barns*
Tin Ceilings 72
Tin, Pierced 106
Tinting Colors 126
Toilet Seats, Wooden 96
Toilets, Period Styles 96
Tools .... 131 - 136
Towel Racks 92
Towers, Roof — *see Cupolas*
Training Courses & Workshops 150
Transoms 58
Transom Hardware 107
Treads & Risers, Staircase 71
Tree Grates 65
Trellis 62
Trompe l'Oeil Painting Services 148
Trompe l'Oeil Wallpaper 90
Trunk Hardware 106
Trunk Repair — *see Furniture Restoration*
Tung Oil 129
Turnbuckle Stars 65
Turnings, Custom 150
Turn-Of-The-Century Furniture 86

U

Umbrella Stands & Coat Racks 90
Upholstering, Furniture — *see Furniture Restoration*
Upholstery Tools & Supplies 135
Urns & Vases, Garden 62

V

Varnishes 35, 130
Vases & Urns, Garden 62
Velvet 85
Veneers & Inlays 74
Venetian Blinds, Wood 91
Ventilating Equipment 111
Victorian Furniture 86
Vinyl Flooring, Period Patterns — *see Linoleum*
Vinyl Wallcovering, Embossed 89

W

Wainscotting 74
Wall Canvas 131
Wall Panelling, Wood 75
Wall Washers — *see Turnbuckle Stars*
Wallcoverings Other Than Wallpaper 89
Wallpaper 89, 90
Wallpaper Borders 90
Wallpaper Cleaners 130
Wallpaper, Custom Duplication 90
Wallpaper Hanging 148
Wallpaper, Period Reproduction 90
Wallpaper, Restoration 148
Wallpaper, Scenic 90
Wallpaper, Victorian 90
Wallpapering & Decorating Tools 135
Washers & Anchors, Plaster 135
Water Heaters — Alternate Fuels 111
Waterproofing Compounds 34
Waxes, Specialty 130
Weatherstripping 111
Weathervanes 64
Whitewash 129
Wicker Furniture 86
Wicker Repair Materials 131
Wicker Restoration — *see Furniture Restoration*
Wicks & Oil, Lamp 121
Wide-Board Flooring 69
Window Balances 54
Window Coverings, Insulating 111
Window Frames & Sash, Metal 54
Window Frames & Sash, Wood 54
Window Framing, Interior 66
Window Glass, Block — *see Glass Block*
Window Glass — Curved 57, 79
Window Glass — Handmade 57
Window Grilles 60
Window Hardware 107
Window Inserts, Double-Glazed 57
Window Screens & Blinds 91
Windows, Special Architectural Shapes 58
Windows, Storm 112
Wood Baskets 110
Wood Carving 150
Wood Fillers 130
Wood Flooring 69
Wood Grain Fillers 130
Wood Mouldings — Custom 50, 82
(see also Architectural Millwork)
Wood Patching Materials 128, 130
Wood Preservatives 35
Wood Sealers 128
Wood Shakes & Shingles 38, 40
(see also Concrete Roofing Tiles)
Wood Stains 35, 129
Wood Turning 150
Woodworking, Custom 143, 145, 150
(see also Millwork, Architectural; Furniture, Reproduction — Custom-Made)
Woodworking Tools 135
Workshops, Training 150
Woven Rugs 88
Wrought Iron, Custom 60
Wrought Iron Ornament 60

Advertisers' Index

18th Century Hardware Company ... 105

A-Ball Plumbing ... 94
AA Abbingdon Affiliates, Inc. ... 72
AFC/A Nortek Company ... 67
Abatron ... 36, 128
Acorn Manufacturing ... 103
Adams & Swett ... 88
Aged Woods ... 68
Ahren's Chimney Technique ... 109
Alfresco Fine Outdoor Furniture ... 63
Allentown Paint Company ... 127
Allied Window ... 112
Amazon Drygoods ... 84
American Chimney Lining Systems ... 109
American Heritage Shutters ... 106
Anthony Wood Products ... 46
Antique Baths & Kitchens ... 62, 95
Antique Hardware Store ... 92
Architectural Accents ... 141
Architectural Antiques ... 141
Architectural Antiques Exchange ... 139
Architectural Components ... 58
Architectural Iron Company ... 61
Architectural Originals ... 91
Architectural Salvage Co. ... 138
Architectural Sculpture ... 77
Art Directions Antiques, Inc. ... 139
Art Glass Studio, Inc. ... 78
Authentic Designs ... 115

Ball & Ball ... 100, 115, 148
Barclay Products ... Inside Back Cover
Barnstable Stove Shop ... 111
Beech River Mill Company ... 51
Bendheim Glass ... 56
Benjamin Moore Paints ... 127
Bentley Brothers ... 89
Besco Plumbing ... 97
Biggs Company ... 83
Blaine Window Hardware ... 106
Blenko Glass Co., Inc. ... 57
Boatech, Inc. ... 109
Bona Decorative Hardware ... 101
Bradbury & Bradbury ... 90, Inside Front Cover
Bradford Consultants ... 121
Sylvan Brandt, Inc. ... 139
Brass Knob ... 136
Brass Light Gallery ... 64F
Brass Tree ... 106
Brasslight, Inc. ... 118
Brownstone Graphics ... 91
Brunschwig & Fils ... 85
Bryant Stoveworks ... 111
Buckingham-Virginia Slate Corp. ... 39
J.R. Burrows & Company ... 76, 85, 89
Butcher Polish Company ... 130
By Gone Era ... 138

Campbellsville Industries ... 43
Cane and Basket Supply ... 131
John Canning, Decorator ... 149
Carlisle Restoration Lumber ... 69
Carpenter and Smith Restorations ... 144
Carter Canopies ... 83
Cathedral Stone ... 146
Charles Street Supply ... 135
Chelsea Decorative Metal Co. ... 73
Chemical Products ... 126
Cherry Creek ... 79
City Knickerbocker ... 120
City Lights ... 114
Classic Accents ... 64D
Classic Architectural Specialties ... 47
Classic Ceilings ... 73
Coastal Trade, Inc. ... 35
Colonial Restoration Products ... 59
Color People ... 149
Commodity Traders Consulting ... 34
Conant Custom Brass ... 101
Conklin Metal Industries ... 38
Copper House ... 64
Copper Specialties ... 37
Corner Store ... 84
Country Curtains ... 84
Country Iron Foundry ... 111
Country Mouse ... 63
Country Shutters ... 105
Craftsman Lumber ... 74
Crawford's Old House Store ... 77
Crispin Treadway Floral Products ... 84
Crystal Mountain Prisms ... 120
Cumberland General Store ... 108
Cumberland Woodcraft ... 46, 64B
Custom Ironwork, Inc. ... 62
Custom Millwork, Inc. ... 40

D.E.A. Bathroom Machineries ... 96
D.H.M. Cabinets ... 86
Daly's Finishing Products ... 124
Dancing Cactus Enterprises ... 96
DeWeese Woodworking ... 96
Decorator's Supply Co. ... 45
Designer's Brass ... 93
Designs in Tile ... 76
Devenco Louver Products ... 105
J.D. Dewell & Company ... 77
Diedrich Chemicals ... 34
Drums Sash and Door ... 54
Dutch Products and Supply Co. ... 76

Easy Time Wood Refinishing Prod. ... 129
Jon Eklund Restorations ... 145
Elephant Hill Ironworks ... 59
Emporium, Inc. ... 41
Enlightened Restorations ... 142

Family Heirloom Weavers ... 88
Felber Studios, Inc. ... 43
Finish Feeder ... 130
Florida Victorian ... 136
Flue Works ... 145
Peter Franklin, Cabinetmaker ... 83
Frameworks ... 132
Fuller-O'Brien Paints ... 127

Garrett Wade Co. ... 133
Gaslight Time ... 116
Gates Moore ... 122
Germantown Restoration Supplies ... 140
Jamie Gibbs and Associates ... 146
Golden Age Glassworks ... 78
Good Directions ... 64
Good Impressions ... 91
Great American Salvage Co. ... 137
Green & Associates, Inc. ... 142
Green Enterprises ... 64
Greg's Antique Lighting ... 121

Haas Wood & Ivory Works, Inc. 143
Hautwork Inc. ... 146
Heads Up ... 93
Hearth Realities ... 110
Heritage Home Designers ... 132
Heritage Lanterns ... 120
Heritage Mantels ... 80
W.P. Hickman Company ... 64F
Allen Charles Hill, A.I.A. ... 143
Hilltop Slate, Inc. ... 37
Hisrich Manufacturing Co. ... 50
Historic Housefitters ... 102
Historic Preservation Alternatives ... 142
Historic Windows ... 105
Historical Replications ... 132
Alvin Holm, A.I.A. ... 142
House of Vermillion ... 83
House of Webster ... 111
Lyn Hovey Studio ... 78
Hydrotherm, Inc. ... 107

Iron Shop ... 71

J&M Custom Cabinets & Millwork ... 104
Johnson Paint Company ... 129
The Joinery ... 66

Kayne & Son Forged Hardware 102
Kenmore Industries 57
King's Chandelier Company ... 114
G. Krug & Son 60

Lamp Doctor 147
Lampco 65
Lamplight Industries, Inc. 65
James Lea Cabinetmaker 86
Brian F. Leo Custom Hardware 107
Joe Ley Antiques 138
Lisa-Victoria Brass Beds 87
London Country 81
London Venturers Company ... 118
Lyemance International 108

M-H Lamp & Fan Company ... 118
Machin Designs, Inc. 63
Daniel Mack Rustic Furnishings 86
Stephen Mack Associates 133
Mad River Woodworks 48
Maizefield Mantels 81
Marvin Windows 54, 64A
Materials Unlimited 137
Maurer & Shepherd Joyners 53
Mechanick's Workbench 133
Mel-Nor Marketing 65
Mendocino Millwork 48
Michael's Fine Colonial Products 54
Mile Hi Crown 89
Montclair Restoration Craftsmen 144
E.T. Moore, Jr. Company 74
Matthew Mosca 148
Moultrie Manufacturing Co. 44
Mountain Lumber Company 74
David G. Mulder 70
Muralo Company 135

NET 62
National Supaflu Products 108
C. Neri Antiques 64C
New England Firebacks 110
New England Woodturners 150
Newe Daisterre Glas 78
Newstamp Lighting Company .. 122
Newton Millham Blacksmith 58
Nixalite of America 34
W.F. Norman Corporation 38, 64, 73
North Pacific Joinery 52
Nowell's, Inc. 120

Oak Crest Manufacturing, Inc. .. 39
Ocean View Lighting 119
C.A. Ohman 72
Old Carolina Brick 35
Old House Inspection Co. 144
Old Wagon Factory 52
Olde Bostonian Antiques 138

PRG 131
Pagliacco Turning & Milling 44
Past Patterns 84
Pennsylvania Firebacks 110
Period Lighting Fixtures 122
Perma Ceram Enterprises, Inc. 150
Perma-Chink Systems, Inc. 36
Phoneco 141
Pietra Dura 147
Pratt and Lambert 126
Premier Communications Co. .. 136
Putnam Rolling Ladder 104

Quaker City Manufacturing Co. 54
Quality Woods, Inc. 67

REM Associates 105
Raleigh, Inc. 150
Rastetter Woolen Mill 88
Readybuilt Products 64D
Rejuvenation House Parts 119
Remodelers & Renovators Supplies 51
Renovation Concepts 140
Renovator's Supply 64H
Restoration Millworks 57
Restorations Unlimited 144
Restore-A-Tub & Brass, Inc. 94
Richcraft Custom Kitchens 104, 64B
Richmond Doors 66
Rinder's New York Flooring ... 148
Dana Robes Wood Craftsmen, Inc. 53
J.M. Roe-Medusa 149
Roman Marble Company 81
Roy Electric Company 95, 117

Saltbox 115
Schlitz Studios 64E, 77
Schwerd Manufacturing Co. 42
Security Home Inspection Inc. 145
Selrite Millwork 55
Shanker Steel Ceiling Co. 72
Shingle Mill 40
Shuttercraft 50
Silver Dollar Trading 63
Silver Tree Farms 39
Silverton Victorian Millworks ... 50
Sink Factory 98
Skyline Engineers of Maryland 144
W.A. Smoot Co., Inc. 82
South Coast Shingle Company .. 40
Southington Specialty Wood Co. 70
St. Louis Antique Lighting 118
H.F. Staples & Co. 126
Stanley Galleries 113
Starbuck Goldner Studios 76
W.P. Stephens Lumber Co. 50
Steptoe & Wife 71
Stewart Manufacturing Co. 60
John Stortz & Son, Inc. 133
Structural Slate Co. 39
Stulb Company 126, 128
Sun Designs 131
Sunrise Specialty 95
Superior Clay Corp. 61
Supradur Manufacturing Co. .. 64G
Swan Wood Products 93
M. Swift & Sons, Inc. 125

Tiresias 69
Traditional Line Ltd. 143
Transylvania Mountain Forge .. 103
Tremont Nail Company 133
Travis Tuck Inc. 64

United House Wrecking 48, 53, 77, 81, 141

Vermont Structural Slate 39
Victorian Collectibles 90
Victorian Construction Company 132
Victorian Glassworks 79
Victorian Interior Restoration .. 140
Victorian Lightcrafters 116
Victorian Lighting Co. 121
Victorian Lighting Works 116
Victorian Warehouse 140
Vintage Lumber Co. 69
Vintage Plumbing Specialties ... 98
Vintage Tub & Sink Restoration 98
Vintage Woodworks 49

Albert J. Wagner and Sons 48
Walker Mercantile 99
Wallace & Hinz 88
Jack Wallis' Doors 53
Washington Copper Works 115
Watercolors 93
W.T. Weaver & Sons, Inc. 75
Otto Wendt & Company 65
Wes-Pine Millwork 55
Whitco/Vincent Whitney Co. 67
Williams Art Glass Studio 79
Williamsburg Blacksmiths 101
Windy Hill Forge 60
Wolf Paints & Wallpapers 123
Woodcare Corporation 125
Woods American Company 74
Woodstone Company 58
Worthington Group, Ltd. 45

Yestershades 87

Company Listing By State

ALABAMA

Alexander City — Robinson Iron Corporation
Birmingham — Fairmont Foundry Co., Inc.
Birmingham — Lawler Machine & Foundry
Cullman — Southern Accents Architectural Antiques
Madison — Olde & Oak Antiques
Montgomery — American Furniture Galleries
Montgomery — Martha M. House Furniture
Northport — Nutt, Craig, Fine Wood Works
Troy — Henderson Black & Greene, Inc.

ARIZONA

Phoenix — Dancing Cactus Enterprises
Phoenix — Direct Safety Company
Phoenix — The New Victorians, Inc. of Arizona
Pinetop — Crowfoot's Inc.

ARKANSAS

Fayetteville — Sunshine Architectural Woodworks
Little Rock — Architectural Antiques, Ltd.
Rogers — House of Webster
Stuttgart — Potlatch Corp. — Townsend Unit
Wheeler — The Corner Store

CALIFORNIA

Alhambra — Bel-Air Door Co.
Anaheim — Russell & Company Victorian Bathrooms
Arcata — Mad River Wood Works
Arcata — Wallace & Hinz
Auburn — Victorian Warehouse
Benicia — Bradbury & Bradbury Wallpapers
Berkeley — Caning Shop
Berkeley — Classic Illumination Inc.
Berkeley — Ocean View Lighting
Berkeley — Ohmega Salvage
Berkeley — The Sink Factory
Berkeley — Sunrise Specialty Co., Inc.
Berkeley — Winans Construction
Bethel Island — Lena's Antique Bathroom Fixtures
Burbank — J.P. Weaver Co.
Campbell — Walton Stained Glass
City of Industry — CasaBlanca Fan Co.
Corona — La Haye Bronze, Inc.
Corte Madera — Shades of the Past
Costa Mesa — Master's Stained and Etched Glass Studio
Covina — Barnard Chemical Co.
Culver City — Beveled Glass Industries
Cupertino — Billard's Old Telephones
Davenport — Lundberg Studios, Inc. Contemporary Art Glass
Drytown — Sierra Lamp Company
Escondido — The Crowe Company Ltd.
Eureka — Houseparts
Eureka — North Pacific Joinery
Ferndale — Victorian Glass Works
Fortuna — Hexagram
Foster City — Designs in Tile
Fullerton — Classic Ceilings
Glendale — Plexacraft Metals Co.
Granada Hills — Vintage Plumbing Specialties

Grass Valley — Deer Creek Pottery
Gualala — Ritter & Son Hardware
Hanford — Gravity - Randall
Hollywood — Linoleum City
Huntington Beach — Cloyd Laibe
Huntington Beach — Frank's Cane and Rush Supply
Industry — Mansion Industries, Inc.
La Canada — Transylvania Mountain Forge
Lafayette — Clocks, Etc.
Laguna Beach — Off The Wall, Architectural Antiques
Long Beach — South Coast Shingle Co.
Los Angeles — Albert Van Luit & Co.
Los Angeles — Brass Bed Company of America
Los Angeles — Cane & Basket Supply Company
Los Angeles — Classic Wicker
Los Angeles — Designer Resource
Los Angeles — Greg's Antique Lighting
Los Angeles — Rumplestiltskin Designs
Los Angeles — Swan Brass Beds
Manhattan Beach — Melvyn Green and Associates, Inc.
Mendocino — Mendocino Millwork
Monrovia — Howard Refinishing Products
Murphys — D.E.A./Bathroom Machineries
Newport Beach — Architectural Originals
North Hollywood — Helen Williams—Delft Tiles
Northridge — Wikkmann House
Oakland — Bartleys Mill
Oakland — Finishing Touch
Oakland — Selva — Borel
Oakland — Arthur Stern Studios Arch. Glass
Orange — Allen Foundry
Pasadena — Arroyo Restoration
Pasadena — Knickerbocker Guild
Ramona — Homestead Products
Rancho Cordova — Sign of the Crab
Riverside — Doors of Distinction
Riverside — Quali-Craft Constructors
Rough & Ready — 19th Century Company
Sacramento — Mac the Antique Plumber
San Bruno — Designer's Brass
San Diego — Burdoch Silk Lampshade Co.
San Diego — Ferris, Robert Donald, Architect, Inc.
San Francisco — Architectural Resources Group
San Francisco — Artistic License in San Francisco
San Francisco — Bay City Paint Company
San Francisco — Larry Boyce & Associates, Inc.
San Francisco — Bob Buckter, Color Consultant
San Francisco — Circecast, Inc.
San Francisco — The Day Studio — Workshop Inc.
San Francisco — Haas Wood & Ivory Works, Inc.
San Francisco — Meyer, Kenneth Co.
San Francisco — San Francisco Color Service
San Francisco — San Francisco Victoriana
San Francisco — Swan Wood
San Jose — Anglo-American Brass Co.
San Jose — Cedar Valley Shingle Systems
San Mateo — A.S.L. Associates
San Mateo — Dura Finish of San Mateo
San Pedro — Coppa Woodworking
Sanger — Kings River Casting
Santa Barbara — Antique Baths and Kitchens
Santa Barbara — Architectural Salvage of Santa Barbara
Santa Barbara — Moriarty's Lamps
Santa Monica — Jadis Moderne
Sausalito — Nowell's, Inc.
Sausalito — Whitco — Vincent Whitney Co.
Sherman Oaks — Canterbury Designs, Inc.
South Gate — Artistic Brass/A MASCO Company
St. Helena — JMR Products
Temecula — Heads Up
Torrance — Abaroot Mfg., Co.
Torrance — Antique Hardware Co.
Torrance — Barbara Vantrease Beall Studio
Tuolumne — Wendall's Wood Stoves
Van Nuys — House of Moulding
Van Nuys — Universal Clamp Corp.
Visalia — Boomer Resilvering
Wilmington — California Glass Bending Company
Winters — Winters Textile Mill
Woodacre — Pagliacco Turning & Milling Architectural Wood Turning

COLORADO

Bayfield — Restoration Millworks
Bayfield — Sunflake/Restoration Millwork
Boulder — Boulder Stained Glass Studios
Boulder — Community Services Collaborative
Colorado Springs — Kingsway Victorian Restoration Materials
Colorado Springs — Kroeck's Roofing
Denver — Cherry Creek Ent. Inc.
Denver — The Color People—Restoration Graphics
Denver — Custom & Historic Millwork
Denver — Grammar of Ornament
Denver — Grandpa Snazzy's Hardware
Denver — Hosek Manufacturing Co.
Denver — The Jasmine Company
Denver — Mile Hi Crown, Inc.
Denver — Rose, Barry
Durango — Alfresco Fine Furniture Since 1976
Durango — Shades of Victoriana
Fort Collins — Point Five Windows
Ft. Collins — Colorado Front Range Bldg. Inspection Service
Hillrose — Windy Lane Fluorescents, Inc.
Ignacio — Kirby Millworks
Loveland — Shady Lady
Montrose — Woodpecker Products Inc.
Silverton — Brueggeman Roofing Co.
Silverton — Klinke & Lew Contractors
Silverton — Silverton Victorian Millworks

A company's name in boldface means there is an advertisement that you can consult for more information. See page 22.

CONNECTICUT

Ansonia — Nomaco Decorative Products, Inc.
Ashford — Jerard Paul Jordan Gallery
Avon — Darworth Co.
Avon — Harry's Closet
Bethel — Bix Process Systems, Inc.
Bloomfield — Mirror Patented Stove Pipe Co.
Branford — Breakfast Woodworks Mackall & Dickinson
Branford — Smithy Hearth Products
Bristol — Blaschke Cabinet Glass
Brooklyn — Native Wood Products, Inc.
Chester — Period Lighting Fixtures
Cornwall Bridge — Strobel Millwork
Cromwell — Custom House
Cromwell — Horton Brasses
Danielson — Pine & Palette Studio
Deep River — Advanced Materials, Inc.
E. Haddam — Earthwise Design
East Lyme — S. & C. Huber, Accoutrements
East Windsor Hill — Early New England Rooms & Exteriors Inc.
Easton — Pollitt, E., AIA
Essex — Country Designs
Essex — Essex Forge
Fairfield — Gunther Mills, Inc.
Glastonbury — Dahlke Stairs
Glastonbury — Maurer & Shepherd, Joyners
Granby — William H. Parsons & Associates
Guilford — Shuttercraft
Hartford — Brewster's Lumberyard
Hartford — Hydrochemical Techniques, Inc.
Hartford — M. Swift & Sons, Inc.
Harwinton — The Country Mouse
Kent — Howland, John — Metalsmith
Manchester — Connecticut Cane & Reed Co.
Meriden — Colonial Casting Co., Inc.
New Hartford — Hitchcock Chair Co.
New Haven — J.D. Dewell & Company
New Haven — H.B. Ives
New Haven — RWL/Welsbach Lighting
Niantic — Connecticut Cupola & Weathervane
Norwalk — Architectural Woodworking
Norwalk — Gates Moore
Norwalk — Midget Louver Co.
Old Lyme — Bullfrog Hollow
Old Saybrook — C & D Distributors Hearth Mate
Old Saybrook — Ryther — Purdy Lumber Co., Inc.
Plantsville — Southington Specialty Wood Co.
Putnam — Hearth-glo
Shelton — Dimension Hardwood Inc.
Short Beach — New England Woodturners
Simsbury — Studio Workshop, Ltd.
Southbury — Henderson Lighting
Southington — Canning, John, Ornamental Painter
Southport — Heritage Mantels
Stamford — Chadwick Studio
Stamford — Good Directions, Inc.
Stamford — Historic Neighborhood Preservation Program
Stamford — Machin Designs (USA), Inc.
Stamford — MarLe Company
Stamford — United House Wrecking Corp.
Stonington — Wick York
Terryville — Colonial Lock Company
Washington — Washington Copper Works
West Simsbury — Richards, R.E., Inc.
West Suffield — Old Home Building & Restoration
Westbrook — Architectural Preservation Trust
Willimantic — The Frame Works
Wilton — Enlightened Restorations
Winchester Center — Maclean Restoration Services
Woodbury — New England Firebacks
Woodbury — Ramase
Woodbury — Woodbury Blacksmith & Forge Co.

DELAWARE

Hockessin — D. C. Mitchell Reproductions
Winterthur — Winterthur Museum and Gardens

DISTRICT OF COLUMBIA

Washington — Nelson Beck of Washington, Inc.
Washington — The Brass Knob
Washington — Canal Co.
Washington — Cathedral Stone Company, Inc.
Washington — Gold Leaf Studios, Inc.
Washington — Oehrlein & Associates
Washington — Park Place
Washington — Victorian Glassworks
Washington — Weaver, W. T. & Sons, Inc.

FLORIDA

Boca Raton — Classique French Imports, Inc.
Fort Lauderdale — Epifanes/Coastal Trade, Inc.
Gainesville — D.V.H. Co.
Green Cove Springs — David J. Lassiter
Jacksonville — DS Locksmithing Company
Jasper — Heart-Wood, Inc.
Key Largo — Backlund Moravian Tile Works
Miami — Entol Industries, Inc.
Miami — Window Components Mfg. A Harrow Co.
Sanford — Florida Victorian Architectural Antiques
Tampa — The 509 Studio
Tampa — San Do Designs/Spanish Tile Factoria
Winter Park — Burke and Bales Associates, Inc.

GEORGIA

Atlanta — Architectural Accents
Atlanta — ByGone Era Architectural Antiques
Atlanta — Conklin Metal Industries
Atlanta — Cross Industries, Inc.
Atlanta — Focal Point, Inc.
Atlanta — Hartmann-Sanders Column Co.
Atlanta — Hearth Realities
Atlanta — Magnolia Hall
Atlanta — Sandy Springs Galleries
Atlanta — Worthington Group Ltd.
Atlanta — Wrecking Bar of Atlanta
Brunswick — Fuller O'Brien Paints
Chamblee — Norcross Galleries
Dalton — Belcher, Robert W.
Danielsville — Broadnax Refinishing Products, Inc.
Decatur — Devenco Products, Inc.
Macon — Second Chance
Marietta — American Folk Art
Marietta — Rocker Shop of Marietta, GA
Marietta — W. P. Stephens Lumber Co.
Moultrie — Moultrie Manufacturing Company
Norcross — TrimbleHouse Corporation
Roswell — The Willow Place
Savannah — Nostalgia
Toccoa — Habersham Plantation Corp.

HAWAII

Aiea — Greg Monk Stained Glass

IDAHO

Boise — Remodelers & Renovators

ILLINOIS

Addison — Craftsman Wood Service Co.
Belvidere — Raleigh, Inc.
Carol Stream — Woodbridge Manufacturing, Inc.
Cary — B&B Glass Etching
Chicago — Barclay Products Ltd.
Chicago — Bird — X, Inc.
Chicago — Cleveland Wrecking Co.
Chicago — Colonial Brick Co., Inc.
Chicago — Consumer Supply Co.
Chicago — Decorators Supply Corp.
Chicago — Downstate Restorations
Chicago — Frog Tool Co., Ltd.
Chicago — Hasbrouck/Hunderman Architects
Chicago — Historic Boulevard Services
Chicago — M — H Lamp & Fan Company
Chicago — Renovation Source, Inc., The
Chicago — Roman Marble Co.
Chicago — Salvage One
Chicago — Stanley Galleries
Chicago — Sterline Manufacturing Corp.
Chicago — Sternberg Lanterns, Inc.
Chicago — USG Corporation
Chicago — Wagner, Albert J., & Son
Des Plaines — Chicago Faucet Co.
East Moline — Nixalite of America
Elmhurst — Midwest Spiral Stair Company, Inc.
Evanston — Botti Studio of Architectural Arts
Evanston — Dalton-Gorman, Inc.
Evanston — Hendershot, Judith
Evanston — Recommended Builders
Freeport — Pyfer, E.W.
Galena — Bassett & Vollum Wallpapers
Geneva — The Country Store
Gilberts — Abatron, Inc.
Glen Ellyn — Easy Time Wood Refinishing Products Corp.
Highland Park — Carpenter and Smith Restorations
Joliet — Reproduction Distributors, Inc.
Joliet — Spiess Antique Building Materials
Lake Forest — The Bartley Collection, Ltd.
Lake Forest — Sweet William House
Melrose Park — Cedar Gazebos, Inc.
Morton — Iron-A-Way, Inc.
Morton Grove — Floors By Juell
Mount Carroll — Campbell Center for Historic Preservation Studies
Naperville — Squaw Alley, Inc.
New Lenox — Johnson Woodworks Inc.
Rantoul — Caradco
Savanna — Facemakers, Inc.
Skokie — Braun, J.G. Co.
Springfield — Melotte-Morse Studios
Wilmette — Perkowitz Window Fashions
Winnetka — Arch Associates/ Stephen Guerrant AIA

INDIANA

Akron — Akron Foundry, Inc.
Auburn — Smith-Cornell, Inc.
Bloomington — Gaston Wood Finishes, Inc.
Decatur — Gilpin, Inc.
Gary — FerGene Studio
Indianapolis — Acquisition and Restoration Corp.
Indianapolis — Brandt Bros. General Contractors
Indianapolis — Haines Masonry Specialties
Jasper — Kimball Furniture Reproductions, Inc.
Jeffersonville — Lyemance International, Inc.
Mishawaka — Troyer, Le Roy and Associates
Newburgh — Sunburst Stained Glass Co.
Noblesville — Sedgwick House
South Bend — J.C. Lauber Co.
South Bend — Midland Engineering Company

IOWA

Ames — Jennings, Gottfried, Cheek/ Preservationists
Cedar Falls — Econol Stairway Lift Corp.
Davenport — Amazon Vinegar & Pickling Works Drygoods
Davenport — Midwest Wood Products
Des Moines — Craftsman's Corner Woodcraft Collection
Des Moines — Knudsen, Mark
Des Moines — Sherman Hill Antiques
Dubuque — Adams Company
Iowa City — Max-Cast
Iowa City — Oak Leaves Woodcarving Studio
Iowa Falls — Competition Chemicals, Inc.
Marshalltown — Marshalltown Trowel Co.
Mt. Pleasant — Heatilator Inc.
Orange City — Master Products, Inc.
Pella — Pella Windows & Doors
Richland — Reliance Industries, Inc.
Waterloo — Sundance Studios

KANSAS

Burlington — Industrial Solar
Kansas City — ProSoCo, Inc.
Lawrence — Prairiewind Traditionals
Manhattan — Hall Associates
Prairie Village — Goodman - Southern Fabrications
Wichita — Lesco, Inc.

KENTUCKY

Berea — Berea College Crafts
Campbellsville — Campbellsville Industries
Covington — Stewart Manufacturing Company
Lexington — Central Kentucky Millwork
Lexington — Huskisson Masonry & Exterior Building Restoration Co.
Louisville — Bentley Brothers
Louisville — Glass Designs
Louisville — Kentucky Wood Floors, Inc.
Louisville — Joe Ley Antiques, Inc.
Louisville — Louisville Art Glass Studio
Louisville — Metal Sales Manufacturing Corp.
Louisville — Morgan Woodworking Supplies
Louisville — Restore-A-Tub and Brass, Inc.
Murray — Jack Wallis' Doors
Sparta — Wallin Forge
Union — Custom Ironworks Inc.

LOUISIANA

Arabi — Wise Company, The
Baton Rouge — Magnetite Corp.
Baton Rouge — Spiral Manufacturing, Inc.
New Iberia — Iberia Millwork
New Orleans — Bank Architectural Antiques
New Orleans — Brass Menagerie
New Orleans — Gallier House Museum
New Orleans — Lachin, Albert & Assoc., Inc.
New Orleans — Preservation Resource Center of New Orleans
New Orleans — Robinson Lumber Company

MAINE

Brooks — Marsh Stream Enterprise
Denmark — Stephen A. Adams, Furnituremakers/W.H. James Co.
North Vassalboro — York Spiral Stair
Owl's Head — Custom House Foundry
Phippsburg Center — Colonial Weavers
Portland — Jotul U.S.A., Inc.
Portland — Phoenix Studio, Inc.
Rockland — Imagineering, Inc.
Rockport — Lea, James — Cabinetmaker
Round Pond — Pemaquid Floorcloths
Saco — Saco Manufacturing & Woodworking
Sanford — Leeke, John — Woodworker
Thorndike — Bryant Stove Works
Union — Curry, Gerald — Cabinetmaker
Washington — Brick Stove Works
Westbrook — Sturbridge Yankee Workshop
Westbrook — Thompson & Anderson, Inc.
Yarmouth — Heritage Lanterns

MARYLAND

Aberdeen — Chemical Products Co., Inc.
Baltimore — Avalon Forge
Baltimore — Gasworks
Baltimore — Bill Goschen
Baltimore — History Store
Baltimore — Inner Harbor Lumber & Hardware
Baltimore — G. Krug & Son, Inc.
Baltimore — Mosca, Matthew
Baltimore — Munsell Color
Baltimore — Readybuilt Products, Co.
Baltimore — Rockland Industries, Inc. Thermal Products Division
Baltimore — Swiss Foundry, Inc.
Baltimore — George J. Thaler, Inc.
Baltimore — Walbrook Mill & Lumber Co., Inc.
Beltsville — Meredith Stained Glass Studio, Inc.
Boonsboro — Custom Sign Co.
Boyds — Fine Woodworking Co.
Boyds — Finish Feeder Company
Brentwood — Giannetti Studios, Inc.
Brownsville — Woods American Co.
Chestertown — Innerwick Industries
Frederick — Skyline Engineers of Maryland, Inc.
Frederick — Victorian Construction Co.
Frederick — Vintage Lumber Co.
Frederick — Wilson, H. Weber, Antiquarian
Germantown — Country Casual
Hagerstown — Blaine Window Hardware, Inc.
Hagerstown — Duvinage Corporation
Hagerstown — Preservation Associates, Inc.
Havre de Grace — Splendor in Brass
Havre de Grace — Wollon, James Thomas, Jr., A.I.A.
Kensington — Fireplace Mantel Shop, Inc.
Kensington — H & M Stair Builders, Inc.
Libertytown — Harne Plastering Co.
Perry Hall — Windy Hill Forge
Potomac — Claxton Walker & Associates
Princess Anne — Ainsworth Development Corp.
Rockville — Beta Timber Restoration System/Dell Corp.
Rockville — Light Ideas
Severna Park — Floorcloths Incorporated
Silver Spring — Acme Stove Company
Silver Spring — Rollerwall, Inc.
Upper Falls — Paxton Hardware Ltd.
Williamsport — Cushwa Brick Co.

MASSACHUSETTS

Adams — Old Stone Mill Factory Outlet
Amherst — Architectural Portraits
Arlington — R.W. Shattuck Co.
Ayer — The Reggio Register Co.
Barnstable — Cape Cod Bullseye Glass Co.
Barnstable — Seaport Village Associates
Belchertown — Home Fabric Mills, Inc.
Blandford — Chester Granite Co., Inc.
Bolton — Bow House, Inc.
Boston — Adams and Swett
Boston — Besco Plumbing & Heating Sales
Boston — J.R. Burrows & Co.
Boston — Cabot Stains
Boston — Charles St. Supply Co.
Boston — Davenport, Peters
Boston — Faneuil Furniture Hardware
Boston — Glass Arts—The Condon Studios
Boston — Johnson Paint Co.
Boston — Kenmore Industries
Boston — Koeppel/Freedman Studios
Boston — Period Furniture Hardware Co., Inc.
Boston — Perry, Edward K., Co.
Boston — Wayne Towle Inc.
Boylston — Josiah R. Coppersmythe
Braintree — Yankee Pride
Brewster — House Carpenters
Bridgewater — Lemee's Fireplace Equipment
Brighton — ARJ Associates
Cambridge — Anderson-McQuaid Co., Inc.
Cambridge — Bow & Arrow Stove Co.
Cambridge — California Products Corp.
Cambridge — City Lights
Cambridge — Lyn Hovey Studio, Inc.
Cambridge — J.M. Roe
Cambridge — Kruger Kruger Albenberg
Chelmsford — Elcanco Inc.
Chelmsford — A. Greenhalgh & Sons, Inc.
Cohasset — Cohasset Colonials
Colrain — Donald C. Stetson, Sr., Enterprises
Concord — Dee, John W. — Distinctive Painting & Decorating
Concord — Shaker Workshops
Danvers — Washburne, E.G. & Co., Inc.
Dorchester — Olde Bostonian Architectural Antiques
E. Orleans — Guardian National House Inspection and Warranty Corp.
East Weymouth — Allied Resin Corp.
Easthampton — Peter Franklin, Cabinetmaker
Fall River — Building Materials Inc.
Fitchburg — Minuteman International Co., Ltd.
Florence — Curran, Patrick J.
Georgetown — Old Time Stove Co.
Great Barrington — Jenifer House
Greenfield — Contemporary Copper/Matthew Richardson
Groton — Country Bed Shop
Groton — Craftsman Lumber Co.
Groton — Old-Fashioned Milk Paint Co.

Hanover — Hand-Stenciled Interiors
Hanover — Whittemore-Durgin Glass Co.
Hanson — Churchill Forest Products, Inc.
Harvard — Antique Color Supply, Inc.
Harvard — Cornucopia, Inc. At the Appleworks
Harwich — K-D Wood Products
Hatfield — 21st Century Antiques
Hingham — Country Loft
Holyoke — Van Cort Instruments, Inc.
Hudson — Round Oak Metal Specialties
Leverett — Architectural Components
Lexington — Antiquaria
Lowell — Dovetail, Inc.
Ludlow — Vintage Tub & Sink Restoration Service
Lunenburg — Crafts Manufacturing Co.
Lynn — Floortown
Mansfield — Acorn Manufacturing Co., Inc.
Marblehead — Stone Ledge Co.
Marion — The Mechanick's Workbench
Marlborough — The Butcher Polish Co.
Martha's Vineyard — Travis Tuck, Inc. — Metal Sculptor
Medford — LaRoche Stained Glass
Medford — Pompei Stained Glass, Inc.
Millers Falls — The Renovator's Supply
N. Andover — Museum of American Textile History — Cons. Center
New Bedford — AFC/A Nortek Company
New Bedford — Preservation Partnership
Newburyport — Anderson Reconstruction
Newburyport — Atlantic Stairworks
Newton — National Home Inspection Service of New England, Inc.
North Dartmouth — Cape Cod Cupola Co., Inc.
North Easton — Newstamp Lighting Co.
North Marshfield — Simms & Thayer Cabinetmakers
Northampton — Amherst Woodworking & Supply
Northboro — REM Associates
Norwell — Weathervanes
Orleans — Olde Village Smithery
Pelham — LaPointe, Chip, Cabinetmaker
Pembroke — Braid-Aid
Reading — Roger A. Reed Inc.
Rockport — London Venturers Company
Rowley — Cassidy Bros. Forge, Inc.
Sandwich — South Bound Millworks
Scituate — Faire Harbour Ltd.
Scituate — Peg Hall Studios
Shrewsbury — Stencil School
Shutesbury — Sky Lodge Farm
So. Weymouth — Bench Manufacturing Co.
Somerset — Homestead Supply
South Ashburnham — Shingle Mill, Inc.
South Boston — Coran — Sholes Industries
Southbridge — Hyde Manufacturing Company
Stockbridge — Country Curtains
Sturbridge — The Coppersmith—
Sturbridge — Old Sturbridge Village
Sturbridge — Seraph, The
Sudbury — Orr, J.F., & Sons
Turners Falls — Mill River Hammerworks
Tyngsboro — Seitz, Robert/Fine Woodworking
W. Barnstable — Barnstable Stove Shop
W. Yarmouth — Mason & Sullivan Co.
Wakefield — Thomas Strahan Co.
Wales — Country Comfort Stove Works
Walpole — Walpole Woodworkers
Waltham — S.P.N.E.A. Conservation Center
Wareham — Tremont Nail Company
Wayland — Yankee Craftsman
West Hanover — Wes-Pine Wood Windows
Westborough — Maynard House Antiques
Westport — Millham, Newton — Blacksmith
Whately — Bernard Restoration
Williamsburg — Williamsburg Blacksmiths, Inc.
Winchester — Hill, Allen Charles AIA
Woburn — A.J.P. Coppersmith
Woburn — Woodcraft Supply Corp.
Worcester — Lighting by Hammerworks

MICHIGAN

Ann Arbor — Conservatory, The
Ann Arbor — Old House Gardens
Battle Creek — David G. Mulder
Battle Creek — O'Sullivan Co.
Bay City — Gougeon Brothers, Inc.
Belding — Country Roads, Inc.
Blissfield — Riverbend Timber Framing, Inc.
Byron Center — American Chimney Lining Systems, Inc.
East Lansing — Elbinger Laboratories, Inc.
Flint — Tomblinson Harburn Assoc. Arch., Eng., & Planners, Inc.
Frankfort — Barap Specialties
Grand Rapids — Klise Manufacturing Company
Grand Rapids — Past Patterns
Grand Rapids — Village Antique Lighting Co.
Grass Lake — Architectural Salvage Co.
Kingsford — Smith, F.E., Castings, Inc.
Lake Orion — Renaissance Marketing, Inc.
Lansing — Delphi Stained Glass
Mt. Clemens — Artistic Woodworking, Inc.
Niles — Elsie's Exquisiques
Niles — Kool-O-Matic Corp.
Niles — QRB Industries
Oxford — Williams Art Glass Studio, Inc./Sunset Antiques, Inc.
Plymouth — Michael Camp
Southgate — Classic Accents
St. Johns — J & M Custom Cabinet and Millwork
Stanton — Turnbull's Lumber Company
Stevensville — Sawdust Room
Whitmore Lake — Vintage Valances
Ypsilanti — American General Products
Ypsilanti — Materials Unlimited
Zeeland — Howard Miller Clock Co.

MINNESOTA

Bayport — Andersen Corporation
Burnsville — London Country, Ltd.
Cold Spring — Cold Spring Granite Co.
Dundas — Heirloom Enterprises
Maple Grove — D.L. Anderson & Associates, Inc.
Minneapolis — Anderson Pulley Seal Co.
Minneapolis — CW Design, Inc.
Minneapolis — Copper Sales, Inc.
Minneapolis — Pete Holly
Minneapolis — Madhatter Press
Minneapolis — Marvin Windows
Minneapolis — Nelson-Johnson Wood Products, Inc.
Minneapolis — Renovation Concepts, Inc.
Minneapolis — Ring, J. Stained Glass, Inc.
Minneapolis — Thermocrete Chimney Systems, Inc.
Minneapolis — Victorian Lighting Co.
Minneapolis — Victorian Reproductions Enterprises, Inc.
Minneapolis — Visible Glass
New Brighton — Country Shutters
Richfield — Leo, Brian
Rochester — John Kruesel's General Merchandise
St. Paul — Industrial Fabrics Association International
St. Paul — Old House - New House Restorations
St. Paul — Plannja AB International Attn* Richard B. Velleu
St. Paul — Window Grille Specialists
White Bear Lake — Original Woodworks

MISSISSIPPI

Columbus — Backstrom Stained Glass et al
Jackson — Historical Replications, Inc.
Philadelphia — DeWeese Woodworking

MISSOURI

Bridgeton — The Hope Co., Inc.
Chesterfield — Gainsborough Hardware Industry
Cuba — T.J. Bottom Industries, Inc.
Hannibal — River City Restorations
Houston — Pioneer Service Shake Company
Kansas City — Hiles Plating Co., Inc.
Kansas City — Olde Theatre Architectural Salvage Co.
Nevada — Norman, W.F., Corporation
Olathe — The Broadway Collection
St. Charles — The Brass Tree
St. Charles — WSI Distributors/ The Brass Tree
St. Charles — Worthington Trading Company
St. Louis — Art Directions
St. Louis — CIPCO Corp.
St. Louis — Custom Bar Designs
St. Louis — Fellenz Hardware & Antiques
St. Louis — Frenzel Specialty Moulding Co.
St. Louis — St. Louis Antique Lighting Co., Inc.
St. Louis — Julius Seidel & Co.
St. Louis — Shaw Marble Works Mid-America Marble & Granite

NEBRASKA

Broken Bow — Wikco Industries
Lincoln — Hydrozo Coatings Co.

NEVADA

Las Vegas — Tiffany Design Lamps
Sparks — Conservation Materials, Ltd.

NEW HAMPSHIRE

Alexandria — Alexandria Wood Joinery
Alstead — Glass & Aluminum Construction Services, Inc.
Alstead — Howard, David, Inc.
Canaan — Kraatz/Russell Glass
Center Ossipee — Beech River Mill Co.
Claremont — Timberpeg, East Inc.
Dublin — Good & Co. — Floorclothmakers
Durham — Piscatagua Architectural Woodwork, Co.
E. Conway — Country Cupolas
E. Conway — Town & Country Decorative and Functional Metalcraft
Enfield — Dana Robes Wood Craftsmen, Inc.
Epsom — Copper House
Exeter — Interior Decorations
Farmington — Lake Country Brass
Freedom — Iron Craft, Inc.
Gonic — Kane-Gonic Brick Corp.
Hampton — Carpenter Assoc., Inc.
Keene — J.A. Wright & Co.
Kene — Insul Shutter

Manchester — Chimney Relining International, Inc.
Meredith — Hood, R. and Co.
Merrimack — Staples, H. F. & Co., Inc.
Milford — Old Smithy Shop
Milford — Williams & Hussey Machine Co.
New Boston — Yankee Shutter & Sash Co.
North Conway — Yield House, Inc.
Northwood — Buddy Fife's Wood Products
Peterborough — Brookstone Company
Portsmouth — Nancy Borden Period Textile Replicas
Portsmouth — Dodge, Adams, and Roy, Ltd.

Portsmouth — Salamandra Glass
Stoddard — Carlisle Restoration Lumber
Tilton — Country Braid House
Tilton — Wiggins Brothers
W. Lebanon — Woodstock Soapstone Co., Inc.

NEW JERSEY

Basking Ridge — Castle Burlingame
Bayonne — Muralo Company
Boonton — Accents
Bound Brook — AMC Housemaster Home Inspection Svc.
Bound Brook — HouseMaster of America
Butler — Woodcare Corporation Metal & Wood Restoration Prod.
Cinnaminson — The Brass Finial
Clinton — Homestead Chimney
Closter — Pasvalco
Collingswood — Bradford Consultants
E. Rutherford — Allied Roofers Supply
E. Rutherford — Hoboken Wood Floors Corp.

Edison — E & B Marine Supply
Englewood — Authentic Lighting
Englewood — Englewood Hardware Co.
Englewood — Impex Assoc. Ltd., Inc.
Farmingdale — Hautwork, Inc.
Frenchtown — Antique Hardware Store
Harrison — Osborne, C. S. & Co.
Jersey City — Alfred Manufacturing Corp.
Jersey City — Grinling Architectural Period Mouldings
Jersey City — W.J. Hampton Plastering
Jersey City — Max Lumber Co.
Keyport — H & R Johnson, Inc.
Keyport — United Stairs Corp.
Lake Hiawatha — Golden Leaf Timber
Lambertville — Niece Lumber Co.
Lebanon — Polytek Development Corp.
Leonia — Renaissance Decorative Hardware Co.
Linden — Shanker Steel Ceiling Co., Inc.
Mahway — Commodity Traders Consulting Group
Maywood — D. Blumchen & Co., Inc.
Montclair — Eklund, Jon Restorations
Montclair — Montclair Restoration Craftsmen
Montclair — Omnia Industries, Inc.
Montclair — Poor Richard's Service Co.
Montvale — Benjamin Moore Co.
Montvale — Minwax Company, Inc.
Morristown — Firebird, Inc.
Morristown — Terra Designs, Inc.
Neptune — Studio Design, Inc., t/a Rainbow Art Glass
New Brunswick — Donald Stryker Restorations
Newark — Cook & Dunn Paint Corp.
Newton — Historic Preservation Alternatives, Inc.
Northvale — Bendix Mouldings, Inc.
Northvale — Hydrotherm
Palmyra — Littlewood & Maue Museum Quality Restorations
Paramus — Bedlam Brass
Paramus — Bergen Bluestone Co., Inc.
Paterson — Center Lumber Company
Pennington — Lenape Products, Inc.
Pennington — Master Wood Carver
Plainfield — Victorian Accents
Princeton — Arkitektura
Princeton — Design-Cast Corporation
Rancocas Woods — Spencer, William, Inc.
Red Bank — Half Moon Antiques c/o Monmouth Antique Shoppes
Sergeantsville — Sunflower Glass Studio
Ship Bottom — Heritage Flags
Somerville — Alte, Jeff Roofing, Inc.
Somerville — Stair-Pak Products Co., Inc.
South Amboy — Wood Masters, Inc.
Stockton — Country Accents
Trenton — Bailey Architectural Millwork
Union — Red Devil, Inc.
Union — Sellrite Millwork Corp.
Union City — The Finishing Company
Westmont — W.N. Russell and Co.

NEW MEXICO

Albuquerque — Woodworker's Supply of New Mexico
Santa Fe — Spanish Pueblo Doors

NEW YORK

Albany — BOATECH
Albany — Empire Stove & Furnace Co., Inc.
Albany — L'esperance Tile Works
Amityville — Murphy Door Bed Co., Inc.
Amsterdam — Behlen, H. & Bros.
Ballston Spa — Bradford Derustit Corp.
Ballston Spa — Maple Hill Woodworking
Bayside — Priscilla Ceramic Tiles
Brewster — Historic Housefitters Company
Briarcliff Manor — Bronze et al
Bronx — Englander Millwork Corp.
Bronx — Mittermeir, Frank Inc.
Bronx — J.H. Monteath Co. — Arch. Rep.
Brooklyn — AA-Abbingdon Affiliates, Inc.
Brooklyn — Ace Wire Brush Co.
Brooklyn — Air-Flo Window Contracting Corp.
Brooklyn — American Wood Column Corporation
Brooklyn — Antares Forge and Metalworks
Brooklyn — Art Glass Studio Inc.
Brooklyn — A Second Wind for Harmoniums
Brooklyn — Bare Wood Inc.
Brooklyn — Brooklyn Stone Renovating
Brooklyn — Brooklyn Tile Supply
Brooklyn — Brownstone Graphics
Brooklyn — Burt Millwork Corp
Brooklyn — Chandelier Warehouse
Brooklyn — City Barn Antiques
Brooklyn — Craftsmen Decorators
Brooklyn — Dimension Lumber Co.
Brooklyn — Eifel Furniture Stripping
Brooklyn — Gaslight Time Antiques
Brooklyn — Goldenrod Ironworks
Brooklyn — Richard N. Hayton and Associates, Inc.
Brooklyn — International Fireproof Door Co., Inc. (IFD)
Brooklyn — Kaplan/Price Assoc. — Architects
Brooklyn — Lamp Doctor
Brooklyn — Lance Woodcraft Products
Brooklyn — David Linker Ltd.
Brooklyn — Mead Associates Woodworking, Inc.
Brooklyn — Nast, Vivian Glass and Design
Brooklyn — Ohman, C.A.
Brooklyn — Old House Inspection Co., Inc.
Brooklyn — Old-House Journal
Brooklyn — Ornamental Design Studios
Brooklyn — Michael Pangia
Brooklyn — Puccio
Brooklyn — Puma Iron Works
Brooklyn — Renaissance Woodcarving, Inc.
Brooklyn — Restorations, Inc.
Brooklyn — Mario Rodriguez Cabinetmaker
Brooklyn — Ross, Douglas — Woodworker
Brooklyn — Roy Electric Co., Inc.
Brooklyn — Security Home Inspection, Inc.
Brooklyn — Shadovitz Bros. Distributors, Inc.
Brooklyn — Star Metal
Brooklyn — TAG Architect & Laurence Carpentry
Buffalo — Glass Roots
Buffalo — Pierce & Stevens Chemical Corp.
Buffalo — Pratt & Lambert
Buffalo — Restoration Works, Inc.
Cambridge — Cambridge Textiles
Cambridge — Paul J. Foster
Chappaqua — Decorative Hardware Studio
Cherry Valley — Rocco V. De Angelo
Chester — NET
Chester — New England Tool Co., Ltd.
Cobleskill — Wigen Restorations
ColdSpring on Hudson — Stencilsmith
Cooperstown — Architectural Stairbuilding and Handrailing
Cooperstown — Restoration Treasures
Corona — George Studios
Deansboro — Old Lamplighter Shop
Deansboro — Schwartz's Forge & Metalworks, Inc.
Dewitt — Christmas Treasures
Douglaston — Manor Art Glass Studio
E. Northport — Armor Products
East Nassau — Eastfield Village
Eastchester — Lieberman, Howard, P.E.
Farmingdale — National Guild of Professional Paperhangers, Inc.
Farmingdale — Old World Moulding & Finishing Co., Inc.
Florida — Vulpiani
Flushing — Dusty Splinters Enterprises
Freeport — Sentry Electric Corp.
Garden City Park — S & W Framing Supplies, Inc.
Garnerville — Chromatic Paint Corp.
Garrison on Hudson — Watercolors, Inc.
Glenwood — International Building Components
Granville — Evergreen Slate Co.
Granville — O'Brien Bros. Slate Co., Inc.
Great Neck — Finishing School
Great Neck — Glass Artisan, Inc.
Greenlawn — Stevens, John R., Associates
Hauppauge — Elmont Manufacturing Co., Inc.
High Falls — Wood Classics, Inc.
Huntington — The Ceiling Fan Place
Huntington Station — Fichet Lock Co.
Indian Lake — Backwoods Furnishings
Jamaica — Merit Moulding, Ltd.
Jeffersonville — H. Pfanstiel Hardware Co.
Kingston — Hurley Patentee Lighting
Lake Placid — Adirondack Store & Gallery
Larchmont — Decoration Day
Liverpool — Shaker Carpenter Shop
Long Island City — Bergamo Fabrics, Inc.
Long Island City — Decor International Wallcovering, Inc.
Long Island City — Gould-Mesereau Co., Inc.
Long Island City — Maxwell Lumber
Long Island City — Mazza Frame and Furniture Co., Inc.

Long Island City — Silk Surplus Inc.
Macedon — Wood Finishing Supply Co., Inc.
Mamaroneck — Colonial Maid Curtains
Maspeth — Allstrip
Maspeth — Eastern Safety Equipment Co., Inc.
Mattituck — Russell Restoration of Suffolk
Mecklenburg — Philip M. White & Associates
Middle Granville — Hilltop Slate Co.
Monsey — Traditional Line Ltd.
Mount Vernon — Accurate Metal Weather Strip Co., Inc.
Mount Vernon — Rohlf's Stained & Leaded Glass Studio
Mount Vernon — Walsh Screen Products
New York — Acme Exterminating Co.
New York — Danny Alessandro/Edwin Jackson
New York — American Glass Light Co.
New York — Amsterdam Corporation
New York — Architectural Paneling, Inc.
New York — Architectural Preservation Consultants
New York — Architectural Sculpture Ltd.
New York — Bendheim, S.A. Co., Inc.
New York — Joan Bogart
New York — Brunschwig & Fils, Inc.
New York — Castle Roofing Co., Inc.
New York — City Knickerbocker, Inc.
New York — Clarence House Imports, Ltd.
New York — Country Floors, Inc.
New York — Couristan, Inc.
New York — Cowtan & Tout, Inc. D&D Building
New York — Daniel Mack Rustic Furnishings
New York — Elon, Inc. A & D Building
New York — Evergreene Painting Studios, Inc.
New York — Fifty / 50 Gallery
New York — Garrett Wade Company
New York — Gazebo
New York — Gem Monogram & Cut Glass Corp.
New York — Halina Gemes
New York — Jamie Gibbs & Associates
New York — Gold Leaf & Metallic Powders, Inc.
New York — Great American Salvage
New York — Greenland Studio, Inc., The
New York — Theodore Grunewald, Urban Archaeologist
New York — Guerin, P.E. Inc.
New York — Harrison, Elaine
New York — Hess Repairs
New York — Hinson & Co.
New York — Hunrath , Wm. Co., Inc.
New York — Import Specialists, Inc.
New York — Isabel Brass Furniture
New York — Jackson, Wm. H. Co.
New York — Janovic/Plaza, Inc.
New York — Karl Mann Associates
New York — Katrina, Inc.
New York — Katzenbach and Warren, Inc.
New York — Lee Jofa
New York — Lost City Arts
New York — Louis W. Bowen Fine Wallcoverings
New York — Lovelia Enterprises, Inc.
New York — Lynn Goodpasture
New York — Marble Technics Ltd.
New York — Mattia, Louis
New York — Metropolis
New York — Metropolitan Lighting Fixture Co., Inc.
New York — Museum of the City of New York
New York — Navedo Woodcraft, Inc.
New York — New York Carved Arts Co.
New York — New York Marble Works, Inc.
New York — H.C. Oswald Supply Co., Inc.
New York — Patterson, Flynn & Martin, Inc.
New York — Peiser Floors
New York — Frank Pellitteri Inc.
New York — Pietra Dura, Inc.
New York — Putnam Rolling Ladder Co., Inc.
New York — Quaker Lace Co.
New York — Raintree Designs, Inc.
New York — Rambusch
New York — Retinning & Copper Repair
New York — Rinder's New York Flooring
New York — Timothy G. Riordan
New York — Roth Painting, Co., Inc.
New York — Scalamandre, Inc.
New York — F. Schumacher & Co.
New York — Bess Schuyler Ceramics
New York — Sculpture Associates, Ltd.
New York — Sculpture House
New York — Sepp Leaf Products
New York — Skyline Windows
New York — Standard Trimming Co.
New York — Stark Carpet Corp.
New York — William H. Straus
New York — Stroheim & Romann
New York — TALAS
New York — Tromploy Inc.
New York — United Ceramic Tile Arch. Design Div.
New York — Urban Archaeology
New York — Welles Fireplace Company
New York — The Wicker Garden
New York — Wolchonok, M. and Son, Inc.
New York — Wolf Paints And Wallpapers
New York — Zetlin, Lorenz — Muralist
North Java — Select Interior Door, Ltd.
North Salem — Crispin Treadway Floral Products
Nyack — Brasslight, Inc.
Nyack — Brown, T. Robins
Pawling — Ship 'n Out
Pearl River — Full Circle Glass Company
Plainview — Cassen, Henry Inc.
Plainview — U.S. General Supply Corp.
Port Chester — Zina Studios, Inc.
Port Jervis — Gillinder Brothers, Inc.
Port Washington — Bertin Tile Studio
Poughkeepsie — David Woods Plaster Restoration
Poughkeepsie — Sedgwick Lifts, Inc.
Rego Park — Dentro Plumbing Specialties
Rochester — Pike Stained Glass Studios, Inc.
Rockville Centre — Antiquity Reprints
Rockville Centre — Gaudio Custom Furniture
Rye — Supradur Mfg. Corp.
Sag Harbor — Copper Specialties, Ltd.
Salt Point — Michael's Fine Colonial Products
Saugerties — Mangione Plaster
Schuyerville — Adirondak Chair Co.
Slate Hill — Victorian Lightcrafters, Ltd.
Smithtown — Perma Ceram Enterprises, Inc.
Staten Island — Antique Brass Works
Suffern — The Old-House Gold Leaf People
Syracuse — Pelnik Wrecking Co., Inc.
Tappan — Edward Fitzgerald Associates
Tarrytown — Restoration Workshop Nat Trust For Historic Preservation
Tillson — Sound Beginnings
Valhalla — Ashwood Restoration
Valhalla — Westal Contracting
Walton — National SUPAFLU Systems, Inc.
Warwick — Golden Age Glassworks
Warwick — Historical Miniatures Associates
Warwick — Warwick Refinishers
West Danby — Shelley Signs
West Nyack — Fisher Skylights, Inc.
West Valley — Native American Hardwood Ltd.
Westfield — Crystal Mountain Prisms
Whitehall — H.B. Slate
Wyandanch — Cosmetic Restoration, Inc.
Yonkers — Peerless Rattan and Reed

NORTH CAROLINA

Asheville — Biltmore, Campbell, Smith Restorations, Inc.
Asheville — W.P. Hickman Co.
Boone — Virginia Goodwin
Candler — Kayne & Son Custom Forged Hardware
Charlotte — Porcelain Restoration and Brass
Concord — Ephraim Marsh
Durham — Sutherland Welles Ltd.
Eden — King's Chandelier Co.
Fayetteville — Fasco Industries, Inc.
Fuquay-Varina — Dan Wilson & Company, Inc.
Greensboro — Greensboro Art Foundry & Machine Co.
Greenville — Carriage Trade Antiques & Art Gallery
Hickory — Colonial Canopies
Hickory — Furniture Traditions, Inc.
High Point — Premier Communications
Lemon Springs — Chicago Old Telephone Co.
Lexington — Mid-State Tile Company
Pleasant Garden — Boren Clay Products Company
Salisbury — Old Carolina Brick Co.
Tarboro — The Joinery Co.
Troutman — Carter Canopies
Wilmington — Dorothy's Ruffled Originals

OHIO

Akron — Acorn Oriental Rug Services
Bath — Western Reserve Antique Furniture Kit
Canton — Union Metal Corp.
Cincinnati — Allied Window, Inc.
Cincinnati — Anderson Building Restoration
Cincinnati — Bona Decorative Hardware
Cincinnati — Huseman, Richard J. Co.
Cincinnati — Meierjohan — Wengler, Inc.
Cincinnati — Old World Restorations, Inc.
Cleveland — Antique Trunk Supply Co.
Cleveland — Astrup Company
Cleveland — Ferguson's Cut Glass Works
Cleveland — Fischer & Jirouch Co.
Cleveland — Glidden Coatings & Resins
Cleveland — Hexter, S. M. Company
Cleveland — Leichtung, Inc.
Cleveland Heights — Newe Daisterre Glas
Columbus — Flue Works
Columbus — Image Group, The
Columbus — Plaskolite, Inc.
Columbus — Rumford Fireplaces
Dayton — Beecham Home Improvement Products, Inc.
Dayton — DAP, Inc.
Dayton — The Farm Forge
Dover — The Hisrich Manufacturing Co.
East Sparta — United States Ceramic Tile Company
Eaton — Brubaker Metalcrafts
Elyria — LampLight Industries, Inc.
Fairfield — Pease Industries
Franklin — Architectural Reclamation, Inc.
Glenmont — Briar Hill Stone Co.
Hudson — The Flood Company
Kidron — Lehman Hardware & Appliances
Mansfield — Marshall Imports
Middletown — You Name It, Inc.
Milford — Lt. Moses Willard, Inc.

Millersburg — Rastetter Woolen Mill
New Lexington — Ludowici-Celadon Co.
Newark — Holophane Division
South Euclid — Lampco
Tallmadge — Walker's
Terrace Park — Wiebold Art Conservation Lab.
Uhrichsville — Superior Clay Corporation
Washington C.H. — Willis Lumber Co.
Washington C.H. — Wood Designs
Wellington — Century House Antiques
Worthington — John Morgan Baker, Framer
Xenia — Xenia Foundry & Machine Co. Specialty Castings Dept.

OKLAHOMA

Carter — Elk Valley Woodworking Company
Oklahoma City — Architectural Antiques
Oklahoma City — The Fan Man
Tulsa — Amenities

OREGON

Boring — Architectural Reproductions, Inc.
Eugene — Old'N Ornate
Eugene — Oregon Wooden Screen Door Co.
Eugene — Restech Industries
Eugene — States Industries
Gates — Silver Tree Farms
Portland — 1874 House
Portland — A-Ball Plumbing Supply
Portland — Cline Glass Company
Portland — Hippo Hardware & Trading Co.
Portland — Lignomat USA
Portland — Ostrom & Co., Inc.
Portland — Portland Willamette, Division Thomas Industries
Portland — Rejuvenation House Parts Co.
Portland — Restoration A Specialty
Portland — R. Wagner Co. Painted Finishes
Portland — Wood Moulding & Millwork Producers Association
Portland — Yestershades

PENNSYLVANIA

Adamstown — Pratt's House of Wicker
Allentown — Allentown Paint Mfg. Co., Inc.
Allentown — Lehigh Portland Cement Co.
Ardmore — Felber Studios, Inc.
Ardmore — Finnaren & Haley, Inc.
Bethlehem — Campbell, Marion
Bethlehem — Starbuck Goldner
Broomall — The Iron Shop
Bucks County — Heritage Rugs
Carlisle — Cumberland Woodcraft Co., Inc.
Centre Hall — Victorian Lighting Works, Inc.
Delta — Aged Woods
Derry — 18th Century Hardware Co.
Douglassville — Merritt's Antiques, Inc.
Doylestown — Moravian Pottery & Tile Works
Drums — Drums Sash & Door Co., Inc.
Easton — Archive
Elizabethville — Restorations Unlimited, Inc.
Emmaus — Gerlachs of Lecha
Emmaus — Homespun Weavers
Erie — Lake Shore Markers
Erie — Sadowski, Robert
Exton — Architectural Shapes, Inc.
Exton — Ball and Ball
Ft. Littleton — JGR Enterprises, Inc.
Gibsonia — Masonry Specialty Co.
Green Lane — Flaharty, David — Sculptor
Harrisburg — Tomas Spiers & Associates
Hustontown — Potomac Products
Kittanning — Continental Clay Company
Lancaster — Forbo N.A., Inc.
Lancaster — Saltbox
Landenberg — Lauria, Tony
Lansdale — American Olean Tile Company
Latrobe — Homecraft Veneer
Leesport — Loose, Thomas — Blacksmith/ Whitesmith
Lima — Restoration Fraternity
Lionville — British-American Marketing Services, Ltd.
Lititz — Sylvan Brandt
Lumberville — Delaware Quarries, Inc.
Media — Permagrain Products, Inc.
Milford — Architectural Iron Company
Neffsville — The Tin Bin
New Castle — Amish Country Collection
New Hope — Purcell, Francis J., II
Newtown — The Antique Restoration Co.
Norristown — Pennsylvania Dutch Quilts
Norristown — The Stulb Co.
North Wales — Colonial Restoration Products
Paoli — The Country Iron Foundry
Pen Argyl — Bangor Cork Co., Inc.
Pen Argyl — Structural Slate Company
Penndel — Langhorne Carpet Co.
Perkasie — Perkasie Industries Corp.
Philadelphia — Aetna Stove Company
Philadelphia — American Architectural Art Company
Philadelphia — Angelo Brothers Co.
Philadelphia — Architectural Antiques Exchange
Philadelphia — Bangkok Industries, Inc.
Philadelphia — Beirs, John — Glass Studio
Philadelphia — Bioclean
Philadelphia — Clio Group, Inc.
Philadelphia — Colonial Wallpaper Company
Philadelphia — Dalton Pavilions Inc.
Philadelphia — Ed's Antiques, Inc.
Philadelphia — Gargoyles, Ltd.
Philadelphia — Germantown Restoration Supplies
Philadelphia — Harvey M. Stern & Co./ Antique Lighting
Philadelphia — Holm, Alvin AIA Architect
Philadelphia — David M. LaPenta, Inc.
Philadelphia — Lester H. Berry & Company
Philadelphia — Luigi Crystal
Philadelphia — Neri, C./Antiques
Philadelphia — Pennsylvania Firebacks, Inc.
Philadelphia — Rosenau, Marion, Sculptor
Philadelphia — Samuel B. Sadtler, Importers
Philadelphia — Stortz, John & Son, Inc.
Philadelphia — Willet Stained Glass Studio, Inc.
Phoenixville — Vixen Hill Manufacturing
Pittsburgh — Eljer Plumbingware
Pittsburgh — Heckler Bros.
Pittsburgh — Koppers Co.
Pittsburgh — Pittsburgh Corning
Pittsburgh — A.F. Schwerd Manufacturing Co.
Pittsburgh — Terra Cotta Productions, Inc.
Pittsburgh — Victorian Interior Restoration
Reading — Baldwin Hardware Mfg. Corp.
Red Lion — Family Heir-Loom Weavers
Robesonia — Rich Craft Custom Kitchens, Inc.
Scranton — United Gilsonite Laboratories
Sharon Hill — Quaker City Manufacturing Co.
Shoemakersville — Glen — Gery Corporation
Slatington — Penn Big Bed Slate Co., Inc.
Somerset — Somerset Door & Column Co.
Spring City — Spring City Electrical Mfg. Co
Stewartstown — Fypon, Inc.
Stroudsburg — Oliver, Bradley C.
Susquehanna — Conklin's Authentic Antique Barnwood
Trevose — Jones & Erwin, Inc.
Troy — John Hinds & Co.
Villanova — Alpha Technical Systems, Inc.
Warminster — Morgan Bockius Studios, Inc.
West Chester — Arden Forge
West Chester — Campbell-Lamps
West Chester — Dilworthtown Country Store
West Chester — Monroe Coldren and Sons
Yardley — Dutch Products & Supply Co.
Yardley — Oberndorfer & Assoc.
York — Lewis, John N.
York — Tioga Mill Outlet

RHODE ISLAND

Ashaway — Stephen P. Mack
N. Scituate — Keddee Woodworkers
Newport — Cosmopolitan International
Newport — Rue de France
Newport — St. Luke's Studio
Rumford — Heirloom Rugs
W. Kingston — Chapin Townsend

SOUTH CAROLINA

Charleston — Historic Charleston Reproductions
Clemson — Fibertech Corp.
Florence — Driwood Moulding Company
Liberty — Flexi-Wall Systems
Orangeburg — Tiresias, Inc.
Pawleys Island — Pawley's Island Hammock Co.
Timmonsville — W. S. Lockhart Designs

SOUTH DAKOTA

Sioux Falls — Ahrens Chimney Technique Inc.
Sioux Falls — C & H Roofing

TENNESSEE

Bellevue — Walker Mercantile Company
Clarksville — Clarksville Foundry & Machine Works
Crossville — Cumberland General Store
Johnson City — Harris — Tarkett, Inc.
Knoxville — Oak Crest Mfg., Inc.
Maryville — Douglas Cooperative, Inc. Window Blanket Division
McMinnville — B & P Lamp Supply Co., Inc.
Memphis — American Heritage Shutters
Memphis — Archicast
Memphis — Chapman Chemical Co.
Memphis — Hunter Fan Company
Memphis — Memphis Hardwood Flooring Co.
Memphis — Tennessee Fabricating Co.
Nashville — Davis Cabinet Co.
Nashville — Tennessee Tub Inc. & Tubliner Co.
Pulaski — Wrisley, Robert T.

TEXAS

Austin — Antique Street Lamps, Inc.
Austin — Westlake Architectural Antiques
Austin — Whit Hanks at Treaty Oak
Bandera — Gerry Sharp Trunk Doctor
Dallas — Bruce Hardwood Floors
Dallas — Classic Architectural Specialties
Dallas — Clay Suppliers
Fort Worth — Bombay Company, The
Fort Worth — Custom Castings
Fredericksburg — Vintage Wood Works
Garland — C.U. Restoration Supplies
Hillsboro — Anthony Wood Products
Houston — Berridge Manufacturing Co.
Houston — Chelsea Decorative Metal Co.
Houston — The Emporium, Inc.
Houston — Great Expectations Quilts, Inc.
Houston — Mel-Nor Marketing
Houston — Metal Building Components, Inc.
Irving — American Lamp Parts, Inc.
Jefferson — Ceilings, Walls & More, Inc.
Pasadena — Larry W. Garnett & Associates, Inc.
Salado — J Hall Building Restoration
San Antonio — Allen and Allen Company
San Elizario — Silver Dollar Trading Co.
Spearman — Charolette Ford Trunks
Spring — Otto Wendt & Co.
Wharton — Heritage Home Designers

UTAH

Kearns — House of Vermillion
Salt Lake City — Alfa Lite
Salt Lake City — Stanfield Shutter Co.

VERMONT

Arlington — Chem-Clean Furniture Restoration Center
Barre — Smith, Whitcomb & Cook Co.
Barre — Trow & Holden Co.
Bennington — Whitten Enterprises, Inc.
Brattleboro — Appropriate Technology Corporation
Bristol — Folkheart Rag Rugs
Bristol — Plain and Fancy
Burlington — Conant Custom Brass
Burlington — Great Northern Construction, Inc.
Cambridge — Cambridge Smithy
Center Rutland — Gawet Marble & Granite
Chester — Weird Wood
Cuttingsville — Vermont Industries, Inc.
Essex — The Aged Ram
Fair Haven — Hubbardton Forge Corp.
Fair Haven — Vermont Structural Slate Co.
Granville — Granville Mfg. Co., Inc.
Moretown — Anderson, Townsend
Moretown — Congdon, Johns/Cabinetmaker
Perkinsville — Vermont Soapstone Co.
Poultney — Iron Horse Antiques, Inc.
Proctor — Carl Schilling Stoneworks
Proctor — Vermont Marble Co.
Putney — Ian Eddy — Blacksmith
Putney — Natural Fiber Fabrics
Putney — Neuman Studios
Randolph — Vermont Castings, Inc.
Rutland — Rutland Products
South Woodstock — The Barn People, Inc.
Springfield — Lavoie, John F.
Sudbury — Mr. Slate - Smid Incorporated
Tunbridge — Elephant Hill Iron Works
W. Rupert — Authentic Designs Inc.
Waterbury — Vermont Iron
West Brattleboro — Broad-Axe Beam Co.
West Pawlet — Rising & Nelson Slate Co.
Westminster — Woodstone Co.
Weston — Vermont Country Store
Wolcott — Smithy, The

VIRGINIA

Abingdon — Old Abingdon Weavers
Alexandria — The Smoot Lumber Company
Berryville — Custom Millwork, Inc.
Bremo Bluff — Cain-Powers, Inc. Architectural Art Glass
Charlottesville — Traditional American Concepts
Clarksville — The Old Wagon Factory
Fairfax — Masterworks, Inc.
Fairfax — Robson Worldwide Graining
Floyd — DHM Cabinets
Fredericksburg — Joy Construction, Inc.
Hamilton — Green Enterprises
Hampton — Electric Glass Co.
Harrisonburg — Historic Windows
Harrisonburg — Shenandoah Manufacturing Co.
Lovingston — Frederick Wilbur, Carver
Manassas — Wood and Stone, Inc.
Martinsville — Poxywood, Inc.
Mechanicsville — Durvin, Tom & Sons
Middleburg — Artifacts, Inc.
Montebello — Blue Ridge Shingle Co.
Norfolk — Herman, Frederick, R.A., Architect
Petersburg — Lisa — Victoria Brass Beds
Richmond — Biggs Company
Richmond — Buckingham-Virginia Slate Corporation
Richmond — Dugwood Turners
Richmond — Hudson Venetian Blind Service, Inc.
Richmond — Moore, E.T., Jr. Co.
Riverton — Riverton Corporation
Ruckersville — Mountain Lumber Company, Inc.
Springfield — PRG
Springfield — Preservation Resource Group
Stephens City — "Rustic Barn" Wood Products
Suffolk — National Screen Co.
Washington — Washington House Reproductions
Waynesboro — Virginia Metalcrafters
Williamsburg — Colonial Williamsburg Foundation
Williamsburg — Hobt, Murrel Dee, Architect

WASHINGTON

Bellevue — Olympic Stain
Bellingham — Creative Openings
Bellingham — Price & Visser Millwork
Edmonds — Sheppard Millwork, Inc.
Everett — Washington Stove Works
Friday Harbor — Homestead Design
Mount Vernon — Weavers Unlimited
Port Townsend — Maizefield Mantels
Puyallup — Gazebo and Porchworks
Redmond — Hearth Shield
Redmond — Perma-Chink Systems, Inc.
Redmond — Sammamish Woodworks
Seattle — Daly's Wood Finishing Products
Seattle — Kaymar Wood Products, Inc.
Seattle — Millwork Supply Company
Seattle — Victorian Homes
Seattle — Vintage Storm Window Co.
Spokane — Zappone Manufacturing
Winlock — Shakertown Corporation

WEST VIRGINIA

Follansbee — Follansbee Steel
Milton — Blenko Glass Co., Inc.
Shirley — Good Impressions Rubber Stamps
Williamstown — Fenton Art Glass Company

WISCONSIN

Algoma — Monarch Range Co. Consumer Prod. Div.
Boscobel — Art Safe Inc.
Burlington — Antique Building Restoration
Colfax — Bjorndal Woodworks
Delafield — Sun Designs
Fond du Lac — Combination Door Co.
Franklin — American Building Restoration
Galesville — Phoneco
Hurley — Gibbons Sash and Door
Janesville — Woodmart
Little Chute — Vande Hey Raleigh
Madison — Arlan Kay & Associates
Manitowoc — J. Goddard & Sons, Ltd.
Milwaukee — A-B Manufacturing Co.
Milwaukee — Brass Light Gallery
Milwaukee — Experi-Metals
Milwaukee — La Lune Collection
Milwaukee — Millen Roofing Co.
Milwaukee — Schlitz Studios
Milwaukee — Victorian Collectibles Ltd.
Oak Creek — Diedrich Chemicals-Restoration Technologies, Inc.
Rice Lake — Tomahawk Foundry
Sister Bay — McGivern, Barbara — Artist
Turtle Lake — Turtle Lake Telephone Co.
Waukesha — Crawford's Old House Store
Waukesha — Dovetail Woodworking
Wausau — Nanik
Wauwatosa — Building Conservation
Wisconsin Rapids — Preway, Inc.

CANADA

Cambridge, Ontario — A & M Wood Specialty, Inc.
Elmira, Ontario — Elmira Stove Works
Lunenberg, Nova Scot — Lunenburg Foundry & Engineering, Ltd.
Ottawa, ONT — Architectural Antique Warehouse, The
Ottawa, OT — Cohen's Architectural Heritage
Ottawa, Ontario — Association for Preservation Technology
Ottawa, Ontario — Lee Valley Tools, Ltd.
Toronto — Turn-of-the-Century Lighting
Toronto, ON — Carson, Dunlop & Associates, Ltd.
Toronto, ON — Steptoe and Wife Antiques Ltd.
Toronto, ON — Steptoe's Old House Store, Ltd.
Toronto, OT — Balmer Architectural Art Limited
Vancouver, BC — Nye's Foundry Ltd.

ENGLAND

London, England — Colefax and Fowler
Stoke-on-Trent, Engl — H & R Johnson Tile Ltd./ Highgate Tile Works
Horsmonden, Kent — Chilstone Garden Ornament
Maldon, Essex — Verine Products & Co.

The Product & Service Directory

The Product & Service Directory tells who makes the product you're looking for. Products and services are logically grouped in broad categories, but there are thousands of products listed. To find exactly the right page, consult the yellow-pages General Index (page **14**) first.

To help you locate companies in your area, a two-letter state abbreviation follows each company name. The full address, telephone number, and a brief description of each company can be found in the alphabetical Company Directory, beginning on page **151** – the grey-edged section.

Bold-face type anywhere in the book denotes a company who has placed a display ad. The Advertisers' Index starts on page 22.

Exterior Building Materials & Supplies

Building Maintenance Materials & Supplies

Abatron, Inc. (IL)

BASEMENT WATERPROOFING PAINTS & COMPOUNDS

Abatron, Inc. (IL)
Benjamin Moore Co. (NJ)
Rutland Products (VT)
USG Corporation (IL)
United Gilsonite Laboratories (PA)

BIRD & PEST CONTROL PRODUCTS

Acme Exterminating Co. (NY)
D.L. Anderson & Associates, Inc. (MN)
Bird — X, Inc. (IL)
Commodity Traders Consulting Group (NJ)
Nixalite of America (IL)

MASONRY CLEANERS & PAINT STRIPPERS

Alpha Technical Systems, Inc. (PA)
American Building Restoration (WI)
Diedrich Chemicals-Restoration Technologies, Inc. (WI)
Hydrochemical Techniques, Inc. (CT)
ProSoCo, Inc. (KS)
Restech Industries (OR)
Vermont Marble Co. (VT)

MASONRY SEALERS

Abatron, Inc. (IL)
Alpha Technical Systems, Inc. (PA)
American Building Restoration (WI)
Building Materials Inc. (MA)
Diedrich Chemicals-Restoration Technologies, Inc. (WI)
Hydrozo Coatings Co. (NE)
ProSoCo, Inc. (KS)
Red Devil, Inc. (NJ)
Rutland Products (VT)
USG Corporation (IL)
United Gilsonite Laboratories (PA)
Wood and Stone, Inc. (VA)

PAINTS, EXTERIOR—MASONRY

Alpha Technical Systems, Inc. (PA)
Cabot Stains (MA)
USG Corporation (IL)

PRESERVATIVES, WOOD

American Building Restoration (WI)
D.L. Anderson & Associates, Inc. (MN)
Beecham Home Improvement Products, Inc. (OH)
Cabot Stains (MA)
Chapman Chemical Co. (TN)
DAP, Inc. (OH)
Darworth Co. (CT)
E & B Marine Supply (NJ)
The Flood Company (OH)
Hydrozo Coatings Co. (NE)
Koppers Co. (PA)
Minwax Company, Inc. (NJ)
Olympic Stain (WA)
United Gilsonite Laboratories (PA)

STAINS, EXTERIOR

Alpha Technical Systems, Inc. (PA)
D.L. Anderson & Associates, Inc. (MN)
Barnard Chemical Co. (CA)
Cabot Stains (MA)
DAP, Inc. (OH)
Darworth Co. (CT)
The Flood Company (OH)
Olympic Stain (WA)
Restech Industries (OR)

VARNISHES, EXTERIOR

E & B Marine Supply (NJ)
Epifanes/Coastal Trade, Inc. (FL)
The Flood Company (OH)
United Gilsonite Laboratories (PA)

Masonry & Supplies

BRICKS, HANDMADE

(1) New
(2) Salvage

Boren Clay Products Company (NC) *1*
Colonial Brick Co., Inc. (IL) *2*
Colonial Restoration Products (PA) *1*
Continental Clay Company (PA) *1*
Cushwa Brick Co. (MD) *1*
Glen — Gery Corporation (PA) *1*
Haines Masonry Specialties (IN) *2*
The Joinery Co. (NC) *2*
Kane-Gonic Brick Corp. (NH) *1*
Moore, E.T., Jr. Co. (VA) *2*
Old Carolina Brick Co. (NC) *1*
Ramase (CT) *2*
Sky Lodge Farm (MA) *2*

See Company Directory for Addresses & Phone Numbers on page 151

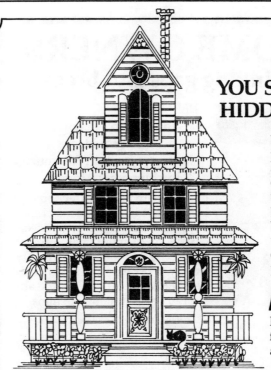

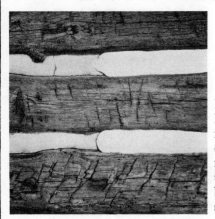

SPECIALTY MORTARS & CEMENTS

Abatron, Inc. (IL)
Colonial Restoration Products (PA)
Lehigh Portland Cement Co. (PA)
Perma-Chink Systems, Inc. (WA)
Riverton Corporation (VA)
Wood and Stone, Inc. (VA)

STONE

(1) Bluestone
(2) Granite
(3) Limestone
(4) Marble
(5) Sandstone (Brownstone)
(6) Slate
(7) Other Stone

Bergen Bluestone Co., Inc. (NJ) *1,2,6*
Briar Hill Stone Co. (OH) *5*
Building Materials Inc. (MA) *1*
Carl Schilling Stoneworks (VT) *1,2,3,4,5,6*
Cathedral Stone Company, Inc. (DC) *3,5*
Chester Granite Co., Inc. (MA) *2*
Cold Spring Granite Co. (MN) *2*
Delaware Quarries, Inc. (PA) *2,3,5,6*
Evergreen Slate Co. (NY) *6*
Gawet Marble & Granite (VT) *2,4*
H.B. Slate (NY) *6*
Haines Masonry Specialties (IN) *3,6*
Hilltop Slate Co. (NY) *6*
Stephen P. Mack (RI) *2,5,7*
Marble Technics Ltd. (NY) *2*
Mr. Slate - Smid Incorporated (VT) *6*
Old World Restorations, Inc. (OH) *4,7*
Pasvalco (NJ) *5*
Penn Big Bed Slate Co., Inc. (PA) *6*
Pietra Dura, Inc. (NY) *1,2,3,4,5,6*
Rising & Nelson Slate Co. (VT) *6*
W.N. Russell and Co. (NJ) *1,2,3,4,5,6*
Sculpture Associates, Ltd. (NY) *4*
Shaw Marble Works Mid-America Marble & Granite (MO) *4*
Structural Slate Company (PA) *6*
Supradur Mfg. Corp. (NY) *6*
Vermont Marble Co. (VT) *4*
Vermont Soapstone Co. (VT) *7*
Vermont Structural Slate Co. (VT) *5,6*
Wood and Stone, Inc. (VA) *1,2,3,4,5,6*

STUCCO PATCHING MATERIALS

Abatron, Inc. (IL)
Building Materials Inc. (MA)
USG Corporation (IL)

Roofing Materials & Supplies

METAL ROOFING

(1) Galvanized and Zinc
(2) Terne
(3) Other

Berridge Manufacturing Co. (TX) *1,2,3*
Conklin Metal Industries (GA) *1,2,3*
Copper Specialties, Ltd. (NY) *3*
Follansbee Steel (WV) *2,3*
W.P. Hickman Co. (NC) *1*
Metal Building Components, Inc. (TX)
Metal Sales Manufacturing Corp. (KY)
Norman, W.F., Corporation (MO) *1,3*
Plannja AB International Attn* Richard B. Velleu (MN) *1*
Round Oak Metal Specialties (MA) *3*
Zappone Manufacturing (WA) *3*

For more information on METAL ROOFING see the W. P. Hickman ad in the Color Section.

See Company Directory for Addresses & Phone Numbers on page 151

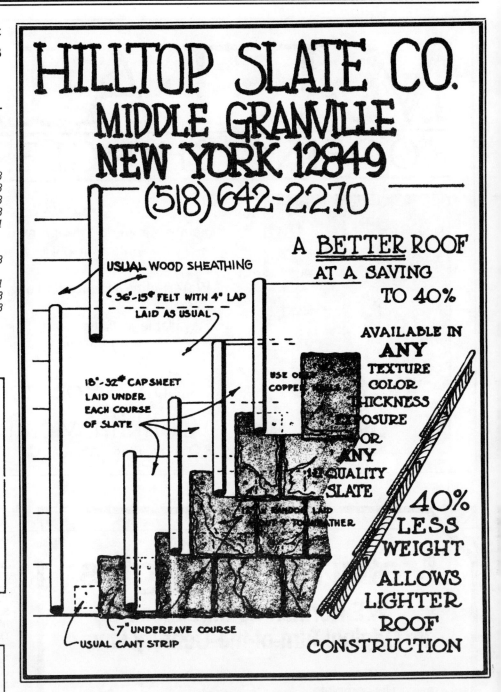

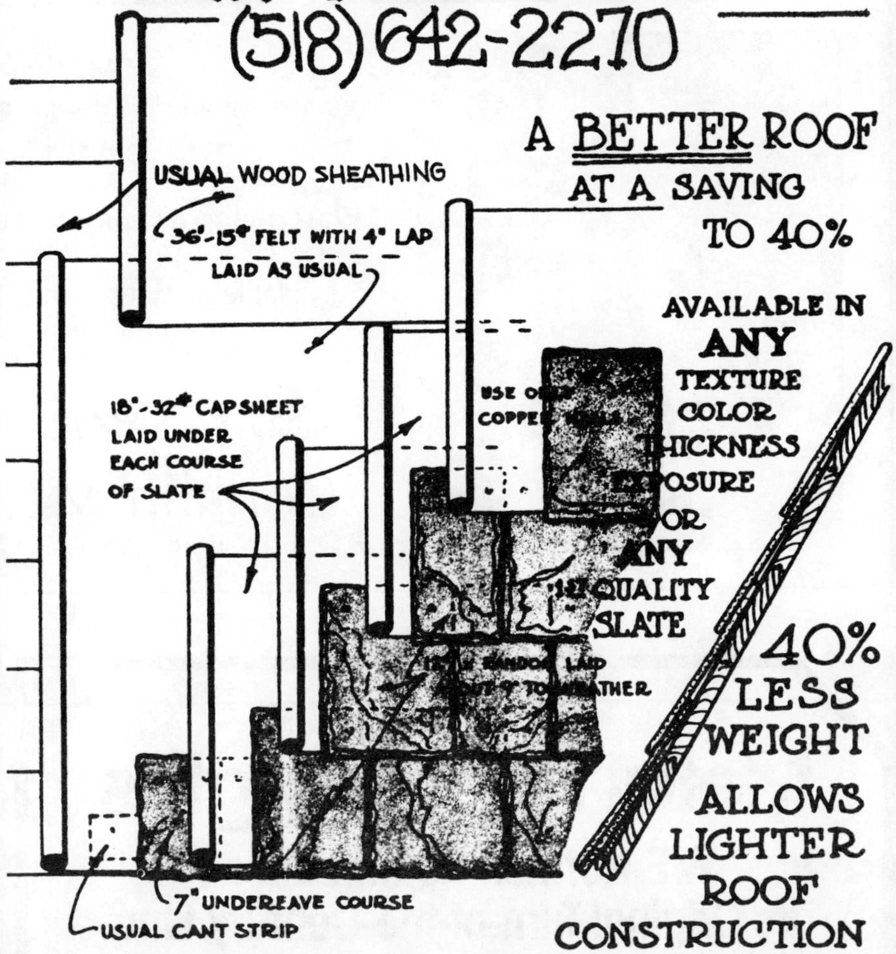

SHAKES & SHINGLES, WOOD

(1) Handsplit
(2) Machine Cut

Amherst Woodworking & Supply (MA) ... *2*
Blue Ridge Shingle Co. (VA) ... *2*
Brewster's Lumberyard (CT) ... *2*
Cedar Valley Shingle Systems (CA) ... *1,2*
Stephen P. Mack (RI) ... *2*
Mad River Wood Works (CA) ... *2*
Oak Crest Mfg., Inc. (TN) ... *1*
The Renovator's Supply (MA)
Julius Seidel & Co. (MO) ... *2*
Shakertown Corporation (WA) ... *2*
Shingle Mill, Inc. (MA) ... *2*
Silver Tree Farms (OR) ... *1,2*
South Coast Shingle Co. (CA) ... *2*
Southington Specialty Wood Co. (CT) ... *2*

SHINGLES, METAL

Berridge Manufacturing Co. (TX)
Conklin Metal Industries (GA)
Norman, W.F., Corporation (MO)
Zappone Manufacturing (WA)

SNOW GUARDS

Antique Hardware Store (NJ)
Millen Roofing Co. (WI)
Round Oak Metal Specialties (MA)
Windy Hill Forge (MD)

TILES, ASBESTOS — CEMENT

Supradur Mfg. Corp. (NY)

TILES, SLATE

Buckingham-Virginia Slate Corporation (VA)
Carl Schilling Stoneworks (VT)
Colonial Restoration Products (PA)
Evergreen Slate Co. (NY)
H.B. Slate (NY)
Hilltop Slate Co. (NY)
Ludowici-Celadon Co. (OH)
Midland Engineering Company (IN)
Millen Roofing Co. (WI)
Mr. Slate - Smid Incorporated (VT)
O'Brien Bros. Slate Co., Inc. (NY)
Penn Big Bed Slate Co., Inc. (PA)
Rising & Nelson Slate Co. (VT)
Structural Slate Company (PA)
Vermont Structural Slate Co. (VT)

TILES, TERRA COTTA & CERAMIC

Allied Roofers Supply (NJ)
Amsterdam Corporation (NY)
Ludowici-Celadon Co. (OH)
Midland Engineering Company (IN)
Paul J. Foster (NY)
Starbuck Goldner (PA)
Supradur Mfg. Corp. (NY)
Terra Cotta Productions, Inc. (PA)

TILES, CONCRETE

Vande Hey Raleigh (WI)

OTHER ROOFING

Raleigh, Inc. (IL)

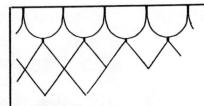

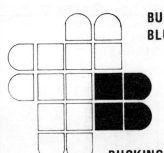

See Company Directory for Addresses & Phone Numbers on page 151

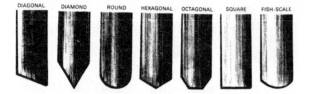

Siding Materials & Supplies

CLAPBOARDS, BEADED EDGE AND OTHER OLD STYLES

(1) Salvage
(2) New

Amherst Woodworking & Supply (MA) ... *2*
Carlisle Restoration Lumber (NH) *2*
Colonial Restoration Products (PA) *2*
Craftsman Lumber Co. (MA) *2*
Custom Millwork, Inc. (VA) *2*
Granville Mfg. Co., Inc. (VT) *2*
Homestead Supply (MA) *2*
Stephen P. Mack (RI) *2*
Remodelers & Renovators (ID) *2*
Silverton Victorian Millworks (CO) *2*
Sky Lodge Farm (MA) *2*
Walker's (OH) *1*
Woods American Co. (MD) *2*

SHINGLES, SPECIAL ARCHITECTURAL SHAPES

Cedar Valley Shingle Systems (CA)
Colonial Restoration Products (PA)
Kingsway Victorian Restoration Materials (CO)
Mad River Wood Works (CA)
Julius Seidel & Co. (MO)
Shakertown Corporation (WA)
Shingle Mill, Inc. (MA)
Silver Tree Farms (OR)
South Coast Shingle Co. (CA)
Vintage Wood Works (TX)

SHAKES & SHINGLES, CUSTOM-CUT

Homestead Supply (MA)
Mad River Wood Works (CA)
Oak Crest Mfg., Inc. (TN)
Pioneer Service Shake Company (MO)
Shakertown Corporation (WA)
Shingle Mill, Inc. (MA)
Silver Tree Farms (OR)
Vintage Wood Works (TX)

SIDING, BARN

(1) Salvage
(2) New

Architectural Antiques (OK)
The Barn People, Inc. (VT) *1*
Belcher, Robert W. (GA) *1*
Conklin's Authentic Antique Barnwood (PA) *1*
Stephen P. Mack (RI) *1,2*
Mad River Wood Works (CA) *2*
Old Home Building & Restoration (CT) ... *1*
Vintage Lumber Co. (MD) *2*
Walker's (OH)

OTHER SIDING

Granville Mfg. Co., Inc. (VT)
Supradur Mfg. Corp. (NY)

Other Exterior Restoration & Maintenance Materials

Bioclean (PA)
Maxwell Lumber (NY)

SALVAGE BUILDING MATERIALS (BOARDS, BEAMS, POSTS, ETC.)

Architectural Accents (GA)
Architectural Preservation Trust (CT)
The Barn People, Inc. (VT)
Belcher, Robert W. (GA)
Cleveland Wrecking Co. (IL)
Conklin's Authentic Antique Barnwood (PA)
Custom Millwork, Inc. (VA)
Florida Victorian Architectural Antiques (FL)
Stephen P. Mack (RI)
Moore, E.T., Jr. Co. (VA)
Old Home Building & Restoration (CT)
Pelnik Wrecking Co., Inc. (NY)
Ramase (CT)
Sky Lodge Farm (MA)
Vintage Lumber Co. (MD)
Walker's (OH)
Woods American Co. (MD)

Exterior Ornament & Architectural Details

ARCHITECTURAL MILLWORK

(1) Stock Items
(2) Custom Fabrication

Abaroot Mfg., Co. (CA) ... *2*
Allen and Allen Company (TX) ... *1*
Amherst Woodworking & Supply (MA) ... *2*
Anderson-McQuaid Co., Inc. (MA) ... *2*
Anthony Wood Products (TX) ... *1,2*
Architectural Components (MA) ... *2*
Architectural Woodworking (CT) ... *2*
Art Directions (MO) ... *2*
Ashwood Restoration (NY) ... *2*
Bailey Architectural Millwork (NJ) ... *2*
Bartleys Mill (CA) ... *2*
Bjorndal Woodworks (WI) ... *2*
Breakfast Woodworks Mackall & Dickinson (CT) ... *2*
Burt Millwork Corp (NY) ... *1*
Campbell, Marion (PA) ... *2*
Carpenter Assoc., Inc. (NH) ... *2*
Carpenter and Smith Restorations (IL) ... *2*
Center Lumber Company (NJ) ... *1,2*
Classic Architectural Specialties (TX) ... *1,2*
Crawford's Old House Store (WI) ... *1*
The Crowe Company Ltd. (CA) ... *1,2*
Cumberland Woodcraft Co., Inc. (PA) ... *1*
Custom & Historic Millwork (CO) ... *2*
Custom Millwork, Inc. (VA) ... *2*
Dimension Lumber Co. (NY) ... *2*
Dodge, Adams, and Roy, Ltd. (NH) ... *2*
Dovetail Woodworking (WI) ... *2*
Driwood Moulding Company (SC) ... *2*
The Emporium, Inc. (TX) ... *1*
Fireplace Mantel Shop, Inc. (MD) ... *1,2*
Frenzel Specialty Moulding Co. (MO) ... *2*
Gunther Mills, Inc. (CT) ... *2*
House Carpenters (MA) ... *2*
House of Moulding (CA) ... *1*
J & M Custom Cabinet and Millwork (MI) ... *2*
The Joinery Co. (NC) ... *1*
Kaymar Wood Products, Inc. (WA) ... *2*
Keddee Woodworkers (RI) ... *2*
Kingsway Victorian Restoration Materials (CO) ... *1*
Knudsen, Mark (IA) ... *2*
David J. Lassiter (FL) ... *2*
Leeke, John — Woodworker (ME) ... *2*
Mad River Wood Works (CA) ... *2*
Maple Hill Woodworking (NY) ... *2*
Maurer & Shepherd, Joyners (CT) ... *2*
Max Lumber Co. (NJ) ... *2*
Mendocino Millwork (CA) ... *1,2*
Merit Moulding, Ltd. (NY) ... *2*
Michael's Fine Colonial Products (NY) ... *2*
Millwork Supply Company (WA) ... *1,2*
Mountain Lumber Company, Inc. (VA) ... *2*
Navedo Woodcraft, Inc. (NY) ... *2*
Nelson-Johnson Wood Products, Inc. (MN) ... *2*
New England Woodturners (CT) ... *2*
North Pacific Joinery (CA) ... *2*
Old House - New House Restorations (MN) ... *1,2*
Pagliacco Turning & Milling Architectural Wood Turning (CA) ... *1,2*
Piscatagua Architectural Woodwork, Co. (NH) ... *1,2*
Price & Visser Millwork (WA) ... *1,2,2*
Renovation Concepts, Inc. (MN)
San Francisco Victoriana (CA) ... *1*
Sellrite Millwork Corp. (NJ) ... *1,2*
Sheppard Millwork, Inc. (WA) ... *2*
Silverton Victorian Millworks (CO) ... *2*
Somerset Door & Column Co. (PA) ... *2*
W. P. Stephens Lumber Co. (GA) ... *1,2*
Strobel Millwork (CT) ... *2*
Vintage Wood Works (TX) ... *1,2*
Walbrook Mill & Lumber Co., Inc. (MD) ... *2*
Wood Designs (OH) ... *2*
Woods American Co. (MD) ... *1,2*
Woodstone Co. (VT) ... *1,2*

SCHWERD'S

Quality Wood Columns

the standard of quality since 1860

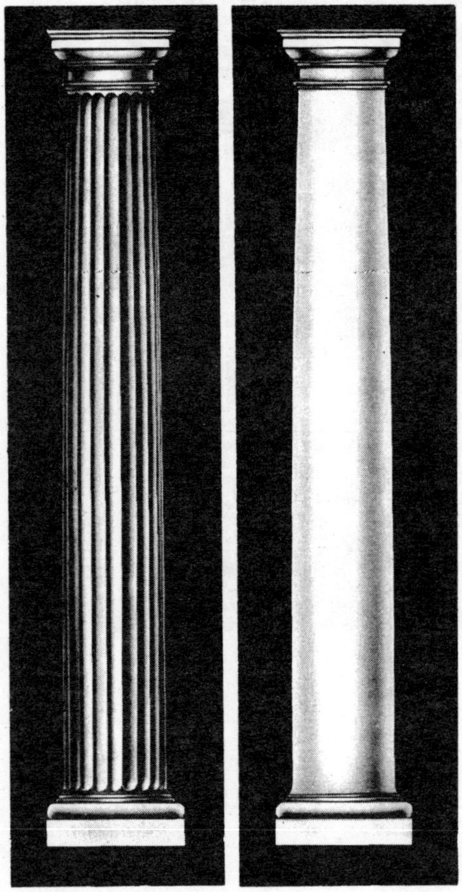

COLUMNS – Schwerd columns are durable.
Our 100+ years of experience in manufacturing wood columns has proven that the durability of a wood column depends upon the strength of the joint and the quality and thickness of the wood. Schwerd column construction was developed to meet each specific requirement. The wood is the highest quality, thoroughly seasoned Northern White Pine. The pride of craftsmanship and skilled techniques acquired by 100 years of specialized experience is applied. The resulting product is a "Schwerd Quality Column" specified by architects with complete confidence. Both standard and detail columns can be furnished from 4 in. to 50 in. in diameter and up to 40 ft. in length with matching pilasters.

If you are one of our old customers during the many years since our beginning in 1860 you know our product, if not, send us your inquiries and orders and join our list of satisfied customers.

SEND FOR OUR FREE CATALOG

Schwerd's complete aluminum bases
are available for 8, 10, 12, 14, 16, 18, 20, 22, 24, 26, 28, and 30 in. dia. columns.

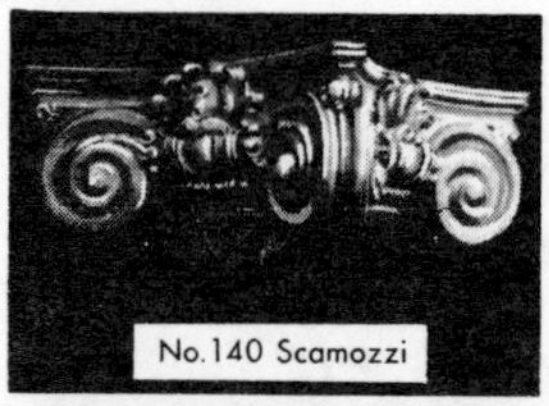
No. 140 Scamozzi

No 141 Roman Ionic

No. 142 Greek Ionic

No 152 Temple of Winds

No. 150 Roman Corinthian

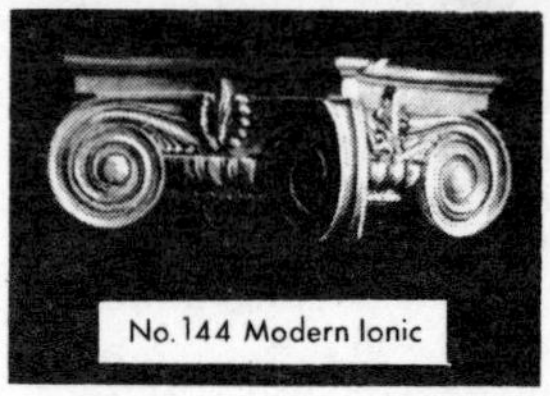
No. 144 Modern Ionic

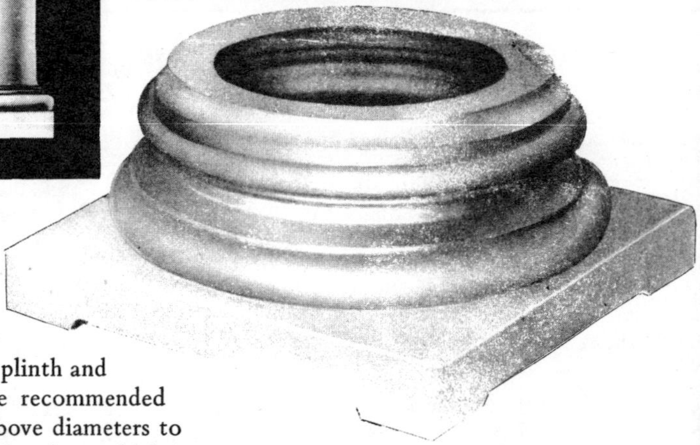

Schwerd's—Aluminum ventilated plinth and aluminum turned member base recommended for all exterior columns in the above diameters to provide a maintenance free, seamless base which is guaranteed against deterioration for a lifetime. Manufactured of 1/4 in. thick metal and a load-bearing capacity of 22,000 lbs.

A. F. SCHWERD MANUFACTURING COMPANY

telephone: 412-766-6322

3215 McClure Avenue Pittsburgh, Pa. 15212

BRACKETS, BUTTRESSES & CORBELS—EXTERIOR

(1) Stone
(2) Stamped Metal
(3) Wood
(4) Composition/Other

American Architectural Art Company (PA) *4*
Anthony Wood Products (TX) *3*
Archicast (TN) *4*
Architectural Reproductions, Inc. (OR) *4*
Art Directions (MO)
ByGone Era Architectural Antiques (GA)
Carl Schilling Stoneworks (VT) *1*
Chester Granite Co., Inc. (MA) *1*
Classic Architectural Specialties (TX) *3*
The Crowe Company Ltd. (CA) *3*
Cumberland Woodcraft Co., Inc. (PA) *3*
Fypon, Inc. (PA) *4*
Koeppel/Freedman Studios (MA) *4*
Mad River Wood Works (CA) *3*
Materials Unlimited (MI)
Mendocino Millwork (CA) *3*
Navedo Woodcraft, Inc. (NY) *3*
Michael Pangia (NY) *1*
Pietra Dura, Inc. (NY) *1*
W.N. Russell and Co. (NJ) *1*
Silverton Victorian Millworks (CO) *3*
United House Wrecking Corp. (CT) *3*
Vintage Wood Works (TX) *3*

BUSYBODIES

Spencer, William, Inc. (NJ)

COLUMNS & CAPITALS—EXTERIOR

(1) Wood
(2) Stone
(3) Plaster
(4) Iron
(5) Fiberglass
(6) Metal
(7) Composition

American Architectural Art Company (PA) *5,7*
American Wood Column Corporation (NY) *1*
Archicast (TN) *2,3,5,7*
Architectural Reproductions, Inc. (OR) *5,6,7*
ByGone Era Architectural Antiques (GA)
Campbellsville Industries (KY) *6*
Carl Schilling Stoneworks (VT) *2*
Chester Granite Co., Inc. (MA) *2*
Chilstone Garden Ornament (UK) *2*
Classic Architectural Specialties (TX) *1*
Custom Castings (TX) *7*
Decorators Supply Corp. (IL) *3*
Design-Cast Corporation (NJ) *2*
Designer Resource (CA) *1,3,6*
Dovetail, Inc. (MA) *3*
Elk Valley Woodworking Company (OK) . *1*
Felber Studios, Inc. (PA) *3*
Goldenrod Ironworks (NY) *6*
Hartmann-Sanders Column Co. (GA) *1,5*
Henderson Black & Greene, Inc. (AL) *1*
International Building Components (NY) *1,5,6*
Koeppel/Freedman Studios (MA) *5*
Lachin, Albert & Assoc., Inc. (LA) *2*
Leeke, John — Woodworker (ME) *1*
Mad River Wood Works (CA) *1*
Moore, E.T., Jr. Co. (VA) *1*
Moultrie Manufacturing Company (GA) . *6*
New England Woodturners (CT) *1*
Pagliacco Turning & Milling Architectural Wood Turning (CA) *1*
Michael Pangia (NY) *2,7*
Pietra Dura, Inc. (NY) *2*
Renovation Concepts, Inc. (MN) *1*
Russell Restoration of Suffolk (NY) *3,5*
W.N. Russell and Co. (NJ) *2*
Saco Manufacturing & Woodworking (ME) *1*
St. Luke's Studio (RI) *2*
San Francisco Victoriana (CA) *3*
A.F. Schwerd Manufacturing Co. (PA) *1,6,7*
Somerset Door & Column Co. (PA) *1*
Tennessee Fabricating Co. (TN) *4*
Verine Products & Co. (UK) *5*
Worthington Group Ltd. (GA) *1*

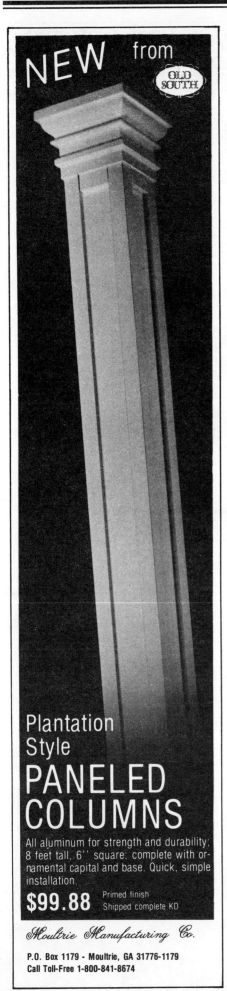

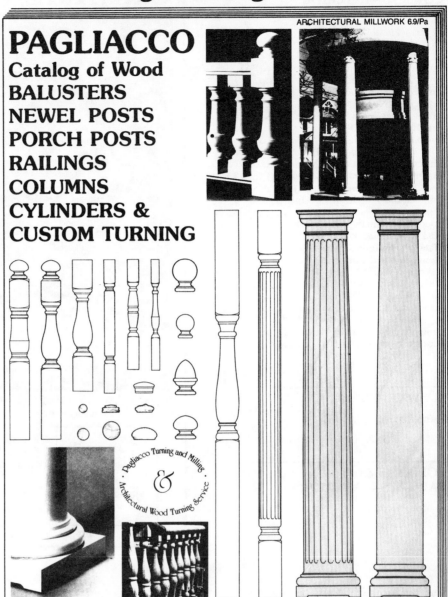

CORNICES—EXTERIOR

(1) Wood
(2) Stamped Metal
(3) Fiberglass, Composition

American Architectural Art Company (PA) ... *3*
Archicast (TN) ... *3*
Campbellsville Industries (KY) ... *2*
Cumberland Woodcraft Co., Inc. (PA) ... *1*
Custom Millwork, Inc. (VA) ... *1*
Design-Cast Corporation (NJ) ... *3*
Designer Resource (CA) ... *1*
Downstate Restorations (IL) ... *2,3*
Fibertech Corp. (SC) ... *3*
Fypon, Inc. (PA) ... *3*
Greensboro Art Foundry & Machine Co. (NC) ... *2*
House of Moulding (CA) ... *1*
Koeppel/Freedman Studios (MA) ... *3*
J.C. Lauber Co. (IN) ... *2*
Mad River Wood Works (CA) ... *1*
Mendocino Millwork (CA) ... *1*
Michael Pangia (NY) ... *1*
Round Oak Metal Specialties (MA) ... *2*
Russell Restoration of Suffolk (NY) ... *3*
Wagner, Albert J., & Son (IL) ... *2*

FINIALS

(1) Composition
(2) Metal
(3) Wood

Archicast (TN) ... *1*
Architectural Reproductions, Inc. (OR) ... *1,2*
Classic Architectural Specialties (TX) ... *1,3*
Crawford's Old House Store (WI) ... *3*
Custom Castings (TX) ... *1*
Goldenrod Ironworks (NY) ... *2*
Greensboro Art Foundry & Machine Co. (NC) ... *2*
Koeppel/Freedman Studios (MA) ... *1*
Lawler Machine & Foundry (AL) ... *2*
Moultrie Manufacturing Company (GA) ... *2*
NET (NY) ... *2,3*
New England Tool Co., Ltd. (NY) ... *2*
Norman, W.F., Corporation (MO) ... *2*
Saco Manufacturing & Woodworking (ME) ... *3*
Vintage Wood Works (TX) ... *3*
Windy Hill Forge (MD) ... *2*
Worthington Group Ltd. (GA) ... *3*

See Company Directory for Addresses & Phone Numbers on page 151

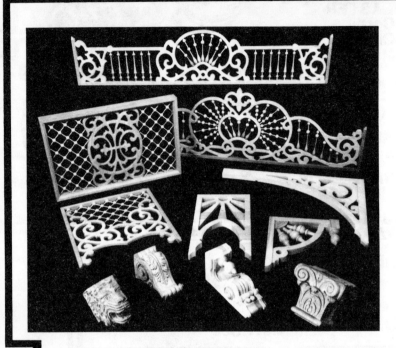

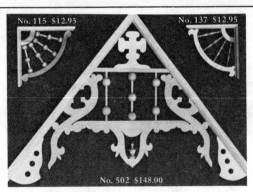

GINGERBREAD TRIM—WOOD

(1) Stock Items
(2) Custom Fabrication

Amherst Woodworking & Supply (MA) ... *2*
Anthony Wood Products (TX) *1,2*
Classic Architectural Specialties (TX) *1*
Cumberland Woodcraft Co., Inc. (PA) *1*
Custom Millwork, Inc. (VA) *2*
The Emporium, Inc. (TX) *1*
Gazebo and Porchworks (WA) *1*
Pete Holly (MN) *2*
David J. Lassiter (FL) *2*
Mad River Wood Works (CA) *2*
Marsh Stream Enterprise (ME) *2*
Mendocino Millwork (CA) *1,2*
North Pacific Joinery (CA) *2*
Rejuvenation House Parts Co. (OR) *1*
Renovation Concepts, Inc. (MN) *1*
Silverton Victorian Millworks (CO) *1,2*
United House Wrecking Corp. (CT) *1*
Vintage Wood Works (TX) *1,2*

GLASS, BLOCK

Pittsburgh Corning (PA)
Salamandra Glass (NH)

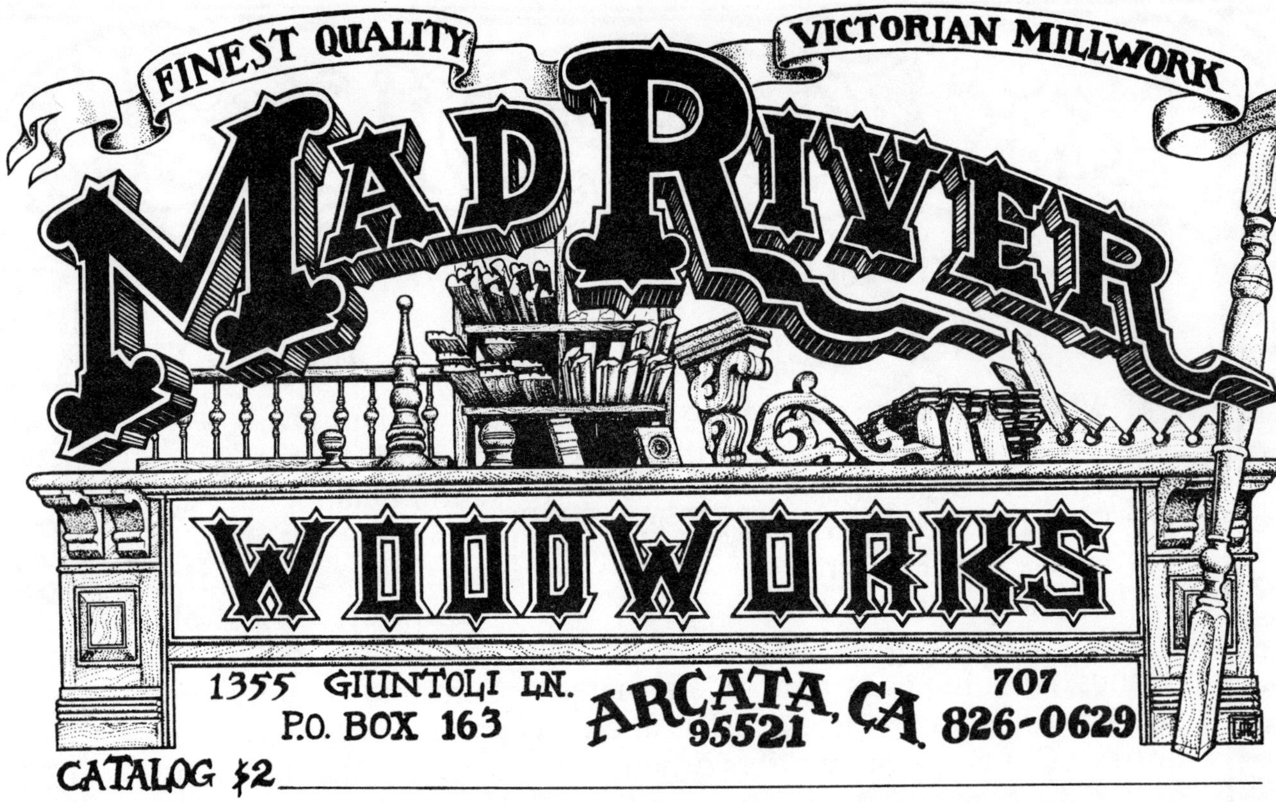
FINEST QUALITY
VICTORIAN MILLWORK
MAD RIVER
WOODWORKS
1355 GIUNTOLI LN.
P.O. BOX 163
ARCATA, CA 95521
707 826-0629
CATALOG $2

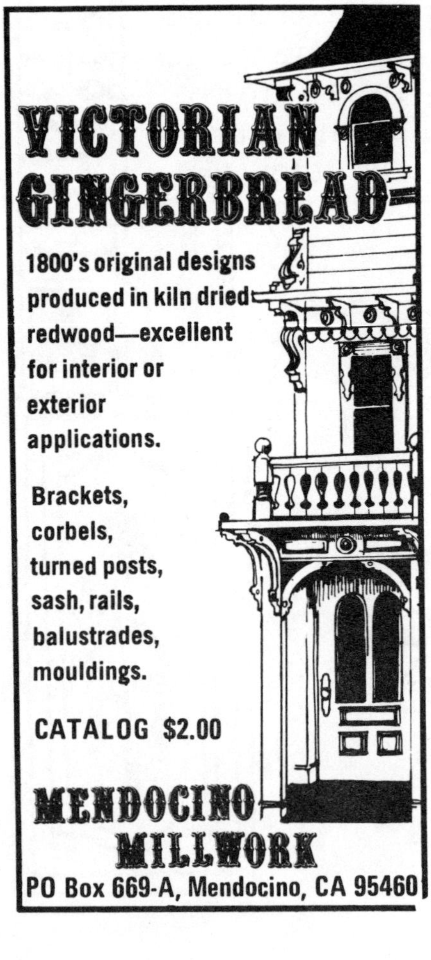
VICTORIAN GINGERBREAD
1800's original designs produced in kiln dried redwood—excellent for interior or exterior applications.
Brackets, corbels, turned posts, sash, rails, balustrades, mouldings.
CATALOG $2.00
MENDOCINO MILLWORK
PO Box 669-A, Mendocino, CA 95460

See Company Directory for Addresses & Phone Numbers on page 151

GUTTERS, LEADERS & LEADER BOXES

(1) Wood
(2) Copper
(3) Lead
(4) Other

Alte, Jeff Roofing, Inc. (NJ) *2*
Conklin Metal Industries (GA) *2,4*
Copper Sales, Inc. (MN) *2,4*
Davenport, Peters (MA) *1*
J.C. Lauber Co. (IN) *4*
Mad River Wood Works (CA) *1*
Round Oak Metal Specialties (MA) *2*
Wagner, Albert J., & Son (IL) *2*

OUR CATALOG... includes 50 pages of custom-length spandrels & shelves, brackets, running trims, fret work, fans, gable decorations, corbels, porch posts, balusters, railings, signs, a gazebo, and much more! Authentic solid wood reproductions for Interior & Exterior. Buy direct and save, with SATISFACTION GUARANTEED!

The Celebrated
VINTAGE WOOD WORKS
Dept. 653, 513 S. Adams • Fredericksburg, TX 78624 • 512/997-9513
AUTHENTIC
Victorian Gingerbread
"You were courteous, professional, prompt and honest. It's been super doing business with you!" — P. Hughes, Ohio
- WE SHIP PROMPTLY NATIONWIDE -
$2.00
Catalog #7
©COPYRIGHT 1986 VINTAGE WOOD WORKS

...YOUR COPY
WILL BE RUSHED
BY 1ST CLASS MAIL

Please Send $2.00 to: Vintage Wood Works, Dept. 653, 513 S. Adams, Fredericksburg, Texas 78624

MOULDINGS, EXTERIOR WOOD

(1) Stock Items
(2) Custom-Made

Allen and Allen Company (TX) *2*
American Wood Column Corporation (NY) *2*
Amherst Woodworking & Supply (MA) ... *2*
Anderson-McQuaid Co., Inc. (MA) *2*
Bailey Architectural Millwork (NJ) *2*
Bendix Mouldings, Inc. (NJ) *1*
Bjorndal Woodworks (WI) *2*
Center Lumber Company (NJ) *2*
Central Kentucky Millwork (KY) *1,2*
Colonial Restoration Products (PA) *2*
Designer Resource (CA) *1,2*
Dimension Lumber Co. (NY) *2*
Driwood Moulding Company (SC) *1*
Drums Sash & Door Co., Inc. (PA) *2*
Fireplace Mantel Shop, Inc. (MD) *1,2*
Homestead Supply (MA) *2*
House of Moulding (CA) *1*
International Building Components (NY) . *2*
Keddee Woodworkers (RI) *2*
Leeke, John — Woodworker (ME) *2*
Mad River Wood Works (CA) *2*
Maple Hill Woodworking (NY) *2*
Maxwell Lumber (NY) *1*
Mendocino Millwork (CA) *1*
Merit Moulding, Ltd. (NY) *2*
Michael's Fine Colonial Products (NY) *2*
Millwork Supply Company (WA) *1,2*
Navedo Woodcraft, Inc. (NY) *2*
North Pacific Joinery (CA) *2*
Old House - New House Restorations (MN) *1,2*
Piscatagua Architectural Woodwork, Co. (NH) *1,2*
Price & Visser Millwork (WA) *2*
Salvage One (IL) *2*
Silverton Victorian Millworks (CO) *1,2*
The Smoot Lumber Company (VA) *1,2*
W. P. Stephens Lumber Co. (GA) *1,2*
Walbrook Mill & Lumber Co., Inc. (MD) .. *2*
Wood Designs (OH) *2*
Wood Masters, Inc. (NJ) *2*
Woods American Co. (MD) *1,2*

MOULDINGS, EXTERIOR

(1) Ceramic
(2) Fiberglass
(3) Plaster
(4) Terra Cotta
(5) Stone
(6) Composition
(7) Other

The 509 Studio (FL) *3,7*
American Architectural Art Company (PA) *2*
Archicast (TN) *2,3,5,6*
Architectural Reproductions, Inc. (OR) *2,3,6*
Architectural Shapes, Inc. (PA) *6*
Carl Schilling Stoneworks (VT) *5*
Custom Castings (TX) *6*
Decorators Supply Corp. (IL) *3*
Design-Cast Corporation (NJ) *5*
Designer Resource (CA) *3*
Felber Studios, Inc. (PA) *2,3*
Fypon, Inc. (PA) *7*
Koeppel/Freedman Studios (MA) *2*
Lachin, Albert & Assoc., Inc. (LA) *5*
Michael Pangia (NY) *6*
Pietra Dura, Inc. (NY) *5*
Russell Restoration of Suffolk (NY) *2,3*
W.N. Russell and Co. (NJ) *5*
Urban Archaeology (NY) *4*

PORCH PARTS

(1) Stock Items
(2) Custom Work

Abaroot Mfg., Co. (CA) *2*
Anthony Wood Products (TX) *1,2*
Classic Architectural Specialties (TX) *1,2*
Cumberland Woodcraft Co., Inc. (PA) .. *1,2*
Custom Millwork, Inc. (VA) *2*
Dugwood Turners (VA) *2*
Gazebo and Porchworks (WA) *1,2*
Great American Salvage (NY) *1*
Henderson Black & Greene, Inc. (AL) *1*
Pete Holly (MN) *2*
Lance Woodcraft Products (NY) *2*
Mad River Wood Works (CA) *2*
Mansion Industries, Inc. (CA) *1*
Mendocino Millwork (CA) *1,2*
Michael's Fine Colonial Products (NY) *2*
New England Woodturners (CT) *2*
North Pacific Joinery (CA) *2*
Pagliacco Turning & Milling Architectural Wood Turning (CA) *1,2*
Michael Pangia (NY) *2*
Price & Visser Millwork (WA) *2*
Remodelers & Renovators (ID) *1*
Renovation Concepts, Inc. (MN) *1*
Saco Manufacturing & Woodworking (ME) *2*
Vintage Wood Works (TX) *1*

See Company Directory for Addresses & Phone Numbers on page 151

SHUTTERS & BLINDS, EXTERIOR WOOD

(1) New (Stock Items)
(2) Custom-Made

American Heritage Shutters (TN) *1,2*
Architectural Components (MA) *2*
Bank Architectural Antiques (LA) *1*
Beech River Mill Co. (NH) *2*
Central Kentucky Millwork (KY) *1,2*
Custom Millwork, Inc. (VA) *2*
Dovetail Woodworking (WI) *2*
The Hisrich Manufacturing Co. (OH) *2*
Iberia Millwork (LA) *2*
International Building Components (NY) . *2*
LaPointe, Chip, Cabinetmaker (MA) *2*
Maurer & Shepherd, Joyners (CT) *2*
Michael's Fine Colonial Products (NY) *2*
Monroe Coldren and Sons (PA) *1,2*
Piscatagua Architectural Woodwork, Co. (NH) *2*
REM Associates (MA) *2*
Restoration Fraternity (PA) *2*
Shuttercraft (CT) *1*
Stanfield Shutter Co. (UT) *2*
Vintage Wood Works (TX) *1,2*
Yankee Shutter & Sash Co. (NH) *2*

EXTERIOR DOORS, REPRODUCTION

(1) Early American
(2) Victorian
(3) Turn-of-Century
(4) Custom-Made
(5) Other

Air-Flo Window Contracting Corp. (NY) .. *4*
Amherst Woodworking & Supply (MA) ... *4*
Architectural Antiques (OK)
Architectural Components (MA) *1,2,2*
Bel-Air Door Co. (CA) *1,2,3,5*
Bjorndal Woodworks (WI) *4*
Central Kentucky Millwork (KY) *1,4*
Classic Architectural Specialties (TX) *2,3*
Colonial Restoration Products (PA) *1*
Custom Millwork, Inc. (VA) *1,2,3,4*
Dodge, Adams, and Roy, Ltd. (NH) *4*
Doors of Distinction (CA) *1,2,3*
Dovetail Woodworking (WI) *2*
Driwood Moulding Company (SC) *4*
Drums Sash & Door Co., Inc. (PA) .. *1,2,3,4*
Early New England Rooms & Exteriors Inc. (CT) *1*
Englander Millwork Corp. (NY) *4*
Gibbons Sash and Door (WI) *3,4*
Keddee Woodworkers (RI) *4*
Kingsway Victorian Restoration Materials (CO) *2*
Kirby Millworks (CO)
Maple Hill Woodworking (NY) *4*
Materials Unlimited (MI) *2,4*
Maurer & Shepherd, Joyners (CT) *4*
Meredith Stained Glass Studio, Inc. (MD) *2*
Millwork Supply Company (WA) *4*
North Pacific Joinery (CA) *4*
Oak Leaves Woodcarving Studio (IA) *4*
Ohmega Salvage (CA) *5*
Old'N Ornate (OR) *2,4*
Piscatagua Architectural Woodwork, Co. (NH) *1,4*
Pompei Stained Glass, Inc. (MA) *2,3*
Price & Visser Millwork (WA) *4*
Renovation Concepts, Inc. (MN) *2,3*
Restoration Fraternity (PA) *4*
Dana Robes Wood Craftsmen, Inc. (NH) . *1*
Salvage One (IL) *4*
Sellrite Millwork Corp. (NJ) *4*
Sheppard Millwork, Inc. (WA) *4*
Spanish Pueblo Doors (NM) *4*
Strobel Millwork (CT) *1,2,3,4*
United House Wrecking Corp. (CT)
Jack Wallis' Doors (KY) *2,4*
Wood Designs (OH) *4*
Woodpecker Products Inc. (CO) *1,4*
Woodstone Co. (VT) *1,2,3,4*
Yankee Shutter & Sash Co. (NH) *1,4*

See Company Directory for Addresses & Phone Numbers on page 151

EXTERIOR DOORS, ANTIQUE (SALVAGE)

Architectural Accents (GA)
Architectural Antique Warehouse, The (CAN)
Architectural Antiques (OK)
Architectural Antiques Exchange (PA)
Architectural Salvage Co. (MI)
Artifacts, Inc. (VA)
Bank Architectural Antiques (LA)
Bare Wood Inc. (NY)
ByGone Era Architectural Antiques (GA)
Canal Co. (DC)
Florida Victorian Architectural Antiques (FL)
Joe Ley Antiques, Inc. (KY)
Materials Unlimited (MI)
Monroe Coldren and Sons (PA)
Off The Wall, Architectural Antiques (CA)
Ohmega Salvage (CA)
Olde Bostonian Architectural Antiques (MA)
Salvage One (IL)
United House Wrecking Corp. (CT)
Walker's (OH)
Westlake Architectural Antiques (TX)

SCREEN DOORS

Classic Architectural Specialties (TX)
Combination Door Co. (WI)
Coppa Woodworking (CA)
Creative Openings (WA)
Doors of Distinction (CA)
JMR Products (CA)
Mad River Wood Works (CA)
Old'N Ornate (OR)
The Old Wagon Factory (VA)
Oregon Wooden Screen Door Co. (OR)
Remodelers & Renovators (ID)
Restoration Fraternity (PA)

ENTRYWAYS & DOOR FRAMING WOODWORK—REPRODUCTION

(1) Early American
(2) Victorian
(3) Stock Items
(4) Salvage
(5) Custom-Made

Architectural Components (MA) *2,5*
Bare Wood Inc. (NY) *1,2,5*
Burt Millwork Corp (NY) *5*
Central Kentucky Millwork (KY) *1,5*
Colonial Restoration Products (PA) *1*
Custom Millwork, Inc. (VA) *1,2,5*
Doors of Distinction (CA) *5*
Drums Sash & Door Co., Inc. (PA) *1,2,5*
Early New England Rooms & Exteriors Inc. (CT) *1*
Fireplace Mantel Shop, Inc. (MD) *1,2*
Fypon, Inc. (PA) *1*
Gibbons Sash and Door (WI) *5*
Glass & Aluminum Construction Services, Inc. (NH) *3*
Great American Salvage (NY) *4*
Henderson Black & Greene, Inc. (AL) ... *1,3*
International Building Components (NY) . *3*
Kenmore Industries (MA) *1,3*
Kingsway Victorian Restoration Materials (CO) *2*
Kirby Millworks (CO) *3*
Mad River Wood Works (CA) *2*
Materials Unlimited (MI) *4*
Maurer & Shepherd, Joyners (CT) *5*
Michael's Fine Colonial Products (NY) *5*
Nostalgia (GA) *4*
Piscatagua Architectural Woodwork, Co. (NH) *1,5*
Ramase (CT) *4*
Restoration Fraternity (PA) *5*
Somerset Door & Column Co. (PA) *5*
Strobel Millwork (CT) *5*
United House Wrecking Corp. (CT) *4*
Jack Wallis' Doors (KY) *5*
Wood Designs (OH) *5*
Woodstone Co. (VT) *1,2,3,5*

WINDOW BALANCES (REPLACEMENT CHANNELS)

Blaine Window Hardware, Inc. (MD)
Quaker City Manufacturing Co. (PA)

WINDOW FRAMES & SASH—PERIOD

(1) Early American
(2) Victorian
(3) New (Stock Items)
(4) Salvage
(5) Custom-Made

Air-Flo Window Contracting Corp. (NY) *5,5*
Andersen Corporation (MN) ... *3*
Architectural Components (MA) ... *5*
Bjorndal Woodworks (WI) ... *5*
Bow House, Inc. (MA) ... *1*
Burt Millwork Corp (NY) ... *5*
Caradco (IL) ... *3*
Central Kentucky Millwork (KY) ... *1,5*
Colonial Restoration Products (PA) ... *1,3*
Custom Millwork, Inc. (VA) ... *1,2,4,5*
D.V.H. Co. (FL) ... *3,5*
Dodge, Adams, and Roy, Ltd. (NH) ... *5*
Dovetail Woodworking (WI) ... *2*
Drums Sash & Door Co., Inc. (PA) ... *5*
Early New England Rooms & Exteriors Inc. (CT) ... *1*
Englander Millwork Corp. (NY) ... *3,5*
Gibbons Sash and Door (WI) ... *5*
Glass & Aluminum Construction Services, Inc. (NH) ... *5*
Greenland Studio, Inc., The (NY) ... *5*
International Building Components (NY) . *5*
International Fireproof Door Co., Inc. (IFD) (NY) ... *3,5*
Keddee Woodworkers (RI) ... *5*
Kenmore Industries (MA) ... *3*
Kingsway Victorian Restoration Materials (CO) ... *2*
Lavoie, John F. (VT) ... *2*
Marvin Windows (MN) ... *3,5*
Maurer & Shepherd, Joyners (CT) ... *5*
Max Lumber Co. (NJ) ... *5*
Mendocino Millwork (CA) ... *3*
Michael's Fine Colonial Products (NY) .. *1,5*
Midwest Wood Products (IA) ... *4,5*
Millwork Supply Company (WA) ... *5*
Pella Windows & Doors (IA) ... *3*
Piscatagua Architectural Woodwork, Co. (NH) ... *1,5*
Point Five Windows (CO) ... *5*
Price & Visser Millwork (WA) ... *5*
Restoration Fraternity (PA) ... *5*
Restoration Millworks (CO)
Sellrite Millwork Corp. (NJ) ... *5*
Silverton Victorian Millworks (CO) ... *5*
Somerset Door & Column Co. (PA) ... *5*
Strobel Millwork (CT) ... *1,2,5*
Sunflake/Restoration Millwork (CO) ... *3*
Vintage Storm Window Co. (WA) ... *5*
Wes-Pine Wood Windows (MA) ... *3,5*
Window Grille Specialists (MN) ... *3*
Wood Designs (OH) ... *5*
Woodstone Co. (VT) ... *2*
Yankee Shutter & Sash Co. (NH) ... *5*

WINDOW FRAMES AND SASH, METAL

Skyline Windows (NY)

S. A. Bendheim Introduces...

RESTORATION GLASS™

Hand made glass...

mouth blown in the same manner since the Middle Ages.

For fine restorations, there is no substitute for authenticity... and for *true* authenticity, there is no substitute for Restoration Glass.™ This unique, hand-crafted glass is created by skilled fifth and sixth generation artisans in one of Europe's oldest glass blowing factories. Each sheet of Restoration Glass™ is mouth blown, according to a time-honored tradition unchanged since the Middle Ages. The slight distortions and imperfections make it ideal for restoration work; it has been chosen, over and over again, for use in America's finest restorations and antique reproductions. Restoration Glass™ is imported exclusively by S.A. Bendheim. For more information please write or call.

Old Sturbridge Village Photo
by Henry E. Peach

RESTORATION GLASS™

DESCRIPTION
A mouthblown glass resembling glasses made during the colonial period. Slight distortions, occasional pits and imperfections make it the ideal choice for restoration work. Available in two varieties: the "Full" is thicker and more distorting; the "Light" is thinner and less distorting.

USAGE
Restoration glass—for use in historic properties, commercial buildings, residential work, reproduction and antique furniture.

SIZE & THICKNESS

Full— Approx. 1/8″ thickness
Sheet Size: Approx. 24″ × 36″

Light— Approx. 3/32″ thickness
Sheet Size: Approx. 42″ × 42″

Bendheim

S.A. Bendheim Co., Inc. 122 Hudson Street, NY NY 10013
Call Toll-Free 1-800-221-7379 In New York State: 212-226-6370

WINDOW GLASS, CLEAR—HANDMADE

(1) New
(2) Antique (Salvage)

Bendheim, S.A. Co., Inc. (NY) *1*
Blenko Glass Co., Inc. (WV) *1*
Colonial Restoration Products (PA) *1*
Custom Millwork, Inc. (VA) *2*
Englander Millwork Corp. (NY) *1*
Glass & Aluminum Construction Services, Inc. (NH) *1*
Glass Designs (KY) *1*
Kraatz/Russell Glass (NH) *1*
Midwest Wood Products (IA)
Point Five Windows (CO) *1*
Ramase (CT) *2*
Vintage Lumber Co. (MD) *2*

WINDOW GLASS, CURVED

California Glass Bending Company (CA)
Shadovitz Bros. Distributors, Inc. (NY)
Visible Glass (MN)

WINDOW INSERTS, DOUBLE-GLAZED

Restoration Millworks (CO)

WINDOWS, SPECIAL ARCHITECTURAL SHAPES (ROUNDS, OVALS, FANLIGHTS, TRANSOMS, ETC.)

Architectural Components (MA)
Bare Wood Inc. (NY)
Bjorndal Woodworks (WI)
Cape Cod Bullseye Glass Co. (MA)
Custom Millwork, Inc. (VA)
D.V.H. Co. (FL)
Dovetail Woodworking (WI)
Golden Age Glassworks (NY)
Lyn Hovey Studio, Inc. (MA)
International Building Components (NY)
Kenmore Industries (MA)
Kraatz/Russell Glass (NH)
Lavoie, John F. (VT)
North Pacific Joinery (CA)
Ohmega Salvage (CA)
Point Five Windows (CO)
Pompei Stained Glass, Inc. (MA)
Salamandra Glass (NH)
Select Interior Door, Ltd. (NY)
Strobel Millwork (CT)
Woodstone Co. (VT)
Yankee Shutter & Sash Co. (NH)

Hardware, Exterior

DOOR HARDWARE, EXTERIOR

(1) Brass & Bronze
(2) Wrought Iron
(3) Door Knockers
(4) Rim Locks
(5) Mortised Locks
(6) Latches, Hand Forged
(7) Mail Slots
(8) Hinges
(9) Strap Hinges

18th Century Hardware Co. (PA) *3,6,9*
Acorn Manufacturing Co., Inc. (MA) .. *2,8,9*
Antique Hardware Store (NJ) *5*
Arden Forge (PA) *1,2,4,5,6,8,9*
Baldwin Hardware Mfg. Corp. (PA) *1,3,4,5,6,7*
Ball and Ball (PA) *1,2,3,4,5,6,8,9*
Bona Decorative Hardware (OH) *1,3,5*
The Brass Finial (NJ) *1,3,4,8*
Broad-Axe Beam Co. (VT) *6,8,9*
The Broadway Collection (MO) *1,3*
Canal Co. (DC) *1*
Cirecast, Inc. (CA) *1,5,7,8*
Colonial Lock Company (CT) *4*
Colonial Restoration Products (PA) *3,6,8,9,9*
Crawford's Old House Store (WI) *1,1,2,3,3,4,4,5,6,7,8,8,9*
DHM Cabinets (VA) *1,4,5,7,8*
DS Locksmithing Company (FL) *1,4,5,8*
Decorative Hardware Studio (NY) *1,3,4,7*
J.D. Dewell & Company (CT) *1,2,9*
Elephant Hill Iron Works (VT) *2,3,6,8,9*
Englewood Hardware Co. (NJ) *5*
Florida Victorian Architectural Antiques (FL) *1,3,4,5,8*
Goldenrod Ironworks (NY) *1*
Guerin, P.E. Inc. (NY) *1,3*
Historic Housefitters Company (NY) .. *1,3,6*
Horton Brasses (CT) *3*
Houseparts (CA) *3*
Hunrath , Wm. Co., Inc. (NY)
Kayne & Son Custom Forged Hardware (NC) *1,2,3,6,9*
Materials Unlimited (MI) *1*
Merritt's Antiques, Inc. (PA) *7*
Mill River Hammerworks (MA) *6,8,9*
Millham, Newton — Blacksmith (MA) *2,3,6,8,9*
D. C. Mitchell Reproductions (DE) *1,2,3,8*
Old Smithy Shop (NH) *2,6,8*
The Old Wagon Factory (VA) *1,2,6,9*
Omnia Industries, Inc. (NJ) *3*
H. Pfanstiel Hardware Co. (NY) *1,3*
Plexacraft Metals Co. (CA) *1*
Remodelers & Renovators (ID) *1*
The Renovator's Supply (MA)
Reproduction Distributors, Inc. (IL) *8*
Restoration Works, Inc. (NY) *3,5,7*
Salvage One (IL) *1*
Samuel B. Sadtler, Importers (PA) *1,5*
Sign of the Crab (CA) *1*
Smithy, The (VT) *2,3,6,8,9*
Town & Country Decorative and Functional Metalcraft (NH) *2,3,6,8*
Transylvania Mountain Forge (CA) *1,2,3,6,7,8,9*
Virginia Metalcrafters (VA) *1,8*
Wallin Forge (KY) *2,3,6,8,9*
Washburne, E.G. & Co., Inc. (MA) *1,2*
Weaver, W. T. & Sons, Inc. (DC) *1,3,4*
Williamsburg Blacksmiths, Inc. (MA) *2,3,6,8,9*
Windy Hill Forge (MD) *1,2,3,4,6,8,9*
Wise Company, The (LA) *3,8*
Wolchonok, M. and Son, Inc. (NY) ... *1,3,4,5*

EXTERIOR HARDWARE, CUSTOM-MADE

(1) Cast Brass & Bronze
(2) Hand-Forged Iron
(3) Cast Iron

18th Century Hardware Co. (PA) *1,2*
Arden Forge (PA) *1,2,2*
Ball and Ball (PA) *1,2,3*
Berea College Crafts (KY) *2*
Bronze et al (NY) *1*
Cassidy Bros. Forge, Inc. (MA) *2*
Circecast, Inc. (CA) *1*
Conant Custom Brass (VT) *1*
DHM Cabinets (VA) *1*
Elephant Hill Iron Works (VT) *2*
Goldenrod Ironworks (NY) *1,2,3*
Kayne & Son Custom Forged Hardware (NC) *1,2*
G. Krug & Son, Inc. (MD) *2*
Leo, Brian (MN) *1*
Mill River Hammerworks (MA) *2*
Millham, Newton — Blacksmith (MA) ... *2*
Plexacraft Metals Co. (CA) *1*
Schwartz's Forge & Metalworks, Inc. (NY) *2*
Smithy, The (VT) *2*
Tennessee Fabricating Co. (TN) *3*
Wallin Forge (KY) *2,2*
Windy Hill Forge (MD)
Woodbury Blacksmith & Forge Co. (CT) .. *2*

DOORBELLS—PERIOD DESIGNS

(1) Electric
(2) Mechanical

Ball and Ball (PA)
Bona Decorative Hardware (OH) *2*
Circecast, Inc. (CA) *1*
Crawford's Old House Store (WI) *2*
Cumberland General Store (TN) *2*
Period Furniture Hardware Co., Inc. (MA) *1*
The Renovator's Supply (MA)
Restoration Works, Inc. (NY) *1,2*
Sign of the Crab (CA) *2*
Victorian Reproductions Enterprises, Inc. (MN) *2*

SHUTTER HARDWARE (HINGES, HOLDBACKS, ETC.)

Acorn Manufacturing Co., Inc. (MA)
Antique Hardware Store (NJ)
Arden Forge (PA)
Ball and Ball (PA)
Cassidy Bros. Forge, Inc. (MA)
Colonial Restoration Products (PA)
Elephant Hill Iron Works (VT)
Fairmont Foundry Co., Inc. (AL)
Millham, Newton — Blacksmith (MA)
Plexacraft Metals Co. (CA)
The Renovator's Supply (MA)
Smithy, The (VT)
Weaver, W. T. & Sons, Inc. (DC)
Williamsburg Blacksmiths, Inc. (MA)
Windy Hill Forge (MD)

Ironwork, Exterior

BALUSTERS & HANDRAILS, IRON—PERIOD DESIGNS

(1) Cast Iron
(2) Wrought Iron

Berea College Crafts (KY) *2*
Braun, J.G. Co. (IL) *1*
Cassidy Bros. Forge, Inc. (MA) *2*
Fairmont Foundry Co., Inc. (AL) *1*
Gilpin, Inc. (IN) *1*
Goldenrod Ironworks (NY) *1*
Greensboro Art Foundry & Machine Co. (NC) *1*
G. Krug & Son, Inc. (MD) *1,2*
Lawler Machine & Foundry (AL) *1*
NET (NY) *1,2*
New England Tool Co., Ltd. (NY) *2*
Nostalgia (GA) *1*
Puma Iron Works (NY) *2*
Schwartz's Forge & Metalworks, Inc. (NY) *2*
Smith, Whitcomb & Cook Co. (VT) *2*
Tennessee Fabricating Co. (TN) *1*
Tomahawk Foundry (WI) *1*
Windy Hill Forge (MD) *1,2*

CAST ALUMINUM, EXTERIOR ORNAMENTAL

Braun, J.G. Co. (IL)
Campbellsville Industries (KY)
Circecast, Inc. (CA)
Clarksville Foundry & Machine Works (TN)
Fairmont Foundry Co., Inc. (AL)
Lawler Machine & Foundry (AL)
Moultrie Manufacturing Company (GA)
Norcross Galleries (GA)
Swiss Foundry, Inc. (MD)

See Company Directory for Addresses & Phone Numbers on page 151

CAST IRON, EXTERIOR ORNAMENTAL

Architectural Iron Company (PA)
G. Krug & Son, Inc. (MD)
Lawler Machine & Foundry (AL)
Nye's Foundry Ltd. (CAN)
Oliver, Bradley C. (PA)
Pennsylvania Firebacks, Inc. (PA)
Robinson Iron Corporation (AL)
Smith, Whitcomb & Cook Co. (VT)
Stewart Manufacturing Company (KY)
Swiss Foundry, Inc. (MD)
Tennessee Fabricating Co. (TN)
Tomahawk Foundry (WI)
Windy Hill Forge (MD)

CAST IRON, CUSTOM CASTING

Architectural Iron Company (PA)
Clarksville Foundry & Machine Works (TN)
Goldenrod Ironworks (NY)
Greensboro Art Foundry & Machine Co. (NC)
G. Krug & Son, Inc. (MD)
Robinson Iron Corporation (AL)
Rocco V. De Angelo (NY)
Smith, Whitcomb & Cook Co. (VT)
Swiss Foundry, Inc. (MD)
Tomahawk Foundry (WI)
Windy Hill Forge (MD)
Xenia Foundry & Machine Co. Specialty Castings Dept. (OH)

CRESTING

(1) Cast Iron
(2) Fiberglass
Archicast (TN) *2*
Architectural Iron Company (PA) *1*
Goldenrod Ironworks (NY) *1*
Greensboro Art Foundry & Machine Co. (NC) *1*
Rejuvenation House Parts Co. (OR) *1*
Robinson Iron Corporation (AL) *1*
Smith, Whitcomb & Cook Co. (VT) *1*
Tennessee Fabricating Co. (TN) *1*
Tomahawk Foundry (WI) *1*
Windy Hill Forge (MD) *1*

RAILINGS, BALCONIES & WINDOW GRILLES

(1) Cast Iron
(2) Wrought Iron
(3) Other
Architectural Antiques Exchange (PA)
Berea College Crafts (KY) *2*
Braun, J.G. Co. (IL) *3*
Cassidy Bros. Forge, Inc. (MA)
Fairmont Foundry Co., Inc. (AL) *1*
Goldenrod Ironworks (NY) *1*
Hubbardton Forge Corp. (VT) *2*
Lawler Machine & Foundry (AL) *1*
Mill River Hammerworks (MA) *1,2*
New England Tool Co., Ltd. (NY) *2,3*
Nostalgia (GA) *1*
Puma Iron Works (NY) *2*
Robinson Iron Corporation (AL) *1*
Schwartz's Forge & Metalworks, Inc. (NY) *2*
Smith, Whitcomb & Cook Co. (VT) *1*
Steptoe and Wife Antiques Ltd. (CAN) ... *1*
Swiss Foundry, Inc. (MD) *1*
Tennessee Fabricating Co. (TN) *1*
Tomahawk Foundry (WI) *1*
Windy Hill Forge (MD) *1,2*

WROUGHT IRON ORNAMENTS, STOCK ITEMS

New England Tool Co., Ltd. (NY)
Puma Iron Works (NY)
Tennessee Fabricating Co. (TN)
Town & Country Decorative and Functional Metalcraft (NH)

WROUGHT IRON, CUSTOM FABRICATION

Antares Forge and Metalworks (NY)
Architectural Iron Company (PA)
Arden Forge (PA)
Cambridge Smithy (VT)
Cassidy Bros. Forge, Inc. (MA)
Colonial Restoration Products (PA)
Elephant Hill Iron Works (VT)
Goldenrod Ironworks (NY)
Kayne & Son Custom Forged Hardware (NC)
G. Krug & Son, Inc. (MD)
Millham, Newton — Blacksmith (MA)
NET (NY)
New England Tool Co., Ltd. (NY)
Puma Iron Works (NY)
Schwartz's Forge & Metalworks, Inc. (NY)
Smithy, The (VT)
Star Metal (NY)
Tremont Nail Company (MA)
Vermont Industries, Inc. (VT)
Wallin Forge (KY)
Windy Hill Forge (MD)
Woodbury Blacksmith & Forge Co. (CT)

Other Exterior Ornament & Details

AWNINGS

Air-Flo Window Contracting Corp. (NY)
Astrup Company (OH)
T.J. Bottom Industries, Inc. (MO)
Gilpin, Inc. (IN)
Industrial Fabrics Association International (MN)
Pease Industries (OH)

AWNING HARDWARE

Astrup Company (OH)
T.J. Bottom Industries, Inc. (MO)
Gilpin, Inc. (IN)
Whitco — Vincent Whitney Co. (CA)

BALUSTRADES, ROOF

Campbellsville Industries (KY)
Fibertech Corp. (SC)
Lachin, Albert & Assoc., Inc. (LA)
Mad River Wood Works (CA)

CHIMNEY POTS

Clay Suppliers (TX)
Superior Clay Corporation (OH)
Terra Cotta Productions, Inc. (PA)
Victorian Reproductions Enterprises, Inc. (MN)

CUPOLAS

Antique Hardware Store (NJ)
Campbellsville Industries (KY)
Cape Cod Cupola Co., Inc. (MA)
Connecticut Cupola & Weathervane (CT)
Copper House (NH)
Copper Specialties, Ltd. (NY)
The Coppersmith— (MA)
Country Cupolas (NH)
Good Directions, Inc. (CT)
International Building Components (NY)
Kool-O-Matic Corp. (MI)
Sun Designs (WI)

See Company Directory for Addresses & Phone Numbers on page 151

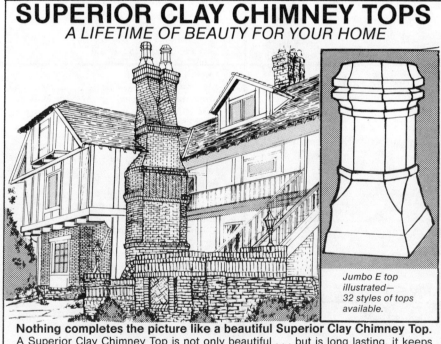

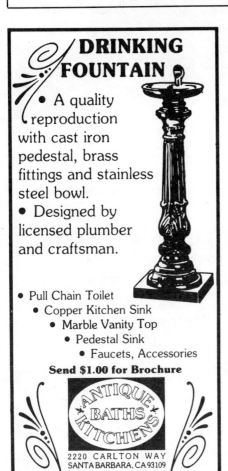

FENCES & GATES—PERIOD DESIGNS

(1) Cast Iron
(2) Wrought Iron
(3) Wood
(4) Antique
(5) Cast Aluminum

Architectural Accents (GA) *4*
Architectural Antiques Exchange (PA) *1*
Architectural Iron Company (PA) *1,2*
Belcher, Robert W. (GA) *3,4*
ByGone Era Architectural Antiques (GA) *4*
Canal Co. (DC) *4*
Cassidy Bros. Forge, Inc. (MA) *2*
Custom Ironworks Inc. (KY) *1,2*
Custom Millwork, Inc. (VA) *3*
Fairmont Foundry Co., Inc. (AL) *1,5*
Goldenrod Ironworks (NY) *1,5*
Hubbardton Forge Corp. (VT) *2*
G. Krug & Son, Inc. (MD) *2*
Lawler Machine & Foundry (AL) *1,5*
Joe Ley Antiques, Inc. (KY) *4*
Mad River Wood Works (CA) *3*
Moultrie Manufacturing Company (GA) . *5*
NET (NY) *1,2*
New England Tool Co., Ltd. (NY) *2*
The Old Wagon Factory (VA) *3*
Oliver, Bradley C. (PA) *4*
Robinson Iron Corporation (AL) *1*
Salvage One (IL) *4*
Schwartz's Forge & Metalworks, Inc. (NY) *2*
Smith, F.E., Castings, Inc. (MI) *1*
Smith, Whitcomb & Cook Co. (VT) *1*
Southern Accents Architectural Antiques (AL) *1,5*
Stewart Manufacturing Company (KY) ... *2*
United House Wrecking Corp. (CT) *4*
Westlake Architectural Antiques (TX) *2,4*
Windy Hill Forge (MD) *1,2*
Wrecking Bar of Atlanta (GA) *2,4*

FLAGS & POLES, PERIOD

(1) Flags
(2) Permanent (in-ground) poles
(3) Temporary
(4) Patriotic Decorations

Heritage Flags (NJ) *1,2,3*
Ryther — Purdy Lumber Co., Inc. (CT) ... *2*
Washburne, E.G. & Co., Inc. (MA) *1,2*

GARDEN ORNAMENT

(1) Fountains
(2) Statuary
(3) Planters
(4) Urns & Vases
(5) Trellis
(6) Other

American Architectural Art Company (PA) *2,3,4*
Antique Baths and Kitchens (CA) *1*
Bench Manufacturing Co. (MA) *3*
Chilstone Garden Ornament (UK) *2,3,4,6*
Contemporary Copper/Matthew Richardson (MA) *1*
Country Casual (MD) *3*
Cross Industries, Inc. (GA) *5*
Dan Wilson & Company, Inc. (NC) *3*
Good Directions, Inc. (CT) *6*
Green Enterprises (VA) *6*
Greensboro Art Foundry & Machine Co. (NC) *2*
Lachin, Albert & Assoc., Inc. (LA) *1*
Lawler Machine & Foundry (AL) *3,4*
Joe Ley Antiques, Inc. (KY) *2,6*
Machin Designs (USA), Inc. (CT) *3*
Moultrie Manufacturing Company (GA) *1,3,4*
NET (NY) *4*
New England Tool Co., Ltd. (NY) *3,6*
Norcross Galleries (GA) *1,4*
The Old Wagon Factory (VA) *3*
Park Place (DC) *1,2,3,4*
Robinson Iron Corporation (AL) *1,2,3,4*
Roman Marble Co. (IL) *2*
Silver Dollar Trading Co. (TX) *1*
Southern Accents Architectural Antiques (AL) *1,2*
Sturbridge Yankee Workshop (ME) *3*
Tennessee Fabricating Co. (TN) *1,2,3,4*
United House Wrecking Corp. (CT) *1,2,3,4,6*
Verine Products & Co. (UK) *3*
Otto Wendt & Co. (TX) *1,3,4*
Windy Hill Forge (MD) *4*

GAZEBOS AND OUTBUILDINGS

Architectural Preservation Trust (CT)
Cedar Gazebos, Inc. (IL)
Cumberland Woodcraft Co., Inc. (PA)
Dalton Pavilions Inc. (PA)
Gazebo and Porchworks (WA)
K-D Wood Products (MA)
Machin Designs (USA), Inc. (CT)
RWL/Welsbach Lighting (CT)
Southern Accents Architectural Antiques (AL)
Vintage Wood Works (TX)
Vixen Hill Manufacturing (PA)

GREENHOUSES AND CONSERVATORIES

Glass & Aluminum Construction Services, Inc. (NH)
Machin Designs (USA), Inc. (CT)
Seaport Village Associates (MA)

HAMMOCKS

Pawley's Island Hammock Co. (SC)

LAWN AND PORCH FURNITURE

(1) Cast Iron
(2) Wood
(3) Wicker
(4) Wrought Iron
(5) Cast Aluminum

Alfresco Fine Furniture Since 1976 (CO) .. *2*
British-American Marketing Services, Ltd. (PA) *2,5*
Country Casual (MD) *2*
The Country Iron Foundry (PA) *1*
Dan Wilson & Company, Inc. (NC) *2*
Fairmont Foundry Co., Inc. (AL) *1,5*
Gazebo and Porchworks (WA) *2*
Goldenrod Ironworks (NY) *1,5*
Gravity - Randall (CA) *4*
Green Enterprises (VA) *2*
Imagineering, Inc. (ME) *2*
Kings River Casting (CA) *5*
Lawler Machine & Foundry (AL) *1,5*
Moultrie Manufacturing Company (GA) . *5*
New England Tool Co., Ltd. (NY) *4*
Norcross Galleries (GA) *5*
Nye's Foundry Ltd. (CAN) *1,5*
The Old Wagon Factory (VA) *2*
Park Place (DC) *2,2,5*
Pratt's House of Wicker (PA) *3*
Putnam Rolling Ladder Co., Inc. (NY) *2*
Robinson Iron Corporation (AL) *1*
Rocker Shop of Marietta, GA (GA) *2*
Southern Accents Architectural Antiques (AL) *1,5*
Stone Ledge Co. (MA) *1*
Tennessee Fabricating Co. (TN) *1,5*
Vermont Industries, Inc. (VT) *4*
Otto Wendt & Co. (TX) *5*
Wikco Industries (NE) *1*
Windy Hill Forge (MD) *1,4*
Wood Classics, Inc. (NY) *2*

LIGHTNING RODS, OLD-FASHIONED

Victorian Reproductions Enterprises, Inc. (MN)

MAIL BOXES — PERIOD DESIGNS

Antique Hardware Store (NJ)
The Country Mouse (CT)
Crawford's Old House Store (WI)
Mel-Nor Marketing (TX)
Norcross Galleries (GA)
Park Place (DC)
Sign of the Crab (CA)
Silver Dollar Trading Co. (TX)

PLAQUES & HISTORIC MARKERS

Allen Foundry (CA)
John Hinds & Co. (PA)
La Haye Bronze, Inc. (CA)
Lake Shore Markers (PA)
Max-Cast (IA)
Meierjohan — Wengler, Inc. (OH)
Smith-Cornell, Inc. (IN)
Sturbridge Yankee Workshop (ME)
Sweet William House (IL)
Town & Country Decorative and Functional Metalcraft (NH)
Weaver, W. T. & Sons, Inc. (DC)
Xenia Foundry & Machine Co. Specialty Castings Dept. (OH)

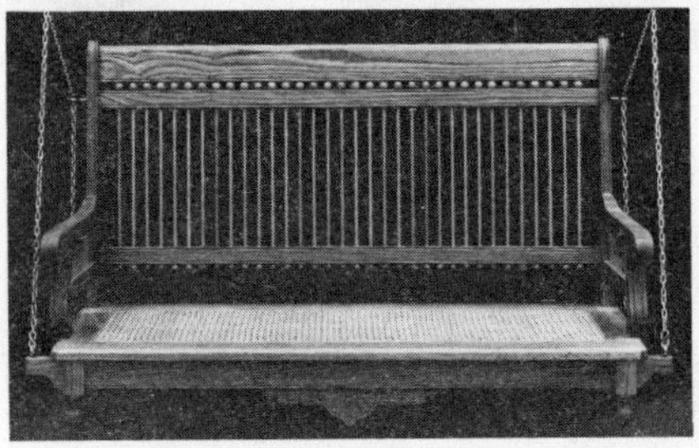

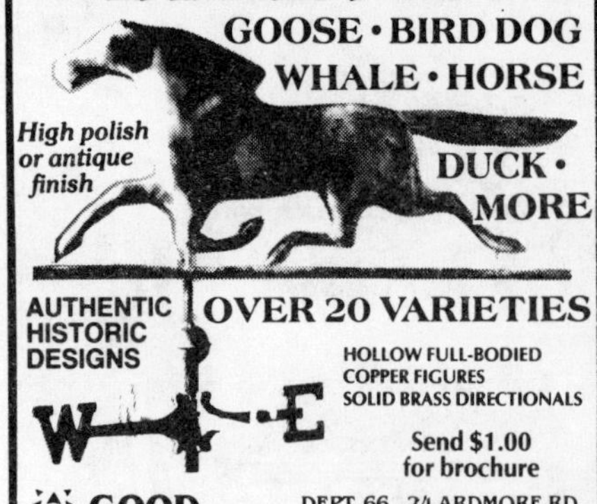

PORCH SWINGS

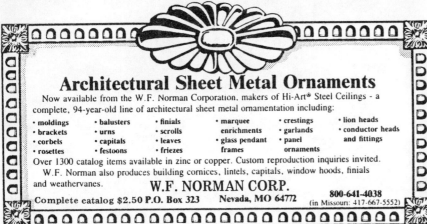

Alfresco Fine Furniture Since 1976 (CO)
Classic Architectural Specialties (TX)
Cumberland General Store (TN)
Green Enterprises (VA)
Wood Classics, Inc. (NY)

SHEET METAL ORNAMENT, EXTERIOR

Authentic Designs Inc. (VT)
Campbellsville Industries (KY)
J.C. Lauber Co. (IN)
Norman, W.F., Corporation (MO)
Wagner, Albert J., & Son (IL)

SIGNS, OLD-FASHIONED

Crawford's Old House Store (WI)
Custom Sign Co. (MD)
Max-Cast (IA)
Ryther — Purdy Lumber Co., Inc. (CT)
Shelley Signs (NY)
Smith-Cornell, Inc. (IN)
Vintage Wood Works (TX)

SKYLIGHTS

Fisher Skylights, Inc. (NY)
Glass & Aluminum Construction Services, Inc. (NH)

WEATHERVANES—NEW & REPRODUCTION

Cambridge Smithy (VT)
Campbellsville Industries (KY)
Cape Cod Cupola Co., Inc. (MA)
Cassidy Bros. Forge, Inc. (MA)
Connecticut Cupola & Weathervane (CT)
Contemporary Copper/Matthew Richardson (MA)
Copper House (NH)
Copper Specialties, Ltd. (NY)
The Coppersmith— (MA)
Crawford's Old House Store (WI)
Cumberland General Store (TN)
Good Directions, Inc. (CT)
Iron Craft, Inc. (NH)
Kayne & Son Custom Forged Hardware (NC)
New England Tool Co., Ltd. (NY)
Period Furniture Hardware Co., Inc. (MA)
The Renovator's Supply (MA)
Sign of the Crab (CA)
Smithy, The (VT)
Town & Country Decorative and Functional Metalcraft (NH)
Travis Tuck, Inc. — Metal Sculptor (MA)
United House Wrecking Corp. (CT)
Washburne, E.G. & Co., Inc. (MA)
Weathervanes (MA)
Windy Hill Forge (MD)

Nostalgia of the past blended with the present and future.

Rich Craft Custom Kitchens knows exactly how to inspire a special atmosphere in the heart of the home. Your kitchen, designed by craftsmen for its supreme quality, is enhanced by top grade woods in soft, natural tones, distinct designs to fill your personal tastes and numerous hand crafted accessories that reflect the Rich Craft high standard of workmanship.

Rich Craft Kitchens knows what makes a kitchen beautiful and this priceless knowledge is inherent in every cabinet built exclusively for the heart of your home . . . your new Rich Craft Kitchen.

Rich Craft
Custom Kitchens, Inc.
141 West Penn Ave., Robesonia, PA 19551
Telephone: 215 - 693-5871

VICTORIAN MILLWORK, ARCHITECTURAL TRIM, CARVINGS

19th Century Victorian designs re-created in solid oak and poplar from the world's leading manufacturer. Fretwork gingerbread and lots more for interior and exterior use; most complete line available.

- Unlimited quantities for total design freedom.
- Precision manufactured so that product groups are compatible with each other for total unity.
- Save with factory-to-you pricing.

Send $3.75 for full-color, 36-page product and design idea catalog & price list. Free if requested on company letterhead.

Cumberland Woodcraft Co. INC.
Post Office Drawer 609, Carlisle, PA 17013
PH: (717) 243-0063
Dept. 153

Artistry in Solid Wood

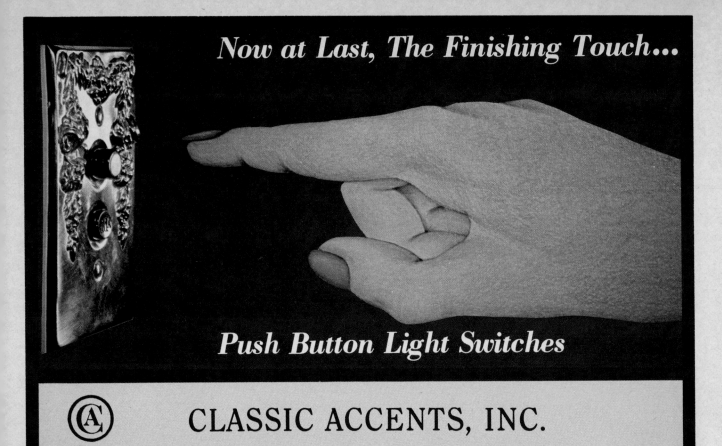

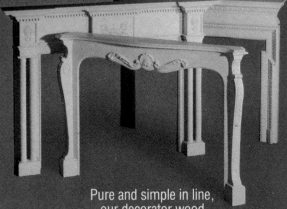

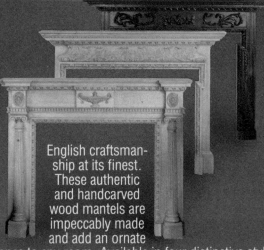

SCHLITZ STUDIOS

Creators in Glass and Bronze

Schlitz Studios manufactures more than 100 authentic Tiffany lamp recreations and over 75 bronze Tiffany base designs, ranging from the most exotic to the more simplistic. In order to achieve superb craftsmanship, every aspect of the piece, from the actual glass manufacturing to the cast bronze and patina, is done at Schlitz Studios under Mr. Schlitz's personal direction.

Not only has Mr. Schlitz recreated the finest of Tiffany's work, but he has also proven his artistic ability by creating original designs for lamps, windows and mosaics.

Prices start at $1,000.00. Accessories begin at $200.00.

Price list and photos are available at $4.00.

245 N. Water Street
Milwaukee, WI 53202
(414) 277-0742

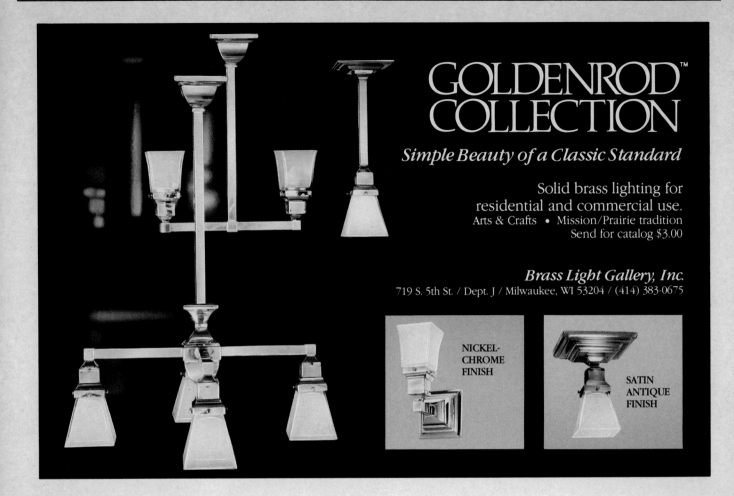

Supradur®
mineral fiber
roofing shingles

OVER 30 YEARS OF
BUILDING PROTECTION

Searching for an Authentic replacement for Slate?

Here's what one restoration specialist had to say about Supradur's Supra-Slate...

To the Editors:

IN AN ISSUE of OHJ sometime last spring, I came across an article on roofing materials which mentioned Supra-Slate by Supradur. I was restoring an 1870 house that originally had a fine hexagonal slate roof, and I was disappointed in the roofing materials available today. Real slate was too expensive, but anything else looked all wrong for the house. I contacted Supradur, and they sent me a sample—just what we needed.

WE'VE CUT the Supra-Slate to match the original hexagonal shingles* It is spectacular. The material resembles slate in texture and color, and behaves like slate in its application. Our roofers, who had never seen it, were surprised and pleased.

Nancy O'Neil
Hartford, Conn.

Reprinted with permission of the Old-House Journal 69A 7th Ave., Brooklyn, NY 11217. Tel. 212-636-4514 Subscriptions $16.00 per annum.

*See photo above (center right).

Supradur Manufacturing Corporation
P.O. Box 908, Rye, New York 10580
Tel.: 1-800-223-1948 ☐ In New York (914) 967-8230

All the comforts of home. . .

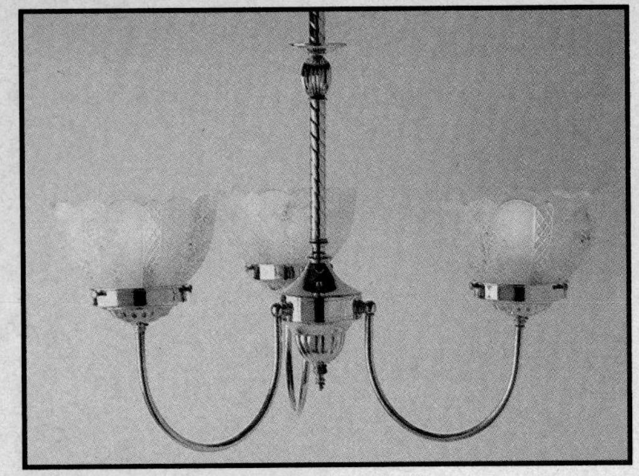

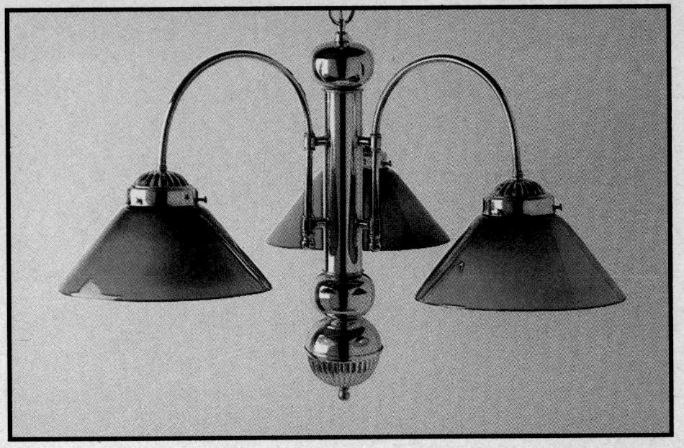

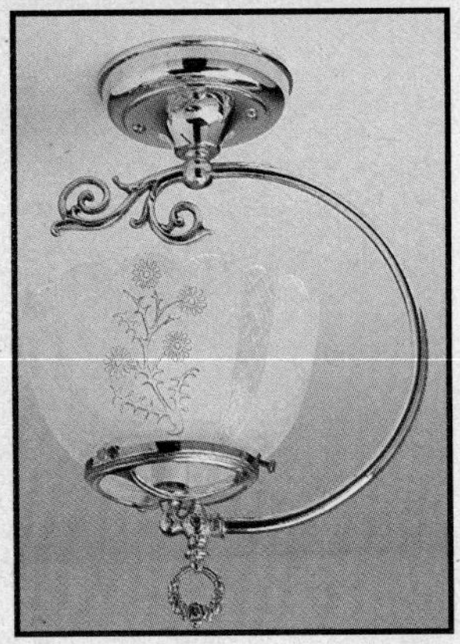

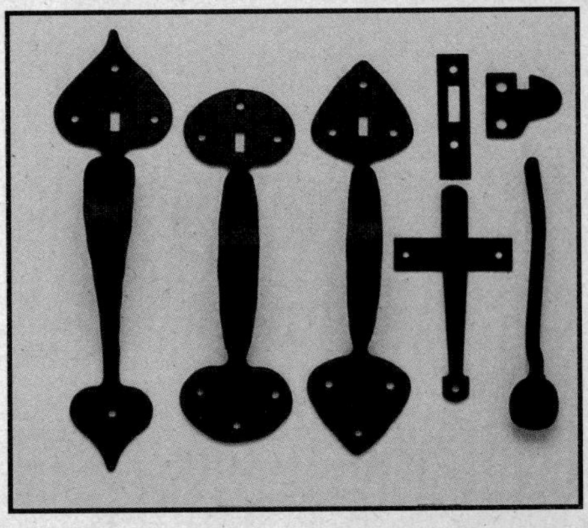

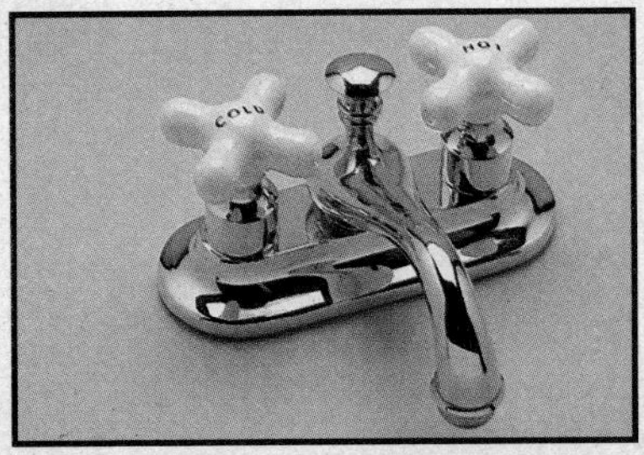

We have everything you need to add comfort, value and elegance to your home. Hundreds of products in many styles—Shaker, Colonial, Victorian, and Country:

sinks & switchplates • chandeliers & candleholders
locks & latches • hooks & hangers • knobs & knockers

All crafted from the finest quality materials:

solid oak • gleaming porcelain • classy brass
rugged wrought iron • solid copper

For full-color catalog, send $3 to:

RENOVATOR'S SUPPLY®

4552 Renovator's Old Mill
Millers Falls, MA 01349

Restaurants • Housing Projects • Condominiums
Genuine Antique Lamps
Create the warmth and glamour of the past with charm and utility through genuine antique street lighting.
• These are not reproduction units.
• Authentic historic outdoor lighting units from the 1920's.
• Made of high quality ductile cast iron, tapered cast steel column, cast aluminum lantern
• Certificate of authenticity with each lamp.
Send for free brochure and price list (Quantity discounts available)
Customized lenses - acrylic or glass.
Flexible heights - 10' to 22'.
Adaptable - multiple energy sources
Easy installation - standard footers - complete instructions.
F.O.B. Elyria, Ohio
SUPPLY LIMITED
Lamp Light IND. INC.
135 Yorkshire Court
Elyria, Ohio 44035
(216) 365-4954
Show Homes • Shopping Centers • Cities • Counties • Schools • Churches • Restaurants
Homeowners Associations • Housing Projects
Shopping Centers • Cities • Counties • Schools • Churches • Homeowners Associations

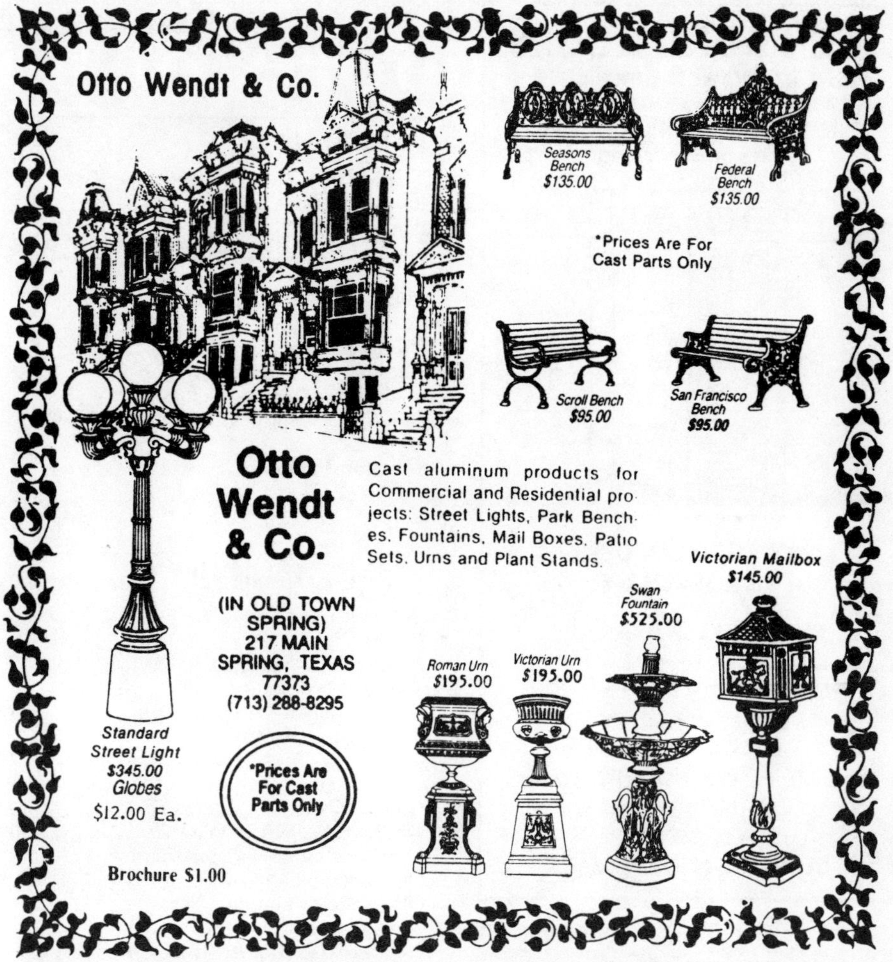

Otto Wendt & Co.
Seasons Bench $135.00
Federal Bench $135.00
*Prices Are For Cast Parts Only
Scroll Bench $95.00
San Francisco Bench $95.00
Otto Wendt & Co.
Cast aluminum products for Commercial and Residential projects: Street Lights, Park Benches, Fountains, Mail Boxes, Patio Sets, Urns and Plant Stands.
Victorian Mailbox $145.00
(IN OLD TOWN SPRING)
217 MAIN
SPRING, TEXAS
77373
(713) 288-8295
Swan Fountain $525.00
Roman Urn $195.00
Victorian Urn $195.00
Standard Street Light $345.00
Globes $12.00 Ea.
*Prices Are For Cast Parts Only
Brochure $1.00

STREETSCAPE EQUIPMENT

(1) Bollards and Stanchions
(2) Promenade Benches
(3) Street Clocks
(4) Tree Grates
(5) Street Lamps

Abaroot Mfg., Co. (CA) *5*
Antique Street Lamps, Inc. (TX) *5*
Bench Manufacturing Co. (MA) *2,3,5*
Canterbury Designs, Inc. (CA) *2,3,4*
Cassidy Bros. Forge, Inc. (MA) *4*
Chilstone Garden Ornament (UK) *2*
Country Shutters (MN) *5*
Fairmont Foundry Co., Inc. (AL) *1*
Gravity - Randall (CA) *2*
Koppers Co. (PA) *5*
Lampco (OH) *5*
LampLight Industries, Inc. (OH) *5*
Mel-Nor Marketing (TX) *1,2,5*
Norcross Galleries (GA) *5*
Nye's Foundry Ltd. (CAN) *1,4,5*
Olde & Oak Antiques (AL) *5*
Park Place (DC) *2,5*
RWL/Welsbach Lighting (CT) *1,5*
Roy Electric Co., Inc. (NY) *5*
Ryther — Purdy Lumber Co., Inc. (CT) ... *5*
A.F. Schwerd Manufacturing Co. (PA) *5*
Sentry Electric Corp. (NY) *5*
Southern Accents Architectural Antiques (AL) *2,4,5*
Spring City Electrical Mfg. Co (PA) *1,5*
Union Metal Corp. (OH) *5*
Vermont Iron (VT) *2*
Otto Wendt & Co. (TX) *2,5*

TURNBUCKLE STARS

Ainsworth Development Corp. (MD)
Windy Hill Forge (MD)

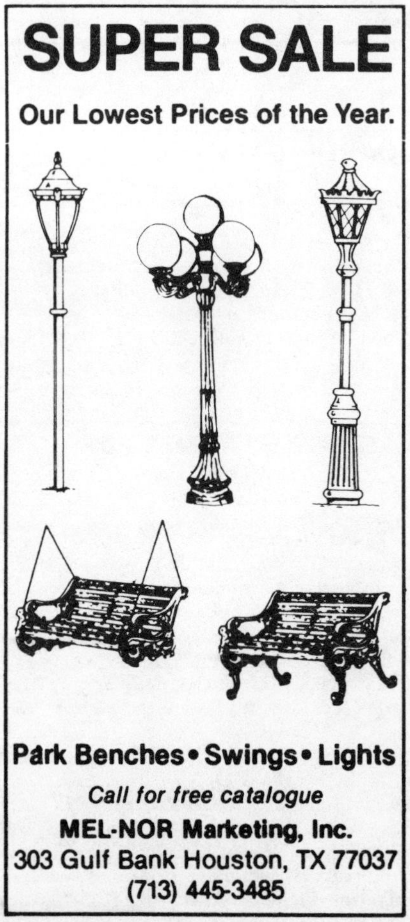

Lampco
STANDARD & CUSTOM DESIGN
Classic Lighting
PRACTICAL
Designed and manufactured to combine economy and durability in any setting - indoors or out.
DISTINCTIVE
Classic turn-of-the-century styling in bronze or aluminum castings. Custom fitting and designing available.
For data contact:
Lampco Inc.
P.O. Box 21680
South Euclid, OH 44121
Phone: (216) 765-2377
Lampco

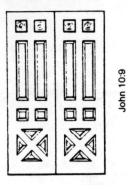

Building Materials For Interiors

BASEBOARDS

Amherst Woodworking & Supply (MA)
Bangkok Industries, Inc. (PA)
Bartleys Mill (CA)
Bendix Mouldings, Inc. (NJ)
Classic Architectural Specialties (TX)
Custom Millwork, Inc. (VA)
Dovetail Woodworking (WI)
Drums Sash & Door Co., Inc. (PA)
House of Moulding (CA)
Mad River Wood Works (CA)
Old World Moulding & Finishing Co., Inc. (NY)
Silverton Victorian Millworks (CO)

BEAMS, HAND-HEWN

(1) Antique (Recycled)
(2) New

Architectural Antiques (OK) 1
The Barn People, Inc. (VT) 1
Belcher, Robert W. (GA) 1
Broad-Axe Beam Co. (VT) 2
ByGone Era Architectural Antiques (GA) 1
Central Kentucky Millwork (KY) 2
Granville Mfg. Co., Inc. (VT) 2
Moore, E.T., Jr. Co. (VA) 1
Mountain Lumber Company, Inc. (VA) .. 1
Old Home Building & Restoration (CT) ... 1
Old World Moulding & Finishing Co., Inc. (NY) 2
Pagliacco Turning & Milling Architectural Wood Turning (CA) 1,2
Ramase (CT) 1
Southington Specialty Wood Co. (CT) 2

BOARDS, SALVAGE

Aged Woods (PA)
The Barn People, Inc. (VT)
The Joinery Co. (NC)
Mountain Lumber Company, Inc. (VA)
Old Home Building & Restoration (CT)
Vintage Lumber Co. (MD)
Woods American Co. (MD)

CASINGS & FRAMES FOR DOORS & WINDOWS

(1) Stock Items
(2) Custom Made

Amherst Woodworking & Supply (MA) ... 2
Architectural Components (MA) 2
Central Kentucky Millwork (KY) 1,2
Custom Millwork, Inc. (VA) 2
Dovetail Woodworking (WI) 2
Drums Sash & Door Co., Inc. (PA) 2
Early New England Rooms & Exteriors Inc. (CT) 2
House of Moulding (CA) 1
Kirby Millworks (CO) 1
Michael's Fine Colonial Products (NY) 2
Restoration Fraternity (PA) 2
"Rustic Barn" Wood Products (VA) 1
San Francisco Victoriana (CA) 1,2
Silverton Victorian Millworks (CO) 2

CABLE, ARMORED ELECTRICAL

AFC/A Nortek Company (MA)

CEILINGS, WOOD—CUSTOM MANUFACTURED

Architectural Paneling, Inc. (NY)
Cumberland Woodcraft Co., Inc. (PA)
Heart-Wood, Inc. (FL)
Wood Designs (OH)

CHAIR RAILS

(1) Stock Items
(2) Custom Made

Amherst Woodworking & Supply (MA) ... 2
Architectural Components (MA) 2
Bartleys Mill (CA) 2
Bendix Mouldings, Inc. (NJ) 1
Central Kentucky Millwork (KY) 1,2
Classic Architectural Specialties (TX) 1
Cumberland Woodcraft Co., Inc. (PA) 1
Custom Millwork, Inc. (VA) 2
Dimension Lumber Co. (NY) 2
Dovetail Woodworking (WI) 2
Drums Sash & Door Co., Inc. (PA) 2
Fireplace Mantel Shop, Inc. (MD) 1
Heart-Wood, Inc. (FL) 2
House of Moulding (CA) 1
Mad River Wood Works (CA) 2
Maurer & Shepherd, Joyners (CT) 2
Michael's Fine Colonial Products (NY) 2
Old World Moulding & Finishing Co., Inc. (NY) 1
Piscatagua Architectural Woodwork, Co. (NH) 1,2
Renovation Concepts, Inc. (MN) 1
"Rustic Barn" Wood Products (VA) 1
San Francisco Victoriana (CA) 1,2
Ship 'n Out (NY) 1
Silverton Victorian Millworks (CO) 2
States Industries (OR) 1
Wood Designs (OH) 2

See Company Directory for Addresses & Phone Numbers on page 151

DOORS, INTERIOR

(1) Antique (Salvage)
(2) Reproduction
(3) Early American
(4) Victorian
(5) Turn-of-Century
(6) Custom-Made
(7) Other

Amherst Woodworking & Supply (MA) ... *6*
Architectural Accents (GA) *1*
Architectural Antique Warehouse, The (CAN) *1*
Architectural Antiques (OK) *1,1*
Architectural Components (MA) *2*
Architectural Salvage Co. (MI) *1*
Art Directions (MO) *1*
Bare Wood Inc. (NY) *1*
Beech River Mill Co. (NH) *6*
Bel-Air Door Co. (CA) *2*
Bjorndal Woodworks (WI) *6*
Bow House, Inc. (MA) *3*
ByGone Era Architectural Antiques (GA) *1*
Canal Co. (DC) *1*
Central Kentucky Millwork (KY) *2,3,6*
Cohen's Architectural Heritage (CAN) *1*
Country Shutters (MN) *2*
Custom Millwork, Inc. (VA) *2,3,4,5,6*
Doors of Distinction (CA) *2,3,4,5*
Dovetail Woodworking (WI) *6*
Driwood Moulding Company (SC) *6*
Drums Sash & Door Co., Inc. (PA) *6*
Early New England Rooms & Exteriors Inc. (CT) *3*
Fireplace Mantel Shop, Inc. (MD) *2*
Florida Victorian Architectural Antiques (FL) *1*
Great American Salvage (NY) *1*
International Building Components (NY) . *6*
Keddee Woodworkers (RI) *6*
Leeke, John — Woodworker (ME) *6*
Joe Ley Antiques, Inc. (KY) *1*
Maple Hill Woodworking (NY) *6*
Materials Unlimited (MI) *1,2,2*
Maurer & Shepherd, Joyners (CT) *6*
Millwork Supply Company (WA) *6*
Monroe Coldren and Sons (PA) *1*
Oak Leaves Woodcarving Studio (IA) *6*
Olde Bostonian Architectural Antiques (MA) *1*
Pelnik Wrecking Co., Inc. (NY) *1*
Piscatagua Architectural Woodwork, Co. (NH) *3,6*
Pompei Stained Glass, Inc. (MA) *4,5*
Renovation Concepts, Inc. (MN) *2,4,5*
Restoration Fraternity (PA) *6*
Salvage One (IL) *1,2*
Second Chance (GA) *1*
Select Interior Door, Ltd. (NY) *2*
Sheppard Millwork, Inc. (WA) *6*
Somerset Door & Column Co. (PA) *6*
W. P. Stephens Lumber Co. (GA) *6*
Strobel Millwork (CT) *2,3,4,5,6*
United House Wrecking Corp. (CT) *1*
Walker's (OH) *1*
Jack Wallis' Doors (KY) *2,4,5,6*
Westlake Architectural Antiques (TX) .. *1,4,5*
Wood Designs (OH) *6*
Woodpecker Products Inc. (CO) *3,6*
Woodstone Co. (VT) *2,3,5,6*
Yankee Shutter & Sash Co. (NH) *2,3*

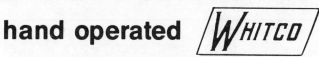

DUMBWAITERS & BUILT-INS

Econol Stairway Lift Corp. (IA)
Iron-A-Way, Inc. (IL)
Murphy Door Bed Co., Inc. (NY)
Sedgwick Lifts, Inc. (NY)
Whitco — Vincent Whitney Co. (CA)

FLOORING, LINOLEUM

Bangor Cork Co., Inc. (PA)
Floortown (MA)
Forbo N.A., Inc. (PA)
Lauria, Tony (PA)
Linoleum City (CA)

Dear Readers of Old-House Journal Catalog:

Are you looking for that "LOOK"? The "LOOK" and the charm of a bygone era can be yours. This can be done by calling our toll free number.

800-233-9307
In PA **717-843-8104**

Just by calling this number you may have found the look that only high quality antique building material, such as ours, can give.

We carry all sorts of wonderful materials. From Peach-Bottom blue roofing slate, which historically has been recorded as the absolute finest slate ever mined in the world, to some of the most beautiful antique wood floors, such as American Chestnut, White Pine, Yellow Pine, Mixed Oaks, Hemlock and some speciality woods never seen before.

So if I have been able to stir those creative images that you may have had for a while, and just did not really know where to find them. Well folks, figuratively speaking, your home. So come on home to **AGED WOODS**®, feel and see that look and charm of **AGED WOODS**® building materials, which come from buildings 100 to over 200 years old.

Please use our toll free number or write for our free brochure and we will give you the information you are looking for, plus you will be able to find out what all we handle.

Most Sincerely,

Donald M. Sprenkle Jr.

Donald M. Sprenkle, Jr.

P.S. Because the main part of our business is milling and reshaping of authentic antique flooring, our floors are now in the process of being distributed nationwide, through local established flooring distributors and dealers. Please call for the distributor or dealer in your area. Thank you.

Aged Woods®

147 West Philadelphia St., York, PA 17401
1 (800) 233-9307 · (717) 843-8104

FLOORING, STONE & CERAMIC

(1) Slate, Marble & Other Stone
(2) Ceramic Tile

American Olean Tile Company (PA) *1,2*
Bergen Bluestone Co., Inc. (NJ) *1*
Brooklyn Tile Supply (NY) *2*
Cold Spring Granite Co. (MN) *1*
Country Floors, Inc. (NY) *2*
Marble Technics Ltd. (NY) *1*
Mid-State Tile Company (NC) *2*
Mr. Slate - Smid Incorporated (VT) *1*
New York Marble Works, Inc. (NY) *1*
Penn Big Bed Slate Co., Inc. (PA) *1*
Permagrain Products, Inc. (PA) *1*
Puccio (NY) *1*
Structural Slate Company (PA) *1*
United Ceramic Tile Arch. Design Div. (NY) *1,2*
Vermont Marble Co. (VT) *1*
Vermont Structural Slate Co. (VT) *1*

FLOORING, WOOD

(1) Hardwood Strip
(2) Heart Pine
(3) Parquet
(4) Wide Board
(5) Other

Aged Woods (PA) *4*
Amherst Woodworking & Supply (MA) . *1,4*
Architectural Accents (GA) *2*
Bangkok Industries, Inc. (PA) *1,3,4*
Broad-Axe Beam Co. (VT) *4*
Bruce Hardwood Floors (TX) *1,3*
ByGone Era Architectural Antiques (GA) *2*
Carlisle Restoration Lumber (NH) *4*
Castle Burlingame (NJ) *4*
Churchill Forest Products, Inc. (MA) *4*
Conklin's Authentic Antique Barnwood (PA) *1,2,4*
Craftsman Lumber Co. (MA) *4*
Dimension Hardwood Inc. (CT) *4*
Floors By Juell (IL) *1*
Florida Victorian Architectural Antiques (FL) *2*
Golden Leaf Timber (NJ) *1,3*
Granville Mfg. Co., Inc. (VT) *2,4*
Harris — Tarkett, Inc. (TN) *3,4*
Heart-Wood, Inc. (FL) *2*
Hoboken Wood Floors Corp. (NJ) *1,4*
The Joinery Co. (NC) *2*
Kentucky Wood Floors, Inc. (KY) *1,3,4*
Maurer & Shepherd, Joyners (CT) *5*
Memphis Hardwood Flooring Co. (TN) *1,3,4*
Moore, E.T., Jr. Co. (VA) *2*
Mountain Lumber Company, Inc. (VA) *2,4*
Peiser Floors (NY) *3*
Permagrain Products, Inc. (PA) *1,3*
Robinson Lumber Company (LA) *2*
"Rustic Barn" Wood Products (VA) *1*
Southington Specialty Wood Co. (CT) *4*
Stark Carpet Corp. (NY) *1,3*
Tiresias, Inc. (SC) *2,4*
Vintage Lumber Co. (MD) *2,4*
Walker's (OH) *4*
Woods American Co. (MD) *1,2,4*

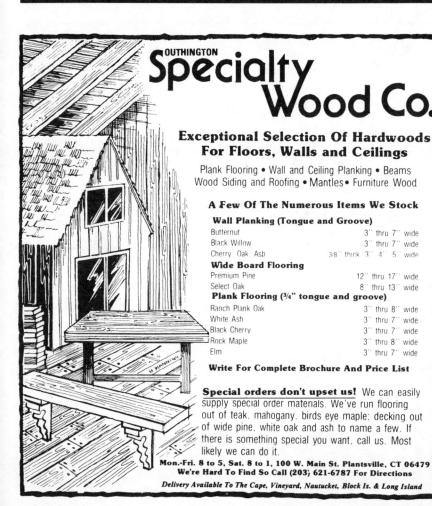

GRILLES FOR HOT-AIR REGISTERS

(1) New
(2) Antique (Original)

A-Ball Plumbing Supply (OR) *1*
Antique Hardware Store (NJ) *1*
Bow & Arrow Stove Co. (MA) *1*
Bryant Stove Works (ME) *2*
Materials Unlimited (MI) *2*
Minuteman International Co., Ltd. (MA) *1*
The Reggio Register Co. (MA) *1*
The Renovator's Supply (MA) *1*

HARDWOODS SUPPLIERS

A & M Wood Specialty, Inc. (CAN)
Allen and Allen Company (TX)
Amherst Woodworking & Supply (MA)
Anderson-McQuaid Co., Inc. (MA)
Center Lumber Company (NJ)
Churchill Forest Products, Inc. (MA)
Craftsman Lumber Co. (MA)
Dimension Lumber Co. (NY)
Golden Leaf Timber (NJ)
Heart-Wood, Inc. (FL)
Kaymar Wood Products, Inc. (WA)
Koppers Co. (PA)
Maxwell Lumber (NY)
J.H. Monteath Co. — Arch. Rep. (NY)
Morgan Woodworking Supplies (KY)
Native American Hardwood Ltd. (NY)
Potlatch Corp. — Townsend Unit (AR)
Southington Specialty Wood Co. (CT)
Turnbull's Lumber Company (MI)
Weird Wood (VT)
Willis Lumber Co. (OH)

OVERDOOR TREATMENTS

Driwood Moulding Company (SC)
Fypon, Inc. (PA)
Kenmore Industries (MA)
Verine Products & Co. (UK)

SPIRAL STAIRCASES

(1) Wood
(2) Metal

American General Products (MI)
Atlantic Stairworks (MA) *1*
Cassidy Bros. Forge, Inc. (MA) *2*
Duvinage Corporation (MD) *1,2*
H & M Stair Builders, Inc. (MD) *1*
International Building Components (NY) *1,2*
The Iron Shop (PA) *1,2*
Midwest Spiral Stair Company, Inc. (IL) *1,2*
David G. Mulder (MI) *1*
Schwartz's Forge & Metalworks, Inc. (NY) *2*
Spiral Manufacturing, Inc. (LA) *1,2*
Stair-Pak Products Co., Inc. (NJ) *1*
Steptoe and Wife Antiques Ltd. (CAN) ... *2*
United Stairs Corp. (NJ) *1*
Urban Archaeology (NY) *2*
Whitten Enterprises, Inc. (VT) *2*
Woodbridge Manufacturing, Inc. (IL) *2*
York Spiral Stair (ME) *1*

STAIRCASE PARTS

(1) Balusters, Antique (Original)
(2) Balusters, New
(3) Balusters, Custom-Made
(4) Handrails
(5) Newel Posts
(6) Other

Abaroot Mfg., Co. (CA) *3,5*
Architectural Accents (GA) *1*
Architectural Stairbuilding and Handrailing (NY) *4*
Bailey Architectural Millwork (NJ) *4*
Bank Architectural Antiques (LA) *4,5*
Bare Wood Inc. (NY) *2,4,5*
Bartleys Mill (CA) *2,3,4,5*
ByGone Era Architectural Antiques (GA) *1,4,5*
Canal Co. (DC) *1,5*
Central Kentucky Millwork (KY) *2,3,4,5*
Classic Architectural Specialties (TX) .. *2,4,5*
The Crowe Company Ltd. (CA) *2,3,4,5*
Cumberland Woodcraft Co., Inc. (PA) *2,2,4,4,5*
Custom Millwork, Inc. (VA) *3,4,5,6*
Drums Sash & Door Co., Inc. (PA) *6*
Dugwood Turners (VA) *3,5*
Elk Valley Woodworking Company (OK) . *2*
Florida Victorian Architectural Antiques (FL) *1,4,5*
Gazebo and Porchworks (WA) *2*
Great American Salvage (NY) *1*
Gunther Mills, Inc. (CT) *3*
H & M Stair Builders, Inc. (MD) *2,4,5*
Haas Wood & Ivory Works, Inc. (CA) . *3,4,5*
Harris — Tarkett, Inc. (TN) *6*
Henderson Black & Greene, Inc. (AL) *2*
House of Moulding (CA) *2,4,5*
Kingsway Victorian Restoration Materials (CO) *2,5,6*
Lance Woodcraft Products (NY) *3,5*
David J. Lassiter (FL) *3*
Lawler Machine & Foundry (AL) *5*
Leeke, John — Woodworker (ME)
Joe Ley Antiques, Inc. (KY) *5*
Mad River Wood Works (CA) *2*
Mansion Industries, Inc. (CA) *2,4,5*
Materials Unlimited (MI) *1*
Michael's Fine Colonial Products (NY) *3,4,5*
Millwork Supply Company (WA) *3*
David G. Mulder (MI) *3,4,5*
Nelson-Johnson Wood Products, Inc. (MN) *2,4,5*
North Pacific Joinery (CA) *3,4,5*
Olde Bostonian Architectural Antiques (MA) *5*
Pagliacco Turning & Milling Architectural Wood Turning (CA) *2,3,5*
Saco Manufacturing & Woodworking (ME) *3,5*
Second Chance (GA) *1,5*
Somerset Door & Column Co. (PA) *3,5*
Urban Archaeology (NY) *5*
Vintage Wood Works (TX) *2,5*

See Company Directory for Addresses & Phone Numbers on page 151

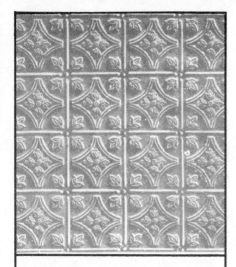

STAIRCASES

Anderson, Townsend (VT)
Architectural Antiques (OK)
Architectural Stairbuilding and Handrailing (NY)
Dahlke Stairs (CT)
Driwood Moulding Company (SC)
Drums Sash & Door Co., Inc. (PA)
H & M Stair Builders, Inc. (MD)
New England Woodturners (CT)
Steptoe and Wife Antiques Ltd. (CAN)
United Stairs Corp. (NJ)

TIN CEILINGS

AA-Abbingdon Affiliates, Inc. (NY)
Architectural Antiques (OK)
Ceilings, Walls & More, Inc. (TX)
Chelsea Decorative Metal Co. (TX)
Classic Ceilings (CA)
Country Shutters (MN)
Designer Resource (CA)
J.D. Dewell & Company (CT)
The Emporium, Inc. (TX)
Kingsway Victorian Restoration Materials (CO)
Klinke & Lew Contractors (CO)
Norman, W.F., Corporation (MO)
Ohman, C.A. (NY)
Remodelers & Renovators (ID)
Renovation Concepts, Inc. (MN)
Shanker Steel Ceiling Co., Inc. (NJ)
Steptoe and Wife Antiques Ltd. (CAN)

W. F. NORMAN Hi-Art Steel Ceilings TIN CEILINGS

Calif., Arizona & Nevada distributor.
Send $3.00 for reprint of 1909 catalog.
Free layout service.

CROWN ANAGLYPTA® AND LINCRUSTA®
family of wallcoverings - imported from England. West coast distributor.
Send for color brochure.

Classic Ceilings

"The quality of yesteryear"

902 E. Commonwealth Ave.
Fullerton, Ca. 92631

166 Waverly Dr.
Pasadena, Ca. 91105

California customers call toll free (800)992-8700
Other states call collect (818)796-5618

HAVE A CEILING YOUR PATRONS WILL LOOK UP TO

18 PATTERNS AVAILABLE

GIVE YOUR RESTAURANT THE RIGHT LOOK WITH

TIN CEILINGS

VICTORIAN TO ART DECO

FREE CATALOG:
CHELSEA DECORATIVE METAL CO.
6115 CHEENA DR., DEPT. OHJ
HOUSTON, TEXAS 77096
713-721-9200

Decorative Metal Ceilings

Original turn-of-the-century patterns

Using eighty year old dies, the W. F. Norman Corporation is once again producing metal plates for the design of ceilings and wall coverings. Their growing popularity stems not only from nostalgia but from their beauty, permanence, fireproofing and economy.

The fullness of the Hi-Art™ line — including center plates, corner plates, border plates, cornice and filler plates — permits classic designs to be produced that are architecturally proportioned for an exact fit.

Write for reproduction copy of 72 page illustrated catalog. Price $3.

W.F. Norman Corporation

P.O. Box 323 • Nevada, Missouri 64772 • 1-800-641-4038

VENEERS & INLAYS

A & M Wood Specialty, Inc. (CAN)
Gaston Wood Finishes, Inc. (IN)
Homecraft Veneer (PA)
J.H. Monteath Co. — Arch. Rep. (NY)
Morgan Woodworking Supplies (KY)

WAINSCOTTING

(1) Antique (Salvage)
(2) New

Amherst Woodworking & Supply (MA) ... *2*
Art Directions (MO) ... *1*
Bare Wood Inc. (NY) ... *2*
Bartleys Mill (CA) ... *2*
Carlisle Restoration Lumber (NH) ... *2*
Central Kentucky Millwork (KY) ... *2*
Craftsman Lumber Co. (MA) ... *2*
Cumberland Woodcraft Co., Inc. (PA) ... *2*
Custom Millwork, Inc. (VA) ... *2*
J.D. Dewell & Company (CT) ... *2*
Dimension Hardwood Inc. (CT) ... *2*
Dovetail Woodworking (WI) ... *2*
Florida Victorian Architectural Antiques (FL) ... *1*
Heart-Wood, Inc. (FL) ... *2*
Mad River Wood Works (CA) ... *2*
Materials Unlimited (MI) ... *1*
Maurer & Shepherd, Joyners (CT) ... *2*
Old World Moulding & Finishing Co., Inc. (NY) ... *2*
Olde Bostonian Architectural Antiques (MA) ... *1*
Renovation Concepts, Inc. (MN)
Restoration Fraternity (PA) ... *2*
Robinson Lumber Company (LA) ... *2*
"Rustic Barn" Wood Products (VA) ... *2*
San Francisco Victoriana (CA) ... *2*
Silverton Victorian Millworks (CO) ... *2*
States Industries (OR) ... *2*
Sunshine Architectural Woodworks (AR) . *2*
Wood Designs (OH)
Woodpecker Products Inc. (CO) ... *2*

Decorative Interior Materials & Supplies

WALL PANELLING, WOOD—PERIOD

(1) Antique (Salvage)
(2) New—Stock Items
(3) Custom-Made

Aged Woods (PA) *1*
Amherst Woodworking & Supply (MA) ... *3*
Architectural Antiques Exchange (PA) *1*
Architectural Components (MA) *3*
Architectural Paneling, Inc. (NY) *3*
Art Directions (MO) *1*
Bangkok Industries, Inc. (PA) *2*
Bare Wood Inc. (NY) *3*
Broad-Axe Beam Co. (VT) *2*
Carlisle Restoration Lumber (NH) *3*
Central Kentucky Millwork (KY) *2,3*
Craftsman Lumber Co. (MA) *3*
Cumberland Woodcraft Co., Inc. (PA) *2*
Dovetail Woodworking (WI) *3*
Driwood Moulding Company (SC) *3*
Early New England Rooms & Exteriors Inc. (CT) *3*
Floors By Juell (IL) *3*
Heart-Wood, Inc. (FL) *3*
LaPointe, Chip, Cabinetmaker (MA) *3*
Leeke, John — Woodworker (ME) *3*
Mad River Wood Works (CA) *3*
Maurer & Shepherd, Joyners (CT) *3*
Moore, E.T., Jr. Co. (VA) *3*
Mountain Lumber Company, Inc. (VA) .. *1*
Niece Lumber Co. (NJ) *2*
Old World Moulding & Finishing Co., Inc. (NY) *2,3*
Frank Pellitteri Inc. (NY) *3*
Piscatagua Architectural Woodwork, Co. (NH) *3*
Restoration Fraternity (PA) *3*
Restorations Unlimited, Inc. (PA) *3*
Salvage One (IL) *1*
Somerset Door & Column Co. (PA) *3*
Southington Specialty Wood Co. (CT) *2*
States Industries (OR) *2*
W. P. Stephens Lumber Co. (GA) *3*
Sunshine Architectural Woodworks (AR) *2,3*
Tiresias, Inc. (SC) *2*
United House Wrecking Corp. (CT) *1*
Urban Archaeology (NY) *1*
Woods American Co. (MD) *1,3*

OTHER INTERIOR STRUCTURAL MATERIALS

Ceilings, Walls & More, Inc. (TX)
J.D. Dewell & Company (CT)

See Company Directory for Addresses & Phone Numbers on page 151

BRACKETS & CORBELS—INTERIOR

ARJ Associates (MA)
American Architectural Art Company (PA)
ByGone Era Architectural Antiques (GA)
Classic Architectural Specialties (TX)
Cumberland Woodcraft Co., Inc. (PA)
Custom Millwork, Inc. (VA)
Decorators Supply Corp. (IL)
Dovetail, Inc. (MA)
Elk Valley Woodworking Company (OK)
Grinling Architectural Period Mouldings (NJ)
Haas Wood & Ivory Works, Inc. (CA)
House of Moulding (CA)
Koeppel/Freedman Studios (MA)
Mendocino Millwork (CA)
United House Wrecking Corp. (CT)
Vintage Wood Works (TX)

CEILING MEDALLIONS

(1) Non-Plaster
(2) Plaster

ARJ Associates (MA) *2*
American Architectural Art Company (PA) *2*
American Lamp Parts, Inc. (TX) *1*
Archicast (TN) *1,2*
Architectural Reproductions, Inc. (OR) .. *1,2*
Architectural Sculpture Ltd. (NY) *2*
Balmer Architectural Art Limited (CAN) .. *2*
Crawford's Old House Store (WI) *1*
Custom Castings (TX) *1*
Decorators Supply Corp. (IL) *2*
Design-Cast Corporation (NJ) *1*
Designer Resource (CA) *1,2*
J.D. Dewell & Company (CT) *1,2*
Dovetail, Inc. (MA) *2*
Entol Industries, Inc. (FL) *1*
Felber Studios, Inc. (PA) *2*
Fischer & Jirouch Co. (OH) *2*
Focal Point, Inc. (GA) *1*
Giannetti Studios, Inc. (MD) *1,2*
Grinling Architectural Period Mouldings (NJ) *1*
History Store (MD) *2*
Hosek Manufacturing Co. (CO) *2*
House of Moulding (CA) *1*
Koeppel/Freedman Studios (MA) *1,2*
Lachin, Albert & Assoc., Inc. (LA) *2*
Nomaco Decorative Products, Inc. (CT) ... *1*
Nostalgia (GA) *2*
Ornamental Design Studios (NY) *2*
Park Place (DC) *1,2*
Renovation Concepts, Inc. (MN) *1,2*
Restoration Works, Inc. (NY) *1*
Russell Restoration of Suffolk (NY) *2*
San Francisco Victoriana (CA) *2*
J.P. Weaver Co. (CA) *1*
Weaver, W. T. & Sons, Inc. (DC) *1*

CERAMIC TILE

(1) Antique
(2) Dutch
(3) Encaustic
(4) Hand-Painted
(5) Period Styles—New
(6) Small White Hexagonal (Bathroom)
(7) Custom-Made

ARJ Associates (MA) *4,7*
American Olean Tile Company (PA) *5*
Amsterdam Corporation (NY) *2,4*
Backlund Moravian Tile Works (FL) *4,5,7*
Barbara Vantrease Beall Studio (CA) *4,7*
Bertin Tile Studio (NY) *4,5,7*
Brooklyn Tile Supply (NY) *6*
J.R. Burrows & Co. (MA) *5*
Country Floors, Inc. (NY) *5*
Deer Creek Pottery (CA) *4,5,7*
Designs in Tile (CA) *2,3,4,5,7*
Dutch Products & Supply Co. (PA) *2,4*
Elon, Inc. A & D Building (NY) *4*
FerGene Studio (IN) *5*
Firebird, Inc. (NJ) *4,7*
H & R Johnson Tile Ltd./ Highgate Tile Works *3,5,7*
Jackson, Wm. H. Co. (NY) *4*
L'esperance Tile Works (NY) *3,4,6,7*
Moravian Pottery & Tile Works (PA) *4,5*
Paul J. Foster (NY) *4,6*
Priscilla Ceramic Tiles (NY) *4,7*
San Do Designs/Spanish Tile Factoria (FL) *4,7*
Second Chance (GA) *1*
Starbuck Goldner (PA) *4,5,7*
Terra Designs, Inc. (NJ) *4,5,7*
United States Ceramic Tile Company (OH)
Victorian Collectibles Ltd. (WI) *5*
Helen Williams—Delft Tiles (CA) *1,2*

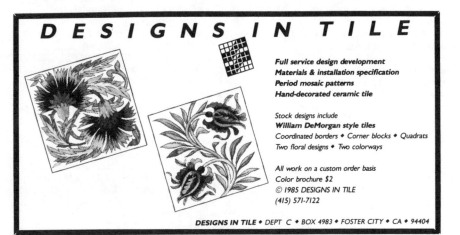

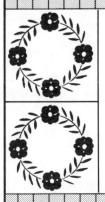

See Company Directory for Addresses & Phone Numbers on page 151

COLUMNS & CAPITALS—INTERIOR

(1) Composition
(2) Plaster
(3) Wood

American Architectural Art Company (PA)
American Wood Column Corporation (NY) *3*
Archicast (TN) *1,2*
Architectural Accents (GA) *3*
Architectural Antiques Exchange (PA) *3*
Architectural Reproductions, Inc. (OR) .. *1,2*
Architectural Sculpture Ltd. (NY) *2*
Balmer Architectural Art Limited (CAN) *1,2*
Bare Wood Inc. (NY) *3*
ByGone Era Architectural Antiques (GA) *3*
Classic Architectural Specialties (TX) *3*
Cumberland Woodcraft Co., Inc. (PA) *3*
Custom Castings (TX) *1*
Decorators Supply Corp. (IL) *2,3*
Designer Resource (CA) *1,2,3*
J.D. Dewell & Company (CT) *2,3,3*
Dovetail, Inc. (MA) *2*
Elk Valley Woodworking Company (OK) . *3*
Felber Studios, Inc. (PA) *2*
Fischer & Jirouch Co. (OH) *2*
Florida Victorian Architectural Antiques (FL) *1,3*
Giannetti Studios, Inc. (MD) *1,2*
Haas Wood & Ivory Works, Inc. (CA) *3*
Hartmann-Sanders Column Co. (GA) *3*
Kingsway Victorian Restoration Materials (CO) *1*
Koeppel/Freedman Studios (MA) *1,2*
Lachin, Albert & Assoc., Inc. (LA) *2*
David J. Lassiter (FL) *3*
Pagliacco Turning & Milling Architectural Wood Turning (CA) *3*
Renaissance Woodcarving, Inc. (NY) *3*
Renovation Concepts, Inc. (MN) *2,3*
Russell Restoration of Suffolk (NY) *2*
A.F. Schwerd Manufacturing Co. (PA) .. *1,3*
Second Chance (GA) *3*
United House Wrecking Corp. (CT) *3*
Worthington Group Ltd. (GA) *3*

CORNER BEAD MOULDING

Central Kentucky Millwork (KY)
Classic Architectural Specialties (TX)
Crawford's Old House Store (WI)
Wood Designs (OH)

FRETWORK & GRILLES, WOOD

Architectural Antiques Exchange (PA)
ByGone Era Architectural Antiques (GA)
Cumberland Woodcraft Co., Inc. (PA)
The Emporium, Inc. (TX)
Gazebo and Porchworks (WA)
Mad River Wood Works (CA)
North Pacific Joinery (CA)
Renovation Concepts, Inc. (MN)
Victorian Reproductions Enterprises, Inc. (MN)
Vintage Wood Works (TX)
Woodstone Co. (VT)

GLASS, CURVED—FOR CHINA CABINETS

Blaschke Cabinet Glass (CT)
Shadovitz Bros. Distributors, Inc. (NY)

GLASS, ART—ANTIQUE (STAINED, BEVELLED, ETCHED, ETC.)

Architectural Accents (GA)
Architectural Antiques (OK)
Architectural Salvage Co. (MI)
Art Directions (MO)
Bank Architectural Antiques (LA)
ByGone Era Architectural Antiques (GA)·
Canal Co. (DC)
Cohen's Architectural Heritage (CAN)
Electric Glass Co. (VA)
Florida Victorian Architectural Antiques (FL)
Glass Arts—The Condon Studios (MA)
Great American Salvage (NY)
Master's Stained and Etched Glass Studio (CA)
Materials Unlimited (MI)
Maurer & Shepherd, Joyners (CT)
Ohmega Salvage (CA)
Old World Restorations, Inc. (OH)
Pelnik Wrecking Co., Inc. (NY)
Salvage One (IL)
Spiess Antique Building Materials (IL)
Splendor in Brass (MD)
United House Wrecking Corp. (CT)
Victorian Glassworks (DC)
Westlake Architectural Antiques (TX)
Williams Art Glass Studio, Inc./Sunset Antiques, Inc. (MI)
Wilson, H. Weber, Antiquarian (MD)
Wrecking Bar of Atlanta (GA)

GLASS, ETCHED—NEW

(1) Stock
(2) Custom

Backstrom Stained Glass et al (MS)	*2*
Bel-Air Door Co. (CA)	*1*
Boulder Stained Glass Studios (CO)	*2*
CW Design, Inc. (MN)	*2*
The Crowe Company Ltd. (CA)	*1*
Curran, Patrick J. (MA)	*2*
Full Circle Glass Company (NY)	
Glass Designs (KY)	*1,2*
Greenland Studio, Inc., The (NY)	*1,2*
Lyn Hovey Studio, Inc. (MA)	*2*
Louisville Art Glass Studio (KY)	*2*
Manor Art Glass Studio (NY)	
Master's Stained and Etched Glass Studio (CA)	*2*
Meredith Stained Glass Studio, Inc. (MD)	*1*
Morgan Bockius Studios, Inc. (PA)	*2*
Nast, Vivian Glass and Design (NY)	*2*
Neuman Studios (VT)	*2*
New York Carved Arts Co. (NY)	*2*
Newe Daisterre Glas (OH)	*2*
Ostrom & Co., Inc. (OR)	*2*
Park Place (DC)	*1,2*
Pompei Stained Glass, Inc. (MA)	*2*
Ring, J. Stained Glass, Inc. (MN)	*2*
Shadovitz Bros. Distributors, Inc. (NY)	*1*
Studio Workshop, Ltd. (CT)	*2*
Sunburst Stained Glass Co. (IN)	*1,2*
Visible Glass (MN)	*2*

GLASS, LEADED & STAINED—NEW

(1) New Work
(2) Restoration & Repair

Architectual Salvage Co. (MI) *1,2*
Art Glass Studio Inc. (NY) *1,2*
Backstrom Stained Glass et al (MS) *1*
Beirs, John — Glass Studio (PA) *1*
Bel-Air Door Co. (CA) *1*
Botti Studio of Architectural Arts (IL) *1,2*
Boulder Stained Glass Studios (CO) *1,2*
Chadwick Studio (CT) *1,2*
The Crowe Company Ltd. (CA) *1*
Curran, Patrick J. (MA) *1*
Full Circle Glass Company (NY) *2*
Glass Artisan, Inc. (NY) *1,2*
Glass Arts—The Condon Studios (MA) .. *1,2*
Glass Designs (KY) *1*
Glass Roots (NY) *2*
Golden Age Glassworks (NY) *1,2*
Greenland Studio, Inc., The (NY) *1,2*
Greg Monk Stained Glass (HI) *1,2*
Lyn Hovey Studio, Inc. (MA) *1,2*
Lake Country Brass (NH) *1*
LaRoche Stained Glass (MA) *1,2*
Louisville Art Glass Studio (KY) *1*
Manor Art Glass Studio (NY) *1,2*
Master's Stained and Etched Glass Studio (CA) *1*
Materials Unlimited (MI) *1*
Melotte-Morse Studios (IL) *1,2*
Meredith Stained Glass Studio, Inc. (MD) *1*
Morgan Bockius Studios, Inc. (PA) *1,2*
Nast, Vivian Glass and Design (NY) *1*
Neuman Studios (VT) *1,2*
Newe Daisterre Glas (OH) *1,2*
Park Place (DC) *1*
Phoenix Studio, Inc. (ME) *1,2*
Pike Stained Glass Studios, Inc. (NY) *1,2*
Pompei Stained Glass, Inc. (MA) *1,2*
Rambusch (NY) *2*
Ring, J. Stained Glass, Inc. (MN) *1,2*
Rohlf's Stained & Leaded Glass Studio (NY) *1,2*
St. Luke's Studio (RI) *1,2*
Salamandra Glass (NH)
Schlitz Studios (WI)
Shadovitz Bros. Distributors, Inc. (NY) *1*
Spiess Antique Building Materials (IL) *1*
Arthur Stern Studios Arch. Glass (CA) *1*
Studio Workshop, Ltd. (CT) *2*
Sunburst Stained Glass Co. (IN) *1,2*
Sunflower Glass Studio (NJ) *1,2*
United House Wrecking Corp. (CT) *1*
Victorian Glassworks (DC) *1,2*
Jack Wallis' Doors (KY) *1*
Walton Stained Glass (CA) *1*
Willet Stained Glass Studio, Inc. (PA) *1,2*
Williams Art Glass Studio, Inc./Sunset Antiques, Inc. (MI) *1,2*
Wilson, H. Weber, Antiquarian (MD) *1,2*

See Company Directory for Addresses & Phone Numbers on page 151

GLASS, SPECIALTY—NEW

(1) Bevelled
(2) Carved & Cut
(3) Engraved
(4) Glue-Chip
(5) Slumping & Bending

The Antique Restoration Co. (PA) *1*
B&B Glass Etching (IL) *3*
Beirs, John — Glass Studio (PA) *1*
Bel-Air Door Co. (CA) *1*
Beveled Glass Industries (CA) *1*
Boulder Stained Glass Studios (CO) *1,5*
Cain-Powers, Inc. Architectural Art Glass (VA) *1*
Cherry Creek Ent. Inc. (CO) *1*
Coran — Sholes Industries (MA) *4*
The Crowe Company Ltd. (CA) *1*
Curran, Patrick J. (MA) *1,5*
Electric Glass Co. (VA) *1*
Ferguson's Cut Glass Works (OH) *1,3*
Full Circle Glass Company (NY) *1,3,4*
Glass Arts—The Condon Studios (MA) .. *1,5*
Glass Designs (KY) *2*
Glass Roots (NY) *1*
Lyn Hovey Studio, Inc. (MA) *1,5*
Louisville Art Glass Studio (KY) *1*
Manor Art Glass Studio (NY) *2*
Master's Stained and Etched Glass Studio (CA) *1*
Meredith Stained Glass Studio, Inc. (MD) *1*
Morgan Bockius Studios, Inc. (PA) *1,2,5*
Neuman Studios (VT) *5*
Newe Daisterre Glas (OH) *1,5*
Nostalgia (GA) *1*
Park Place (DC) *1,2*
Point Five Windows (CO) *4*
Pompei Stained Glass, Inc. (MA) *1,5*
Ring, J. Stained Glass, Inc. (MN) *1,3,5*
Shadovitz Bros. Distributors, Inc. (NY) *1,4,5*
Spiess Antique Building Materials (IL) *1*
Studio Workshop, Ltd. (CT) *4*
Sunburst Stained Glass Co. (IN) *1*
Visible Glass (MN) *5*
Walton Stained Glass (CA) *1*
Williams Art Glass Studio, Inc./Sunset Antiques, Inc. (MI) *1,4*

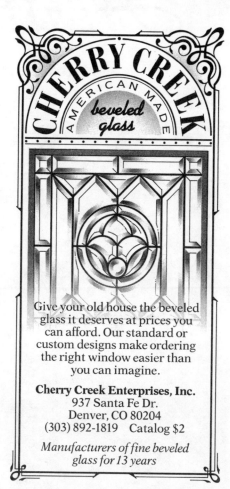

MANTELS

(1) Antique (Original)
(2) New (Reproduction)
(3) Cast Iron
(4) Marble
(5) Slate
(6) Wood
(7) Custom
(8) Other

Danny Alessandro/Edwin Jackson (NY) *1,2,4,6,6*
Architectural Accents (GA) *1*
Architectural Antiques (OK) *1,3,6,1,4,6*
Architectural Components (MA) *2,6*
Architectural Paneling, Inc. (NY) *2,6*
Architectural Salvage Co. (MI) *1*
Art Directions (MO) *1*
Artifacts, Inc. (VA) *1,2*
Bank Architectural Antiques (LA) *1*
Bare Wood Inc. (NY) *1,2,6*
Bartleys Mill (CA) *2,6*
Bjorndal Woodworks (WI) *2,6*
ByGone Era Architectural Antiques (GA) *1,3,4,5,6*
Canal Co. (DC) *1*
Central Kentucky Millwork (KY) *2,6,7*
Cohen's Architectural Heritage (CAN) *1*
Crawford's Old House Store (WI) *2*
Custom Millwork, Inc. (VA) *2,6,7*
Dalton-Gorman, Inc. (IL) *4*
Decorators Supply Corp. (IL) *2*
Designer Resource (CA) *6,8*
Driwood Moulding Company (SC) *2,7*
Drums Sash & Door Co., Inc. (PA) *2*
Early New England Rooms & Exteriors Inc. (CT) *6,7*
Fireplace Mantel Shop, Inc. (MD) *2,6*
Florida Victorian Architectural Antiques (FL) *1*
Gazebo and Porchworks (WA) *6*
Great American Salvage (NY) *1*
Gunther Mills, Inc. (CT) *4*
Heart-Wood, Inc. (FL) *2,6*
Henderson Black & Greene, Inc. (AL) *2*
Heritage Mantels (CT) *2,4*
History Store (MD) *1*
Jackson, Wm. H. Co. (NY) *6*
Joe Ley Antiques, Inc. (KY) *1*
London Country, Ltd. (MN) *1*
Maizefield Mantels (WA) *2,6,7*
Maple Hill Woodworking (NY) *7*
Materials Unlimited (MI) *1*
Millwork Supply Company (WA) *6*
Monroe Coldren and Sons (PA) *1*
Moore, E.T., Jr. Co. (VA) *6*
New York Marble Works, Inc. (NY) *4*
Off The Wall, Architectural Antiques (CA) *1*
Old Carolina Brick Co. (NC) *2,8*
Old World Moulding & Finishing Co., Inc. (NY) *2*
Olde Bostonian Architectural Antiques (MA) *1*
Olde & Oak Antiques (AL) *1,6*
Pelnik Wrecking Co., Inc. (NY) *1*
Puccio (NY) *4*
Purcell, Francis J., II (PA) *1*
Ramase (CT) *1*
Readybuilt Products, Co. (MD) *2,6*
Remodelers & Renovators (ID) *2*
Renaissance Woodcarving, Inc. (NY) *2,6,7*
Renovation Concepts, Inc. (MN) *2*
Restoration Fraternity (PA) *2*
Roman Marble Co. (IL) *1,4*
Salvage One (IL) *1*
Second Chance (GA) *1*
Sheppard Millwork, Inc. (WA) *2,6,7*
Southington Specialty Wood Co. (CT) *6*
Spiess Antique Building Materials (IL) *1*
Sunshine Architectural Woodworks (AR) *2,6*
United House Wrecking Corp. (CT) *1,6*
Verine Products & Co. (UK) *2*
Westlake Architectural Antiques (TX) *1,3,4,5,6*
Williams Art Glass Studio, Inc./Sunset Antiques, Inc. (MI) *1*
Wrecking Bar of Atlanta (GA) *1*

MARBLE, REPLACEMENT (FINISHED PIECES)

Marble Technics Ltd. (NY)
New York Marble Works, Inc. (NY)
Pietra Dura, Inc. (NY)
Puccio (NY)
Shaw Marble Works Mid-America Marble & Granite (MO)
Vermont Marble Co. (VT)

See Company Directory for Addresses & Phone Numbers on page 151

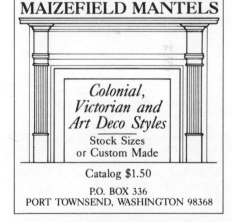

ORNAMENTS

(1) Composition
(2) Wood
(3) Plaster

American Wood Column Corporation (NY) *1,2*
Archicast (TN) *1,3*
Architectural Sculpture Ltd. (NY) *3*
Balmer Architectural Art Limited (CAN) .. *1*
Bendix Mouldings, Inc. (NJ) *2*
Custom Castings (TX) *1*
Decorators Supply Corp. (IL) *1,2,3*
Dovetail, Inc. (MA) *3*
Entol Industries, Inc. (FL) *1,2*
Felber Studios, Inc. (PA) *3*
Fischer & Jirouch Co. (OH) *3*
Focal Point, Inc. (GA) *1*
Giannetti Studios, Inc. (MD) *1,3*
Haas Wood & Ivory Works, Inc. (CA) *2*
Hosek Manufacturing Co. (CO) *3*
House of Moulding (CA) *2*
Kingsway Victorian Restoration Materials (CO) *3,3*
Koeppel/Freedman Studios (MA) *1,1,3,3,3*
Lachin, Albert & Assoc., Inc. (LA) *3*
David J. Lassiter (FL) *2*
Mendocino Millwork (CA) *2*
Nelson-Johnson Wood Products, Inc. (MN) *2*
Nostalgia (GA) *3*
Russell Restoration of Suffolk (NY) *3*
Silverton Victorian Millworks (CO) *2*
J.P. Weaver Co. (CA) *1*
Weaver, W. T. & Sons, Inc. (DC) *1,2*

MOULDINGS & CORNICES—INTERIOR DECORATIVE

(1) Composition
(2) Plaster
(3) Wood
(4) Custom

American Architectural Art Company (PA) *1,2*
American Wood Column Corporation (NY) *1,3*
Archicast (TN) *1,2,4*
Architectural Paneling, Inc. (NY) *3*
Architectural Sculpture Ltd. (NY) *2,4*
Architectural Shapes, Inc. (PA) *1,4*
Balmer Architectural Art Limited (CAN) *1,2*
Bare Wood Inc. (NY) *3,4*
Bartleys Mill (CA) *3*
Bendix Mouldings, Inc. (NJ) *3*
Central Kentucky Millwork (KY) *3,4*
Classic Architectural Specialties (TX) *3*
Colonial Restoration Products (PA) *4*
Country Shutters (MN) *3*
Cumberland Woodcraft Co., Inc. (PA) *3*
Custom Castings (TX) *1,4*
Custom Millwork, Inc. (VA) *3,4*
Decorators Supply Corp. (IL) *1,2,3*
Design-Cast Corporation (NJ) *1*
Designer Resource (CA) *1,2,3*
J.D. Dewell & Company (CT) *2,3,3*
Dimension Lumber Co. (NY) *3*
Dovetail, Inc. (MA) *2*
Dovetail Woodworking (WI) *3*
Driwood Moulding Company (SC) *3*
Elk Valley Woodworking Company (OK)
Englewood Hardware Co. (NJ) *2*
Entol Industries, Inc. (FL) *1*
Felber Studios, Inc. (PA) *2,4*
Fireplace Mantel Shop, Inc. (MD) *3*
Fischer & Jirouch Co. (OH) *2*
Focal Point, Inc. (GA) *1*
Frenzel Specialty Moulding Co. (MO) *3,4*
Giannetti Studios, Inc. (MD) *1,2,4*
Glass & Aluminum Construction Services, Inc. (NH) *3*
Greensboro Art Foundry & Machine Co. (NC) *4*
Grinling Architectural Period Mouldings (NJ) *1*
Gunther Mills, Inc. (CT) *3*
Haas Wood & Ivory Works, Inc. (CA) *3*
Heart-Wood, Inc. (FL) *3,4*
Homestead Supply (MA) *3,4*
Hosek Manufacturing Co. (CO) *2*
House of Moulding (CA) *3*
Kingsway Victorian Restoration Materials (CO) *3*
Klise Manufacturing Company (MI) *3*
Koeppel/Freedman Studios (MA) *4*
Lachin, Albert & Assoc., Inc. (LA) *2,4*
David J. Lassiter (FL) *3*
Maxwell Lumber (NY) *3*
Mendocino Millwork (CA) *3*
Merit Moulding, Ltd. (NY) *3*
Michael's Fine Colonial Products (NY) .. *3,4*
J.H. Monteath Co. — Arch. Rep. (NY) *3*
Moore, E.T., Jr. Co. (VA) *3*
Navedo Woodcraft, Inc. (NY) *3*
Nelson-Johnson Wood Products, Inc. (MN) *3*
Niece Lumber Co. (NJ) *3*
Nomaco Decorative Products, Inc. (CT) ... *1*
Nostalgia (GA) *2*
Old House - New House Restorations (MN) *3,4*
Old World Moulding & Finishing Co., Inc. (NY) *3*
Ornamental Design Studios (NY) *2,4*
Park Place (DC) *2,4*
Frank Pellitteri Inc. (NY) *3*
Piscatagua Architectural Woodwork, Co. (NH) *3*
Price & Visser Millwork (WA) *3*
Reliance Industries, Inc. (IA) *3,4*
Renovation Concepts, Inc. (MN) *2,3*
Russell Restoration of Suffolk (NY) *2,4*
San Francisco Victoriana (CA) *2,3,4*
Sheppard Millwork, Inc. (WA) *3*
Silverton Victorian Millworks (CO) *3*
The Smoot Lumber Company (VA) *3*
W. P. Stephens Lumber Co. (GA) *3*
Sunshine Architectural Woodworks (AR) . *3*
Victorian Collectibles Ltd. (WI) *2*
Walbrook Mill & Lumber Co., Inc. (MD) .. *3*
J.P. Weaver Co. (CA) *1*
Wood Designs (OH) *3*
Wood Masters, Inc. (NJ) *3,4*
Wood Moulding & Millwork Producers Association (OR) *3*
Woods American Co. (MD) *3,3,4*

See Company Directory for Addresses & Phone Numbers on page 151

Furniture & Furnishings

BED HANGINGS

(1) Netted Bed Canopies
(2) Bed Curtains
(3) Quilts & Coverlets

Biggs Company (VA) *1*
Nancy Borden Period Textile Replicas (NH) *2*
Carter Canopies (NC) *1,2,3*
Cohasset Colonials (MA) *1*
Colonial Canopies (NC) *1*
Colonial Weavers (ME) *3*
Country Curtains (MA) *2,3*
The Country Store (IL) *3*
Ephraim Marsh (NC) *1*
Family Heir-Loom Weavers (PA) *3*
Gazebo (NY) *3*
Virginia Goodwin (NC) *1,3*
Great Expectations Quilts, Inc. (TX) *3*
House of Vermillion (UT) *2*
S. & C. Huber, Accoutrements (CT) *1,2*
Natural Fiber Fabrics (VT) *3*
Old Abingdon Weavers (VA) *1,3*
Pennsylvania Dutch Quilts (PA) *3*
Plain and Fancy (VT) *3*
Quaker Lace Co. (NY) *3*
Winters Textile Mill (CA) *3*
Yankee Pride (MA) *3*

CANDLESTANDS & HOLDERS

(1) Candlestands
(2) Candelabra
(3) Candlesticks

Brubaker Metalcrafts (OH) *2*
Cohasset Colonials (MA) *1*
Colonial Casting Co., Inc. (CT) *3*
Colonial Restoration Products (PA) *1,2,3*
Colonial Williamsburg Foundation (VA) *1,2,3*
Crafts Manufacturing Co. (MA) *3*
Essex Forge (CT) *1*
Historic Charleston Reproductions (SC) ... *3*
Hood, R. and Co. (NH) *1,3*
Hurley Patentee Lighting (NY) *1,2,3*
Kayne & Son Custom Forged Hardware (NC) *1*
Loose, Thomas — Blacksmith/ Whitesmith (PA) *3*
Millham, Newton — Blacksmith (MA) ... *1*
Olde Village Smithery (MA) *3*
The Renovator's Supply (MA)
Saltbox (PA) *1*
Sign of the Crab (CA) *2*
Donald C. Stetson, Sr., Enterprises (MA)
The Tin Bin (PA) *3*
Vermont Industries, Inc. (VT) *3*
Washington Copper Works (CT) *2*
Windy Hill Forge (MD) *1,2*
Winterthur Museum and Gardens (DE) ... *1*
Wolchonok, M. and Son, Inc. (NY) *3*

CHAIRS, EARLY AMERICAN REPRODUCTION

(1) Colonial Wooden Side Chairs
(2) Rockers
(3) Other

Stephen A. Adams, Furnituremakers/W.H. James Co. (ME) *1,2*
Michael Camp (MI) *1*
Cohasset Colonials (MA)
Colonial Williamsburg Foundation (VA) ... *1*
Cornucopia, Inc. At the Appleworks (MA) *1,2*
Country Bed Shop (MA) *1*
Ephraim Marsh (NC) *1,2*
Peter Franklin, Cabinetmaker (MA) *1*
Furniture Traditions, Inc. (NC) *1*
Habersham Plantation Corp. (GA) *1,2*
Hitchcock Chair Co. (CT)
Lea, James — Cabinetmaker (ME) *1*
Rocker Shop of Marietta, GA (GA) *2*
Shaker Workshops (MA) *1,2*
Yield House, Inc. (NH) *1*

See Company Directory for Addresses & Phone Numbers on page 151

CHAIRS, VICTORIAN REPRODUCTION

(1) Morris
(2) Turn-of-Century Oak
(3) Rockers
(4) Other

Magnolia Hall (GA) *2,3*
Martha M. House Furniture (AL) *4*
Rocker Shop of Marietta, GA (GA) *3*
Victorian Reproductions Enterprises, Inc. (MN) *3*

CHAIRS, TWENTIETH-CENTURY REPRODUCTION

Arkitektura (NJ)
Fifty / 50 Gallery (NY)
Metropolis (NY)

CHRISTMAS DECORATIONS

Amazon Vinegar & Pickling Works Drygoods (IA)
D. Blumchen & Co., Inc. (NJ)
Christmas Treasures (NY)
Crispin Treadway Floral Products (NY)
Gerlachs of Lecha (PA)
Hurley Patentee Lighting (NY)
Museum of the City of New York (NY)
Victorian Accents (NJ)

CLOCKS

(1) Traditional (Assembled)
(2) Kits

Armor Products (NY)
Clocks, Etc. (CA) *1*
The Corner Store (AR) *1*
Cumberland General Store (TN) *1*
Magnolia Hall (GA) *1*
Mason & Sullivan Co. (MA) *1*
Merritt's Antiques, Inc. (PA) *1,2*
Howard Miller Clock Co. (MI) *1*
Selva — Borel (CA) *1,2*
Sign of the Crab (CA) *1*
Winterthur Museum and Gardens (DE) *1*

CLOTHING, PERIOD

(1) Patterns
(2) Custom-Made
(3) Ready-To-Wear

Amazon Vinegar & Pickling Works Drygoods (IA) *1,3*
Madhatter Press (MN) *1*
Past Patterns (MI) *1*
Shaker Workshops (MA) *1*

DRAPERY HARDWARE

(1) Wood Poles, Brackets or Finials
(2) Metal Poles & Brackets
(3) Decorative Tie-Backs

Antique Hardware Store (NJ) *3*
Ball and Ball (PA) *2,3*
Cohasset Colonials (MA) *1*
Country Curtains (MA) *1*
Decoration Day (NY) *3*
Decorative Hardware Studio (NY) *2,3*
Gould-Mesereau Co., Inc. (NY) *1,2,3*
Guerin, P.E. Inc. (NY) *2,3*
Hunrath , Wm. Co., Inc. (NY) *2*
Kayne & Son Custom Forged Hardware (NC) *3*
Perkowitz Window Fashions (IL) *1,2*
South Bound Millworks (MA) *1,2*
Standard Trimming Co. (NY) *3*

DRAPERY TRIMMINGS

Colonial Williamsburg Foundation (VA)
Decoration Day (NY)
Elsie's Exquisiques (MI)
Goodman - Southern Fabrications (KS)
Meyer, Kenneth Co. (CA)
Scalamandre, Inc. (NY)
Silk Surplus Inc. (NY)
Standard Trimming Co. (NY)

DRAPERY & CURTAINS

(1) Curtains, Ready-Made
(2) Curtains, Custom-Made
(3) Drapes, Custom-Made

Nelson Beck of Washington, Inc. (DC) .. *2,3*
Nancy Borden Period Textile Replicas (NH) *2*
J.R. Burrows & Co. (MA) *1*
Cassen, Henry Inc. (NY) *2*
Cohasset Colonials (MA) *1*
Colonial Maid Curtains (NY) *1*
Country Curtains (MA) *1*
Dorothy's Ruffled Originals (NC) *1,2*
Goodman - Southern Fabrications (KS) *3*
Home Fabric Mills, Inc. (MA) *3*
House of Vermillion (UT) *2*
Maynard House Antiques (MA) *2,3*
Olde & Oak Antiques (AL) *2,3*
Quaker Lace Co. (NY) *1*
Rue de France (RI) *2,3*
Vintage Valances (MI) *2,3*

DRAPERY & CURTAIN PATTERNS—PERIOD DESIGNS

Colonial Weavers (ME)

FABRIC, REPRODUCTION

(1) Early American
(2) Victorian
(3) Turn-of-Century
(4) Twentieth-Century

Amazon Vinegar & Pickling Works Drygoods (IA) *2*
Bergamo Fabrics, Inc. (NY) *3*
Nancy Borden Period Textile Replicas (NH) *1,2*
Brunschwig & Fils, Inc. (NY) *1,2,3,4*
Clarence House Imports, Ltd. (NY) *1,2*
Cohasset Colonials (MA) *1*
Colonial Williamsburg Foundation (VA) ... *1*
Cowtan & Tout, Inc. D&D Building (NY) *2,3*
Elsie's Exquisiques (MI) *2*
Hexter, S. M. Company (OH) *1*
Hinson & Co. (NY) *1*
Historic Charleston Reproductions (SC) ... *2*
Lee Jofa (NY) *1,2*
Scalamandre, Inc. (NY) *1,2,3*
Silk Surplus Inc. (NY) *1,2,3,4*
Victorian Collectibles Ltd. (WI) *2*

FABRIC, TRADITIONAL

(1) Tapestry
(2) Crewel
(3) Handwoven
(4) Linen, Cotton
(5) Horsehair
(6) Silk, Velvet, Damask
(7) Lace

Bergamo Fabrics, Inc. (NY) *4,6*
Brunschwig & Fils, Inc. (NY) *1,4,5,6*
J.R. Burrows & Co. (MA) *7*
Classique French Imports, Inc. (FL) *1*
Colonial Williamsburg Foundation (VA) . *4,6*
Cowtan & Tout, Inc. D&D Building (NY) . *6*
Elsie's Exquisiques (MI) *4,6,7*
Hinson & Co. (NY) *4,6*
Home Fabric Mills, Inc. (MA) *6,7*
Homespun Weavers (PA) *4*
Lee Jofa (NY) *2,4*
Lovelia Enterprises, Inc. (NY) *1*
Natural Fiber Fabrics (VT) *1,4,6*
Quaker Lace Co. (NY) *7*
Rue de France (RI) *7,7*
Scalamandre, Inc. (NY) *2,4,5,6*
Silk Surplus Inc. (NY) *1,2,4,6*
Stroheim & Romann (NY) *5*
Tioga Mill Outlet (PA) *1,2,6,7*
Winterthur Museum and Gardens (DE) *4,6*

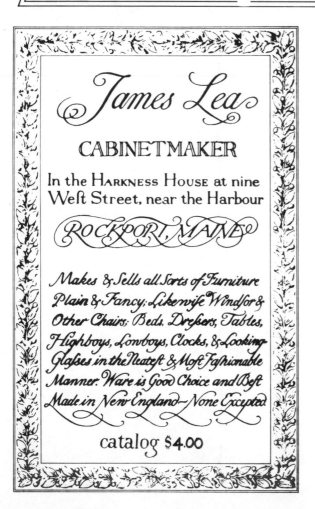

FURNITURE, REPRODUCTION — CUSTOM-MADE

Alexandria Wood Joinery (NH)
Artistic Woodworking, Inc. (MI)
Biggs Company (VA)
Campbell, Marion (PA)
Carpenter and Smith Restorations (IL)
Congdon, Johns/Cabinetmaker (VT)
Crowfoot's Inc. (AZ)
Curry, Gerald — Cabinetmaker (ME)
Custom Millwork, Inc. (VA)
DHM Cabinets (VA)
Daniel Mack Rustic Furnishings (NY)
Fifty / 50 Gallery (NY)
Peter Franklin, Cabinetmaker (MA)
Gaudio Custom Furniture (NY)
Granville Mfg. Co., Inc. (VT)
LaPointe, Chip, Cabinetmaker (MA)
Lea, James — Cabinetmaker (ME)
David Linker Ltd. (NY)
Maple Hill Woodworking (NY)
Master Wood Carver (NJ)
Mazza Frame and Furniture Co., Inc. (NY)
Mead Associates Woodworking, Inc. (NY)
Nutt, Craig, Fine Wood Works (AL)
Orr, J.F., & Sons (MA)
Renaissance Woodcarving, Inc. (NY)
Vulpiani (NY)
Wood Designs (OH)
Wrisley, Robert T. (TN)

FURNITURE & ACCESSORIES — PERIOD STYLES

(1) Country Primitive
(2) Wicker
(3) Early American
(4) Victorian
(5) Turn-of-Century
(6) Brass Beds
(7) Murphy Beds
(8) Kits & Patterns
(9) Rustic
(10) Art Deco and Moderne
(11) Twentieth-Century

21st Century Antiques (MA) *10,11,5*
Stephen A. Adams, Furnituremakers/W.H. James Co. (ME) *3*
Adirondack Store & Gallery (NY) *9*
Adirondak Chair Co. (NY) *8,9*
Alfresco Fine Furniture Since 1976 (CO) .. *9*
American Folk Art (GA) *9*
American Furniture Galleries (AL) *4*
Amish Country Collection (PA) *9*
Antiquaria (MA) *4*
Arkitektura (NJ) *10*
Artistic Woodworking, Inc. (MI) *4*
Avalon Forge (MD) *1*
Backwoods Furnishings (NY) *9*
The Bartley Collection, Ltd. (IL) *3,8*
Bedlam Brass (NJ) *4,6*
Berea College Crafts (KY) *3*
Bombay Company, The (TX) *4*
Brass Bed Company of America (CA) *6*
Michael Camp (MI) *3*
Cane & Basket Supply Company (CA) *8*
Chapin Townsend (RI) *3*
Classic Wicker (CA) *2*
Cohasset Colonials (MA) *1,3*
Colonial Williamsburg Foundation (VA) ... *3*
Congdon, Johns/Cabinetmaker (VT) *3*
Cornucopia, Inc. At the Appleworks (MA) *1,3*
Country Bed Shop (MA) *1,3*
Country Loft (MA) *1,3*

Craftsman's Corner Woodcraft Collection (IA) 8
Crawford's Old House Store (WI) 4,5
Cumberland General Store (TN) 4
Custom Bar Designs (MO) 8
Daniel Mack Rustic Furnishings (NY) 9
Davis Cabinet Co. (TN) 3,4
Ephraim Marsh (NC) 3
Fifty / 50 Gallery (NY) 11
Peter Franklin, Cabinetmaker (MA) 3
Furniture Traditions, Inc. (NC) 3
Gravity - Randall (CA) 4
Habersham Plantation Corp. (GA) 1,3
Historic Charleston Reproductions (SC) 3
Hitchcock Chair Co. (CT) 3
Hood, R. and Co. (NH) 1,3
Imagineering, Inc. (ME) 9
Innerwick Industries (MD) 3
Isabel Brass Furniture (NY) 6
Jadis Moderne (CA) 10
Jenifer House (MA) 3
Kimball Furniture Reproductions, Inc. (IN) 4
La Lune Collection (WI) 9
Lawler Machine & Foundry (AL) 8
Lea, James — Cabinetmaker (ME) 1,3
Lisa — Victoria Brass Beds (VA) 6
Magnolia Hall (GA) 4,5
Martha M. House Furniture (AL) 4
Maynard House Antiques (MA) 3
Mazza Frame and Furniture Co., Inc. (NY)
Metropolis (NY) 10
Morgan Woodworking Supplies (KY) 8
Murphy Door Bed Co., Inc. (NY) 7
Neri, C./Antiques (PA) 4
Peg Hall Studios (MA) 8
Piscatagua Architectural Woodwork, Co. (NH) 3
Pratt's House of Wicker (PA) 2,4,5
Dana Robes Wood Craftsmen, Inc. (NH) . 1
Rocker Shop of Marietta, GA (GA) 1,9
Mario Rodriguez Cabinetmaker (NY) 3
Rue de France (RI) 4
Seraph, The (MA)
Shaker Carpenter Shop (NY) 1
Shaker Workshops (MA) 3,8
Simms & Thayer Cabinetmakers (MA) 1,3
Splendor in Brass (MD) 6
Sturbridge Yankee Workshop (ME) 3,4,6
Swan Brass Beds (CA) 6
Victorian Reproductions Enterprises, Inc. (MN) 4
Vulpiani (NY) 5
Walpole Woodworkers (MA) 2,9
Western Reserve Antique Furniture Kit (OH) 3,8
The Wicker Garden (NY) 2
The Willow Place (GA) 9
Winterthur Museum and Gardens (DE) 3
Wolchonok, M. and Son, Inc. (NY) 4,5
Wood Classics, Inc. (NY) 8,9
Yankee Craftsman (MA) 1,3
Yield House, Inc. (NH) 3
You Name It, Inc. (OH) 4

See Company Directory for Addresses & Phone Numbers on page 151

LAMP SHADES — FRINGE

Burdoch Silk Lampshade Co. (CA)
Golden Age Glassworks (NY)
Rumplestiltskin Designs (CA)
Shady Lady (CO)

LAMP SHADES — PERIOD STYLES

Alfa Lite (UT)
Burdoch Silk Lampshade Co. (CA)
Century House Antiques (OH)
Custom House (CT)
Dilworthtown Country Store (PA)
Lamp Doctor (NY)
Light Ideas (MD)
Lundberg Studios, Inc. Contemporary Art Glass (CA)
Shades of Victoriana (CO)
Shady Lady (CO)
Splendor in Brass (MD)
Tiffany Design Lamps (NV)
Victorian Reproductions Enterprises, Inc. (MN)
Yestershades (OR)

NEEDLEWORK KITS

(1) Crewel Chair Kits
(2) Rug Braiding & Hooking
(3) Needlepoint and Cross Stitch
(4) Quilt Patterns and Kits

Braid-Aid (MA) *2,4*
Colonial Williamsburg Foundation (VA) . *1,3*
Shaker Workshops (MA) *3*

OLD-FASHIONED RESTAURANT FITTINGS

Architectural Antiques Exchange (PA)
Art Directions (MO)
Bare Wood Inc. (NY)
Bedlam Brass (NJ)
Bona Decorative Hardware (OH)
Brass Menagerie (LA)
The Broadway Collection (MO)
Gargoyles, Ltd. (PA)
Lake Country Brass (NH)
Joe Ley Antiques, Inc. (KY)
Metropolis (NY)
Ship 'n Out (NY)
Spiess Antique Building Materials (IL)
United House Wrecking Corp. (CT)
Urban Archaeology (NY)
Wallace & Hinz (CA)

PEDESTALS & PLANT STANDS

(1) Cast Iron
(2) Marble
(3) Wood
(4) Wrought Iron

Cassidy Bros. Forge, Inc. (MA) *4*
Lake Country Brass (NH)
Magnolia Hall (GA) *3*
New York Marble Works, Inc. (NY) *2*
Roman Marble Co. (IL) *2*
Wolchonok, M. and Son, Inc. (NY) *1,3,4*

PICTURE FRAMES

John Morgan Baker, Framer (OH)
Newe Daisterre Glas (OH)
Sedgwick House (IN)
Shadovitz Bros. Distributors, Inc. (NY)
Sundance Studios (IA)

PICTURE HANGERS — PERIOD STYLES

Alfred Manufacturing Corp. (NJ)
Classic Accents (MI)
S & W Framing Supplies, Inc. (NY)
Shadovitz Bros. Distributors, Inc. (NY)
R.W. Shattuck Co. (MA)

PRINTS & ORIGINAL ART

Architectural Portraits (MA)
Brownstone Graphics (NY)
Facemakers, Inc. (IL)
Historical Miniatures Associates (NY)
McGivern, Barbara — Artist (WI)
Prairiewind Traditionals (KS)
Bess Schuyler Ceramics (NY)
Shaker Workshops (MA)
Sundance Studios (IA)
Victorian Homes (WA)

RUGS & CARPETS

(1) Ingrain
(2) Oriental
(3) Traditional
(4) Documentary Reproductions
(5) Custom-Made
(6) Other

Adams and Swett (MA) *4*
J.R. Burrows & Co. (MA) *3,4,5*
Colefax and Fowler *3,5*
Couristan, Inc. (NY) *2,4*
Family Heir-Loom Weavers (PA) *1*
Langhorne Carpet Co. (PA) *3,4,5*
Patterson, Flynn & Martin, Inc. (NY) *3,4*
Rastetter Woolen Mill (OH) *3*
Scalamandre, Inc. (NY) *1,3*
Stark Carpet Corp. (NY) *2,6*
Victorian Collectibles Ltd. (WI) *4*

RUGS, FOLK

(1) Braided
(2) Floorcloths
(3) Straw Matting
(4) Hooked
(5) Needlework
(6) Woven
(7) Other

Adams and Swett (MA) *1,4*
The Aged Ram (VT) *4*
Cornucopia, Inc. At the Appleworks (MA) *1*
Country Braid House (NH) *1*
Floorcloths Incorporated (MD) *2*
Folkheart Rag Rugs (VT) *6*
Gazebo (NY) *1,4,6*
Good & Co. — Floorclothmakers (NH) *2*
Goodman - Southern Fabrications (KS) *6*
Heirloom Rugs (RI) *4*
Heritage Rugs (PA) *6*
S. & C. Huber, Accoutrements (CT) *4,5,6*
Import Specialists, Inc. (NY) *3*
Natural Fiber Fabrics (VT) *6*
Pemaquid Floorcloths (ME) *2*
Prairiewind Traditionals (KS) *2*
Rastetter Woolen Mill (OH) *4,6*
Sturbridge Yankee Workshop (ME) *1*
R. Wagner Co. Painted Finishes (OR) *2*
Weavers Unlimited (WA) *6*
Yankee Pride (MA) *1,4*

WALLCOVERINGS (OTHER THAN WALLPAPER)

(1) Embossed Paper
(2) Leather, Genuine
(3) Embossed Linseed-based
(4) Embossed Vinyl
(5) Other

Bentley Brothers (KY) *1,3,4*
J.R. Burrows & Co. (MA) *1,3,4*
Classic Ceilings (CA) *1,3,4*
Crawford's Old House Store (WI) *1,4*
Decor International Wallcovering, Inc. (NY) *1*
J.D. Dewell & Company (CT) *1,2,3*
Flexi-Wall Systems (SC) *5*
Hinson & Co. (NY) *2,4*
Mile Hi Crown, Inc. (CO) *1,3,4*
Olde & Oak Antiques (AL) *1,4*
Rejuvenation House Parts Co. (OR) *1*
San Francisco Victoriana (CA) *1*
Scalamandre, Inc. (NY) *2,3*
Steptoe and Wife Antiques Ltd. (CAN) . *1,3*
Winterthur Museum and Gardens (DE) ... *2*

See Company Directory for Addresses & Phone Numbers on page 151

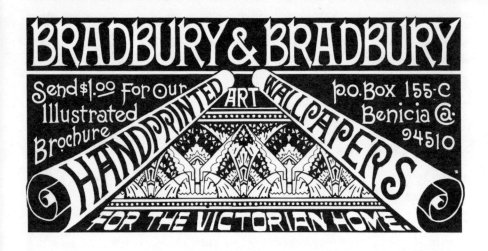

WALLPAPER, EARLY AMERICAN

(1) Documentary Reproduction
(2) Scenic Antique
(3) Scenic Reproduction
(4) Other

Albert Van Luit & Co. (CA) *3*
Brunschwig & Fils, Inc. (NY) *1*
Colonial Wallpaper Company (PA)
Colonial Williamsburg Foundation (VA) ... *1*
Hexter, S. M. Company (OH) *1*
Hinson & Co. (NY) *1*
Jones & Erwin, Inc. (PA) *1*
Katzenbach and Warren, Inc. (NY) *1*
Scalamandre, Inc. (NY) *1*
F. Schumacher & Co. (NY) *1*
Winterthur Museum and Gardens (DE) ... *1*

WALLPAPER, CUSTOM DUPLICATION

Bradbury & Bradbury Wallpapers (CA)
Hexter, S. M. Company (OH)
Old Stone Mill Factory Outlet (MA)
Scalamandre, Inc. (NY)
Victorian Collectibles Ltd. (WI)
Zina Studios, Inc. (NY)

WALLPAPER, SPECIALTY

(1) Murals
(2) Imported Oriental
(3) Borders & Panels
(4) Custom-Made
(5) Trompe-l'oeil
(6) Ceiling Papers

Albert Van Luit & Co. (CA) *2,3*
Bassett & Vollum Wallpapers (IL) *3*
Bradbury & Bradbury Wallpapers (CA) . *3,6*
Brunschwig & Fils, Inc. (NY) *3*
J.R. Burrows & Co. (MA) *1,3,6*
Cowtan & Tout, Inc. D&D Building (NY) . *3*
Karl Mann Associates (NY) *5,6*
Katrina, Inc. (NY) *3*
Louis W. Bowen Fine Wallcoverings (NY) *1,2,3,5*
Raintree Designs, Inc. (NY) *3,6*
San Francisco Victoriana (CA) *3*
Scalamandre, Inc. (NY) *3,5*
Silk Surplus Inc. (NY) *3*
Victorian Collectibles Ltd. (WI) *3,6*

WALLPAPER, TRADITIONAL

(1) Early American Patterns
(2) Victorian Design
(3) Art Nouveau
(4) Other

Albert Van Luit & Co. (CA) *1,2*
Bradbury & Bradbury Wallpapers (CA) ... *2*
Brunschwig & Fils, Inc. (NY) *2*
J.R. Burrows & Co. (MA) *2*
Colonial Wallpaper Company (PA) *1*
Colonial Williamsburg Foundation (VA) ... *1*
Cowtan & Tout, Inc. D&D Building (NY) . *2*
J.D. Dewell & Company (CT) *2,2*
Hexter, S. M. Company (OH) *1*
Hinson & Co. (NY) *1,2*
Katrina, Inc. (NY) *3*
Katzenbach and Warren, Inc. (NY)
Scalamandre, Inc. (NY) *1,2,4*
F. Schumacher & Co. (NY) *1,2*
Silk Surplus Inc. (NY) *1,2,3*
Thomas Strahan Co. (MA) *1,2*
Victorian Collectibles Ltd. (WI) *2,3*
Wolf Paints And Wallpapers (NY) *1,2*

WALLPAPER, VICTORIAN

(1) Documentary Reproduction
(2) Hand-Printed Reproduction
(3) Other

Bradbury & Bradbury Wallpapers (CA) . *1,2*
Brunschwig & Fils, Inc. (NY) *2*
Colonial Wallpaper Company (PA)
Cowtan & Tout, Inc. D&D Building (NY) . *2*
J.D. Dewell & Company (CT) *1*
Katzenbach and Warren, Inc. (NY) *1*
Scalamandre, Inc. (NY) *1,2*
F. Schumacher & Co. (NY) *1*
Silk Surplus Inc. (NY) *1,2*
Victorian Collectibles Ltd. (WI) *1,2*
Zina Studios, Inc. (NY) *1*

UMBRELLA STANDS & COAT RACKS

(1) Umbrella Stands
(2) Coat Racks

Bedlam Brass (NJ) *2*
Brass Bed Company of America (CA) *2*
Isabel Brass Furniture (NY) *1,2*
Kayne & Son Custom Forged Hardware (NC) *2*
Lake Country Brass (NH) *2*
Lemee's Fireplace Equipment (MA) *1*
Magnolia Hall (GA) *1*
The Renovator's Supply (MA) *2*
Ship 'n Out (NY) *1,2*
Sturbridge Yankee Workshop (ME) *1,2*
Swan Brass Beds (CA) *2*

WINDOW SCREENS & BLINDS

Blaine Window Hardware, Inc. (MD)
Devenco Products, Inc. (GA)
Goodman - Southern Fabrications (KS)
Hudson Venetian Blind Service, Inc. (VA)
Iberia Millwork (LA)
Nanik (WI)
Perkowitz Window Fashions (IL)
Walsh Screen Products (NY)

SHADES, WINDOW

Goodman - Southern Fabrications (KS)
Perkowitz Window Fashions (IL)

MISCELLANEOUS DECORATIVE ORNAMENT

(1) Armor & Heraldry
(2) Sculpture
(3) Other
Historical Miniatures Associates (NY) *3*
Van Cort Instruments, Inc. (MA) *2*

OTHER DECORATIVE ACCESSORIES

Akron Foundry, Inc. (IN)
Amazon Vinegar & Pickling Works Drygoods (IA)
Architectural Originals (CA)
Bullfrog Hollow (CT)
Crafts Manufacturing Co. (MA)
Decoration Day (NY)
Good Impressions Rubber Stamps (WV)
Granville Mfg. Co., Inc. (VT)
Historical Miniatures Associates (NY)
Lewis, John N. (PA)
Winterthur Museum and Gardens (DE)

See Company Directory for Addresses & Phone Numbers on page 151

Interior Hardware, Plumbing & House Fittings

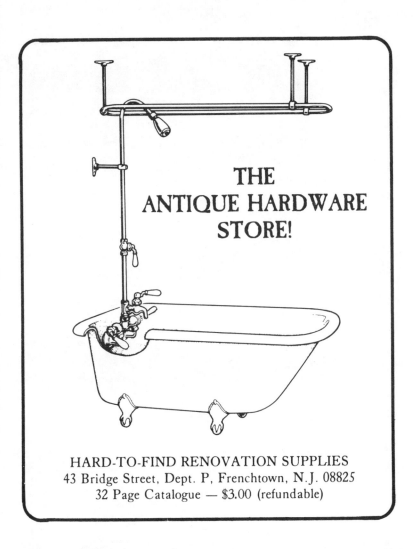

See Company Directory for Addresses & Phone Numbers on page 151

For more information on BATHROOM FIXTURES — and — BATH HARDWARE see the ad for Barclay Products inside the Back Cover.

BATHROOM ACCESSORIES

(1) Soap Dishes, Etc.
(2) Towel Racks, Etc.
(3) Medicine Cabinets
(4) Other

A-Ball Plumbing Supply (OR) *1*
Acorn Manufacturing Co., Inc. (MA) .. *1,2,4*
Antique Baths and Kitchens (CA) *1,2,3*
Antique Hardware Store (NJ) *1,2,3*
Artistic Brass/A MASCO Company (CA) .. *2*
Baldwin Hardware Mfg. Corp. (PA) *1,2,4*
Barclay Products Ltd. (IL) *1,2,3,4*
Bona Decorative Hardware (OH) *2*
Brass Menagerie (LA) *2*
The Broadway Collection (MO) *2*
Buddy Fife's Wood Products (NH) *1,2*
Canal Co. (DC) *3*
Crawford's Old House Store (WI) *1,2,3*
DS Locksmithing Company (FL) *1,2,4*
Dancing Cactus Enterprises (AZ) *3*
Decorative Hardware Studio (NY) *1,2*
Designer's Brass (CA) *1,2*
DeWeese Woodworking (MS) *1,2,3*
J.D. Dewell & Company (CT) *1,2*
Ian Eddy — Blacksmith (VT) *2,4*
Englewood Hardware Co. (NJ) *3*
Guerin, P.E. Inc. (NY) *2*
Half Moon Antiques c/o Monmouth Antique Shoppes (NJ) *1,2*
Harry's Closet (CT) *2*
Heads Up (CA) *2,3*
Historic Housefitters Company (NY) *2*
Houseparts (CA) *1,2*
John Kruesel's General Merchandise (MN) *1,2*
Kayne & Son Custom Forged Hardware (NC) *2*
Lenape Products, Inc. (NJ) *1,2*
Lena's Antique Bathroom Fixtures (CA) . *1,2*
Mac the Antique Plumber (CA) *1,2*
Off The Wall, Architectural Antiques (CA) *1,2*
H. Pfanstiel Hardware Co. (NY) *2*
Restoration Works, Inc. (NY) *1,2,4*
Roy Electric Co., Inc. (NY) *1,2*
San Do Designs/Spanish Tile Factoria (FL) *1,2,4*
Sign of the Crab (CA)
Smithy, The (VT) *2*
Southern Accents Architectural Antiques (AL) *3*
Sturbridge Yankee Workshop (ME) *1,2*
Sunrise Specialty Co., Inc. (CA) *1,2*
Swan Wood (CA) *3*
Tennessee Tub Inc. & Tubliner Co. (TN) *1,2,4*
Tremont Nail Company (MA) *1,2*
United House Wrecking Corp. (CT) *1,2*
Walker Mercantile Company (TN) *1,2,3*
Watercolors, Inc. (NY) *1,2*

VICTORIAN MEDICINE CABINET

Handcrafted solid oak with brass hardware. Mirrored door. Adj. glass shelves. 26-1/2 x 17-1/2 x 7-1/2. Specify unstained, dark or golden oak. Send $185 (add 6% sales tax in Calif.) plus $15 handling to:

SWAN WOOD PRODUCTS
1513 Golden Gate Avenue
San Francisco, CA 94115

For custom orders or additional information call **(415) 567-3263.**
(Corner cabinets available.)

WATERCOLORS

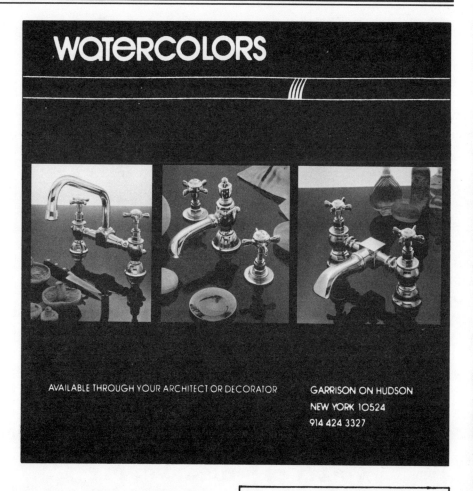

AVAILABLE THROUGH YOUR ARCHITECT OR DECORATOR

GARRISON ON HUDSON
NEW YORK 10524
914 424 3327

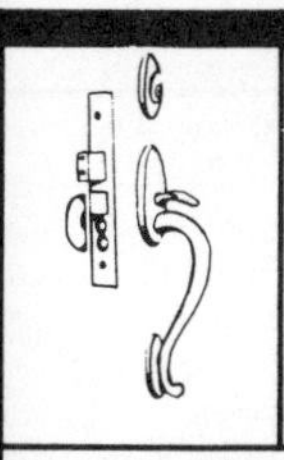

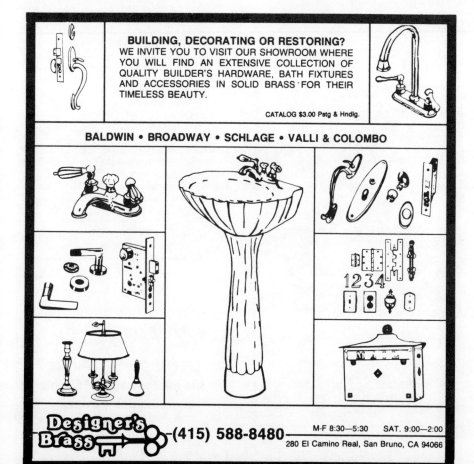

BUILDING, DECORATING OR RESTORING?

WE INVITE YOU TO VISIT OUR SHOWROOM WHERE YOU WILL FIND AN EXTENSIVE COLLECTION OF QUALITY BUILDER'S HARDWARE, BATH FIXTURES AND ACCESSORIES IN SOLID BRASS FOR THEIR TIMELESS BEAUTY.

CATALOG $3.00 Pstg & Hndlg.

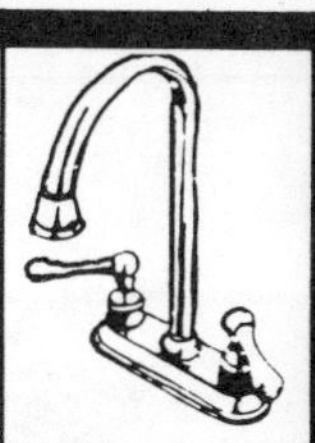

BALDWIN • BROADWAY • SCHLAGE • VALLI & COLOMBO

Designer's Brass **(415) 588-8480**

M-F 8:30—5:30 SAT. 9:00—2:00

280 El Camino Real, San Bruno, CA 94066

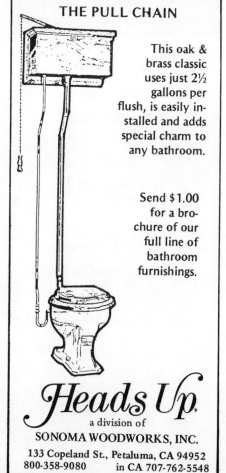

THE PULL CHAIN

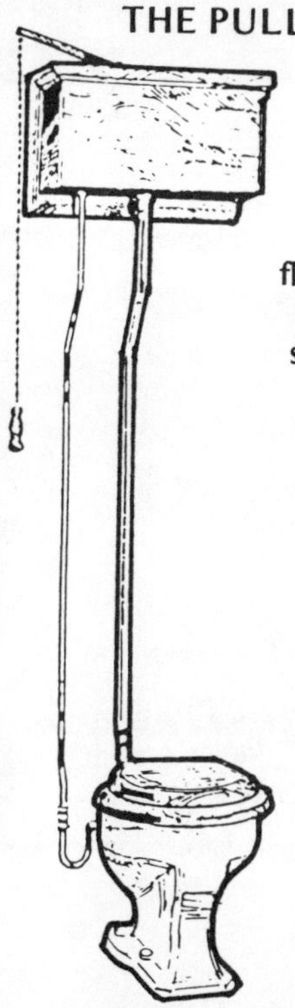

This oak & brass classic uses just 2½ gallons per flush, is easily installed and adds special charm to any bathroom.

Send $1.00 for a brochure of our full line of bathroom furnishings.

Heads Up
a division of
SONOMA WOODWORKS, INC.
133 Copeland St., Petaluma, CA 94952
800-358-9080 in CA 707-762-5548

BATHROOM FAUCETS & FITTINGS

(1) Antique (Salvage)
(2) Reproduction
(3) Old Faucet Parts

A-Ball Plumbing Supply (OR) ... *2*
Antique Baths and Kitchens (CA) ... *2*
Architectural Antique Warehouse, The (CAN) ... *1,2*
Architectural Antiques (OK) ... *1*
Architectural Salvage Co. (MI) ... *1*
Artistic Brass/A MASCO Company (CA) .. *2*
Barclay Products Ltd. (IL) ... *2*
Besco Plumbing & Heating Sales (MA) ... *1*
Bona Decorative Hardware (OH) ... *2*
The Brass Finial (NJ) ... *2*
Brass Menagerie (LA) ... *2*
Chicago Faucet Co. (IL) ... *2*
Consumer Supply Co. (IL) ... *2*
Crawford's Old House Store (WI) ... *2*
DS Locksmithing Company (FL) ... *2*
Decorative Hardware Studio (NY) ... *2*
Dentro Plumbing Specialties (NY) ... *3*
The Emporium, Inc. (TX) ... *1*
Englewood Hardware Co. (NJ) ... *2*
Guerin, P.E. Inc. (NY) ... *2*
Hippo Hardware & Trading Co. (OR) ... *1*
History Store (MD) ... *1,2*
Houseparts (CA) ... *2*
Hunrath , Wm. Co., Inc. (NY) ... *2*
Innerwick Industries (MD) ... *2*
John Kruesel's General Merchandise (MN) ... *1*
Lena's Antique Bathroom Fixtures (CA) ... *1*
Mac the Antique Plumber (CA) ... *1,2*
Masterworks, Inc. (VA) ... *2*
Materials Unlimited (MI) ... *1,2,2*
Off The Wall, Architectural Antiques (CA) ... *2,3*
Ohmega Salvage (CA) ... *1*
H. Pfanstiel Hardware Co. (NY) ... *2*
Porcelain Restoration and Brass (NC) ... *2*
Remodelers & Renovators (ID) ... *2*
The Renovator's Supply (MA) ... *2*
Restore-A-Tub and Brass, Inc. (KY) ... *2*
Roy Electric Co., Inc. (NY) ... *1*
Salvage One (IL) ... *1*
Sign of the Crab (CA)
Southern Accents Architectural Antiques (AL)
Sunrise Specialty Co., Inc. (CA) ... *2*
Tennessee Tub Inc. & Tubliner Co. (TN) .. *2*
United House Wrecking Corp. (CT) ... *1,2*
Walker Mercantile Company (TN) ... *2*
Watercolors, Inc. (NY) ... *2*
Wolchonok, M. and Son, Inc. (NY) ... *2*

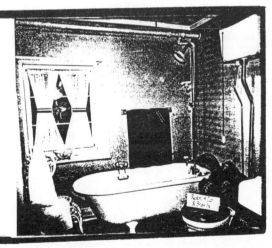

See Company Directory for Addresses & Phone Numbers on page 151

For more information on PERIOD HARDWARE — and — BATHROOM FITTINGS see the Renovators' Supply ad in the Color Section page 64H.

ANTIQUE PLUMBING FIXTURES

Claw Tubs • Brass & Chrome Showers • Shower Rings • Pedestal Sinks • Faucets • Oak High Tank Toilets • Cage Showers • Cross Handles Porcelain • Hard-to-Find Parts • A Huge Selection of Accessories • Expert Advice

Plumbing Catalog $5.00

VICTORIAN
AND TURN OF THE CENTURY
Chandeliers, Sconces & Fixtures

- Design
- Contract
- Manufacturer
- Restoration
- Replacement Parts & Glass Shades

THE MOST COMPLETE SOURCE FOR ANTIQUE AND REPRODUCTION GAS, OIL AND ELECTRIC LIGHTING

Lighting Catalog $3.00

THE FINEST LAMP & FIXTURE RESTORATION AVAILABLE

ROY ELECTRIC CO., INC. **(718) 339-6311**

SHOWROOM: **1054 Coney Island Ave., Brooklyn, NY 11230**

PULL CHAIN TOILET

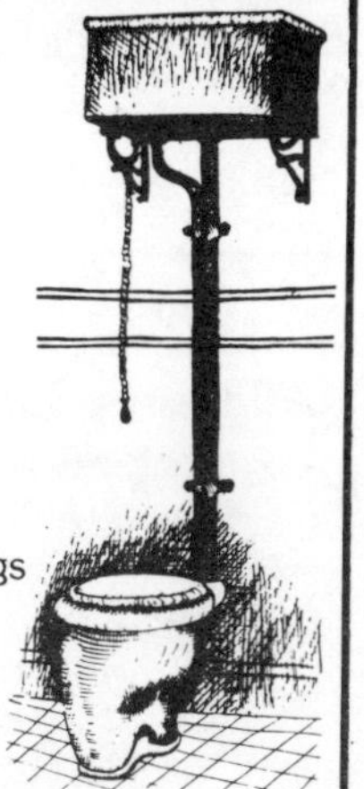

*Handcrafted oak tank with durable stainless steel liner, brass pipe and fittings
*Designed by licensed plumber and craftsman

*Copper Kitchen Sinks
*Marble Vanity Top
*Drinking Fountain
*Faucets, Accessories, Parts
*Send $1.00 for Brochure

ANTIQUE BATHS KITCHENS

2220 CARLTON WAY
SANTA BARBARA, CA 93109
805-962-8598

SUNRISE SPECIALTY CO.

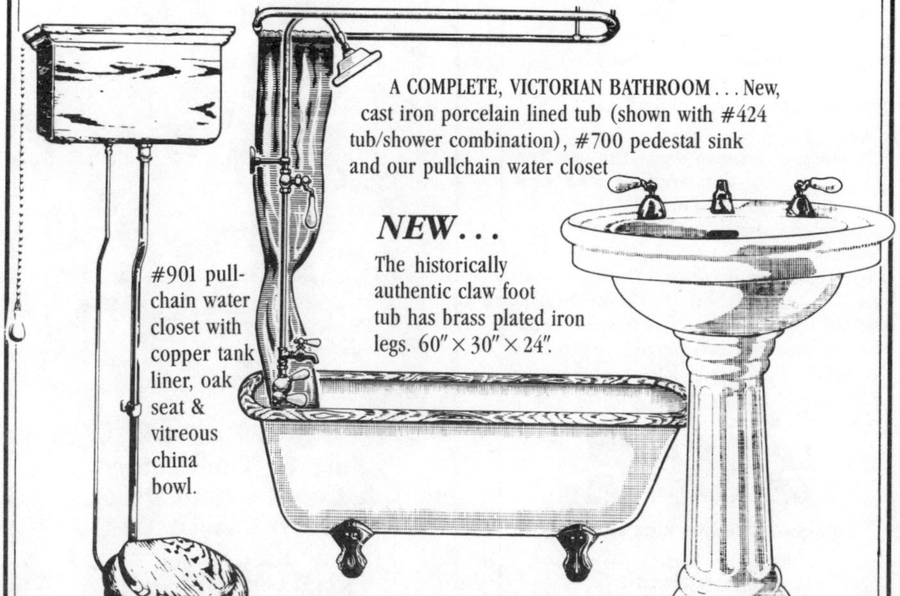

A COMPLETE, VICTORIAN BATHROOM . . . New, cast iron porcelain lined tub (shown with #424 tub/shower combination), #700 pedestal sink and our pullchain water closet

NEW . . .
The historically authentic claw foot tub has brass plated iron legs. 60″ × 30″ × 24″.

#901 pull-chain water closet with copper tank liner, oak seat & vitreous china bowl.

Write or call for beautiful, full color catalog. $2.00

2204 San Pablo Ave., Berkeley, CA 94702
415-845-4751

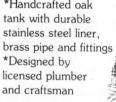

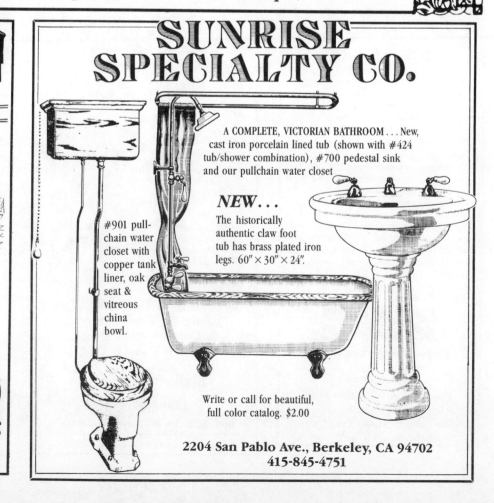

BATHROOM TOILETS & SEATS — PERIOD STYLES

(1) High-Tank Toilets (New)
(2) High-Tank Toilets (Salvage)
(3) Toilets, Period Styles
(4) Toilets, Period Styles (Salvage)
(5) Toilet Parts
(6) Wooden Toilet Seats

A-Ball Plumbing Supply (OR) *3*
Antique Baths and Kitchens (CA) *1,3,5*
Antique Hardware Store (NJ) *1,5*
Architectural Antiques (OK) *4*
Architectural Salvage Co. (MI) *2,4*
Barclay Products Ltd. (IL) *1,6*
Besco Plumbing & Heating Sales (MA) ... *1*
Brass Menagerie (LA) *3*
Buddy Fife's Wood Products (NH) *6*
Crawford's Old House Store (WI) *1,3,5,6*
Cumberland General Store (TN) *1*
D.E.A./Bathroom Machineries (CA) .. *1,2,3,4*
Dancing Cactus Enterprises (AZ) *1*
DeWeese Woodworking (MS) *6*
The Emporium, Inc. (TX) *4*
Florida Victorian Architectural Antiques (FL) *4*
Heads Up (CA) *1,3*
Hippo Hardware & Trading Co. (OR) *4*
John Kruesel's General Merchandise (MN) *2*
Lena's Antique Bathroom Fixtures (CA) . *2,4*
Mac the Antique Plumber (CA) *1,2,5,6*
Ohmega Salvage (CA) *4*
Restoration Works, Inc. (NY) *6*
Restore-A-Tub and Brass, Inc. (KY) *2,4*
Russell & Company Victorian Bathrooms (CA) *1,6*
Southern Accents Architectural Antiques (AL) *4*
Sunrise Specialty Co., Inc. (CA) *1*
Tennessee Tub Inc. & Tubliner Co. (TN) .. *1*
Vintage Plumbing Specialties (CA) *2,4*
Walker Mercantile Company (TN) *1,2,3,4,5,6*

See Company Directory for Addresses & Phone Numbers on page 151

Today's
Potters
Making
Tomorrow's
Antiques
Potters of hand crafted vitreous china for the bathroom • Victorian and modern style pedestal sinks • Full line of bathroom accessories and brass or chrome faucets by Chicago • Colors and floral design application available • Custom work welcome
THE SINK FACTORY
2140 San Pablo Avenue, Berkeley, California 94702
(415) 540-8193
Send $3.00 for Catalog

Unusual, Fancy,
Pull Chain Toilets,
Claw Foot Bathtubs,
Pedestal Lavatories,
Showers, Foot Tubs,
Sitz Tubs, Etc., Etc.
— ALL OLD
— BOUGHT & SOLD
Vintage
Plumbing &
Sanitary Specialties
Send for FREE FLYER
17800 Minnehaha St. Granada Hills, CA 91344
(818) 368-1040

ANTIQUE
TUBS
PEDESTAL SINKS
COMPLETE RESTORATIONS
RESTORE YOURS OR BUY OURS
(413) 589-0769
Call Today or Send $2.00 for Our Brochure
Vintage Tubs & Sink Restoration Service
701 Center St., Ludlow, MA 01056

See Company Directory for Addresses & Phone Numbers on page 151

BATHTUBS & SINKS — PERIOD STYLES

(1) Tubs & Sinks, Antique (Salvage)
(2) Sinks, Period Styles — New
(3) Sink Replacement Bowls
(4) Tubs, Period Styles — New
(5) Tub Parts & Fittings
(6) Sink Parts & Fittings
(7) Shower Rings
(8) Shower Curtains, Extra-Size

A-Ball Plumbing Supply (OR) *2,5,6,7*
Antique Baths and Kitchens (CA) *2,5,6*
Antique Hardware Store (NJ) *1*
Architectural Antiques (OK) *1,1*
Architectural Salvage Co. (MI) *1*
Barclay Products Ltd. (IL) *2,4,5,6,7*
Besco Plumbing & Heating Sales (MA) *1,2,7,8*
Brass Menagerie (LA) *2,3*
The Broadway Collection (MO) *2,3*
Cleveland Wrecking Co. (IL) *1*
Crawford's Old House Store (WI) *2,3,4,5,6,7*
Cumberland General Store (TN) *4*
D.E.A./Bathroom Machineries (CA) *1,3,4*
Dancing Cactus Enterprises (AZ) *2*
Decorative Hardware Studio (NY) *3*
J.D. Dewell & Company (CT) *1*
Eljer Plumbingware (PA) *2*
The Emporium, Inc. (TX) *1*
Englewood Hardware Co. (NJ) *2*
Florida Victorian Architectural Antiques (FL) *1*
Great American Salvage (NY) *1*
Guerin, P.E. Inc. (NY) *2*
Hippo Hardware & Trading Co. (OR) *1*
John Kruesel's General Merchandise (MN) *1*
Lena's Antique Bathroom Fixtures (CA) ... *1*
Mac the Antique Plumber (CA) *1,2,5,6,7*
Masterworks, Inc. (VA) *2,3*
Off The Wall, Architectural Antiques (CA) *1*
Ohmega Salvage (CA) *1*
Period Furniture Hardware Co., Inc. (MA) *2,3*
Puccio (NY) *2*
Remodelers & Renovators (ID) *2,3*
Renovation Concepts, Inc. (MN) *2*
Restoration Works, Inc. (NY) *5,6,7*
Restore-A-Tub and Brass, Inc. (KY) *1*
Roy Electric Co., Inc. (NY) *1*
The Sink Factory (CA) *2,3*
Southern Accents Architectural Antiques (AL) *1,5,7*
Sterline Manufacturing Corp. (IL) *5,7*
Sunrise Specialty Co., Inc. (CA) *2,5,7*
Tennessee Tub Inc. & Tubliner Co. (TN) *1,2,5,6,7*
United House Wrecking Corp. (CT) *1*
Vintage Plumbing Specialties (CA) *1*
Vintage Tub & Sink Restoration Service (MA) *1*
Walker Mercantile Company (TN) *2,3,4,5*
Weaver, W. T. & Sons, Inc. (DC) *3*

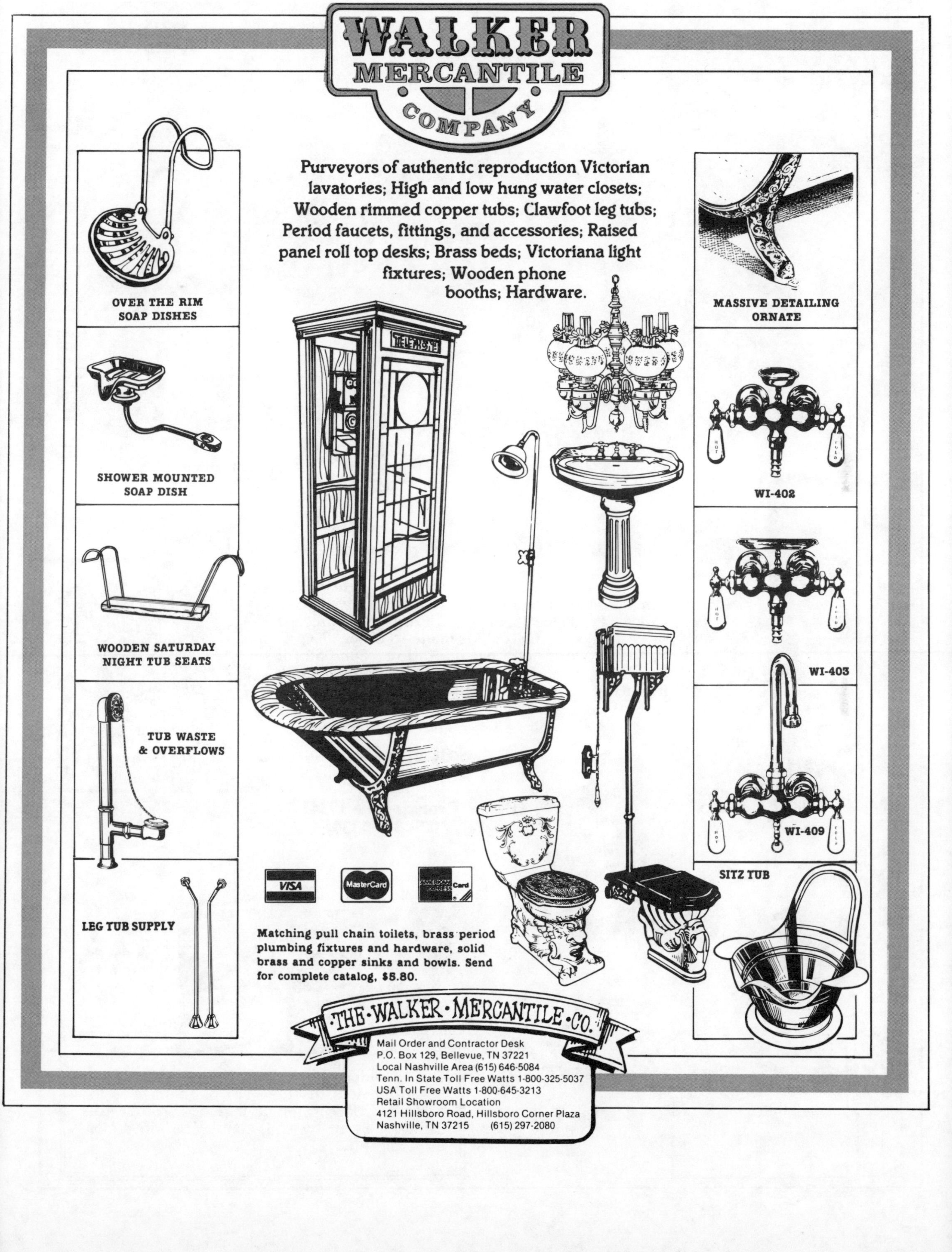
WALKER
MERCANTILE
COMPANY
Purveyors of authentic reproduction Victorian lavatories; High and low hung water closets; Wooden rimmed copper tubs; Clawfoot leg tubs; Period faucets, fittings, and accessories; Raised panel roll top desks; Brass beds; Victoriana light fixtures; Wooden phone booths; Hardware.
OVER THE RIM SOAP DISHES
SHOWER MOUNTED SOAP DISH
WOODEN SATURDAY NIGHT TUB SEATS
TUB WASTE & OVERFLOWS
LEG TUB SUPPLY
MASSIVE DETAILING ORNATE
WI-402
WI-403
WI-409
SITZ TUB
TELEPHONE
VISA
MasterCard
AMERICAN EXPRESS Card
Matching pull chain toilets, brass period plumbing fixtures and hardware, solid brass and copper sinks and bowls. Send for complete catalog, $5.80.
THE·WALKER·MERCANTILE·CO.
Mail Order and Contractor Desk
P.O. Box 129, Bellevue, TN 37221
Local Nashville Area (615) 646-5084
Tenn. In State Toll Free Watts 1-800-325-5037
USA Toll Free Watts 1-800-645-3213
Retail Showroom Location
4121 Hillsboro Road, Hillsboro Corner Plaza
Nashville, TN 37215 (615) 297-2080

EVERYTHING for your restoration!
House, cabinet & furniture hardware, lighting fixtures, fireplace equipment and decorative accessories. Produced from brass, bronze, handforged or cast iron, from stock or made to order. Repair and copy work done per quotation. Send $5 for our latest catalog. 108 pgs., 1500 items, including many "new" Victorian period reproductions.
Ball and Ball
463 W. Lincoln Highway
Exton, Pennsylvania 19341
Tel. (215) 363-7330
GOLDEN GLOW BRASS POLISH
GOLDEN GLOW BRASS POLISH
Our "Golden Glow" Brass Polish is shipped in minimum lots of three (3) one-pint cans for $18.00, U.P.S. shipping included. (Sorry this cannot be sent by U.S. mail.) Visa/MC/Amer. Exp. accepted.

CABINET & FURNITURE HARDWARE — PERIOD

1874 House (OR)
18th Century Hardware Co. (PA)
19th Century Company (CA)
Acorn Manufacturing Co., Inc. (MA)
Anglo-American Brass Co. (CA)
Antique Hardware Co. (CA)
Antique Hardware Store (NJ)
Arden Forge (PA)
B & P Lamp Supply Co., Inc. (TN)
Ball and Ball (PA)
Bona Decorative Hardware (OH)
The Brass Finial (NJ)
The Brass Tree (MO)
The Broadway Collection (MO)
C.U. Restoration Supplies (TX)
Cirecast, Inc. (CA)
Cloyd Laibe (CA)
Conant Custom Brass (VT)
Craftsman Wood Service Co. (IL)
Crawford's Old House Store (WI)
DHM Cabinets (VA)
DS Locksmithing Company (FL)
Decorative Hardware Studio (NY)
Designer's Brass (CA)
The Emporium, Inc. (TX)
Englewood Hardware Co. (NJ)
Faneuil Furniture Hardware (MA)
Gainsborough Hardware Industry (MO)
Gaston Wood Finishes, Inc. (IN)
Guerin, P.E. Inc. (NY)
Heirloom Enterprises (MN)
Hippo Hardware & Trading Co. (OR)
Historic Housefitters Company (NY)
Hood, R. and Co. (NH)
Horton Brasses (CT)
Houseparts (CA)
Hunrath , Wm. Co., Inc. (NY)
Impex Assoc. Ltd., Inc. (NJ)
Klise Manufacturing Company (MI)
Lesco, Inc. (KS)
Materials Unlimited (MI)
D. C. Mitchell Reproductions (DE)
Morgan Woodworking Supplies (KY)
Old Smithy Shop (NH)
Omnia Industries, Inc. (NJ)
Paxton Hardware Ltd. (MD)
Period Furniture Hardware Co., Inc. (MA)
H. Pfanstiel Hardware Co. (NY)
Plexacraft Metals Co. (CA)
Potomac Products (PA)
Remodelers & Renovators (ID)
Renaissance Decorative Hardware Co. (NJ)
The Renovator's Supply (MA)
Restoration Works, Inc. (NY)
Ritter & Son Hardware (CA)
Squaw Alley, Inc. (IL)
Transylvania Mountain Forge (CA)
WSI Distributors/ The Brass Tree (MO)
Weaver, W. T. & Sons, Inc. (DC)
Williamsburg Blacksmiths, Inc. (MA)
Windy Hill Forge (MD)
Wise Company, The (LA)
Wolchonok, M. and Son, Inc. (NY)

See Company Directory for Addresses & Phone Numbers on page 151

CARPET RODS

Acorn Oriental Rug Services (OH)
Baldwin Hardware Mfg. Corp. (PA)
Ball and Ball (PA)
Decorative Hardware Studio (NY)
Englewood Hardware Co. (NJ)
Guerin, P.E. Inc. (NY)
Hunrath , Wm. Co., Inc. (NY)
Impex Assoc. Ltd., Inc. (NJ)
H. Pfanstiel Hardware Co. (NY)
Renaissance Decorative Hardware Co. (NJ)
The Renovator's Supply (MA)
Wolchonok, M. and Son, Inc. (NY)

COAT HOOKS

19th Century Company (CA)
Anglo-American Brass Co. (CA)
Baldwin Hardware Mfg. Corp. (PA)
C.U. Restoration Supplies (TX)
Cloyd Laibe (CA)
Harry's Closet (CT)
Houseparts (CA)
Kayne & Son Custom Forged Hardware (NC)
Merritt's Antiques, Inc. (PA)
Old Smithy Shop (NH)
Omnia Industries, Inc. (NJ)
The Renovator's Supply (MA)
Sign of the Crab (CA)
Smithy, The (VT)
Transylvania Mountain Forge (CA)
Weaver, W. T. & Sons, Inc. (DC)
Wise Company, The (LA)

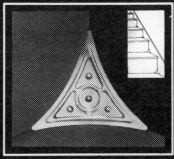

DOOR LATCHES—WROUGHT IRON

(1) New—Stock Items
(2) Custom-Made

18th Century Hardware Co. (PA) *1*
Acorn Manufacturing Co., Inc. (MA) *1*
Antares Forge and Metalworks (NY) *2*
Antique Hardware Store (NJ) *1*
Arden Forge (PA) *2*
Ball and Ball (PA) *1,2*
Bona Decorative Hardware (OH) *1*
The Broadway Collection (MO) *1*
Colonial Restoration Products (PA) *1*
Crawford's Old House Store (WI) *1*
Elephant Hill Iron Works (VT) *1,2*
Historic Housefitters Company (NY) *1*
Hood, R. and Co. (NH) *1*
Horton Brasses (CT) *1*
Kayne & Son Custom Forged Hardware (NC) *1*
Loose, Thomas — Blacksmith/ Whitesmith (PA) *1*
Mill River Hammerworks (MA) *2*
Millham, Newton — Blacksmith (MA) . *1,2*
Old Smithy Shop (NH) *1*
Period Furniture Hardware Co., Inc. (MA) *1*
Potomac Products (PA) *1*
The Renovator's Supply (MA) *1*
Smithy, The (VT) *2*
Transylvania Mountain Forge (CA) *1*
Tremont Nail Company (MA)
Wallin Forge (KY) *2*
Williamsburg Blacksmiths, Inc. (MA) *1*
Windy Hill Forge (MD) *2*
Woodbury Blacksmith & Forge Co. (CT) .. *2*

DOOR LOCKS

(1) Brass & Bronze
(2) Iron
(3) Rim Locks
(4) Mortised Locks
(5) Early American
(6) Victorian
(7) Turn-of-Century
(8) Other

Acorn Manufacturing Co., Inc. (MA) *5*
Antique Hardware Store (NJ) *1,2,3,5,6*
Arden Forge (PA) *1,2,3,4*
Baldwin Hardware Mfg. Corp. (PA) *1,3,4*
Ball and Ball (PA) *1,2,3,4,5,6,7,8*
Bona Decorative Hardware (OH) *1,2,3,4,5*
The Brass Finial (NJ) *3*
Brass Menagerie (LA) *1*
The Broadway Collection (MO) *1*
Circecast, Inc. (CA) *1,4,6*
Colonial Lock Company (CT) *2,3*
Crawford's Old House Store (WI) *1,2,3,4,5,6,7,8*
DHM Cabinets (VA) *1,3,4,8*
DS Locksmithing Company (FL) ... *1,3,4,5,6,7*
Decorative Hardware Studio (NY) *4*
Designer's Brass (CA)
Elephant Hill Iron Works (VT) *2,5*
Garrett Wade Company (NY) *1*
Guerin, P.E. Inc. (NY) *1,4,8*
JGR Enterprises, Inc. (PA)
Kayne & Son Custom Forged Hardware (NC) *2,3,5*
Millham, Newton — Blacksmith (MA) . *2,5*
Omnia Industries, Inc. (NJ) *1,4*
Period Furniture Hardware Co., Inc. (MA) *1,3,3,4,5*
H. Pfanstiel Hardware Co. (NY) *1*
The Renovator's Supply (MA) *1,2,4,5*
Reproduction Distributors, Inc. (IL) *3*
Samuel B. Sadtler, Importers (PA) *1,4*
Sign of the Crab (CA) *1,4,5,6*
Transylvania Mountain Forge (CA) *2*
Virginia Metalcrafters (VA) *3*
Washburne, E.G. & Co., Inc. (MA) *1*
Weaver, W. T. & Sons, Inc. (DC) *3*
Williamsburg Blacksmiths, Inc. (MA) . *2,4,5*
Windy Hill Forge (MD) *1,2,3,5*
Wise Company, The (LA) *1,2*

DOOR HINGES

(1) Brass & Bronze
(2) Iron
(3) Early American
(4) Victorian
(5) Turn-of-Century
(6) Custom-Cast Brass & Bronze
(7) Custom-Wrought Iron
(8) Other

18th Century Hardware Co. (PA) *3*
Acorn Manufacturing Co., Inc. (MA) *2,3*
Antares Forge and Metalworks (NY) *7*
Antique Hardware Store (NJ) *1,3,4*
Arden Forge (PA) *2,3,6,7*
Baldwin Hardware Mfg. Corp. (PA) *1*
Ball and Ball (PA) *1,2,3,5*
Bona Decorative Hardware (OH) *1,3*
The Brass Finial (NJ) *1*
The Broadway Collection (MO) *1*
C.U. Restoration Supplies (TX) *1,4,5*
Cassidy Bros. Forge, Inc. (MA) *2,7*
Circecast, Inc. (CA) *1,4*
Colonial Restoration Products (PA) *2,3*
Crawford's Old House Store (WI) .. *1,2,4,5,6*
DHM Cabinets (VA) *1,6*
DS Locksmithing Company (FL) *1,4,5*
Elephant Hill Iron Works (VT) *2,3,7,7*
The Farm Forge (OH) *7*
Garrett Wade Company (NY) *1*
Guerin, P.E. Inc. (NY) *1,5,6*
Horton Brasses (CT) *2*
Kayne & Son Custom Forged Hardware (NC) *2,3*
Lee Valley Tools, Ltd. (CAN) *1,2,4,5*
Leo, Brian (MN) *4,6*
Loose, Thomas — Blacksmith/ Whitesmith (PA) *2,3*
Mill River Hammerworks (MA) *1,2,3,6,7*
Millham, Newton — Blacksmith (MA) *2,3,7*
Old Smithy Shop (NH) *2,3*
Omnia Industries, Inc. (NJ) *1,3,4*
Period Furniture Hardware Co., Inc. (MA) *1,2*
H. Pfanstiel Hardware Co. (NY) *1,5*
Plexacraft Metals Co. (CA) *1*
Potomac Products (PA) *1*
Renovation Concepts, Inc. (MN) *1*
The Renovator's Supply (MA) *2,3*
Sign of the Crab (CA) *1,3,4*
Smithy, The (VT) *7*
Transylvania Mountain Forge (CA) *1,2*
Virginia Metalcrafters (VA) *1*
Wallin Forge (KY) *7*
Washburne, E.G. & Co., Inc. (MA) *1,2*
Williamsburg Blacksmiths, Inc. (MA) ... *2,3*
Windy Hill Forge (MD) *1,2,3*
Wise Company, The (LA) *1*
Wolchonok, M. and Son, Inc. (NY) *1*
Woodbury Blacksmith & Forge Co. (CT) .. *7*

See Company Directory for Addresses & Phone Numbers on page 151

DOORKNOBS & ESCUTCHEONS

(1) Brass & Bronze
(2) Porcelain & Glass Knobs

Acorn Manufacturing Co., Inc. (MA) *2*
Anglo-American Brass Co. (CA) *1*
Antique Hardware Co. (CA) *1*
Antique Hardware Store (NJ) *1,2*
Baldwin Hardware Mfg. Corp. (PA) *1*
The Brass Finial (NJ) *1,2*
The Broadway Collection (MO)
C.U. Restoration Supplies (TX) *1*
Cirecast, Inc. (CA) *1*
Crawford's Old House Store (WI) *1,2*
DHM Cabinets (VA) *1*
DS Locksmithing Company (FL) *1*
Decorative Hardware Studio (NY) *1,2*
Englewood Hardware Co. (NJ)
Gainsborough Hardware Industry (MO) *1,2*
Garrett Wade Company (NY) *1*
Guerin, P.E. Inc. (NY)
Hippo Hardware & Trading Co. (OR)
Historic Housefitters Company (NY) *1*
Houseparts (CA) *1,2*
Hunrath , Wm. Co., Inc. (NY) *1*
Impex Assoc. Ltd., Inc. (NJ)
Lee Valley Tools, Ltd. (CAN) *1*
Leo, Brian (MN) *1*
Omnia Industries, Inc. (NJ) *1,2*
Plexacraft Metals Co. (CA) *1,2*
Renaissance Decorative Hardware Co. (NJ) *1*
Renovation Concepts, Inc. (MN) *1*
The Renovator's Supply (MA)
Reproduction Distributors, Inc. (IL)
Transylvania Mountain Forge (CA) *1*
Washburne, E.G. & Co., Inc. (MA) *1*
Weaver, W. T. & Sons, Inc. (DC) *1*
Wise Company, The (LA) *1*

DRY SINKS & LINERS

Orr, J.F., & Sons (MA)

See Company Directory for Addresses & Phone Numbers on page 151

FANS, CEILING

Bow & Arrow Stove Co. (MA)
CasaBlanca Fan Co. (CA)
The Ceiling Fan Place (NY)
Cumberland General Store (TN)
The Fan Man (OK)
Fasco Industries, Inc. (NC)
Homestead Products (CA)
Hunter Fan Company (TN)
M — H Lamp & Fan Company (IL)
Newstamp Lighting Co. (MA)
Southern Accents Architectural Antiques (AL)
Worthington Trading Company (MO)

HARDWARE, ANTIQUE (OLD)

Antique Hardware Store (NJ)
Architectural Accents (GA)
Arden Forge (PA)
Blaine Window Hardware, Inc. (MD)
J.D. Dewell & Company (CT)
J.D. Dewell & Company (CT)
The Emporium, Inc. (TX)
Fellenz Hardware & Antiques (MO)
Grandpa Snazzy's Hardware (CO)
Hippo Hardware & Trading Co. (OR)
History Store (MD)
H.B. Ives (CT)
Lee Valley Tools, Ltd. (CAN)
Materials Unlimited (MI)
Monroe Coldren and Sons (PA)

HARDWARE, INTERIOR—CUSTOM DUPLICATION

(1) Cast Brass & Bronze
(2) Cast Iron
(3) Wrought Iron

18th Century Hardware Co. (PA)
Acorn Manufacturing Co., Inc. (MA) *3*
Anglo-American Brass Co. (CA) *1*
Antares Forge and Metalworks (NY) *3*
Arden Forge (PA) *3*
Ball and Ball (PA) *1*
Blaine Window Hardware, Inc. (MD) *1*
Brass Menagerie (LA) *1*
Bronze et al (NY) *1*
Cassidy Bros. Forge, Inc. (MA) *3*
Cirecast, Inc. (CA) *1*
Conant Custom Brass (VT) *1*
Elephant Hill Iron Works (VT) *3*
Experi-Metals (WI) *1*
The Farm Forge (OH) *3*
Guerin, P.E. Inc. (NY) *1*
Hippo Hardware & Trading Co. (OR) *1*
JGR Enterprises, Inc. (PA)
Kayne & Son Custom Forged Hardware (NC) *1,3*
Leo, Brian (MN) *1*
Plexacraft Metals Co. (CA) *1*
Smithy, The (VT) *3*
Donald C. Stetson, Sr., Enterprises (MA) *3*
Swiss Foundry, Inc. (MD) *1*
Tremont Nail Company (MA) *3*
Wallin Forge (KY) *3*
Windy Hill Forge (MD) *3*

HOOSIER HARDWARE

19th Century Company (CA)
Antique Hardware Store (NJ)

ICE BOX HARDWARE

19th Century Company (CA)
Anglo-American Brass Co. (CA)
Antique Hardware Co. (CA)
C.U. Restoration Supplies (TX)
The Renovator's Supply (MA)
Ritter & Son Hardware (CA)

KEY BLANKS—FOR ANTIQUE LOCKS

18th Century Hardware Co. (PA)
19th Century Company (CA)
Ball and Ball (PA)
C.U. Restoration Supplies (TX)
DS Locksmithing Company (FL)
Kayne & Son Custom Forged Hardware (NC)
Wise Company, The (LA)

KITCHEN CABINETS

Custom Millwork, Inc. (VA)
Dovetail Woodworking (WI)
Eklund, Jon Restorations (NJ)
J & M Custom Cabinet and Millwork (MI)
Restorations Unlimited, Inc. (PA)
Rich Craft Custom Kitchens, Inc. (PA)

KITCHEN FAUCETS & FITTINGS, OLD STYLES

(1) Antique (Salvage)
(2) Reproduction

Antique Hardware Store (NJ) *1,2*
Chicago Faucet Co. (IL) *2*
Hippo Hardware & Trading Co. (OR) *1*
Sunrise Specialty Co., Inc. (CA) *2*

KITCHEN SINKS, OLD STYLES

(1) Antique (Salvage)
(2) Reproduction

Antique Baths and Kitchens (CA) *2*
Hippo Hardware & Trading Co. (OR) *1*
Vermont Soapstone Co. (VT) *2*
Vintage Tub & Sink Restoration Service (MA) *1*

LIBRARY LADDERS

Putnam Rolling Ladder Co., Inc. (NY)

RADIATORS — PERIOD STYLES

(1) Antique (Salvage)
(2) New

Consumer Supply Co. (IL) *1*

SHUTTERS & BLINDS, INTERIOR

(1) New—Stock Items
(2) Custom-Made

American Heritage Shutters (TN) *1,2*
Architectural Components (MA) *1*
Bank Architectural Antiques (LA)
Beech River Mill Co. (NH) *2*
Bjorndal Woodworks (WI) *2*
Classic Architectural Specialties (TX) *1*
Country Shutters (MN) *1*
Custom Millwork, Inc. (VA) *2*
Devenco Products, Inc. (GA) *2*
Dovetail Woodworking (WI) *2*
Goodman - Southern Fabrications (KS) *2*
Historic Windows (VA) *2*
Iberia Millwork (LA) *2*
Insul Shutter (NH)
LaPointe, Chip, Cabinetmaker (MA) *2*
Maurer & Shepherd, Joyners (CT) *2*
Michael's Fine Colonial Products (NY) *2*
Nanik (WI) *1*
Perkowitz Window Fashions (IL) *1*
Piscatagua Architectural Woodwork, Co. (NH) *2*
REM Associates (MA) *2*
Restoration Fraternity (PA) *2*
Stanfield Shutter Co. (UT) *2*
Sunshine Architectural Woodworks (AR)
Vintage Wood Works (TX)

SHUTTER HARDWARE

(1) Brass & Bronze
(2) Iron
(3) Custom-Made

Acorn Manufacturing Co., Inc. (MA) *2*
Arden Forge (PA) *2,3*
Ball and Ball (PA) *1,2,3*
Kayne & Son Custom Forged Hardware (NC) *2*
Millham, Newton — Blacksmith (MA) ... *2*
Period Furniture Hardware Co., Inc. (MA) *2*
Plexacraft Metals Co. (CA) *1*
The Renovator's Supply (MA)
Smithy, The (VT) *2*
Windy Hill Forge (MD) *2,3*

SLIDING DOOR TRACKS & HARDWARE

Blaine Window Hardware, Inc. (MD)
JGR Enterprises, Inc. (PA)

SWITCH PLATES, PERIOD DESIGNS

A-Ball Plumbing Supply (OR)
Acorn Manufacturing Co., Inc. (MA)
Arden Forge (PA)
The Brass Finial (NJ)
Decorative Hardware Studio (NY)
Gainsborough Hardware Industry (MO)
Guerin, P.E. Inc. (NY)
The Renovator's Supply (MA)
Sign of the Crab (CA)
Weaver, W. T. & Sons, Inc. (DC)
Wise Company, The (LA)
Wolchonok, M. and Son, Inc. (NY)

TIN, PIERCED

Country Accents (NJ)

TRUNK HARDWARE

Antique Trunk Supply Co. (OH)
The Brass Tree (MO)
C.U. Restoration Supplies (TX)
Charolette Ford Trunks (TX)
Kayne & Son Custom Forged Hardware (NC)
Gerry Sharp Trunk Doctor (TX)
WSI Distributors/ The Brass Tree (MO)

WINDOW HARDWARE

(1) Brass & Bronze
(2) Iron
(3) Custom-Made
(4) Transom

Ball and Ball (PA) *1,2,3*
Blaine Window Hardware, Inc. (MD) ... *1,1*
Bona Decorative Hardware (OH) *1*
CIPCO Corp. (MO) *4*
Circecast, Inc. (CA) *1,2*
Crawford's Old House Store (WI) *1,4*
Elephant Hill Iron Works (VT) *2,3*
Garrett Wade Company (NY) *1*
Grandpa Snazzy's Hardware (CO) *4*
Guerin, P.E. Inc. (NY) *1*
Hippo Hardware & Trading Co. (OR) *1*
Kayne & Son Custom Forged Hardware (NC) *1,2,3*
Leo, Brian (MN) *3*
Period Furniture Hardware Co., Inc. (MA) *1*
Quaker City Manufacturing Co. (PA)
The Renovator's Supply (MA) *1*
Smithy, The (VT) *2*
Transylvania Mountain Forge (CA) *1,2*
Whitco — Vincent Whitney Co. (CA) *4*
Window Components Mfg. A Harrow Co. (FL) *1,3,4*
Windy Hill Forge (MD) *2,3*

OTHER INTERIOR HARDWARE & FITTINGS

Armor Products (NY)

See Company Directory for Addresses & Phone Numbers on page 151

Heating Systems, Fireplaces & Stoves, and Energy-Saving Devices

AUXILIARY FIREPLACE DEVICES TO INCREASE HEAT DISTRIBUTION

Cumberland General Store (TN)
Iron Craft, Inc. (NH)
Preway, Inc. (WI)
Shenandoah Manufacturing Co. (VA)
Vermont Castings, Inc. (VT)

CENTRAL HEATING SYSTEMS

(1) Wood Fired
(2) Coal Fired
(3) Combination
(4) Other Fuels

Heckler Bros. (PA) *2*
Hydrotherm (NJ) *4*
Shenandoah Manufacturing Co. (VA) *1*

CHIMNEY BRUSHES

Ace Wire Brush Co. (NY)
C & D Distributors Hearth Mate (CT)
Iron Craft, Inc. (NH)
Minuteman International Co., Ltd. (MA)
Woodmart (WI)

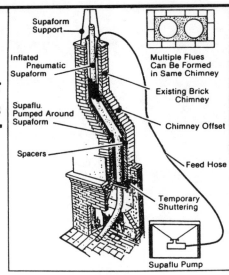

CHIMNEY LININGS

Ahrens Chimney Technique Inc. (SD)
American Chimney Lining Systems, Inc. (MI)
BOATECH (NY)
Bow & Arrow Stove Co. (MA)
C & D Distributors Hearth Mate (CT)
Chimney Relining International, Inc. (NH)
Flue Works (OH)
Homestead Chimney (NJ)
Iron Craft, Inc. (NH)
Mirror Patented Stove Pipe Co. (CT)
National SUPAFLU Systems, Inc. (NY)
Superior Clay Corporation (OH)
Terra Cotta Productions, Inc. (PA)
Thermocrete Chimney Systems, Inc. (MN)

COAL GRATES

(1) Coal-Burning
(2) Simulated
Bryant Stove Works (ME) *1*
Cumberland General Store (TN) *1*
Hearth Realities (GA) *1,2*
Heckler Bros. (PA) *1*
Lemee's Fireplace Equipment (MA) *1*

FIREPLACES, CUSTOM-BUILT

Rumford Fireplaces (OH)
Vermont Soapstone Co. (VT)

FIREPLACES, MANUFACTURED

Acme Stove Company (MD)
Heatilator Inc. (IA)
Jotul U.S.A., Inc. (ME)
Preway, Inc. (WI)
Readybuilt Products, Co. (MD)
Rumford Fireplaces (OH)

FIREPLACE SURROUNDS

Acquisition and Restoration Corp. (IN)
London Country, Ltd. (MN)
Minuteman International Co., Ltd. (MA)
Old Carolina Brick Co. (NC)

FIREPLACE DAMPERS & STRUCTURAL PARTS

Heatilator Inc. (IA)
Homestead Chimney (NJ)
Lyemance International, Inc. (IN)

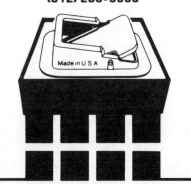

See Company Directory for Addresses & Phone Numbers on page 151

Restore, strengthen, seal and protect.

Ahrens unique two-liner chimney lining process.

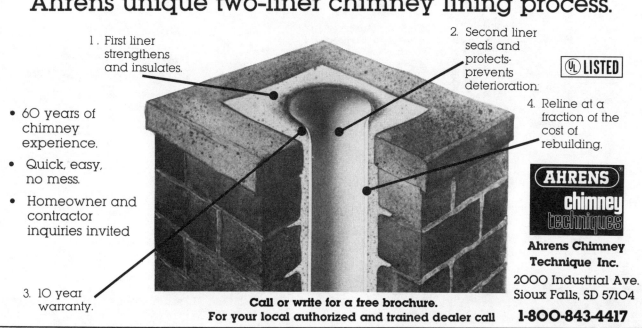

1. First liner strengthens and insulates.
2. Second liner seals and protects-prevents deterioration.
3. 10 year warranty.
4. Reline at a fraction of the cost of rebuilding.

(UL) LISTED

- 60 years of chimney experience.
- Quick, easy, no mess.
- Homeowner and contractor inquiries invited

AHRENS® chimney techniques

Ahrens Chimney Technique Inc.
2000 Industrial Ave.
Sioux Falls, SD 57104

Call or write for a free brochure.
For your local authorized and trained dealer call **1-800-843-4417**

RESTORES chimney to vent your heating appliance or fireplace **SAFELY.**

(UL) listed

VENTINOX™ CHIMNEY SYSTEM

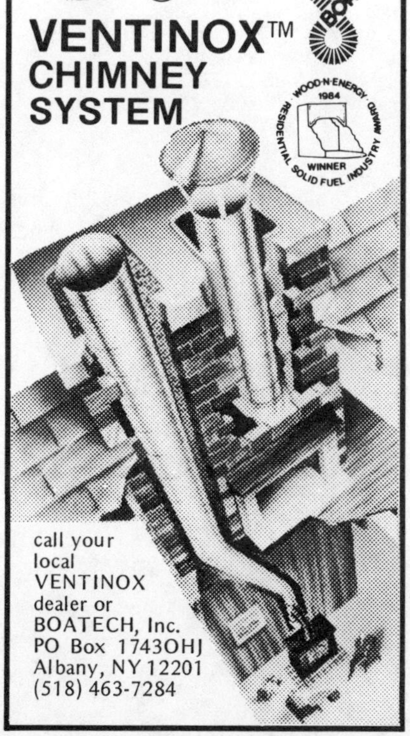

WOOD-N-ENERGY 1984
RESIDENTIAL SOLID FUEL INDUSTRY AWARD
WINNER

call your local VENTINOX dealer or
BOATECH, Inc.
PO Box 17430HJ
Albany, NY 12201
(518) 463-7284

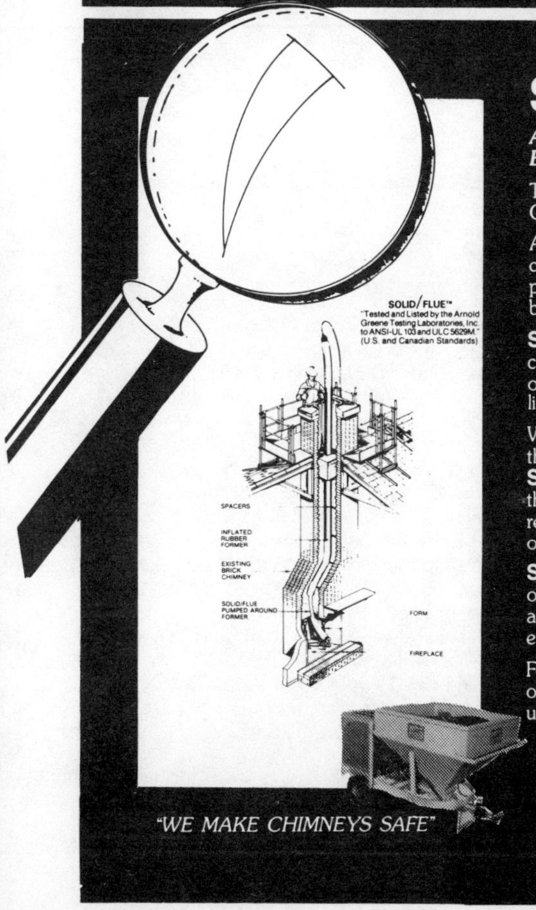

SOLID/FLUE™
"Tested and Listed by the Arnold Greene Testing Laboratories, Inc. to ANSI-UL 103 and ULC 5629M." (U.S. and Canadian Standards)
SPACERS
INFLATED RUBBER FORMER
EXISTING BRICK CHIMNEY
SOLID/FLUE PUMPED AROUND FORMER
FORM
FIREPLACE

"WE MAKE CHIMNEYS SAFE"

SOLID/FLUE®

ATTENTION: Architects, Contractors, Building Professionals.

Take a closer look: at **SOLID/FLUE®**, America's Chimney Restoration & Lining System.

At **SOLID/FLUE®**, we can provide you with a cast in place **pumped** chimney lining system as a perfect compliment to your particular contracting business.

SOLID/FLUE® is a tested system that gives chimneys a continuous, smooth, one piece lining of specially formulated, highly insulative flue lining mix.

We'll customize a system to fit your needs and then completely train you in how to use it. **SOLID/FLUE®** reduces the need to break through the chimney or walls of your building or restoration projects. It also elimintes the problems of corrosion that's prevalent in steel liners.

SOLID/FLUE® provides you with the satisfaction of giving your customers the best product available and doing it with the most economical & efficient equipment.

For additional dealership information or the name of the **SOLID/FLUE®** contractor nearest you, give us a call.

American Chimney Lining Systems, Inc.
9797 Clyde Park, S.W.
Byron Center, Michigan 49315
(616) 878-3577 Ask For Dept. J

SOLID FLUE

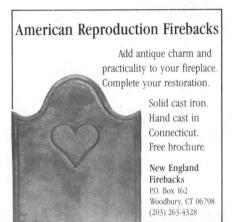

FIREPLACE ACCESSORIES

(1) Andirons
(2) Bellows
(3) Coal Scuttles
(4) Cranes
(5) Fenders
(6) Firebacks
(7) Firegrates
(8) Firescreens
(9) Pokers & Fireplace Tools
(10) Wood Baskets

Acme Stove Company (MD)
Acorn Manufacturing Co., Inc. (MA) *9*
Adams Company (IA) *1,10,6,8,9*
Danny Alessandro/Edwin Jackson (NY) *1,10,5,8,9*
Arden Forge (PA) *1,4,9*
Ball and Ball (PA) *1,4,5,8,9*
Berea College Crafts (KY) *9*
Bona Decorative Hardware (OH) *1,7,8,9*
Boren Clay Products Company (NC)
Cassidy Bros. Forge, Inc. (MA) ... *1,4,6,7,8,9,9*
Colonial Restoration Products (PA) *1,4,5,6,7,9*
Colonial Williamsburg Foundation (VA)
The Country Iron Foundry (PA) *1,6*
DHM Cabinets (VA) *1,10,2,3,5,6,8,9*
Dalton-Gorman, Inc. (IL) *1,5,8,9*
Ian Eddy — Blacksmith (VT) *9*
Elephant Hill Iron Works (VT) *1,4,9*
Essex Forge (CT) *1,9*
Hearth Realities (GA) *7*
Historic Housefitters Company (NY) *9*
Iron Craft, Inc. (NH) *1,2,3,7,9*
Jackson, Wm. H. Co. (NY) *1,5,7,9*
Kayne & Son Custom Forged Hardware (NC) *1,4,5,7,8,9*
Lawler Machine & Foundry (AL) *1,7*
Lehman Hardware & Appliances (OH) .. *3,9*
Lemee's Fireplace Equipment (MA) *1,2,3,4,6,7,8,9*
Mill River Hammerworks (MA) *1*
Millham, Newton — Blacksmith (MA) . *1,4*
Minuteman International Co., Ltd. (MA) *8,9*
Monroe Coldren and Sons (PA) *1,4,9*
New England Firebacks (CT) *6*
New England Tool Co., Ltd. (NY) *8,9*
Old Smithy Shop (NH) *4*
Pennsylvania Firebacks, Inc. (PA) *6*
Period Furniture Hardware Co., Inc. (MA) *1,5,6,8,9*
Pine & Palette Studio (CT) *2*
Portland Willamette, Division Thomas Industries (OR) *1,10,5,7,8,9*
The Renovator's Supply (MA) *1,9*
Schwartz's Forge & Metalworks, Inc. (NY) *9*
Smithy, The (VT) *9*
Smithy Hearth Products (CT) *8*
Donald C. Stetson, Sr., Enterprises (MA)
Vermont Castings, Inc. (VT) *10*
Vermont Industries, Inc. (VT) *1,10,7,8,9*
Virginia Metalcrafters (VA) *1,4,8,9*
Washburne, E.G. & Co., Inc. (MA)
Washington Stove Works (WA) *3*
Westlake Architectural Antiques (TX) .. *1,5,8*
Helen Williams—Delft Tiles (CA) *6*
Windy Hill Forge (MD) *1,4,8*
Woodbury Blacksmith & Forge Co. (CT) *1,4,9*

FURNACE PARTS

Heckler Bros. (PA)
H.C. Oswald Supply Co., Inc. (NY)

GAS LOGS

Readybuilt Products, Co. (MD)

HEAT SHIELDS FOR FREE-STANDING STOVES

Advanced Materials, Inc. (CT)
Hearth Shield (WA)
USG Corporation (IL)

STOVES

(1) Heating
(2) Cooking (Kitchen)
(3) Wood-Burning
(4) Coal-Burning
(5) Antique

Acme Stove Company (MD) *3,4*
Aetna Stove Company (PA) *5*
Barnstable Stove Shop (MA) *1,2,3,4,5*
Bow & Arrow Stove Co. (MA) *3,4*
Brick Stove Works (ME) *1,2,3*
Bryant Stove Works (ME) *2,4,5*
C & D Distributors Hearth Mate (CT) *3,4*
Country Comfort Stove Works (MA) ... *3,4,5*
Cumberland General Store (TN) *2,3,4*
Elmira Stove Works (CAN) *3,4*
Empire Stove & Furnace Co., Inc. (NY) . *3,4*
House of Webster (AR) *2*
Jotul U.S.A., Inc. (ME) *1,3,4*
Lehman Hardware & Appliances (OH) *1,2,3,4*
Lunenburg Foundry & Engineering, Ltd. (CAN) *1*
Monarch Range Co. Consumer Prod. Div. (WI)
Old Time Stove Co. (MA) *3,4,5*
Shenandoah Manufacturing Co. (VA) *1,3*
Stone Ledge Co. (MA) *3,4*
Vermont Castings, Inc. (VT) *1,3,4*
Vermont Iron (VT) *3*
Washington Stove Works (WA) *1,2,3,4*
Wendall's Wood Stoves (CA) *1,2,3,4,5*
Woodstock Soapstone Co., Inc. (NH) *3*
Worthington Trading Company (MO) ... *3,4*

See Company Directory for Addresses & Phone Numbers on page 151

STOVE PARTS

(1) Stove Pipe & Fittings
(2) Isinglass For Stove Doors
(3) Parts For Antique Stoves

Aetna Stove Company (PA) 1,2,3
Akron Foundry, Inc. (IN) 3
Architectural Iron Company (PA) 3
Barnstable Stove Shop (MA) 2,3
BOATECH (NY) 1
Bow & Arrow Stove Co. (MA) 1
Brick Stove Works (ME)
Bryant Stove Works (ME) 2,3
Country Comfort Stove Works (MA)
Cumberland General Store (TN) 1
Empire Stove & Furnace Co., Inc. (NY) . 2,3
Hearth Shield (WA)
Heckler Bros. (PA) 3
Iron Craft, Inc. (NH) 2
Jotul U.S.A., Inc. (ME) 1
Lunenburg Foundry & Engineering, Ltd. (CAN) 3
Max-Cast (IA) 3
Monarch Range Co. Consumer Prod. Div. (WI) 3
Nye's Foundry Ltd. (CAN) 3
H.C. Oswald Supply Co., Inc. (NY) 3
Smith, F.E., Castings, Inc. (MI) 3
Smith, Whitcomb & Cook Co. (VT) 3
George J. Thaler, Inc. (MD) 3
Thompson & Anderson, Inc. (ME) 1
Tomahawk Foundry (WI) 3
Wendall's Wood Stoves (CA) 3
Worthington Trading Company (MO) 2
Xenia Foundry & Machine Co. Specialty Castings Dept. (OH) 3

OTHER HEATING EQUIPMENT

Cumberland General Store (TN)

VENTILATING EQUIPMENT

Fasco Industries, Inc. (NC)
Fypon, Inc. (PA)
Kool-O-Matic Corp. (MI)
Midget Louver Co. (CT)
Sammamish Woodworks (WA)

WATER HEATERS—ALTERNATE FUELS

Cumberland General Store (TN)

WINDOW COVERINGS, INSULATING

Appropriate Technology Corporation (VT)
T.J. Bottom Industries, Inc. (MO)
Bow & Arrow Stove Co. (MA)
Douglas Cooperative, Inc. Window Blanket Division (TN)
Insul Shutter (NH)
The Jasmine Company (CO)
Magnetite Corp. (LA)
Restoration Millworks (CO)
Rockland Industries, Inc. Thermal Products Division (MD)

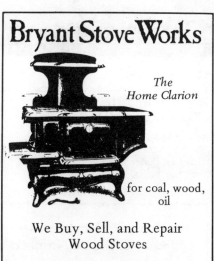

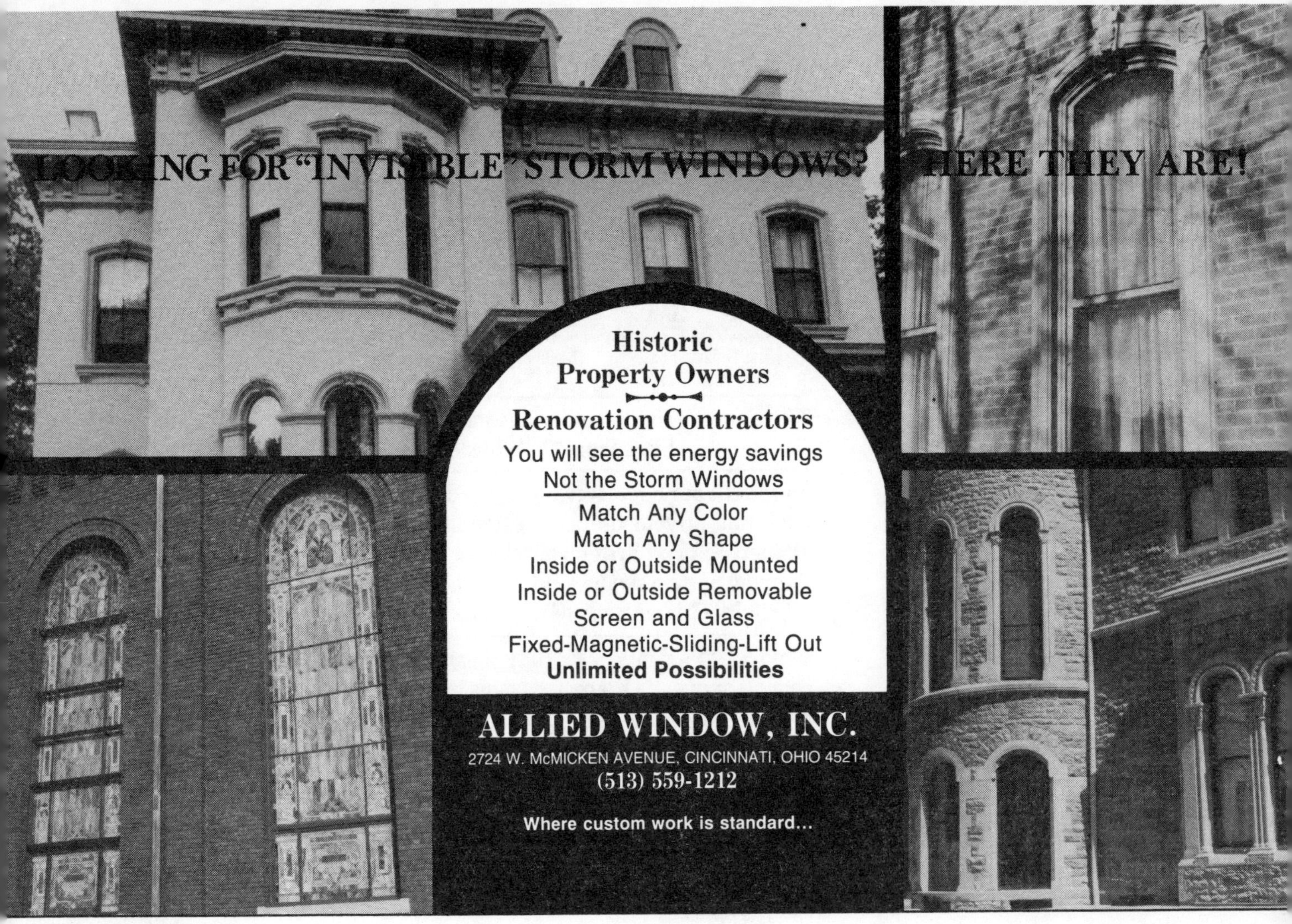

STORM WINDOWS, WOOD

(1) Outside Mounting
(2) Inside Mounting

Allied Window, Inc. (OH) *1,2*
Bjorndal Woodworks (WI) *1,2*
Combination Door Co. (WI) *1*
D.V.H. Co. (FL) *1,2*
Drums Sash & Door Co., Inc. (PA) *1*
Glass & Aluminum Construction Services, Inc. (NH)
International Fireproof Door Co., Inc. (IFD) (NY) *1*
Marvin Windows (MN) *1*
National Screen Co. (VA) *1*
Wes-Pine Wood Windows (MA)

STORM WINDOWS, METAL & PLASTIC

(1) Outside Mounting
(2) Inside Mounting

Air-Flo Window Contracting Corp. (NY) *1,2*
Allied Window, Inc. (OH) *1,2*
Elmont Manufacturing Co., Inc. (NY) *1,2*
Glass & Aluminum Construction Services, Inc. (NH)
The Jasmine Company (CO) *1,2*
Perkasie Industries Corp. (PA) *2*
Plaskolite, Inc. (OH) *2*

WEATHERSTRIPPING PRODUCTS (INTEGRAL)

Accurate Metal Weather Strip Co., Inc. (NY)
Anderson Pulley Seal Co. (MN)

See Company Directory for Addresses & Phone Numbers on page 151

Lighting Fixtures & Parts

LIGHTING FIXTURES & LAMPS—ANTIQUE

1874 House (OR)
21st Century Antiques (MA)
Alfa Lite (UT)
American Glass Light Co. (NY)
Architectural Accents (GA)
Architectural Antiques (OK)
Architectural Antiques Exchange (PA)
Architectural Salvage Co. (MI)
Art Directions (MO)
Bernard Restoration (MA)
Joan Bogart (NY)
Brass Light Gallery (WI)
Brass Menagerie (LA)
ByGone Era Architectural Antiques (GA)
Canal Co. (DC)
Century House Antiques (OH)
City Barn Antiques (NY)
City Knickerbocker, Inc. (NY)
City Lights (MA)
Cleveland Wrecking Co. (IL)
Conservatory, The (MI)
The Emporium, Inc. (TX)
Fellenz Hardware & Antiques (MO)
Gaslight Time Antiques (NY)
Gem Monogram & Cut Glass Corp. (NY)
Great American Salvage (NY)
Greg's Antique Lighting (CA)
Half Moon Antiques c/o Monmouth Antique Shoppes (NJ)
Harvey M. Stern & Co./ Antique Lighting (PA)
Hexagram (CA)
Hippo Hardware & Trading Co. (OR)
History Store (MD)
John Kruesel's General Merchandise (MN)
LampLight Industries, Inc. (OH)
Joe Ley Antiques, Inc. (KY)
London Venturers Company (MA)
Mattia, Louis (NY)
Moriarty's Lamps (CA)
Neri, C./Antiques (PA)
Ocean View Lighting (CA)
Old Lamplighter Shop (NY)
Olde Bostonian Architectural Antiques (MA)
Olde & Oak Antiques (AL)
Oliver, Bradley C. (PA)
Rejuvenation House Parts Co. (OR)
Roy Electric Co., Inc. (NY)
St. Louis Antique Lighting Co., Inc. (MO)
Sandy Springs Galleries (GA)
Sherman Hill Antiques (IA)
Squaw Alley, Inc. (IL)
Stanley Galleries (IL)
William H. Straus (NY)
Turn-of-the-Century Lighting (CAN)
United House Wrecking Corp. (CT)
Wilson, H. Weber, Antiquarian (MD)
Wrecking Bar of Atlanta (GA)
Yankee Craftsman (MA)

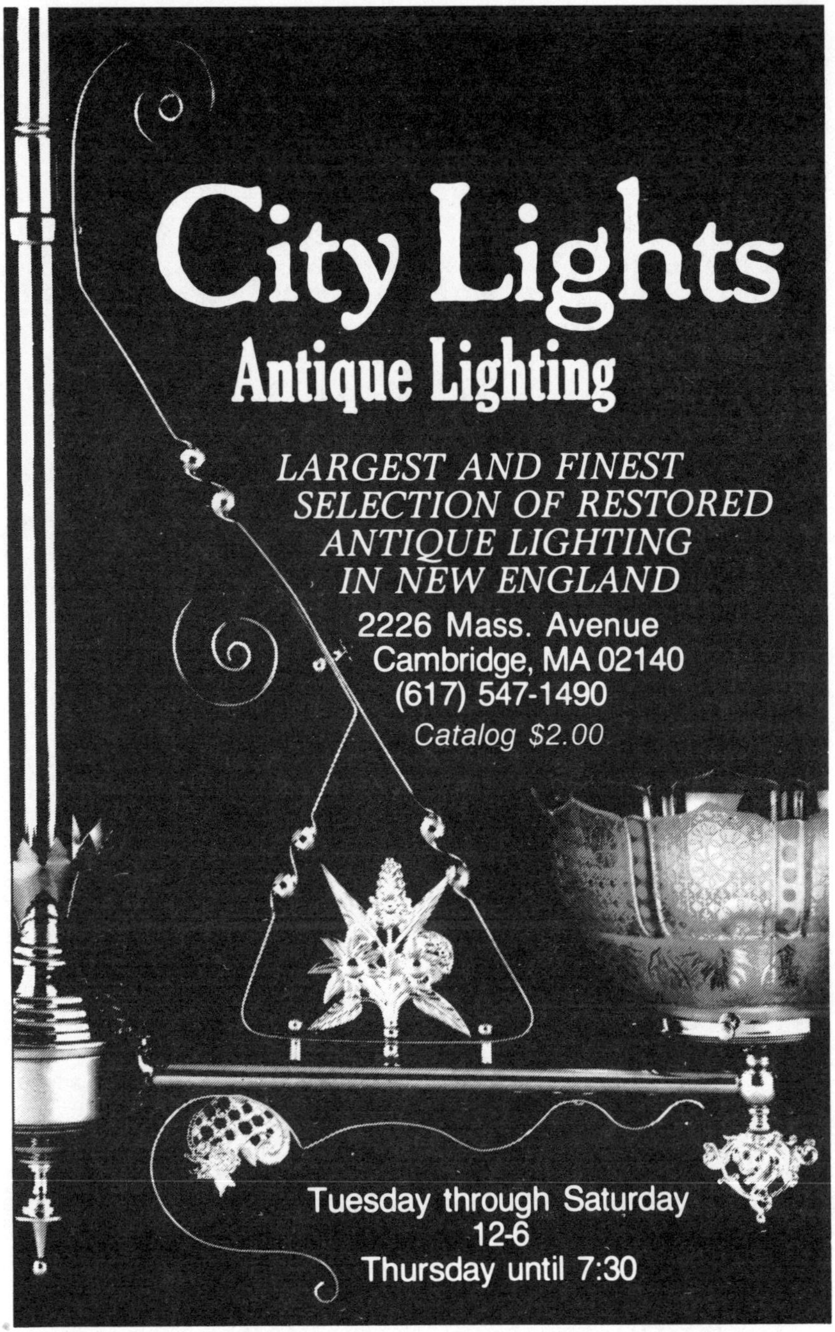

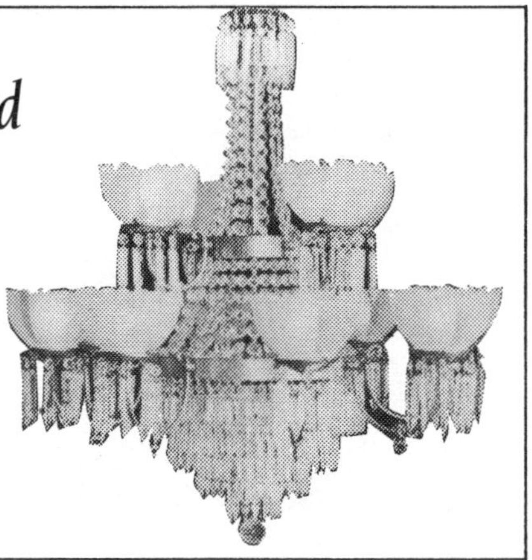

LIGHTING FIXTURES, REPRODUCTION—EARLY AMERICAN

(1) Ceiling & Wall Fixtures
(2) Lamps

A.J.P. Coppersmith (MA) *1*
Alfa Lite (UT) *1,2*
Authentic Designs Inc. (VT) *1,2*
Authentic Lighting (NJ) *2*
Baldwin Hardware Mfg. Corp. (PA) *1,2*
Ball and Ball (PA) *1*
Brass Menagerie (LA)
Brubaker Metalcrafts (OH) *1,2*
Cassidy Bros. Forge, Inc. (MA) *1,2*
Chandelier Warehouse (NY) *1*
Cohasset Colonials (MA) *1,2*
Colonial Casting Co., Inc. (CT) *1*
Colonial Restoration Products (PA) *1*
Colonial Williamsburg Foundation (VA) ... *1*
Copper House (NH) *1*
The Coppersmith— (MA) *1,2*
Josiah R. Coppersmythe (MA) *1,2*
Country Loft (MA) *1,2*
The Country Store (IL) *1*
Dutch Products & Supply Co. (PA) *1*
Essex Forge (CT) *1*
Gates Moore (CT) *1*
Hearth-glo (CT) *1*
Henderson Lighting (CT) *1*
Heritage Lanterns (ME) *1,2*
Hippo Hardware & Trading Co. (OR) *1*
Historic Charleston Reproductions (SC) ... *2*
Hood, R. and Co. (NH) *1,2*
Hubbardton Forge Corp. (VT) *1*
Hurley Patentee Lighting (NY) *2*
Kayne & Son Custom Forged Hardware (NC) *1*
King's Chandelier Co. (NC) *1*
Lester H. Berry & Company (PA) *1,2*
Lighting by Hammerworks (MA) *1,2*
Loose, Thomas — Blacksmith/ Whitesmith (PA) *1*
MarLe Company (CT) *1*
Metropolitan Lighting Fixture Co., Inc. (NY) *1*
Newstamp Lighting Co. (MA) *1,2*
Nostalgia (GA) *1,2*
Olde Village Smithery (MA) *1*
Period Furniture Hardware Co., Inc. (MA) *1,2*
Period Lighting Fixtures (CT) *1,2*
The Renovator's Supply (MA) *1*
Saltbox (PA) *1,2*
Spencer, William, Inc. (NJ) *1*
Sturbridge Yankee Workshop (ME) *1,2*
The Tin Bin (PA) *1*
Virginia Metalcrafters (VA) *1,2*
Washington Copper Works (CT) *1,2*
Lt. Moses Willard, Inc. (OH) *1,2*
Windy Hill Forge (MD) *1,2*

See Company Directory for Addresses & Phone Numbers on page 151

Liting the Way™, a tradition at THE SALTBOX™

★ Lanterns · Postlights · Chandeliers of Tin, Copper, Brass ★

Authentic Reproductions for primitive·country·formal homes

BROCHURE OF LIGHTING FIXTURES $1.00

AMERICAN PERIOD Period™ COLLECTION LIGHTING FIXTURES

Recreated by Dedicated Craftsmen

Recommended by Homeowners and Restorations

THE SALTBOX™ 3004 Columbia Ave., Lancaster, PA 17603 ★ 1747 Riverside Dr., Suamico, WI 54173

Iron Chandeliers

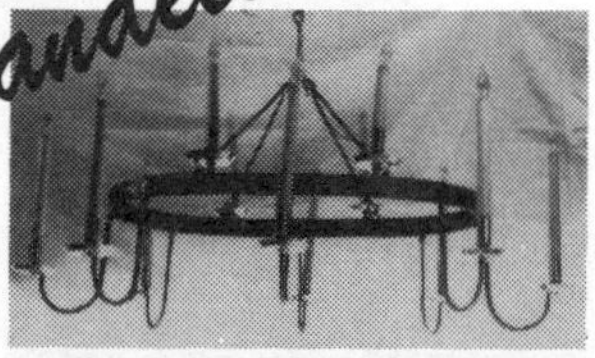

We combine the simplicity of hand forged iron with the beauty of polished brass, creating a chandelier that will add to any decor in a subtle manner.

Call or write for your **Free Mini-Catalog** of Quality House and Furniture Hardware. Or send $5.00 for our complete 108 page Catalog, now including many new Victorian Products.

BALL and BALL

Finest Quality Reproductions

463 W. Lincoln Hwy., Exton, PA 19341
(215) 363-7330

Hand-Crafted Copper Lanterns

Catalogue $3.00, refundable with order

The Washington Copper Works

Washington, Connecticut 06793

COLONIAL AND EARLY AMERICAN LIGHTING FIXTURES

AUTHENTIC DESIGNS

The Mill Road
West Rupert; Vermont 05776-0011
Tel (802) 394-7713

Catalogue $3.00

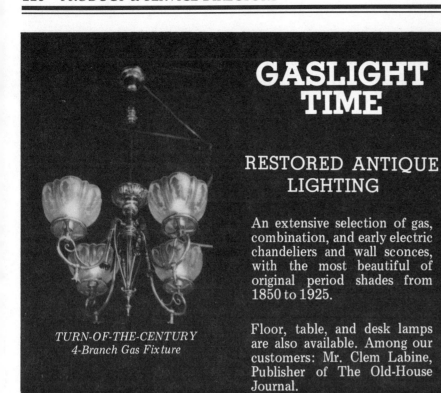

LIGHTING FIXTURES, REPRODUCTION—VICTORIAN

(1) Ceiling & Wall Fixtures
(2) Lamps

Alfa Lite (UT) *1,2*
Authentic Lighting (NJ) *1,2*
B & P Lamp Supply Co., Inc. (TN) *1,2*
Brass Light Gallery (WI) *1*
Brass Menagerie (LA) *2*
Brasslight, Inc. (NY) *1,2*
Chandelier Warehouse (NY) *1*
City Knickerbocker, Inc. (NY) *1,2*
Classic Illumination Inc. (CA) *1,2*
Crawford's Old House Store (WI) *1*
Fenton Art Glass Company (WV) *2*
Gaslight Time Antiques (NY)
Golden Age Glassworks (NY) *1,2*
Henderson Lighting (CT) *1*
Hippo Hardware & Trading Co. (OR) *1*
King's Chandelier Co. (NC) *1*
Light Ideas (MD) *1,2*
London Venturers Company (MA) *1*
Luigi Crystal (PA) *1,2*
M — H Lamp & Fan Company (IL) *1,2*
Magnolia Hall (GA) *2*
Martha M. House Furniture (AL) *1,2*
Metropolitan Lighting Fixture Co., Inc. (NY) *1*
Nowell's, Inc. (CA) *1,2*
Ocean View Lighting (CA) *1*
Park Place (DC) *1,2*
Rejuvenation House Parts Co. (OR) *1*
Remodelers & Renovators (ID) *1*
The Renovator's Supply (MA) *1*
Roy Electric Co., Inc. (NY) *1,2*
St. Louis Antique Lighting Co., Inc. (MO) *1,2*
Schlitz Studios (WI) *1,2*
Sign of the Crab (CA) *2*
Spencer, William, Inc. (NJ) *1*
United House Wrecking Corp. (CT) *1*
Victorian Lightcrafters, Ltd. (NY) *1*
Victorian Lighting Co. (MN) *1,2*
Victorian Lighting Works, Inc. (PA) *1,2*
Village Antique Lighting Co. (MI) *1,2*
Washington House Reproductions (VA) . *1,2*
Windy Lane Fluorescents, Inc. (CO) *1*

See Company Directory for Addresses & Phone Numbers on page 151

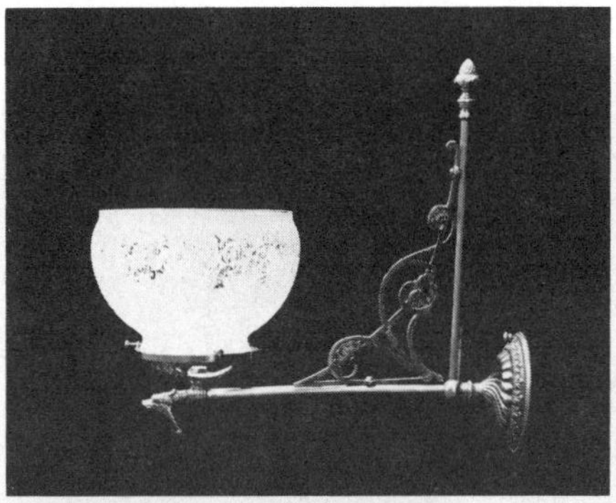
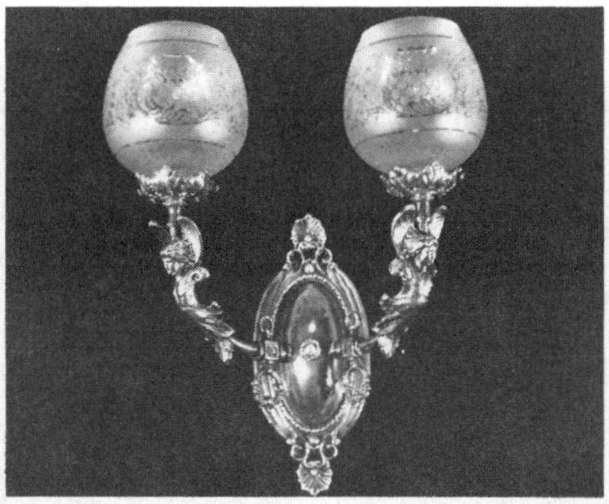

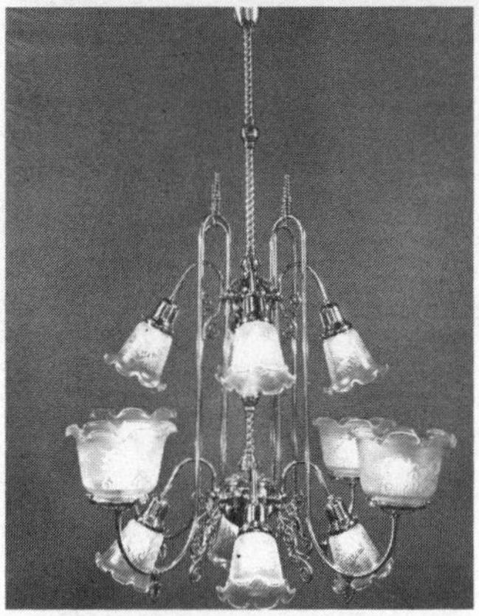

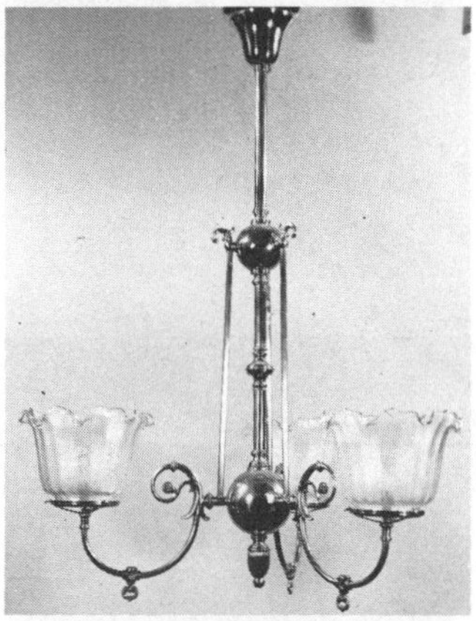
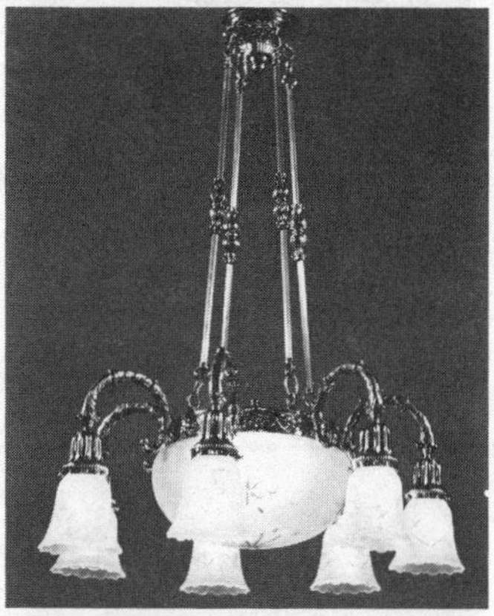

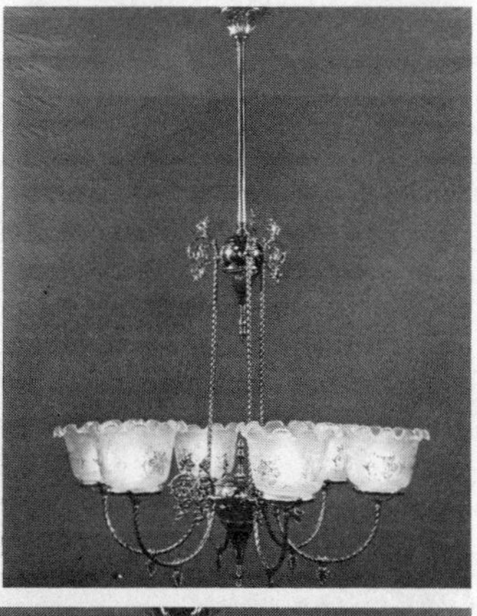

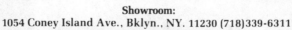

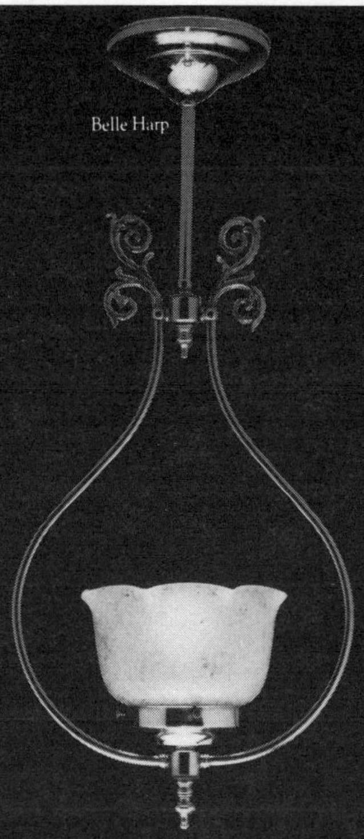
Belle Harp

Introducing
the New Classics...

The Brasslight Collection.

A totally original line of desk lamps, ceiling fixtures and wall sconces, hand made from solid American brass. Meticulously polished and lacquered by hand for lasting beauty and easy care. Available with a variety of interchangeable glass shades.

Send $3 for details on the complete collection.

Cavalier

Brasslight
Dept. H
90 Main Street
Nyack, New York
10960
(Wholesale prices to dealers on request.)

St. Louis Antique Lighting Company

Restore or decorate with fine old gas, electric or combination fixtures. Exquisitely handcrafted solid brass reproduction ceiling fixtures, sconces and lamps; along with an excellent shade selection. We also have added a fine Mission style oak and art glass ceiling fixture. 12-page color catalog; $3.00. All fixtures U.L. Listed; and Restoration Services available.

St. Louis Antique Lighting Co., Inc.
801 N. Skinker, St. Louis, MO 63130
(314) 863-1414

SOLID BRASS ANTIQUE

- Desk Lamps
- Wall Sconces
- Chandeliers
- Restored Antique Ceiling Fans

LIGHTING REPRODUCTIONS
Catalog: $3.00

M–H LAMP & FAN CO.

7231½ North Sheridan, Chicago, IL 60626
(312) 743-2225

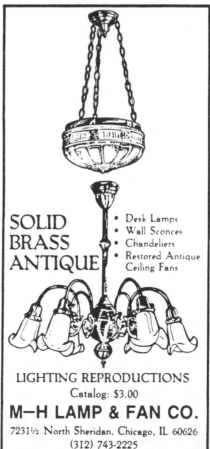

ORIGINAL GAS, OIL AND EARLY ELECTRIC LIGHTING FIXTURES

1800 - 1910

restored, wired, and ready to hang
catalog $2.00
we ship anywhere

THE LONDON VENTURERS COMPANY
ROCKPORT, MASSACHUSETTS 01966
(617) 546-7161

LIGHTING FIXTURES, REPRODUCTION—EARLY 20TH CENTURY

(1) Ceiling & Wall Fixtures
(2) Lamps

Alfa Lite (UT) *1,2*
American Glass Light Co. (NY) *1,2*
Arroyo Restoration (CA) *1,2*
Art Directions (MO)
B & P Lamp Supply Co., Inc. (TN) *1,2*
Brass Light Gallery (WI) *1*
Brass Menagerie (LA)
Brasslight, Inc. (NY) *1,2*
Chandelier Warehouse (NY) *1*
Classic Illumination Inc. (CA) *1,2*
Curran, Patrick J. (MA) *2*
Golden Age Glassworks (NY) *1,2*
Heirloom Enterprises (MN) *1*
Hippo Hardware & Trading Co. (OR) *1*
History Store (MD) *1,2*
Jadis Moderne (CA) *1,2*
Light Ideas (MD) *1,2*
London Venturers Company (MA) *1*
Lundberg Studios, Inc. Contemporary Art Glass (CA) *2*
M — H Lamp & Fan Company (IL) *1*
Metropolis (NY) *2*
Metropolitan Lighting Fixture Co., Inc. (NY) *1*
Ocean View Lighting (CA) *1*
Old Lamplighter Shop (NY) *2*
Rambusch (NY) *1*
Rejuvenation House Parts Co. (OR) *1*
Renaissance Marketing, Inc. (MI) *2*
Roy Electric Co., Inc. (NY) *1*
St. Louis Antique Lighting Co., Inc. (MO) *1,2*
Sierra Lamp Company (CA) *2*
Squaw Alley, Inc. (IL) *1,2*
Tiffany Design Lamps (NV) *2*
Victorian Lightcrafters, Ltd. (NY) *1*
Victorian Lighting Co. (MN) *1,2*
Village Antique Lighting Co. (MI) *1,2*

For more
REPRODUCTION
LIGHTING FIXTURES
see the ad for Brass Light
Gallery in the Color Section

See Company Directory for
Addresses & Phone Numbers
on page 151

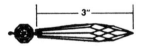

LIGHTING FIXTURE PARTS—GLASS

(1) Globes
(2) Shades
(3) Prisms
(4) Other (Specify)

Alfa Lite (UT) *1,2,3*
American Lamp Parts, Inc. (TX) *1,2,3*
Angelo Brothers Co. (PA) *1,2*
B & P Lamp Supply Co., Inc. (TN) *1,2,3*
Blenko Glass Co., Inc. (WV) *2*
Boulder Stained Glass Studios (CO) *2*
Brasslight, Inc. (NY) *1,2*
Campbell-Lamps (PA) *1,2*
Century House Antiques (OH) *1,2*
City Knickerbocker, Inc. (NY) *1,2*
Crystal Mountain Prisms (NY) *3*
Cumberland General Store (TN) *1,2*
Gaslight Time Antiques (NY) *2*
Gem Monogram & Cut Glass Corp. (NY) . *3*
Gillinder Brothers, Inc. (NY) *2*
Golden Age Glassworks (NY) *2*
Greg's Antique Lighting (CA) *1,2*
Hexagram (CA) *2*
Hippo Hardware & Trading Co. (OR) *1,2*
Holophane Division (OH) *2*
Lyn Hovey Studio, Inc. (MA) *2*
Light Ideas (MD) *2*
Luigi Crystal (PA) *1,2,3*
Lundberg Studios, Inc. Contemporary Art Glass (CA) *2*
Moriarty's Lamps (CA) *2*
Nowell's, Inc. (CA) *1,2*
Ocean View Lighting (CA) *1*
Old Lamplighter Shop (NY) *1,2,3*
Old World Restorations, Inc. (OH)
Paxton Hardware Ltd. (MD) *2,3*
Pyfer, E.W. (IL) *1,2*
Renaissance Marketing, Inc. (MI) *2*
The Renovator's Supply (MA) *2*
Roy Electric Co., Inc. (NY) *1,2*
St. Louis Antique Lighting Co., Inc. (MO) *2*
Salamandra Glass (NH)
Tiffany Design Lamps (NV) *2*
Victorian Lightcrafters, Ltd. (NY) *2*
Victorian Lighting Co. (MN) *1,2,3*
Victorian Reproductions Enterprises, Inc. (MN) *2*

LIGHTING FIXTURE PARTS—METAL

American Lamp Parts, Inc. (TX)
B & P Lamp Supply Co., Inc. (TN)
Barap Specialties (MI)
Campbell-Lamps (PA)
Century House Antiques (OH)
Craftsman Wood Service Co. (IL)
Cumberland General Store (TN)
Holophane Division (OH)
Lundberg Studios, Inc. Contemporary Art Glass (CA)
Moriarty's Lamps (CA)
Old Lamplighter Shop (NY)
Paxton Hardware Ltd. (MD)
Roy Electric Co., Inc. (NY)
Squaw Alley, Inc. (IL)
Victorian Lighting Co. (MN)
Village Antique Lighting Co. (MI)

LIGHTING FIXTURES—GAS BURNING

(1) Antique (Original)
(2) New Reproduction

Joan Bogart (NY) *1*
City Barn Antiques (NY) *1*
Greg's Antique Lighting (CA) *1*
Hexagram (CA) *1*
Materials Unlimited (MI) *1*
Neri, C./Antiques (PA) *1*
Norcross Galleries (GA) *2*
Nowell's, Inc. (CA) *1,2*
Roy Electric Co., Inc. (NY) *1,2*
Sherman Hill Antiques (IA) *1*
Stanley Galleries (IL) *1*
William H. Straus (NY) *1*
TrimbleHouse Corporation (GA) *2*
Turn-of-the-Century Lighting (CAN) *1*
Yankee Craftsman (MA) *1*

GAS MANTLES AND BOBECHES

Bradford Consultants (NJ)
Gasworks (MD)
Nowell's, Inc. (CA)

KEROSENE LAMPS & LANTERNS

B & P Lamp Supply Co., Inc. (TN)
Campbell-Lamps (PA)
Cumberland General Store (TN)
DS Locksmithing Company (FL)
Dutch Products & Supply Co. (PA)
Heritage Lanterns (ME)
Lehman Hardware & Appliances (OH)
Moriarty's Lamps (CA)
Nowell's, Inc. (CA)
Old Lamplighter Shop (NY)
Sandy Springs Galleries (GA)
Sign of the Crab (CA)
Washington Copper Works (CT)
Worthington Trading Company (MO)
Yankee Craftsman (MA)

For more on ANTIQUE LIGHTING see the ad for C. Neri Antiques in the Color Section

ELECTRIC CANDLES

Elcanco Inc. (MA)
Spencer, William, Inc. (NJ)

LAMP POSTS & STANDARDS, REPRODUCTION

Abaroot Mfg., Co. (CA)
Antique Street Lamps, Inc. (TX)
Hearth-glo (CT)
Lampco (OH)
MarLe Company (CT)
Park Place (DC)
RWL/Welsbach Lighting (CT)
Saco Manufacturing & Woodworking (ME)
Saltbox (PA)
A.F. Schwerd Manufacturing Co. (PA)
Silver Dollar Trading Co. (TX)
Spring City Electrical Mfg. Co (PA)
Sternberg Lanterns, Inc. (IL)
Tennessee Fabricating Co. (TN)
TrimbleHouse Corporation (GA)
United House Wrecking Corp. (CT)
Otto Wendt & Co. (TX)

LAMP WICKS & LAMP OIL

Campbell-Lamps (PA)
Cumberland General Store (TN)
Lehman Hardware & Appliances (OH)

LIGHT BULBS, CARBON FILAMENT

Bradford Consultants (NJ)
City Knickerbocker, Inc. (NY)
Victorian Lightcrafters, Ltd. (NY)
Victorian Lighting Co. (MN)

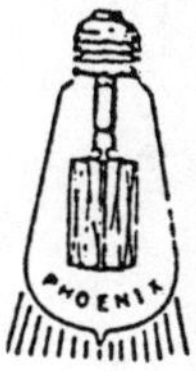

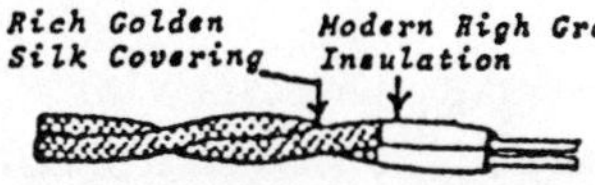

See Company Directory for Addresses & Phone Numbers on page 151

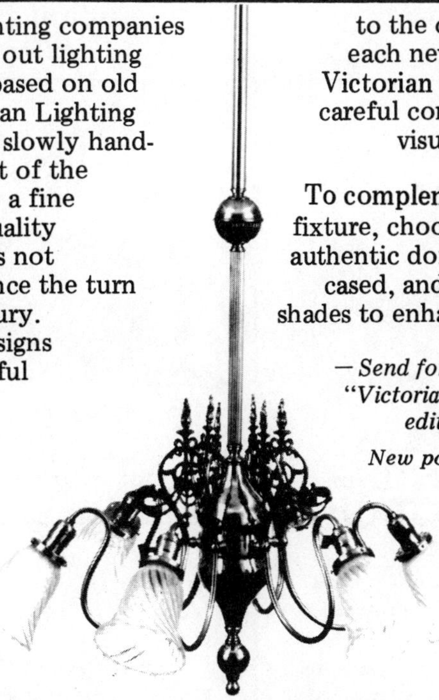

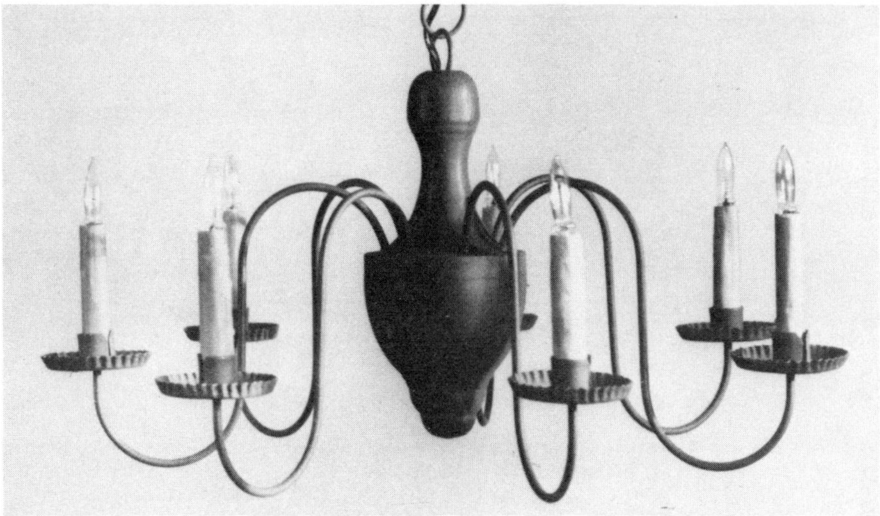

As Shown $165 plus U.P.S. and handling. Dia. 24" H. 11"

HANDCRAFTED

To The Drip On The Tapered Candles

Early American Lighting since 1938; chandeliers, copper lanterns, and wall sconces. Catalog $2 (refundable).

Knowledgeable collectors, Restorations and Museums have been buying our fine fixtures for over 30 years. A list available on request.

GATES MOORE

2 River Rd., Silvermine, Norwalk, Conn. 06850 Tel. (203) 847-3231

HANDMADE PERIOD LIGHTING REPRODUCTIONS

Entirely handmade 17th and 18th century lanterns, chandeliers and sconces in copper, pewter, distressed tin and wood. Carefully researched designs and detailed craftsmanship reflect the original warmth and charm of early lighting.

•catalogues (refundable) $3.00

PERIOD LIGHTING FIXTURES

1 Main Street, Dept. OJ7
Chester, CT 06412 (203) 526-3690

Beautiful and Unusual Lighting Catalog

- Colonial and Traditional Styles
- For indoor and outdoor use.
- Visit our factory store.
- Send $2.00 for idea-packed 28 page catalog

NEWSTAMP LIGHTING
Dept. OH87
227 Bay Road, N. Easton, MA 02356

For more information on
PUSH-BUTTON ELECTRIC SWITCHES
see Classic Accents' ad in the Color Section

LAMPS & LANTERNS, EXTERIOR—REPRODUCTION

A.J.P. Coppersmith (MA)
Authentic Designs Inc. (VT)
Ball and Ball (PA)
British-American Marketing Services, Ltd. (PA)
Cassidy Bros. Forge, Inc. (MA)
Contemporary Copper/Matthew Richardson (MA)
The Coppersmith— (MA)
Dutch Products & Supply Co. (PA)
Essex Forge (CT)
Gates Moore (CT)
Henderson Lighting (CT)
Heritage Lanterns (ME)
Lampco (OH)
LampLight Industries, Inc. (OH)
Lighting by Hammerworks (MA)
MarLe Company (CT)
Newstamp Lighting Co. (MA)
Norcross Galleries (GA)
Nostalgia (GA)
Park Place (DC)
Period Lighting Fixtures (CT)
RWL/Welsbach Lighting (CT)
Rambusch (NY)
Saltbox (PA)
Sign of the Crab (CA)
Silver Dollar Trading Co. (TX)
Sternberg Lanterns, Inc. (IL)
Travis Tuck, Inc. — Metal Sculptor (MA)
TrimbleHouse Corporation (GA)
United House Wrecking Corp. (CT)
Washburne, E.G. & Co., Inc. (MA)
Washington Copper Works (CT)
Lt. Moses Willard, Inc. (OH)

SWITCHES, ELECTRIC PUSH-BUTTON

Classic Accents (MI)

OTHER LIGHTING FIXTURES & PARTS

Bradford Consultants (NJ)
Industrial Solar (KA)

See Company Directory for Addresses & Phone Numbers on page 151

Paints, Finishes, Removers & Supplies

BLEACH, WOOD

Behlen, H. & Bros. (NY)
Cabot Stains (MA)
Chapman Chemical Co. (TN)
Chem-Clean Furniture Restoration Center (VT)
Daly's Wood Finishing Products (WA)
Janovic/Plaza, Inc. (NY)
Johnson Paint Co. (MA)
Wolf Paints And Wallpapers (NY)
Wood Finishing Supply Co., Inc. (NY)

BRASS LACQUER

Behlen, H. & Bros. (NY)
Janovic/Plaza, Inc. (NY)
Wolf Paints And Wallpapers (NY)

BRONZING & GILDING LIQUIDS

Behlen, H. & Bros. (NY)
Gold Leaf & Metallic Powders, Inc. (NY)
Janovic/Plaza, Inc. (NY)
Wolf Paints And Wallpapers (NY)
Wood Finishing Supply Co., Inc. (NY)

CLEANERS & POLISHES, METAL

(1) Brass & Copper
(2) Silver
(3) Stove Polish and Finish
19th Century Company (CA)
Bradford Derustit Corp. (NY)
The Butcher Polish Co. (MA)
Colonial Restoration Products (PA) *1*
Competition Chemicals, Inc. (IA) *1,2*
Cumberland General Store (TN) *1,1,2,3*
Easy Time Wood Refinishing Products Corp. (IL) *1*
J. Goddard & Sons, Ltd. (WI) *1,2*
The Hope Co., Inc. (MO) *3*
Howard Refinishing Products (CA) *1,2*
Iron Craft, Inc. (NH) *3*
Ship 'n Out (NY) *1*
Staples, H. F. & Co., Inc. (NH) *3*
Woodcare Corporation Metal & Wood Restoration Prod. (NJ) *1,3*
J.A. Wright & Co. (NH) *1,2*

FINISH REVIVERS

19th Century Company (CA)
Behlen, H. & Bros. (NY)
Broadnax Refinishing Products, Inc. (GA)
Cornucopia, Inc. At the Appleworks (MA)
Daly's Wood Finishing Products (WA)
Easy Time Wood Refinishing Products Corp. (IL)
Finish Feeder Company (MD)
Finishing Touch (CA)
The Hope Co., Inc. (MO)
Howard Refinishing Products (CA)
O'Sullivan Co. (MI)
Restech Industries (OR)
United Gilsonite Laboratories (PA)
Woodcare Corporation Metal & Wood Restoration Prod. (NJ)

FLATTING OILS

Behlen, H. & Bros. (NY)
Janovic/Plaza, Inc. (NY)
Johnson Paint Co. (MA)

"Here's My Secret..."
DALY'S
SeaFin Teak Oil
ProFin
HARD DRYING QUICK SET OIL FINISH
DALY'S
Ben Matte Clear
Danish Tung-Oil Finish

GLAZING STAINS & LIQUIDS

Bay City Paint Company (CA)
Behlen, H. & Bros. (NY)
Benjamin Moore Co. (NJ)
Daly's Wood Finishing Products (WA)
Gaston Wood Finishes, Inc. (IN)
Janovic/Plaza, Inc. (NY)
Johnson Paint Co. (MA)
Wolf Paints And Wallpapers (NY)
Wood Finishing Supply Co., Inc. (NY)

GOLD LEAF

Behlen, H. & Bros. (NY)
Gold Leaf & Metallic Powders, Inc. (NY)
Janovic/Plaza, Inc. (NY)
Johnson Paint Co. (MA)
The Old-House Gold Leaf People (NY)
Sepp Leaf Products (NY)
M. Swift & Sons, Inc. (CT)
United Gilsonite Laboratories (PA)
Wolf Paints And Wallpapers (NY)
Wood Finishing Supply Co., Inc. (NY)

LACQUERS, CLEAR & COLORED

Barap Specialties (MI)
Bay City Paint Company (CA)
Behlen, H. & Bros. (NY)
Gaston Wood Finishes, Inc. (IN)
Janovic/Plaza, Inc. (NY)
Wolf Paints And Wallpapers (NY)
Wood Finishing Supply Co., Inc. (NY)

MARBLE CLEANERS, SEALERS & POLISHES

Gawet Marble & Granite (VT)
ProSoCo, Inc. (KS)
Sculpture Associates, Ltd. (NY)
TALAS (NY)
Wolf Paints And Wallpapers (NY)

OIL FINISHES, NATURAL

19th Century Company (CA)
Barap Specialties (MI)
Behlen, H. & Bros. (NY)
Bix Process Systems, Inc. (CT)
Broadnax Refinishing Products, Inc. (GA)
Cabot Stains (MA)
Cohasset Colonials (MA)
Daly's Wood Finishing Products (WA)
Easy Time Wood Refinishing Products Corp. (IL)
Gaston Wood Finishes, Inc. (IN)
The Hope Co., Inc. (MO)
Minwax Company, Inc. (NJ)
Pierce & Stevens Chemical Corp. (NY)
Wood Finishing Supply Co., Inc. (NY)
Woodcare Corporation Metal & Wood Restoration Prod. (NJ)
Woodworker's Supply of New Mexico (NM)

PORCELAIN REFINISHING MATERIALS

Abatron, Inc. (IL)
Janovic/Plaza, Inc. (NY)

PAINTS—PERIOD COLORS

(1) Exterior
(2) Interior

Allentown Paint Mfg. Co., Inc. (PA) *1,2*
Barnard Chemical Co. (CA) *2*
Benjamin Moore Co. (NJ) *1,2*
California Products Corp. (MA) *1,2*
Cohasset Colonials (MA) *2*
Colonial Williamsburg Foundation (VA) . *1,2*
Cook & Dunn Paint Corp. (NJ) *1,2*
Finnaren & Haley, Inc. (PA) *1,2*
Fuller O'Brien Paints (GA) *1,2*
Glidden Coatings & Resins (OH) *1*
Janovic/Plaza, Inc. (NY) *1,2*
Munsell Color (MD)
Muralo Company (NJ) *1*
Pratt & Lambert (NY) *1,2*
Shaker Workshops (MA) *1,2*
The Stulb Co. (PA) *1,2*
Wolf Paints And Wallpapers (NY) *1,2*

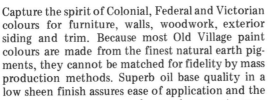

PAINT STRIPPING CHEMICALS, INTERIOR

Behlen, H. & Bros. (NY)
Bix Process Systems, Inc. (CT)
Chem-Clean Furniture Restoration Center (VT)
Chemical Products Co., Inc. (MD)
Easy Time Wood Refinishing Products Corp. (IL)
Howard Refinishing Products (CA)
Master Products, Inc. (IA)
ProSoCo, Inc. (KS)
QRB Industries (MI)
Red Devil, Inc. (NJ)
Staples, H. F. & Co., Inc. (NH)
United Gilsonite Laboratories (PA)
Wood Finishing Supply Co., Inc. (NY)
Woodcare Corporation Metal & Wood Restoration Prod. (NJ)

PIGMENTS & TINTING COLORS

Behlen, H. & Bros. (NY)
Benjamin Moore Co. (NJ)
Janovic/Plaza, Inc. (NY)
Johnson Paint Co. (MA)
Wood Finishing Supply Co., Inc. (NY)

Fuller-O'Brien Paints Is Proud To Offer You

The Palette of

Cape May Victorian COLORS™

This Fuller-O'Brien Palette of Cape May Victorian Colors has received the endorsement and full support of the Cape May Historic District Commission of the City of Cape May, New Jersey.

FULLER O'BRIEN® PAINTS

THIS RICH, BOLD COLLECTION OF 70 AUTHENTIC VICTORIAN COLORS WAS FORMULATED SPECIALLY FOR HOUSES OF THE VICTORIAN ERA.

This Palette is designed to provide appropriate colors related to that period for use both on exterior and interior surfaces. Architects, designers and homeowners have sought for and used these colors more and more for period structures that are being restored and preserved.

The Cape May Victorian Color Palette is available to subscribers of **The Old House Journal** at one half the regular price. For your own copy, send $1.50 with your name and address to:

FULLER-O'BRIEN PAINTS
P. O. Box 864, Brunswick, GA 31521

VICTORIAN RESTORATIONS

breathe new life into old cities

Breinig's Ready-Mixed Oil Paint

puts new life into old wood. This linseed oil paint set the standard for exterior durability. It's available again in 12 ready-mixed cottage shades originally produced in the Victorian Era. Two coats of Breinig's will protect original wood up to 10 years.

QUALITY PAINTS SINCE 1855

ALLENTOWN PAINT
MANUFACTURING COMPANY, INC.
Graham & E. Allen Sts. P.O. Box 597
Allentown, PA 18105

Authentic American colors look fresh & natural today

Quality finishes in historically-inspired colors from Benjamin Moore Paints.

Inside: Choose authentic historical colors for walls, trim and accents that reflect the dignity and warmth of past generations. Use them naturally, in traditional or colonial settings, or as inspiration for your own style. Outside: You'll find documented 18th & 19th century color combinations that restore the charm of yesterday, with finishes formulated to provide maximum protection today.

See your Benjamin Moore dealer for courteous service & expert advice, to help you create a personal look that is historically correct.

Benjamin Moore® PAINTS

PUTTY, COLORED

Behlen, H. & Bros. (NY)
Daly's Wood Finishing Products (WA)
Darworth Co. (CT)
Staples, H. F. & Co., Inc. (NH)

ROT PATCHING & RESTORING MATERIALS

Abatron, Inc. (IL)
Allied Resin Corp. (MA)
Beecham Home Improvement Products, Inc. (OH)
Beta Timber Restoration System/Dell Corp. (MD)
E & B Marine Supply (NJ)
Gougeon Brothers, Inc. (MI)
Poxywood, Inc. (VA)

RUST & CORROSION REMOVERS

Bradford Derustit Corp. (NY)
C.U. Restoration Supplies (TX)
DAP, Inc. (OH)
Woodcare Corporation Metal & Wood Restoration Prod. (NJ)

SEALERS, WOOD

Beecham Home Improvement Products, Inc. (OH)
Behlen, H. & Bros. (NY)
Benjamin Moore Co. (NJ)
Broadnax Refinishing Products, Inc. (GA)
DAP, Inc. (OH)
Daly's Wood Finishing Products (WA)
Garrett Wade Company (NY)
Gaston Wood Finishes, Inc. (IN)
Gougeon Brothers, Inc. (MI)
Pierce & Stevens Chemical Corp. (NY)
Sutherland Welles Ltd. (NC)
United Gilsonite Laboratories (PA)
Wood Finishing Supply Co., Inc. (NY)
Woodcare Corporation Metal & Wood Restoration Prod. (NJ)

SPECIALTY PAINTS & FINISHES

(1) Calcimine
(2) Casein
(3) Whitewash
(4) Texture Paints
(5) Milk Paint
(6) Metallic Paints, Custom

Antique Color Supply, Inc. (MA) *5*
Bay City Paint Company (CA) *2,4*
Benjamin Moore Co. (NJ) *4*
Chromatic Paint Corp. (NY)
Dusty Splinters Enterprises (NY) *5*
Janovic/Plaza, Inc. (NY) *2,3,4*
Johnson Paint Co. (MA) *1,5*
Muralo Company (NJ) *1,4*
Old-Fashioned Milk Paint Co. (MA) *5*
The Stulb Co. (PA) *5*
Sutherland Welles Ltd. (NC)
USG Corporation (IL) *4*
United Gilsonite Laboratories (PA) *4*
Wolf Paints And Wallpapers (NY) *2*

STAINS, WOOD

D.L. Anderson & Associates, Inc. (MN)
Barnard Chemical Co. (CA)
Beecham Home Improvement Products, Inc. (OH)
Behlen, H. & Bros. (NY)
Benjamin Moore Co. (NJ)
Bix Process Systems, Inc. (CT)
Cabot Stains (MA)
Cohasset Colonials (MA)
DAP, Inc. (OH)
Daly's Wood Finishing Products (WA)
Darworth Co. (CT)
Garrett Wade Company (NY)
Gaston Wood Finishes, Inc. (IN)
Master Products, Inc. (IA)
Minwax Company, Inc. (NJ)
Olympic Stain (WA)
Restech Industries (OR)
Sutherland Welles Ltd. (NC)
United Gilsonite Laboratories (PA)
Wood Finishing Supply Co., Inc. (NY)
Woodcare Corporation Metal & Wood Restoration Prod. (NJ)

TEXTILE CLEANERS

J. Goddard & Sons, Ltd. (WI)
TALAS (NY)

TUNG OIL

Behlen, H. & Bros. (NY)
Bix Process Systems, Inc. (CT)
Broadnax Refinishing Products, Inc. (GA)
Daly's Wood Finishing Products (WA)
Easy Time Wood Refinishing Products Corp. (IL)
Garrett Wade Company (NY)
The Hope Co., Inc. (MO)
Sutherland Welles Ltd. (NC)
United Gilsonite Laboratories (PA)
Wolf Paints And Wallpapers (NY)
Wood Finishing Supply Co., Inc. (NY)
Woodcare Corporation Metal & Wood Restoration Prod. (NJ)

VARNISHES

Barnard Chemical Co. (CA)
Behlen, H. & Bros. (NY)
Benjamin Moore Co. (NJ)
Bix Process Systems, Inc. (CT)
DAP, Inc. (OH)
Daly's Wood Finishing Products (WA)
Epifanes/Coastal Trade, Inc. (FL)
Garrett Wade Company (NY)
Minwax Company, Inc. (NJ)
Pierce & Stevens Chemical Corp. (NY)
The Stulb Co. (PA)
Sutherland Welles Ltd. (NC)
United Gilsonite Laboratories (PA)
Wood Finishing Supply Co., Inc. (NY)

WALLPAPER CLEANERS

TALAS (NY)

WAXES, MICROCRYSTALLINE & OTHER SPECIALTY

Behlen, H. & Bros. (NY)
The Butcher Polish Co. (MA)
Conservation Materials, Ltd. (NV)
Finish Feeder Company (MD)
J. Goddard & Sons, Ltd. (WI)
Janovic/Plaza, Inc. (NY)
Marshall Imports (OH)
O'Sullivan Co. (MI)
Roger A. Reed Inc. (MA)
Staples, H. F. & Co., Inc. (NH)
Wolf Paints And Wallpapers (NY)
Wood Finishing Supply Co., Inc. (NY)
Woodcare Corporation Metal & Wood Restoration Prod. (NJ)

WOOD FILLERS & PATCHING MATERIALS

Abatron, Inc. (IL)
Allied Resin Corp. (MA)
Beecham Home Improvement Products, Inc. (OH)
Beta Timber Restoration System/Dell Corp. (MD)
DAP, Inc. (OH)
Darworth Co. (CT)
Poxywood, Inc. (VA)
Staples, H. F. & Co., Inc. (NH)
United Gilsonite Laboratories (PA)
Wolf Paints And Wallpapers (NY)
Wood Finishing Supply Co., Inc. (NY)

WOOD GRAIN FILLERS

Barap Specialties (MI)
Behlen, H. & Bros. (NY)
Benjamin Moore Co. (NJ)
Daly's Wood Finishing Products (WA)
Garrett Wade Company (NY)
Gaston Wood Finishes, Inc. (IN)
Janovic/Plaza, Inc. (NY)
Wolf Paints And Wallpapers (NY)
Wood Finishing Supply Co., Inc. (NY)

OTHER FINISHES & SUPPLIES

Behlen, H. & Bros. (NY)
The Butcher Polish Co. (MA)
C.U. Restoration Supplies (TX)
DAP, Inc. (OH)
Garrett Wade Company (NY)
The Hope Co., Inc. (MO)
Rutland Products (VT)
Sutherland Welles Ltd. (NC)
Wood Finishing Supply Co., Inc. (NY)

See Company Directory for Addresses & Phone Numbers on page 151

Tools & Other Supplies

ADZES, FROES & HAND HEWING TOOLS

Avalon Forge (MD)
Cumberland General Store (TN)
Frog Tool Co., Ltd. (IL)
Garrett Wade Company (NY)
Kayne & Son Custom Forged Hardware (NC)
Stortz, John & Son, Inc. (PA)
Woodcraft Supply Corp. (MA)

CANVAS

Janovic/Plaza, Inc. (NY)
Wolf Paints And Wallpapers (NY)

CHAIR SEAT REPAIR

(1) Caning, Wicker, Etc.
(2) Chair Tapes
(3) Pressed Fiber Replacement Seats
(4) Leather Seats
(5) Other Chair Repair Supplies

19th Century Company (CA) *1*
Barap Specialties (MI) *1*
The Brass Tree (MO) *1,3*
C.U. Restoration Supplies (TX) *1,5*
Cane & Basket Supply Company (CA) *1*
Caning Shop (CA) *1,2,3,5*
Connecticut Cane & Reed Co. (CT) *1,2,5*
Craftsman Wood Service Co. (IL) *1*
Finishing Touch (CA) *1,4*
Frank's Cane and Rush Supply (CA) *1,5*
Morgan Woodworking Supplies (KY) *1*
Original Woodworks (MN) *1,2*
Paxton Hardware Ltd. (MD) *1*
Peerless Rattan and Reed (NY) *1*
Poor Richard's Service Co. (NJ) *1*
Pyfer, E.W. (IL) *1*
The Renovator's Supply (MA) *3,4*
Shaker Workshops (MA) *2*
Squaw Alley, Inc. (IL) *3*
WSI Distributors/ The Brass Tree (MO) .. *1,3*
Wise Company, The (LA) *1*
Woodcraft Supply Corp. (MA) *1*

CONSERVATOR'S TOOLS

(1) Contour Gauges
(2) Magnifiers, Portable
(3) Measuring Instruments
(4) Moisture Meters
(5) Telltales

Conservation Materials, Ltd. (NV)
Direct Safety Company (AZ) *4*
Lignomat USA (OR) *4*
PRG (VA) *1,2,4*

GAZEBO & OUTBUILDING PLANS

A.S.L. Associates (CA)
Architectural Preservation Trust (CT)
Bow House, Inc. (MA)
Building Conservation (WI)
Country Designs (CT)
Homestead Design (WA)
Native Wood Products, Inc. (CT)
Sun Designs (WI)
Victorian Accents (NJ)

GRAINING TOOLS

Bay City Paint Company (CA)
Janovic/Plaza, Inc. (NY)
Johnson Paint Co. (MA)
Master Products, Inc. (IA)
Wolf Paints And Wallpapers (NY)

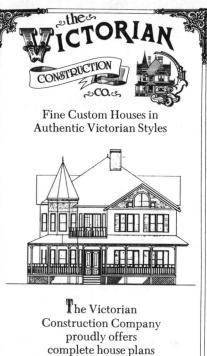

HOUSE PLANS, PERIOD DESIGNS

(1) Early American
(2) Victorian
(3) Turn-of-Century

Antiquity Reprints (NY)
Bow House, Inc. (MA) *1*
Country Designs (CT) *1*
The Frame Works (CT) *1*
Larry W. Garnett & Associates, Inc. (TX) *1,2*
Heritage Home Designers (TX) *1,2*
Historical Replications, Inc. (MS) *2,3*
Homestead Design (WA) *1*
House Carpenters (MA) *1*
Howard, David, Inc. (NH) *1*
W. S. Lockhart Designs (SC) *1*
Stephen P. Mack (RI) *1*
Native Wood Products, Inc. (CT) *1*
The New Victorians, Inc. of Arizona (AZ) *2*
Pollitt, E., AIA (CT) *1*
Timberpeg, East Inc. (NH) *1*
Traditional American Concepts (VA) *1*
Victorian Construction Co. (MD) *1,2*

LEADED, ETCHED, & STAINED GLASS SUPPLIES & KITS

(1) Tools & Supplies
(2) Lamp Shade Kits

Blenko Glass Co., Inc. (WV) *1*
Cline Glass Company (OR) *1*
Coran — Sholes Industries (MA) *1,2*
Delphi Stained Glass (MI) *1*
Greg Monk Stained Glass (HI) *1*
Meredith Stained Glass Studio, Inc. (MD) *1*
Ring, J. Stained Glass, Inc. (MN) *1*
Shadovitz Bros. Distributors, Inc. (NY) *1*
Studio Design, Inc., t/a Rainbow Art Glass (NJ) *1,2*
Timberpeg, East Inc. (NH)
Whittemore-Durgin Glass Co. (MA) *1,2*

SUPPLIES FOR MOULDS AND CASTS

(1) Mould-Making Materials
(2) Casting Plastics & Related Materials
(3) Casting Plaster
(4) Casting Repair Kits

Abatron, Inc. (IL) *1,2*
Archicast (TN) *2*
Conservation Materials, Ltd. (NV) *2*
Polytek Development Corp. (NJ) *1,2*
Rutland Products (VT) *3*
Sculpture Associates, Ltd. (NY) *1,2,3*
Sculpture House (NY) *3*
USG Corporation (IL) *3*

NAILS, HAND-MADE

Arden Forge (PA)
Colonial Restoration Products (PA)
Elephant Hill Iron Works (VT)
Kayne & Son Custom Forged Hardware (NC)
Stephen P. Mack (RI)
Millham, Newton — Blacksmith (MA)
Old Smithy Shop (NH)
Tremont Nail Company (MA)

PAINT BRUSHES, SPECIALTY

Johnson Paint Co. (MA)
The Old-House Gold Leaf People (NY)
Sepp Leaf Products (NY)
Wolf Paints And Wallpapers (NY)

PAINT STRIPPING TOOLS

(1) Heat Stripping Devices
(2) Mechanical Scrapers
(3) Rotary Tools
Easy Time Wood Refinishing Products Corp. (IL) *1*
Hyde Manufacturing Company (MA) *1*
Old-House Journal (NY) *1*
Red Devil, Inc. (NJ) *2*
Sculpture Associates, Ltd. (NY) *1,2*
Stortz, John & Son, Inc. (PA) *2*
Wolf Paints And Wallpapers (NY) *1,1,2*
Woodcraft Supply Corp. (MA) *2*

PLANES, WOOD-MOULDING

Frog Tool Co., Ltd. (IL)
Garrett Wade Company (NY)
Iron Horse Antiques, Inc. (VT)
The Mechanick's Workbench (MA)
Williams & Hussey Machine Co. (NH)
Woodcraft Supply Corp. (MA)

PLASTERING & MASONRY TOOLS

Colonial Restoration Products (PA)
Hyde Manufacturing Company (MA)
Marshalltown Trowel Co. (IA)
Masonry Specialty Co. (PA)
Mittermeir, Frank Inc. (NY)
Red Devil, Inc. (NJ)
Sculpture Associates, Ltd. (NY)
Sculpture House (NY)
Stortz, John & Son, Inc. (PA)
Trow & Holden Co. (VT)
Wolf Paints And Wallpapers (NY)

See Company Directory for Addresses & Phone Numbers on page 151

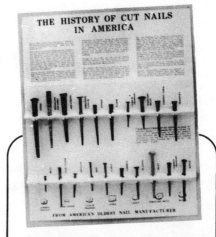

THE PAINT-STRIPPING HEAT GUN

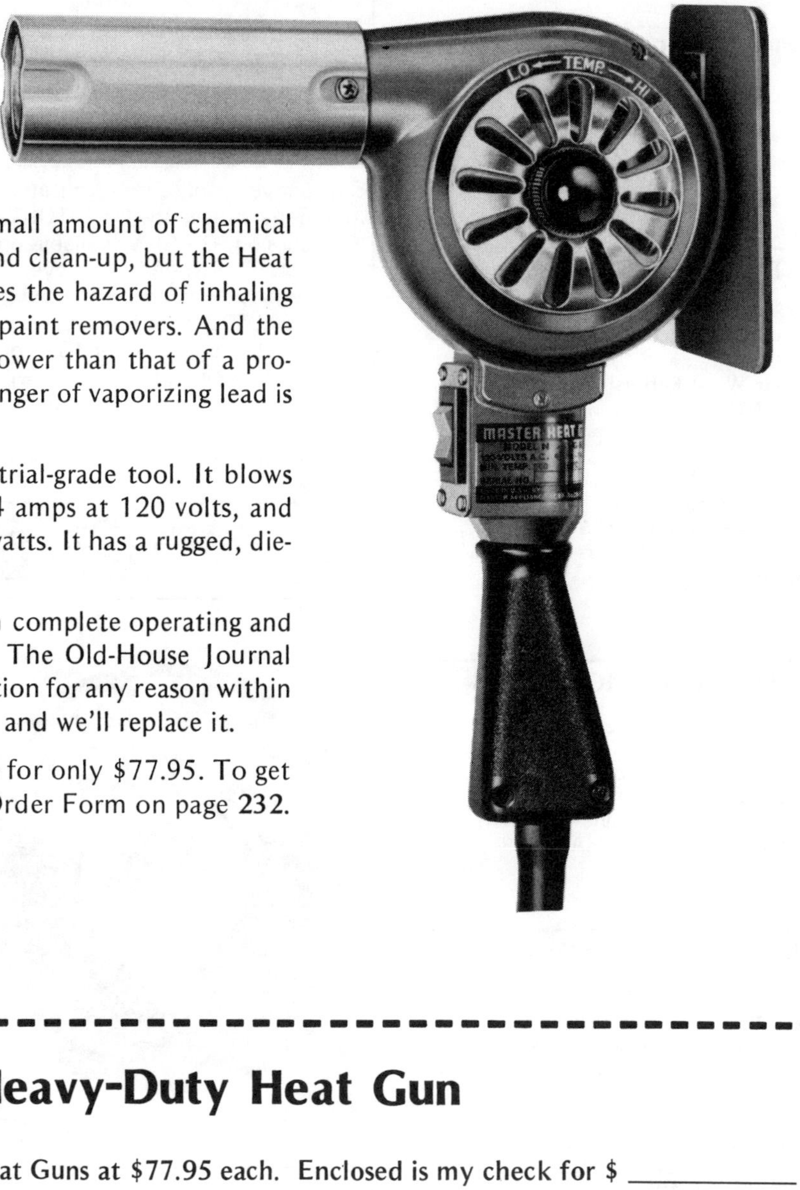

Nearly 10,000 OHJ subscribers have bought **the Heavy-Duty Heat Gun,** and discovered the best tool for stripping paint from interior woodwork. This electric-powered heat gun softens paint in a uniform way, so it can be scraped off with a knife. A small amount of chemical cleaner is suggested for tight crevices and clean-up, but the Heat Gun does most of the work. It reduces the hazard of inhaling methylene chloride vapors present in paint removers. And the Heat Gun's operating temperature is lower than that of a propane torch or blowtorch. Thus, the danger of vaporizing lead is minimized.

The Heavy-Duty Heat Gun is an industrial-grade tool. It blows at 23 cubic feet per minute, draws 14 amps at 120 volts, and operates at 500 to 750 degrees, 1650 watts. It has a rugged, die-cast aluminum body — no plastics.

The Heavy-Duty Heat Gun comes with complete operating and safety instructions, and is backed by The Old-House Journal Guarantee: If your unit should malfunction for any reason within two months of purchase, return it to us and we'll replace it.

The Heavy-Duty Heat Gun is available for only $77.95. To get yours, use the coupon below or the Order Form on page **232**.

The Heavy-Duty Heat Gun

Please send me _____ Heavy-Duty Heat Guns at $77.95 each. Enclosed is my check for $ __________

(NY State residents please add applicable sales tax.)

NAME ______________________________

ADDRESS ______________________________

CITY ____________________ STATE ______________ ZIP __________

Mail to: The Old-House Journal, 69A Seventh Avenue, Brooklyn, NY 11217.

PLASTER PATCHING MATERIALS

Muralo Company (NJ)
Rutland Products (VT)
USG Corporation (IL)
Wolf Paints And Wallpapers (NY)

PLASTER WASHERS & ANCHORS

Charles St. Supply Co. (MA)

SAFETY EQUIPMENT

Art Safe Inc. (WI)
Direct Safety Company (AZ)
Eastern Safety Equipment Co., Inc. (NY)
Masonry Specialty Co. (PA)

SLATE ROOFING TOOLS

Evergreen Slate Co. (NY)
Kayne & Son Custom Forged Hardware (NC)
Lehman Hardware & Appliances (OH)
Stortz, John & Son, Inc. (PA)

SPECIALTY POWER TOOLS

Dusty Splinters Enterprises (NY)
Garrett Wade Company (NY)
Sculpture Associates, Ltd. (NY)
Trow & Holden Co. (VT)
U.S. General Supply Corp. (NY)
Universal Clamp Corp. (CA)
Weaver, W. T. & Sons, Inc. (DC)
Woodcraft Supply Corp. (MA)

STENCILLING SUPPLIES

(1) Brushes
(2) Stencil Paper
(3) Stencils, Drawn or Pre-Cut
(4) Stencil Kits

Behlen, H. & Bros. (NY) *1*
Chromatic Paint Corp. (NY)
Crafts Manufacturing Co. (MA)
Hand-Stenciled Interiors (MA) *3*
Hood, R. and Co. (NH) *1,3*
S. & C. Huber, Accoutrements (CT) *1,2*
Janovic/Plaza, Inc. (NY) *1,2*
Johnson Paint Co. (MA) *1*
Peg Hall Studios (MA)
Stencil School (MA) *3*
Wolf Paints And Wallpapers (NY) *1,3*

UPHOLSTERY TOOLS & SUPPLIES

(1) Upholstery Supplies, Webbing, Batting, Etc.
(2) Upholstery Tools

Barap Specialties (MI)
Osborne, C. S. & Co. (NJ) *2*

WALLPAPERING & DECORATING TOOLS

Hyde Manufacturing Company (MA)
Red Devil, Inc. (NJ)
Rollerwall, Inc. (MD)
Wolf Paints And Wallpapers (NY)

WOODWORKING TOOLS, HAND

19th Century Company (CA)
Armor Products (NY)
Brookstone Company (NH)
Cumberland General Store (TN)
Dusty Splinters Enterprises (NY)
Frog Tool Co., Ltd. (IL)
Garrett Wade Company (NY)
Iron Horse Antiques, Inc. (VT)
Lehman Hardware & Appliances (OH)
Leichtung, Inc. (OH)
The Mechanick's Workbench (MA)
Mittermeir, Frank Inc. (NY)
Sculpture Associates, Ltd. (NY)
Sculpture House (NY)
Stortz, John & Son, Inc. (PA)
U.S. General Supply Corp. (NY)
Universal Clamp Corp. (CA)
Wikkmann House (CA)
Woodcraft Supply Corp. (MA)
Woodworker's Supply of New Mexico (NM)

OTHER RESTORATION TOOLS & SUPPLIES

Conservation Materials, Ltd. (NV)
Wikkmann House (CA)

SECURITY FEATURES

(1) Steel Doors
(2) Fire & Burglar Alarms
(3) Locks

Ball and Ball (PA) *3*
Colonial Lock Company (CT) *3*
Fichet Lock Co. (NY) *3*
JGR Enterprises, Inc. (PA) *3*
D. C. Mitchell Reproductions (DE) *3*
Pease Industries (OH) *1*
Premier Communications (NC) *2*
Reproduction Distributors, Inc. (IL) *3*

See Company Directory for Addresses & Phone Numbers on page 151

Antique & Recycled House Parts

ANTIQUE & RECYCLED HOUSE PARTS

1874 House (OR)
Architectural Accents (GA)
Architectural Antique Warehouse, The (CAN)
Architectural Antiques (OK)
Architectural Antiques Exchange (PA)
Architectural Antiques, Ltd. (AR)
Architectural Preservation Trust (CT)
Architectural Salvage Co. (MI)
Architectural Salvage of Santa Barbara (CA)
Art Directions (MO)
Artifacts, Inc. (VA)
Backstrom Stained Glass et al (MS)
Bank Architectural Antiques (LA)
Bare Wood Inc. (NY)
Sylvan Brandt (PA)
The Brass Knob (DC)
ByGone Era Architectural Antiques (GA)
Canal Co. (DC)
Cohen's Architectural Heritage (CAN)
Conservatory, The (MI)
Florida Victorian Architectural Antiques (FL)
Gargoyles, Ltd. (PA)
Great American Salvage (NY)
Hippo Hardware & Trading Co. (OR)
History Store (MD)
Jerard Paul Jordan Gallery (CT)
Joe Ley Antiques, Inc. (KY)
Lost City Arts (NY)
Stephen P. Mack (RI)
Materials Unlimited (MI)
Merritt's Antiques, Inc. (PA)
Nostalgia (GA)
Off The Wall, Architectural Antiques (CA)
Old Home Building & Restoration (CT)
Olde Bostonian Architectural Antiques (MA)
Olde Theatre Architectural Salvage Co. (MO)
Olde & Oak Antiques (AL)
Oliver, Bradley C. (PA)
Pelnik Wrecking Co., Inc. (NY)
Rejuvenation House Parts Co. (OR)
Renovation Source, Inc., The (IL)
Restoration Treasures (NY)
Salvage One (IL)
Second Chance (GA)
Southern Accents Architectural Antiques (AL)
Spiess Antique Building Materials (IL)
United House Wrecking Corp. (CT)
Urban Archaeology (NY)
Vintage Plumbing Specialties (CA)
Walker's (OH)
Westlake Architectural Antiques (TX)
Whit Hanks at Treaty Oak (TX)
Wigen Restorations (NY)
Williams Art Glass Studio, Inc./Sunset Antiques, Inc. (MI)
Wilson, H. Weber, Antiquarian (MD)
Wrecking Bar of Atlanta (GA)
You Name It, Inc. (OH)

Behind our Doors

a world of rare architectural treasure awaits your inspection

Materials Unlimited offers an extensive collection of both new and restored architectural antiques beautifully displayed in 30,000 sq. ft. of showrooms. The new and antique treasures of the highest quality are carefully selected from throughout the country and are ready for installation in your residence or commercial establishment. Materials Unlimited's extensive inventory includes: doors, entrance sets, stained and beveled glass windows, fireplace mantels, lighting, bars, bathroom fixtures, staircases, hardware, fine antique furnishings and accompaniments. Materials Unlimited offers complete design and fabrication services and can assist you with any project from concept through completion.

LITERATURE AVAILABLE:
Please inquire about our Company Brochure, $3.00
Or, the Reproduction Product Line Package, $8.00

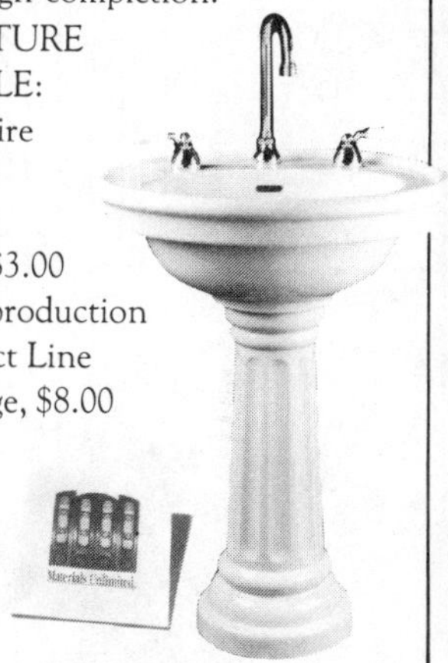

Materials Unlimited.

Two West Michigan Avenue
Ypsilanti, Michigan 48197 (313) 483-6980
Open Daily 10-5

Great American Salvage Co.

Architectural Antiques

Acquired recently was this 1903 mansion built by Solomon Dresser.

Entryways, columns, mantels, stained glass, stone and iron work, pedestal sinks, tubs, and lighting from buildings of another time.

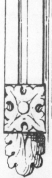

34 Cooper Square, New York, New York 10003 (212) 505-0070
3 Main Street, Montpelier, Vermont 05602 (802) 223-7711
Main and Madison, Sag Harbor, New York 11963 (516) 725-2272
1630 San Marco Blvd., Jacksonville Fl. 32207 (904) 396-8081
PO Box 1892; 97 Crown St. New Haven Ct. 06508 (203) 624-1009

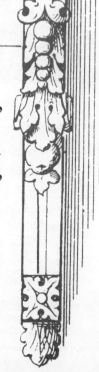

See Company Directory for Addresses & Phone Numbers on page 151

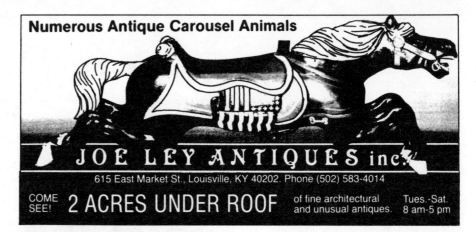

RECYCLED HOUSES, BARNS & OTHER STRUCTURES

Architectural Preservation Trust (CT)
Art Directions (MO)
The Barn People, Inc. (VT)
Belcher, Robert W. (GA)
Sylvan Brandt (PA)
The Frame Works (CT)
Stephen P. Mack (RI)
Old Home Building & Restoration (CT)
Riverbend Timber Framing, Inc. (MI)
Vintage Lumber Co. (MD)
Walker's (OH)
Wigen Restorations (NY)

Art Directions

Architectural Antiques
•also•
CUSTOM BUILT
BAR & LIGHTING FIXTURES

- 12,000 Sq. Ft. Showroom
- Stained and Beveled Glass Windows and Entrance Sets
- Antique Lighting Fixtures Residential and Commercial Scale
- Saloon Front and Back Bars
- Architectural Bronze
- Millwork • Mantles
- Doors and Entrance Ways
- Columns, Cornices and Brackets

Send $3.00 for brochures

6120 Delmar Blvd.
St. Louis, Mo. 63112
314·863·1895

LOG HOUSES. . .and other 18th & 19th century building materials salvaged from old houses, grist mills, and barns:

• hand hewn logs •
• flooring •
• windows •
• doors •
• hardware •

Sylvan Brandt

653 Main Street Lititz, PA 17543
(717) 626-4520

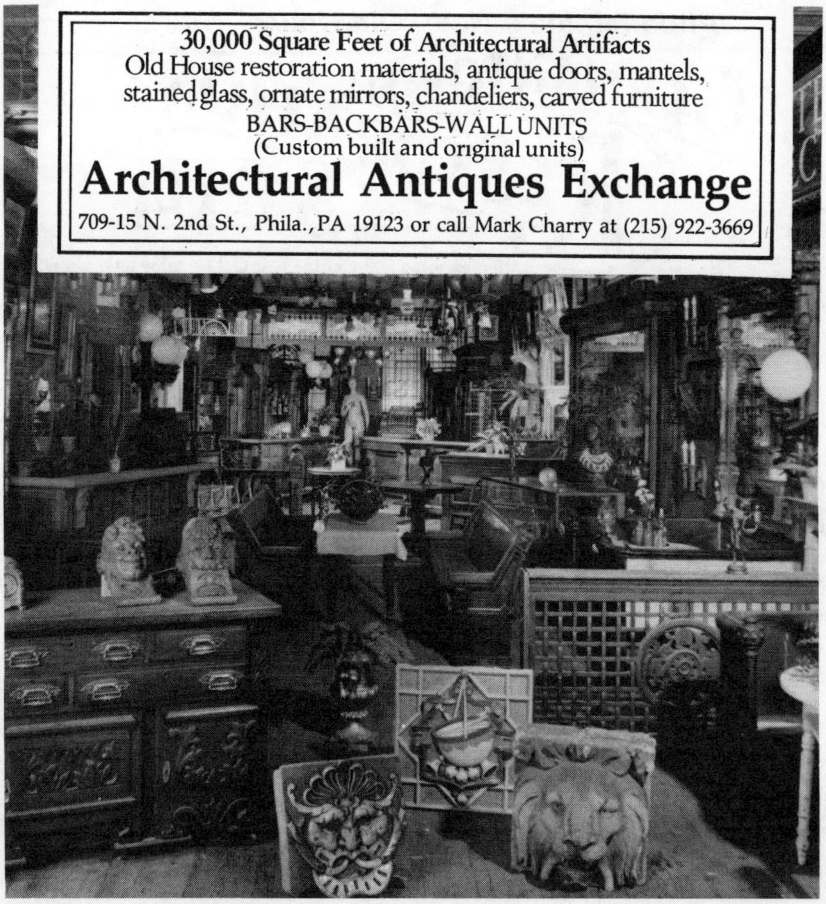

30,000 Square Feet of Architectural Artifacts
Old House restoration materials, antique doors, mantels,
stained glass, ornate mirrors, chandeliers, carved furniture
BARS-BACKBARS-WALL UNITS
(Custom built and original units)
Architectural Antiques Exchange
709-15 N. 2nd St., Phila., PA 19123 or call Mark Charry at (215) 922-3669

RENOVATION & RESTORATION SUPPLY STORES

(1) Walk-In Stores
(2) Mail-Order Suppliers

19th Century Company (CA) *1,2*
Amenities (OK) *1*
Antique Hardware Store (NJ) *1,2*
Architectural Antique Warehouse, The (CAN) *2*
Ball and Ball (PA) *2*
C.U. Restoration Supplies (TX) *2*
Classic Architectural Specialties (TX) *1,2*
Colonial Restoration Products (PA) *2*
Conservatory, The (MI) *1*
Crawford's Old House Store (WI) *2*
The Emporium, Inc. (TX) *1*
Germantown Restoration Supplies (PA) .. *1*
Hippo Hardware & Trading Co. (OR) *1,2*
History Store (MD) *1*
Hood, R. and Co. (NH) *2*
Houseparts (CA) *1,2*
Inner Harbor Lumber & Hardware (MD) . *1*
Stephen P. Mack (RI) *1,2*
Original Woodworks (MN) *2*
Rejuvenation House Parts Co. (OR) *1,2*
Remodelers & Renovators (ID) *1,2*
Renovation Concepts, Inc. (MN) *1,2*
Renovation Source, Inc., The (IL) *1*
The Renovator's Supply (MA) *2*
Restoration Works, Inc. (NY) *1,2*
Squaw Alley, Inc. (IL) *1*
Steptoe's Old House Store, Ltd. (CAN) . *1,2*
Urban Archaeology (NY) *1*
Vermont Country Store (VT) *1,2*
Victorian Interior Restoration (PA) *1,2*
Victorian Reproductions Enterprises, Inc. (MN) *2*
Victorian Warehouse (CA) *2*
Weaver, W. T. & Sons, Inc. (DC) *2*
Wise Company, The (LA) *2*
Woodworker's Supply of New Mexico (NM) *2*

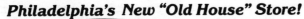

See Company Directory for Addresses & Phone Numbers on page 151

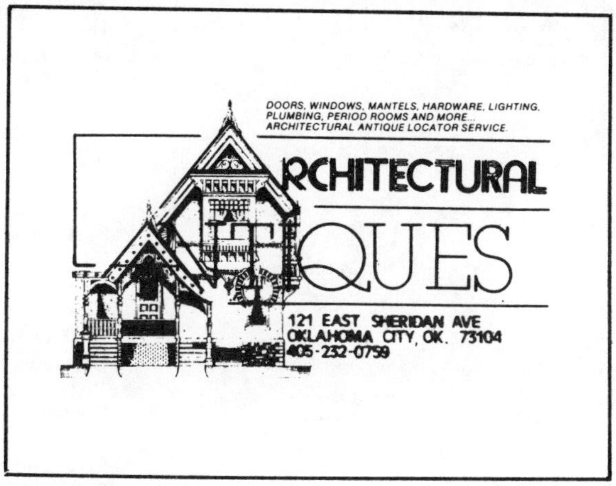

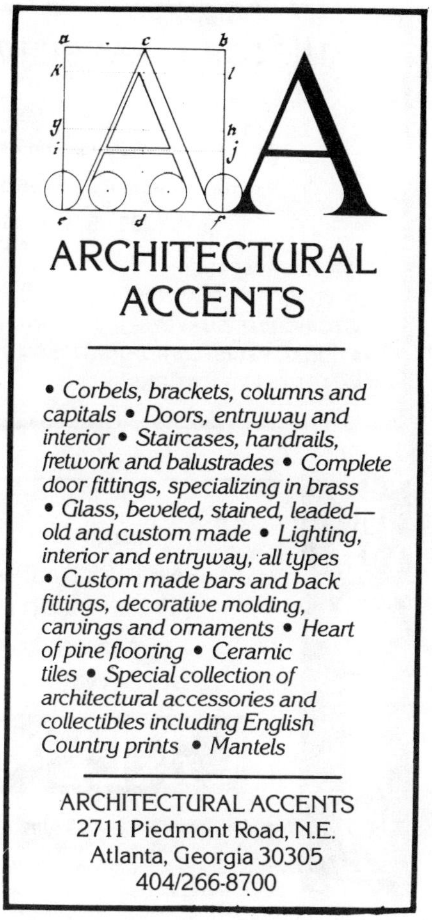

Restoration & Decorating Services

ANTIQUE REPAIR & RESTORATION

(1) Ceiling Fan Restoration
(2) Clock Repair & Parts
(3) Furniture Restoration
(4) Porcelain, Glass, & China Repair
(5) Stove Restoration
(6) Telephone Repair & Parts
(7) Textile Restoration

Aetna Stove Company (PA) 5
Alexandria Wood Joinery (NH) 3
Antique Hardware Co. (CA) 3
Architectural Antiques, Ltd. (AR) 3,4
Artistic Woodworking, Inc. (MI) 3
Bare Wood Inc. (NY) 3
Barnstable Stove Shop (MA) 5
Nelson Beck of Washington, Inc. (DC) 3
Billard's Old Telephones (CA) 6
Bjorndal Woodworks (WI)
Bryant Stove Works (ME) 5
California Glass Bending Company (CA) 4
Cambridge Textiles (NY) 7
Carriage Trade Antiques & Art Gallery (NC) 3
Chicago Old Telephone Co. (NC) 6
Country Roads, Inc. (MI) 3
Ed's Antiques, Inc. (PA) 3
Eifel Furniture Stripping (NY) 3
Finishing Touch (CA) 3
Gaudio Custom Furniture (NY) 3
George Studios (NY) 3,4
Glass Designs (KY) 4
Gold Leaf Studios, Inc. (DC) 3
Harrison, Elaine (NY) 3
Hess Repairs (NY) 4
Innerwick Industries (MD) 6
Lamp Doctor (NY) 2
Light Ideas (MD) 1
David Linker Ltd. (NY) 3
M — H Lamp & Fan Company (IL) 1
Montclair Restoration Craftsmen (NJ) 3
Museum of American Textile History — Cons. Center (MA) 7
Old Time Stove Co. (MA) 5
Old World Restorations, Inc. (OH) 3,4
Original Woodworks (MN) 3
Phoneco (WI) 6
Poor Richard's Service Co. (NJ) 3
Restorations, Inc. (NY) 7
Timothy G. Riordan (NY) 3
Mario Rodriguez Cabinetmaker (NY) 3
Ross, Douglas — Woodworker (NY) 3
Sawdust Room (MI) 3
Selva — Borel (CA) 2
Studio Workshop, Ltd. (CT) 3
Sutherland Welles Ltd. (NC) 1
Turtle Lake Telephone Co. (WI) 6
Victorian Glass Works (CA) 3
Vulpiani (NY) 3
Wiebold Art Conservation Lab. (OH) 4
Wrisley, Robert T. (TN) 3

ARCHEOLOGICAL SURVEYS & INVESTIGATIONS

Historic Preservation Alternatives, Inc. (NJ)

See Company Directory for Addresses & Phone Numbers on page 151

ARCHITECTURAL DESIGN & CONSULTING SERVICES

(1) Architectural Design—Restoration
(2) Consulting Services
(3) Historical Research
(4) Lectures & Seminars

ARJ Associates (MA) *1*
Acquisition and Restoration Corp. (IN) .. *1,2*
Anderson, Townsend (VT) *2*
Arch Associates/ Stephen Guerrant AIA (IL) *1*
Architectural Accents (GA) *1*
Architectural Preservation Consultants (NY) *2,3*
Architectural Reclamation, Inc. (OH) *2*
Architectural Resources Group (CA) *1,2*
Architectural Woodworking (CT) *2*
Archive (PA) *1,2,3,4*
Arlan Kay & Associates (WI) *1,2,3*
Artistic License in San Francisco (CA)
The Barn People, Inc. (VT) *1,2*
Beta Timber Restoration System/Dell Corp. (MD) *2*
Nancy Borden Period Textile Replicas (NH) *2*
Breakfast Woodworks Mackall & Dickinson (CT) *1*
Brown, T. Robins (NY) *2,3*
Burke and Bales Associates, Inc. (FL) *1*
Carpenter and Smith Restorations (IL) *2*
Clio Group, Inc. (PA) *2,3*
The Color People—Restoration Graphics (CO) *1*
Colorado Front Range Bldg. Inspection Service (CO) *2*
Community Services Collaborative (CO) *1,2,3*
Cosmetic Restoration, Inc. (NY) *2*
Cosmopolitan International (RI) *2*
Dodge, Adams, and Roy, Ltd. (NH) ... *1,2,3*
Donald Stryker Restorations (NJ) *2*
Downstate Restorations (IL) *2*
Earthwise Design (CT) *1*
Enlightened Restorations (CT) *2,3*
Ferris, Robert Donald, Architect, Inc. (CA) *1,2*
Gallier House Museum (LA) *4*
Melvyn Green and Associates, Inc. (CA) . *1*
Theodore Grunewald, Urban Archaeologist (NY) *3*
Hall Associates (KS) *1*
J Hall Building Restoration (TX) *1*
Hasbrouck/Hunderman Architects (IL) . *1,2,3*
Richard N. Hayton and Associates, Inc. (NY) *1*
Heritage Home Designers (TX)
Herman, Frederick, R.A., Architect (VA) *1,2,4*
Hill, Allen Charles AIA (MA) *1,2,3,4*
Historic Boulevard Services (IL) *2,4*
Historic Neighborhood Preservation Program (CT) *1,2,3,4*
Historic Preservation Alternatives, Inc. (NJ) *1,2,3,4*
History Store (MD) *3*
Hobt, Murrel Dee, Architect (VA) *1,2,3*
Holm, Alvin AIA Architect (PA) *1,2*
Image Group, The (OH) *1,2*
Interior Decorations (NH) *2,4*
Jennings, Gottfried, Cheek/ Preservationists (IA) *2,3*
Kaplan/Price Assoc. — Architects (NY) *1*
Knickerbocker Guild (CA) *2*
Koeppel/Freedman Studios (MA) *1*
Kruger Kruger Albenberg (MA) *1,2*
David M. LaPenta, Inc. (PA) *1*
Leeke, John — Woodworker (ME) *2*

Stephen P. Mack (RI) *1,2*
Oehrlein & Associates (DC) *2,3*
Old House Gardens (MI) *4*
William H. Parsons & Associates (CT) *2*
Preservation Associates, Inc. (MD) *2,3*
Preservation Partnership (MA) *1,2,3,4*
Preservation Resource Center of New Orleans (LA) *3*
Preservation Resource Group (VA) *2,3,4*
Quali-Craft Constructors (CA) *1*
Renovation Source, Inc., The (IL) *1,2*
Restoration A Specialty (OR) *2*
Restoration Fraternity (PA)
Restoration Workshop Nat Trust For Historic Preservation (NY) *2*
Restorations, Inc. (NY) *4*
Restorations Unlimited, Inc. (PA) *2,3*
Richards, R.E., Inc. (CT) *1*
River City Restorations (MO) *2*
S.P.N.E.A. Conservation Center (MA) . *2,3,4*
Tomas Spiers & Associates (PA) *1,2,3*
Stevens, John R., Associates (NY) *1*
TAG Architect & Laurence Carpentry (NY) *1,2*
Tomblinson Harburn Assoc. Arch., Eng., & Planners, Inc. (MI) *1,3*
Traditional American Concepts (VA) *1,2*
Traditional Line Ltd. (NY) *1,2*
Troyer, Le Roy and Associates (IN) *1*
Victorian Interior Restoration (PA) *2*
Wilson, H. Weber, Antiquarian (MD) *2,4*
Winans Construction (CA)
Wollon, James Thomas, Jr., A.I.A. (MD) *1,2,4*
Wick York (CT) *1,2,3,4*

CABINETMAKING & FINE WOODWORKING

Amherst Woodworking & Supply (MA)
Architectural Accents (GA)
Architectural Components (MA)
Architectural Reclamation, Inc. (OH)
Artistic Woodworking, Inc. (MI)
Ashwood Restoration (NY)
Bjorndal Woodworks (WI)
Campbell, Marion (PA)
Carpenter and Smith Restorations (IL)
Congdon, Johns/Cabinetmaker (VT)
Crowfoot's Inc. (AZ)
Custom & Historic Millwork (CO)
Custom Millwork, Inc. (VA)
Dovetail Woodworking (WI)
Early New England Rooms & Exteriors Inc. (CT)
Eklund, Jon Restorations (NJ)
Fine Woodworking Co. (MD)
Floors By Juell (IL)
Haas Wood & Ivory Works, Inc. (CA)
Johnson Woodworks Inc. (IL)
LaPointe, Chip, Cabinetmaker (MA)
Lea, James — Cabinetmaker (ME)
Leeke, John — Woodworker (ME)
Maurer & Shepherd, Joyners (CT)
Mead Associates Woodworking, Inc. (NY)
Moore, E.T., Jr. Co. (VA)
Nutt, Craig, Fine Wood Works (AL)
Old House - New House Restorations (MN)
Frank Pellitteri Inc. (NY)
Renaissance Woodcarving, Inc. (NY)
Restorations Unlimited, Inc. (PA)
Rich Craft Custom Kitchens, Inc. (PA)
Ross, Douglas — Woodworker (NY)
Roth Painting, Co., Inc. (NY)
Seitz, Robert/Fine Woodworking (MA)
Wood Designs (OH)
Woods American Co. (MD)

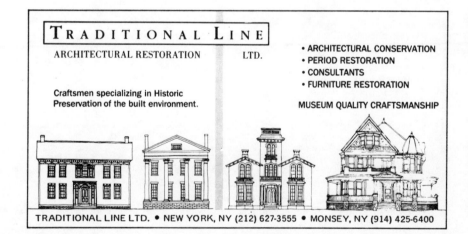

CONTRACTING SERVICES—RESTORATION

Acquisition and Restoration Corp. (IN)
American Building Restoration (WI)
Anderson Building Restoration (OH)
Anderson, Townsend (VT)
Antique Building Restoration (WI)
Architectural Reclamation, Inc. (OH)
Arroyo Restoration (CA)
Beta Timber Restoration System/Dell Corp. (MD)
Brandt Bros. General Contractors (IN)
Burke and Bales Associates, Inc. (FL)
Carpenter and Smith Restorations (IL)
Custom & Historic Millwork (CO)
Dodge, Adams, and Roy, Ltd. (NH)
Donald Stryker Restorations (NJ)
Downstate Restorations (IL)
Early New England Rooms & Exteriors Inc. (CT)
Eklund, Jon Restorations (NJ)
The Finishing Company (NJ)
Great Northern Construction, Inc. (VT)
Haines Masonry Specialties (IN)
Richard N. Hayton and Associates, Inc. (NY)
Historic Boulevard Services (IL)
Huseman, Richard J. Co. (OH)
Joy Construction, Inc. (VA)
Klinke & Lew Contractors (CO)
Knickerbocker Guild (CA)
Koeppel/Freedman Studios (MA)
David M. LaPenta, Inc. (PA)
Stephen P. Mack (RI)
Montclair Restoration Craftsmen (NJ)
Old House - New House Restorations (MN)
William H. Parsons & Associates (CT)
Preservation Associates, Inc. (MD)
Quali-Craft Constructors (CA)
Rambusch (NY)
Recommended Builders (IL)
Restoration A Specialty (OR)
Restoration Fraternity (PA)
Restoration Workshop Nat Trust For Historic Preservation (NY)
Restorations Unlimited, Inc. (PA)
Richards, R.E., Inc. (CT)
River City Restorations (MO)
Rose, Barry (CO)
Skyline Engineers of Maryland, Inc. (MD)
Stevens, John R., Associates (NY)
Victorian Interior Restoration (PA)
Winans Construction (CA)

FIREPLACE & CHIMNEY RESTORATION

Acquisition and Restoration Corp. (IN)
American Chimney Lining Systems, Inc. (MI)
Chimney Relining International, Inc. (NH)
Durvin, Tom & Sons (VA)
Flue Works (OH)
Haines Masonry Specialties (IN)
Huskisson Masonry & Exterior Building Restoration Co. (KY)
National SUPAFLU Systems, Inc. (NY)
William H. Parsons & Associates (CT)
Rumford Fireplaces (OH)
Welles Fireplace Company (NY)

CARPENTRY

Acquisition and Restoration Corp. (IN)
Anderson Reconstruction (MA)
Bare Wood Inc. (NY)
Beta Timber Restoration System/Dell Corp. (MD)
Custom & Historic Millwork (CO)
Eklund, Jon Restorations (NJ)
Fine Woodworking Co. (MD)
Bill Goschen (MD)
Homestead Supply (MA)
House Carpenters (MA)
Joy Construction, Inc. (VA)
Knudsen, Mark (IA)
Montclair Restoration Craftsmen (NJ)
Old House - New House Restorations (MN)
Ross, Douglas — Woodworker (NY)
Roth Painting, Co., Inc. (NY)
Skyline Engineers of Maryland, Inc. (MD)

CASTING, CUSTOM—PLASTER, FIBERGLASS, COMPO, ETC.

The 509 Studio (FL)
ARJ Associates (MA)
Advanced Materials, Inc. (CT)
Archicast (TN)
Architectural Shapes, Inc. (PA)
Custom Castings (TX)
Design-Cast Corporation (NJ)
Felber Studios, Inc. (PA)
Giannetti Studios, Inc. (MD)
Koeppel/Freedman Studios (MA)
Ludowici-Celadon Co. (OH)
Ornamental Design Studios (NY)
Rosenau, Marion, Sculptor (PA)
J.P. Weaver Co. (CA)

HOUSE INSPECTION SERVICES

AMC Housemaster Home Inspection Svc. (NJ)
Acquisition and Restoration Corp. (IN)
Anderson Reconstruction (MA)
Arch Associates/ Stephen Guerrant AIA (IL)
Carson, Dunlop & Associates, Ltd. (CAN)
Claxton Walker & Associates (MD)
Colorado Front Range Bldg. Inspection Service (CO)
Donald Stryker Restorations (NJ)
Edward Fitzgerald Associates (NY)
Guardian National House Inspection and Warranty Corp. (MA)
Haines Masonry Specialties (IN)
Historic Preservation Alternatives, Inc. (NJ)
HouseMaster of America (NJ)
Lieberman, Howard, P.E. (NY)
National Home Inspection Service of New England, Inc. (MA)
Oberndorfer & Assoc. (PA)
Old House Inspection Co., Inc. (NY)
Preservation Associates, Inc. (MD)
Preservation Partnership (MA)
Security Home Inspection, Inc. (NY)
Wick York (CT)

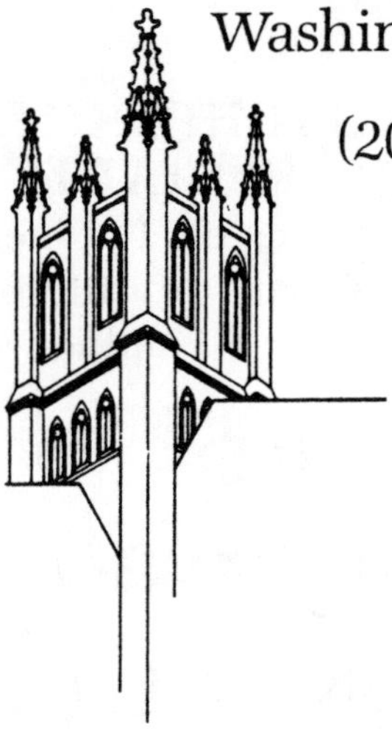

HOUSE MOVING

Architectural Preservation Trust (CT)
The Barn People, Inc. (VT)
Stephen P. Mack (RI)
Wigen Restorations (NY)

LANDSCAPE GARDENING—PERIOD DESIGN

Jamie Gibbs & Associates (NY)
Richard N. Hayton and Associates, Inc. (NY)
Old House Gardens (MI)
Philip M. White & Associates (NY)

LIGHTING FIXTURE RESTORATION & WIRING

Alfa Lite (UT)
The Antique Restoration Co. (PA)
Authentic Lighting (NJ)
Bernard Restoration (MA)
Boulder Stained Glass Studios (CO)
Century House Antiques (OH)
Chandelier Warehouse (NY)
Conant Custom Brass (VT)
Ed's Antiques, Inc. (PA)
Golden Age Glassworks (NY)
Harvey M. Stern & Co./ Antique Lighting (PA)
Hexagram (CA)
Kayne & Son Custom Forged Hardware (NC)
Lamp Doctor (NY)
Littlewood & Maue Museum Quality Restorations (NJ)
M — H Lamp & Fan Company (IL)
Mattia, Louis (NY)
Moriarty's Lamps (CA)
Old Lamplighter Shop (NY)
Pyfer, E.W. (IL)
Rambusch (NY)
Roy Electric Co., Inc. (NY)
St. Louis Antique Lighting Co., Inc. (MO)
Sherman Hill Antiques (IA)
Squaw Alley, Inc. (IL)
Stanley Galleries (IL)
Turn-of-the-Century Lighting (CAN)
Victorian Lighting Co. (MN)
Victorian Lighting Works, Inc. (PA)
Victorian Reproductions Enterprises, Inc. (MN)
Village Antique Lighting Co. (MI)
Washington House Reproductions (VA)
Yankee Craftsman (MA)

MASONRY REPAIR & CLEANING

Acquisition and Restoration Corp. (IN)
American Building Restoration (WI)
Anderson Building Restoration (OH)
Bioclean (PA)
Cathedral Stone Company, Inc. (DC)
Downstate Restorations (IL)
Durvin, Tom & Sons (VA)
Haines Masonry Specialties (IN)
Harne Plastering Co. (MD)
Huskisson Masonry & Exterior Building Restoration Co. (KY)
William H. Parsons & Associates (CT)
Pietra Dura, Inc. (NY)
River City Restorations (MO)
Russell Restoration of Suffolk (NY)
Skyline Engineers of Maryland, Inc. (MD)

METAL CASTING—CUSTOM

Allen Foundry (CA)
Greensboro Art Foundry & Machine Co. (NC)
La Haye Bronze, Inc. (CA)
Rocco V. De Angelo (NY)
Round Oak Metal Specialties (MA)
Tomahawk Foundry (WI)

METAL POLISHING & REPLATING

Antique Brass Works (NY)
Bernard Restoration (MA)
CIPCO Corp. (MO)
Harvey M. Stern & Co./ Antique Lighting (PA)
Hautwork, Inc. (NJ)
Hiles Plating Co., Inc. (MO)
Lamp Doctor (NY)
Old World Restorations, Inc. (OH)
Poor Richard's Service Co. (NJ)
Pyfer, E.W. (IL)

See Company Directory for Addresses & Phone Numbers on page 151

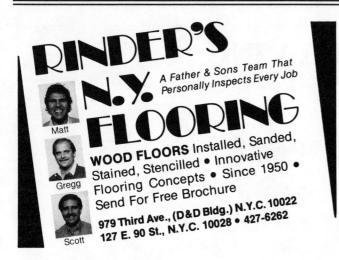

METALWORK REPAIRS

18th Century Hardware Co. (PA)
Antique Brass Works (NY)
The Antique Restoration Co. (PA)
Architectural Antiques, Ltd. (AR)
Arden Forge (PA)
Authentic Designs Inc. (VT)
Authentic Lighting (NJ)
Ball and Ball (PA)
Bernard Restoration (MA)
Bronze et al (NY)
Cambridge Smithy (VT)
Cassidy Bros. Forge, Inc. (MA)
Conant Custom Brass (VT)
Dura Finish of San Mateo (CA)
Experi-Metals (WI)
Hautwork, Inc. (NJ)
Hiles Plating Co., Inc. (MO)
Howland, John — Metalsmith (CT)
Kayne & Son Custom Forged Hardware (NC)
Moriarty's Lamps (CA)
Old World Restorations, Inc. (OH)
Retinning & Copper Repair (NY)
Star Metal (NY)
Westal Contracting (NY)
Windy Hill Forge (MD)

WALLPAPER RESTORATION

Larry Boyce & Associates, Inc. (CA)
Bill Goschen (MD)

MIRROR RESILVERING

The Antique Restoration Co. (PA)
Boomer Resilvering (CA)
Curran, Patrick J. (MA)
Ferguson's Cut Glass Works (OH)
Old World Restorations, Inc. (OH)
Ring, J. Stained Glass, Inc. (MN)

MUSICAL INSTRUMENT RESTORATION

A Second Wind for Harmoniums (NY)
Sadowski, Robert (PA)

PAINTING & DECORATING—PERIOD

(1) Decorating Contractor
(2) Gilding
(3) Glazing
(4) Graining
(5) Marbleizing
(6) Murals & Frescoes
(7) Stencilling
(8) Trompe l'oeil
(9) Wallpaper Hanging

ARJ Associates (MA) *4,5,7*
Acquisition and Restoration Corp. (IN) *2,3,4,5,6,7,8*
Archive (PA)
Artistic License in San Francisco (CA) *1,2,3,4,5,7,9*
Biltmore, Campbell, Smith Restorations, Inc. (NC) *1,2,4,5,6,7,9*
Larry Boyce & Associates, Inc. (CA) *2,3,6,7,9*
Canning, John, Ornamental Painter (CT) *3,4,5,6,7,8*
Craftsmen Decorators (NY) *2,3,4,5,7*
Custom Sign Co. (MD) *2,3,5,8*
Dee, John W. — Distinctive Painting & Decorating (MA) *1,9*
Evergreene Painting Studios, Inc. (NY) *2,3,4,5,6,7,8*
Halina Gemes (NY) *6,7,8*
George Studios (NY) *2,5,6*
Gold Leaf Studios, Inc. (DC) *2*
Bill Goschen (MD) *1,2,3,4,5,6,7,8*
Grammar of Ornament (CO) *4,5,7*
A. Greenhalgh & Sons, Inc. (MA) *1,7,9*
Hand-Stenciled Interiors (MA) *7*
Hendershot, Judith (IL) *7*
J.M. Roe (MA) *3,4,5,8*
Knickerbocker Guild (CA)
Koeppel/Freedman Studios (MA) *3,5,6,7,8*
Lynn Goodpasture (NY) *2,3,4,5,7,7*
Maclean Restoration Services (CT) *1,3,5*
National Guild of Professional Paperhangers, Inc. (NY) *9*
Perry, Edward K., Co. (MA) *2,3,4,5,7,8*
Rambusch (NY) *1,2,4,5,6,7*
Robson Worldwide Graining (VA) *2,3,4,5,7*
Roth Painting, Co., Inc. (NY) ... *1,2,3,4,5,6,7,8*
Skyline Engineers of Maryland, Inc. (MD) *2*
Stencilsmith (NY) *2,3,4,5,6,7,8*
Tromploy Inc. (NY) *4,5,6,7,8*
R. Wagner Co. Painted Finishes (OR) *2,3,4,5,7,8*
Wiggins Brothers (NH) *5,6,7*
Zetlin, Lorenz — Muralist (NY) *5,6,8*

See Company Directory for Addresses & Phone Numbers on page 151

PAINT AND COLOR SERVICES

(1) Paint and Materials Analysis
(2) Color Consulting

- Accents (NJ) *2*
- Architectural Resources Group (CA) *1*
- Artistic License in San Francisco (CA) *1*
- Bob Buckter, Color Consultant (CA) *2*
- **Colonial Restoration Products (PA)** *1*
- **The Color People—Restoration Graphics (CO)** *2*
- Community Services Collaborative (CO) .. *1*
- Grammar of Ornament (CO) *1*
- **Mosca, Matthew (MD)** *1,2*
- Munsell Color (MD) *1*
- Oehrlein & Associates (DC) *1*
- Preservation Partnership (MA) *1*
- San Francisco Color Service (CA) *2*
- Wick York (CT) *1,2*

PAINT STRIPPING SERVICES

- Alexandria Wood Joinery (NH)
- Allstrip (NY)
- American Building Restoration (WI)
- Anderson Building Restoration (OH)
- **Bare Wood Inc. (NY)**
- Bioclean (PA)
- Cosmetic Restoration, Inc. (NY)
- Downstate Restorations (IL)
- Dura Finish of San Mateo (CA)
- Eifel Furniture Stripping (NY)
- Eklund, Jon Restorations (NJ)
- Haines Masonry Specialties (IN)
- Johnson Woodworks Inc. (IL)
- **Montclair Restoration Craftsmen (NJ)**
- William H. Parsons & Associates (CT)
- Poor Richard's Service Co. (NJ)
- Timothy G. Riordan (NY)
- River City Restorations (MO)
- Warwick Refinishers (NY)
- Wayne Towle Inc. (MA)

PARQUET REPAIR & INSTALLATION

- Floors By Juell (IL)
- Peiser Floors (NY)
- **Rinder's New York Flooring (NY)**

PHOTO RESTORATION

- Elbinger Laboratories, Inc. (MI)

PLASTERING, ORNAMENTAL

- **ARJ Associates (MA)**
- Acquisition and Restoration Corp. (IN)
- David Woods Plaster Restoration (NY)
- Eklund, Jon Restorations (NJ)
- **Felber Studios, Inc. (PA)**
- Flaharty, David — Sculptor (PA)
- W.J. Hampton Plastering (NJ)
- Harne Plastering Co. (MD)
- Koeppel/Freedman Studios (MA)
- Mangione Plaster (NY)
- Ornamental Design Studios (NY)
- Rosenau, Marion, Sculptor (PA)
- Russell Restoration of Suffolk (NY)
- J.P. Weaver Co. (CA)

TRAINING COURSES & WORKSHOPS

Association for Preservation Technology (CAN)
Campbell Center for Historic Preservation Studies (IL)
Custom House Foundry (ME)
The Day Studio — Workshop Inc. (CA)
Eastfield Village (NY)
Finishing School (NY)
Historic Neighborhood Preservation Program (CT)
Old Sturbridge Village (MA)
Restoration Workshop Nat Trust For Historic Preservation (NY)
Winterthur Museum and Gardens (DE)

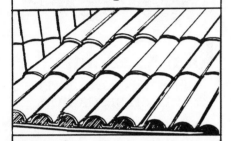

PORCELAIN REFINISHING

Perma Ceram Enterprises, Inc. (NY)
Porcelain Restoration and Brass (NC)
Tennessee Tub Inc. & Tubliner Co. (TN)
Vintage Tub & Sink Restoration Service (MA)

ROOFERS, SPECIALTY

Alte, Jeff Roofing, Inc. (NJ)
Brueggeman Roofing Co. (CO)
C & H Roofing (SD)
Castle Roofing Co., Inc. (NY)
Copper Specialties, Ltd. (NY)
Haines Masonry Specialties (IN)
Midland Engineering Company (IN)
Millen Roofing Co. (WI)
Raleigh, Inc. (IL)
Restorations Unlimited, Inc. (PA)
Skyline Engineers of Maryland, Inc. (MD)
Skyline Engineers of Maryland, Inc. (MD)
Wagner, Albert J., & Son (IL)
Westal Contracting (NY)

SANDSTONE (BROWNSTONE) REPAIR

Brooklyn Stone Renovating (NY)
Carl Schilling Stoneworks (VT)
Cathedral Stone Company, Inc. (DC)
Haines Masonry Specialties (IN)
William H. Parsons & Associates (CT)

STAIRCASE REPAIR

Anderson, Townsend (VT)

TERRA COTTA RESTORATION & CASTING

Clay Suppliers (TX)
Haines Masonry Specialties (IN)
Ludowici-Celadon Co. (OH)
Terra Cotta Productions, Inc. (PA)

TURNINGS, CUSTOM

A-B Manufacturing Co. (WI)
American Wood Column Corporation (NY)
Bare Wood Inc. (NY)
Bartleys Mill (CA)
Cumberland Woodcraft Co., Inc. (PA)
Dugwood Turners (VA)
Pete Holly (MN)
Johnson Woodworks Inc. (IL)
Kaymar Wood Products, Inc. (WA)
Knudsen, Mark (IA)
David J. Lassiter (FL)
Leeke, John — Woodworker (ME)
Michael's Fine Colonial Products (NY)
Navedo Woodcraft, Inc. (NY)
Nelson-Johnson Wood Products, Inc. (MN)
New England Woodturners (CT)
Nutt, Craig, Fine Wood Works (AL)
Pagliacco Turning & Milling Architectural Wood Turning (CA)
Sawdust Room (MI)
Sheppard Millwork, Inc. (WA)
Sound Beginnings (NY)
Walbrook Mill & Lumber Co., Inc. (MD)
Woodstone Co. (VT)

WOOD CARVING

Bare Wood Inc. (NY)
Bjorndal Woodworks (WI)
Knudsen, Mark (IA)
Lea, James — Cabinetmaker (ME)
Master Wood Carver (NJ)
Nutt, Craig, Fine Wood Works (AL)
Oak Leaves Woodcarving Studio (IA)
Shelley Signs (NY)
Frederick Wilbur, Carver (VA)
Wrisley, Robert T. (TN)

The Company Directory

The Company Directory that follows is an alphabetical listing of all 1423 companies whose products and services are listed in this book. Look here when you know what company you want to contact.

If you don't know who makes the product you need, look up the product in the yellow-pages General Index on page 14, which will refer you to the proper page in the Product & Service Directory.

A bullet (•) next to a company name means that company has placed a display advertisement. Use the Advertisers' Index on page 22 to find the ad quickly.

1874 House
8070 S.E. 13th Ave. Dept. OHJ
Portland, OR 97202
(503) 233-1874
RS/O
Specialists in architectural fragments, antique hardware for doors, cabinets, furniture, antique Victorian lighting fixtures, antique plumbing fixtures, antique sinks, replacement parts and pieces for almost everything. Walk-in shopping only. No literature.

• **18th Century Hardware Co.**
131 East 3rd St. Drawer OH
Derry, PA 15627
(412) 694-2708
MO RS/O
Reproduction hardware in brass, porcelain, and black iron covering the Early American and Victorian periods. Pulls, knobs, casters, hinges, hooks, latches, door knockers, and other brass accessories. Also, authentic hand-painted cast-aluminum fire marks. Will duplicate & repair hardware, brass lamps, and locks. Catalog, $3., by third class mail.

19th Century Company
P.O. Box 599 Dept. O
Rough & Ready, CA 95975
(916) 432-1040
MO RS/O
Manufacturer and distributor of hard-to-find parts and hardware for antique furniture and vintage homes. They carry a complete line of cast brass including Victorian and Chippendale period items through Art Deco and English hardware of the early 20th century. They also offer desk hardware, oak and walnut dowels and knobs, and much more. They now carry a line of wood finishes as well as caning supplies. Wholesale and retail. Illustrated catalog, $2.

21st Century Antiques
11-1/2 Main St., Box 70 Dept. OHJ
Hatfield, MA 01038
(413) 247-9396
MO RS/O
A mail-order source for original 20th-century decorative art objects (Art-Deco, Arts & Crafts Movement, '50s, etc.). Also a large selection of reference books about the objects and the time period. Replicas of some lines. $4 mailing list charge for catalogs as published.

The 509 Studio
PO Box 18623 Dept. OHJ
Tampa, FL 33679
(813) 875-0701
RS/O
Ornamental restoration, model and mold makers. Concrete, plaster, bronze, and resin casting. Interior and exterior sculpture, balluster, cartouche, decorative plaster, urns, and concrete production. Free information sheet.

KEY TO ABBREVIATIONS

MO	sells by Mail Order
RS/O	sells through Retail Store or Office
DIST	sells through Distributors
ID	sells only through Interior Designers or Archtects

A

• **AA-Abbingdon Affiliates, Inc.**
2149 Utica Avenue Dept. OHJ
Brooklyn, NY 11234
(718) 258-8333
RS/O . MO
21 patterns of hard-to-find embossed tin panels, and tin cornices in 10 patterns for metal ceiling installation. Popular 50-100 years ago, metal ceilings are an economical way to decorate in period style. Illustrated brochure $1.

A-B Manufacturing Co.
1168 N. 50th Place Dept. OHJ
Milwaukee, WI 53208
(414) 258-1308
RS/O
Custom wood turning. Will duplicate any item to your specifications. No literature.

• **A-Ball Plumbing Supply**
1703 W. Burnside St. Dept. OHJ
Portland, OR 97209
(503) 228-0026
RS/O MO
Various plumbing supplies and hardware, including shower set-ups, high-tank toilets, faucets, waste & overflow, metal and tile cleaners, epoxy tub-resurfacing kit, cast aluminum reproduction grates, old-fashioned soap dishes, customized shower rings and rods, hand-held showers for built-in and clawfoot tubs, safety rails for clawfoot tubs. They also carry pedastal basins and 2-hole mixing faucet for old sinks, as well as toilet parts for those who want to restore old ones. Free catalog.

• **AFC/A Nortek Company**
55 Samuel Barnet Blvd. Dept. OHJ
New Bedford, MA 02745
(617) 998-1131
DIST
AFC is a leading manafacturer of armored electrical cables, conduits, and systems, with headquarters in New Bedford, MA and plants in New Bedford and Bensalem, PA. Free literature on every product. "Electric Wiring & Lighting in Historic American Buildings" book — $9.95.

A.J.P. Coppersmith
20 Industrial Pkwy. Dept. M
Woburn, MA 01801
(617) 245-1223
MO RS/O
Long-established company offers an extensive line of authentic Colonial lighting fixtures. Chandeliers, sconces, post or wall lanterns are hand-crafted with a choice of finishes: Copper (antique or verdigris), Brass, Pewter-type (lead-coated copper or terne). A distinctive collection by three generations of craftsmen — send $2. for 32-page color catalog.

A & M Wood Specialty, Inc.
358 Eagle St., N. Dept. OHJ
Cambridge, Ontario, Canada N3H456
(519) 653-9322
MO RS/O
This company sells domestic and foreign hardwoods, veneers, timbers, plywoods, and instrument parts, retail and wholesale. Free literature.

AMC Housemaster Home Inspection Svc.
421 W. Union Ave. Dept. OHJ
Bound Brook, NJ 08805
(201) 469-6050
RS/O
House inspections and warranty service working in New Jersey. Free brochure.

ARJ Associates
310 Washington St. Dept. OHJ
Brighton, MA 02135
(617) 783-0467
RS/O MO
Custom design and restoration of ornamental plasterwork for old and new buildings, specializing in decorative cornices and moldings. They execute specialist wall and surface effects including: murals, stencilling, marbling, ragging and gilding. Collection of traditional designs hand painted on ceramic tile for bath, kitchen, and fireplaces; also custom tile work. Free catalogue and literature available.

A.S.L. Associates
P.O. Box 6296 Dept. OHJ
San Mateo, CA 94403
(415) 344-5044
MO
Plans for building a gazebo. The set consists of three 17" x 22" sheets, and includes full construction details and a materials list. The finished gazebo is 8 ft. in diameter and has an inside height of 7 ft. 4 in. clear. Price — $10. Free flyer.

Abaroot Mfg., Co.
21757-1/2 S. Western Ave. Dept. OHJ
Torrance, CA 90501
(213) 320-8172
RS/O
Hand woodturning in Los Angeles since 1932. Manufacture columns, newels, balusters, lamp posts, and porch posts. Will work in hard or soft woods. No literature.

• **Abatron, Inc.**
141 Center Drive Dept. OH
Gilberts, IL 60136
(312) 426-2200
MO
Manufactures epoxies and plastic resins for restoration, repair, patching, coating, resurfacing, and maintenance of wood, masonry, metal, and most rigid surfaces. Shrink-free wood fillers and consolidants. Casting resins for moulds and patterns. Laminating resings for fiberglass. Structural adhesives. Porcelain refinishing materials. Also sealants and waterproof coatings. Dealer inquiries welcomed. Free brochures.

Accents
312 Spruce Street Dept. OHJ
Boonton, NJ 07005
(201) 334-7767
RS/O
Victorian and Colonial housepainting, both interior and exterior. Leans towards the "Painted Lady" look; projects are entire homes/buildings or highlighting detail. Clientele consists of homeowners and contractors. References, but no literature.

Accurate Metal Weather Strip Co., Inc.
725 South Fulton Ave. Dept. OHJ
Mount Vernon, NY 10550
(914) 668-6042
MO
Integral weatherstripping in a variety of metals and sizes designed to fit casement or double-hung windows (wood & metal). Interlocking weatherstrip for doors, bronze & aluminum thresholds. Free catalog.

Ace Wire Brush Co.
30 Henry St. Dept. OHJ
Brooklyn, NY 11201
(718) 624-8032
MO
All types of chimney brushes: wire, fiber, nylon. Free catalog.

Acme Exterminating Co.
460 9th Avenue Dept. OHJ
New York, NY 10018
(212) 594-9230
RS/O
Exterminating company providing general pest control services in the New York Metropolitan area, Rockland, New Jersey, and Westchester. Free brochure.

Acme Stove Company
9315 Georgia Avenue Dept. OHJ
Silver Spring, MD 20910
(301) 585-0240
RS/O MO
Major supplier of pre-fab fireplaces, wood-stoves, and woodburning accessories in the Mid-Atlantic area. Also chimney systems, efficient heat-circulating systems, fireplace accessories. Professional counselors will design complementary systems in townhouses and multifamily restorations. 6 locations; call or write for information.

• **Acorn Manufacturing Co., Inc.**
457 School St., PO Box 31 Dept. OJC
Mansfield, MA 02048
(617) 339-4500
MO DIST RS/O
Selection of forged-iron reproduction Colonial hardware. Butterfly, strap, H and H-L hinges. Cabinet, door, and shutter hardware. Also hurricane lamps, and sconces, bath accessories, fireplace tools, and decorative wall plates. Catalog, $2.

Acorn Oriental Rug Services
2001 Harlem Road Dept. OHJ
Akron, OH 44320
(216) 745-6097
MO
One-piece solid brass stair rods with finials are available. Stock size fits 27 in. or under-stair runner, custom sizes also available; both maintain authentic early 1900s look. $14.95. Quantity discounts available. They welcome all inquiries.

Acquisition and Restoration Corp.
423 Massachusetts Avenue Dept. OHJ
Indianapolis, IN 46204
(317) 637-1266
RS/O
Experienced general contractors, construction managers, consultants, and real estate developers in architectural restoration. Building inspection, historical research, financing and property-tax abatement consultation. Reproductions of English cast-iron fireplace surrounds produced in plaster. 614 residential and commercial projects completed. No fee for initial correspondence. Restoration, renovation, and preservation projects undertaken throughout continental U.S. No literature.

Adams Company
100 E. 4th St. Dept. OHJ
Dubuque, IA 52001
(319) 583-3591
MO DIST
Manufactures a line of fireplace furnishings of heavy-gauge steel, solid brass, and cast iron. Sold through distributors and mail order, free descriptive brochure is available.

• See Advertisers' Index
on page 22
for more details.

Stephen A. Adams, Furnituremakers/W.H. James Co.
Mill Hill Rd. Box 130 Dept. OHJ
Denmark, ME 04022
(207) 452-2444
MO
Handmade Colonial reproduction furniture, including Windsor chairs, rockers, and benches; bannister back chairs; dropleaf, trestle, extension, bedside, hall, and tilt-top tables; highboys, blanket chests, china cabinets, and pencil-post beds. Hand-rubbed finish or milk paint. Catalog, $3.

• **Adams and Swett**
380 Dorchester Ave. Dept. OHJ
Boston, MA 02127
(617) 268-8000
RS/O MO
A portfolio of rugs selected for old houses. They include hand and machine-made braided rugs, rag rugs, oriental designs, dhurries, berbers and other hand woven and machine made accent and room-sized rugs. Portfolio and price list, $2.

Adirondack Store & Gallery
109 Saranac Ave. Dept. OHJ
Lake Placid, NY 12946
MO RS/O
Original rustic pieces, retrieved from old camps in the Adirondacks; some reproduction pieces handmade by local craftspeople. Free brochure.

Adirondak Chair Co.
Box 1257 Dept. OHJ
Schuyerville, NY 12871
(518) 695-6923
MO
Pre-cut and drilled kits for assembling pine Adirondack chairs, $33.50.

Advanced Materials, Inc.
PO Box 917 Dept. OHJ
Deep River, CT 06417
(203) 526-9755
MO RS/O
Fiberglass-reinforced cement that can be cast to resemble marble, granite, or wood: cornices, moulding, mantels, etc. They also stock protective back panels and platforms for stoves, plus cast-iron decorative poles. Pole and stove-shield flyers, free; call or write for custom-casting information.

Aetna Stove Company
S.E. Cor. 2nd & Arch Streets Dept. OHJ
Philadelphia, PA 19106
(215) 627-2008
RS/O MO
One of the oldest stove repair parts companies in the U.S., servicing and providing parts for gas and electric stoves, wood and coal ranges, etc. Large diversified stock of antique parts. Also supplies stove black, isinglass (Mica) (mica windows). Please call or write for information. Prepaid shipments via UPS can be arranged.

The Aged Ram
PO Box 201 Dept. OHJ
Essex, VT 05451
(802) 878-4530
MO
The Aged Ram is devoted to hooking rugs in the folk tradition of early New England. Their production is limited and most rugs are custom designed and created by special order.

• **Aged Woods**
R.D. 3, Box 80 Dept. OHJ
Delta, PA 17314
(800) 233-9307
MO RS/O
This company specializes in the disassembly of old buildings and factorys to procure woods that are anywhere from 100 to over 200 years old. They then remill the woods into random-width wide-plank flooring in white and yellow pines or assorted oaks. They also carry a rare American Chestnut for flooring. Besides flooring, they can make paneling, and carry a full line of hand-hewn beams, rafters, Peach-Bottom Blue Roofing Slate. Inside Penn. call (717) 456-7617. Free brochure.

• **Ahrens Chimney Technique Inc.**
2000 Industrial Ave. Dept. OHJ
Sioux Falls, SD 57104
(800) 843-4417
DIST RS/O
A lining and relining process for masonry chimneys. Ahrens first liner restores, strengthens, and insulates. The second liner glazing seals, protects, and prevents future deterioration. Ahrens system is U.L. listed and offers a 10 year warranty. Specializing in residential and commercial applications. Dealer inquiries invited.

Ainsworth Development Corp.
Beckford Dept. OHJ
Princess Anne, MD 21853
(301) 651-3219
MO
Manufactures turnbuckle stars for reinforcing masonry walls. Will design & supply tension member for determining tension being applied by turnbuckle. For literature, send stamped self-addressed envelope.

Air-Flo Window Contracting Corp.
194 Concord St. Dept. OHJ
Brooklyn, NY 11201
(718) 875-8600
RS/O
Fabricates and installs wood and metal prime windows and vinyl and metal storm windows in 10 historically correct colors. Double-hung and casements available. Styles to suit old houses: doors and windows conform to Landmark Commission standards. Can be glazed with Thermopane, Lexan, or Solar- Cool as well as single-pane glass. Custom window-boxes and awnings also available. Free literature available on request, or call for more information.

Akron Foundry, Inc.
501 Main, PO Box 37 Dept. OHJ
Akron, IN 46910
(219) 893-4548
MO RS/O
A small, family owned factory that does both custom loose-pattern work and production runs of wood-burning ranges and heating stoves, sad irons, anvils, book ends. Pattern-making and pattern repair service available. Prices very competitive.

Albert Van Luit & Co.
4000 Chevy Chase Dr. Dept. OHJ
Los Angeles, CA 90039
(818) 247-8840
DIST
Hand-screened wallcoverings and related fabrics in historical designs including florals, scenics, and chinoiseries. Some of their designs are for the Winterthur Museum collection. Free literature.

Danny Alessandro/Edwin Jackson
1156 Second Ave. Dept. OHJ
New York, NY 10021
(212) 421-1928
MO RS/O
Fireplace specialists since 1879, this antique dealer sells antique and reproduction 18th-century limestone, marble, and wood mantels, club fenders, andirons, firescreens, and other hearth accessories, both antique and reproduction.

Alexandria Wood Joinery
Plumer Hill Road Dept. OHJ
Alexandria, NH 03222
(603) 744-8243
RS/O
Custom woodworking, antique repair and restoration, furniture stripping and chair seating. Serving Northern New England. Furniture design & manufacture. No literature.

Alfa Lite
380 E. 1700 South Dept. OHJ
Salt Lake City, UT 84115
(801) 487-3451
MO RS/O
Restoration and reproduction of antique lamps and shades. Repair and refurbishing of chandeliers, wall mounts. Replacement glass and parts. Custom lighting. Victorian lampshades in stock.

Alfred Manufacturing Corp.
350 Warren St. Dept. OHJ
Jersey City, NJ 07302
(201) 332-9100
MO
Mail-order source for inexpensive Victorian-style picture-hangers with tassels. In natural off-white or gold. (Not silk.) Packed in boxes of 6 only, at $1.75 each hanger. Postage is $2.50 per order.

• **Alfresco Fine Furniture Since 1976**
PO Box 1336 Dept. OHJ
Durango, CO 81301
(303) 247-9739
MO RS/O
Porch swings, Adirondack chairs, and tables constructed of redwood. Available unfinished or finished with a penetrating oil. Mastercharge or Visa accepted. Free brochure. Also (303) 259-5743.

Allen Foundry
1024 No. Parker Dept. OHJ
Orange, CA 92667
(714) 532-3630
MO ID
Custom cast plaques in bronze or aluminum: historic markers, addresses, numbers. Also horse hitching posts. Free brochure.

Allen and Allen Company
PO Box 5140 Dept. OHJ
San Antonio, TX 78284
(512) 733-9191
MO RS/O
A retail/wholesale lumber & hardware company that has been in business since 1931. They specialize in hardwood lumber along with many different types of mouldings. Also, a wide array of commercial, residential, & decorative hardware. No literature.

• See Advertisers' Index
on page 22
for more details.

• **Allentown Paint Mfg. Co., Inc.**
E Allen & N Graham, Box 597 Dept. OHJ
Allentown, PA 18105
(215) 433-4273
RS/O DIST MO
Oldest ready-made paint company in U.S. (established 1855); offers a line of oil-based or latex exterior paints in colors appropriate for Colonial and Victorian era houses. Many colors and formulations date from the 1860s, with the exception of additives for easy application and color fastness. Literature available through local paint stores, or contact Allentown office for name of distributor.

Allied Resin Corp.
Weymouth Industrial Park Dept. OHJ
East Weymouth, MA 02189
(617) 337-6070
MO
A mail-order source for epoxies, polyester resins, silicones & pressure sensitive tapes. Will ship nation wide. Free literature.

Allied Roofers Supply
Rt. 17 N., PO Box 511 Dept. OHJ
E. Rutherford, NJ 07073
(201) 935-0800
RS/O MO
Distributor for new terra-cotta roofing tiles from Ludowici-Celadon. Will ship orders of over 600 pieces (300 sq. ft.) anywhere. Customers can pick up any smaller orders. Please call — no literature.

• **Allied Window, Inc.**
2724 W. McMicken Ave. Dept. OHJ
Cincinnati, OH 45214
(513) 559-1212
MO DIST RS/O
Manufactures and installs aluminum, plastic (PVC), steel, or wood storm windows that fit flush with house's windows; inside or outside mounted, a variety of colors, screen or glass panels. Arched, eyebrow, Gothic, or custom shapes available. Fixed, magnetic, sliding, or lift-out designs. Free 8-page catalog and color flyer.

Allstrip
60-17A 56th Road Dept. OHJ
Maspeth, NY 11378
(718) 326-0124
RS/O
Will come and do paint stripping of architectural woodwork in your home. Also provides full range of wood refinishing services. References available. Serves NYC metropolitan area. No literature; call for appointment and estimate.

Alpha Technical Systems, Inc.
PO Box 281 Dept. OHJ
Villanova, PA 19085
(215) 269-9125
MO DIST RS/O
Alpha Technical Systems, Inc. manufactures cleaners, strippers, stains, and water repellants for rejuvenating and protecting masonry. These products are suited for historic preservation work. Alpha Restoratives clean limestone, brick, & concrete of atmospheric pollutants without damaging the substrate. Gamma Clears and Stains resist dirt and repel rainwater. Power Sigma Strippers lift or soften old paint on masonry/wood for removal by scraping or power washing. Alpha will custom formulate especially difficult stripping projects.

Alte, Jeff Roofing, Inc.
PO Box 639 Dept. OHJ
Somerville, NJ 08876
(201) 526-2111
RS/O
General roofing contractors and roofing consultants serving Central and Northern New Jersey. Repair and reroofing of churches and older houses, including slate and cedar shingle work. Expertise and equipment to handle copper gutters, leaders, built-in gutters: their metal shop can fabricate gutters, ridge caps, etc. No literature; please call for appointment.

• **Amazon Vinegar & Pickling Works Drygoods**
2218 E. 11th Street Dept. OC
Davenport, IA 52803
(309) 786-3504
MO
A purveyor of items to create a 19th-century impression, 1750-1927. Emphasis on the hoop skirt and bustle era. Items include: Period clothing & fabric for men, women, and children (patterns & ready-made); military accessories; and books on clothing, history, period interiors, land-scaping and architecture. Victorian toys, cards & decorations for all holidays. 40-page catalog, $2. Illustration of all 309 clothing patterns not included in catalog, $4.

Amenities
8102A South Lewis Dept. OHJ
Tulsa, OK 74137
(918) 298-2636
RS/O
A decorative building and restoration supply store that carries brass door and cabinet hardware, bathroom fittings, brass and pedestal sinks, bevelled glass, wood carved mouldings, fireplace mantels, staircase parts, and hand-crafted hardwood shutters. Free brochure.

American Architectural Art Company
1910 N Marshall St. Dept. OHJ
Philadelphia, PA 19122
(215) 236-6492
RS/O
Professional artists and craftsmen will custom sculpt and fabricate architectural accents (mouldings, copings, medallions, etc.) for interior or exterior remodeling or historic reconstruction. They can reproduce from historic originals or from your drawing specifications. The casts are fabricated in lightweight polymerized fiberglass reinforced gypsum, Design-Cast®, or fiberglass reinforced polyester. They can simulate wood, terra cotta, metal or masonry. Call or write for your specific needs. Free literature.

American Building Restoration
9720 So. 60th St. Dept. OHJ
Franklin, WI 53132
(414) 761-2440
MO DIST
Manufacturer of chemicals for paint stripping and cleaning historical buildings. Sold direct, through distributors and dealers. Also exterior restoration contractors. Works throughout the U.S. Video presentation showing chemical systems and projects restored since 1970. Free color brochure.

• **American Chimney Lining Systems, Inc.**
9797 Clyde Park, SW Dept. OHJ
Byron Center, MI 49315
(616) 878-3577
MO RS/O
One-piece "solid-flue" poured-in-place masonry chimney lining system for restoring old, damaged chimneys. Free brochure.

American Folk Art
354 Kennesaw Ave. Dept. OHJ
Marietta, GA 30060
(404) 344-5985
MO RS/O
They have been making rustic furniture for some 100 years, including bent-willow porch and lawn pieces. Catalog, $2.

American Furniture Galleries
P.O. Box 60 Dept. OHJ
Montgomery, AL 36101
(800) 547-5240
DIST RS/O ID
Manufacturer of the two most widely known lines of Victorian reproduction furniture, Carlton McLendon and Capitol Victorian. All pieces are hand crafted from solid Honduras mahogany. Products are available at retail dealers throughout the U.S. & Canada. Brochures, $1.

American General Products
1735 Holmes Rd., PO Box 395 Dept. OHJ
Ypsilanti, MI 48197
(313) 483-1833
MO DIST RS/O
Spiral and circular stairs. Spiral stairs are available in all wood, wood and steel designs, and all steel. All are available in a variety of styles, diameters and in any floor to floor height. Circular stairs are for interior use and shipped assembled; spirals are shipped knocked down. 800-STAIRS-1. Literature available, $1.

American Glass Light Co.
37 W. 72 St. Dept. OHJ
New York, NY 10023
(212) 874-6189
MO RS/O DIST
Limited and unlimited editions of antique and reproduction lighting fixtures. Art Deco lamps and fixtures, turn-of-the-century ceiling fixtures with ribbed-glass shades. Free color brochure.

• **American Heritage Shutters**
2549 Lamar Ave. Dept. OHJ
Memphis, TN 38114
(901) 743-2800
RS/O
Constructed of white pine with 2-in.-wide movable louvers, American Heritage's shutters are available in custom sizes designed to fit circular windows. Free brochure.

American Lamp Parts, Inc.
200 S. Beltline Rd. Dept. OHJ
Irving, TX 75060
(214) 790-1004
DIST
Wholesale distributor of a wide variety of lamp and lighting fixture parts: Art Nouveau lamp bases, Victorian-style plastic ceiling plates, prisms, ornate bobeches and arms, chimneys, glass globes and shades. Wholesale only — they cannot sell to consumers, but their catalog is free and they can provide names of distributors.

American Olean Tile Company
P.O. Box 271 Dept. OHJ
Lansdale, PA 19446
(215) 855-1111
DIST
A major tile manufacturer, makes the 1-inch square & 1-inch Hexagon white ceramic mosaic floor tiles and Bright White & Gloss Black glazed wall tiles used in early 20th century bathrooms. A terra-cotta quarry tile and a rough-textured tile are appropriate for rustic kitchens. Also marble tiles that have a polished surface, bevelled edges and come in ten colors. Decorating Ideas Brochure No. 761—$.50; Ceramic Mosaics Sheet 1846—Free; Quarry Tile Sheet 1334—Free; Primitive Encore Sheet 1384—Free; Bright and Matte Sheet 1389—Free; Quarry Naturals Sheet 1645—Free.

American Wood Column Corporation
913 Grand Street Dept. OHJ
Brooklyn, NY 11211
(718) 782-3163
MO
Produces stock and custom wooden exterior and interior columns, capitals, and bases. Also wood turnings, and mouldings of any description and ornamental work to sketch or detail. Free brochure available.

Amherst Woodworking & Supply
Box 575, Hubbard Avenue Dept. OHJ
Northampton, MA 01061
(413) 584-3003
RS/O
Produces commercial and residential architectural woodwork. Doors, mouldings, windows, furniture, cabinets, flooring, raised and flat panelling, etc. Works primarily for contractors; custom work, no stock items. Will bid work if plans are provided. No literature.

Amish Country Collection
RD 5 Sunset Valley Rd. Dept. OHJ
New Castle, PA 16105
(412) 656-1755
MO RS/O
Rustic furniture, made of oak and hickory twigs selected by Amish craftspeople in nearby woods. Chairs, tables, accessories. Full color catalog, $5., refundable.

Amsterdam Corporation
150 E. 58th St. Dept. OHJ
New York, NY 10155
(212) 644-1350
DIST RS/O
Large selection of imported hand-painted tiles including embossed and Delft tiles. A set of 3 brochures featuring Delft tiles is $5. Also available, hand-formed white ceramic cornice tiles, each 4 in. long. New line of imported decorated tiles for kitchens and baths; literature available for $5.

Andersen Corporation
Box 12 Dept. OHJ
Bayport, MN 55003
(612) 439-5150
DIST
Established 1903. Nation's largest manufacturer of wood windows; some appropriate for old houses, including arched windows. Top-quality materials. Free brochures: insulating glass, patio doors, window and door installation, arched windows.

D.L. Anderson & Associates, Inc.
10650 Highway 152 Dept. OHJ
Maple Grove, MN 55369
(800) 328-9493
MO DIST
U.S. Sikkens distributor, manufacturer of advanced technology transparent interior and exterior wood finishes, an insecticide that can be mixed with stain, wood-preserving stains, etc. Free brochure.

Anderson Building Restoration
923 Marion Avenue Dept. OHJ
Cincinnati, OH 45229
(513) 281-5258
RS/O
Exterior restoration contractors specializing in chemical paint removal and chemical cleaning of historic masonry structures. They provide expert tuck-pointing, caulking, epoxy consolidation, and painting. A member of The Association for Preservation Technology, the company takes great pride in using only the safest, most gentle methods. They work in the Ohio, Kentucky, and Southeastern Indiana areas. Free literature available.

Anderson-McQuaid Co., Inc.
170 Fawcett St. Dept. OHJ
Cambridge, MA 02138
(617) 876-3250
MO RS/O
Since 1946 the craftsmanship of this company has been heralded through-out the architectural millwork trade. Their millwork includes: custom and restoration mouldings, picture frame mouldings, flooring and panelling as well as hardwood lumber. Hardwood lumber price list available.

Anderson Pulley Seal Co.
920 W. 53rd St. Dept. OHJ
Minneapolis, MN 55419
(612) 827-1117
MO
Manufacture the Anderson Pulley Seal for windows with sash cords. The Seal will reduce heat loss. Free flyer.

Anderson Reconstruction
42 Boardman St. Dept. OHJ
Newburyport, MA 01950
(617) 465-9622
RS/O
Services for houses built before 1850 including house inspection. White pine clapboards with graduated spacing, wooden downspouts, exterior and interior work. Replaces rotted corner posts, beams and sills with new or old wood. Wide pine floors and beaded sheathing. No literature.

Anderson, Townsend
RD 1, Box 860 Dept. OHJ
Moretown, VT 05660
(802) 244-5095
RS/O
Restoration services for historic properties including research and congruent design, consultation, on-site management, period landscape design, finish joinery, and architectural parts designed and built to appropriate specifications, tax credit certification. Recent work includes restoration of the 1804 John Warren House in Middlebury, recipient of a 1984 National Trust Preservation Honor Award. Historic preservation experts working throughout northern New England. Inquiries are welcomed and promptly answered.

Angelo Brothers Co.
10981 Decatur Rd. Dept. OHJ
Philadelphia, PA 19154
(215) 632-9600
DIST
Primarily a wholesaler, this company has the largest selection of glass shades and globes for replacements on 19th century lighting fixtures. Angelo Master Catalog is $15. It can also be viewed at your local dealer.

KEY TO ABBREVIATIONS

- MO sells by Mail Order
- RS/O sells through Retail Store or Office
- DIST sells through Distributors
- ID sells only through Interior Designers or Archtects

Anglo-American Brass Co.
PO Box 9487 Dept. OHJ
San Jose, CA 95157
(408) 246-0203
MO DIST RS/O
Authentic sandcast, die cast, and stamped solid brass reproduction hardware for the restoration of furniture, doors, cupboards, etc. Included are bails, handle sets, knobs, drops, hinges, catches, lock sets, ice box sets, door knobs and back-plates, kitchen hardware, escutcheons, coat hooks, etc. Since they are manufacturers, they can also custom-produce articles for builders, wholesalers or manufacturers. Color catalog No. 125, $1.50. Also, (408) 246-3232.

Antares Forge and Metalworks
501 Eleventh St. Dept. OHJ
Brooklyn, NY 11215
(718) 499-5299
RS/O
Design and forging of architectural and ornamental ironwork, domestic implements, fireplace equipment, etc. All work is custom. No literature.

• **Anthony Wood Products**
PO Box 1081 S Dept. OHJ
Hillsboro, TX 76645
(817) 582-7225
MO RS/O
Complete line of hand-crafted wooden gingerbread. Catalog, $2.

Antiquaria
11 Whittier Rd. Dept. OHJ
Lexington, MA 02173
(617) 862-9073
MO
This company sells a changing inventory of antique American Victorian furniture and accessories, specializing in Rococo, Renaissance Revival and Eastlake styles, through an illustrated quarterly mail order catalog, $3.

• **Antique Baths and Kitchens**
2220 Carlton Way Dept. OHJ
Santa Barbara, CA 93109
(805) 962-8598
MO RS/O
For 12 years, this company has produced high quality reproductions for old kitchens and bathrooms. Their products include oak pull chain toilets, low tank toilets, pedestal basins, medicine chests, copper kitchen sinks, kitchen and bath faucets, brass and china basins, and drinking fountains. New for this year are marble vanity tops of 1-1/4-in.-thick marble carved with period patterns. They also have toilet parts and specialize in custom work. Brochure — $1.

Antique Brass Works
290 Port Richmond Avenue Dept. OHJ
Staten Island, NY 10302
(718) 447-1262
MO RS/O
Restoration services offered for lighting fixtures, gas lamp fixtures, bathroom hardware, brass beds, all types of brass and copper housewares. Manufacturer of exterior Colonial and Victorian lighting fixtures. Specialists in no-tarnish epoxy clear coating for all non-ferrous metal finishes. Complete metal spinning facilities for duplicating damaged and missing (lamp-bed) parts. Total restoration services on premises. Metal plating; silver, gold, brass, copper and nickel. Free flyer.

Antique Building Restoration
505 Storle Ave. Dept. OHJ
Burlington, WI 53105
(414) 763-8822
RS/O
Large or small restoration jobs including trim repair or replacement, exterior & interior painting & detailing, paint stripping and refinishing, carpentry to match or rebuild, custom built French and beveled glass doors, sash and storm repair, structural antiques installed, much more. Will travel. Free information sheet. Send SASE.

Antique Color Supply, Inc.
PO Box 711 Dept. OHJ
Harvard, MA 01451
(617) 582-6426
MO DIST
Authentic powdered milk paint for use on antique restorations, reproductions, and stencilling projects. Package sizes: 1 ounce, 6 ounces (makes 1 pint), and 12 ounces. Free information with SASE.

Antique Hardware Co.
PO Box 1592 Dept. OHJ
Torrance, CA 90505
(213) 378-5990
MO
Manufactures a collection of authentic handcrafted reproduction antique hardware. Drawer pulls, Armoire pulls, tear drop pulls, knobs, hooks, ice box hardware, locks, hinges, etc. Catalog, $2.

• **Antique Hardware Store**
43 Bridge Street Dept. P
Frenchtown, NJ 08825
(201) 996-4040
MO DIST RS/O
Restoration supplies including brass cabinet hardware, weathervanes, bathroom fixtures including pedestal sinks, and antique lighting. Will also sell wholesale. Catalog, $3.

The Antique Restoration Co.
440 E. Centre Ave. Dept. OHJ
Newtown, PA 18940
(215) 968-2343
RS/O
They specialize in quality restoration and repairs by dedicated craftspeople, each a specialist in his field. Brass or bronze casting, mirror resilvering, glass bevelling, furniture refinishing, stripping & repairs, gold leafing, special parts machined, brass & copper sheet metal work. Also, brass, copper, & silver polishing; bronze patinas & repairs; and light fixture repairs. No literature.

Antique Street Lamps, Inc.
8412 S. Congress Ave. Dept. OHJ
Austin, TX 78745
(512) 282-9780
MO RS/O
Manufactures old-fashioned street lamps in a variety of styles. Constructed of cast iron or high-strength fiberglass with Lexan globes. Authentic reproductions of old cast-iron street lamps used in early 1900s. Suitable for driveways, entrances, townhouses, and offices. Free flyer and price list.

Antique Trunk Supply Co.
3706 W. 169th St. Dept. OHJ
Cleveland, OH 44111
(216) 941-8618
MO
Trunk repair parts, handles, nails, rivets, corners, etc. Catalog, $1. Instruction and repair manual $4. Price and identification guide to antique trunks, $4.50.

Antiquity Reprints
PO Box 370 Dept. OHJ
Rockville Centre, NY 11571
(516) 766-5585
MO
Publishes a wide selection of reprinted 19th-century titles, including a large selection of house plan books; also vintage bird-house plans, household hints. Brochure, $2.

Appropriate Technology Corporation
PO Box 975, Technology Dr. Dept. OHJ
Brattleboro, VT 05301
(802) 257-4501
DIST
Manufactures Window Quilt and Window Showcase insulating window shades that can cut household heat loss and heat gain by as much as 79%. The product is available through a national network of about 2000 dealers. Approximate retail prices range from $125. to $200. for a 3 x 5 window, depending on style. Complete information package, including regional dealer list, available on request.

Arch Associates/ Stephen Guerrant AIA
824 Prospect Avenue Dept. OHJ
Winnetka, IL 60093
(312) 446-7810
RS/O
Chicago-area firm that specializes in restoration and rehabilitation. Will provide measured drawings and building surveys as well as full architectural services. Maintains extensive materials resource catalog file. Will also inspect old houses on a fixed fee basis. No literature.

Archicast
1316 Madison Dept. OHJ
Memphis, TN 38104
(901) 725-9620
MO DIST
Casts in almost any material: plaster, lightweight concrete, fiberglass, reinforced concrete, a variety of composites, polymer concrete (reproduces stone). Will repair old pieces or reproduce from drawings or photos. Makes quality moulds which can be used by do-it-yourselfers. Also casts signs in stone. Free brochure.

• **Architectural Accents**
2711 Piedmont Rd., NE Dept. OHJ
Atlanta, GA 30305
(404) 266-8700
RS/O
Architectural antiques and design consultants. Large selection of mantels from England, France and America; doors and entryways; columns (fluted and plain). Cabinetry, stained and bevelled glass, light fixtures, decorative hardware, ephemera, etc. for commercial or residential applications. No literature. Call or write with your specific needs.

KEY TO ABBREVIATIONS

MO	sells by Mail Order
RS/O	sells through Retail Store or Office
DIST	sells through Distributors
ID	sells only through Interior Designers or Archtects

Architectural Antique Warehouse, The
P. O. Box 3065 Stn 'D' Dept. OHJ
Ottawa, ONT, Canada K1P6H6
(613) 526-1818
MO RS/O
Antique architectural accessories, interior and exterior. Antique plumbing & lighting, and Victorian spiral staircases. Full range of bathroom fittings including unusual tubs, pedestal sinks, towel bars, mirrors, and soap dishes. No literature.

• **Architectural Antiques**
121 East Sheridan Dept. OHJ
Oklahoma City, OK 73104
(405) 232-0759
MO RS/O
20,000 sq. ft. of architectural antiques, primarily American. Doors, windows, store fronts, back bars, complete rooms, light fixtures, hardware, plumbing, columns, store fixtures, and other items. Complete restoration and installation services. Free architectural antique locator service. No literature, but responds to all inquiries.

• **Architectural Antiques Exchange**
709-15 N. 2nd Street Dept. OHJ
Philadelphia, PA 19123
(215) 922-3669
RS/O MO
Antique and recycled saloon fixtures and restaurant decor including bars, backbars, fretwork, ironwork doors, cabinets, counters, and carved wall units. Also antique and recycled house parts; interior and exterior doors, fences and gates, iron railings and window grills, wall panelling, mantels, ceiling and wall fixtures, and stained bevelled, and etched glass. Literature, $3.

Architectural Antiques, Ltd.
1321 E. 2nd St. Dept. OHJ
Little Rock, AR 72202
(501) 372-1744
MO RS/O
Over 36,000 square feet of architectural antiques complete panelled rooms, store fronts, and interiors, bevelled and stained-glass doors, windows, complete entries, mantels, doors, front and back bars, street lights, chandeliers, etc. Commercial and residential. Also complete restoration and design shops for stained and bevelled glass, furniture, and architectural pieces, and metal restorations. Free brochure and flyers.

• **Architectural Components**
PO Box 249 Dept. OHJ
Leverett, MA 01054
(413) 367-9441
MO RS/O
Produces and supplies 18th and 19th century architectural millwork. Interior and exterior doors; small pane window sashes; plank window frames and a variety of reproduction mouldings patterned after Connecticut Valley architecture. Also custom work: panelled fireplace walls, pediments, shutters, fan lights, French doors, period entrances, etc. Send $3 for brochure or call.

• **Architectural Iron Company**
Box 126, Route 6 West Dept. OHJ
Milford, PA 18337
(717) 296-7722
RS/O MO
A full service restoration company specializing in 19th-century cast and wrought iron work. They make their own castings in their own foundry and fabricate wrought work with historically accurate techniques. They will also make custom castings and fabrications for individuals or other firms. In NY, call (212) 243-2664. Consulting services are available; to receive a catalog and services information, send $3. to cover first class postage.

• **Architectural Originals**
PO Box 8023J Dept. OHJ
Newport Beach, CA 92658
(714) 551-4325
MO DIST RS/O
Architectural Originals is dedicated to preserving and displaying the images of historic architecture on quality products. They specialize in a select line of stationery, home decorating and gift items centering on a theme of historic architecture, including note cards, calendars, rubber stamps, posters, casual apparel, toys, and more.

Architectural Paneling, Inc.
979 Third Avenue, Suite 1518 Dept. OHJ
New York, NY 10022
(212) 371-9632
RS/O MO
Reproduces in carved wood English and French paneling and mantels and built-in cabinets and ceilings. Installations throughout the western hemisphere. Fireplaces, carvings and mouldings are also available. $5 for brochure.

Architectural Portraits
110 Sand Hill Rd. Dept. OHJ
Amherst, MA 01002
(413) 549-4121
MO
Architectural portraits of homes, historic sites, and businesses. Will work from photos or on site. You'll receive an original pen and ink drawing suitable for framing, approximately 17 x 22, and a photostat for reproductions on stationery. Portfolio and samples free on request.

Architectural Preservation Consultants
125 Cedar Street Dept. OHJ
New York, NY 10006
(212) 227-1271
RS/O
Architectural preservation consultants providing such preservation services as: restoration, preservation & rehabilitation programs and planning; maintenance programs; architectural and historical research and analysis; architectural surveys; feasibility studies; photographic documentation; and assistance with National Register nominations, local landmark status and Tax Act certification. No literature.

Architectural Preservation Trust
152 Old Clinton Road Dept. OHJ
Westbrook, CT 06498
(203) 669-1776
RS/O
They disassemble, reconstruct, and restore 17th through 19th century buildings. They also sell kits for building outbuildings like privies, wagon sheds, and corn cribs with all timber, pegs, instructions, siding, and roof boards. Will also do custom duplication of existing buildings. Also stock recycled building parts; will crate and ship anywhere. Free flyer.

Architectural Reclamation, Inc.
312 S. River St. Dept. OHJ
Franklin, OH 45005
(513) 746-8964
RS/O
Complete contracting services for restoration/adaptive reuse and repair of log, timber frame, balloon frame, and masonry structures. Custom woodworking; reuse of salvaged materials and architectural antiques. Design and construction of functional modern facilities compatible in style with historic homes. Serving Southwestern OH. No literature.

Architectural Reproductions, Inc.
19402 S.E. Foster Dept. OHJ
Boring, OR 97009
(503) 658-6400
MO RS/O
Manufacturer and contractor of decorative architectural elements for interior and exterior. Based upon project requirements and budgets, parts can be crafted from plaster, cast metals, fiberglass, or cast stone. Products range from an individually sculpted rosette to computer-formed sheet metal cornices. Most work custom; limited inventory of stock shapes and profiles also available. Free 4-page brochure with photos of recent work.

Architectural Resources Group
Pier 9, The Embarcardero Dept. OHJ
San Francisco, CA 94111
(415) 421-1680
RS/O
Professional architectural & urban planning services related to historic preservation, downtown revitalization, materials analysis and conservation, restoration & rehabilitation. Free literature.

• **Architectural Salvage Co.**
103 W. Michigan Ave. POBox 401 Dept. OHJ
Grass Lake, MI 49240
(517) 522-8516
MO RS/O
Retail outlet for architectural antiques specializing in doors, hardware, woodwork, stained glass, fixtures, mantles, columns etc. Also offer services including: Stained glass repair and reconditioning, expert carpentry, installation. Free brochure.

Architectural Salvage of Santa Barbara
726 Anacapa St. Dept. OHJ
Santa Barbara, CA 93101
(805) 965-2446
RS/O
This company offers a wide range of fixtures, ornaments, and other salvaged house parts. Specializes in Spanish-style wrought iron. No literature.

• **Architectural Sculpture Ltd.**
242 Lafayette Street Dept. OHJ
New York, NY 10012
(212) 431-5873
RS/O MO
Custom-order and in-stock cast plaster ornament — medallions, mouldings, brackets, capitols, plaques, sculptures, etc. Specializing in Neo classic and turn-of-the-century restoration ornament. They have replicated pieces for many landmark NYC interiors. Showroom hours T-F, 10-6, Sat. 12-5. Catalog is $2.

Architectural Shapes, Inc.
Suite 216 Marsh Creek Ctr. Dept. OHJ
Exton, PA 19341
(215) 363-0466
MO RS/O
They make a glass-reinforced gypsum that can be moulded into corners, coves, mouldings and the like; the surface can be painted, stained, or covered with wallpaper, metal, or ceramic tiles. Call or write for more information.

• See Advertisers' Index on page 22 for more details.

Architectural Stairbuilding and Handrailing
62 Pioneer St. Dept. OHJ
Cooperstown, NY 13326
(607) 547-2675
RS/O MO
Provides professional, individualized custom stair and handrail work. All phases of common, intricate, straight, curved, new and alteration work. Stair and handrail work matched or copied. All woods, all work special order only. Material shipped anywhere F.O.B. Cooperstown, N.Y. Planning, layout design and consulting services available.

Architectural Woodworking
347 Flax Hill Rd. Dept. OHJ
Norwalk, CT 06854
(203) 866-0943
RS/O MO
Fine architectural woodwork. Cost estimates provided upon receipt of detailed material specifications. Consultation services available. No literature.

Archive
32 N. Second St., Library Hall Dept. OHJ
Easton, PA 18042
(215) 258-3193
RS/O
Restoration design and development consulting services. Specialists in sensitive restorations of and additions to historically or architecturally significant residential properties. Preparation of master plan work to that end. Interior and exterior color and decorative design recommendations. Measured drawings, histories, and architectural services relating to Department of the Interior tax credit projects. Architectural illustrations and identity programs. No literature.

Arden Forge
301 Brinton's Bridge Rd. Dept. OHJ
West Chester, PA 19382
(215) 399-1530
MO RS/O
Specializing in accurate reproductions of period iron work, hand-forged from original examples. Interior & exterior hardware, household accessories for kitchen, fireplace, etc. Also, Victorian hardware, and new-old hardware. Will also restore antique metalwork.

Arkitektura
PO Box 210 Dept. OHJ
Princeton, NJ 08540
(313) 646-0097
DIST
A collection of furniture and accessories designed by Eliel and Eero Saarinen for the Cranbrook Educational Community in Bloomfield Hills, Michigan. Furniture designs are authorized reproductions and available to the public for the first time. The designs are dated from 1925-1930; prices range from $1750 for a cigarette table to $15,000 for a credenza. Free folder woth color photos.

Arlan Kay & Associates
110 King Street Dept. OHJ
Madison, WI 53703
(608) 251-7515
RS/O
This is a full service architectural firm with emphasis on building recycling and restoration. They'll do inspection, historic certification, documentation, architectural and interior design, contract documents, and construction management. They have completed over 500 recycling/restoration projects. Free literature.

Armor Products
P.O. Box 445 Dept. OHJ
E. Northport, NY 11731
(516) 462-6228
MO RS/O
Sells clock movements for restoring grandfather, mantel and banjo clocks. Also plans for those who wish to make their own. Other items include lamp parts, specialty hardware, butler tray and ice box hinges, brassware, wood turnings, and wood toy parts. Catalog, $1.

Arroyo Restoration
78 N. Marengo, No. 29 Dept. OHJ
Pasadena, CA 91001
(818) 796-6345
RS/O
A total restoration company specializing in Craftsman/ Bungalow era (although they're happy to work on Victorians, too). Everything from plumbing, electricity, woodwork refinishing to reproduction Greene and Greene lighting fixtures (catalog, $3; $1.50 if picked up in person). Also, (818) 795-4926.

• **Art Directions**
6120 Delmar Blvd. Dept. OHJ
St. Louis, MO 63112
(314) 863-1895
RS/O MO
12,000 sq. ft. of architectural antiques — stained and beveled glass windows and entrance ways; hundreds of light fixtures including large-and small-scale bronze, brass, crystal, gas, and electric; front and back bars; custom-built millwork; paneled rooms, columns, bronze work bank cages, architectural woodwork, mantels, trim, corbels. Comprehensive catalog, $4.

• **Art Glass Studio Inc.**
333 Flatbush Ave. Dept. OHJ
Brooklyn, NY 11217
(718) 857-6888
RS/O
Original creations in stained, sandblasted, carved, and leaded glass, custom work. Stained & leaded glass repair. Free estimates with stamped self-addressed envelope. Send dimensions. No literature.

Art Safe Inc.
Box 185 Dept. OHJ
Boscobel, WI 53805
MO
A supplier of safety equipment all of which has been chosen to fulfill the special needs of artists, craftspeople, and related fields. Also, literature pertaining to safety and health in the arts. Free brochure.

KEY TO ABBREVIATIONS

MO sells by Mail Order
RS/O sells through Retail Store or Office
DIST sells through Distributors
ID sells only through Interior Designers or Archtects

Artifacts, Inc.
PO Box 1787 Dept. OHJ
Middleburg, VA 22117
(703) 364-2722
MO RS/O
Specializing in early country mantels and doors. Photographs furnished upon request.

Artistic Brass/A MASCO Company
4100 Ardmore Avenue Dept. OHJ
South Gate, CA 90280
(213) 564-1100
DIST
Manufacturers of decorative, solid brass fittings for the lavatory, tub, shower, bidet, and bar. Matching accessories in Wedgwood, crystal, porcelain, onyx, gemstones, marble, and solid ash wood. Backed by a 5-year limited warranty on parts and finish, each fitting made of solid brass is polished, assembled, and tested by hand. A complete illustrated catalog is available for $5.00.

Artistic License in San Francisco
855 Alvarado St. Dept. OHJ
San Francisco, CA 94114
(415) 285-4544
RS/O
A guild of 22 artisans specializing in Victorian restoration. They are trained in all areas of Victorian architectural and decorative art restoration/design. They'll give slide presentations to the general public specifically interested in the Vicorrian period. Free brochure.

Artistic Woodworking, Inc.
163 Grand Ave. Dept. OHJ
Mt. Clemens, MI 48043
(313) 465-5700
MO RS/O
Specialist in furniture and cabinetmaking. Will reproduce a piece from a drawing or photograph — Victorian, Rococo, Renaissance, and Eastlake styles. Also, furniture restoration. Free literature.

A Second Wind for Harmoniums
256 Carroll Street Dept. OHJ
Brooklyn, NY 11231
(718) 852-1437
RS/O
Restoration, appraisal, voicing, tuning & general rehabilitation of reed organs, melodeons, and harmoniums. In-home service available. Greater NY area, unless the job is extensive & merits travel. Prefers telephone consultation (a.m. & eves).

Ashwood Restoration
Hammond House, Grasslands Rd. Dept. OHJ
Valhalla, NY 10595
(914) 592-2258
RS/O
A small company specializing in custom millwork and fine carpentry as well as structural problems in historic houses. References include Sunnyside, Phillipsburg Manor, Van Cortlant Manor. Call for more information.

Association for Preservation Technology
Box 2487, Station D Dept. OHJ
Ottawa, Ontario, Canada K1P5W6
(613) 238-1972
RS/O MO
Prior to the yearly APT conference, several coinciding 3-day technical training seminars are held. Also "Home Restoration" seminars upon request. They have also started 3-day technical, professional development workshops on rehabilitating historic buildings. The workshops are held in the South, Midwest, West, Mid-Atlantic, and New England. U.S. Office: 1100 17th St., NW, Suite 1000, Washington, DC 20036. Free information.

Astrup Company
2937 W. 25th St. Dept. OHJ
Cleveland, OH 44113
(216) 696-2800
DIST
This 110 year old company makes fine fabric and the hardware for awnings. Window awnings not only keep a room cooler and save on air conditioning costs, but add an appropriate decorative feature to late 19th and turn-of-the-century houses. Write for free information.

Atlantic Stairworks
PO Box 244 Dept. OHJ
Newburyport, MA 01950
(617) 462-7502
MO RS/O
Custom-made free-standing and spiral stairs in traditional and contemporary styles. Steps and handrails are solid hardwood in a variety of finishes; stringers are fine hardwood. Free brochure.

• **Authentic Designs Inc.**
The Mill Road Dept. H
W. Rupert, VT 05776
(802) 394-7713
MO DIST RS/O
Handcrafted recreations of 18th and 19th century lighting fixtures. Chandeliers, sconces, table lamps: all fixtures made of solid American brass, Vermont maple turnings. Electrified and for candles. Finishes available include hand burnished antique brass, polished and lacquered brass, antique pewter plating, gunmetal plating, and paint to order. Also outdoor post and wall-mounted lanterns. Modifications and custom work. 64-page catalog for $3.

Authentic Lighting
558 Grand Avenue Dept. OHJ
Englewood, NJ 07631
(201) 568-7429
MO RS/O
Reproduction and restoration of all types of lighting fixtures. Services include fixture cleaning, rewiring, mounting of lamps, polishing. Also metal polishing for beds, tables, fixtures, etc. Crystal in stock. Reproduction sconces and fixtures at reasonable prices. No literature; please call or write with specific request.

Avalon Forge
409 Gun Road Dept. OHJ
Baltimore, MD 21227
(301) 242-8431
MO
Authentic replicas of 18th century goods for living history and restorations. Emphasis on military and primitive goods. Examples - Hornware: snuffboxes, dippers, cups, combs. Tinware: cups, canteens, plates. Leather: cartridge boxes, handmade shoes, buckets. Tools: pitchforks, axes, bill hooks, tomahawks. Woodware: bowls, trenchers, spoons. Cookware: cast iron pots, spiders. Printed matter: maps, cards, books. Illustrated catalog $2.

• See Advertisers' Index on page 22 for more details.

B

B&B Glass Etching
6408 Hilly Way Dept. OHJ
Cary, IL 60013
(312) 639-3017
RS/O
Glass panel engraving, popular from 1860 to early 1900s. Duplicate missing or broken panels used as door glass, sidelights, transoms. Not a simulation, but the original process. Design is carved into a frosted glass panel, then polished.

B & P Lamp Supply Co., Inc.
Route 3 Dept. OHJ
McMinnville, TN 37110
(615) 473-3016
MO DIST
Manufacturers and wholesalers of reproduction lighting fixtures and parts. Selection includes hand-blown and hand-decorated glass shades, solid brass parts, and UL approved wiring components. Also specialize in reproductions of and parts for — "Gone with the Wind", Handel, Tiffany, Aladdin, and Emeraldlite fixtures. Complete color catalog and price list for dealers only $5., refundable.

Backlund Moravian Tile Works
46 Ocean Drive Dept. OHJ
Key Largo, FL 33037
(305) 852-5865
MO DIST
Over 300 hand-painted embossed tiles copied from an interesting variety of sources: medieval churches, Mexican and Yucatan codices, coats of arms, etc. Custom work also, even to life size mosaics made in the manner of a jig saw puzzle. Illustrated 4 color catalog with wholesale and/or retail price lists — $1.25.

Backstrom Stained Glass et al
PO Box 2311 Dept. OHJ
Columbus, MS 39704
(601) 329-1254
MO RS/O
Architectural antiques and custom-made stained glass windows — your pattern scaled up or down. Repairs and glass etching too. No literature available.

Backwoods Furnishings
Box 161 Route 28 Dept. OHJ
Indian Lake, NY 12842
(518) 251-3327
MO RS/O
Rustic furniture, such as tables and chairs made of twigs, custom-made to specifications. Rockers, four-poster beds, desks. Color flyer is free.

Bailey Architectural Millwork
125 Slack Ave. Dept. OHJ
Trenton, NJ 08648
(609) 392-5137
RS/O
Custom millwork including stair rail duplication. No literature.

John Morgan Baker, Framer
PO Box 149 Dept. OHJ
Worthington, OH 43085
(614) 885-7040
MO
Custom-made frames of solid curly or birdseye maple for paintings, watercolors, needlework; elegant mirrors for decorative/architectural purposes (entry hall, bath, bedroom). Options available in any combination: mitered or hard-to-find block corners, dark or light stains, antique gold inner liner, many others. Stand-up table frames in standard sizes; custom options available. $1 for brochure, color photos.

Baldwin Hardware Mfg. Corp.
841 Wyomissing Blvd. Box 82 Dept. OHJ
Reading, PA 19603
(215) 777-7811
DIST
Solid brass exterior and interior latches, knobsets and handsets for period houses. Lighting fixtures, candlesticks, and accessories adapted from Early American designs. Bath accessories including towel bars, towel rings, tissue roll holders, robe hooks, soap dishes, toothbrush/tumbler holders, and glass shelves in solid brass with maintenance free, baked-on enamel finish. Color brochures available: hardware, $2; lighting, $3; bath, $.75.

• **Ball and Ball**
463 W. Lincoln Hwy. Dept. OHJ
Exton, PA 19341
(215) 363-7330
RS/O MO
Vast selection of reproduction hardware for 18th and 19th century houses. In addition to all types of hardware for doors, windows and shutters, the company also supplies security locks with a period appearance, lighting fixtures, and will also repair locks and repair or reproduce any item of metal hardware. Call or write for free mini-catalog or send $5 for complete 108-page catalog — revised in 1984. Close to 200 Victorian items now included.

Balmer Architectural Art Limited
69 Pape Avenue Dept. OHJ
Toronto, OT, Canada M4M2V5
(416) 466-6306
RS/O MO
Quality fibrous plaster and gypsum composition ornament. Cornices, ceiling centers, columns, pilasters, niches, domes, mantel and mantel ornament, restoration, sand sculpture, rib wall, panel mouldings and corners. Brochure free; full catalog $14.00; ceiling center brochure and cornice brochure, each $1.00.

Bangkok Industries, Inc.
Gillingham & Worth Streets Dept. OHJ
Philadelphia, PA 19124
(215) 537-5800
RS/O MO DIST
A wide variety of exotic hardwood flooring in pre-finished and unfinished plank, strip and parquet patterns—many of which can be used in period houses. Of special interest are 8 ornamental border patterns. Custom colored pre-finished parquet. Can be completely installed in one day. Free consultation available. Architectural grade paneling historically correct for period dens, formal drawing rooms, etc. Free illustrated brochures.

Bangor Cork Co., Inc.
William & D Streets Dept. OHJ
Pen Argyl, PA 18072
(215) 863-9041
DIST
True linoleum imported from Holland. Available in 8 colors, Battleship Linoleum is homogeneous through to the backing to resist indentation from dynamic and static loads. Free literature.

Bank Architectural Antiques
1824 Felicity St. Dept. OHJ
New Orleans, LA 70113
(504) 523-2702
RS/O
They offer a wide variety of original and reproduction building materials. Always in stock are bevelled and stained glass, brass hardware, mantels, millwork, doors, shutters, brackets, and columns. In addition they offer wood stripping and carry reproduction shutters, French doors, stair railings, interior and exterior spindles, and newels. No literature.

Barap Specialties
835 Bellows Ave. Dept. OHJ
Frankfort, MI 49635
(616) 352-9863
MO
Mail-order catalog supplies for cane & caning tools. Also, brass hardware, lamp parts, finishing materials, turned wood parts and other do-it-yourself supplies. Catalog, $1.

• **Barclay Products Ltd.**
424 N. Oakley Blvd. Dept. OHJ
Chicago, IL 60612
(312) 243-1444
MO
Full line of quality Victorian and turn-of-century reproduction bathroom accessories. Includes many models for the CONVERTO SHOWERS, which allows a shower to be added to existing bath tubs. Other products are cast iron enameled sinks, Chicago Faucet Renaissance Collection, Speakman d'Elegance Collection, claw footed bathtubs, brass and copper sinks, brass fittings for exposed plumbing, custom size shower curtains and brass bathroom accessories. All items available for immediate delivery. Free catalog.

Bare Wood Inc.
106 Ferris St. Dept. OHJ
Brooklyn, NY 11231
(212) 875-9037
MO RS/O
Custom manufacture 18th and 19th century architectural Millwork, interior and exterior. Selection of antique doors, mantels, staircase parts, etc. Their trained craftsmen include hand-carvers, turners, and cabinetmakers. Specialize in custom restoration or duplication of moulding or other details in your choice of wood. Consulting services available. Inquiries should be specific. Free flyer.

The Barn People, Inc.
P.O. Box 4 Dept. OHJ
South Woodstock, VT 05071
(802) 457-3943
RS/O MO
Offer 18th and 19th century Vermont barns, and frames of post and beam construction which have been dismantled, repaired/restored, shipped to any new site, anywhere in the United States and reassembled. Stock of salvaged building materials. Barn moving. Also design related and consulting services, such as residential design and feasibility cost studies for restoration or relocation of barns in the Northeast. Portfolio (inventory, photo, etc.) is $10.

Barnard Chemical Co.
P.O. Box 1105 Dept. OHJ
Covina, CA 91722
(213) 331-1223
DIST
Manufactures fire retardant paints, coatings and varnishes. Coatings, for example, can add fire resistance to fine interior wood panel or exterior shakes and shingles. Will direct inquirers to nearest distributor or will fill orders direct from their warehouse when necessary. Free brochures.

• **Barnstable Stove Shop**
Box 472, Rt. 149 Dept. OHJ
W. Barnstable, MA 02668
(617) 362-9913
MO RS/O
This store buys, sells and restores antique wood and coal stoves. Will do foundry, recasting, nickel plating, and complete rebuilds of your stove or choose from inventory of over 300 stoves. Large inventory of parts. Brochure available $1; write or call with your needs.

The Bartley Collection, Ltd.
747 Oakwood Avenue Dept. OHJ
Lake Forest, IL 60045
(312) 634-9510
MO
The Bartley Collection offers 130 authentic Queen Anne and Chippendale style furniture reproductions available either hand made or in kit form. Many of these pieces are exact reproductions of 18th-century originals. The furniture is hand-crafted from solid Honduras mahogany and Pennsylvania cherry. Kits include instructions and wipe-on finishing materials. Price range: $65 to $1600. Free 16-page color catalog.

Bartleys Mill
8515 San Leandro St. Dept. OHJ
Oakland, CA 94621
(415) 569-5533
MO DIST RS/O
Old mouldings reproduced. Custom mouldings in all woods. All phases of restoration projects: consultation; moulding design & selection, fabrication, millwork, turnings and on-site installations. Sales offices in Oakland and San Francisco. Free informational letter.

Bassett & Vollum Wallpapers
217 N. Main St. Dept. OHJ
Galena, IL 61036
(815) 777-2460
RS/O
Specializes in reproductions of traditional border designs suitable for restoration. Borders, with matching sidewall papers, are available in widths from 1 to 21 inches. Folder describing their border patterns is available free. Available in stock colorings and/or as special orders.

Bay City Paint Company
2279 Market Street Dept. OHJ
San Francisco, CA 94114
(415) 431-4914
MO RS/O
Since 1937, Bay City Paint Co. has supplied professional painters, artists, finishers, and "do-it-yourselfers" with specialty paints and brushes. They stock Japan colors, caseins, aniline dye stains, and glaze coat plus woodgraining tools including metal and rubber combs, rubber rollers, pipe-over grainers, floggers, badger blenders, and French round sash brushes for wall glazing. Inventory includes leafing supplies and such hard to find items as bronze powders, lacquer sticks, orange shellac flakes, cotton waste and granular hide glues.

Barbara Vantrease Beall Studio
20309 Gramercy Place Dept. OHJ
Torrance, CA 90501
(213) 618-8878
MO DIST RS/O
Custom hand-painted tile, custom-colored field tile, and various handmade tiles in landscape, floral, nautical, etc. patterns.

Nelson Beck of Washington, Inc.
920 U St. NW Dept. OHJ
Washington, DC 20001
(202) 387-4114
ID
Upholstered furniture restored and reupholstered. Period draperies - various types of poles, wood and metal. Custom finials for poles. Tab curtains, Austrian shades. Will supply fabrics or will use client's fabrics. Trade shop only - no literature.

Bedlam Brass
137 Route 4 Westbound Dept. OH
Paramus, NJ 07652
(201) 368-3500
RS/O
Complete bar rail systems for commercial or residential use. Individual components can be purchased. Also, solid- brass furniture — reproductions of antique designs, but in today's sizes. Bed and accessories catalog, $3. Bar & handrail catalog, $1. Data sheet of parts for repairing antique brass or cast-iron beds, $1.

• **Beech River Mill Co.**
Old Rt. 16 Dept. OHJ
Center Ossipee, NH 03814
(603) 539-2636
MO
Housed in Smart's Mill (established in 1856), this company manufactures custom exterior and interior, louvered or panelled shutters using the mill's original water-powered machinery. They use traditional mortise-and- tenon joinery, and can duplicate any shutter for the restoration of old buildings. They also make louvered doors, room dividers and vents. Send $2 for brochure.

Beecham Home Improvement Products, Inc.
PO Box 277 Dept. OHJ
Dayton, OH 45401
(513) 667-4461
MO DIST RS/O
Manufacturer of caulks, sealants, wood fillers and repair products, coatings, wood preservatives and stains, adhesives that are available in most hardware stores or through their offices. Brands include: DAP, Dow-Corning, Derusto, Broma, Touch 'n Tone, Tuff 'n Easy, Woodlife, Weldwood, and PermaBond.

Behlen, H. & Bros.
Rt. 30 North Dept. OHJ
Amsterdam, NY 12010
(518) 843-1380
DIST
The largest stock of traditional and old world finishing supplies and products for hardwood finishing and paintings. Among the 90-year-old company's specialities: bronze powder and paste, lacquer tinting colors, wood fillers and glue, various lacquers, stains (including dry aniline) specialty waxes, hard-to-find brushes and tools, and varnish. Complete line of gilding supplies. Sold through distributors only.

Beirs, John — Glass Studio
225 Race St. Dept. OHJ
Philadelphia, PA 19106
(215) 923-8122
MO RS/O
Leaded and bevelled glass. No literature.

KEY TO ABBREVIATIONS

MO	sells by Mail Order
RS/O	sells through Retail Store or Office
DIST	sells through Distributors
ID	sells only through Interior Designers or Archtects

Bel-Air Door Co.
322 S. Date Ave., PO Box 829 Dept. OHJ
Alhambra, CA 91802
(213) 283-3731
MO DIST
Handcrafted carved exterior wood doors (with designed panels and openings) in fir and mahogany, and oak; and a collection of bevelled, leaded, and etched glass. Several are suitable for Victorian, Tudor-style, Chippendale, and turn-of-the-century influenced houses. Security and fire-rated doors available. Standard door size: 30 in., 32 in., 36 in. x 80 in. x 1-3/4 in. Special sizes upon request. Illustrated brochures $1.50. Also, (818) 576-2545.

Belcher, Robert W.
2505 West Hillview Dr. Dept. OHJ
Dalton, GA 30720
(404) 259-3482
RS/O
Has a supply of old weathered chestnut rails for zig-zag stacked rail fences. Supplies old barnboards, 55-gal. oak barrels and old yellow poplar and oak beams. Also has old hand hewn log houses, and consults on log house restoration. No literature; call for prices.

Bench Manufacturing Co.
390 Pond Street Dept. OHJ
So. Weymouth, MA 02190
(617) 436-3080
MO
Promenade benches in many styles, planters, trash receptacles, and street post clocks. Ornamental cast-iron street light poles and fixtures. Please specify your interest for a free brochure.

• **Bendheim, S.A. Co., Inc.**
122 Hudson St. Dept. OHJ
New York, NY 10013
(212) 226-6370
MO RS/O
Supplier for replacement colonial-type window glass including mouth-blown panes. Also imported and domestic stained glass, rondells, crown bullions, bull's-eye, etc. Literature available.

Bendix Mouldings, Inc.
235 Pegasus Ave. Dept. OHJ
Northvale, NJ 07647
(201) 767-8888
MO DIST
Supplies a diversified assortment of unfinished decorative wood mouldings, metal and plastic mouldings plus an extensive stock of pre-finished, authentic and carefully crafted picture frame mouldings. Also carved wood ornaments, pearl beadings, open fretwork, dentils, rosettes, crowns, cornices, "Instalead" self adhesive lead reels and glass paint for stained glass effect, and scalloped plywood moulding. Illustrated catalog and price lists $2. Specify unfinished or pre-finished mouldings.

• **Benjamin Moore Co.**
51 Chestnut Ridge Road Dept. OHJ
Montvale, NJ 07645
(201) 573-9600
RS/O DIST
This major paint manufacturer has exterior and interior paints for early American houses — Historical Color Collection and Cameo Collection. There are free leaflets about these lines as well as these useful booklets — "Interior Wood Finishing", "Painting Walls, Ceilings and Trim" and "How To Paint The Outside of Your House."

• **Bentley Brothers**
918 Baxter Ave. Dept. OHJ
Louisville, KY 40204
(800) 824-4777
MO RS/O
Direct importers of Crown high-relief wallcoverings, including Anaglypta, Supaglypta, and newly introduced period Lincrusta designs. (Lincrusta is a registered trademark of Crown). Their store has a complete display of these products, including room settings. Catalog, $2.

Berea College Crafts
CPO No. 2347 Dept. OHJ
Berea, KY 40404
(606) 986-9341
RS/O MO
Reproductions of simple, classic period furniture - Empire armchairs, rope leg dining table, ladder back chairs, goose neck rocker. Also handcrafted decorative accessories and custom wrought iron work. Catalog, $2.

Bergamo Fabrics, Inc.
37-20 34th Street Dept. OHJ
Long Island City, NY 11101
(718) 392-5000
ID
Importers of fine fabrics. Available through interior designers. No literature.

Bergen Bluestone Co., Inc.
404 Rt. 17, PO Box 67 Dept. OHJ
Paramus, NJ 07652
(201) 261-1903
RS/O
A large supplier of bluestone, slate, granite, veneer stone, and landscaping stone. Showroom displays different uses. Inquiries welcome, but they can't generally ship stone. Free brochure.

Bernard Restoration
81 State Rd./Routes 5 & 10 Dept. OHJ
Whately, MA 01093
(413) 665-4425
RS/O MO
Silver, copper, nickel replating. Silver and pewter items cleaned and repaired. All types of brass and copper cleaned and polished; lamps rewired and refinished. Old fashioned hand-wiped tinning on copper and brass cookware (excluding teakettles). Large inventory of restored period lighting fixtures. Literature available upon request.

Berridge Manufacturing Co.
1720 Maury Dept. OHJ
Houston, TX 77026
(713) 223-4971
RS/O MO DIST
Manufactures metal roofing products, including Victorian classic and fish-scale metal shingles. Standing seam and batten seam metal roof systems are offered. These products are available in pre-finished galvanized steel, Galvalume, and copper. Catalog free.

Bertin Tile Studio
10 St. John Place Dept. OHJ
Port Washington, NY 11050
(516) 944-6964
RS/O
Handmade ceramic wall, floor, and fireplace tiles. Molds made to specifications. Custom size, design, and color. Handmade glazes. Restorations. Please call or write. No literature.

• **Besco Plumbing & Heating Sales**
729 Atlantic Ave. Dept. OHJ
Boston, MA 02111
(617) 423-4535
MO RS/O
This company specializes in plumbing supplies for repairing and restoring bathrooms including old fixtures, pedestal sinks, high tank toilets, tubs, faucets, and shower accessories in brass or nickel plate. They do installations, find pieces, buy, sell and trade. Complete catalog, $5.

Beta Timber Restoration System/Dell Corp.
PO Box 1462 Dept. OHJ
Rockville, MD 20850
(301) 279-2612
DIST
General contracting and carpentry services for all aspects of restoration. Consulting and training services in wood and timber restoration available. North American distributor for Beta Timber Restoration System. A system using epoxy mortar with specially fabricated polyfiber reinforcement rods. Information and/or list of licensed applicators of the Beta system is available. Experienced contractors wishing to be trained in epoxy techniques, contact Dell Corporation.

Beveled Glass Industries
6006 W. Washington Bl. Dept. OHJ
Culver City, CA 90232
(213) 657-1462
MO
Leaded and beveled glass panel inserts for doors and windows. Available through distributors, decorators, contractors, or architects. Showroom at D&D Building, Suite 825, 979 Third Avenue, New York, NY 10022. (212) 753-1380. For a full catalog, please send $5. Also, (800) 421-0518. In CA, (800) 231-4939.

• **Biggs Company**
105 E. Grace St. Dept. OHJ
Richmond, VA 23219
(804) 644-2891
MO
Reproductions of 18th century furniture. Several expensive lines are authentic historic reproductions licensed by Old Sturbridge Village, Independence National Historic Park. 82 pg. catalog and price list — $5.

Billard's Old Telephones
21710C Regnart Rd. Dept. OHJ
Cupertino, CA 95014
(408) 252-2104
MO RS/O
Old telephones and parts. Brass and oak sets. Old phones converted to modern use. Do-it-yourself kits available. Replica in oak of 1892 Kellogg crank phone, a working dial set. Their private museum also buys unusual telephones. Complete restoration parts catalog, $1., refundable on purchase.

• See Advertisers' Index
on page 22
for more details.

Biltmore, Campbell, Smith Restorations, Inc.
One Biltmore Plaza Dept. OHJ
Asheville, NC 28803
(704) 274-1776
RS/O
A company offering complete decorative restoration services: Stencilling, graining, gilding, and marbleizing. Will also clean and restore murals and interior stonework. Other services include cloth & paper hanging, wood & stone carving, and stained glass repair. Free literature.

Bioclean
1511 N. Philip St. Dept. OHJ
Philadelphia, PA 19122
(215) 739-6061
RS/O
Exterior building cleaning. Cleaning of all types of masonry. Paint removal from masonry and wood surfaces. Specialists in historic building work. Brochure available.

Bird — X, Inc.
730 W. Lake St. Dept. OHJ
Chicago, IL 60606
(312) 642-6871
MO
Supplier of complete line of bird-repelling products. Products include electronic ultrasonic bird repellers, bird lites, and chemical and steel needle roost inhibitors, bird netting, and lifelike, moving replica of the Pigeon Hawk. Free brochures and consultation service available.

Bix Process Systems, Inc.
PO Box 3091 Dept. OHJ
Bethel, CT 06801
(203) 743-3263
MO
Manufactures semi-paste and liquid paint removers. Also tung oil stains and varnishes. Sells portable units for on-site stripping of houses and furniture. Established business for 27 years. Complete illustrated catalog and discount price list, $1.

Bjorndal Woodworks
Rt. 1, Box 110 Dept. OHJ
Colfax, WI 54730
(715) 962-4389
MO
Custom millwork, sash & doors, baseboard, casing, plinth blocks, coves, cabinetmaking, and fine woodworking of all styles. For quote: specific style (sample preferred), quantity in linear feet, and wood desired. All inquiries answered promptly. No literature.

• Blaine Window Hardware, Inc.
1919 Blaine Dr. Dept. OHJ
Hagerstown, MD 21740
(301) 797-6500
MO RS/O
Large selection of contemporary replacement hardware for windows, closet doors, sliding doors, and patio doors. Hard-to-find and obsolete hardware is a specialty. Antique security and safety screens. Custom design, casting, and duplication available. Send sample for free identification and quotation. 64-page catalog, $2, refundable.

• See Advertisers' Index on page 22 for more details.

Blaschke Cabinet Glass
670 Lake Avenue Dept. OHJ
Bristol, CT 06010
(203) 584-2566
MO RS/O
Curved china cabinet glass — all sizes in stock. Literature available, call for appointment.

• Blenko Glass Co., Inc.
P.O. Box 67 Dept. OHJ
Milton, WV 25541
(304) 743-9081
RS/O MO
Clear or colored window glass, antique-style sheet glass for use in restoration work for the windows in old houses. Hurricane shades for use with candleholders. Price list free. Tableware catalog available, museum and wholesale outlet at factory. Factory brochure available. Tours encouraged.

Blue Ridge Shingle Co.
Dept. OHJ
Montebello, VA 24464
(703) 377-6635
MO
White oak shingles taper-sawn smooth today just as they were over 100 years ago (see article in OHJ Oct. 1984, pp 184). Historic authenticity. Exceptional durability. Authentic appearance is unique and quickly identifiable as White Oak. Ages rapidly to natural antique color and texture. Especially important for quality historic restorations. Supplied in 18 in. and 24 in. lengths. Free flyer and specs.

D. Blumchen & Co., Inc.
PO Box 929J Dept. OHJ
Maywood, NJ 07607
(201) 843-5251
MO
A high-quality line of reproduction Christmas decorations, including Victorian bead "icicles," blown-glass figural ornaments, and miniature hat boxes trimmed with gold embossed paper. Also many die-cut greeting cards; all items are exact reproductions. Catalog, $1. They also have a line of Easter cards and decorations.

• BOATECH
PO Box 1743 Dept. OHJ
Albany, NY 12201
(518) 463-7284
DIST
Manufacturer of the Ventinox stainless-steel chimney lining system, which is sold and installed by trained dealers nationwide. UL listed type 321 stainless, continuously welded. Ventinox reduces creosote formation; increases efficiency of heating appliance; improves safety. Good installer servicing and guarantee. Also sells stove connector for safe installation of fireplace insert stoves. Free literature.

Joan Bogart
Box 265 Rockville Centre Dept. OHJ
New York, NY 11571
(516) 764-0529
MO RS/O
Specializes in Victorian lighting, gas chandeliers, Argand, Astral lamps. Showroom, by appointment: 617 Seaman Ave., Baldwin, NY.

Bombay Company, The
Box 79186, 5678 Bl. Mnd. Rd. Dept. OHJ
Fort Worth, TX 76179
(817) 232-5650
MO RS/O
A selection of English and traditional antique reproductions, wine, butler-, coffee-, end-, and occasional-tables. Furnishings are mahogany finished; offered at a affordable price. Free color catalog. Call toll free (800) 535-6876. In Texas call (817) 232-5650; Dept. 9263.

• Bona Decorative Hardware
3073 Madison Rd. Dept. OHJ
Cincinnati, OH 45209
(513) 321-7877
RS/O MO
Decorative hardware — mostly formal French and English in style. Bathroom fittings and accessories- several designs are appropriate for period houses. Also black iron door & cabinet hardware, brass rim locks, porcelain door knobs, fireplace tools, and accessories. Also of interest are their brass bar rail hardware and brass sliding door pulls; faucets for footed tubs and brass sinks. Illustrated catalog and price list, $2.

Boomer Resilvering
603 N. Court St. Dept. OHJ
Visalia, CA 93291
(209) 734-2188
MO RS/O
Specialize in resilvering antique mirrors; cost $8./sq. ft. Out-of-town customers can crate & ship mirrors for resilvering. For local customers they offer custom woodworking services including replacement parts for furniture, re-veneering, and refinishing. No literature.

Nancy Borden Period Textile Replicas
PO Box 4381 Dept. OHJ
Portsmouth, NH 03801
(603) 436-4284
MO RS/O
Custom historic fabric replications of window treatments, bed hangings, slip casings, upholstery all to specific desired period. Specializes in museum-documented fabrics, their appropriate household uses, 17th, 18th and 19th century. Travel U.S. for in-home consultation (per diem basis). Write directly with specific interests.

Boren Clay Products Company
PO Box 368 Dept. OHJ
Pleasant Garden, NC 27313
(919) 674-2255
DIST RS/O
One of the largest manufacturers of clay face brick in the U.S. No literature.

Botti Studio of Architectural Arts
919 Grove St. Dept. OHJ
Evanston, IL 60201
(312) 869-5933
MO RS/O
Designers, fabricators & installers of original stained & faceted glass windows. Will do extensive remodling and restoration throughout the U.S. The firm has been continually in business over 150 years. Free literature.

T.J. Bottom Industries, Inc.
PO Box 546; Hy. 19 South Dept. OHJ
Cuba, MO 65453
(800) 322-3270
MO DIST
Stock and custom sizes and colors of window awnings and door canopies. Made from Textilene Sunsure fabric that gives additional cooling.

Boulder Stained Glass Studios
1920 Arapahoe Ave. Dept. OHJ
Boulder, CO 80302
(303) 449-9030
MO RS/O
Designs and manufactures high-quality, handcrafted reproductions of Victorian and Art Nouveau window panels to fit any opening. Colored and bevelled glass. Specialists in reproducing etched glass — sandblasted or acid etched finish. Replacement of bent, colored glass panels in antique lampshades. Also appraisals & expert repair of antique windows and lampshades.

Bow & Arrow Stove Co.
11 Hurley St. Dept. OHJ
Cambridge, MA 02141
(617) 492-1411
MO RS/O
Replacement parts for Vermont Castings, Jotul, Lange, Godin, Coalbrookdale, and Waterford stoves. Distributors of "Vitroliner" stainless steel and enamel coated chimney liners, and prefabricated chimneys such as Selkirk Metalbestos which are adequate for use with coal fuel. They also distribute Abingdon tin ceilings and Hunter ceiling fans. Also store at 885 Main St., Cape Cod, Osterville, MA 02655. Free literature.

Bow House, Inc.
PO Box 228 Dept. OHJ
Bolton, MA 01740
(617) 779-6464
MO
An architect-designed package that offers the buyer an authentic reproduction of a bow-roof Cape Cod house. The package supplies to the builder those items necessary for the period character of the house: roof and siding materials, trim, windows, doors, hardware, stairs, glass, etc; specifications working drawings, manual and detail book. Illustrated brochure — $5.00. Also — a belvedere or gazebo of classic and generous proportions is available in kit form. Illustrated brochure $2.

Larry Boyce & Associates, Inc.
PO Box 421507 Dept. OHJ
San Francisco, CA 94142
(415) 923-1366
RS/O
An organization of artists trained in architectural ornamental painting. They are most renowned for elaborate 19th & 20th century room stencillings, but they also do (and restore) gilding and leafing, secco, in-fill painting, glazing, and decoupage wallpapering. Their work has been featured in major publications such as Smithsonian Magazine, the New York Times, and Historic Preservation. Flyer available upon request.

• **Bradbury & Bradbury Wallpapers**
PO Box 155-C Dept. OHJ
Benicia, CA 94510
(707) 746-1900
MO
Designers and handprinters of Victorian style wallpapers for decorators, homeowners, museums, and commercial interiors. A small firm willing to work directly with clients. They handprint reasonably-priced, hard-to-find specialties: borders, friezes, ceiling decorations, multi-design roomsets, and Morris papers. Available by mail order. Catalog, with black & white and color illustrations, is $2 bulk-rate or $3 first-class.

• **Bradford Consultants**
16 E. Homestead Ave. Dept. OHJ
Collingswood, NJ 08108
(609) 854-1404
MO
Phoenix lightbulbs — the perfect bulbs for period fixtures. "Edison" style: carbon loop bulbs — 1880 to 1918. "Mazda" style: zig-zag cage filament in a straight side bulb — 1909 to 1930. "Apollo" Golden Lamp Cord, authentic twisted, silk-covered cord for all reproduction and original period lamps. Free literature.

Bradford Derustit Corp.
Curtis Ind. Pk., RFD 3 Rt. 67 Dept. OHJ
Ballston Spa, NY 12020
(518) 885-4307
MO DIST
B.P. Metal Cleaner: a biodegradable, non-corrosive rust and oxide remover that does not harm metal, finishes or normal skin. Liquid or paste formulas. Also B-P No. 1 Brightner — a metal cleaner for quick, economical removal of heat stains, discoloration and tarnish from stainless steel, chrome, nickel, copper or brass. Free literature.

Braid-Aid
466 Washington St. Dept. OHJ
Pembroke, MA 02359
(617) 826-6091
RS/O MO DIST
96-page color catalog featuring all the tools, materials & accessories needed for rug braiding and rug hooking. Wool by the yard and remnant poundage, kits, patterns, designs, instruction and rug backing. A full line of supplies for quilting, shirret, spinning and weaving. Illustrated and detailed catalog with color and "how-to-do-it" tips. $3 (U.S. funds) ppd. Also, (617) 826-2560.

Brandt Bros. General Contractors
8141 S. Talbot Ave. Dept. OHJ
Indianapolis, IN 46227
(317) 881-5929
RS/O
Primarily carpentry contractor but full complement of sub-contractors available if desired. Interior and exterior work. List of renovation projects in Indianapolis area can be furnished. No literature.

• **Sylvan Brandt**
653 Main St. Dept. OHJ
Lititz, PA 17543
(717) 626-4520
RS/O
Parts from loghouses and barns including antique glass, hardware, shutters, flooring, doors, and hand-hewn logs. Also, millstones and equipment. No literature.

Brass Bed Company of America
2801 East 11th St. Dept. OHJ
Los Angeles, CA 90023
(213) 269-9495
DIST
Over 500 brass and iron-and-brass bed styles, cheval mirrors, cradles, cribs, night stands, coat racks, entry hall stand. Also oak daybeds and tables, rattan beds, etc.

KEY TO ABBREVIATIONS

MO	sells by Mail Order
RS/O	sells through Retail Store or Office
DIST	sells through Distributors
ID	sells only through Interior Designers or Archtects

The Brass Finial
2408 Riverton Road Dept. OHJ-7
Cinnaminson, NJ 08077
(609) 786-9337
MO
Offers fine quality brass products including hard-to-find door and cabinet hinges, door lever sets, and replicas of Victorian plumbing fixtures. Also has a selection of interior accessories in coordinating styles to finish any restoration project. Generous quantity discounts and a variety of metal finishes along with a complete guarantee of satisfaction. Catalog, $1.

• **The Brass Knob**
2311 18th St. N.W. Dept. OHJ
Washington, DC 20009
(202) 332-3370
MO RS/O
Architectural antiques, specializing in brass hardware; lighting fixtures; mantels; firebacks; columns; doors; stained, etched, and leaded glass; bathroom fixtures; corbel brackets; ironwork; marble; tiles, and garden ornaments.

• **Brass Light Gallery**
719 S. 5th St. Dept. OHJ
Milwaukee, WI 53204
(414) 383-0675
MO DIST RS/O
Manufactures solid brass Mission/Prairie lighting fixtures. Also original commercial Holophane lights in various sizes. Restored antique fixtures: Victorian, Classical Revival, Art Deco, etc., ceiling, table, floor, or wall lighting. No literature on antique fixture; Mission/Prairie catalog, $3.

Brass Menagerie
524 St. Louis Street Dept. OHJ
New Orleans, LA 70130
(504) 524-0921
RS/O
Solid brass hardware & locks of all periods, antique & reproduction. Porcelain & wrought iron hardware, rim locks, unusual hardware: bar rails, solid brass drapery & curtain hardware, fireplace hooks, chandeliers, wall brackets and sconces. Bathroom fixtures & accessories of American and European design, including period toilets, with wall hung tanks, decorated sink bowls and turn-of- century pedestal type sinks. Send for free brochure.

• **The Brass Tree**
308 North Main St. Dept. OHJ
St. Charles, MO 63301
(314) 947-7707
MO RS/O
Brass hardware including door, furniture, Hoosier, ice box, desk and trunk hardware. They also sell furniture restoration supplies: wood and porcelain casters, furniture locks, fiber and wood chair seats, caning and weaving supplies, wood veneer, and wood ornaments. Catalog, $2.

• **Brasslight, Inc.**
90 Main Street Dept. H
Nyack, NY 10960
(914) 353-0567
MO DIST
Solid, brass desk lamps, wall sconces, and ceiling fixtures. A variety of interchangeable glass shades in green, brown, white, frosted, etc. Stylings include Edwardian and late Victorian. Some variations of style available on quantity purchases. All lamps and fixtures are polished and lacquered. Catalog, $3.

Braun, J.G. Co.
7540 McCormick, PO Box 66 Dept. OHJ
Skokie, IL 60076
(312) 761-4600
MO DIST
Complete selection of architectural metal extrusions & castings in aluminum, bronze, and steel. Featuring railing systems and component parts. Catalog, $1.

Breakfast Woodworks Mackall & Dickinson
50 Maple St. Dept. OHJ
Branford, CT 06405
(203) 488-8364
RS/O
Mackall & Dickinson, architects, and Breakfast Woodworks are two companies that work together to provide extensive architectural design and woodworking services. Almost any wooden element can be created. Design expertise allows for complete restoration or renovation services. Specialize in passive solar retrofit and additions. For more information, write or call.

Brewster's Lumberyard
211 Murphy Rd. Dept. OHJ
Hartford, CT 06100
(203) 549-4800
RS/O MO
Source for white-cedar roof shingles, clear and extra quality grade. Two yard locations: Milford, CT and Hartford. Will send shingles anywhere, but customer must call for particular shipping charges and delivery specifics. No shingle literature.

Briar Hill Stone Co.
PO Box 398 Dept. OHJ
Glenmont, OH 44628
(216) 276-4011
MO DIST RS/O
Quarriers of sandstone. Colors range from light buff and gray through tans, browns, chocolates, and reds. Sills, lintels, steps, balusters, and coping. Free information brochure. Full-color, 32-page fireplace book, $2.

Brick Stove Works
374 Nelson Ridge Rd. Dept. OHJ
Washington, ME 04574
(207) 845-2440
MO RS/O
The Brick Stove Works specializes in the design and construction of masonry stoves (Finnish or Russian) throughout New England. Also distributes and installs Tulikivi soapstone heaters/fireplaces. Brik-Doorsɸ evolved from the need to offer traditional design cast-iron clean outs that matched the beauty of the stoves. The Brik- Doors brochure and Masonry Stove brochure are free.

British-American Marketing Services, Ltd.
251 Welsh Pool Rd. Dept. OHJ
Lionville, PA 19353
(215) 363-0400
MO DIST RS/O ID
Solid teak benches from England, in historical 19th and early 20th designs with traditional mortise-and- tenon construction. Also Victorian street lighting in copper and brass with cast iron bases and wall brackets with posts of solid steel. All fittings UL approved. A limited number of antique posts taken from the streets of London are available. Brochure $.50. Also, (800) 344-0259.

Broad-Axe Beam Co.
RD 2, Box 417 Dept. OHJ
West Brattleboro, VT 05301
(802) 257-0064
MO
Authentically produced hand-hewn beams of white pine. Two types — structural and decorative — in standard 8, 12, 14 and 16 ft. lengths. Structural beams (7-1/2 in. square) $5.90 per linear ft.; decorative beams (3-1/2 x 7-1/2 in.), $4.00 per linear ft. Custom hewing done, plus random-width white pine flooring and panelling, hand-forged latches and hinges. Illustrated brochure and price list, $1.

Broadnax Refinishing Products, Inc.
P.O. Box 322 Dept. OHJ
Danielsville, GA 30633
(404) 795-2659
MO
Distributes Broadnax Furniture Refinisher for stripping old wood finishes, Lemon Oil for reviving old wood, and Tung Oil to seal and preserve. They have a book on refinishing furniture which includes helpful hints on cleaning and repairing finishes, preserving brass from tarnish, controlling bathroom mildew, etc. Customers receive periodic newsletter. Free flyer.

The Broadway Collection
250 N. Troost Dept. OHJ
Olathe, MO 66061
(800) 255-6365
DIST MO RS/O
Solid brass, porcelain, crystal, and wood bathroom fixtures/fittings. Standing lavatories; door hardware, cabinet hardware, and switch plates for Colonial & Victorian style architecture. Also decorative hardware of formal French/English derivation. Brass bar rail. 90-page illustrated catalog, $5.

Bronze et al
Holbrook Road Dept. OHJ
Briarcliff Manor, NY 10510
(914) 941-1015
MO RS/O
Restoration and patina service for bronze, brass, copper, and other non-ferrous metals. Capacities range from repairs on art sculpture (fixing scratches, dents, holes, damaged patina, remounting, fabrication and replacement of missing parts) to replication of antique hardware including 're-patina' (hinges, knobs, drawer pulls, latches, railings, ornamentation). Free literature.

Brooklyn Stone Renovating
458 Baltic St. Dept. OHJ
Brooklyn, NY 11217
(718) 875-8232
RS/O
Has expert masons who specialize in restoring brownstone stoops and facades. Will recreate carved ornament in brownstone stucco. Their services are in great demand, so you have to be persistent and prepared to wait awhile. No literature; call for appointment.

Brooklyn Tile Supply
184 4th Ave. Dept. OHJ
Brooklyn, NY 11217
(718) 875-1789
RS/O
Carries small white hexagonal bathroom tiles, 6 x 3 white tile, American Olean tiles, Mexican terra cotta, quarry tiles, and ceramic bathroom fixtures. No literature. Sells through store only.

Brookstone Company
709 Vose Farm Road Dept. 596A
Peterborough, NH 03458
(603) 924-7181
RS/O MO
High-quality, hard-to-find tools such as a wooden smoothing plane, a chamfer spokeshave, a flexible sole plane, extra-long drill bits. Free illustrated catalog.

Brown, T. Robins
12 First Avenue Dept. OHJ
Nyack, NY 10960
(914) 358-5229
RS/O
Consultant in architectural history and historic preservation, restoration, and renovation. Services available in the Middle Atlantic states and Conn. National Register and historic Preservation Tax Incentives applications. Historic sites survey work. Historic research. Preparation of walking tours and other publications about an area's architecture. No literature.

• **Brownstone Graphics**
106 Berkeley Place Dept. OHJ
Brooklyn, NY 11217
(718) 230-0510
MO RS/O
House portraits on fine quality stationery for letterheads, note cards, holiday cards, invitations, etc... Calligraphy available. Exterior or interior, drawn from photographs. Original pen-and-ink artwork available for framing. Complete information package with samples, free.

Brubaker Metalcrafts
209 N. Franklin St. Dept. OHJ
Eaton, OH 45320
(513) 456-5834
MO
Specializing in 18th-century reproductions of tin and brass wall sconces, candlemolds, chandeliers, and Paul Revere lanterns. Free brochure.

Bruce Hardwood Floors
16803 Dallas Parkway Dept. OHJ
Dallas, TX 75248
(214) 931-3000
RS/O
World's largest manufacturer of hardwood flooring with more 140 prefinished and unfinished flooring products. Choose from including 3/4 in. solid oak plank, 3/4 in. solid oak parquet, 3/8 in. laminated oak plank, 3/8 in. laminated oak parquet, and 5/16 in. solid oak parquet. Serves entire United States and Canada. Free information.

Brueggeman Roofing Co.
PO Box 63 Dept. OHJ
Silverton, CO 81433
(303) 387-5640
RS/O
Second- and third-generation roofers. Specialties include red-cedar shingles, Victorian restorations, flat ceramic roof tiles, copper flashing. Will travel throughout southwest and provide consulting and design services. Call or write for information; no literature.

• See Advertisers' Index on page 22 for more details.

• **Brunschwig & Fils, Inc.**
979 Third Avenue Dept. OHJ
New York, NY 10022
(212) 838-7878
ID
Museums, restoration and historical agencies use the fine reproductions of 18th, 19th and some 20th century fabric trimming and wallpaper made by this firm. A recent collection inspired by the Muse des Arts Deoratifs, coordinates chintzes and wallpapers in the French chinoiserie tradition. Their products are sold only through interior designers. No literature.

• **Bryant Stove Works**
R.F.D. 2, Box 2048 Dept. OHJ
Thorndike, ME 04986
(207) 568-3665
RS/O MO
Family-owned business restores and then sells antique cast-iron cookstoves and parlor heaters. They specialize in old kitchen ranges. Search service finds rare stoves for museums and historic restorations. Large stock of antique parts. Also The Bryant Stove Museum is a collection of rare ornate stoves, many one-of-a-kind. Shipping can be arranged anywhere. Free flyers. Catalog, 24 pages, $10.

• **Buckingham-Virginia Slate Corporation**
Box 11002, 4110 Fitzhugh Ave. Dept. OHJ
Richmond, VA 23230
(804) 355-4351
MO DIST
Excellent quality VA-region slate. Roofing slate available. Out-of-state shipping possible on orders. Samples and literature available upon request.

Bob Buckter, Color Consultant
3877 20th St. Dept. OHJ
San Francisco, CA 94114
(415) 922-7444
MO RS/O
Consultant for exterior paint colors of historic homes. Send preferences, photos, and an idea of what your neighborhood looks like for a paint-by-number scheme, recommendations about surface preparation; will travel to job site, can work with blueprints and provide color sequences for tracts or blocks.

Buddy Fife's Wood Products
9 Main St. Dept. OHJ
Northwood, NH 03261
(603) 942-8777
MO DIST RS/O
Handcrafted solid wood toilet seats. Also, bathroom vanities and wooden accessories. Custom-made items to order. Free catalog.

KEY TO ABBREVIATIONS

MO	sells by Mail Order
RS/O	sells through Retail Store or Office
DIST	sells through Distributors
ID	sells only through Interior Designers or Archtects

Building Conservation
2204 Ludington Ave. Dept. OHJ
Wauwatosa, WI 53226
MO
Plans are available in authentic Victorian styles for houses, gazebos, cottages, stables, garages, sheds, kennels and birdhouses in Gothic, Italianate, Stick, Queen Anne, Eastlake, & Colonial Revival. Featured are designs for energy-saving Victorian Solar Bay Window. Plans include dimensions, construction details and ornamental patterns using modern materials. Sizes are expandable to meet your needs. Send $5 for illustrated brochure.

Building Materials Inc.
139 Front St., PO Box 888 Dept. OHJ
Fall River, MA 02722
(617) 675-7809
RS/O
Supplier of various masonry supplies specializing in brick, bluestone, cement blocks, asphalt roofing, adhesives, waterproofings, lumber, and repair materials for masonry buildings. No literature.

Bullfrog Hollow
Halls Rd. Dept. OHJ
Old Lyme, CT 06371
(203) 434-8106
MO RS/O
Specialize in country decorative items for the home, especially the kitchen: tinware, cast iron, linens, wood, primatives, baskets, pottery, etc. Catalog, $1.

Burdoch Silk Lampshade Co.
11120 Roselle St. - Suite G Dept. OHJ
San Diego, CA 92121
(619) 458-1005
MO
Embroidered, hand-sewn fabric shades and lamp bases in Victorian, turn-of-the-century, and Art Deco styles. These highly decorative shades come in many colors including burgundy, honey beige, medium peach, and dark green. Can be used on table or floor-lamp bases. Send stamped, self-addressed envelope plus $2. for color flyer.

Burke and Bales Associates, Inc.
1330 Palmetto Ave. Dept. OHJ
Winter Park, FL 32789
(305) 647-1223
RS/O
This architectural firm has a restoration department capable of handling large renovation/restoration projects from residential to commercial, including creative adaptive use. Can provide architectural services for renovations or pure restoration for tax credit and assist the client in applying for a National Register of Historic Places Listing and/or tax credit eligibility. Also historic interior design services. Free brochure.

• **J.R. Burrows & Co.**
PO Box 418 Cathedral Station Dept. OHJ
Boston, MA 02118
(617) 451-1982
MO RS/O
Showroom and importer of a wide variety of Victorian reproductions, including wallpaper (embossed vinyl, imitation leather, Bradbury & Bradbury), Nottingham lace (both yards and finished panels), and traditional and documentary reproduction carpets. Also Minton reproduction pictorial tiles. Lace brochure, $2. Tile brochure, $2.

Burt Millwork Corp
1010 Stanley Ave. Dept. OHJ
Brooklyn, NY 11208
(718) 257-4601
RS/O
They manufacture wood windows and doors; also distribute other millwork products. Free list of products stocked & manufactured.

• **The Butcher Polish Co.**
120 Bartlett St. Dept. OH
Marlborough, MA 01752
(617) 481-5700
MO RS/O
Since 1880, Butcher's Paste Waxes for cleaning, protecting, and beautifying wood floors, furniture, antiques, and paneling have been a standard of quality. Literature: how-to Booklet: "More Handy Tips of Wood Care" — $.50.

• **ByGone Era Architectural Antiques**
4783 Peachtree Rd. Dept. OHJ
Atlanta, GA 30341
(404) 458-3016
RS/O MO
25,000 square feet of architectural antiques: lighting, stained and bevelled glass, staircases, doors, mantels, and columns. Specializing in bars, offices, restaurant furnishings. Always on hand: 200 stained glass windows, hundreds of doors and mantels, footed tubs, pedestal sinks, along with original fretwork and panelling. Stock constantly changing. Company will crate and ship. Call or write your needs.

C

C & D Distributors Hearth Mate
PO Box 766 Dept. OHJ
Old Saybrook, CT 06475
(203) 388-3408
MO DIST
Sells Hearth Mate wood, catalytic, and wood/coal stoves in both freestanding and fireplace models. They also make an add-on wood/coal hot air furnace and an Ultra-Burn Catalytic retrofit for top or rear exhaust. Also chimney cleaning equipment and stove accessories. Free brochures.

C & H Roofing
1713 South Cliff Ave. Dept. OHJ
Sioux Falls, SD 57105
(605) 332-5060
MO RS/O
In business for 10 years, this company specializes in steam-bent cedar shingle roofs (imitative of the English & cottage thatch style). Manufacture of bent wood shingles which can be installed by others. Also specializing in custom cedar shake and shingle roofs. Will travel for installation. References. Free information.

C.U. Restoration Supplies
1414 Cranford Dr. Dept. OHJ
Garland, TX 75041
(214) 271-0319
MO RS/O
A mail-order source for all types of products for the restoration and refinishing of antiques. Their "Everything for Antiques" Catalog includes brass furniture and house hardware, cane and rush seating supplies, pressed fibre seats, wood furniture parts, veneers, books, chemicals, tools, etc. Also, trunk parts, imported European hardware, and wood trims and replacement parts. Catalog, $2. Dealers send business card.

CW Design, Inc.
1618 Central Ave., NE Dept. OHJ
Minneapolis, MN 55413
(612) 789-5685
MO RS/O
Carved and chipped glass as well as acid etching on glass and/or mirrors using standard or custom designs or submitting your own black and white art work. Applications include windows, sidelights, doors, transoms, cabinet doors, bar or fireplace mirrors. For more information, please contact.

Cabot Stains
1 Union Street Dept. OHJ
Boston, MA 02108
(617) 723-7740
DIST
The first company to manufacture wood stains, including a line of weather stains, they make products primarily for exterior & interior wood surfaces . . . paneling, siding, clapboard, shingles and shakes. Free brochures and color cards.

Cain-Powers, Inc. Architectural Art Glass
Rt. 1, Box AAA Dept. OHJ
Bremo Bluff, VA 23022
(804) 842-3984
MO RS/O
Doors with bevelled glass inserts. Carved glass — period designs such as Victorian or Art Nouveau, Art Deco, as well as contemporary. In-house custom design available. Free flyer.

California Glass Bending Company
320 East 'B' Street Dept. OHJ
Wilmington, CA 90744
(213) 549-5255
RS/O
Specialize in bending glass for china cabinets, secretaries, show cases, Victorian style curved windows, etc. Free literature.

California Products Corp.
169 Waverly St., PO Box 569 Dept. OHJ
Cambridge, MA 02139
(617) 547-5300
DIST
Interior and exterior house paints, including Ox-Line, Colorizer, and California Paints brand names. California and Colorizer lines include Historic Newport Colors for exteriors. Company also distributes ColorGenie, a computer that can "look" at any paint sample and create a matching color. Available through most paint stores.

Cambridge Smithy
Dept. OHJ
Cambridge, VT 05444
(802) 644-5358
RS/O
Metal antique restoration; handwrought items; lighting fixtures; custom weathervanes. No literature.

KEY TO ABBREVIATIONS

MO sells by Mail Order
RS/O sells through Retail Store or Office
DIST sells through Distributors
ID sells only through Interior Designers or Archtects

Cambridge Textiles
Dept. OHJ
Cambridge, NY 12816
(518) 677-2624
RS/O MO
Professional conservation, preservation, and restoration of textiles: American samplers, quilts, Coptic, archeological textiles, tapestries, rugs, silk pictures. Safe, spacious studios. By appointment or ship insured parcel post, registered mail, or UPS. Free protocol flyer.

Michael Camp
636 Starkweather Dept. OHJ
Plymouth, MI 48170
(313) 459-1190
MO RS/O
Authentic replicas of 17th- and 18th-century furniture, hand-crafted by Michael Camp. They use carefully researched period methods (dovetailing, hand-planing and scraping), wide pine secondary woods. Beds, chairs, tables, low and highboys, desks, chests, cupboards. Details and catalog, $3.

Campbell Center for Historic Preservation Studies
PO Box 66 Dept. OHJ
Mount Carroll, IL 61053
(815) 244-1173
RS/O
Preservation training workshops are held on a variety of subjects related to Architectural Preservation, Furniture Conservation and Care of Museum Collections. The visiting faculty is composed of leading experts in the field. Courses are geared towards professionals and interested laypersons active in the preservation field. Phone or write for current schedule.

Campbell-Lamps
1108 Pottstown Pike, Dept. 25 Dept. OHJ
West Chester, PA 19380
(215) 696-8070
RS/O MO
New gas and electric shades from original molds. Lamp chimneys, lantern globes, and misc. glass lamp parts. Wholesale and retail. Cased glass shades including student shades and gas and electric. Solid cast brass parts for gas and electric lights. Distributor of Aladdin kerosene lamps and full line of replacement parts for most kerosene heaters. Aladdin catalog, $.75.

Campbell, Marion
39 Wall St. Dept. OHJ
Bethlehem, PA 18018
(215) 865-2522
RS/O
Architectural woodwork and furniture in American period styles designed and built to order. Authentic details and finest materials are used to match or recreate old work. Projects include, but are not limited to, mantels, paneling, cornices, valances, doors and door ways, shutters, built-in cabinets, chests, desks, tables, stands, bookcases., etc. Finishing and installation. Appointment necessary. Brochure $.50.

• **Campbellsville Industries**
PO Box 278 Dept. OHJ
Campbellsville, KY 42718
(502) 465-8135
MO
Manufacturers of aluminum cupolas, domes, steeples, weathervanes, cornices, louvers, balustrades, and columns for exterior ornamental use. (Columns are load- bearing.) Aluminum balustrades and railings have been reproduced in exact detail for historic buildings — also a selection of standard components. (Balustrades are primarily for roofs.) Free brochure available — please specify your interest.

Canal Co.
1612 14th St., N.W. Dept. OHJ
Washington, DC 20009
(202) 234-6637
RS/O
Architectural antiques including fully restored lighting fixtures from the 1860's thru the 1930's; fireplace mantels; stained and leaded glass; interior and exterior doors; medicine cabinets; handrails, newel posts, and balusters; columns; brass door hardware; pedestal sinks; iron fencing & window guards. No literature.

• **Cane & Basket Supply Company**
1283 South Cochran Avenue Dept. OJ
Los Angeles, CA 90019
(213) 939-9644
RS/O MO
Every supply necessary to re-cane, re-rush and re-splint chair seats. Related tools and supplies. Also furniture kits for a side chair and 3 stools. Illustrated catalog with price list — $1.

Caning Shop
926 Gilman St. Dept. OHJ
Berkeley, CA 94710
(415) 527-5010
MO RS/O
Cane webbing, chair cane, round and flat reeds, ash splints, Danish cord, rawhide, rattan, pressed fiber seats, Shaker tapes, how-to books. Authors of The Caner's Handbook. Basketry supplies include hoops and handles, classes, and how-to books. Catalog $1, refundable.

• **Canning, John, Ornamental Painter**
132 Meeker Rd. Dept. OHJ
Southington, CT 06489
(203) 621-2188
RS/O
John Canning apprenticed in Scotland, U.K., as house and church decorator. Skilled in the techniques used in decorative restoration, i.e. graining, marbleizing, stencilling, glazing, murals, trompe l'oiel and "faux" finishes. Services also include the investigation, paint analysis and conservation of historic decoration. No literature.

Canterbury Designs, Inc.
PO Box 5730 Dept. OHJ
Sherman Oaks, CA 91413
(213) 936-7111
RS/O MO
Company has a line of streetscape and mall furnishings — some pieces in period style. Of special interest are 4-faced outdoor clocks; oak and iron or aluminum benches; an 1890 hexagonal bench; and cast aluminum tree grates. (17-ft. 4-faced Victorian street clock is approximately $18,000.) Color catalog—free. Prices on specific request.

Cape Cod Bullseye Glass Co.
Box 533 Dept. OHJ
Barnstable, MA 02630
(617) 362-6808
MO
Hand-blown, bull's-eye glass window panes, with rough pontil mark, thicker concentric circle in center. Can be cut to size, for transoms, sidelights, or small sash: available in 10" x 10", 12" x 12", and 14" x 14". Free flyer.

Cape Cod Cupola Co., Inc.
78 State Road Dept. OHJ
North Dartmouth, MA 02747
(617) 994-2119
RS/O MO DIST
Wooden cupolas in a variety of sizes and styles. Over 200 weathervane designs in a choice of finishes and sizes. Illustrated catalog and price list — $1.00.

Caradco
PO Box 920 Dept. OHJ
Rantoul, IL 61866
(217) 893-4444
MO DIST
Caradco offers a complete line of wood windows, both double-hung and casement, some of which are appropriate for old houses. Free brochure.

Carl Schilling Stoneworks
61 Main St. Dept. OHJ
Proctor, VT 05765
(802) 459-2000
MO RS/O
Restoration, reconstruction, and carving of stone by a company in operation since 1882. Also exterior cladding and thin tile available in marble, limestone, and Brownstone Russet (a.k.a. New York brownstone) from their quarries. A company with bases in West Germany and the U.S. Free flyer.

• **Carlisle Restoration Lumber**
Rt. No. 123 Dept. OHJ
Stoddard, NH 03464
(603) 446-3937
RS/O MO
Restoration lumber dealer selling wide pine or oak boards, ship-lapped boards, feather-edge clapboards. Free brochure — please specify your needs for a price quote. Will also consult on and design wood flooring and panelling; serves the Maryland to Maine region. No literature; call or write for appointments.

Carpenter Assoc., Inc.
40 Timber Swamp Rd. Dept. OHJ
Hampton, NH 03842
(603) 926-3801
RS/O MO
They produce custom designs as well as reproduction pieces of any wood product with an historic architectural reference. Any type custom millwork including stairways, kitchens, turnings, windows, doors and entrances, mantels, all types of period wall paneling, and much more. Forward your specific needs for price quotations. Call for more information.

• **Carpenter and Smith Restorations**
Box 504 Dept. OHJ
Highland Park, IL 60035
(312) 831-5047
RS/O
A woodworking shop specializing in restoration and custom woodworking. Commercial and residential structural repair and design consultant. Interior and exterior renovation — large and small scale. Quality cabinetmaking services — adaptations and reproductions. Antique refurbishing with related leatherwork and metalwork. Furniture restored, designed, and built to order. No literature.

Carriage Trade Antiques & Art Gallery
402 Student St. Dept. OHJ
Greenville, NC 27834
(919) 757-1982
MO RS/O
Unique services for the collector: they will search for you on a cost-plus basis. Their refinishing department does all work by hand; also custom restoration and relining of antique trunks. Interior design consultation, and cataloging & appraisal of household items of value. No literature. References available.

Carson, Dunlop & Associates, Ltd.
597 Parliament St., Ste. B-5 Dept. OHJ
Toronto, ON, Canada M4X1W3
(416) 964-9415
RS/O
A certified professional engineering company (APEO), members of the American Society of Home Inspectors. Prepurchase home inspection services available in the greater Toronto area. Written report includes analyses of structure, heating, plumbing, wiring, insulation, interior and exterior finishes. Budget figures are also offered for recommended improvements. Purchasers are invited to attend inspection. Brochure available on request.

• **Carter Canopies**
PO Box 808 Dept. OH5
Troutman, NC 28166
(704) 528-4071
MO
Custom hand-tied fishnet bed canopies, in natural or white, 100% cotton, hand washable. Also supplies custom dust ruffles. Free brochure; dealer inquiries welcome.

CasaBlanca Fan Co.
450 N. Baldwin Park Blvd. Dept. OHJ
City of Industry, CA 91746
(800) 423-1821
DIST
Manufacturers of a full line of quality ceiling fans. Sold through distributors nationwide. Write for name of nearest retailer.

Cassen, Henry Inc.
245 Newtown Road Dept. OHJ
Plainview, NY 11803
(516) 249-3100
ID
Irish point, lace embroidered, net, and tambour curtains. No literature, but will answer specific inquiries from the trade.

Cassidy Bros. Forge, Inc.
U.S. Route 1 Dept. O83
Rowley, MA 01969
(617) 948-7611
MO RS/O
Cassidy Bros. Forge is a manufacturer of standard and custom-made forged reproduction hardware, lighting devices, fireplace accessories and architectural metalwork. Catalog, $1.

Castle Burlingame
R.D. 1, Box 352 Dept. OHJ
Basking Ridge, NJ 07920
(201) 647-3885
RS/O
Specialists exclusively in antique wide-board flooring, both soft eastern white pine & hard long leaf yellow pine. Three booklets available: "Where to find and how to select antique flooring"; "How to install antique flooring — step by step"; "How to sand and finish antique flooring." $5.99 each plus $1.50 for postage & handling.

Castle Roofing Co., Inc.
107 W. 26th St., No. 2 Dept. OHJ
New York, NY 10001
(212) 989-2029
RS/O
Castle Roofing Co. works exclusively installing slate and copper roofs. High quality, high tech. Artistic, and challenging installations are our forte. No literature.

• **Cathedral Stone Company, Inc.**
2505 Reed St., N.E. Dept. OHJ
Washington, DC 20018
(202) 832-1135
MO DIST RS/O
Suppliers of building stone (limestone and sandstone) for structural use as well as ornamental carving, lettering, etc. They supply for both restoration and additions and can duplicate existing or original features in stone. Also do on-site masonry repair and restoration. Literature available.

Cedar Gazebos, Inc.
10432 Lyndale Avenue Dept. OHJ
Melrose Park, IL 60164
(312) 455-0928
MO
Pre-fabricated gazebo kits. Modular units are made of heartwood cedar; each wall and roof panel is handcrafted and comes pre-assembled. Four styles available: Bell-shaped, Pagoda (either 6- or 8-sided), South Seas Classic, and Midwestern Classic (both 6-, 8-, or 10-sided). Optional features: counter ledges, double entry door, and full lattice panels. Brochures and price list, $1.

Cedar Valley Shingle Systems
985 S. Sixth St. Dept. OHJ
San Jose, CA 95112
(408) 998-8550
MO RS/O
Manufacturers of red cedar shingles for roofs, mansards, and sidewalls. Free literature.

The Ceiling Fan Place
20 Round Swamp Rd. Dept. OHJ
Huntington, NY 11743
(516) 367-3835
MO RS/O
Specializes in Hunter Ceiling fans. Catalog and price list, $3, refundable.

Ceilings, Walls & More, Inc.
Box 494, 124 Walnut St. Dept. O
Jefferson, TX 75657
(214) 665-2221
RS/O MO DIST
Old tin ceiling panels reproduced in light-weight, high-impact polymer materials. The 24 by 24 in. panels are easily installed in a suspended grid system or glued directly onto sheetrock or plaster ceilings. The decorative patterns are appropriate to any decor and especially to rooms of the Victorian period. Free literature and price list on request. Sample kits $7.50.

Center Lumber Company
85 Fulton Street, Box 2242 Dept. OHJ
Paterson, NJ 07509
(201) 742-8300
RS/O
Distributors of both domestic and imported hardwood, 1-in. thru 4-in. thicknesses. Special architectural millwork, including custom hardwood mouldings. Operate dry kilns. No literature.

• See Advertisers' Index on page 22 for more details.

Central Kentucky Millwork
2623 Regency Road Dept. OHJ
Lexington, KY 40503
(606) 277-1755
MO RS/O
A wide selection of authentic Colonial and Federal reproduction woodwork: panelled doors, entry framing, shutters, arched windows, window framing, mantels (34 styles, some full-wall), panelled wall sections, some 150 styles of moulding, newels, balusters, and handrails. Choice of 10 different woods, and they have extensive custom capabilities. Two catalogs: 103 pages and 20 pages; $7, refundable. Also, videotape: $30, refundable.

Century House Antiques
46785 Rt. 18 Dept. OHJ
Wellington, OH 44090
(216) 647-4092
RS/O
Antique store specializing in antique lamps and lamp repair. Also old shades plus custom-made shades, pierced tin lamps, a complete line of replacement parts, and metal stripping & buffing. Free flyer with SASE.

Chadwick Studio
89 Northill St. Dept. OHJ
Stamford, CT 06907
(203) 348-3237
RS/O
The studio specializes in repair and restoration of Tiffany lamps and will do custom new work. They also work on windows and are experienced with delicate and high-style pieces. Quotations on request, no literature.

Chandelier Warehouse
40 Withers St. Dept. OHJ
Brooklyn, NY 11211
(718) 388-6800
MO RS/O
Large stock of period-style chandeliers, specializing in crystal chandeliers. Also restoration of antique fixtures, and distributor of Focal Point ceiling medallions. Catalog — $5.

Chapin Townsend
PO Box 628, James Trail Dept. OHJ
W. Kingston, RI 02892
(401) 783-6614
MO DIST
Chapin Townsend was founded to produce fine examples of eighteenth-century American furniture. Each piece is chosen for its rarity and aesthetic and historical importance. The furniture is totally handmade in the manner of the early masters, and faithfully duplicates the designs, details, construction techniques, authentic woods, and finishes of the originals. Their furniture is made for those who admire the originals. Brochure, $2.

Chapman Chemical Co.
PO Box 9158 Dept. OHJ
Memphis, TN 38109
(901) 396-5151
MO DIST
A large selection of wood preservatives and water repellents such as Woodguard™. Also other specialty coatings. Free literature. Call toll free (800) 238-2523.

• **Charles St. Supply Co.**
54 Charles St. Dept. OHJ
Boston, MA 02114
(617) 367-9046
MO
This retail store has agreed to ship plaster washers to OHJ readers who can't find them locally. Price is $1.35 per dozen (ppd.), minimum order 3 dozen, or by the pound, approx. 23 dozen, $20.00 ppd. No literature.

Charolette Ford Trunks
Box 536 Dept. OH
Spearman, TX 79081
(806) 659-3027
MO
Antique trunk hardware and supplies. 40 page catalog, $1.50.

• **Chelsea Decorative Metal Co.**
6115 Cheena Drive Dept. OHJ
Houston, TX 77096
(713) 721-9200
MO RS/O
Embossed metal for ceilings are stamped with the original dies that date back as far as the Civil War and as recently as the Art-Deco era. There are eighteen designs and they come in 2′ x 8′ sheets. They are 26 gauge and have a silvery tin finish. Metal cornice comes in 4 ft. lengths, but the widths vary. Also, 2 ft. x 2 ft. plastic panels for suspended ceilings. Catalog free.

Chem-Clean Furniture Restoration Center
Historic Route 7A Dept. OHJ
Arlington, VT 05250
(802) 375-2743
RS/O MO
Wood finishing products for floors, stairs, fine furniture — paint and varnish removers, bleach, brush cleaner, satin finish polyurethane varnish. Brochure and price list — $.25.

• **Chemical Products Co., Inc.**
P.O. Box 400 Dept. OHJ
Aberdeen, MD 21001
(301) 272-0100
DIST
Supplies chemicals in commercial quantities for professional vat strippers. Write for literature.

• **Cherry Creek Ent. Inc.**
937 Santa Fe Drive Dept. OHJ
Denver, CO 80204
(303) 892-1819
MO RS/O
One of the largest manufacturers of machine bevelled parts, as well as fine quality hand bevelled pieces and wheel engraving. They supply standard beveled, leaded windows, skylights, door panels, etc. Also, custom design capabilities. Catalog, $2.

Chester Granite Co., Inc.
Algerie Road Dept. OHJ
Blandford, MA 01008
(413) 269-4287
RS/O
Stone masons specializing in using traditional techniques and hand tools to produce architectural details such as door steps, pillars, quoins, window sills, and lintels. Available in granite, marble, or brownstone. They are also a source for quarried blue-gray granite. Work is done from architectural drawings or samples. No literature.

Chicago Faucet Co.
2100 South Nuclear Dr. Dept. OHJ
Des Plaines, IL 60018
(312) 694-4400
DIST
Elegant brass faucets copied from turn-of-the-century designs with minor changes to meet modern plumbing codes. Sold through nationwide distributors. "The Renaissance Collection" brochure, $1.

Chicago Old Telephone Co.
PO Box 189 Dept. OHJ
Lemon Springs, NC 28355
(919) 774-6625
MO
Chicago Old Telephone has been collecting old telephones for 20 years. Each is restored with authentic parts, from dial to cord, and works (can be plugged into outlets of modern systems). Durable materials and a one-year guarantee. SASE for color brochure (and many more are available than are listed in their catalog).

Chilstone Garden Ornament
Sprivers Estate Dept. OHJ
Horsmonden, Kent, UK
(089) 272-3553
RS/O MO DIST
Handsome garden ornaments — exact copies of 16th, 17th, and 18th century models — in cast stone. Urns, planters, benches, statuary, obelisks, pedestals, balls and bases, columns, balustrades — all by noted designers. Catalog — $6.00.

Chimney Relining International, Inc.
P.O. Box 4035 Dept. OHJ
Manchester, NH 03108
(603) 668-5195
DIST
Chimneys easily lined, new or old, straight or crooked, residential or industrial, using European pumped refractory process. Also restores fire-damaged chimneys in summer or winter. Tested to ANSI/UL Standard #103. BOCA Evaluated (Report 82-23). Homeowner, architect, contractor inquiries welcomed, indicate interest. Free literature.

Christmas Treasures
PO Box 53 HJ Dept. OHJ
Dewitt, NY 13214
MO
Goose-feather Christmas trees, a popular tradition at the turn-of-the-century, have been reproduced with strong wire limbs, a wooden dowel trunk, and feathers treated with fire retardant dye. Heights range from two to three feet, with 3, 4 or 5 tiers. Also period decorations (Santa Claus, etc.) Catalog, $2.

Chromatic Paint Corp.
PO Box 105 Dept. OHJ
Garnerville, NY 10923
(914) 947-3210
DIST
Manufacturer of specialty paints such as Japan colors, sign paints, automotive finishes and industrial coatings. Also gold sizes. Free color card and information sheet.

Churchill Forest Products, Inc.
Dept. OHJ
Hanson, MA 02341
(800) 446-1002
MO RS/O
Sells kiln-dried lumber, including domestic hardwoods, western white pine, mahogany, and teak. Specializes in wide pine flooring. In MA, (800) 322-2243.

CIPCO Corp.
22nd & Cole St. Dept. OHJ
St. Louis, MO 63106
(314) 436-0011
DIST
CIPCO has produced transom operators since 1919; they have updated the technology only slightly and left the appearance unchanged. A variety of heights (36 to 72 inches) and finishes (brass, bronze or zinc plate) are available. They recently opened their plating (brass, bronze, and nickel) and polishing department to the public for restoring door and window hardware. No literature.

• Circast, Inc.
380 7th St. Dept. OHJ
San Francisco, CA 94103
(415) 863-8319
MO DIST
An outstanding collection of reproduction hardware, late 1870s to mid 1880s. Bronze doorknobs, hinges, escutcheons, keyholes, and sash lifts reproduced from original patterns using the lost-wax process. Other metals offered. Write for your nearest dealer.

City Barn Antiques
362 Atlantic Ave. Dept. OHJ
Brooklyn, NY 11217
(718) 855-8566
MO RS/O
A large selection of restored brass antique gas lighting fixtures with original etched glass shades. 1860 — 1910. No literature, no advice on decorating.

• City Knickerbocker, Inc.
781 Eighth Ave. Dept. OHJ
New York, NY 10036
(212) 586-3939
RS/O
A large selection of 19th century lighting fixtures and lamps. Reproduction cased glass Emeralite Shades. Restores, rewires, adds antique or reproduction glass shades. Also, the "Tee" series — seven reproduction variations in the green glass shade type of fixture. "Tee" series brochure free.

• City Lights
2226 Massachusetts Ave. Dept. OHJ
Cambridge, MA 02140
(617) 547-1490
RS/O MO
Dealer in fully restored antique lighting. Fixtures are repaired, rewired, cleaned, polished, and lacquered and have all antique glass shades. Fixtures displayed at shop. Catalog available for $2.

Clarence House Imports, Ltd.
211 East 58th St. Dept. OHJ
New York, NY 10022
(212) 752-2890
ID
Re-creation of antique textile designs in fine fabrics and wallcoverings. Used by museums, including the Frick and Metropolitan museums in New York City. Specializing in 18th and 19th century hand printed cottons and wallpaper as well as fine silks, leathers, horsehair, mohair and woven textures. Through interior designers and architects only.

Clarksville Foundry & Machine Works
P.O. Box 786 Dept. OHJ
Clarksville, TN 37040
(615) 647-1538
MO RS/O
Gray iron and aluminum foundry and machine shop in operation since 1854. They produce a wide range of rough and finished castings in volumes of one piece to several hundred. They have many old patterns, and can produce quality castings using a customer's sample as a pattern. Custom and jobbing work a specialty. No literature.

• See Advertisers' Index on page 22 for more details.

• Classic Accents
PO Box 1181 Dept. OHJ
Southgate, MI 48195
(313) 282-5525
MO
Classic Accents manufactures push button light switches inlaid with mother of pearl. They look like the originals, but are completely modernized replications. These 120 volt, 20 amp switches were designed by an electrical engineer and meet code in most areas. These unusual light switches have not been made in over 25 years. Classic Accents also has several styles of reproduction cover plates as well as picture hangers in gold or ivory Free literature.

• Classic Architectural Specialties
5302 Junius Dept. OHJ
Dallas, TX 75214
(214) 827-5111
MO RS/O
Restoration/renovation products source. Common items such as corner brackets & mouldings, and turnings in stock. Showroom and retail store with special-order service for a variety of other materials: custom made and stock screen doors, gingerbread, fretwork, Victorian design porch swings, park benches, entry doors, gargoyles, newels, balusters, shingles, chair rails, mantels, metal ceilings, window sash, cupolas. Design consultation available to customers. Catalog, $2.

• Classic Ceilings
902 E. Commonwealth Ave. Dept. OHJ
Fullerton, CA 92631
(714) 526-8062
MO RS/O
West-Coast distributor of Anaglypta, Lincrusta (a Crown trademark), W.F. Norman tin ceilings. Also, in CA, (800) 992-8700.

Classic Illumination Inc.
2743 Ninth St. Dept. OHJ
Berkeley, CA 94710
(415) 849-1842
DIST
Manufacturers of authentic handcrafted solid brass Victorian and early-20th century lighting including Art Deco, and the bronze griffin and Craftsman collection, plus etched-glass fixtures made from original Art Deco moulds. These U.L. listed electric and gas-style chandeliers, wall sconces and table lamps are available with a variety of shades, lengths and finishes (custom variations available). Wholesale inquiries invited. Write for illustrated catalogue ($3) and nearest dealers.

Classic Wicker
8532 Melrose Ave. Dept. OHJ
Los Angeles, CA 90069
(213) 659-1121
MO RS/O
Manufactures reproduction Victorian wicker furniture, with a crew of some 20 craftspeople recreating high-style, intricate pieces. Free brochure with price list.

Classique French Imports, Inc.
6069 Glendale Drive Dept. OHJ
Boca Raton, FL 33433
(305) 392-5558
MO
Classique is an importer of French tapestries in traditional (reproductions of those hanging in European museums) and contemporary images (signed, limited editions). They import also French damask cloth tapestry material for restoration work on period boudoir furniture and other applications. Catalog $10, refundable.

Claxton Walker & Associates
10000 Falls Road Dept. OHJ
Potomac, MD 20854
(301) 299-2755
RS/O
House inspection services in Washington, D.C., and surrounding Virginia and Maryland. Newly expanded service to Annapolis. Free brochure and price list of books and articles on home inspection and maintenance. Also, (301) 867-7447 in Annapolis, MD.

Clay Suppliers
102 N. Windomere Dept. OHJ
Dallas, TX 75208
(214) 942-4608
MO DIST
This company imports chimney pots from England. Over 100 styles are available in red terra cotta, buff fireclay, or black slate. Sizes range from six inches to six feet. Standard models, $50 to $350 (more for custom work). Brochure with current inventory, price list, and drawings is free; manufacturer's color catalog, $3.

Cleveland Wrecking Co.
3801 Milwaukee Ave. Dept. OHJ
Chicago, IL 60641
(312) 685-1100
RS/O
Architectural items of all types, including plumbing and lighting fixtures, new and used lumber. 11 offices around the country: Boston, Philadelphia, Cincinnati, Indianapolis, Charleston, Louisville, St. Louis, Dallas, Los Angeles, San Francisco, Portland. Two in Canada: Vancouver and Calgary. No literature.

Cline Glass Company
1135 S.E. Grand Dept. OHJ
Portland, OR 97214
1-800-547-8417
MO RS/O
An established stained glass wholesale-retail specialty house, carrying supplies for every facet of stained glass procedure. Call toll free. Free supply catalog available.

Clio Group, Inc.
3961 Baltimore Ave. Dept. OHJ
Philadelphia, PA 19104
(215) 386-6276
RS/O
Consultants in architectural and land use history providing a full range of restoration and preservation services. Preparation of National Register Nomination forms; applications for Tax Certification; counseling for adaptive re-use projects. Specialists in archival, demographic and property research; interpretation of historic structures. Survey drawings. Free brochure.

KEY TO ABBREVIATIONS

MO	sells by Mail Order
RS/O	sells through Retail Store or Office
DIST	sells through Distributors
ID	sells only through Interior Designers or Archtects

Clocks, Etc.
3401-C Mt. Diablo Blvd. Dept. OHJ
Lafayette, CA 94549
(415) 284-4720
RS/O MO
Restore, trade, buy and sell old and new clocks and watches. Nationwide clock locating service for specific antique timepieces. Photos available; please specify your wants or needs. Will ship anywhere. Brochures about new grandfather and wall clocks, $1.

Cloyd Laibe
PO Box 5485 Dept. OHJ
Huntington Beach, CA 92646
(714) 962-3265
MO
Solid brass hardware, sand cast, for turn-of-century American furniture. Over 50 items — all handmade, using the original technique. Send SASE for brochure.

Cohasset Colonials
643X Ship St. Dept. OHJ
Cohasset, MA 02025
(617) 383-0110
MO
Manufactures and sells, by mail, exact reproductions of early American furniture both in kits and assembled finished. Assembly of kits is easy and does not require special tools. Stain, glue, hardware included with kits. Choose from Shaker, Queen Anne, Chippendale, Country. Catalog includes reproduction fabric, paint, lighting fixtures, brass, pewter. 32-page color catalog, $2.

Cohen's Architectural Heritage
35 Armstrong Dept. OHJ
Ottawa, OT, Canada K1Y2Z4
(613) 729-4427
RS/O
Architectural antiques and authentic period pieces. Stained-glass windows and window sets in Victorian, Art Nouveau, and Art Deco styles. Complete restoration facility. Exterior and interior doors, gingerbread, mantels, stair parts, decorative plaster, bath fixtures, iron fences, light fixtures. Also, woodworking facility for custom crafting. Will ship anywhere. One-page flyer, $1.

Cold Spring Granite Co.
202 South 3rd Ave. Dept. OHJ
Cold Spring, MN 56320
(800) 328-5040
DIST RS/O
The manufacturer produces a line of marble, stone and granite tiles in a variety of patterns, textures and colors; the tiles come in 3/8 in. through 6 in. thicknesses. In Minnesota, call (612) 685-3621. Free color brochure.

Colefax and Fowler
39 Brook St. Dept. OHJ
London, England, W1Y1AU
01-493-2231
DIST RS/O
Thirty designs of Brussels and Wilton weave carpets. They are based on 18th- and 19th-century English patterns. The designs are in narrow widths (27 in.) and can be used with coordinating borders. Colors can be made to match customer swatches. Available in U.S. through Patterson, Flynn, & Martin, 950 3rd Ave., New York, NY 10021. Free brochure.

Colonial Brick Co., Inc.
977 W. Cermak Road Dept. OHJ
Chicago, IL 60623
(312) 927-0700
MO RS/O
Company specializing in Chicago used common brick and antique street pavers. For samples and further information, please call. Free literature.

Colonial Canopies
Box 927 Dept. OHJ
Hickory, NC 28603
MO
Hand-tied fishnet canopies in six different patterns. Also available as valances, table overskirts, fringed dust ruffles. Free color flyer.

Colonial Casting Co., Inc.
443 South Colony St. Dept. OHJ
Meriden, CT 06450
(203) 235-5189
MO DIST
Handcrafted pewter candlesticks and sconces in Early American and Queen Anne styles. Also; Plates, mugs, ash trays & goblets. Catalog and price list — $1.00.

Colonial Lock Company
172 Main St. Dept. OHJ
Terryville, CT 06786
(203) 584-0311
MO
Box type rim locks based on the old-fashioned style but with modern engineering. A maximum dead bolt security lock. Send $.25 for catalog.

Colonial Maid Curtains
Depot Plaza Dept. OHJ
Mamaroneck, NY 10543
(914) 698-6136
MO
Authentic Colonial curtains in a variety of sizes. Includes ruffled, fringed, smocked, balloon styles; lace, eyelet, sheer fabrics, mostly no-iron. Bedspreads and dust ruffles also available. 56-page full color catalog, free.

• **Colonial Restoration Products**
405 E. Walnut St. Dept. OHJ
North Wales, PA 19454
(215) 699-3133
MO
Their mail-order catalog contains a wide variety of quality reproductions for restoring a Colonial home. All items are made with 18th-century methods, and range from doors, nails, and mortar to hardware and andirons. Mortar matching service—send three-inch sample, and they'll mix appropriate Type O (soft) mortar. Free catalog.

Colonial Wallpaper Company
707 E. Passyunk Ave. Dept. OHJ
Philadelphia, PA 19147
(215) 922-1472
MO RS/O
Distributor of Victorian and Early American wallpapers, including Hamilton-Weston (circa 1690 to 1840), Crown's Anaglypta and Lincrusta (registered trademarks), Bradbury & Bradbury, Sanderson (William Morris hand-blocked papers, traditional borders). Also Victorian reproduction tile, fabrics, carpets, and lace. Free Sanderson brochure, Crown brochure, $.25.

Colonial Weavers
Box 16 Dept. OHJ
Phippsburg Center, ME 04562
(207) 389-2033
MO RS/O
Handwoven reproductions of antique coverlets in Colonial Overshot or summer & winter techniques. Coverlets are woven to order in a wide choice of traditional patterns and colors. Drapery fabric woven to match coverlets or tablecloths and runners. A reproduction of an antique Maine coverlet was purchased by the Renwick Gallery of the Smithsonian Institution for their 'Crafts Multiples' show. Also tablecloths, placemats. Catalog, $2.

Colonial Williamsburg Foundation
PO Box C Dept. OHJ
Williamsburg, VA 23187
(804) 229-1000
RS/O MO
WILLIAMSBURG Reproductions: More than 2,500 examples of fine home furnishings approved by the Colonial Williamsburg Foundation as being authentic reproductions, adaptations, and interpretations of antiques at Williamsburg. The 286-page full color catalog and price list, $8.95 ppd, a must for those interested in eighteenth and early nineteenth-century furnishing styles. Also, historic paint colors — color card, $1.25.

• **The Color People—Restoration Graphics**
1672 Madison St. Dept. OHJ
Denver, CO 80206
(303) 388-8686
MO
Restoration Graphics does color consulting and exterior design for buildings. They do exterior color schemes for all styles of new and old buildings, but specialize in Victorians. (They do not do paint analysis.) Free color brochure.

Colorado Front Range Bldg. Inspection Service
PO Box 9614 Dept. OHJ
Ft. Collins, CO 80525
(303) 482-1976
RS/O
Retired general contractor with extensive experience with old buildings, both residential and commercial. Provides real estate inspection service. Will travel anywhere. Several brochures available for $1 each. Write for titles. Over 5,000 inspections performed to date. Also phone, toll-free, (800) 321-8387 x 229.

Combination Door Co.
P.O. Box 1076 Dept. JC
Fond du Lac, WI 54935
(414) 922-2050
DIST MO
Manufacturers (since 1912) of wood combination storm and screen doors. Plain wood screen doors, wood combination doors in many styles, wood combination windows, wood basement and garage windows, available through distributors and lumber dealers in 24 states, and direct to consumers in those states without distributors. Write for free brochures and name of your distributor.

• **Commodity Traders Consulting Group**
PO Box 538 Dept. OHJ
Mahway, NJ 07430
MO
Makers of a guaranteed mouse trap; no poison, no jaws; patent applied for. $12.50 ppd.

KEY TO ABBREVIATIONS

MO	sells by Mail Order
RS/O	sells through Retail Store or Office
DIST	sells through Distributors
ID	sells only through Interior Designers or Archtects

Community Services Collaborative
1315 Broadway Dept. OHJ
Boulder, CO 80302
(303) 442-3601
MO
National practice with complete consulting and architectural services for historic preservation and restoration. Property surveys, interior/exterior design, specifications, construction management, and historic development research. Economic and adaptive use studies and plans and full Tax Act services. Consultant to National Park Service. Historic materials laboratory; including paint, mortar and plaster analysis. Literature available on request.

Competition Chemicals, Inc.
P.O. Box 820 Dept. OHJ
Iowa Falls, IA 50126
(515) 648-5121
DIST
Importers of SIMICHROME POLISH for all metals (brass, pewter, copper, etc.). Sold through distributors/dealers. Literature available from distributors/dealers or from main office at above address.

• **Conant Custom Brass**
PO Box 1523, 270 Pine St. Dept. OHJ
Burlington, VT 05401
(802) 658-4482
MO RS/O
They work with brass, bronze, and copper offering a variety of services including polishing, repair, restoration, chrome & nickel stripping, soldering, brazing, spinning, and custom fabrication. They also buy and sell brass antiques, specializing in fully restored lighting fixtures. They can bring most brass items back to their original condition. Also authentically designed, solid brass "dust corners," designed to simplify cleaning of staircase corners and originally developed in the 1890s. Free brochure.

Congdon, Johns/Cabinetmaker
RFD 1, Box 350 Dept. OHJ
Moretown, VT 05660
(802) 485-8927
RS/O MO
Fine cabinetwork in period styles. Authentic reproductions, or original designs in appropriate period fashion. All work done by hand; all solid woods; fine brass hardware. Custom design service built on a sound knowledge of 18th century furniture. Prefers personal consultation with customers, but will work through mail or by phone if necessary. Photos and references to serious inquiries. Catalog, $3.

• **Conklin Metal Industries**
PO Box 1858 Dept. OHJ
Atlanta, GA 30301
(404) 688-4510
RS/O MO
Manufactures metal roofing shingles, including one pattern typical of late 19th century houses. Available in galvanized steel, copper, TCS or terne. Also supplies galvanized roofing sheets, gutters and leaders. Flyer "Metal Shingles" $3.

Conklin's Authentic Antique Barnwood
RD 1, Box 70 Dept. OHJ
Susquehanna, PA 18847
(717) 465-3832
RS/O
Wholesaler of authentic barn siding and hand-hewn beams. Sells to construction industry. Also planks are pine and hemlock flooring. Various sizes, woods, and colors (grey, silver-grey, red, brown) to choose from; some 75,000 square feet of barnwood and 9,000 feet of beams maintained in stock. Timber is trimmed, denailed, and ready for use. Shipping by common carrier or trailer in lots. Free flyer. Wood samples, $5 applied to first order.

Connecticut Cane & Reed Co.
Box 762 Dept. OHJ
Manchester, CT 06040
(203) 646-6586
MO RS/O
Dealer in chair seating, wicker repair, and basketry materials. Chair cane, rush, and splint seating, tape for shaker chairs, oak and ash splint stocked. Large stock/prompt delivery. Basketry kits and many patterns of pre-woven cane webbing in stock. Brochure, $.50.

Connecticut Cupola & Weathervane
PO Box 204 Dept. OHJ
Niantic, CT 06357
(203) 739-6360
MO
Standard Colonial-style cupolas in clear pine or redwood; removable louvers, separate bases for easy mounting. Also complete custom cupola and steeple service. A line of 108 hand-hammered weathervanes in traditional designs. Free literature.

Conservation Materials, Ltd.
240 Freeport Blvd., Box 2884 Dept. OHJ
Sparks, NV 89431
(702) 331-0582
MO
A mail order company that supplies products and tools for professional conservation work. Items include paint, brushes, and mounting supplies. Also Renaissance wax and acid-free wax. Renaissance wax brochure, $.50; complete catalog, $4.

Conservatory, The
111 W. Liberty St. Dept. OHJ
Ann Arbor, MI 48104
(313) 994-4443
RS/O
Shop offers antique and contemporary products for the older home, including selected architectural artifacts, restored gas lighting fixtures, Victorian hardware, as well as new designer hardware. Of special interest is the catalog center, featuring the catalogs and brochures of numerous fine companies. No literature.

Consumer Supply Co.
1110 W. Lake Dept. OHJ
Chicago, IL 60607
(312) 666-6080
MO RS/O
A large selection of used radiators and plumbing fixtures in period styles. Call or write with your specifications. No literature.

Contemporary Copper/Matthew Richardson
Box 69 Dept. OHJ
Greenfield, MA 01302
(413) 773-9242
MO
Craftsman producing contemporary interpretations of the traditional metalsmith's art. Copper and brass range hoods and canopies, windvanes, garden ornament, fountains, interior & exterior lighting, original wall art. Pieces are compatible with a broad range of historical styles. Custom work is considered. Catalog, $3.

• See Advertisers' Index on page 22 for more details.

Continental Clay Company
PO Box 1013 Dept. OHJ
Kittanning, PA 16201
(412) 543-2611
DIST RS/O
Founded in 1896, Continental Clay Co. has been manufacturing brick and tile products continously from world renowned Kittanning, PA clay and shale. Traditional building products are made in a variety of colors and shapes in both glazed and unglazed brick and tile. They'll custom match sizes and colors for restoration projects. Free literature.

Cook & Dunn Paint Corp.
PO Box 117 Dept. OHJ
Newark, NJ 07101
(201) 589-5580
ID
Exterior and interior paints and stains, including a collection of historic colors for colonial to Victorian houses. Both latex and oil-based. Free color card.

Coppa Woodworking
1231 Paraiso Ave. Dept. OHJ
San Pedro, CA 90731
(213) 548-4142
MO RS/O
Wood screen doors in styles not strictly Victorian, but appropriate for most old houses. Reasonably priced with stock and custom sizes. The largest manufacturer of wood screen doors in California. Brochure, $.50.

• **Copper House**
RFD 1, Rt. 4 Dept. OHJ
Epsom, NH 03234
(603) 736-9798
MO RS/O
Handmade copper weathervanes. Copper lighting/lanterns for post wall, or hanging indoor/outdoor. Authentic reproductions. A variety of styles and sizes are available. Flagpole balls and eagles; weathervane parts. Cupolas - in pine - from 16 to 54 in. wide; three roof styles, by their division New Hampshire Cupola. Three catalogs, $2.

Copper Sales, Inc.
2220 Florida Ave., South Dept. OHJ
Minneapolis, MN 55426
(800) 426-7737
RS/O DIST
A mill distributor for copper gutters. Selection includes half-round and O.G.K. style gutters and round, square, or corrugated copper downspouts and sheet copper. Free literature.

• **Copper Specialties, Ltd.**
RD 2, Box 440 Dept. OHJ
Sag Harbor, NY 11963
(516) 725-1002
MO RS/O
Custom work in copper: specialties include cupolas and ornament. Also consulting on slate and copper roofing. Free brochure.

The Coppersmith—
Box 755, Route 20 Dept. OHJ
Sturbridge, MA 01566
(617) 347-7038
MO RS/O
Hand-crafted reproductions of Colonial lanterns, chandeliers, sconces, cupolas, 15 styles of weathervanes, in copper, tin, and brass. Catalog, $2.

Josiah R. Coppersmythe
80 Stiles Rd. Dept. OHJ
Boylston, MA 01505
(617) 869-2769
MO
They offer 75 styles of Early American light fixtures, hand crafted in copper and brass. Several finishes and custom work available. Mostly "town crier" style wall and hanging lanterns; some chandeliers and sconces. Color brochure, 14 pages, $2.

Coran — Sholes Industries
509 East 2nd Street Dept. OHJ
South Boston, MA 02127
(617) 268-3780
RS/O MO
Manufactures and distributes lead, glass, tools, equipment, pattern books to the stained glass artisan. A very complete line of Tiffany-style lamp kits. Illustrated catalog with price list — $3.00.

• **The Corner Store**
Mount Comfort Rd. Dept. OHJ
Wheeler, AR 72775
(501) 521-5108
MO
A variety of country items, including a reproduction Victorian clock, $170 ppd. Send SASE and $1 for catalog.

Cornucopia, Inc. At the Appleworks
P.O. Box 44-OHJ Dept. OHJ
Harvard, MA 01451
(617) 772-0023
MO RS/O
Handmade country primitive and Early American furniture. A nice variety of settees, rockers, windsor chairs, pine and cherry dining tables, and reproduction hutches. The company also sells a furniture dressing for restoration of old pieces and wool hand-braided rugs. Catalog, $2.

Cosmetic Restoration, Inc.
1500 Straight Path Dept. OHJ
Wyandanch, NY 11798
(516) 491-1616
RS/O
Large scale paint stripping services to restore wood and masonry buildings to their original surface. Specializes in old houses and churches. Can also spray on textured coatings for ceilings. Restoration consultant. Literature free.

Cosmopolitan International
PO Box 3844 Dept. OHJ
Newport, RI 02840
(401) 849-0092
MO RS/O
Formal 18th & 19th century American & European furniture. Interior design & appraisal services available for the owners of turn-of-the-century, Neo-Classical and Colonial homes. Branch offices located in NY, CT, & RI. Please write or call with specific request.

Country Accents
RD 2, Box 293 Dept. OHJ
Stockton, NJ 08559
(201) 996-2885
MO RS/O
This company specializes in handcrafted pierced tin for furniture and decorative accessories. Kits available. 100-page catalog, $3. Sixteen sample swatches of metal finishes, each approximately 3 inches by 5 inches, $7.95 postpaid.

Country Bed Shop
Box 222H Dept. OHJ
Groton, MA 01450
(617) 448-6336
RS/O MO
Custom-made furniture — hand-made in traditional American, country, and high styles from the 17th and 18th centuries. Numerous styles of beds including pencil-post and other tall posts with canopy frames, low post styles, folding beds, trundle beds, and cradles. Windsor chairs, chests, tables and cupboards. Illustrated 28 pg. catalog, $4. Pencil-post bed folder, $.50. Stamps OK.

Country Braid House
Clark Rd., RFD 2, Box 29 Dept. OHJ
Tilton, NH 03276
(603) 286-4511
RS/O MO
Traditional New England Colonial braided rugs. Hand-laced all-wool rugs are made to order. They'll also make up custom kits for you to lace yourself. Free company brochure. Prices quoted on your requested size and style — or phone ahead to visit the shop.

Country Casual
17317 Germantown Rd. Dept. OHJ-6
Germantown, MD 20874
(301) 540-0040
MO RS/O
Direct importers of Charles Verey, Lister, and other fine English garden and leisure furniture including benches, tables and chairs, and planters. They also specialize in cherry and oak swings from U.S. manufacturers in Victorian, traditional, and contemporary styles.

Country Comfort Stove Works
Union Road Dept. OHJ
Wales, MA 01081
(413) 245-7396
RS/O
Professional restorers of antique wood and coal burning kitchen ranges and parlor stoves. Totally restored stoves, will also do total or partial restoration of your stove. Can provide refractory liners for most stoves. Hours 12-6 pm weekdays, all day Sat. & Sun.

Country Cupolas
Main St. Dept. OHJ
E. Conway, NH 04037
(603) 939-2698
MO DIST RS/O
A small company with 87 in-stock cupolas in 7 roof styles, 260 stock options, plus custom designs. All stock models available fully assembled or in kits. Free literature.

• **Country Curtains**
At The Red Lion Inn Dept. 4576OHJ
Stockbridge, MA 01262
(413) 243-1300
RS/O MO
Curtains in cotton muslin, permanent-press and other fabrics, some with ruffles, others with fringe, braid or lace trim. Also bedspreads, dust ruffles, canopy covers and tablecloths. Tab curtains and wooden rods. Lined and insulated curtains. Eight retail shops: in Stockbridge, Sturbridge, Salem, Braintree, Boston; Avon, CT, Providence, RI, and Newington, NH. Free 56-page catalog includes illustrations and color photographs.

Country Designs
Box 774 Dept. OHJ
Essex, CT 06426
MO
Building plans for "country" barns, sheds, garages, and cottages: saltbox garages, two-horse barns with cupolas, bungalow-style pool houses, plus Victorian well houses, playhouses, gazebos, and a folio of fence plans are available. Illustrated 24-page catalog, $3.

Country Floors, Inc.
300 East 61st St. Dept. OHJ
New York, NY 10021
(212) 758-7414
RS/O MO DIST
Handmoulded and handpainted ceramic tiles for walls and floors from Holland, Portugal, France, Italy, Spain, England, Finland, Mexico & Peru as well as specialty tiles from American artisans. 96-page full color catalog, $10. Represented in most major U.S. cities, Canada, and Australia.

• **The Country Iron Foundry**
PO Box 600 Dept. OHJ-6
Paoli, PA 19301
(215) 296-7122
MO RS/O
Antique iron firebacks, hand-cast from original design which date back to Early American and European periods. Prices range from $75 to $400, depending on size. Illustrated and informative brochure, $1. Showroom at 1792 E. Lancaster Pike, Paoli, displays firebacks. Also a catalog of assorted cast iron reproductions: banks, footscrapers, garden furniture, andirons, in Victorian and Colonial designs.

Country Loft
South Shore Park Dept. OHJ
Hingham, MA 02043
(617) 749-7766
MO
Furnishings and decorative accessories with an Early American flavor. Many attractive housewares appropriate for the country or Colonial home. 48-page color catalog, free.

• **The Country Mouse**
Box 176 Dept. OHJ
Harwinton, CT 06791
MO
Among other country-style items they sell a cedar mailbox shaped like a Dutch barn ($39). It can be engraved with your name; other models are available—free brochure.

Country Roads, Inc.
1122 South Bridge St. Dept. OHJ
Belding, MI 48809
(616) 794-3550
MO DIST RS/O
This company restores old theater seats. Repair and refinishing of wood parts, metal refinishing, and reupholstering done on-site or in their shop. Their "Mobile Plant" — a renovation facility on wheels — goes anywhere to provide quick service for public buildings. Free brochure.

KEY TO ABBREVIATIONS

MO	sells by Mail Order
RS/O	sells through Retail Store or Office
DIST	sells through Distributors
ID	sells only through Interior Designers or Archtects

• See Advertisers' Index on page 22 for more details.

• **Country Shutters**
Box 12384 1255 Old Hwy. 8 Dept. OHJ
New Brighton, MN 55112
(612) 871-7071
DIST RS/O
They make interior shutters in an unusual arched shape—the fan-shaped top has radiating louvers. Standard shapes and a variety of stains available. Stock and custom hand-carved doors, some with leaded glass. Also suppliers of moulding and cornices (can be finished in gold leaf), tin ceilings, and exterior lamp posts. Free catalogs.

The Country Store
28 James St. Dept. OHJ
Geneva, IL 60134
(312) 879-0098
MO RS/O
Reproduction Early American pierced-tin lighting fixtures. Also Whig Rose pattern afghans in ten colors, plus assorted country accessories. 20-page catalog, $2.

Couristan, Inc.
919 Third Avenue Dept. OHJ
New York, NY 10022
(212) 371-4200
DIST RS/O
America's largest supplier of Oriental design area rugs. Also supplies hand-knotted Orientals, contemporary rugs, as well as fine broadloom. Free brochure on hand-hooked rugs or full-color catalogues on Oriental design rugs available: Kashimar $3; Omar $2; Summa Sino $1.

Cowtan & Tout, Inc. D&D Building
979 Third Avenue Dept. OHJ
New York, NY 10022
(212) 753-4488
ID
Domestic and imported glazed chintzes, wovens and silks; fine, handblocked wallpapers; wallcoverings with coordinating fabrics. Custom colorings available. Specialists in European 18th and 19th century patterns. No literature.

Crafts Manufacturing Co.
72 Massachusetts Ave. Dept. OHJ
Lunenburg, MA 01462
(617) 342-1717
MO RS/O
Stencilling supplies, also candleholders, etc., in Early American painted tinware. Also available unpainted, with painting instructions. Includes a Chippendale-style switch plate. Catalog and price list, $1.25.

• **Craftsman Lumber Co.**
PO Box 222, 436 Main St. Dept. OHJ
Groton, MA 01450
(617) 448-6336
RS/O MO
Specializing in kiln-dried, wide pine board flooring, 12 in. to 24 in. wide. Also, wide oak flooring, 4 in. to 9 in. wide, and Victorian wainscotting (custom-made). Custom-made panelling & flooring. Also cut nails and Watco Danish Oil for floors. Leaflet and price list $.60. Stamps are OK.

Craftsman Wood Service Co.
1735 W. Cortland Court Dept. OHJ
Addison, IL 60101
(312) 629-3100
MO RS/O
Woodworkers' one-stop source for supplies, featuring domestic and imported hardwood lumber and veneer. Some listed items are mouldings, trims, lamp parts, upholstery supplies including chair cane, furniture hardware, finishing material, books, power and hand tools, clock movements, musical movements, dowel rods and pins, etc. Free 144-page catalog with over 4000 items.

Craftsman's Corner Woodcraft Collection
4012 NE 14th St., PO Box AP Dept. OHJ
Des Moines, IA 50302
(515) 265-3239
MO
Craftsman's Corner's product line consists primarily of oak "turn-of-the-century" antique reproduction in kit form: classic oak roll-top desk, swivel chairs, file cabinets, and barrister bookshelves. Other kits include a dry sink, bookcase, chest of drawers, night stand, steamer trunk, small accent tables and wall accessories, some clocks and music boxes made from walnut, cherry and oak. Free catalog.

Craftsmen Decorators
2611 Ocean Avenue Dept. OHJ
Brooklyn, NY 11229
(718) 769-1024
RS/O
Specializes in graining, glazing, gilding, antiquing, stencilling and traditional decorating techniques. Restorations a particular specialty. No literature.

• **Crawford's Old House Store**
301 McCall St. Room 86
Waukesha, WI 53186
(414) 542-0685
MO
A wide variety of old-house items, including authentic Victorian reproduction door and window hardware, lighting and plumbing supplies, reproduction marble fireplace mantels, wood corner blocks, finials, door stops, corner beads, and reference books. Illustrated catalog, $2, refundable with purchase.

Creative Openings
PO Box 4204 Dept. OHJ
Bellingham, WA 98227
(206) 671-6420
RS/O MO
Hand-crafted hardwood screen and storm doors, for Victorian or other style houses. Solid brass mesh screen. Your choice of oak, mahogany, ash. Bent laminations, hand-turned spindles. Brochure sent upon request; send $3 for color design catalog.

• **Crispin Treadway Floral Products**
Bogtown Rd. Dept. OHJ
North Salem, NY 10560
(914) 669-5865
MO
Goosefeather Christmas trees, wreaths, and hedges. Many are replicas of Victorian originals. Various old-fashioned tree bases are available, painted red or white; gold accents cost an additional $2. Also pre-decorated trees and custom work. Brochure, $1.50.

Cross Industries, Inc.
5262 Peachtree Rd. Dept. OHJ
Atlanta, GA 30341
(404) 451-4531
DIST RS/O
Producers of PVC (polyvinylchloride) lattice for trellises etc. that never needs paint, will not rot or split, and comes in nine colors and white. Two sizes, thicknesses, and designs available, appropriate for old houses. Free brochures; products also available from distributors.

The Crowe Company Ltd.
1478 W. Mission Rd. Dept. OHJ
Escondido, CA 92025
(619) 741-2069
MO RS/O
Custom and production woodturning and stairparts. Architectural millwork: mouldings, panelling, wainscotting, and mantels. Art glass: stained, leaded, bevelled, etched, and carved. Windows, doors, mirrors, skylights, and lamps. No literature.

Crowfoot's Inc.
Box 1297 Dept. OHJ
Pinetop, AZ 85935
(602) 367-5336
RS/O MO
Fine woodworking, cabinetmaking, turnings, furniture reproduction, Victorian and Early American. Works mainly in Southwest area. Will supply photos of work done to serious inquirers.

• **Crystal Mountain Prisms**
PO Box 31 Dept. OHJ
Westfield, NY 14787
(716) 326-3676
MO RS/O
Prisms, pendants, bobeches, chains, pendelogues, plug drops, kite pendants, and prism pins are some of the items offered by this company. Send SASE for the complete list of sizes, shapes, and colors.

• **Cumberland General Store**
Route 3 Dept. OH-87
Crossville, TN 38555
(615) 484-8481
RS/O MO
"Complete outfitters: goods in endless variety for man and beast." From chamber pots to covered wagons — over 10,000 items, many available only here and all new goods. Of particular interest are the period kitchen utensils and implements, period bathtubs, and wood-burning cookstoves. The interesting, illustrated 250 pg. catalog makes fascinating browsing for $3 plus $.75 postage and handling.

• **Cumberland Woodcraft Co., Inc.**
PO Drawer 609 Dept. 105
Carlisle, PA 17013
(717) 243-0063
RS/O MO
Leading manufacturer of Victorian millwork faithfully duplicates the intricate designs of the Victorian era. Will provide millwork to duplicate any period decor. Full line includes: architectural hand carvings, brackets, corbels, grilles, fretwork, turnings, plus special treatments. Also available: raised-panel ceiling treatments, bars, partitions, wainscotting. All crafted from solid oak or poplar. Unlimited quantities available. Complete 36-page, full-color catalog and price list, $3.75.

Curran, Patrick J.
30 No. Maple St. Dept. OHJ
Florence, MA 01060
(413) 584-5761
MO
Custom stained, bevelled, and etched glass. Also, four styles and sizes of opalescent glass table lamps. Several lamp bases also offered. Some stained and painted glass restoration as well as bent glass repairs for bent panel lamps. Slide portfolio available.

Curry, Gerald — Cabinetmaker
Pound Hill Road Dept. OHJ
Union, ME 04862
(207) 785-4633
MO
Small shop specializing 18th-century furniture reproductions. Design, construction, and materials are faithfully copied from the originals. Fine craftsmanship combined with years of study results in the museum-quality reproductions. An illustrated brochure is free.

Cushwa Brick Co.
PO Box 160, Rt. 68 Dept. OHJ
Williamsport, MD 21795
(301) 223-7700
MO DIST
Established 1872. Manufacturers and distributors of distinctive "Calvert" machine-molded and custom handmade molded brick. Specialize in matching old brick and special brick designs for color, texture, and size. Complete line of brick available in numerous colors. Restoration work includes Independence Hall, Monticello, and Betsy Ross House. Brochure available for $2. prepaid.

Custom Bar Designs
7504 Devonshire Dept. OHJ
St. Louis, MO 63119
(314) 781-7911
MO
This company sells plans for antique-style bars, back bars, mantels, and furniture. They also sell brass rails and wood carvings. Catalog, $3.

Custom Castings
3324 Stuart Dr. Dept. OHJ
Fort Worth, TX 76110
(817) 927-2707
MO RS/O
They produce glass-reinforced concrete, moulded in rubber for column capitals, etc., that looks like terra cotta, limestone, brownstone, or many other materials. Their glass-reinforced gypsum has interior applications like columns, moulding, ceilings. Call for free estimates. Free brochures.

Custom & Historic Millwork
5310 Tennyson St. Dept. OHJ
Denver, CO 80212
(303) 480-1617
MO DIST RS/O
Custom woodworking, duplication of special items needed in restoration, contracting of entire buildings. Cabinet work, mouldings to match. Victorian era specialists.

Custom House
6 Kirby Rd. Dept. OHJ
Cromwell, CT 06416
(203) 828-6885
MO RS/O
Silk lampshades: Custom designs and recovering old frames. Hardback lampshades: hand made from new or antique fabric. Also, pierced & botanical lampshades. All shades made by a staff of skilled craftsmen. Write your specific needs for further details.

Custom House Foundry
South Shore Drive, PO Box 38 Dept. OHJ
Owl's Head, ME 04854
(207) 594-5985
MO RS/O
Third-generation blacksmith with over 25 years of experience custom casts iron-&-brass door, shutter, & cabinet hardware, replacement trivets for cookstoves, family crests and shields (send copy of crest for free price quote). Mantel & cornice ornaments in lightweight metals. Also gates & fences plus garden statuary and ornament forged & cast.

• **Custom Ironworks Inc.**
PO Box 99 Dept. OHJ
Union, KY 41091
(606) 384-4486
MO DIST RS/O
This company manufactures reproduction cast and wrought iron fencing. Will travel to install. Brochure $1.

• **Custom Millwork, Inc.**
PO Box 562 Dept. OHJ
Berryville, VA 22611
(703) 955-4988
MO RS/O
Custom Millwork specializes in all phases of restoration woodwork for historic preservation projects. Most items are designed or reproduced specifically for each particular project. Products include, but are not limited to, the following: mouldings, casework, staircases & stair parts, windows, doors, exterior woodwork, flooring, panelling, raised panel wainscotting, turnings of all varieties and hand-carved complements. Antique lumber is also available. Free brochure.

Custom Sign Co.
111 Potomac St. Dept. OHJ
Boonsboro, MD 21713
(301) 432-5792
RS/O
Hand-lettered gold leaf numbers in period styles, painted on your transom. Also, antique reproduction signs, gilding, and trompe l'oeil. Free price list. Prefer Washington DC suburbs or Frederick MD vicinity.

D

DAP, Inc.
PO Box 277 Dept. OHJ
Dayton, OH 45401
(513) 667-4461
DIST RS/O
Do-it-yourself home repair and maintenance products — caulks, adhesives, glazing compounds, spackle, putty, deglosser, primer-sealer, plumbers putty, rust preventive paints, galvanized metal paint. Free folder.

• **D.E.A./Bathroom Machineries**
495 Main St., Box 1020-OH Dept. OHJ
Murphys, CA 95247
(209) 728-3860
MO RS/O
Brass, porcelain, and oak, antique and reproduction bathroom fixtures. Catalog, $2.

• **DHM Cabinets**
PO Box 173, Route 4 Dept. OHJ
Floyd, VA 24091
(703) 745-3825
MO RS/O
Custom made reproduction furniture. Specializing in Chippendale, Regency, Sheridan, and Queen Anne. However, can do all types of custom furniture. Also: Brassware imported from Scotland, including architectural, cabinet, lighting, and fireplace brassware. All are cast from original moulds. Literature available.

DS Locksmithing Company
220 East Sixth St. Dept. OHJ
Jacksonville, FL 32206
(904) 356-5396
MO
Bonded locksmiths who offer authentic reproduction Colonial and Victorian padlocks, cabinet locks, and door locks. Very well made, they provide better security than most modern locks. A wide variety of solid brass hardware is also available. Lock Catalog, $1; Brass Hardware Catalog, $2; Kerosene Lamp Brochure, $.25 & SASE.

D.V.H. Co.
15 S.W. 3rd Ave. Dept. OHJ
Gainesville, FL 32607
(904) 377-0438
MO RS/O
A millshop specializing in stock and custom size windows in Ponderosa pine; other woods by request. Also, custom wood storms & screens, and a replacement kit for double-hung sash. Also, custom moldings. Literature, $2.50.

Dahlke Stairs
122 Naubuc Ave. Dept. OHJ
Glastonbury, CT 06033
(203) 659-1887
RS/O
Custom stairbuilding. Reproductions, architects' plans, or will custom design to clients' specifications. No stair parts are stocked. All parts are fabricated in their shop or supplied by manufacturers. All work is quoted per job. Free brochure.

Dalton-Gorman, Inc.
1508 Sherman Ave. Dept. OHJ
Evanston, IL 60201
(312) 869-5575
MO RS/O
La Chemine marble mantels — reproductions of 17th to 19th century marble mantels at affordable prices. Complete line of comlementary brass fireplace accessories including screens, tool sets, fenders, andirons. Free literature.

Dalton Pavilions Inc.
7260-68 Oakley St. Dept. OHJ
Philadelphia, PA 19111
(215) 342-9804
MO RS/O
Gazebos: open and screened, prefabricated or installed on your property. Several styles and sizes, all Western red cedar. Free catalog and price list.

• **Daly's Wood Finishing Products**
3525 Stone Way North Dept. OHJ
Seattle, WA 98103
(206) 633-4200
RS/O MO DIST
Manufacturing and marketing of wood finishing products including brasswire brushes and a wooden scraping tool; bleaches and stain removers; BenMatte Danish finishing oil, clear and stain; Floor Fin treatment. A complete guide to wood finishing: 'Class Notes,' $2. Free descriptive literature; free guidance in solving wood finishing problems.

Dan Wilson & Company, Inc.
PO Box 566 Dept. OHJ
Fuquay-Varina, NC 27526
(919) 552-4945
RS/O MO DIST
Custom-made garden furniture, handcrafted from selected hardwoods. Chinese Chippendale planters with removable galvanized liners, Chippendale garden benches, tables and chairs. Catalog, $2.

• **Dancing Cactus Enterprises**
7727 W. Mulberry Dept. OHJ
Phoenix, AZ 85033
(602) 849-0783
MO RS/O
A complete line of oak bathroom fixtures, cabinetry and accessories. This includes high-tank toilets and a low-tank oak conversion kit. Also, old-time pedestal sinks, decorative ceramic or brass basins, and decorative faucets. Product catalog and literature, $2.

• **Daniel Mack Rustic Furnishings**
225 W. 106th St. Dept. OHJ
New York, NY 10025
(212) 866-5746
RS/O
Rustic furniture, both custom-made and stock. Uses twigs and branches, fine woodworking techniques. Can design furniture to suit. Free brochure.

Darworth Co.
P.O. Box K, Tower Lane Dept. OHJ
Avon, CT 06001
(203) 677-7721
DIST
Manufactures FI:X®, a wood patch which is made from wood and stains like wood. Also, their Flix Touch Up-Stik effectively hides nail holes, small cracks, and scratches on finished wood surfaces. Their Cuprinol® wood preservative and stain shields wood siding and trim, decks, lawn furniture and fences from inclement weather. And their POLYSEAMSEAL® Adhesive Caulking seals both interior and exterior cracks. Free literature. Call (800) 624-7767.

Davenport, Peters
129 South Street Dept. OHJ
Boston, MA 02111
(617) 542-1811
DIST
This company, founded in 1811, stocks wood gutters (Douglas Fir) in the traditional Boston pattern. 4x5, 4x6, and 3x4, lengths up to 40 feet. Call to find local distributors.

David Woods Plaster Restoration
129 Academy St. Dept. OHJ
Poughkeepsie, NY 12601
(914) 471-9832
RS/O
All facets of plaster restoration, from framing, lathing, and flat work (ceilings and walls) to ornamental work. Period techniques. No literature, but references.

Davis Cabinet Co.
Box 60444 Dept. OHJ
Nashville, TN 37206
(615) 244-7100
DIST
Solid wood bedroom, dining room, and occasional items. Booklet available for $2.00 that illustrates manufacturer's production method and displays several collections — Victorian, American Traditional, English, French, and Oriental. The Lillian Russell Victorian Collection is the oldest collection in continuous manufacture in the United States.

KEY TO ABBREVIATIONS

MO sells by Mail Order
RS/O sells through Retail Store or Office
DIST sells through Distributors
ID sells only through Interior Designers or Archtects

The Day Studio — Workshop Inc.
1504r Bryant St. Dept. OHJ
San Francisco, CA 94103
(415) 626-9300
MO RS/O
Two-day seminars on glazing, gilding, and marbleizing held in San Francisco, Los Angeles, New York, and Atlanta. Also one- or two-week hands-on workshops in San Francisco and New York. Videotapes also available.

Decor International Wallcovering, Inc.
37-39 Crescent St. Dept. OHJ
Long Island City, NY 11101
(718) 392-4990
DIST
They offer an inexpensive embossed paper wallcovering called "The Classic Coverup". Available in 6 designs, it is a heavily embossed paintable wallpaper designed for problem walls/ceilings. Literature and samples. Available across the country in paint and wallpaper stores.

Decoration Day
2076 Boston Post Rd. Dept. OHJ
Larchmont, NY 10538
(914) 834-9252
MO RS/O
This company deals in antiques, silk and dried flower arrangements, tassels in all sizes and colors, old kitchenware, and reproduction accessories.

Decorative Hardware Studio
PO Box 627, 160 King Street Dept. OHJ
Chappaqua, NY 10514
(914) 238-5251
MO DIST RS/O
Fine decorative hardware and fittings. Crystal, brass, porcelain accessories. Furniture hardware, faucets, sinks, locksets, door hardware, drapery hardware, etc. Styles from Colonial to contemporary. Showrooms: Patterson, Flynn, Martin, Chicago, IL; Delk-Morrison, New Orleans, LA; Royce Allen Wall, Houston, TX; Boyd-Levinson & Co., Dallas, TX. Extensive catalog, in binder, $10 plus freight.

• **Decorators Supply Corp.**
3610-12 S. Morgan St., rear Dept. OHJ
Chicago, IL 60609
(312) 847-6300
RS/O MO
Thousands of composition and wood fibre ornaments for woodwork, furniture and architectural trim; hundreds of plaster ornaments, composition capitals and brackets; 15 wood mantels in Colonial, French and English styles. 5 illustrated catalogs and price lists. Plaster Ornaments — $3.00, Capitals & Brackets — $3.00 Mantels — $2.00, Wood Fibre Carvings — $2.00, Woodwork-Furniture Ornaments — $15.00.

Dee, John W. — Distinctive Painting & Decorating
PO Box 152 Dept. OHJ
Concord, MA 01742
(617) 369-8897
RS/O
Interior & exterior painting. Wallcovering installation. Home remodelling & repairs. Paint-failure analysis & trouble shooting. Quality restoration. Craftsmanship, integrity. No literature.

• See Advertisers' Index on page 22 for more details.

Deer Creek Pottery
305 Richardson St. Dept. OHJ
Grass Valley, CA 95945
(916) 272-3373
DIST ID
They reproduce ceramic tile, using original moulds (they have a collection of 500 moulds). Styles range from Victorian to Art Deco. Tiles are hand pressed, low fired, and hand inlaid. Custom colors available. Call for nearest distributor; free list of showrooms.

Delaware Quarries, Inc.
River Rd. Dept. OHJ
Lumberville, PA 18933
(215) 297-5647
DIST RS/O
Producers of an extensive line of building stone. Specialists in the matching of stone from old, unavailable sources. Custom fabrication of slate, limestone, granite, and sandstone for a variety of uses in the home. Free building stone brochure.

Delphi Stained Glass
2116 E. Michigan Ave. Dept. OHJ
Lansing, MI 48912
(800) 248-2048
MO RS/O
Stained glass tools and supplies, including hundreds of glass types. Also instructional videos. Catalog, $2.

Dentro Plumbing Specialties
63-16 Woodhaven Blvd. Dept. OHJ
Rego Park, NY 11374
(718) 672-6882
MO
Supplies modern or obsolete faucet & shower stems or spindles only. Cannot supply porcelain faucet handles or complete faucets. Must have the old one for a sample. No diagrams or sketches. Complete line of Case parts for tanks, and original drainboards. No catalogs or other literature available.

Design-Cast Corporation
PO Box 134 Dept. OHJ
Princeton, NJ 08540
(609) 890-1010
RS/O ID
Custom-moulded fireproof man-made stone laminates designed for non-loadbearing applications. They can be colored with pigments and moulded to match marble, granite, sandstone, masonry, wood, and metals. No price list—custom work, quoted individually. No literature.

Designer Resource
5160 Melrose Ave. Dept. OHJ
Los Angeles, CA 90038
(213) 465-9235
MO RS/O
Complete selection of period and hard-to-find architectural detail. Stock and custom designs in columns, mantels, metal ceilings, composition ornament, architectural plaster detail, carved, embossed wood mouldings, metal mouldings, plaster cornices, etc. Designer Resource sells to designers, architects, and builders, but will sell to the serious individual restoring a period home. Extensive catalogs are available, please write or call for list.

• **Designer's Brass**
280 El Camino Real Dept. OHJ
San Bruno, CA 94066
(415) 588-8480
RS/O
A complete selection of quality builder's hardware, bathroom fixtures and accessories in a diversity of design and a full range of finishes. Call for availability of literature.

• **Designs in Tile**
PO Box 4983 Dept. CO3 Dept. 2OHJC
Foster City, CA 94404
(415) 571-7122
MO DIST
Historic reproduction ceramic tile or traditional or contemporary patterns. Stock line includes Anglo-Japanese, Folk (Pennsylvania Dutch and Northern European), Arts & Crafts, and Art Nouveau. From $8 per tile. Styles and techniques suitable for residential and commercial applications on walls, floors, exteriors. Custom work including encaustic, from $15 to $250 per foot. Mail orders welcome. Color brochure, $2.

• **Devenco Products, Inc.**
PO Box 700 Dept. OHJ
Decatur, GA 30031
(404) 378-4597
RS/O MO
Specialists in Colonial wooden blinds, movable louver and raised-panel shutters, all custom manufactured to window specifications. Devenco uses Ponderosa pine and cedar and can stain or paint any tone. Wood Finish by Minwas is used exclusively for a finish. Mail orders accepted and shipment arranged. Please write or telephone for specific information and free color brochure.

• **DeWeese Woodworking**
P.O. Box 576 Dept. OHJ
Philadelphia, MS 39350
(601) 656-4951
MO DIST RS/O
Since 1976, DeWeese has grown to be the country's foremost producer of oak commode seats. They also offer other bathroom accessories: towel bars, tissue roll holder, magazine rack, toothbrush/tumbler holder, and our original towel clip. They have a 30 day "no hassle" return policy. Free color brochure.

• **J.D. Dewell & Company**
1008 State Street Dept. OHJ
New Haven, CT 06511
(203) 624-0803
RS/O
Extensive line of original and reproduction interior building and decorative materials for restorationists. Baldwin Brass and H.B. Ives hardware (latches and strap hinges), period wallcoverings (Anaglypta, Lincrusta, Schumacher, Waverly, Bradbury and Bradbury), Victorian bathroom accessories, architectural details (cornice mouldings, columns and tin ceilings). If they don't have what you're looking for, they can probably find it. Call to get on their mailing list.

• **Diedrich Chemicals-Restoration Technologies, Inc.**
300 A East Oak Street Dept. OHJC
Oak Creek, WI 53154
(414) 764-0058
DIST MO RS/O
Professional restoration chemicals for building exteriors: masonry restorer-cleaner, water-repellent preservative sealers. Paint removers for both wood and masonry. Chemicals sold only to distributors/contractors nationwide. Products specified and used on over 100 buildings in the National Register of Historic Places. Movie demonstrating products is available. New-guidebook for cleaning technology. Write for free brochure and name of your nearest distributor/contractor. Also (800) 323-3565.

Dilworthtown Country Store
275 Brinton's Bridge Rd. Dept. OHJ
West Chester, PA 19380
(215) 399-0560
MO RS/O
Built in 1758 as a general store and saddlery, it is believed to be one of the oldest continously operated general stores in the country. They offer American country gifts, accessories and folk art along with antiques, herbs & dried flowers, 18th century reproductions and upholstered furniture from Angel House Designs. Catalog, $2.

Dimension Hardwood Inc.
113 Canal St., PO Box 825 Dept. OHJ
Shelton, CT 06484
(203) 735-3343
MO DIST RS/O
Dimension Hardwood is a custom manufacturer of fancy plank and wideboard flooring, and related solid wood products like v-bevelled wall panelling; specifically catering to the renovation and restoration market. Free literature.

Dimension Lumber Co.
517 Stagg St. Dept. OHJ
Brooklyn, NY 11237
(718) 497-7585
MO RS/O
Complete milling facilities for custom fabrication of mouldings and trim, dressed four sides in any hardwood and most softwoods. They can match original mouldings with samples, plaster casts, and blue prints. Also mills hardwood to your specifications. No minimum amounts. No literature available. Also (718) 497-1680.

Direct Safety Company
7815 S. 46th St. Dept. OHJ
Phoenix, AZ 85044
(602) 968-7009
MO
A large assortment of mail-order safety equipment from goggles to leak detectors to asbestos-removal gloves. Free catalog. Toll-free, (800) 528-7405.

Dodge, Adams, and Roy, Ltd.
Stoodley's Tavern, Hancock St. Dept. OHJ
Portsmouth, NH 03801
(603) 436-6424
RS/O
Consultants and contractors specializing in restoration and preservation of buildings. Survey work, research, and documentation are aspects of their consulting services. Roofing, interior and exterior woodwork, masonry, and foundation work are contracting specialties. They'll travel anywhere.

KEY TO ABBREVIATIONS

MO sells by Mail Order
RS/O sells through Retail Store or Office
DIST sells through Distributors
ID sells only through Interior Designers or Archtects

Donald Stryker Restorations
154 Commercial Ave. Dept. OHJ
New Brunswick, NJ 08901
(201) 828-7022
MO RS/O
Provides interior and exterior restoration services for residential and small-scale commercial buildings, with special emphasis on 19th century residential structures. Also offer "Historic Property Analysis" that describes present condition, immediate repairs needed, maintenance cycles, suggested restoration plans, and restoration resources available. No literature. Please include phone number in correspondence.

Doors of Distinction
2988 Fairmount Blvd. Dept. OHJ
Riverside, CA 92501
(714) 788-9514
MO
Custom carving of entry doors in four period styles: Colonial, Federdl, Gothic, and Queen Anne. Period designs in screen doors also available, plus custom door casings and pediments. Descriptive flyer and price list, $1.

Dorothy's Ruffled Originals
6721 Market Street Dept. OHJ
Wilmington, NC 28405
(800) 334-2593
MO
Curtains and accessories: ruffled curtains, valances, tiers, balloon-style curtains are just a few. "Custom Home Decorating" catalog, vol. I, $4, (refundable). In NC, (800) 672-2924.

Douglas Cooperative, Inc. Window Blanket Division
320 Everett High Rd. Dept. OHJ
Maryville, TN 37801
(615) 983-5522
MO
Insulated window curtains: Channel quilted tab or track installation window covering. Made of 100% polished cotton with soil-resistant finish. Filled with lightweight polyester fiberfill for sound-absorption and energy- savings. Fade resistant, water-repellent insulated cotton lining. Standard size 45" wide x 84" long. Custom lengths available. Easy to install on cafe or dowel rods, or track which is included. Free color brochure and fabric swatches.

Dovetail, Inc.
PO Box 1569-102 Dept. OHJ
Lowell, MA 01853
(617) 454-2944
RS/O MO
Traditional medallions, cornices, brackets, and complete ceiling designs that are strong, lightweight, and fire-resistant. All items designed with ease of installation in mind. Prompt efficient attitude combined with quality plaster castings and custom-drawn mouldings. Specialty work and consulting service available. Color catalog: $3.

• See Advertisers' Index on page 22 for more details.

Dovetail Woodworking
550 Elizabeth St. Dept. OHJ
Waukesha, WI 53186
(414) 544-5859
MO RS/O
A high quality millwork shop specializing in hard to find architectural woodwork. Products include all types & shapes sash, custom doors, louvered shutters, cabinetry to match any period, and a line of Victorian kitchen cabinets. They also have over 1000 moulding patterns bought from several old mills. Our clients include, State Historical Societies, architects, commercial renovations and private restorations.

Downstate Restorations
2773 North Kenmore Dept. OHJ
Chicago, IL 60614
(312) 929-5588
RS/O
Building restoration firm specializing in facade restoration. Extensive masonry cleaning and chemical paint removal experience. Ornamental cornice fabrication and repair — metal, fiberglass, and plaster. Also full line of painting services, consulting, field testing, and research. Specification preparation and nomination to the National Register. Serving Illinois and the Midwest as contractors, consulting nationally. Site inspections. Free company literature.

Driwood Moulding Company
P.O. Box 1729 Dept. OHJ
Florence, SC 29503
(803) 669-2478
RS/O MO
They have been fabricating embossed hardwood period mouldings for over 50 years. Hundreds of historically authentic designs suitable for ceiling cornices, chair rails, door and window casings, bases, etc. They custom manufacture mantels, doors, and architectural millwork. Custom-made curved wood stairs. Mouldings normally shipped within two to three weeks of purchase order. Two catalogs of mouldings and millwork, $6 credited against order.

• **Drums Sash & Door Co., Inc.**
P. O. Box 207 Dept. OHJ
Drums, PA 18222
(717) 788-1145
MO RS/O
Architectural woodwork company supplying clear white pine custom window sash; stair treads, risers and mouldings; custom hardwood trim (casing, base, cove); wood screen/storm doors, custom interior & exterior doors. Also cabinet fronts in oak, birch, cherry, or poplar. Will supply window glass and other window parts. Catalog/price list: $2.00.

Dugwood Turners
PO Box 634 Dept. OHJ
Richmond, VA 23205
(804) 231-6564
RS/O
One-man turning shop, providing columns, balusters, newels, porch parts, and custom designs. Also offers a line of country-style beds, chairs, and trestle tables. Can make accessories (bowls, doll beds, lamps, stools) and furniture parts. Call for free estimate. Free flyer.

Dura Finish of San Mateo
726 S. Amphlett Blvd. Dept. OHJ
San Mateo, CA 94402
(415) 343-3672
RS/O
Professional paint-stripping company using immersion process on all types of interior/exterior wood and metalwork: stained-glass windows, mouldings, registers, railings, gingerbread, doors, mantels, and pillars. Also metal de-rusting and etching. Specializing in antique repair-restoration-refinishing; and chair caning. Free literature.

Durvin, Tom & Sons
Rt. 6, Box 307 Dept. OHJ
Mechanicsville, VA 23111
(804) 746-3845
RS/O
Family-owned and operated brick contracting business. Services include fireplace and chimney restoration. Small, quality-oriented company with old-house experience. Greater Richmond area. Please phone for free estimate.

Dusty Splinters Enterprises
PO Box 3204-OHJ Dept. OHJ
Flushing, NY 11386
(718) 366-4524
MO
Dusty Splinters is a mail-order woodworker's and refinisher's supplier. As well as selling woodworker's tools, they carry traditional milk paint. Milk paint brochure and color chart, $1, refundable with purchase.

• **Dutch Products & Supply Co.**
166 Lincoln Ave. Dept. OHJ
Yardley, PA 19067
(215) 493-4873
MO DIST RS/O
The complete line — 26 patterns — of Royal Delft Tiles. Colonial chandeliers in solid brass and brass with Delft parts. Also hanging brass oil lamps; wall sconces in brass/pewter, street lamps. Brochure, $1.

Duvinage Corporation
P.O. Box 828 Dept. OHJ
Hagerstown, MD 21740
(301) 733-8255
MO
Manufactures complete lines of spiral and circular stairway systems for residential, commercial, and industrial applications; interior and exterior use. Circular and spiral stairs are custom built to specifications. Steel, aluminum, grating, cast iron, cast aluminum, and stainless steel. Treads covered in wood, carpet, rubber, terrazzo, marble, concrete or tile. Continuous rails of aluminum, steel or wood. Free brochure.

E

E & B Marine Supply
980 Gladys Court, PO Box 747 Dept. OHJ
Edison, NJ 08818
(201) 287-3900
MO DIST
High-performance marine supplies useful for restoration projects. Caulking compounds, exterior finishes, varnishes, rot-patching materials, epoxy fillers, and more. Mail and phone orders are filled promptly (within 48 hours). Major credit cards are accepted. Free discount catalog featuring savings from 20 — 60%.

Early New England Rooms & Exteriors Inc.
PO Box 377 Dept. OHJ
East Windsor Hill, CT 06028
(203) 282-0236
RS/O
Reproduction of 18th-century woodwork: doors (various styles), wainscotting, mantels, sash, cabinetry. Authentic period techniques, adapted to age of the house. Will also undertake complete building restorations. Some stock items, mostly custom. Catalog, $2.

Earthwise Design
PO Box 435, End of Sims Lane Dept. OHJ
E. Haddam, CT 06423
(203) 873-1617
RS/O
Architectural services for historic buildings: measured drawings of existing buildings, feasibility studies, contract drawings for renovation and preservation. Mostly residential scale projects. No literature.

Eastern Safety Equipment Co., Inc.
59-20 56 Ave. Dept. OHJ
Maspeth, NY 11378
(718) 894-7900
DIST
A large selection of safety equipment including respirators for paint stripping and other hazardous fumes. They will not sell direct, however they will put you in contact with your local distributor. Free information.

Eastfield Village
Box 145 R.D. Dept. OHJ
East Nassau, NY 12062
(518) 766-2422
RS/O
Dedicated to Historic Preservation and historical American trades, Eastfield's hands-on workshops employ traditional methods and tools. All of Eastfield's resources, including a study collection of 27 appropriately furnished and outfitted structures of the period 1787-1840, are available to workshop participants. Accommodations and the first-hand experience of early 19th-century living conditions is provided by the Village Tavern. Write or call for a free class schedule and details.

• **Easy Time Wood Refinishing Products Corp.**
PO Box 686 Dept. OHJ
Glen Ellyn, IL 60137
(312) 858-9630
MO DIST RS/O
Company sells a wood refinisher that removes varnish, lacquer, shellac, and light coats of paint, without sanding, scraping, or further preparation. No methylene chloride. Also tung oil penetrating sealer, lemon oil, a lightweight electric heat gun for removing paint, and a metal cleaner and polish. Products distributed through antique and hardware stores, but they will also sell direct. Free brochure for SASE.

Econol Stairway Lift Corp.
2513 Center St. Dept. OHJ
Cedar Falls, IA 50613
(319) 277-4777
DIST RS/O
Manufacturers of residential elevators, wheel chair lifts, stair ride lifts, vertical lifters and dumbwaiters. Write or call for free information.

Ed's Antiques, Inc.
1029 Pine St. Dept. OHJ
Philadelphia, PA 19107
(215) 923-4120
RS/O
Antique shop specializing in repair and rewiring of lighting fixtures, recaning, wood furniture refinishing, and reframing of antique stained glass and bevelled windows repaired. Walk-in shop; no literature.

Ian Eddy — Blacksmith
RD 1, Box 975, Sand Hill Rd. Dept. OHJ
Putney, VT 05346
(802) 387-5991
MO DIST RS/O
A full-time blacksmith-craftsman traditionally forging wrought iron functional objects. Special orders, reproductions, and commission items gladly accepted. Send $3 for brochure.

Eifel Furniture Stripping
69 15th Street Dept. OHJ
Brooklyn, NY 11215
(718) 788-3104
RS/O
This small refinishing service has been in business since 1959. They are equipped to strip doors, mouldings, shutters, etc. without heat or caustics. Specialize in antique and natural wood finishes. Will show samples upon request. Free literature.

• **Eklund, Jon Restorations**
80 Gates Avenue Dept. OHJ
Montclair, NJ 07042
(201) 746-7483
MO RS/O
This company will do interior and exterior restorations of old buildings, as well as design and construction of period conforming structures, expansions, and additions. They specialize in creating/remodeling Victorian and early 20th century kitchens/pantries. On-site stripping and refinishing of interior woodwork, custom millwork, cabinets, doors, sashes. Also plaster restoration, both plain and ornamental. On-site work in NY, NJ area. Custom orders welcome. Call or write for free initial consultation.

Elbinger Laboratories, Inc.
220 Albert St. Dept. OHJ
East Lansing, MI 48823
(517) 332-1430
MO RS/O
Quality copying and restoration of heirloom and historical photographs. Photos are copied on a large-format negative and printed to meet or exceed "archival" standards. Brochure, $2.00.

Elcanco Inc.
60 Chelmsford St. Dept. OHJ
Chelmsford, MA 01824
(617) 256-9972
MO DIST
Their electric, real wax candles "Starlites" and "Morelites" have been used in such prestigious restorations as Mount Vernon, Colonial Williamsburg, Sleepy Hollow, and many private homes. Beeswax candlecovers can be ordered to size. Brochures, $1.

Electric Glass Co.
1 E. Mellen St. Dept. OHJ
Hampton, VA 23663
(804) 722-6200
RS/O MO
They offer new bevelled glass door and window inserts, stained glass panels, new and old art glass, and Tiffany style shades. Beveled Glass Catalog — $3.00.

• **Elephant Hill Iron Works**
RR 1, Box 168 Dept. OHJ
Tunbridge, VT 05077
(802) 889-9444
MO RS/O
A small company producing accurate reproductions of 17th, 18th, and early 19th-century hardware. All items are hand forged and finished to ensure an authentic representation of pieces of the period. In addition to stock items illustrated in the catalog, they welcome your inquiries concerning custom work such as house hardware, gates, railings, and sign brackets. Catalog, $2.

Eljer Plumbingware
3 Gateway Center Dept. OHJ
Pittsburgh, PA 15222
(412) 553-7200
ID
This major manufacturer of plumbing fixtures carries a line of cast-iron enameled sinks similar to those made between 1900 and 1930. Also a line of Victorian reproduction hardware. Sells to the trade only; call for distributor information.

Elk Valley Woodworking Company
Rt. 1, Box 88 Dept. OHJ
Carter, OK 73627
(405) 486-3337
MO RS/O
They specialize in redwood and cedar porch columns and white pine, ash, oak, mahogany, and walnut room columns and balusters. They will also turn to your pattern or duplicate columns for partial replacements. Many decorative brackets are also available. Also custom-built furniture: cabinets, tables, etc. Send $2. for brochure.

Elmira Stove Works
22 Church St., W. Dept. OHJ
Elmira, Ontario, Canada N3B1M3
(519) 669-5103
DIST
Wood- or coal-burning cast iron cookstoves. Also, electric and combination wood/electric cookstoves. Many are copies of turn-of-the-century designs. Also produces fireplace inserts. Color flyers, $1. Distributors throughout Canada and the United States. Color brochure, $1.

Elmont Manufacturing Co., Inc.
175 Kennedy Dr. Dept. OHJ
Hauppauge, NY 11788
(516) 231-7400
DIST
Aluminum storm windows and doors with a baked acrylic paint finish in a variety of colors that will blend with old-house color schemes.

Elon, Inc. A & D Building
150 E. 58th St. Dept. OHJ
New York, NY 10155
(212) 759-6996
DIST RS/O
Source for Elon Carrillo® Mexican handmade glazed and unglazed terra cotta tiles and accessories. Mexican Ironware. Glazed tile from Italy, Culinarios from Portugal, and handmade French tiles. Palace Collection™ of hand-painted English tile, plus panels, and trim. Catalog, $5.

Elsie's Exquisiques
513 Broadway Dept. OHJ
Niles, MI 49120
(800) 742-SILK
MO RS/O
Ribbons, trims, fabrics, and laces for the Victorian house, including 185 shades of silk ribbon. Catalog, $5, refundable. Also, (616) 684-7034.

Empire Stove & Furnace Co., Inc.
793-797 Broadway Dept. OHJ
Albany, NY 12207
(518) 449-5189
RS/O MO
In addition to many wood and coal-burning stoves, this shop (in business since 1901) carries an extensive inventory of parts for old stoves, ranges, furnaces & boilers, and accessories. There are also patterns for many parts that aren't in stock. No literature. For best results phone number above or 449-2590.

• **The Emporium, Inc.**
2515 Morse St. Dept. OHJ
Houston, TX 77019
(713) 528-3808
RS/O MO
Walk-in store carries large stock of Victorian and turn-of-century architectural embellishments, such as tin ceilings, restored antique table fans, mantels, promenade benches, lamp posts, gingerbread, antique stained glass, doors, restored brass lighting fixtures, plumbing fixtures & fittings, antique door and cabinet hardware. Plus gingerbread by mail-order: corbels, fretwork, trim, and brackets. Illustrated 'gingerbread' brochure, $2.

Englander Millwork Corp.
2369 Lorillard Place Dept. OHJ
Bronx, NY 10458
(212) 364-4240
MO RS/O
Manufactures wood windows, doors and mouldings to customer's specifications. Specialty: round and curved windows. Will also duplicate counter-balance, double-hung, and pulley wheel window frames. Glass types available. No literature.

Englewood Hardware Co.
25 No. Dean St. Dept. OHJ
Englewood, NJ 07631
(201) 568-1937
RS/O
A restoration supply/hardware store, well-stocked with reproduction faucets, door and furniture hardware, fine brass fittings, ceiling and ornament and cornice mouldings, etc. Walk-in sales only; mail-order buyers contact Renaissance Decorative Hardware, their subsidiary.

• **Enlightened Restorations**
51 Shadow Lane Dept. OHJ
Wilton, CT 06897
(203) 834-1505
RS/O
Consulting services including house dating, historical research, and the locating of capable crafts people required for your house restoration. Consultation on decoration of period rooms & use of antique artifacts. Available for lectures & seminars also.

Entol Industries, Inc.
8180 NW 36th Ave. Dept. OHJ
Miami, FL 33147
(305) 696-0900
MO DIST
Art Carved® mouldings, medallions, and rosettes. Made of lightweight polyurethane polymers and/or fiberglass reinforced gypsum. Pieces can be primed or pre-finished in white or wood grain (custom finishes are also offered). Literature, $.50.

KEY TO ABBREVIATIONS

MO	sells by Mail Order
RS/O	sells through Retail Store or Office
DIST	sells through Distributors
ID	sells only through Interior Designers or Archtects

Ephraim Marsh
PO Box 266, Dept. 93 Dept. OHJ
Concord, NC 28026
(704) 782-0814
MO
Adaptions and reproductions of 18th century furniture. Also, home and office furniture. Mostly moderate in price. Catalog with price list — $2. Sell direct at below retail prices. Will send wood chips and fabric swatches upon request.

• **Epifanes/Coastal Trade, Inc.**
601 S. Andrews Ave. Dept. OHJ
Fort Lauderdale, FL 33301
(305) 467-8325
MO RS/O
High quality paints and finishes, imported from Holland: varnishes, enamels, one- and two-part urethanes, wood finishes and primers, solvents, and various additives. Also three types of chinese bristle brushes. Free color brochure.

Essex Forge
12 Old Dennison Rd. Dept. OHJ
Essex, CT 06426
(203) 767-1808
MO RS/O
Authentic hand-forged reproductions of early American fireplace accessories; terne, copper and iron chandeliers and sconces, copper and brass exterior lanterns. Illustrated catalog — $2.

Evergreen Slate Co.
68 East Potter Ave. Dept. OHJ
Granville, NY 12832
(518) 642-2530
MO RS/O
Producers of roofing slate in all colors and thicknesses: Semi-Weathering Gray-Green, VT Black & Gray-Black, Unfading Green, Red, Royal Purple, Unfading Mottled Green & Purple, and Rustics. Company also sells 'ESCO' Slate Cutters, Slate Rippers, Slate Hammers, and Slate Hooks for slate repairs. Write or call for free brochure.

Evergreene Painting Studios, Inc.
365 West 36th St. Dept. OHJ
New York, NY 10018
(212) 239-1322
RS/O
An organization of artists, craftsmen, and designers dedicated to preservation. They provide services that include conceptual drawings, research, color samples, models, detailed estimates, and time and cost projections. They will do murals, public art, fine decorative painting, tromp l'oeil, stencilling, architectural decoration, gold leaf, graining, glazing, marbleizing, lettering, frescoes, faux finishes, floorcloths, colored plaster, custom wallpapers, and painted objects. Free literature.

Experi-Metals
524 W. Greenfield Avenue Dept. OHJ
Milwaukee, WI 53204
(414) 384-2167
RS/O MO
Individual craftsman does high-quality custom castings in brass, bronze and related alloys. Excellent reproduction work. Has done custom duplication of hardware through the mail. No literature — you must call or write.

F

Facemakers, Inc.
140 Fifth St. Dept. OHJ
Savanna, IL 61074
(815) 273-3944
RS/O MO
Creates original paintings done to customer specifications. Specializes in period portraits that are done from clients' photographs. Customer can have portrait done in almost any style and in the appropriate costume of the period selected. Paintings done in oils on stretched canvas. Prices start at $1500. Also interior and exterior restoration design service. Send $5.00 for brochure.

Faire Harbour Ltd.
44 Captain Pierce Rd. Dept. OHJ
Scituate, MA 02066
(617) 545-2465
MO RS/O
Distributors of Aladdin kerosene mantle lamps and manufacturers of several old-style kerosene table and bracket lamps. These well-made brass, glass, and aluminum lamps with glass shades and chimneys give a steady light equal to a 75 watt bulb. Optional electric converter. Replacement parts and supplies. Illustrated catalog and price list — $2 by 1st class mail — refundable. Minimum purchase, $5.

Fairmont Foundry Co., Inc.
3125 35th Ave., North Dept. OHJ
Birmingham, AL 35207
(205) 841-6472
DIST
Ornamental fencing and railing in aluminum or grey iron. Decorative castings and components only — you or your contractor must do the designing and fabricating. Also offer garden furniture in both materials. Custom reproduction of ornamental cast iron and aluminum. Free catalog.

• **Family Heir-Loom Weavers**
Meadow View Dr., RD 3, Box 59E Dept. OHJ
Red Lion, PA 17356
(717) 246-2431
MO RS/O
Weavers of coverlets, table runners, and ingrain carpets in historically accurate patterns. Free brochure. Also, (717) 244-5921.

The Fan Man
2721 NW 109 Terrace Dept. OHJ
Oklahoma City, OK 73120
(405) 751-0933
MO RS/O
Restores and sells antique ceiling fans, lighting fixtures, and lamps. Free brochure: "Why buy a restored antique ceiling fan?" with color photos.

Faneuil Furniture Hardware
94-100 Peterborough St. Dept. OHJ
Boston, MA 02215
(617) 262-7516
MO RS/O
They stock extensive selections of pulls, handles, knobs, ornaments, casters, grilles and allied items for all periods of furniture design. A 138-page catalog is available for $3.00.

The Farm Forge
6945 Fishburg Rd. Dept. OHJ
Dayton, OH 45424
(513) 233-6751
MO RS/O
Mr. Wood offers a complete selection of reproduction and restoration hardware, lighting, and architectural iron work, in traditional or contemporary styles. Hand-Forged and custom items. Catalog, $1.

Fasco Industries, Inc.
PO Box 150 Dept. OHJ
Fayetteville, NC 28302
(800) 334-4126
ID
Ceiling fans in a variety of designs, some with custom lighting fixtures attached. "Decorator" collection offers six colors. Also attic, bath, and kitchen ventilation. This major manufacturer provides color brochures.

• **Felber Studios, Inc.**
110 Ardmore Ave., Box 551 Dept. OHJ
Ardmore, PA 19003
(215) 642-4710
MO RS/O
Felber, Inc. maintains a collection of 2,300 plus original antique ornamental models. Ceiling medallions, cornices, cartouches, and niche shells are stocked. Their custom department can create new or restore period plaster mouldings and ornaments. Most castings will be reinforced with glass fibers and making them stronger and lighter than traditional ornamental plaster while maintaining the same intricate detail. Catalogue available, $2.00.

Fellenz Hardware & Antiques
2216 Cherokee Dept. OHJ
St. Louis, MO 63118
(314) 776-8363
RS/O
Antique shop specializing in light fixtures, drawer pulls, door hardware, bathroom & plumbing fixtures, and light switch plates. Walk-in shop. No literature.

Fenton Art Glass Company
700 Elizabeth Street Dept. OHJ
Williamstown, WV 26187
(304) 375-6122
RS/O MO DIST
Handmade glassware and lamps in 19th-century styles, many of which are handpainted and signed by the artists. Also baskets, bells, vases, and figurines. Send $6. for 54-page illustrated catalog and price guide.

FerGene Studio
4320 Washington Street Dept. OHJ
Gary, IN 46408
(219) 884-1119
MO
Reproduction turn-of-century fireplace tiles. Face tiles 6 x 6. Hearth tile 6 x 6, 6 x 3, 6 x 1-1/2 with some special sizes on request. Can color tiles, using modern commercial glazes, to complement other tiles, wallpaper or fabric. Patterns include: vine pattern, morning glory, scrolls, and medieval lady and knight. Flyer $1 (large self-addressed, stamped envelope, please).

• See Advertisers' Index on page 22 for more details.

Ferguson's Cut Glass Works
4292 Pearl Rd. Dept. OHJ
Cleveland, OH 44109
(216) 459-2929
MO RS/O
Ferguson's Cut Glass Works specializes in glass engraving, bevelling and mirror resilvering. The glass is hand-engraved and polished just as it was at the turn-of-the-century, which gives the finished piece a diamond-like appearance. Ferguson's is one of the only companies engraving large pieces of glass, such as door lites, windows, etc., in America. The engraved and bevelled glass can be used as room dividers, mirrors, entrance door and side lites, tabletops, etc. Also offers lead hand-cut crystal tableware. Free brochure.

Ferris, Robert Donald, Architect, Inc.
3776 Front St. Dept. OHJ
San Diego, CA 92103
(714) 297-4659
RS/O
Architectural design services for interior and exterior restoration and rehabilitation of all types of buildings, including public buildings, commercial and residential. All types of construction, including adobe; adaptive re-use studies, feasibility reports and planning. Southern California and Hawaii. No literature.

Fibertech Corp.
PO Box 9 Dept. OHJ
Clemson, SC 29633
(803) 654-2190
MO RS/O
Fabricators of replacement building parts such as cornices, balustrades, columns & facings in fiberglass — reinforced plastic. Custom work. Shipping can be arranged; no installations. Free literature and newsletter. Photographs available of work done on courthouse and opera house in Abbeville, S.C., office renovation in St. Louis, warehouse conversion in Atlanta, cornice restoration in Montgomery and Birmingham, Ala.

Fichet Lock Co.
4 Osage Drive Dept. OHJ
Huntington Station, NY 11746
(516) 673-1818
MO DIST
Fichet is renowned for high security locks since 1825. High-security locking devices that can be adapted to old buildings/doors. Free literature.

Fifty / 50 Gallery
793 Broadway Dept. OHJ
New York, NY 10003
(212) 777-3208
RS/O
Specializing in reproductions of furniture designed by 20th-century architects; will also do custom reproductions. Call or write for more information.

Fine Woodworking Co.
16750 White Store Rd. Dept. OHJ-81
Boyds, MD 20841
(301) 972-8808
RS/O
Quality-conscious company specializing in old-house restoration, custom cabinetwork, and custom millwork. Washington, D.C. metropolitan area. No literature.

• **Finish Feeder Company**
P.O. Box 60 Dept. J
Boyds, MD 20841
(301) 972-1474
RS/O MO DIST
A furniture polish based on an 18th century cabinetmakers' formula. For furniture, wood panelling and floors, colored marble (never white). Free literature. Money back guarantee!

The Finishing Company
209 48th St., B-5 Dept. OHJ
Union City, NJ 07087
(201) 864-7579
MO RS/O
Specialize in stripping, restoration, and duplication of architectural woodwork, cabinetry, and furniture. Stains, varnishes, and hand-rubbed finishes applied. Also, interior painting service that includes plaster repair, plaster moulding replacement, and stencilling. Free consultation.

Finishing School
1 Elm St. Dept. OHJ
Great Neck, NY 11021
(516) 487-2270
RS/O
Courses offered in marbleizing, graining, gilding, wall glazing, strie, wall marbleizing, & other faux finishes. Weekend, 1 and 4-day courses. Call or write for brochure.

Finishing Touch
5636 College Avenue Dept. OHJ
Oakland, CA 94618
(415) 652-4908
MO RS/O
Suppliers of fine reproduction brass hardware. Specialists in antique wicker furniture restoration. Manufacture and sales of genuine leather seats, available in six embossed designs, three shapes and six sizes. Sheet caning supplies and instructions available. Also, "Howard's Restor-A-Finish", for eliminating heat rings, water marks, and scratches in naturally finished wood. Catalog, $.50.

Finnaren & Haley, Inc.
2320 Haverford Road Dept. OHJ
Ardmore, PA 19003
(215) 649-5000
MO DIST RS/O
Interior and exterior paints, both water-based and oil-based, in 30 colors of historic Philadelphia, 10 of which were authenticated through the cooperation of the National Park Service as used in historic Philadelphia buildings. F&H Color Card available upon request; send $.40 in stamps.

Firebird, Inc.
4 Spring St. Dept. OHJ
Morristown, NJ 07960
(201) 267-0414
MO DIST RS/O
Hand-made, hand-painted ceramic tiles. Embossed designs include Victorian flowers, exotic herbs, sea creatures and shells, folk art birds and country buttermolds. All designs in a complete range of colors. Matching plain tiles are also available. Firebird specializes in custom work, and offers a full line of stock tile murals.

Fireplace Mantel Shop, Inc.
4217 Howard Ave. Dept. OHJ
Kensington, MD 20895
(301) 564-1550
RS/O MO
Architectural woodwork, specializing in decorative wood mantels, entrance sets, and cornices/mouldings. Also custom millwork, panels, doors. 22-page "Wood Mouldings & Millwork" catalog, $3.50.

• See Advertisers' Index on page 22 for more details.

Fischer & Jirouch Co.
4821 Superior Avenue Dept. OHJ
Cleveland, OH 44103
(216) 361-3840
MO
Ornaments of fiber-reinforced plaster. They also do restoration work, and can reproduce existing pieces if a good example is supplied. (For example, a foot of moulding in very good condition is needed to make a mould.) Complete catalog of 1500 items with prices and terms is $25.00. Photo-copies of single elements sent free on specific request.

Fisher Skylights, Inc.
50 Snake Hill Road Dept. OHJ
West Nyack, NY 10994
(914) 358-9000
DIST RS/O
They design, manufacture, and install custom and stock aluminum-framed skylights in a variety of shapes including octagonal, pyramidal, and old-fashioned pyramid clusters. Free 28-page color catalog.

Edward Fitzgerald Associates
46 Lawrence St. Dept. OHJ
Tappan, NY 10983
(914) 359-0200
RS/O
Complete house inspections, from basement to roof, including heating, plumbing, and electrical systems; chimneys and fireplaces; septic systems, outbuildings, and termite damage. Written reports provided, lawyer advisement services available, 28 years experience.

Flaharty, David — Sculptor
79 Magazine Rd., R.D. 1 Dept. OHJ
Green Lane, PA 18054
(215) 234-8242
RS/O MO
Specializes in the reproduction and restoration of architectural details and ornaments, especially in plaster and fiberglass. Among his clients are the State Department, the White House, the U.S. Capitol, Georgetown University, Metropolitan Museum of Art. No literature. Photos of work supplied for serious inquiries.

Flexi-Wall Systems
P.O. Box 88 Dept. OHJ
Liberty, SC 29657
(803) 855-0500
MO
They offer a patented, gypsum-impregnated flexible wallcovering, designed for problem wall surfaces (especially masonry). They have passed the rigid fire and toxicity tests required for use in New York City. An ideal finish for the thermal mass walls in the field of passive solar energy. "Scotland Weave" decorative finish. Complete test data, catalog information, and prices are available.

The Flood Company
1213 Barlow Road, PO Box 399 Dept. OHJ
Hudson, OH 44236
(800) 321-3444
ID
A family-owned company that has specialized in wood-care products for over 100 years. Products for preserving shakes and shingles, decks, fences, siding and rustic interiors. Two exterior wood finishes, CWF and Aquatrol, can restore natural color to weathered wood. Wood cleaner, marine finish. Call for information and literature. In OH call collect at (216) 650-4070.

Floorcloths Incorporated
P.O. Box 812 Dept. OHJ
Severna Park, MD 21146
(301) 544-0858
RS/O MO
Reproductions of 18th and 19th century painted canvas floorcoverings. Patterns are documented or adapted from original sources. Finest hand-painting and stencilling techniques. Their trained designers also work from designs supplied by the client. Prices start at $10.00 per square foot. Design portfolios available at $2.00 to cover postage and handling.

Floors By Juell
8137 N. Austin Ave. Dept. OHJ
Morton Grove, IL 60053
(312) 965-6900
RS/O
Hardwood floor specialists, supplying a variety of creative and technical capabilities. Services include: custom designs; installation; refinishing; restoration; cleaning and waxing; antiquing; inlaid borders; custom tables; paneling; cabinetry. No literature available.

Floortown
26 Union St. Dept. OHJ
Lynn, MA 01902
(617) 599-6544
MO RS/O
Battleship linoleum, imported from Holland; in green, gray, terra cotta, brown, and black. Free maintenance sheet.

• **Florida Victorian Architectural Antiques**
901 W. 1 St. (Hwy. 46) Dept. OHJ
Sanford, FL 32771
(305) 321-5767
RS/O
Architectural antiques. Assorted stained, bevelled, leaded glass doors & windows; porch and stair railings, newel posts, columns, and capitals, mantels, backbars, pedestal sinks and tubs. Recycled building and plumbing materials. Can also call (904) 228-3404. Brochure available with SASE.

• **Flue Works**
110 W. Spruce St. Dept. OHJ
Columbus, OH 43215
(614) 221-6918
MO RS/O
Specializes in the restoration of fireplaces and chimneys in old and historic houses as well as the conversion of coal and gas fireplaces to wood-burning. Also manufactures modular, all-masonry Rumford fireplaces. (See article in OHJ, Jan./Feb. 1985, p.8.) Write for more detailed information.

Focal Point, Inc.
2005 Marietta Rd., N.W. Dept. OHC4
Atlanta, GA 30318
(800) 662-5550
MO DIST
Manufactures a handsome line of architecturally accurate ceiling medallions, cornice mouldings, niche caps, overdoor pieces, and more. Made of Endure-All™, a high-quality polymer, the product is resilient and lightweight. Factory-primed to receive paint or stain and is indistinguishable from wood or plaster. Easy to install. 4-color brochure, $3.

Folkheart Rag Rugs
18 Main St. Dept. OHJ
Bristol, VT 05443
(802) 453-4101
MO RS/O
A small handweaving operation that makes 100% cotton rag rugs which are then hand stencilled. Will sell wholesale as well as retail. Color (retail) brochure — $1.

Follansbee Steel
State St. Dept. OHJ
Follansbee, WV 26037
(800) 624-6906
DIST
Manufactures terne roofing and terne-coated stainless for standing-seam metal roofs. One of the oldest types of metal roofing, terne is used on many historic buildings such as Monticello and the Smithsonian Institution. It's a a premium-quality long-lasting material. Free brochures: "Terne Roofing" and "Terne-Coated-Stainless Roofing."

Forbo N.A., Inc.
218 W. Orange St., Suite A Dept. OHJ
Lancaster, PA 17603
(717) 291-5874
DIST
Major Swiss manufacturer of plain battleship linoleum. Made of all natural materials. Solid color throughout, wears well. Through distributors only, though the company offers a free information flyer.

• **The Frame Works**
33 Church St. Dept. OHJ
Willimantic, CT 06226
(203) 456-7885
RS/O
Makers of an adaptable timber post-and-beam frame house 26′ x 36′. Erected on your site; end and side wings available. Authentic 1800s design. Brochure and study plans, $5.

Frank's Cane and Rush Supply
7252 Heil Ave. Dept. OH
Huntington Beach, CA 92647
(714) 847-0707
MO RS/O
A complete supply of cane webbing, strand cane, rush, reeds, natural rattans, basketry rings, wood parts, brass hardware, books, kits and much more. Knowledgeable personnel in all kinds of chair caning and seat weaving, wicker repair and basketry. Buy from a leading supplier and save! Also, write for free catalog.

• **Peter Franklin, Cabinetmaker**
1 Cottage St., PO Box 1166 Dept. OHJ
Easthampton, MA 01027
(413) 527-2127
MO
Hand-crafted reproductions of 18th-century Windsor chairs. Techniques and tools would be familiar to an 18th-century furniture-maker. Also, on request, makes reproductions of any 18th- or early 19th-century American furniture. Catalog and price list, $2.

KEY TO ABBREVIATIONS

MO	sells by Mail Order
RS/O	sells through Retail Store or Office
DIST	sells through Distributors
ID	sells only through Interior Designers or Archtects

Frenzel Specialty Moulding Co.
4911 Ringer Rd. Dept. OHJ
St. Louis, MO 63129
(314) 892-3292
MO
Any available moulding can be reproduced at a reasonable price. For an estimate, send a copy of existing moulding on piece of cardboard.

Frog Tool Co., Ltd.
700 W. Jackson Blvd. Dept. HJ1
Chicago, IL 60606
(312) 648-1270
MO RS/O
An extensive collection of traditional and old-fashioned woodworking tools, including imported tools. Adzes, froes, broad axes, Myford lathes, wood moulding planes, wood finishing materials and wood carving chisels. Books, furniture plans, and many other unusual items. Catalog $2.50 for 3 year subscription refundable with purchase. Mail order catalog available — $2.50.

Full Circle Glass Company
16-18 Railroad Place Dept. OHJ
Pearl River, NY 10965
(914) 735-4137
RS/O
Art glass studio specializing in original ecclesiastic and residential stained, etched, and bevelled glass. Will also restore 19th- and 20th-century windows. Some cut-wheel engraving, vitreous paints, deep-acid etching, glue-chip, etc. Free brochure.

• **Fuller O'Brien Paints**
P.O. Box 864 Dept. OHJ
Brunswick, GA 31521
(912) 265-7650
DIST
Has a handsome collection of Early American, Victorian and Traditional colors for both interior and exterior use. Free color chips include "Heritage" Color Collection, Whisper Whites and their Decorating Guide which has 136 different colors to choose from. The new palette of "Cape May" Victorian colors is available for $1.50.

Furniture Traditions, Inc.
PO Box 5067 Dept. HJ1
Hickory, NC 28603
(704) 324-0611
MO
Early American and traditional furniture for living room, dining room and bedroom. Hand-tailored leather sofas and chairs for home and office. Finely crafted furniture collections ranging from country to formal English, French and American. 32-page catalog, $3.

Fypon, Inc.
Box 365, 22 W. Penna. Ave. Dept. OHJ
Stewartstown, PA 17363
(717) 993-2593
DIST
High density polyurethane millwork that can be nailed, drilled, puttied, painted, and handled with regular carpenter tools. Four lines of entrance features, mouldings, specialty millwork, window features, and most recently, copper-finished bay window roofs. Designs are suitable for Colonial and Victorian style architecture. Free brochures upon request.

G

Gainsborough Hardware Industry
PO Box 569 Dept. OHJ
Chesterfield, MO 63017
(314) 532-8466
DIST
Manufacturers doorknobs and cabinet knobs in porcelain, crystal, brass, wood, stoneware, and polyester acrylic. Switch plates made in porcelain. Also, solid-brass numerals. Free brochure.

Gallier House Museum
1118-32 Royal Street Dept. OHJ
New Orleans, LA 70116
(504) 523-6722
MO RS/O
Films on ornamental plasterwork, cast iron work, and marbling & graining are available for rental. Reproduction glass globes and brass shade rings for 19th-century gasoliers. Please call for more information.

Gargoyles, Ltd.
512 South Third Street Dept. OHJ
Philadelphia, PA 19147
(215) 629-1700
RS/O MO
Architectural antique & reproductions, ironwork, fretwork, ceiling fans, tin ceilings, bars & backbars, leaded glass, mantels, Victorian wall units, complete store interiors, chandeliers, brackets, and anything they can find. Your best bet will be a visit to their warehouse/showroom, but please call & make an appointment if you come from out of town. Weekend hours by special appt.

Larry W. Garnett & Associates, Inc.
3515 Preston Rd., Ste. 200 Dept. OHJ
Pasadena, TX 77505
(713) 487-0427
MO RS/O
A 9-year-old building design firm specializing in single family residential design. Portfolios available: Victorian, French, Garden, Designer, Classical, Project Plans. Prices range from $7 to $12. Write for information.

• **Garrett Wade Company**
161 Avenue of the Americas Dept. OHJ
New York, NY 10013
(212) 807-1155
RS/O MO
A comprehensive selection of quality hand woodworking and carving tools, many imported from Western Europe and Japan. Wood-working benches, plans and hardware, complete line of Behlen finishing supplies, including stains, oils, waxes, and paint removers. Power tools include English and German lathes and INCA Swiss circular saws, bandsaws, jointer/planers. Extensive book list on working with wood. 250-page illustrated catalog with price list, $4. Brass Hardware catalog, $.50.

• **Gaslight Time Antiques**
823 President St. Dept. OHJ
Brooklyn, NY 11217
(718) 789-7185
MO RS/O
This shop sells antique lighting fixtures with glass shades, and reproduction lighting fixtures and glass shades. No literature.

Gaston Wood Finishes, Inc.
7155 E. St. Rd. 46/PO Box 1246 Dept. OHJ
Bloomington, IN 47402
(812) 339-9111
MO RS/O
An excellent selection of traditional wood finishing supplies, reproduction furniture hardware, and veneer. Catalog $1.75.

Gasworks
2409 Madison Ave. Dept. OHJ
Baltimore, MD 21217
(301) 669-3992
MO
Ceramic candles and bobeches for gas chandeliers, produced in white, heat-resistant ceramic that look and function just like the originals. Custom orders a specialty.

• **Gates Moore**
2 River Road, Silvermine Dept. OHJ
Norwalk, CT 06850
(203) 847-3231
RS/O MO
Handmade reproductions of early American lighting fixtures in a variety of finishes: old paint effect, distressed tin, pewter, flat black. Will make anything from drawings or sketch with complete dimensions. Illustrated 29 pg. catalog with price list — $2, refundable.

Gaudio Custom Furniture
21 Harrison Ave. Dept. OHJ
Rockville Centre, NY 11570
(516) 766-1237
RS/O
Specializing in creations constructed with fine veneer inlays of floral marquetry and geometric parquetry. Also: antique reproduction and restoration, bronze ormolu mounts, architectural paneling. No literature.

Gawet Marble & Granite
Dept. OHJ
Center Rutland, VT 05736
(802) 773-8868
MO RS/O
Suppliers of building stone and marble who also carry a line of marble cleaners, poultices, and polishes. Free flyers.

Gazebo
660 Madison Ave. Dept. OHJ
New York, NY 10021
(212) 832-7077
MO RS/O
Handsome, hand-woven rag, hooked, and braided rugs. New appliqued and pieced quilts available in custom colors or from their extensive stock. Also quilted pillows. Designs are based on traditional patterns. Call for location of stores in Beverly Hills, CA, Dallas, TX, and Ardmore, PA. Color catalog with price list, $4.

KEY TO ABBREVIATIONS

MO	sells by Mail Order
RS/O	sells through Retail Store or Office
DIST	sells through Distributors
ID	sells only through Interior Designers or Archtects

Gazebo and Porchworks
728 9th Ave., SW Dept. OHJ
Puyallup, WA 98371
(206) 848-0502
MO RS/O
A small family business offering a wide selection of wood turnings, (spindles, newels, porch posts), corner brackets, corbels, gable trims, porch swings, and mantels. Several arbor kits available along with a plan/instruction book for gazebos. Catalog, $2.

Gem Monogram & Cut Glass Corp.
623 Broadway Dept. OHJ
New York, NY 10012
(212) 674-8962
MO RS/O
Chandeliers, antique & reproduction. They have a loft full of crystal parts, such as prisms and pendants, some dating back to the 18th century. No literature, specify your requirements. Visitors welcome.

Halina Gemes
5 White St. Dept. OHJ
New York, NY 10013
(212) 966-4435
RS/O
Museum-trained European restorer of murals, stencilling, and paintings. Free estimates. Free flyer. Also, (718) 448-0262.

George Studios
45-04 97th Place Dept. OHJ
Corona, NY 11368
(212) 271-2506
RS/O
Will restore wall murals or create one for you. Will also restore or create hand-painted decorations on porcelain, furniture, etc. Other restorations skills — gold leafing, marblizing, and faux finishes. No literature.

Gerlachs of Lecha
PO Box 213 Dept. OHJ
Emmaus, PA 18049
(215) 965-9181
MO RS/O
Seasonal catalogs feature nostalgic antique Victorian and Pennsylvania German replicas in cast iron, tin, pewter, wood and paper. Spring-Easter, Summer-Fall, and Christmas, $2 each. Special blown glass Christmas tree ornaments catalog shows huge selection of exclusive European imports and other rare Christmas tree trimmings, $1.25.

• **Germantown Restoration Supplies**
5445 Germantown Ave. Dept. OHJ
Philadelphia, PA 19144
(215) 849-9050
RS/O
Restoration supply store featuring hand-screened period wallpapers, Lincrusta, (a Crown trademark), moulding, wooden gingerbread, tin ceilings, brass hardware, stains, refinishers, heat guns, and free consulting service.

Giannetti Studios, Inc.
3806 38th Street Dept. OHJ
Brentwood, MD 20722
(301) 927-0033
RS/O MO DIST
Primarily engaged in the design, manufacture and installation of ornamental plaster in the Washington, DC metropolitan area. Some restoration/preservation services. Brochure $3. (refundable on purchase).

Gibbons Sash and Door
Route 1, Box 76 Dept. OHJ
Hurley, WI 54534
(715) 561-3904
MO DIST
Sash & door mill specializing in custom doors and windows. Hardwood French, frame and panel doors. Circular and elliptical windows. Divided windows, thermopane glazing available. Custom work to architectural specifications. Literature, $2.

• **Jamie Gibbs & Associates**
340 E. 93rd St., No. 14C Dept. OHJ
New York, NY 10128
(212) 722-7508
RS/O
Restoration and re-creation of period landscape designs for residential and commercial clients. Specialize in master plans and full specifications. Expert staff with range of talents in design, research, horticulture, and period decoration. All types of garden design, including townhouse, terrace, roofgarden, suburban, and estate. Experience in West, Mid-West, South, and East Coast, along with South America and Europe. References and biographical prospectus free.

Gillinder Brothers, Inc.
Box 1007 Dept. OHJ
Port Jervis, NY 12771
(914) 856-5375
DIST
Manufacturers of glass parts for the lamp and lighting industry. Products include cased glass shades, clear & colored, gas shades, electric shades, lamp bodies . . .Thousands of molds date back to the 1800's. Sales are wholesale only. Their catalog can be seen at many retail lighting fixture stores. No literature available to retail customers.

Gilpin, Inc.
PO Box 471 Dept. OHJ
Decatur, IN 46733
(800) 348-0746
MO DIST RS/O
Gilpin has been producing wrought-iron railing since the 1930s. They've been supplying major chains with sectional ornamental iron railing and are now expanding into new products. Free brochure.

Glass & Aluminum Construction Services, Inc.
PO Box 14, Jct. Rt. 123A & 123 Dept. OHJ
Alstead, NH 03602
(603) 835-2918
RS/O
A major designer, fabricator, and installer of wood, glass and aluminum windows, greenhouses, and entry way systems. Specialize in refurbishing and renovating older and historic structures — both commercial and residential—especially in re-manufacturing original wood doors and window sash. Their primary market is New England; literature is available on request.

Glass Artisan, Inc.
51 Brampton Lane Dept. OHJ
Great Neck, NY 11023
(516) 466-3890
RS/O
Designs and fabricates new stained glass. Also removal, repair/restoration, and re-installation of old stained glass; all size jobs, large or small. Experienced with church restorations; resume upon request.

Glass Arts—The Condon Studios
30 Penniman Road Dept. OHJ
Boston, MA 02134
(617) 782-7760
MO RS/O
Professional glass studio specializing in both antique stained and etched glass windows and lamps as well as in designing and creating glass works in stained, leaded, bevelled, and etched glass — Victorian and other styles. Glass art works and signs (edge-lit or framed). Restoration of leaded windows and lamps. Glass bending and repair services for antique lamps. Matching antique etched glass. Call for information. $3 for bevelled, leaded/etched brochure.

Glass Designs
918 Baxter Ave. Dept. OHJ
Louisville, KY 40204
(502) 589-2939
MO RS/O
Custom designs of stained and leaded glass and mirrors; standard designs also available. They include sidelights, transoms, and cabinet doors. Cathedral glass tub enclosures and beveled and etched glass also available. Etched mirror mantlepieces made to your direction. Catalog, $2.

Glass Roots
191 Allen St. Dept. OHJ
Buffalo, NY 14201
(716) 884-1908
MO RS/O
Stained and bevelled glass; stock, custom, and restoration. Stock lines include Art Nouveau and late-Victorian bevelled designs. Also a series for kitchen cabinets; prices range from $60—200. Free brochures.

Glen — Gery Corporation
PO Box 340, Route 61 Dept. OHJ
Shoemakersville, PA 19555
(215) 562-3076
DIST
Manufacturers of a large array of handmade and moulded colonial brick that looks just like old brick. Free brochure — "Alwine Handmade Brick."

Glidden Coatings & Resins
925 Euclid Ave. Dept. OHJ
Cleveland, OH 44115
(216) 344-8216
RS/O
Their American Legacy exterior paint collection features deep, muted tones of red, green, brown, blue, grey and tan, applicable to any period house. Free brochure with paint chips.

J. Goddard & Sons, Ltd.
PO Box 808 Dept. OHJ
Manitowoc, WI 54220
(414) 684-7137
DIST MO
Manufactures a complete line of fine care products for silver, jewelry, metal, fabric, and furniture articles. An illustrated brochure is available at no charge. Toll free (800) 558-7621.

Gold Leaf & Metallic Powders, Inc.
2 Barclay St. Dept. OHJ
New York, NY 10007
(212) 267-4900
MO RS/O
Distributes a complete line of Genuine and Imitation Gold Leaf and other Leaf products such as XX Deep Gold, Patent Gold, Lemon Gold, White Gold, Composition Gold Leaf, Aluminum Leaf, Copper Leaf, Variegated Leaf. Manufactures metallic pigments in bronze, copper and aluminum with a wide range of shades available in mesh sizes suitable for many applications. Product list and color card available — free.

Gold Leaf Studios, Inc.
PO Box 50156 Dept. OHJ
Washington, DC 20004
(202) 638-4660
MO
Gold Leaf conservation and restoration primarily for frames, but also architecutral, interior, and furniture. Clients include the White House, The State Department Diplomatic Reception Rooms, The Smithsonian Institute, The Hearst Castle at San Simeon, California, the Nebraska State Capitol and many others. They'll also search for appropriate frames for artwork and consult. The Frame in America 1700-1900: A Survey of Fabrication Techniques and Styles, $15.

• **Golden Age Glassworks**
339 Bellvale Rd. Dept. OHJ
Warwick, NY 10990
(914) 986-1487
RS/O MO
Design and manufacture leaded and stained glass windows, lampshades, architectural pieces, skylights, room dividers, etc. Also museum quality Victorian (and other styles) reproductions and restorations. Extensive church and residential experience — in business over 12 years. Will work from your design or help you to create one. Free information; slides showing examples of work, $2/set of 4, please specify style of interest. Also carries imported English antique stained glass.

• **Golden Leaf Timber**
PO Box 205 Dept. OHJ
Lake Hiawatha, NJ 07034
(201) 927-0742
MO RS/O
Teak parquet, prefinished: $1.95 per square foot on orders over 1,000 square feet; $2.25 for 500-1000 square feet. Also, imported T&G plank, T&G strip, plus teak lumber and plywood. Free brochure.

Goldenrod Ironworks
144 Bedford Ave. Dept. OHJ
Brooklyn, NY 11211
(718) 387-5428
RS/O
Designs, fabricates, and installs custom metalwork in iron, steel, brass, bronze, and aluminum. Projects range from handmade hardware (custom-forged door knockers, weathervanes) to staircases, spiral stairs, skylights, gates, grates, furniture, railings, fences. Fully insured. Free flyer.

Good & Co. — Floorclothmakers
Box 387-OHJ Dept. OHJ
Dublin, NH 03444
(603) 672-0490
MO RS/O
Documented and original designs by Nancy Good Cayford are applied to canvas floor cloths — free hand and stenciled. Heavy canvas and oil base paints are used for durability. Finished with varnish for a long lasting, easy to clean carpet. Any color — any size available. Custom orders taken. Prices start at $4. sq./ft. Color catalog $2. Retail showroom at Salzburg Sq., Rt. 101, Amherst, NH.

• See Advertisers' Index on page 22 for more details.

• **Good Directions, Inc.**
24 Ardmore Rd. Dept. OH
Stamford, CT 06902
(203) 348-1836
MO
Weathervane catalog offers 20 varieties of solid copper weathervanes. Many are authentic reproductions with prices starting at $69. Wood cupolas also available. 8-page color catalog, $1.

• **Good Impressions Rubber Stamps**
Dept. OHJ
Shirley, WV 26434
MO
Manufactures Victorian and country style rubber stamps. Hundreds of decorative word and picture stamps offered through illustrated catalogue, $1, refundable with order. General price range for individual stamps $3-$7.50 post paid. Many sets also offered. Custom stamps and options such as rocker mounts available. 8 colors of stamp pads. They also design period style advertising, sell image reproduction rights, and offer Period Wholesale display.

Goodman - Southern Fabrications
PO Box 8164 Dept. OHJ
Prairie Village, KS 66208
(913) 642-1288
MO RS/O
This company provides custom services for window treatments (draperies, shades, blinds, shutters), wall upholstering, hand-woven area rugs, custom quilted white- on-white counterpanes, netted drapery trim, and interior design consultation for historic restoration projects. Free brochure. Also, (816) 942-0832.

Virginia Goodwin
Rt. 2, Box 770 Dept. OHJ
Boone, NC 28607
(704) 264-7704
MO
Weavers since 1812, the Goodwin family uses antique patterns and looms to create coverlets. A specialty is Virginia Goodwin's hand-tied fishnet bed canopies and window valances. Send $1. for further information.

Bill Goschen
PO Box 7454 Dept. OHJ
Baltimore, MD 21227
(301) 242-0049
MO RS/O
Restoration services including glazing, marbleizing, graining, gilding, stencilling, trompe l'oeil, wallpaper restoration, carpentry, exterior house painting. Brass and bronze refinishing. Samples upon request.

Gougeon Brothers, Inc.
PO Box X-908 Dept. OHJ
Bay City, MI 48707
(517) 684-7286
MO DIST
Manufacturer of WEST SYSTEM brand epoxy products, designed for marine, wood-composite structures; for any wood building or repairing project where long term, all-weather durability is a primary concern. Line includes epoxy resins for bonding and primary sealing, fillers used with epoxy resins, reinforcing fabrics and application tools and accessories. Technical assistance, product catalog, technical manual, newsletter, free.

Gould-Mesereau Co., Inc.
21-16 44th Road Dept. OHJ
Long Island City, NY 11101
(718) 361-8120
DIST
Manufactures a complete line of metal and real wood drapeware products, both utility and decorative in extensive variety of styles and finishes to complement every decor. "Sierra", Gould's all wood drapeware/ decorative products line, is available in traverse, pole sets and component parts. All accessories & installation aids. Consumer brochures for Sierra line available; catalogs available to the trade ONLY — both free.

Grammar of Ornament
2626 Curtis Street Dept. OHJ
Denver, CO 80205
(303) 295-2431
DIST RS/O
Period consultation. Murals, glazed finishes, stencil painting, gilding, woodgraining and marbleizing. Examples of services can be found in over 20 sites on the National Register, both residential and commercial. Will do on-site examination and research. Call or write regarding estimates and consultation charges.

Grandpa Snazzy's Hardware
1832 S. Broadway Dept. OHJ
Denver, CO 80210
(303) 935-3269
RS/O MO
An antique store which stocks reproduction hardware from 72 companies as well as antique hardware. They can match patterns of hinges, doorknobs, sash lifts, etc. Transom hardware and hard-to-find parts. Can also match furniture hardware. Mail order welcome. Send needs. They can fabricate any part or piece you are missing. No literature. Also, (303) 778-6508.

Granville Mfg. Co., Inc.
Rt. 100 Dept. OHJ
Granville, VT 05747
(802) 767-4747
MO RS/O
This company is one of the last to produce spruce and pine clapboards, quartersawn to warp less, and wide pine boards for siding and flooring. Custom dimensional lumber such as beams. Other decorative wooden accessories like bootjacks and one-piece hardwood salad bowls. They can also do custom reproduction of furniture and household items; in operation since 1857. Free flyer.

Gravity - Randall
208 N. Douty St., PO Box 1378 Dept. OHJ
Hanford, CA 93232
(209) 584-2216
MO RS/O
Two attractive wood and wrought-iron garden benches in a variety of sizes, plus reproductions of an 1842 wrought-iron English pub table and a Victorian table base. Onyx and marble tops available. Free illustrated brochure and price list.

• See Advertisers' Index on page 22 for more details.

• **Great American Salvage**
34 Cooper Sq. Dept. OHJ
New York, NY 10003
(212) 505-0070
MO RS/O
Five showrooms of antique architectural components, inventoried and accessed by computer. A vast selection of doors, stained glass, lighting fixtures, hardware, pedestal sinks, bathtubs, mantels, gates, newel posts, columns, stonework, bars, and restoration materials. Also design consultation, custom woodworking, metal and glasswork. Other showrooms: Jacksonville, FL; New Haven, CT; Southhampton, NY, and Montpelier, VT 05602 (802) 223-7711. Free newsletter.

Great Expectations Quilts, Inc.
155 Town & Country Village Dept. OHJ
Houston, TX 77024
(713) 465-7622
MO RS/O
New and antique quilts for sale. Custom quilts made. Complete line of quilting supplies including fabric, books and patterns, stencil supplies, and classes. Also, country and folk art gifts. Free literature, photographs of quilts, $5 deposit.

Great Northern Construction, Inc.
199 Church Street Dept. OHJ
Burlington, VT 05401
(802) 862-1463
RS/O
This full service contracting firm specializes in quality restoration of 18th and 19th century buildings, both residential and commercial. Also available for home improvement, custom design/build, new construction additions, commercial establishment design and construction, custom case work: display and counters. All work includes one year free warranty inspection and a client list is available for references.

• **Green Enterprises**
43 S. Rogers St. Dept. OHJ
Hamilton, VA 22068
(703) 338-3606
MO
They manufacture Victorian-style porch swings, tables and wind chimes. They also build architectural and mechanical models, and museum exhibits. Free literature.

• **Melvyn Green and Associates, Inc.**
1145 Artesia Blvd., Ste 204 Dept. OHJ
Manhattan Beach, CA 90266
(213) 374-6424
RS/O
Engineering and architectural firm specializing in historic rehabilitation & restoration.

KEY TO ABBREVIATIONS

MO	sells by Mail Order
RS/O	sells through Retail Store or Office
DIST	sells through Distributors
ID	sells only through Interior Designers or Archtects

A. Greenhalgh & Sons, Inc.
PO Box 400 Dept. OHJ
Chelmsford, MA 01824
(617) 256-3777
RS/O
Interior and exterior painting, wallpapering, & stenciling. Specialists in the restoration of older homes. Stencils are traditional American patterns or are created to fit historical era of home. Interior design consulting available. Serving New England. In NH (603) 880-7887. Brochure available.

Greenland Studio, Inc., The
147 W. 22nd St. Dept. OHJ
New York, NY 10011
(212) 255-2551
RS/O
Stained glass repaired and manufactured. Expert craftsmanship for new work and restoration of all kinds of leaded glass. Tiffany windows and lampshades, painted, etched, bevelled, carved, sandblasted. Museum-quality restoration practices. Conservator for several museum collections; also, architectural wood restoration on landmark buildings such as Washington Square Church; can recreate old window frames and sash. Free literature.

Greensboro Art Foundry & Machine Co.
1201 Park Terrace Dept. OHJ
Greensboro, NC 27403
(919) 299-0106
MO RS/O
Provides precise duplication services in brass, bronze, and iron for architectural hardware, components and sculpture. Shop uses sand and investment casting techniques. In house pattern shop, machine and welding facilities. Information sheets available.

Greg Monk Stained Glass
98-027 Hekaha St., Bldg. 3 Dept. OHJ
Aiea, HI 96701
(808) 488-9538
RS/O MO
Stained glass windows designed and built by Greg Monk, who has fourteen years of experience and has handled commissions from Guam to New York. He can also assist in contacting other glass artists in Hawaii. Custom-designed windows; classes; supplies. Press releases & descriptive literature available.

• **Greg's Antique Lighting**
12005 Wilshire Blvd. Dept. OHJ
Los Angeles, CA 90025
(213) 478-5475
RS/O
Original antique lighting fixtures, 1850-1930. Stock includes floor and table lamps, wall sconces, and chandeliers. Specializes in high-quality gas fixtures from the Victorian period. Primarily supplying the Los Angeles area. No literature. Photos may be sent in response to phoned inquiries.

Grinling Architectural Period Mouldings
192 Christopher Columbus Dr. Dept. OHJ
Jersey City, NJ 07302
(201) 451-0699
MO DIST
This line of architectural mouldings include ceiling medallions, cornices, brackets, corbels, and dados. They are made of hard polyurethane. Write for free brochure.

Theodore Grunewald, Urban Archaeologist
260 E. 10th St. West Store Dept. OHJ
New York, NY 10009
(212) 713-5780
RS/O
Uncovers original documents that aid in accurate and interpretive restorations of older buildings. Digs in building departments, archives, etc. Provides building histories. Call for consultation; no literature.

Guardian National House Inspection and Warranty Corp.
Box 431 Dept. OHJ
E. Orleans, MA 02643
(800) 334-6492
RS/O DIST
Headquarters for the company. Services are currently offered in twenty-two states. Company provides in-depth engineering surveys of all structural and mechanical components of an old or newer house. A highly accepted guarantee is available to back up their survey. Also, a comprehensive program to train qualified representatives is available. Free introductory brochure.

Guerin, P.E. Inc.
23 Jane Street Dept. BD-1
New York, NY 10014
(212) 243-5270
RS/O MO
Fabricators and importers of fine traditional brass decorative hardware since 1857. Some Early American and English designs, but the emphasis is on period French hardware. Among the splendid bathroom fittings, there are several suitable for 19th and turn-of-the-century houses. Over 50,000 models available for custom manufacture. Specialists in careful reproduction from owner's antique examples. Prices are not cheap. 64 pg. (16 in color) illustrated catalog and price list — $5.

Gunther Mills, Inc.
120 Eliot St. Dept. OHJ
Fairfield, CT 06430
(203) 259-4859
MO
A custom millwork who will make stairs, mantels, mouldings, windows, doors, and turnings. Satisfaction guaranteed. Illustrated brochure, $1.

H

H.B. Slate
RD 2, Box 127 Dept. OHJ
Whitehall, NY 12887
(518) 499-0826
RS/O
Manufacturers of slate products including colored flagstone, slate tile, veneer stone, and roofing slate. No literature.

H & M Stair Builders, Inc.
4217 Howard Ave. Dept. OHJ
Kensington, MD 20895
(301) 564-1550
MO RS/O
Large selection of wood staircases and staircase parts. Free brochure. Call for prices.

H & R Johnson, Inc.
State Highway 35 Dept. OHJ
Keyport, NJ 07735
(800) 631-2176
RS/O
Reproduction of 19th-century encaustic & geometric ceramic floor tiles. Custom and stock. Also, 3 x 3 and 6 x 3 tile "murals." Free color brochure. Also, (201) 264-0566.

H & R Johnson Tile Ltd./ Highgate Tile Works
Tunstall Dept. OHJ
Stoke-on-Trent, Engl, ST64JX
0782-85611
MO
Founded in the mid 19th Century, this company specializes in encaustic ceramic tiles. Samples and quotations can be prepared for the restoration of Victorian ceramic wall tiles and encaustic and geometric floors. Literature available.

• **Haas Wood & Ivory Works, Inc.**
64 Clementina St. Dept. OHJ
San Francisco, CA 94105
(415) 421-8273
RS/O MO
They manufacture hand-turned or semi-automatic ornamentation for both new construction and restoration projects. Items include newels, brackets, arches for windows and doors, scrolls, balusters, handrails, mouldings, columns, capitals, caps and hoods, finials. Custom cabinet shop builds a wide variety of hand-constructed and finished pieces for home or business. They work from your plans and specifications, in any type or combination of woods. Write for brochure.

Habersham Plantation Corp.
PO Box 1209 Dept. JR
Toccoa, GA 30577
(404) 886-1476
DIST MO
Manufacturers of 17th and 18th century Colonial reproductions. Furniture is handcrafted from pine, oak, and cherry in the country manner. Each piece is signed and dated. Includes tables, beds, chairs, side boards, and a painted wedding chest. Sold through 200 dealers throughout the U.S. Large catalog, called "The Habersham Workbook," shows complete collection, $10.00.

Haines Masonry Specialties
2747 N. Emerson Ave. Dept. OHJ
Indianapolis, IN 46218
(317) 547-5531
RS/O
One of the oldest and largest masonry restoration companies in Indiana, family owned and operated since 1936. Specialties include building cleaning; tuckpointing, all types of masonry repairing, waterproofing, flashings, slate roofing, chimneys, caulking. They also do some painting and remodeling, serving the complete state of Indiana. They will give free technical advice, inspections, and estimates. "Protection of Masonry Surfaces", $2.50, flyer, $.25.

Half Moon Antiques c/o Monmouth Antique Shoppes
217 W. Front St. Dept. OHJ
Red Bank, NJ 07701
(201) 842-1863
RS/O
Dealers in restored gas & electric lighting, 1860-1930. Solid brass chandeliers and wall sconces with original glass shades. Also original brass bath accessories. Sold at antique shows (write for list), and by appointment. Large-scale refurbishment projects considered. No catalog.

Hall Associates
Rt. 4, Box 339B Dept. OHJ
Manhattan, KS 66502
(913) 776-6010
RS/O MO
Architectural restoration, rehabilitation, and design services for all types of public, commercial, and residential buildings. Energy conservation, measured drawings, feasibility studies, and building surveys. Specialize in adaptive re-use & new uses for historic buildings. Brochure, resume, and list of completed projects available on request.

J Hall Building Restoration
PO Box 328 Dept. OHJ
Salado, TX 76571
(817) 947-8483
RS/O
Building restoration. Resume and references available on request.

W.J. Hampton Plastering
30 Fisk St. Dept. OHJ
Jersey City, NJ 07305
(201) 433-9002
RS/O
Hampton specializes in plain and ornamental plastering, particularly the restoration of ceilings and walls. Also, reproduction and restoration of cornices, medallions, mantels, niches, columns, and all types of interior mouldings in Victorian houses and landmark buildings and churches. NJ, NY area. No literature.

Hand-Stenciled Interiors
590 King Street Dept. OHJ
Hanover, MA 02339
(617) 878-7596
MO
Personal, specialized stencilling service with hundreds of unpublished patterns available and custom stencil designs. Pre-cut patterns individually suited to customer's needs are sent with complete instructions; or professional stenciller will come to your home/business to complete the work. For information, send $1.; no catalog.

Harne Plastering Co.
PO Box 22 Dept. OHJ
Libertytown, MD 21762
(301) 898-5600
RS/O
Over 30 years experience in plaster & stucco restoration. Services include all veneer plastering and exterior "DRYVIT" stucco systems. Call or write for information and advice. Brochure—$3.

Harris — Tarkett, Inc.
P.O. Box 300 Dept. OHJ
Johnson City, TN 37601
(615) 928-3122
DIST
This 80 year old company makes hardwood flooring in 22 parquet and plank patterns — many of which are suitable for period houses. Available in red oak, white oak, fumed oak, yellow pine, walnut, angelique teak, and maple. Plank available V-joint or square joint. Illustrated catalog and technical notes, $1.00 each.

• See Advertisers' Index
on page 22
for more details.

Harrison, Elaine
7 Park Avenue Dept. OHJ
New York, NY 10016
(212) 889-6247
RS/O
Repair and restoration of period painted furniture, reverse glass painting, eglomise, tole trays, and clock dials. No literature.

Harry's Closet
PO Box 1254 Dept. OHJ
Avon, CT 06001
(203) 658-6072
MO
A replica of folding racks as used to dry laundry in the 19th century. Bracket is enameled or brass; the ten hardwood rods fold down when rack is not in use. Free brochure with order form.

Hartmann-Sanders Column Co.
4340 Bankers Circle Dept. OHJ
Atlanta, GA 30360
(404) 449-1561
DIST
Architectural columns of clear heart redwood, or clear poplar. Pilasters and square columns as well as round columns in the Greek orders. Composition capitals; fiberglass bases, caps, and plinths. Finest quality materials, construction, detail (entasis, fluting). Load-bearing. Free color catalog.

Harvey M. Stern & Co./ Antique Lighting
6350 Germantown Ave. Dept. OHJ
Philadelphia, PA 19444
(215) 438-6350
RS/O
Old and unusual lamps and chandeliers. Also does refinishing, repairing, rewiring, and plating. Expert metal refinishing and restoration. Custom lamp mounting. No literature, write for references.

Hasbrouck/Hunderman Architects
711 South Dearborn St. Dept. OHJ
Chicago, IL 60605
(312) 922-7211
RS/O
Architectural firm specializing in historic restorations and adaptive reuse. They prepare feasibility studies, programming, and furnish complete architectural service; the firm has acted as a consultant on numerous National Register properties. No literature.

• **Hautwork, Inc.**
100 Academy St. Dept. OHJ
Farmingdale, NJ 07727
(201) 938-4251
RS/O
Hautwork, Inc. is a custom metal polishing service specializing in the restoration of antique brass and bronze architectural hardware, lighting, etc. Can remove and pick up, deliver and install. They offer ultrasonic cleaning, mirror polishing through patination, lacquer and a clear baked epoxy coating, the finest most durable protection available. Free brochure.

Richard N. Hayton and Associates, Inc.
501 11th St. Dept. OHJ
Brooklyn, NY 11215
(718) 499-5299
RS/O
An architectural and landscape design and construction firm in business for 13 years. Landscape treatments are suitable for old houses. They can provide specially designed alterations of commercial and residential buildings. Free flyer.

• **Heads Up**
PO Box 1210 Dept. OHJ
Temecula, CA 92390
(714) 676-6005
MO RS/O
A complete line of solid oak bathroom furniture and accessories, including medicine cabinets, vanity cabinets, and reproduction high-tank pull-chain toilets. Send $1 for full brochure, can buy direct from factory.

Heart-Wood, Inc.
Rt. 1, Box 97A Dept. OHJ
Jasper, FL 32052
(904) 792-1688
MO RS/O
Quality flooring, panelling, and millwork from new heart pine (not recycled). Specialize in heart pine, heart cypress, select new-growth cypress, and southern red cherry. A sampling of heart pine flooring is available for $5 to cover shipping and handling.

Hearth-glo
53 Pomfret Street Dept. OHJ
Putnam, CT 06260
(203) 928-6818
DIST
Entirely handcrafted Early American lighting fixtures wrought from solid copper, brass, and pewter finish. Their selection includes authentic interior/exterior lanters, wall sconces, chandeliers, and post lanterns most of which are available in several finishes: natural, antique, verde, and pewter. Custom work and design considered. Illustrated catalog, $2.

• **Hearth Realities**
PO Box 38093 Dept. OHJ
Atlanta, GA 30334
(404) 377-6852
MO
The only U.S. manufacturer of cast-iron hanging coal basket grates for metal framed fireplaces. Available in a wide selection of styles and sizes. Also a selection of antique metal frames, grates, hearths, summer screens, etc. Free information.

Hearth Shield
14560 N.E. 91st Court Dept. OHJ
Redmond, WA 98052
(800) 526-5971
DIST RS/O
Hearth Shield mats are installed on either walls or floors to prevent heat and fire damage caused by open hearth fireplaces and stoves. These UL-listed boards are made from decorative, heavy-gauge textured steel laminated to fire-resistant insulation core. Mat allows installation of fire-standing fireplace or stove anywhere in the home without fire hazard. Phone for free literature.

Heatilator Inc.
1915 W. Saunders Rd. Dept. OHJ
Mt. Pleasant, IA 52641
(319) 385-9211
DIST
The original patented heat circulating manufactured fireplace. Available in built-in, zero-clearance, woodburning models. Can be installed by a handy do-it- yourself person. Cost when professionally installed is less expensive than a conventional installation. Also chimney systems and glass doors for the fireplace, woodstoves and fireplace inserts. Brochures — $.50.

Heckler Bros.
4105 Stuebenville Pike Dept. OHJ
Pittsburgh, PA 15205
(412) 922-6811
MO
They have acquired the original patterns for, and will repair/supply parts for the following: Williamson, Economy, Boomer, Leader, and Berger coal furnaces; and for Columbia and Economy coal boilers. Also supply and stock parts for thousands of coal furnaces, coal boilers, coal heating and coal cookstoves. Firebrick and grates for most coal furnaces. Please call or write with your specific request.

Heirloom Enterprises
PO Box 146 Dept. OHJ
Dundas, MN 55019
(507) 645-9341
MO DIST
Manufacturers of authentic early 20th-century chandeliers. Chandeliers are made of solid brass and are available with a variety of shades and styles. They also manufacture solid brass furniture hardware and solid oak furniture, including reproductions of library- style occasional tables and French Provincial reproductions. The table line consists of coffee tables with matching end tables, sculpture pedestals, sofa tables and other accessory items. Free literature.

Heirloom Rugs
28 Harlem Street Dept. OHJ
Rumford, RI 02916
(401) 438-5672
MO DIST
Over 500 hand-drawn hooked rug patterns (on burlap base). Sizes range from chairseats to room-size. Company does not sell hooking materials or accessories. Illustrated catalog shows 297 of the patterns — $1.50.

Hendershot, Judith
1408 Main Street Dept. OHJ
Evanston, IL 60202
(312) 475-6411
RS/O
Decorative stencilling for ceilings, walls and floors. Custom designs created in all periods and styles for medallions, borders, dados, etc. Original Victorian stencilled ceilings restored or recreated. Decorations also designed to match wallpapers, draperies and other patterns. On-premise custom work only; no stencils or stencil kits available. Illustrated brochure is free.

Henderson Black & Greene, Inc.
PO Box 589 Dept. OHJ
Troy, AL 36081
(205) 566-5000
DIST
Manufactures stock millwork items as follows: Columns, turned posts, spindles, balusters, sidelights, mantels, ironing board cabinets and Colonial entrance features. Literature available on all items — please specify.

KEY TO ABBREVIATIONS

MO sells by Mail Order

RS/O sells through Retail Store or Office

DIST sells through Distributors

ID sells only through Interior Designers or Archtects

Henderson Lighting
PO Box 585 Dept. OHJ
Southbury, CT 06488
(203) 264-3037
MO
Recreations and adaptations of early American lanterns in brass and copper. Most are electrical. A classic cornucopia for Victorian entranceways is also available. Catalog, $2., refundable with first order.

Heritage Flags
1919 Long Beach Blvd. Dept. OHJ
Ship Bottom, NJ 08008
(609) 494-2626
MO RS/O
Heritage Flags sells flags of all kinds, including historical, US, state, international, marine, and custom. Also, flag poles in cedar, fiberglass, steel, and aluminum. Free flag and flagpole brochure. 50-page catalog, $2.50.

• **Heritage Home Designers**
650 Kriegel Rd. Dept. OHJ
Wharton, TX 77488
(409) 532-0019
MO
Stock plan service; plans are described in four catalogs of Victorian house plans, $4 - $5. Also will do custom Victorian replicas. Call for details; 9-5 Mon.-Fri.

• **Heritage Lanterns**
70A Main Street Dept. OHJ
Yarmouth, ME 04096
(207) 846-3911
RS/O MO
Wide selection of hand-crafted reproduction lanterns, sconces and chandeliers for interior or exterior use. Available in brass, copper or pewter. 52-page catalog, $2.

• **Heritage Mantels**
PO Box 240 Dept. OHJ
Southport, CT 06490
(203) 335-0552
MO RS/O
Reproductions of antique marble mantels in all periods. Made of pulverized quarried marble, cast from moulds made directly from carved antique marble pieces. Showroom: Market Square, High Point, N.C. Designers kit, showing marble samples, $30, refundable on first order. Color catalog, $3.

Heritage Rugs
P.O. Box 404, Lahaska Dept. OHJ
Bucks County, PA 18931
(215)794-7229
MO RS/O
Heritage Rugs has preserved the old craft of weaving early American rag rugs on their antique looms. These all wool rugs are custom made in sizes up to 15' wide and 35' long. Just send the colors you would like included (by enclosing paint, fabric or wallpaper samples). Each rug is numbered and registered as a Heritage original. Brochure available for $.50.

Herman, Frederick, R.A., Architect
420 West Bute Street Dept. OHJ
Norfolk, VA 23510
(804) 625-6575
RS/O
Restoration architect and historic preservation planner/consultant. Dr. Frederick Herman is available for lectures. No literature; please write or call for more information.

Hess Repairs
200 Park Ave., So. Dept. OHJ
New York, NY 10003
(212) 260-2255
RS/O MO
All types of repairs on fine antiques. Specializes in silver, glass, crystal, porcelain. Supplies missing parts and restores old dresser sets. No literature.

Hexagram
2247 Rohnerville Rd. Dept. OHJ
Fortuna, CA 95540
(707) 725-6223
RS/O MO
Specializing in antique lighting fixtures since 1968. Large selection of brass reproduction desk lamps, sconces, and chandeliers, both gas and electric. They will completely restore, wire, and polish any lighting fixture. Also a big selection of antique glass shades. Free photographs; please call or write. No literature.

Hexter, S. M. Company
2800 Superior Ave. Dept. OHJ
Cleveland, OH 44114
(216) 696-0146
DIST
This company manufactures Greenfield Village fabrics and wallcoverings: Designs are taken from documentary material found at the Henry Ford Museum, Greenfield Village in Dearborn, MI. Several of their books — including "Village Gallery," "Greenfield Village" and "The Countryside Collection" — are widely available at wallcovering stores and interior designers around the country. No literature.

• **W.P. Hickman Co.**
PO Box 15005 Dept. OHJ
Asheville, NC 28813
(704) 272-4000
DIST
Makes Microzine roofing, an architectural sheet metal that weathers to a grey patina without rusting. Self-heals if scratched, does not bleed. Cannot be used in direct contact with acidic woods or metals other than aluminum or galvanized. Weighs less than steel or copper. Free brochure. Also, (800) 438-4897.

Hiles Plating Co., Inc.
2028 Broadway Dept. OHJ
Kansas City, MO 64108
(816) 421-6450
MO RS/O
This company specializes in the restoration of metals including silver plating, gold plating, copper, brass, and pewter refinishing and repairs. They also match finishes of other manufacturers on plumbing fixtures, door hardware, etc. Customers may send items for free estimate. Free silver plating brochure.

• **Hill, Allen Charles AIA**
25 Englewood Road Dept. OHJ
Winchester, MA 01890
(617) 729-0748
RS/O
Preservation architectural firm: services for preservation, restoration, repair, conservation, & expansion, including planning, research, & National Register nominations; design, preparation of construction documents, & building evaluation, analysis, technical consulting, & troubleshooting; lectures & workshops. Jobs range from brief consultations to multi-year phased projects. Literature available; specific inquiries answered.

• Hilltop Slate Co.
Rt. 22A Dept. OHJ
Middle Granville, NY 12849
(518) 642-2270
MO DIST RS/O
NY—VT region slate in all colors and sizes from their 7 quarries. Specializing in roofing slate for restoration and new construction. Shipment arranged. Also structural slate and flagging. Free color brochure.

John Hinds & Co.
55 Railroad Ave. Dept. OHJ
Troy, PA 16947
(717) 297-3995
MO
This company makes National Register Plaques, cast in bronze or aluminum as well as custom plaques. Prices begin at $38 (standard, cast aluminum). Free flyer and price list.

Hinson & Co.
979 Third Ave. Dept. OHJ
New York, NY 10022
(212) 475-4100
ID
Suppliers of traditional fabrics and wallpaper. Call or write for more information.

Hippo Hardware & Trading Co.
201 S.E. 12th Dept. OHJ
Portland, OR 97214
(503) 231-1444
MO RS/O
Called by Historic Preservation League of Oregon the "source of last resort." Can supply almost any kind of door or furniture hardware; has large stock on hand, represents 15 makers of custom pieces. Has 100,000 lighting fixture parts and wide selection of fixtures from Victorian to Art Deco. Also plumbing and fittings, architectural antiques. Will repair/restore lighting fixtures, hardware, and plumbing. Three catalogs, $1.

• The Hisrich Manufacturing Co.
121 W. 4th St. Dept. OHJ
Dover, OH 44622
(216) 343-8834
MO RS/O
Custom-crafted, kiln-dried poplar shutters with fixed or movable louvers. Specifications and fact sheet, $1.

Historic Boulevard Services
1520 West Jackson Blvd. Dept. OHJ
Chicago, IL 60607
(312) 829-5562
RS/O MO
Restoration services, including structural engineering consultation, and general contracting. Will travel, consult, and speak nationally. "Turn-Key" masterbuilding is a specialty. Also have re-issued book on Masonry, Carpentry, and Joinery methods c. 1899; $20 postpaid. No literature available.

Historic Charleston Reproductions
105 Broad St., Box 622 Dept. OHJ
Charleston, SC 29402
(803) 723-8292
MO RS/O
The sale of these reproductions of 18th — early 19th century pieces from historic Charleston generates royalties to further the preservation work of Historic Charleston Foundation. Charleston-made furniture, imported English pieces; porcelains; documentary fabrics; brass accessories; lamps, hand-made mirrors. Silver, glass, pewter. 80-page catalog, $7.50.

• Historic Housefitters Company
Farm To Market Road, Dept. 20 Dept. OHJ
Brewster, NY 10509
(914) 278-2427
MO
A small but high-quality selection of traditional hardware in both hand-wrought iron (latches, fireplace accessories, hooks, towel holders) and detailed, solid brass (door knockers, doorknobs, levers, cabinet-drawer pulls). Catalog, $2.

Historic Neighborhood Preservation Program
78 Webb's Hill Rd. Dept. OHJ
Stamford, CT 06903
(203) 322-6671
RS/O
A non-profit planning & design firm specializing in the restoration of historic structures & communities for government agencies & private developers. Preservation contracting team specializes in the restoration and replication of historic buildings. Carpentry, masonry. National Register nominations & tax act certifications. Historic commercial storefront rehabilitation. Staff training programs & workshops. Location of Tax Act eligible projects. Renee Kahn, Director, lectures on a number of topics. No literature.

• Historic Preservation Alternatives, Inc.
15 Sussex Street Dept. OHJ
Newton, NJ 07860
(201) 579-2525
RS/O
A multidisciplinary firm of planners, architects and historians specializing in preservation planning, historical research, National Register nominations, historic site surveys, adaptive reuse and restoration projects, grant proposals, building inspections, historic district ordinances, site interpretation, and Tax Act certifications. Brochure describing services provided free of charge on request.

• Historic Windows
Box 1172 Dept. OHJ
Harrisonburg, VA 22801
(703) 434-5855
MO
Custom made Early American indoor shutters. Full or half in 3/4" solid hardwoods. An excellent insulator for drafty windows. Birch sample 8 in. x 12 in. is available for $20. (refundable). Send $3. for brochure.

Historical Miniatures Associates
339 Bellvale Rd. Dept. OHJ
Warwick, NY 10990
(914) 986-1487
MO
Traditional painted miniature tin figures that are historically accurate. Favored Victorian cabinet pieces including historical personages of all eras and places. Also miniature painting service, historical dioramas researched and built. Figures start with Adam and Eve. Specify area of interest. Museum and individual inquiries.

• Historical Replications, Inc.
P.O. Box 13529 Dept. OHJ/86
Jackson, MS 39236
(601) 981-8743
MO
Victorian, farmhouse, and traditional house plans: Authentic exteriors of yesteryear updated with modern floorplans designed for energy efficiency and economy of construction. Historical Replications portfolio features Victorian, farmhouse, & traditional styles. Louisiana collection contains Acadian and plantation styles. Classic Cottages portfolio features a variety of authentic designs, all under 2000 square feet. Each portfolio is $12, two portfolios are $20, or all three portfolios for $30.

History Store
1736 Aliceanna St. Dept. OHJ
Baltimore, MD 21231
(301) 342-1676
RS/O
Retail store serving the general public, architects, and contractors. Open Monday through Saturday. Stocks architectural antiques including mantels, doors, shutters, lights, hardware, bathroom fixtures. Reproduction millwork, tin ceilings, plaster, wallpapers, bathroom fixtures, lights, and other high quality products. Tax credit applications, historical research, National Register nominations, house histories. Office in Wilmington, DE, (302) 654-1727.

Hitchcock Chair Co.
PO Box 369 Dept. OHJ
New Hartford, CT 06057
(203) 379-8531
DIST
Manufacturers of high-quality American traditional designs, crafted in solid maple, ash, and cherry. 44-page catalog, $1.

Hoboken Wood Floors Corp.
100 Willow St., PO Box 510 Dept. OHJ
E. Rutherford, NJ 07073
(201) 933-9700
DIST
Manufacturers and wholesalers of hardwood floors in a variety of styles including random width plank, custom designed parquet, strip hardwood flooring, and vinyl- bonded wood veneers. Can also phone (212) 564-6818. A full-color 32 page brochure, $5.00.

Hobt, Murrel Dee, Architect
P.O. Box 322 Dept. OHJ
Williamsburg, VA 23187
(804) 220-0767
RS/O
Architectural services in the areas of historic restoration, conservation, rehabilitation and/or adaptive reuse of vintage buildings. Design of new buildings, structures or additions compatible with older buildings or historic districts. Designs for the reconstruction of period, replica buildings, commercial or residential. Historic surveys and inventories. Literature available describing architectural services and Limited Edition Period House Plans, $5. ppd.

Pete Holly
3111 2nd Ave. Dept. OHJ
Minneapolis, MN 55408
(612) 824-2333
MO RS/O
Victorian embellishments including custom latticework, porch rails, balcony rails, and wood turning. Free brochure.

• Holm, Alvin AIA Architect
2014 Sansom St. Dept. OHJ
Philadelphia, PA 19103
(215) 963-0747
RS/O
Architectural services for historic structures. Design and consultation, preservation, adaptive re-use, appropriate additions. Also historic structures reports, systems analysis, National Register nomination, etc. Registered in PA, NY, DE, and NJ. Serving individuals as well as organizations. Resume on request.

• See Advertisers' Index on page 22 for more details.

Holophane Division
214 Oakwood Ave., PO Box 3004 Dept. OHJ
Newark, OH 43055
(800) 822-2122
DIST
They offer a large selection of classic, ribbed-crystal Holophane light fixtures and shades. Mountings come in pendant, chain or wall-mounted units. Contact company for local sales representative.

Home Fabric Mills, Inc.
PO Box 662, Route 202 Dept. OHJ
Belchertown, MA 01007
(413) 323-6321
MO RS/O
Exclusive decorator fabrics at 'Mill-Store' prices. Their inventory includes velvets, upholstery, prints, antique satins, sheers, all-purpose, and thermal fabrics. Mail orders welcomed. Will custom-make drapes. Stores in Cheshire, Ct; Scotia, NY; and Belchertown, MA. Free brochure.

Homecraft Veneer
901 West Way Dept. OHJ
Latrobe, PA 15650
(412) 537-8435
MO RS/O
Specialists in veneer and veneering supplies — domestic and imported veneers, tools, adhesives, wood finishes, brushes, sanding papers, saw blades, steel wood screws, dowels, dowel pins. 4 pg. illustrated instruction brochure, descriptive literature with price list — $1.00.

Homespun Weavers
530 State Ave. Dept. OHJ
Emmaus, PA 18049
(215) 967-4550
MO RS/O
Cotton homespun fabric woven in authentic Pennsylvania Dutch patterns. Suitable for tablecloths, drapes, bedspreads. Available by-the-yard or in custom-made tablecloths. 10 colors. Also available, 100% cotton kitchen towels in 5 colors. Free color brochure with swatches.

Homestead Chimney
PO Box 5182 Dept. OHJ
Clinton, NJ 08809
(201) 735-7708
RS/O
Clean, inspect, evaluate, repair, reline, and rebuild all types of chimneys and fireplaces. Serve the New York, New Jersey, Connecticut, and Pennsylvania area. Lining unlined or damaged chimneys with either Z-Flex stainless steel liners or PermaFlu poured liners a specialty; both methods have a 10-year guarantee. Free brochures on both methods, plus "Giving Your Chimney the Care It Deserves" and "Lyemance Top Sealing Damper."

Homestead Design
PO Box 988 Dept. OHJ
Friday Harbor, WA 98250
(206) 378-5185
MO
Traditional designs for barns, workshops, garages, and small country homes. 40-page illustrated catalog, $3.

Homestead Products
114 14th St. Dept. OHJ
Ramona, CA 92065
(619) 789-2314
DIST
A wide variety of ceiling fans; 5 and 3 speeds, two directions. Close-to-ceiling baLL mounts, so fans can hang from pitched ceilings. Some with four-bulb light fixtures, with choice of 24 shades. All metal is die-cast zinc. Traditional and contemporary designs. Free brochure.

Homestead Supply
PO Box 525 Dept. OHJ
Somerset, MA 02726
(617) 672-9006
MO
Will do custom Colonial woodworking and carpentry. Can make shaving horses, tool handles, fancy shingles, mouldings, and clapboard. Will travel to sites. No literature, but inquiries are answered promptly and photos can be requested.

Hood, R. and Co.
RFD 3 College Rd. Dept. OHJ
Meredith, NH 03253
(603) 279-8607
RS/O MO
Early American decorating specialists, distributing Williamsburg, Sturbridge reproductions, and other historic paints, wallpaper, fabrics, drapes, furniture, accessories, hardware, lighting fixtures, etc. Free brochure on Colonial hardware — send SASE.

The Hope Co., Inc.
12777 Pennridge Ind. Dr. Dept. OHJ
Bridgeton, MO 63044
(314) 432-5697
DIST RS/O
Manufactures furniture refinishing and care products. 100% Tung Oil — no thinners added; Instant Furniture Refinisher; Tung Oil Varnish; Furniture Cleaner; Lemon Oil contains no wax or polish to build up; and Hope's grill and stove black, a high-heat black finish for BBQ grills, woodburners, etc. Also silver, brass & copper polish. Free brochure & literature on request.

Horton Brasses
PO Box 120 Nooks Hill Rd. Dept. OJ
Cromwell, CT 06416
(203) 635-4400
RS/O MO
Reproduction hardware. No literature.

Hosek Manufacturing Co.
4877 National Western Dr., 205 Dept. OHJ
Denver, CO 80216
(303) 298-7010
RS/O
Originally founded over 50 years ago, this company is still offering traditional plaster castings and ornaments; also, ceiling medallions and mouldings. They also produce FGR column covers and table bases. Please call or write for free brochure or send $3 for catalog.

House Carpenters
Box 217 Dept. OHJ
Brewster, MA 01072
(617) 896-7857
MO RS/O
Custom-fabrication of 18th century millwork, including doors, windows, paneling, and flooring. The House Carpenters build 18th century timber framed houses throughout the Eastern U.S. All work is custom. Information on millwork is free. A brochure of timber framed house designs is available for $4.00.

HouseMaster of America
421 W. Union Ave. Dept. OHJ
Bound Brook, NJ 08805
(201) 469-6565
RS/O
Professional house inspection services through franchised agents in 24 states. Inspection covers nine major structural, electrical, and mechanical elements. Inspection report and warranty on inspected elements. Free brochure. Outside NJ, call toll free (800) 526-3939.

House of Moulding
15202 Oxnard St. Dept. BM
Van Nuys, CA 91411
(818) 781-5300
RS/O MO
An extensive selection of mouldings — softwood, hardwood, embossed, stairway parts, chair rails, cornices, bandsawn & carved corbels. Distributors for Focal Point architectural decorations. Illustrated catalog, $5.

• **House of Vermillion**
PO Box 18642 Dept. OHJ
Kearns, UT 84118
(801) 967-3611
MO RS/O
Custom-made period drapery, bed ensembles. Historically accurate styles; tablecloths, pillows, etc. Catalog and fabric swatches, $4.

• **House of Webster**
Box OH87 Dept. OHJ
Rogers, AR 72756
(501) 636-4640
MO
This 50 year old family business has a mail-order gift catalog. They manufacture old-fashioned COUNTRY CHARM electric cast-iron ranges, wall ovens, microwaves, electric skillets, and kettles. Catalog is $1.

Houseparts
417 Second St. Dept. OHJ
Eureka, CA 95501
(707) 443-3152
MO RS/O
Houseparts offers door and cabinet hardware, kitchen and bath fittings, and a variety of accessories. Formerly Restoration Hardware. Free 20-page catalog.

• **Lyn Hovey Studio, Inc.**
266 Concord Avenue Dept. OHJ
Cambridge, MA 02138
(617) 492-6566
MO RS/O
Stained and leaded glass lighting, windows, walls of glass, doors, and mirrors. Distinctive original designs in Early American, Victorian, and early 20th century styles. The studio features expertise in ancient painting techniques, acid etching, and glass bending as well as custom sashes, metal support bar systems, protective glazing, and restoration. Brochure, $2.00.

KEY TO ABBREVIATIONS

MO	sells by Mail Order
RS/O	sells through Retail Store or Office
DIST	sells through Distributors
ID	sells only through Interior Designers or Archtects

Howard Refinishing Products
411 W. Maple Ave. Dept. OHJ
Monrovia, CA 91016
(818) 357-9545
MO DIST
They sell Restor-A-Finish, which can be used to restore naturally finished wood; eliminates white rings, water marks, scratches, and restores color and luster on all natural wood finishes. They also sell paint- and varnish-stripping chemicals of varying strengths. Free brochure: "How To Use Howard Finish Restorers."

Howard, David, Inc.
P.O. Box 295 Dept. OHJ
Alstead, NH 03602
(603) 835-6356
RS/O MO
Designs and builds old style braced post and beam houses in a variety of sizes and styles. Frame members are pre-fitted, numbered, and shipped to site. Their crew erects the structure. Windows, doors, siding, roofing, hardware, cabinets and stairs can be supplied. Also, imported English 15th & 16th century timber frames. Free introductory brochure. Detailed literature, $8.00.

Howland, John — Metalsmith
Elizabeth St. Dept. OHJ
Kent, CT 06757
(203) 927-3064
RS/O
Restoration and repair of museum-quality metal antiques. He will reproduce or manufacture missing parts, either from original or a sketch. Works in wrought iron, brass, copper, bronze. Restores andirons, lamps, weathervanes, statuary, etc. Can be reached by phone Monday through Friday, 9-4 or by mail. Estimates for work can be given upon visual inspection of the job. No literature. Minimum repair charge, $250.

Hubbardton Forge Corp.
RD H Dept. OHJ
Fair Haven, VT 05743
(802) 273-2047
MO DIST RS/O
Hand wrought iron work including kitchen fixtures, panracks, lamps, chandeliers and sconces, and architectural iron work. Custom designed pieces are available. For file of 8 x 10 photo sheets, send $3.

S. & C. Huber, Accoutrements
82 Plants Dam Rd. Dept. OHJ
East Lyme, CT 06333
(203) 739-0772
RS/O MO
Company produces hand crafted goods of 18th and early 19th century design on its small 1710 farm. They conduct lessons for such crafts as wool dyeing, soap making, candle dipping, paper making, rug braiding, etc. Among items for sale: Spinning wheels and fibers, handspun yarns and fabrics, weaving and textile tools, natural dyes, candles, candle making supplies, handmade soap, stencils and papermaking supplies. Craft books. Wooden treen ware. Charming catalog — $1.50.

Hudson Venetian Blind Service, Inc.
2000 Twilight Lane Dept. OHJ
Richmond, VA 23235
(804) 276-5700
RS/O MO
Since 1947 Hudson has specialized in producing wood blinds to the exact specifications and color finish required to complement the room decor. The custom wood blinds come in 6 slat widths, from 1" to 2-3/8". Stains available in a wide range of wood tones — from natural to black. Free brochure.

Hunrath , Wm. Co., Inc.
153 E. 57th St. Dept. OHJ
New York, NY 10022
(212) 758-0780
RS/O
Shop carries a full line of decorative hardware in brass, bronze, iron. Furniture hardware, door knobs, etc. Free literature.

Hunter Fan Company
PO Box 14775 Dept. OHJ
Memphis, TN 38114
(901) 743-1360
DIST
Manufacturer of "Hunter Originial Ceiling Fan", little changed from models introduced in 1886. Hunter offers two sizes (42" and 52"), seven motor finishes, and four choices of blades. Hardwood blades are mounted on irons, available in colors to match motors, which allows a multitude of combinations. Hunter Ceiling Fan brands also include Original Low Profile, 1886 Limited Edition, Low Profile, Summer Breeze, and Studio Series fans. Illustrated catalog, $1. Brochure free.

Hurley Patentee Lighting
R.D. 7 - Box 98A Dept. OHJ
Kingston, NY 12401
(914) 331-5414
RS/O MO
17th and 18th century lights reproduced from fixtures in museums and private collections. These unusual lights are authentic in appearance due to a special aging process. Over 180 tin, iron and brass bettys, candleholders, sconces, lanterns and chandeliers — electric or candle. Illustrated catalog and price list — $2.

Huseman, Richard J. Co.
2824 Stanton Avenue Dept. OHJ
Cincinnati, OH 45206
(513) 861-7980
RS/O
Company has 45 years of experience in all phases of renovation and re-construction of some of the finest historical homes, churches and institutions in the Cincinnati area. They have their own cabinet shop for duplicating woodwork in every detail. No literature.

Huskisson Masonry & Exterior Building Restoration Co.
Box 949, 148 Jefferson St. Dept. OHJ
Lexington, KY 40587
(606) 252-5011
RS/O
Contracting masonry restoration, renovation, reconstruction, and new masonry construction. Services available in Kentucky only. No literature.

Hyde Manufacturing Company
54 Eastford Road Dept. OHJ
Southbridge, MA 01550
(617) 764-4344
DIST
A long established manufacturer of tools designed to prepare surfaces for painting, decorating and refinishing. Among the tools are — joint knives, paint, wood and wallpaper scrapers, putty knives, seam rollers, craft knives. Illustrated how-to book and catalog — $2.00.

Hydrochemical Techniques, Inc.
P.O. Box 2078 Dept. OHJ
Hartford, CT 06145
(203) 527-6350
MO DIST
Hydroclean is a series of chemical cleaning systems for various kinds of masonry: brick, granite, sandstone, limestone & marble. It's available through restoration contractors nationwide. Free literature.

• **Hydrotherm**
Rockland Ave. Dept. OHJ
Northvale, NJ 07647
(201) 768-5500
DIST
Manufacturer of residential and commercial hydronic and steam heating products for space heating and/or water heating, and air conditioning products for homes with hot water or steam heat. Free literature.

Hydrozo Coatings Co.
P.O. Box 80879 Dept. OHJ
Lincoln, NE 68501
(402) 474-6981
MO DIST
Established manufacturer of clear, water-repellent exterior coatings. Masonry and wood clear coatings protect surface without creating impermeable film. Also manufactures a sealer for wood that protects against rot and fungus. Free literature.

I

Iberia Millwork
500 Jane Street Dept. OHJ
New Iberia, LA 70560
(318) 365-5644
MO RS/O
New custom-made exterior wood rolling-slat shutter: hand stapled w/round crown copper coated staple. Shutters also appropriate for interior use as blinds. Standard fixed-slat shutters are available. Circle head shutters can also be fabricated. Literature available. Photographs and scale drawings available free of charge for serious inquiries.

Image Group, The
398 So. Grant Ave. Dept. OHJ
Columbus, OH 43215
(614) 221-1016
RS/O
Architectural and interior design services in the area of building rehabilitation and restoration as well as specializing in "Theme" restaurant design. Offices across the country. No literature.

Imagineering, Inc.
PO Box 648 Dept. OHJ
Rockland, ME 04841
(207) 596-6483
DIST RS/O
Imagineering, Inc., uses shipbuilding techniques to make reproductions and complementary pieces of furniture originally built for a coastal Maine summer estate at the turn of the century. The furniture is made of white-painted mahogany. Portfolio and year's literature subscription, $10.

Impex Assoc. Ltd., Inc.
25 N. Dean St. Dept. OHJ
Englewood, NJ 07631
(201) 568-2243
DIST
This company carries mostly furniture and door hardware in modern styles, some of the pieces are appropriate for old furniture and houses. No literature.

Import Specialists, Inc.
82 Wall Street Dept. OHJ
New York, NY 10005
(212) 709-9633
DIST
Importers and distributors of various kinds of natural fiber matting and rugs; i.e. sisal, coco, rice straw, seagrass, etc. An extensive selection of cotton rag rugs and dhurries. Distributed nationally to many large department stores and specialty stores like Bloomingdale's, Room & Board, Marshall Field's, etc. You can write for name of nearest retail store, but they do not sell outside of the trade.

Industrial Fabrics Association International
345 Cedar Bldg, Suite 450 Dept. OHJ
St. Paul, MN 55101
(612) 222-2508
MO
They offer a free directory of nationwide awning manufacturers.

Industrial Solar
PO Box 117 Dept. OHJ
Burlington, KA 66839
(316) 364-2662
MO
Small company operated out of owner's home, providing fabric covered wire. Will also help locate replacement parts for old porcelain sockets, wall plugs, etc. Send SASE for information.

Inner Harbor Lumber & Hardware
900 Fleet St. Dept. OHJ
Baltimore, MD 21202
(301) 837-0202
RS/O
Renovation products center in downtown Baltimore & Northern Baltimore (4345 York Rd., (301) 532-2710). Stock includes structural as well as decorative materials. Bricks, framing lumber, flooring, treated lumber, gutters, plumbing & electrical, decorative hardware, Diedrich chemicals, and shutters. Custom orders on replacement window sash. No literature.

Innerwick Industries
Route 1, Box 808-B Dept. OHJ
Chestertown, MD 21620
(301) 348-5862
MO
Bathroom accessories, 18th and 19th century brass hardware, and colonial sconces, are available from this company as well as a line of oak and brass iceboxes and telephones. All items are also offered unfinished for additional savings. Literature, $2 refundable.

Insul Shutter
PO Box 888, 69 Island St. Dept. OHJ
Kene, NH 03431
(603) 352-2726
MO DIST RS/O
InsulShutters are hardwood interior shutters, for doors and windows, that block air and sound infiltration and have a rating of 9.1 thermal blockage. They can be installed over existing frames; when they are closed only the panelled hardwood shutters show. Free flyer.

• See Advertisers' Index on page 22 for more details.

Interior Decorations
48-52 Lincoln Street Dept. OHJ
Exeter, NH 03833
(603) 778-0406
RS/O
17th — 18th — 19th century interior restoration throughout New England by decorator Jane Kent Rockwell. Specializing in period draperies, documentary fabrics, wallcoverings and carpets. Lectures given. No literature.

International Building Components
Box 51 Dept. OHJ
Glenwood, NY 14069
(716) 592-2953
DIST
Hand-crafted custom millwork, windows, custom wood doors, oak and metal door frames, stairways, fireplace mantels, special cornice detailing, cupolas, columns, steeples, bell towers, church pews and pulpits. Sold through distributors, product literature is free — please specify your interest.

International Fireproof Door Co., Inc. (IFD)
76 Lexington Ave. Dept. OHJ
Brooklyn, NY 11238
(718) 783-1310
RS/O
New York dealer for Marvin wood windows and doors. Made to order windows and doors are available in standard and custom sizes. All units are insulated, weather stripped & may be ordered with a variety of interior & exterior options. Specialities include round tops, true divided- lite insulated windows and custom work of all sorts. They specialize in landmark restoration and the rehabilitation of brownstones, townhouses and frame houses.

Iron Craft, Inc.
PO Box 108 Dept. OHJ
Freedom, NH 03836
MO DIST RS/O
Cast iron, aluminum & brass tea kettles, cast iron cookware, novelties, toys, fireplace, stove and barbecue grates and grills. Dutch Oven doors, Colonial hardware, weathervanes and lamps. Kerosene lamps & wicks, isinglass (stove mica) hot water stove front or jacket, maintenance supplies such as chimney cleaner, brushes, polish, pipe, chimney, dampers, and draft aids. Mail-order catalog, $1., refundable.

Iron Horse Antiques, Inc.
R.D. No. 2 Dept. OHJ
Poultney, VT 05764
(802) 287-4050
RS/O MO
Specializes in old and antique tools. Also carries books dealing with restoration, tools, crafts, etc. "The Fine Tool Journal", illustrated, is published 6 times a year, $15. per year. Current issue, $3. Brochure/booklist, free.

KEY TO ABBREVIATIONS

MO sells by Mail Order

RS/O sells through Retail Store or Office

DIST sells through Distributors

ID sells only through Interior Designers or Archtects

• **The Iron Shop**
Box 128, 400 Reed Rd. Dept. OHJ-7
Broomall, PA 19008
(215) 544-7100
MO RS/O
This company manufactures custom-built spiral, curved, and floating stairs. Spiral stair kits in metal and wood also available. Brochure, $1.

Iron-A-Way, Inc.
220 W. Jackson Dept. OHJ
Morton, IL 61550
(309) 266-7232
DIST RS/O
Manufacturers of built-in ironing centers. Several models; many safety features. Free literature.

Isabel Brass Furniture
120 East 32nd St. Dept. OHJ
New York, NY 10016
(800) 221-8523
RS/O MO
Designers and craftsmen in brass. In addition to the 20 styles of handcrafted pure brass beds in the catalog, they can make umbrella stands, hat racks and reproductions of antique bass beds. Also repairs and restoration of antique brass beds. 4 color catalog, price list and booklet — $4.

H.B. Ives
PO Box 1887 Dept. OHJ
New Haven, CT 06508
(203) 772-0310
MO DIST
An extensive line of solid brass hardware; hard-to-find pieces for windows and doors, including Dutch doors. Can be purchased by mail order or from many hardware stores. Free catalog.

J

JGR Enterprises, Inc.
PO Box 32, Rt. 522 Dept. OHJ
Ft. Littleton, PA 17223
(800) 223-7112
DIST
Manufacturers of the Kennaframe sliding and folding door hardware and Kennaframe sliding and folding Mirror doors. Also, Kennaframe security hardware. Specialize in the reproduction of custom replacement hardware. Free "Kennaframe" catalog and literature available.

• **J & M Custom Cabinet and Millwork**
2750 N. Bauer Rd., R 2 Dept. OHJ
St. Johns, MI 48879
(517) 593-2244
MO
Builders of custom kitchen and cabinets for 27 years. Also specialty millwork, such as Victorian trim. Catalog and price sheet $2, refundable with purchase.

JMR Products
115 Main Street Dept. JC
St. Helena, CA 94574
(707) 963-7377
MO
Reproduction Victorian-style screen doors made from #1 clear-heart redwood and decorated with hardwood turnings and filagrees, etc. $195. for standard sizes. Send $.50 for detailed brochure.

• **J.M. Roe**
236 Prospect St. Dept. OHJ
Cambridge, MA 02139
(617) 876-6329
RS/O
Faux Marbre, trompe l'oeil, special painted finishes. For interiors, architecture, & furniture. Free brochure, with samples.

Jackson, Wm. H. Co.
3 E. 47th St. Dept. OHJ
New York, NY 10017
(212) 753-9400
RS/O MO
Manufactures and retails a full line of fine fireplace equipment, carved wood mantels, andirons, fire tools, grates, fenders, hand-painted tiles, bellows, etc. Company established 1827. Their lava gas fire simulates real coal and fits most grates. Also: a full line of antique fireplace equipment, including marble mantels, fenders, fire tools, delft tiles, etc. For a brochure send self-addressed business size envelope.

Jadis Moderne
2701 Main St. Dept. OHJ
Santa Monica, CA 90405
(213) 396-3477
MO RS/O
An extensive line of reproduction Art Deco lamps (standing and table), ceiling and wall fixtures, and furniture: chairs, tables, desks, plus accessories like telephones and ashtrays. Prices range from $65 for a seltzer bottle and $85 for a bar stool to $2500 for an executive desk. Catalog, $5.

Janovic/Plaza, Inc.
1150 Third Avenue Dept. OHJ
New York, NY 10021
(212) 772-1400
RS/O MO
Store has probably the largest stock of specialty painting and decorating supplies in the U.S. Will also service mail orders. Ability to computer match colors in any finish. No literature.

The Jasmine Company
PO Box 7304 Dept. OHJ
Denver, CO 80207
(303) 399-2150
MO
The Jasmine Company is a mail order business based in Denver, CO that sells storm window materials and kits for making insulated shades, with instruction booklets, directly to the public. Their 'Sensible Storm Window' is easy to construct, attractive, very affordable and will fit many different types of windows. Booklet, $3. Shades or storm windows, free flyers.

Jenifer House
New Marlboro Stage Dept. OJ
Great Barrington, MA 01230
(413) 528-1500
MO RS/O
Their 104-page catalog offers fine gifts, decorative accessories, dinnerware, flatware, rugs, lamps, furniture, etc. Also Early American hardware and authentic reproduction of Early American furniture.

• See Advertisers' Index on page 22 for more details.

Jennings, Gottfried, Cheek/ Preservationists
Box 1890 Dept. OHJ
Ames, IA 50010
(515) 292-7192
RS/O
Provides community development and historic preservation services, including architectural, archeological, and historic surveys; cultural resource analysis; preservation planning and implementation through public policy and private initiative; neighborhood conservation planning; public education including volunteer training; preparation of National Register forms and certification applications; rehabilitation guidelines; interior or exterior design consultation; townscape design. No literature.

Jerard Paul Jordan Gallery
PO 71, Slade Acres Dept. OHJ
Ashford, CT 06278
(203) 429-7954
MO RS/O
Jerard Paul Jordan Gallery is a distributor of 18th century building materials including such items as panelling, sheathing, beams, windows, brick, H & HL hinges, butterfly hinges, strap hinges, barn siding, doors, mantels, latches for both the interior and exterior. Catalog, $4.50.

John Kruesel's General Merchandise
22 3rd St., S.W. Dept. OHJ
Rochester, MN 55902
(507) 289-8049
RS/O
Has been in the business of collecting early lighting and plumbing fixtures since he was 8 yrs. old. Will consult, sell, purchase — everything is original. No literature. Photographs available upon request.

• **Johnson Paint Co.**
355 Newbury St. Dept. OHJ
Boston, MA 02115
(617) 536-4838
RS/O MO
A specialty paint distributor catering to the Boston restoration market. They will ship hard-to-find calcimine paint on receipt of a written order. Will ship UPS COD. Minimum order 25 lbs. of powder (makes between 12-15 qts). Please call for current prices & shipping charges before ordering.

Johnson Woodworks Inc.
1030 S. Cedar Dept. OHJ
New Lenox, IL 60451
(815) 485-4262
RS/O
A full service finishing/restoration shop. Paint stripping, staining & finishing, and custom repairs. Also, custom furniture making. Free brochure.

• **The Joinery Co.**
PO Box 518 Dept. OHJ
Tarboro, NC 27886
(919) 823-3306
MO RS/O
Designers and handbuilders of traditional architectural millwork, using period techniques. Specialize in heart pine flooring, hand-hewn beams, pegged raised-panel wainscotting, cabinetry, mantels, moulding, stair parts, and panelled doors. Will grain- and color-match, grind custom cutter heads for restoration projects. 4,500-sq-ft. showroom. Color portfolio, $5.

Jones & Erwin, Inc.
515 Andrews Rd. Dept. OHJ
Trevose, PA 19047
(215) 364-2880
RS/O DIST
Hobe Erwin Editions In Wallpaper, a line of Early American documentary wallpapers. Also Colonial, French and English designs adapted from antique documents. No literature — write for area distributor.

Jotul U.S.A., Inc.
400 Riverside St., PO Box 1157 Dept. OHJ
Portland, ME 04104
(207) 797-5912
DIST
United States subsidiary of A/S Jotul, Oslo, Norway, manufacturer of Jotul and Surdiac cast-iron wood- and coal-burning stoves and fireplaces. All models UL-listed; wood, coal, wood/coal combination and high efficiency stoves. Porcelain enamelled stoves available in red and green. Free brochures and flyers on request.

Joy Construction, Inc.
4803 Courthouse Rd. Dept. OHJ
Fredericksburg, VA 22401
(703) 898-4139
RS/O
General contractors in restoration and renovations of old buildings, in the Fredericksburg, VA area for over 12 years. Recent buildings have included Chatham Manor and Little Whim. All aspects of carpentry and painting, both interior and exterior. Cost estimates provided upon request with detailed material specifications. No literature.

K

K-D Wood Products
527 Main St., Box 348 Dept. OHJ
Harwich, MA 02645
(617) 432-4022
MO
Gazebo kits, with pre-built panels, pre-attached hardware, and 2x4 framing. Two versions: octagon (10-ft.-6-in. diameter) and hexagon (8-ft. diameter), $1000 and $800 respectively. Free color flyer.

Kane-Gonic Brick Corp.
Winter St. Dept. OHJ
Gonic, NH 03867
(603) 332-2861
RS/O MO
Manufacture authentic Harvard water-struck brick. Hand-, and machine-moulded in many sizes and shapes. Can do custom shapes and colors. Numerous restoration projects including South Street Seaport. Will ship nationwide. No brochure.

Kaplan/Price Assoc. — Architects
452 Sixth Avenue Dept. OHJ
Brooklyn, NY 11215
(718) 789-8537
RS/O
Architectural firm specializing in brownstones, townhouses, restoration and adaptive re-use of old buildings and commercial interiors. Metropolitan NYC area. No literature.

Karl Mann Associates
232 E. 59th St. Dept. OHJ
New York, NY 10022
(212) 699-7141
ID
A line of decorative ceiling papers, silkscreened and hand-printed, with Renaissance, Art Deco, etc. motifs. They make trompe l'oeil "decorative plaster" and "beams" for ceilings, on fabric. Call or write for more information.

Katrina, Inc.
122 W. 74th St. Dept. OHJ
New York, NY 10023
(212) 595-9779
DIST
Katrina's World is a coordinated collection of wallpapers, borders, and fabrics, including hard-to-find craftsman- and Art Nouveau-style patterns in period colors. Write for list of local distributors.

Katzenbach and Warren, Inc.
950 Third Ave. Dept. OHJ
New York, NY 10022
(212) 759-5410
ID
Manufacturers of Williamsburg Wallpapers — three collections available with large and small scale designs and coordinating borders (see listing for Craft House, Colonial Williamsburg). Also distributors of Waterhouse Wallcoverings — a collection of documentary patterns from papers found on walls, trunks, bookbindings, etc., mostly in New England. No literature.

Kaymar Wood Products, Inc.
4603 35th S.W., Dept. 23 Dept. OHJ
Seattle, WA 98126
(206) 932-3584
MO RS/O
Kaymar carries 80 exotic and domestic hardwoods, featuring Pacific NW woods. They'll search for hard-to-find species from large resource list. Full milling facilities. Product line includes custom wood turning, speciality flooring and feature strips of exotic hardwoods, marine items and quality survey stakes. Established 1947. Free hardwood price list.

• **Kayne & Son Custom Forged Hardware**
76 Daniel Ridge Rd. Dept. OHJ
Candler, NC 28715
(704) 667-8868
RS/O MO
Custom forged — hinges, latches, bolts, kitchen utensils, fireplace tools, cranes, andirons, dutch-oven doors, hearth accessories, brackets, candlelighting fixtures, drawer/door hardware and accessories. Stock cast brass/bronze interior/exterior hinges, thumb latches, icebox hardware, door knockers, tin lanterns. Repairs and restorations. Custom brass furniture hardware cast from originals. Hand Forged Hardware catalog including fireplace tools—$2; Cast Brass/Bronze Hardware catalog—$2; both $3.50. Also, (704) 665-1988.

KEY TO ABBREVIATIONS

MO	sells by Mail Order
RS/O	sells through Retail Store or Office
DIST	sells through Distributors
ID	sells only through Interior Designers or Archtects

Keddee Woodworkers
RR 2, Box 877 Dept. OHJ
N. Scituate, RI 02857
(401) 934-2000
MO RS/O
Custom only manufacturer of architectural restoration sash and mill work. Will match windows, doors, pediments, mouldings, turnings, brackets, "Gingerbread", carvings, etc. to samples or drawings. Also, will reproduce synthetic marble, casting, etc. Free literature.

• **Kenmore Industries**
One Thompson Square Dept. OHJ
Boston, MA 02129
(617) 242-1711
MO RS/O
A stock line of decorative and historical over-door pieces, and a variety of fanlights (half-round and elliptical). Georgian, Federal, Victorian, and Revival designs. Also several styles of entryway doors: Swans neck broken pediment with pineapple on a pedestal and 15 panel door, Connecticut Valley broken pediment with a pair of doors, and a Federal triangular pediment with a choice of 1/2 round windows. Color brochure, $3.

Kentucky Wood Floors, Inc.
4200 Reservoir Avenue Dept. OHJ
Louisville, KY 40213
(502) 451-6024
DIST
Full line of hardwood flooring, from classic designs to plank and parquet, both prefinished and unfinished. Directed toward the architect, designer, and upper-end consumer. Contemporary designs as well as reproductions of European classics, Colonial America's hand-scraped plank and Jefferson's Monticello parquet. Literature, $2.

Kimball Furniture Reproductions, Inc.
1600 Royal St., PO Box 460 Dept. OHJ
Jasper, IN 47546
(812) 482-1600
DIST
Manufacturers of authentic 19th century Victorian and French reproductions. Company uses hand-carved solid Honduras mahogany, Italian marble, and Belgian fabrics for detailed reproductions. Products include sofas, chairs, tables, and complete dining room sets. A free color brochure is available.

• **King's Chandelier Co.**
Highway 14, PO Box 667 Dept. OHJ-3
Eden, NC 27288
(919) 623-6188
RS/O MO
A huge collection of chandeliers, sconces and candelabra — each assembled from imported and domestic parts that are designed and maintained by the company. There are brass and crystal reproductions of Victorian styles, and elegant formal 18th century crystal ones, including Strass crystal. Also early American brass and pewter ones. 96-page illustrated catlogue — $2.

Kings River Casting
1350 North Ave. Dept. OHJ
Sanger, CA 93657
(209) 875-8250
MO RS/O
Cast aluminum benches, with solid oak slats, in several models including a hanging swing. Also, tractor seat barstool and antique-design ice cream table. Catalog, $1.

Kingsway Victorian Restoration Materials
3575 Merriment Way Dept. OHJ
Colorado Springs, CO 80917
(303) 596-6776
MO
They sell Victorian restoration materials: gingerbread brackets and fretwork, stair parts, door and window casings, panelling, wainscotting, wood shingles, front doors, plaster and composition ornaments, mouldings, wood fiber carvings, and embossed metal ceilings. Catalog, $3. plus $.50 postage.

Kirby Millworks
PO Box 898E Dept. OHJ
Ignacio, CO 81137
(303) 563-9436
RS/O
Offers solid oak doors for interiors with 1-1/4" raised panels. French doors, six-panel, four-panel, prehanging, stock and custom designs as well as custom shapes and sizes (arched, etc.) available. Free product specifications and price list.

Klinke & Lew Contractors
1304 Greene Street Dept. OHJ
Silverton, CO 81433
(303) 387-5713
RS/O MO
Specializing in Victorian construction and restoration. Distributors for W.F. Norman Co. pressed tin ceilings in Western Colorado; W. F. Norman Catalog, $3.

Klise Manufacturing Company
601 Maryland Ave. Dept. OHJ
Grand Rapids, MI 49505
(616) 459-4283
MO DIST
Furniture and cabinet trim. Manufactures decorative carved-wood mouldings and ornaments. Bamboo, ropes, dentils, classical patterns, carved and plain rosettes. Metal furniture grilles of formed or woven wire, brass plated and antiqued. Send two $.22 stamps for Accent Mouldings literature and prices: two stamps for metal-grille catalog.

Knickerbocker Guild
623 N. Catalina Ave. Dept. OHJ
Pasadena, CA 91106
(818) 449-8508
RS/O
A painting and decorating company specializing in authentic restoration work. Restoration consultants, crafts persons who strip, stain, not to mention paint & repair. Free literature.

Knudsen, Mark
1100 E. County Line Rd. Dept. OHJ
Des Moines, IA 50320
(515) 285-6112
RS/O
Wood carver and turner who offers a full range of custom woodworking services. Duplication of moulding, ornament, and gingerbread; fancy joinery; stair parts, porch posts, doors, and windows; repair and reproduction of fine period furniture. Also does machine turning. Please contact for specific information.

Koeppel/Freedman Studios
368 Congress St., 5th Floor Dept. OHJ
Boston, MA 02210
(617) 426-8887
RS/O
This small company specializes in custom architectural restoration and design, including mould making, hand remodeling, and creation of new ornaments for appropriate application within the context of existing architecture. Interior work is cast in reinforced plaster or a combination of plaster and fiberglass. Most exterior work is cast in epoxy-fiberglass, cement, or a combination of these. Color matching, painting services, and consultation also available. Free information.

Kool-O-Matic Corp.
PO Box 310 Dept. OHJ
Niles, MI 49120
(616) 683-2600
DIST
This manufacturer of residential ventilating equipment even makes an attic fan concealed in an Early American cupola. Also roof, gable and 'Energy Saving' whole house ventilators, complete with solid state speed controls and timer features. For complete information send $.25.

Koppers Co.
1900 Koppers Bldg. Dept. OHJ
Pittsburgh, PA 15219
(800) 556-7737
DIST
Wolmanized® and Outdoor® pressure-treated lumber exterior-use wood has lifetime guarantee against termites and rot. Wolmanized lamp post, 30-year guarantee against termites and rot; $25. "How To Build a Deck" and "How To Build Backyard Projects and Fences" guides, $2. Raincoat® (clear) and Wolman stain water repellents protect treated or untreated wood against moisture; 10 shades. Wolman Clear and Green brush-on preservatives also contain water repellent. Flyers free.

Kraatz/Russell Glass
RFD 1/Box 320C/Grist Mill Hill Dept. OHJ
Canaan, NH 03741
(603) 523-4289
MO RS/O
Manufactures hand-blown, wavy bull's-eye window panes with pontil mark in center, appropriate for side lights and transoms in Early American restorations and reproductions. Panes are cut to customer's specifications. Also diamond-pane leaded casement windows, custom-designed leaded panels, and RESTORATION GLASS™. Free brochure.

Kroeck's Roofing
PO Box 38309 Dept. OHJ
Colorado Springs, CO 80937
(303) 528-1223
RS/O
This fourth generation family company, established in Germany in 1885, installs slate roofing. They will do restoration, repairs, and consultations. Serving, but not limited to, the Rocky Mountain region. No literature.

• **G. Krug & Son, Inc.**
415 W. Saratoga St. Dept. OHJ
Baltimore, MD 21201
(301) 752-3166
RS/O
Specializing in custom ornamental ironwork such as gates, fences, tables, etc. Work done to customer's specifications: design services also available. Fancy blacksmithing work and reproduction of antique hardware a specialty. This is the oldest continuously operating iron shop in the country: since 1810. No catalog or regular mail-order procedure.

Kruger Kruger Albenberg
2 Central Square Dept. OHJ
Cambridge, MA 02139
(617) 661-3812
RS/O
Architects, engineers, builders serving the New York Metropolitan area and New England. Office also at 24 Beverly Rd., West Orange, NJ 07052, (201) 325-8040. Services include determination of replacement cost of construction, investigation of construction problems, construction documents for and construction management of repairs and changes. No literature; telephone inquiries welcomed.

L

La Lune Collection
241 N. Broadway Dept. OHJ
Milwaukee, WI 53202
(414) 271-1172
ID
Wide selection of bent willow furniture available in 9 finishes. Couches, chaises lounges, chairs, tables, beds, chests, cabinets, bar stools. Prices range from $210 for an ottoman, $430 for a chair, $3080 for king-size bed. Through trade only; designers can obtain their catalog, list of showrooms, list of recent clients, and samples of canvas and wood. Cabinet supplement should be requested separately.

Lachin, Albert & Assoc., Inc.
618 Piety Street Dept. OHJ
New Orleans, LA 70117
(504) 948-3533
MO RS/O
Architectural sculptors specializing in ornamental plaster and cement work. Ceiling medallions (ornate, 18-60-in.), mouldings, columns and capitals, domes, finials, etc. Reinforced plaster or stone. Custom work. Cement products shop: Columns, finials, fountains, capitals, and balustrades. Free flyer.

La Haye Bronze, Inc.
1346 Railroad St. Dept. OHJ
Corona, CA 91720
(714) 734-1371
MO DIST RS/O
One of the largest (and oldest — 150 years) bronze foundries in America, La Haye offers an unconditional guarantee on their historical markers and plaques. Six styles of National Register plaques and delivery guarantee. They will also do all forms of custom casting of decorative metal, including gates and grillwork, in bronze, copper, nickel, and aluminum. Free flyer.

Lake Country Brass
PO Box 45 Dept. OHJ
Farmington, NH 03835
(800) 535-5002
MO DIST
Lake Country Brass offers a complete line of brass railing in all sizes, plus matching fittings; also prefabricated posts, coat racks, wine racks, plant stands, easels, door hardware, and more. Free color catalog.

Lake Shore Markers
P.O. Box 59 Dept. OHJ
Erie, PA 16512
(800) 458-0463
MO
Make historical markers, date plates and plaques in cast aluminum or bronze. Also special design street name signs and historic district identification. Submit drawings and specifications for quotation. Free literature on request.

• **Lamp Doctor**
1944 Coney Island Ave. Dept. OHJ
Brooklyn, NY 11223
(718) 627-0448
MO RS/O
Restores any kind of lighting fixture. Also brass plating (lighting fixture parts, hardware, fireplace screens and andirons, etc.). Will custom make Victorian and Art Deco lampshades, wire gas fixtures for electricity, repair and restore crystal chandeliers. Also antique clock repairs. Mail orders for shades welcome. Will repair items sent by mail and ship them back.

• **Lampco**
PO Box 21680 Dept. OHJ
South Euclid, OH 44121
(216) 765-2377
MO RS/O
Stock and custom exterior lighting:wall- and post-mounted, bronze or aluminum, can reproduce or create original designs.

• **LampLight Industries, Inc.**
135 Yorkshire Court Dept. OHJ
Elyria, OH 44035
(216) 365-4954
MO RS/O
A historic outdoor lighting company. They carry reconditioned antique lighting units (wall- and post-mounted) and repair parts. Free catalog.

Lance Woodcraft Products
20 Eckford St. Dept. OHJ
Brooklyn, NY 11222
(718) 387-1531
MO RS/O
This company will do custom wood turning of any kind, including baluster spindles, newel posts, and porch posts. No literature.

Langhorne Carpet Co.
PO Box 175 Dept. OHJ
Penndel, PA 19047
(215) 757-5155
ID
Wilton weave carpets in a variety of Victorian patterns. Period reproductions are their specialty. Free descriptive flyer.

David M. LaPenta, Inc.
157 North Third Street Dept. OHJ
Philadelphia, PA 19106
(215) 627-2782
RS/O
Architectural and general contracting services for the renovation and restoration of old buildings for residential and commercial use in the Philadelphia area. No literature.

David J. Lassiter
PO Box 1459 Dept. OHJ
Green Cove Springs, FL 32043
(904) 284-0171
MO
Architectural and furniture-grade woodturning; knobs, porch posts, moulding, gingerbread, corner blocks, rosettes. Does mostly custom work; works from samples, photos, and drawings. Send SASE for brochure on stock corner blocks and rosettes.

J.C. Lauber Co.
504 E. LaSalle Ave. Dept. OHJ
South Bend, IN 46617
(219) 234-4174
RS/O
Founded in 1890, this company will fabricate almost anything in any type of sheet metal — gutters, cornices, finials, steeples, and mouldings. Will also do slate and clay roofing. Specialize in custom and one-of-a-kind work. Free brochure.

Lauria, Tony
RD 2, Box 253B Dept. OHJ
Landenberg, PA 19350
(215) 268-3441
MO
Authentic new battleship linoleum in nine solid colors (beige, terra cotta, dark green, gray, brown, blue, gold, light green and black). It's one-eighth inch thick, burlap- backed and priced at $3/sq. ft. Available in widths up to 79 inches. No literature but they will send samples. Send SASE.

Lavoie, John F.
P.O. Box 15 Dept. OHJ
Springfield, VT 05156
(802) 886-8253
MO RS/O
Manufacturers of historical windows: Rounds, ovals, fanlights, transoms. Frames are clear pine; double-strength glazing. All windows are custom made to customers particular specifications. No stock windows available. Brochure, $2.

Lawler Machine & Foundry
PO Box 2977 Dept. OHJ
Birmingham, AL 35212
(205) 595-0596
MO DIST
Complete line of ornamental metal castings and accessory items (gray iron & aluminum). Designs from Vintage to Modern. Sold as component parts to metalworking shops who fabricate, assemble, and finish for the homeowner. Casting catalog, $4.

• **Lea, James — Cabinetmaker**
Harkness House Dept. OHJ
Rockport, ME 04856
(207) 236-3632
MO RS/O
Handcrafted reproductions of 18th century American master cabinetmakers' furniture and Windsor chairs. Prices compare favorably with commercial reproduction furniture. Illustrated catalog and price list — $3.

Lee Jofa
979 Third Ave. Dept. OHJ
New York, NY 10022
(212) 688-0444
ID
For 100 years, they have provided authentic documentary fabrics, Indian crewel embroideries & authentic Tartan plaids. Also, they offer largest single collection of English chintzes & linens which meticulously duplicate the ancient hand-block printing technique. Leading source to museums, restorations & historical agencies, they maintain an ongoing collection of documentary fabrics & wall coverings derived from authentic designs at the Museum of the American China Trade, Milton, MA. No literature.

• See Advertisers' Index
on page 22
for more details.

Lee Valley Tools, Ltd.
2680 Queensview Dr. Dept. OHJ
Ottawa, Ontario, Canada K2B8H6
(613) 596-0350
MO RS/O
An impressive selection of antique hardware: from the 1800s to date, including much Victorian and Art Deco, all unused and in working order. Also a line of modern brass cabinet hardware from Classic Hardware. Plus a complete selection od woodworking tools including chisels, saws, axes, drawknives, planes, etc. Antique hardware catalog, $3; tool catalog, $4; Classic Hardware catalog, $1.

Leeke, John — Woodworker
RR1, Box 847 Dept. OHJ
Sanford, ME 04073
(207) 324-9597
RS/O
Consulting to homeowners, carpenters, & wood-workers on restoration of architectural woodwork, and columns. Information sheet, $1. Custom woodworking that includes new furniture and cabinet work as well as historic house restoration (doors, raised panelling, stairwork, sash & mouldings for interior & exterior). Turning & carving (even by mail order) are specialities and include architectural column restoration & reproduction.

Lehigh Portland Cement Co.
PO Box 1882 Dept. OHJ
Allentown, PA 18105
(215) 776-2600
DIST
Produces Atlas colored masonry cements available in twelve colors, plus white. All masonry cements meet ASTM specifications. Write for free color chart.

Lehman Hardware & Appliances
PO Box 41J Dept. OHJ
Kidron, OH 44636
(216) 857-5441
MO RS/O
Old-fashioned, unusual, but still useful appliances and tools from the Amish/Mennonite community. Includes wood-coal-electric stoves & gas refrigerators; quality tools like slater's tools and woodworking benches; 19th century style hayforks and apple parers. 88-page catalog, $2. Free reports on gas refrigerators, etc.

Leichtung, Inc.
4944 Commerce Parkway Dept. OHJ
Cleveland, OH 44128
(216) 831-7645
MO RS/O
U.S. distributor of Lervad (Denmark) workbenches, Bracht (Germany) chisels, plus a treasury of fine, difficult-to- find tools from all over the continent. Free 1986 catalog (86 pages).

Lemee's Fireplace Equipment
815 Bedford St. Dept. OHJ
Bridgewater, MA 02324
(617) 697-2672
RS/O MO
Handmade bellows & fireplace accessories & equipment. Also: iron hardware, brass bowls, candlesticks & doorknockers, cast-iron banks & doorstops, black doorknockers, cast-iron firebacks, brass and copper kettles & buckets, black bath accessories, black & brass eagles, lighting fixtures in brass, copper, & black, post lanterns, fireplace cranes, andirons & screens. Plant hooks, black kettles, hooks & umbrella stands. Illustrated catalog & price list of fireplace equipment — $1 deductible with first order.

Lenape Products, Inc.
Pennington Ind. Ctr., Rt. 31 Dept. OHJ
Pennington, NJ 08534
(609) 737-0206
MO DIST
The leading manufacturers of a full range of porcelain wall-mounted switch plates, clip-on bath accessories. Available in white (and 9 other colors), and choice of four patterns. The selection includes a corner soap dish, towel bars, tissue holders, robe hooks, cabinet knobs, drawer pulls, etc. Catalog, $2.

Lena's Antique Bathroom Fixtures
PO Box 1022 Dept. OHJ
Bethel Island, CA 94511
(415) 634-5933
MO RS/O
An extensive selection of antique plumbing fixtures and bathroom accessories. Tubs, toilets, sinks, etc. 90% of the merchandise has been reconditioned and restored, but they also have products for the do-it-yourselfer. No literature, but write with your specific needs and they'll send photos.

• **Leo, Brian**
7520 Stevens Ave., So. Dept. OHJ
Richfield, MN 55423
(612) 861-1473
MO DIST
Domestic & commercial hardware cast in silicon bronze or brass-bronze. Hinges, knobs, doorplates, handles, letter drops, and more. Carefully moulded from antique originals. Shutter hinges in steel, large handles, furniture hardware, and pushplates. Cost-competitive reproduction of hardware original by soft or hard-tooling. Collection of designs is not all Victorian, but includes many styles and periods. Will try complicated jobs. Catalog, $3.

Lesco, Inc.
3409 W. Harry, Box 12209 Dept. OHJ
Wichita, KS 67277
(316) 942-8151
MO
Builders hardware of all kinds, including cast-iron hinges. No literature.

L'esperance Tile Works
240 Sheridan Ave. Dept. OHJ
Albany, NY 12210
(518) 465-5586
MO DIST RS/O
Designs and manufactures tiles. Services include on-site conservation; will identify and appraise ceramic tile, reproduce all forms including encaustic, low-relief, various geometric shapes, floor tile. Specialists in matching glaze and clay colors. Will accept orders for single tiles. Two brochures, Restoration and Custom Designs, with samples: $10 each.

KEY TO ABBREVIATIONS

MO	sells by Mail Order
RS/O	sells through Retail Store or Office
DIST	sells through Distributors
ID	sells only through Interior Designers or Archtects

Lester H. Berry & Company
PO Box 53377 Dept. OHJ
Philadelphia, PA 19105
(215) WA3-2603
MO DIST RS/O
This company carries reproduction 18th-century lighting fixtures: Chandeliers, wall sconces, coach lights, hanging lights. Free literature.

Lewis, John N.
156 Scarboro Drive Dept. OHJ
York, PA 17403
(717) 848-8461
MO RS/O
Antique barometers bought and sold. Mechanical repair and complete restoration for those looking for professional craftsmanship. Unable to ship finished product by way of common carrier — barometers have to be picked up by owner due to the elusiveness of the mercury. No problem with shipping aneroid barometers. No literature.

• **Joe Ley Antiques, Inc.**
615 East Market St. Dept. OHJ
Louisville, KY 40202
(502) 583-4014
MO RS/O
Six buildings house over 2 acres of antiques. Hard-to-find items including mantels, columns, newels. Specializing in light fixtures, restaurant items, doors, garden ornaments, brass hardware, and iron fences/gates. Brochure upon request.

Lieberman, Howard, P.E.
434 White Plains Rd. Dept. OHJ
Eastchester, NY 10709
(914) 779-3773
RS/O
Prepurchase building inspection and consulting, engineering services. No literature.

Light Ideas
1037 Taft St. Dept. OHJ
Rockville, MD 20850
(301) 424-LITE
MO RS/O
This lamp and lighting fixture store makes reproduction Victorian, Art Deco, and Nouveau style lampshades. They will also remake old lampshades. Lighting fixture glass and special wire is available as needed. Also repair & restoration of old ceiling fans. Free brochure.

Lighting by Hammerworks
75D Webster St. Dept. OHJ
Worcester, MA 01603
(617) 755-3434
MO RS/O
A complete line of handmade copper and brass lanterns, chandeliers, and tin, copper,and brass sconces. Custom work available. Catalog, $3.

Lignomat USA
PO Box 30145 Dept. OHJ
Portland, OR 97230
(800) 227-2105
MO
In Oregon, phone (503) 257-8957. Digital and analog moisture meters, beginning with a $1 pocket model. Free flyer.

• See Advertisers' Index
on page 22
for more details.

David Linker Ltd.
109 S. 5th St., 5th floor Dept. OHJ
Brooklyn, NY 11211
(718) 388-9443
RS/O
David Linker uses period methods (no power tools) to do museum-quality furniture restoration. Recent clients have included Gracie Mansion. Also traditional French polish. Paris division can locate or reproduce antique furniture. Free flyer.

Linoleum City
5657 Santa Monica Blvd. Dept. OHJ
Hollywood, CA 90038
(213) 463-1729
RS/O
A supplier of Hollywood props which stocks Dutch battleship linoleum and "Marmoleum," 9x9 and 12x12 black- & white vinyl tiles and old linoleum flooring. Carries a large selection of marbleized and solid color linoleum. Importer of cork tiles for walls and floors. No literature; write with your specific needs.

• **Lisa — Victoria Brass Beds**
17106 So. Crater Rd. - 7 Dept. OHJ
Petersburg, VA 23805
(804) 862-1491
MO
Reasonably priced, custom-made solid brass beds with the emphasis on Victorian styles. Available only by mail-order. Color catalog, $4, refundable with order.

Littlewood & Maue Museum Quality Restorations
PO Box 402 Dept. OHJ
Palmyra, NJ 08065
(609) 829-4615
MO RS/O
Restoration of period lighting fixtures for museums and private collectors. Mr. Littlewood does lectures, slide shows & demonstrates working lamps of the period. Free flyer and references.

W. S. Lockhart Designs
112 S. Warren St. Dept. OHJ
Timmonsville, SC 29161
(803) 346-3531
MO RS/O
W.S. Lockhart Designs has over 1600 home plan designs and sells these designs and the blueprints for the designs by mail and out of the office. These designs and blueprints are sold to individuals, developers, construction companies, builders, etc. The company has been in business for 16 years. Sample portfolios $12. Early American and Deep South editions available.

• **London Country, Ltd.**
13634 Oakwood Curve Dept. OHJ
Burnsville, MN 55337
(612) 894-6266
MO RS/O
Restored Victorian fireplace inserts, imported from England; most with tiles, some Art Nouveau; also mantels, architectural antiques, and reproductions. Free information sheet with color photos.

• **London Venturers Company**
2 Dock Square Dept. OHJ
Rockport, MA 01966
(617) 546-7161
RS/O MO
Specializing in original gas, oil, and early electric lighting fixtures: chandeliers, hall lights, wall sconces and table lamps. Also quality reproductions of gas, oil, and early electric lighting. Illustrated catalog, $2.

Loose, Thomas — Blacksmith/ Whitesmith
Rt. 2, Box 2410 Dept. OHJ
Leesport, PA 19533
(215) 926-4849
MO RS/O
Hand-wrought items for home and hearth, finely decorated with brass and copper inlay. Kitchen and fireplace utensils and lighting devices. Hardware and other items for old home restoration made to your specifications. Brochure available; please enclose a stamp with your request.

Lost City Arts
257 West 10th St. Dept. OHJ
New York, NY 10014
(212) 807-6979
RS/O
Their showroom at 257 W. 10th St. has architectural artifacts such as stained glass, iron fencing, pedestal sinks, mantels, columns, garden urns and sculpture, & upscale light fixtures from some of N.Y.'s unique buildings. No literature.

Louis W. Bowen Fine Wallcoverings
950 Third Ave. Dept. OHJ
New York, NY 10022
(212) 759-5410
ID
Trompe-l'oeil brackets, moulding, swags, and dadoes in wallpaper-border form. Choice of grey, sepia, and gold tones. Also murals depicting early American scenes: West Point, New York in the 1800s, etc., or florals and scenics. No literature.

Louisville Art Glass Studio
1110 Baxter Ave. Dept. OHJ
Louisville, KY 40204
(502) 585-5421
MO RS/O
Leaded glass designs and ornaments for home use, designed and manufactured by a 90-year-old company. Custom stained glass. "Creative Leaded Glass", an 11-page, unbound catalog — $10.00.

Lovelia Enterprises, Inc.
Box 1845, Grand Cen. Sta. Dept. OHJ
New York, NY 10017
(212) 490-0930
MO RS/O
Importers of machine woven tapestries from France, Belgium and Italy in sizes 10 inches to 10 feet. Gobelin and Aubusson tapestries are woven on old looms from original jacquards in either wool or 100% cotton. Some are copies of masterpieces with the signature of the original artist. 20-page color catalog, plus 4 illustrated pages on new uses for tapestries, $4.00.

Ludowici-Celadon Co.
P.O. Box 69 Dept. OHJ
New Lexington, OH 43764
(614) 342-1995
MO RS/O
Manufactures wide range of handsome ceramic roofing tiles. Free product data sheets on each style, which include: Barrel mission style, Spanish and various interlocking roof tiles, also flat ceramic shingle tile. Manufactures terra cotta and cast stone for restoration. Distributes slate.

Luigi Crystal
7332 Frankford Ave. Dept. OHJ
Philadelphia, PA 19136
(215) 338-2978
MO
Painted glass Victorian table lamps, cut crystal chandeliers, hurricane lamps, sconces. Reasonably priced. Imported crystal prisms. Illustrated catalog & price list — $1.00, refunded with order.

Lundberg Studios, Inc. Contemporary Art Glass
131 Marineview Ave., PO Box C Dept. OHJ
Davenport, CA 95017
(408) 423-2532
MO DIST RS/O
They offer a variety of art glass, specializing in lamps and shades imitating Tiffany and Steuben. Over 50 different shades in Art Nouveau, Victorian & Modern styles are available. Metal lamp bases and replacement parts also available. They will buy or trade for original Tiffany lamp bases. Quantity discounts offered to distributors. Individuals can order from $3 catalog.

Lunenburg Foundry & Engineering, Ltd.
Dept. OHJ
Lunenberg, Nova Scot, Canada B0J2C0
(902) 634-8827
MO
Makers of cast-iron stoves and parts, especially small-scale stoves ideal for cottages or boats. The stoves burn wood, oil or coal; the smallest, the "Sardine," is 12 x 11 inches. Free brochure.

• **Lyemance International, Inc.**
PO Box 505 Dept. OHJ
Jeffersonville, IN 47131
(812) 288-9953
DIST
Top-sealing fireplace damper saves energy; reduces heat loss by controlling down drafts when fireplace is not in use. Seals out birds and insects, keeps out rain, sleet and snow and saves on air conditioning costs. The damper is shut by means of a stainless-steel cable that extends down the flue to the firebox, where it is secured to a bracket on the side firebox wall. Installed on chimney tops. Brochure free.

Lynn Goodpasture
42 W. 17th St. Dept. OHJ
New York, NY 10011
(212) 989-5246
RS/O
Custom stencilling, marbleizing, gold leaf, and other painted finishes, for walls, ceilings, floors, furniture, and floorcloths. Authentic reproductions as well as contemporary and adapted designs. No literature.

M

• **M — H Lamp & Fan Company**
7231-1/2 N. Sheridan Road Dept. OHJ
Chicago, IL 60626
(312) 743-2225
MO RS/O
They manufacture solid brass, hand-made, Victorian and early 20th century reproduction light fixtures. Also specialize in complete restoration of antique desk and ceiling fans, and antique light fixtures. They have a limited supply of restored fans, inquiries welcome. Lighting catalog, $3. Restoration service listing free with SASE. Brochure on restored antique ceiling fans free with SASE.

Mac the Antique Plumber
885 57th St. Dept. OHJ
Sacramento, CA 95819
(916) 454-4507
MO DIST RS/O
A wide variety of antique and reproduction plumbing: tubs, porcelain faucets and handles, pedestal lavatories, high-tank toilets, kits to convert standard to high tank; custom shower enclosures, towel bars, soap holders, etc. Will also strip, polish, repair, and refinish old plumbing. Color 24-page catalog, $3.50, refundable.

• **Machin Designs (USA), Inc.**
652 Glenbrook Rd. Dept. OHJ
Stamford, CT 06906
(203) 348-5319
RS/O
High-quality period-style conservatories to complement old houses. Also a range of ornamental garden buildings, including pavilions, covered seats, and planters. Will work with homeowners as well as contractors. Conservatories catalog, $5; ornamental garden buildings catalog, $3.

• **Stephen P. Mack**
Chase Hill Farm Dept. OHJ
Ashaway, RI 02804
(401) 377-8041
MO RS/O
Architectural firm offering services as architects, designers, preservationists, contractors, suppliers of period building materials—new and old. Specialize in 18th-century houses and barns, dismantled, which come with a full set of plans by a staff architect and photographic documentation. Nationwide clientele. No literature.

Maclean Restoration Services
105 Stone House Rd. Dept. OHJ
Winchester Center, CT 06094
(203) 738-0048
RS/O
Interior finish restoration. Paint removal, authentic paints and glazes from period recipes. Graining, marbleizing, simulated aged surfaces. Consultation workshops. Period window treatments, bed hangings. Nine years experience. No literature.

• **Mad River Wood Works**
P.O. Box 163 Dept. OHJ
Arcata, CA 95521
(707) 826-0629
MO DIST
Manufacturers of Victorian millwork in redwood and select hardwoods. Several patterns of ornamental shingles, turnings, ornamental trim, mouldings, old-style screen door replicas, corbels, brackets, balusters and railings, and ornamental pickets. Custom work is also accepted. Catalog, $2.

Madhatter Press
3101 12th Ave. S. Dept. OHJ
Minneapolis, MN 55407
(612) 722-8951
MO
Publish "From the Neck Up: An Illustrated Guide to Hatmaking" — a complete book for making felt, straw, and fabric covered hats. Easy to follow instructions illustrated with 400 photographs and drawings. Includes list of suppliers, 60 modern and historical patterns. Spiral bound. 200 pages. $19.95 $1.25 postage. Quantity discounts.

Magnetite Corp.
8386 Tom Dr. Dept. OHJ
Baton Rouge, LA 70815
(800) MAG-TITE
DIST RS/O
A patented insulated window that attaches magnetically to the insides of windows. Acrylic glazing, magnetized gasket, steel strip with wood frame. Free brochure. Dealer inquiries welcome. In LA, (504) 927-8712.

Magnolia Hall
726 Andover Dr. Dept. OH9
Atlanta, GA 30327
(404) 256-4747
MO
Well-built, solid mahogany, hand-carved Victorian reproduction furniture. Some brass and oak pieces. Collection of highly-carved Louis XIV French sofas, chairs. Also lamps, clocks, mirrors, footstools. Large selection of whatnot stands and wall curio cabinets. 80-page illustrated catalog and fabric samples — $1.00.

• **Maizefield Mantels**
PO Box 336 Dept. OHJ
Port Townsend, WA 98368
(206) 385-6789
MO RS/O
Specializes in the construction of wooden mantels in a variety of styles: colonial, Victorian, Art Deco. Stock sizes and custom-made. Also, fireplace accessories: tools and screens. Send $1.50 for catalog.

Mangione Plaster
21 John St. Dept. OHJ
Saugerties, NY 12477
(914) 246-9863
RS/O
Specializes in the restoration of ornamental plasterwork. Will also reproduce plaster domes and mouldings. Serving New York/Connecticut area. No literature.

Manor Art Glass Studio
20 Ridge Road Dept. OHJ
Douglaston, NY 11363
(212) 631-8029
RS/O MO
Professional craftsmen will restore your antique stained glass windows to their original strength and beauty. Rosalind Brenner has designed windows for homes, fine restaurants and religious institutions throughout the country and will create new windows to blend with the period architecture of your home. Slides available on specific request.

KEY TO ABBREVIATIONS

MO	sells by Mail Order
RS/O	sells through Retail Store or Office
DIST	sells through Distributors
ID	sells only through Interior Designers or Archtects

Mansion Industries, Inc.
PO Box 2220 Dept. OHJ
Industry, CA 91746
(818) 968-9501
DIST
Hemlock and oak stairparts in traditional styles: newel posts, post tops, balusters, and railings. Easy-to-install Promontory line for level or angle runs. Installation instructions, architectural tracing details, reference wall charts, audio-visual training films — all available on request. Contact Customer Service Dept. for direct assistance.

Maple Hill Woodworking
RD 2 Dept. OHJ
Ballston Spa, NY 12020
(518) 885-7258
MO RS/O
Mouldings and millwork made to order for restoration and reproduction of period homes and antique furniture. Softwoods and hardwoods available. They specialize in exact reproduction of existing mouldings in large or small quantities, also mantels. Authentic reproductions of batten doors made to order. No literature.

Marble Technics Ltd.
A & D Bldg. 150 E. 58th St. Dept. OHJ
New York, NY 10155
(212) 750-9189
DIST RS/O
Real marble, limestone, and granite you can install like paneling. Thin, lightweight (similar to ceramic tile) sheets — cut from blocks of stone. 70 colors are stocked in large sizes. May be used as wall covering, flooring, or furniture applications. They also offer some tiles with decorative patterns of multi-colored stone for interior floors. Color catalog and installation information, $1.

MarLe Company
35 Larkin St., PO Box 4499 Dept. OHJ
Stamford, CT 06907
(203) 348-2645
RS/O MO
Individually fabricated lanterns of brass and copper - most for exterior use, but some suitable for interiors. Designs are taken from the 60 year old company's collection of antique lanterns. Primarily early American in style, there are 2 designs specifically for Victorian and turn-of-the-century houses. Also custom-made work. Catalog with photos of 18 lanterns and price list — $2.

Marsh Stream Enterprise
RFD 2, Box 490 Dept. OHJ
Brooks, ME 04921
(207) 722-3575
MO
Nine stencils of original 'Knees' from a turn-of-the-century woodworking mill enable you to make your own gingerbread. Popular designs used on porches, eaves, and gables, ranging in size from 18-in. x 30-in. to 6-in. x 10-in. $9.00 for complete set, including instructions.

Marshall Imports
713 South Main Dept. 15
Mansfield, OH 44907
(419) 756-3814
MO
Sole United States importer of Antiquax, the pure wax polish used by museums. Gives a soft mellow sheen, will not fingerprint, produces a deep patina on both antique and contemporary finishes. Use on woodwork, cabinetry, and furniture. Sold through better stores or by mail. A brochure describing Antiquax products is available at no charge.

Marshalltown Trowel Co.
PO Box 738 Dept. OHJ
Marshalltown, IA 50158
(515) 754-6116
MO DIST
Trowels and other tools for working with cement, brick, concrete block, dry wall and plaster. Free illustrated catalog. A useful 24 pg. booklet "Troweling Tips and Techniques" is available for $1.00.

Martha M. House Furniture
1022 So. Decatur Street Dept. OHJ
Montgomery, AL 36104
(205) 264-3558
RS/O MO
A large mail-order source for Victorian reproduction furniture. Hand-carved solid mahogany pieces; tables with wood or Carrara marble tops. Sofas, chairs, bedroom and dining furniture. Large choice of covers and finishes. "Southern Heirlooms" catalog, $2. Color catalog of yesteryear lamps, pictures and other accessories, $2.

• **Marvin Windows**
8043 24th Ave., S. Dept. OHJ
Minneapolis, MN 55420
(800) 346-5128
DIST
Wood windows and patio doors for replacement and remodeling. Available in standard, retro, and custom sizes. Single, double, and triple glazing and wood storms. All units are weather stripped, and may be ordered bare wood, primed or prefinished. Options include authentic divided lites, leaded glass, Low E glass, or grids. Custom shapes and sizes include round and arched windows. Free brochure. In Minn., (800) 552-1167.

Mason & Sullivan Co.
586 Higgins Crowell Rd. Dept. 4512
W. Yarmouth, MA 02673
(617) 778-1056
MO RS/O
Reproduction clock kits, copies of clocks by Aaron Willard and other great American clock craftsmen. Also movements, dials, assembled clocks, specialty tools, and books. 56-page color catalog, $2.

Masonry Specialty Co.
4430 Gibsonia Rd. Dept. OHJ
Gibsonia, PA 15044
(412) 443-7080
MO DIST
Manufactor/distributor of top quality tools and equipment for the construction trades. Including tools for brick masonry, cement finishing, drywall, tilesetting, and plastering. Free catalog illustrating over 1900 items.

Master Products, Inc.
PO 274, S. Ind. Air Park Dept. OHJ
Orange City, IA 51041
(712) 737-3436
MO DIST
Manufacturers of base paint, decorator wood stains, woodgraining systems, and paint removers & refinishes trademarked with "Old Masters." Sold primarily through paint stores nationwide. Free color chart and how-to booklet; wood graining instructions.$.50.

Master Wood Carver
103 Corrine Dr. Dept. OHJ
Pennington, NJ 08534
(609) 737-9364
MO RS/O
Handcrafts authentic Colonial reproduction pieces in solid wood. Each item is signed and numbered. Antique restoration and repair expertly done. Custom pieces from drawings or pictures. Please call for appointment or send $1. for introductory brochure.

Master's Stained and Etched Glass Studio
729 West 16th St., No. B-1 Dept. OHJ
Costa Mesa, CA 92627
(714) 548-4951
RS/O MO
Painted, leaded, etched and bevelled glass. Residential and commercial commissions. Antique windows. Free brochure.

Masterworks, Inc.
8558 I Lee Highway Dept. OHJ
Fairfax, VA 22031
(703) 532-0234
MO RS/O
Wholesale/retail purveyor of decorative hardware and bathroom fittings. Exclusive agent in Washington D.C. area for authentic design bath fittings from England, and Barclay faucets. Exclusive agent for Watercolors faucets, Brassart door hardware of England. Extensive selection of polished brass lavatory basins, pedestal sinks, and small drop-in china sinks. Brochure on pedestal sinks, free.

• **Materials Unlimited**
2 W. Michigan Ave. Dept. OHJ
Ypsilanti, MI 48197
(313) 483-6980
MO RS/O
The largest collection of restored architectural antiques in the midwest. Three floors of display. Stained & beveled glass doors, windows, entrances; restored brass chandeliers & sconces; mantels; furniture; hardware; decorative accessories; front & back bars. In addition, a complete selection of new building materials is now available. Custom services include: glass beveling, leaded glass repair, custom design, and modification to specification of beveled windows, millwork, and bars. Brochure (antiques), $3. Complete product package (reproductions), $8.

Mattia, Louis
980 2nd Ave. Dept. OHJ
New York, NY 10022
(212) 753-2176
RS/O
This little store is full of turn-of-century lighting fixtures. Mattia restores, rewires, adds antique or reproduction glass shades. Hundreds of wall sconces — wired or for candles. Cannot handle mail orders. No literature.

• **Maurer & Shepherd, Joyners**
122 Naubuc Ave. Dept. OHJ
Glastonbury, CT 06033
(203) 633-2383
RS/O MO
Handcrafted custom-made interior and exterior 18th century architectural trim. Finely-detailed Colonial doors and windows, shutters, wainscot and wall panelling, carved details, pediments, etc. Wide pine flooring, half-lapped. Pegged mortise and tenon joints — authentic work. Also antique glass. Free brochure.

Max-Cast
R3, Box 126 Dept. OHJ
Iowa City, IA 52240
(319) 351-0708
MO
A custom foundry willing to do small runs of appliance and architectural castings in brass, bronze, aluminum, and grey iron. Stove parts a specialty. No literature.

Max Lumber Co.
1112 Garfield Ave. Dept. OHJ
Jersey City, NJ 07304
(201) 333-7700
RS/O
This lumber and millwork company specializes in old houses. Reproduction doors, windows, mouldings, etc. available. No literature.

Maxwell Lumber
25-30 Borden Ave. Dept. OHJ
Long Island City, NY 11101
(212) 929-6088
RS/O
In business for over 60 years, Maxwell Lumber has an extensive line of embossed, carved, and machined mouldings in hard and softwood as well as lumber and plywood. They sell to the trade as well as to homeowners. Second location: 211 W. 18th St., New York, NY 10011. 101-page product manual available for $1.50 plus postage.

Maynard House Antiques
11 Maynard St. Dept. OHJ
Westborough, MA 01581
(617) 366-2073
MO RS/O
They specialize in country sofas and wing chairs, upholstered in fabrics by Greeff, Waverly, Schumacher, and representing the period 1780 to 1820. Catalog, $2. Also, custom-made window treatments for the same period: swags, festoons, etc. Coverlet material by Avery, sold by the yard. Free flyers.

Mazza Frame and Furniture Co., Inc.
35-10 Tenth Street Dept. OHJ
Long Island City, NY 11106
(718) 721-9287
MO ID
Manufacturers of hardwood furniture frames in period styles. Mail orders shipped throughout the U.S. and overseas. Firm sells primarily to decorators and upholstery shops. Can handle variations of standard designs, and custom work. Free brochure; prices and specific photos on request.

McGivern, Barbara — Artist
659 Sunnyside Lane Dept. OHJ
Sister Bay, WI 54234
(414) 762-0849
MO
Will do pen & ink drawing, $10, or full color watercolor, $25, of a home, scene, historic building, etc. Renderings of buildings and sites. Send photo (returnable) and check. Free brochure.

Mead Associates Woodworking, Inc.
63 Tiffany Place Dept. OHJ
Brooklyn, NY 11231
(718) 643-1313
RS/O
Custom cabinetmaking and architectural woodworking. Expert at details in keeping with the restoration of older houses. They make kitchens, library units, offices, commercial interiors and furniture. Also custom-made doors of all types and styles including completely weatherized doors and entrances. Prefer to work from drawings and will consult. Cabinetmakers to the Old-House Journal. No literature, references available; call for appointment.

KEY TO ABBREVIATIONS

MO	sells by Mail Order
RS/O	sells through Retail Store or Office
DIST	sells through Distributors
ID	sells only through Interior Designers or Archtects

• **The Mechanick's Workbench**
PO Box 544 Dept. O
Marion, MA 02738
(617) 748-1680
MO
They specialize in fine quality, antique woodworking tools for craftsmen and collectors. Wooden moulding planes for reproduction of 18th and 19th century mouldings a specialty. Send want list with profiles or samples. Their catalogs have the reputation of being the best in the field and are published 2 or 3 times a year — all different offerings in each. Catalog, $10.

Meierjohan — Wengler, Inc.
10330 Wayne Ave. Dept. OHJ
Cincinnati, OH 45215
(513) 771-6074
MO
Firm has been making cast tablets and markers for over 50 years. Available in a variety of stock shapes or special sizes. Emblems, symbols or crests can be incorporated to create a special one-of-a-kind design. Choice of material: Bronze, aluminum or silver-bronze. Can also do lost-wax casting. Free catalog.

• **Mel-Nor Marketing**
303 Gulfbank Dept. OHJ
Houston, TX 77037
(713) 445-3485
MO
A large selection of Victorian-styled park benches made of cast aluminum and a choice of fir or oak slats. Custom sizes & colors are offered. Also, porch swings, mail-box, and street lamps. Free catalog.

Melotte-Morse Studios
213 South Sixth Street Dept. OHJ
Springfield, IL 62701
(217) 789-9515
RS/O
Melotte-Morse Studios designs, fabricates and renovates stained glass art for ecclesiastical, commercial, and individual clients. A division of Melotte-Morse, Architects and Planners, the Studio also works extensively with existing antique glass works, performing corrective maintenance and restorative repairs or renovations. The studio has refurbished entire stained glass collections for churches as well as individual panels for residential reinstallation. Current newsletter is free.

Memphis Hardwood Flooring Co.
P.O. Box 7253 Dept. OHJ
Memphis, TN 38107
(901) 526-7306
DIST
Hardwood flooring available through distributors. Colorful 12-page catalog available $.50 postpaid.

• **Mendocino Millwork**
PO Box 669A Dept. OHJ
Mendocino, CA 95460
(707) 937-4410
MO
Many stock patterns of sawn wood ornaments, Victorian Gingerbread trim & decorative parts for the house & porch: Applique & mouldings, porch brackets, porch railings, posts & pickets, corbels, baseboards, multi- pane windows, & French doors. Also, custom work. New illustrated catalog with price list — $2.

Meredith Stained Glass Studio, Inc.
5700-F Sunnyside Ave. Dept. OHJ
Beltsville, MD 20705
(301) 345-0433
RS/O MO
Glass, tools, books and supplies for do-it-yourself stained or etched glass. "Restoration" glass for windows or furniture fronts. Solid hardwood exterior doors with stock leaded, bevelled, or etched oval or rectangular lights. Retail/wholesale to trade. Stained glass supply catalog, $2. For wholesale catalog, also send verification of business status. Door information, send SASE. Phone inquiries welcome; showroom open to public. Also, (800) 448-7853.

Merit Moulding, Ltd.
95-35 150th St. Dept. OHJ
Jamaica, NY 11435
(718) 523-2200
RS/O
Manufacturer of custom wood mouldings — short runs a specialty. Also, oak mouldings and trim. No literature.

Merritt's Antiques, Inc.
RD 2 Dept. OHJ
Douglassville, PA 19518
(215) 689-9541
MO RS/O
Large selection of clock repair supplies, including hands, pulleys, keys, dials, movements, and pendulums. Also, a nice selection of wall, shelf, and grandfather clocks (antique, reproduction, and kits). Complete line of antique furniture, glass, china, bric-a-brac and more. Complete line of reproduction items including wicker, furniture, brass, glass etc. Clock supply catalog, $1.50; Clock catalog, $1.

Metal Building Components, Inc.
PO Box 38217 Dept. OHJ
Houston, TX 77238
(713) 445-8555
MO
MBCI offers a large selection of preformed metal roof, wall, and fascia systems available in a variety of colors and gauges. Color-matched trim and accessories also available. Orders generally ready in three days. Free color flyer.

Metal Sales Manufacturing Corp.
10300 Linn Station Rd. Dept. OHJ
Louisville, KY 40223
(502) 426-5215
DIST
They make two types of metal roofing. Their stile line of metal roof panels look like clay tile but resist chipping, chalking, and fading. Five colors, widths up to one meter, lengths to 16 inches. Pro-Panel II standing-seam panels have a painted surface and weather-tight seals. Lengths up to 40 inches, widths up to 36 inches. Free color flyers. Also (800) 321-5833.

Metropolis
100 Wooster St. Dept. OHJ
New York, NY 10012
(212) 226-6117
MO RS/O
Reproductions of Art Deco furniture, including lamps, chairs, couches, bars, and shelves. Free brochure.

• See Advertisers' Index on page 22 for more details.

Metropolitan Lighting Fixture Co., Inc.
1010 Third Ave. Dept. OHJ
New York, NY 10021
(212) 838-2425
DIST ID
A wide selection of reproduction lighting fixtures from traditional pieces in solid brass to Art Deco ceiling fixtures (these are cast from original moulds). Lalique wall fixtures, rustic wooden "antler" chandeliers, Holophane hanging globes, Victorian-style chandeliers with bevelled or etched shades, and chandeliers hung with crystal are some of the options. Full-color, 73-page catalog, $5. They also do elaborate custom work; samples illustrated in the catalog.

Meyer, Kenneth Co.
327 6th Ave. Dept. OHJ
San Francisco, CA 94118
(415) 752-2865
ID
Manufacturers of custom-made trimmings, fringes, tassels, tiebacks for Interior Decorators. No literature.

• **Michael's Fine Colonial Products**
Rte 44, RD1, Box 179A Dept. OHJ
Salt Point, NY 12578
(914) 677-3960
MO
Custom-made millwork appropriate for 19th century as well as Colonial houses: Divided light sash; circle head sash; Gothic, triangle, and segment windows; raised panel blinds & shutters; stock and custom stair parts; doors. Mouldings to pattern. Free flyer with large SASE.

Mid-State Tile Company
PO Box 1777 Dept. OHJ
Lexington, NC 27292
(704) 249-3931
DIST
Quarry and pavers are available in 4" x 8", 6" sq., 8" sq., and 8" hex. Twelve natural colors and matching trim will give you an authentic look in any application. Tough enough for exterior use in areas below the freeze line. Also available in brick-look patterns. Brochures, free.

Midget Louver Co.
800 Main Ave., Rt. 7 Dept. OHJ
Norwalk, CT 06852
(203) 866-2342
MO RS/O
Round midget louvers for ventilating enclosed spaces, 1 to 6 in. in diameter; no screws or nails needed for installation. Free descriptive brochure.

Midland Engineering Company
PO Box 1019 Dept. OHJ
South Bend, IN 46637
(219) 272-0200
MO DIST RS/O
A midwest distributor of Vermont roofing slate and imported clay tiles. Below average retail cost; will sell direct to the consumer. Also roof restoration specialist and consultant for slate and tile roofing. Free brochures, please specify your interest.

Midwest Spiral Stair Company, Inc.
113 Adell Dept. OHJ
Elmhurst, IL 60126
(312) 941-3395
MO RS/O
A complete selection of spiral stairs in both metal and wood, shipped anywhere in the U.S. Flyer available.

Midwest Wood Products
1051 South Rolff St. Dept. OHJ
Davenport, IA 52802
(319) 323-4757
RS/O
A millwork company specializing in wood sash, 1-3/8" standard sizes in stock. Will custom make any size sash required: devided lite, round top, or curved; double hung, fixed, casement or storm sash. Can also provide period store fronts, shutters, doors, screens, storm doors, porch screens and trim. In many cases, sash can be fabricated to accept insulated glass which they can also supply to the customer.

• **Mile Hi Crown, Inc.**
Design Ctr/1801 Wynkoop, 290 Dept. OHJ
Denver, CO 80202
(303) 777-2099
ID
Distributor of England's Crown Decorative Products, including Anaglypta, Supaglypta, and Lincrusta. (All are Crown's registered trademark.) These wallcoverings are available in 112 patterns ranging from Victorian to contemporary. Free info sheet & price list. Color brochure & sample packet $2.

Mill River Hammerworks
65 Canal St. Dept. OHJ
Turners Falls, MA 01376
(413) 863-8388
MO RS/O
Museum experienced metal craftsman offers repair and reproduction services in iron, copper, brass, pewter, and tin. Hardware, lighting devices, kitchen and fireplace accessories, etc. Hand-forged, cast, spun, or fabricated as needed. Also, exterior architectural hardware, gates, railings, and grilles. Difficult or unusual antique repair or reproduction a specialty. Free brochure available.

Millen Roofing Co.
2247 N. 31 St. Dept. OHJ
Milwaukee, WI 53208
(414) 442-1424
MO RS/O
Tile and slate roofing. Large supply of old types of roofing tile and weathered slate for restoration work. Tools, equipment, copper nails, copper clips and fasteners, brass snow guards also available. Does consulting, design, specifications, and inspections. No literature.

Howard Miller Clock Co.
860 E. Main St. Dept. OHJ
Zeeland, MI 49464
(616) 772-9131
DIST
Reproductions and adaptations of antique wall, mantel, and grandfather clocks using the finest of woods, movements, and craftsmanship. Sold through fine furniture distributors. Literature free to the trade.

KEY TO ABBREVIATIONS

MO sells by Mail Order

RS/O sells through Retail Store or Office

DIST sells through Distributors

ID sells only through Interior Designers or Archtects

• **Millham, Newton — Blacksmith**
672 Drift Road Dept. OHJ
Westport, MA 02790
(617) 636-5437
RS/O MO
Offers a wide selection of 17th, 18th and early 19th century architectural house hardware: latches, spring latches, H and strap hinges, bolts, shutter dogs. Household ironware includes: cooking utensils, hearth items, early candleholders, candlestands, rush lights pipe tongs, etc. Illustrated catalog and price list $1.

Millwork Supply Company
2225 1st Ave. South Dept. OHJ
Seattle, WA 98134
(206) 622-1450
MO RS/O
In business at this location for 64 years. They are manufacturers and distributors for stock and custom; wood doors, windows, frames, mouldings, mantels, and stair parts. Free stock moulding sheet.

Minuteman International Co., Ltd.
75 Sawyer Passway Dept. OHJ
Fitchburg, MA 01420
(617) 343-7475
MO DIST RS/O
Fireplace accessories: Cast-metal (cast iron and brass) kettles, trivets, and cast-iron registers and grilles. Also, chimney brushes and rods. Free full color catalog.

Minwax Company, Inc.
102 Chestnut Ridge Plaza Dept. HC
Montvale, NJ 07645
(201) 391-0253
DIST
Easy-to-use stains and woodfinishing products for durable, attractive finishes from a 75-year old company. Their high- performance wood filler can be sanded, planed, painted, or stained. Free literature & color card. Also free: "Tips on Wood Finishing", a 22 page booklet providing do-it-your selfers with information ranging from how to apply a preservative stain to a house exterior to preparing antiques for refinishing.

Mirror Patented Stove Pipe Co.
11 Britton Drive Dept. OHJ
Bloomfield, CT 06002
(203) 243-8358
DIST
A manufacturer of No. 304, 24-gauge stainless steel pipe and flexible stainless tube for chimney relining. No literature, but will put you in contact with a distributor in your area.

D. C. Mitchell Reproductions
RD 1 Box 446 Dept. OHJ
Hockessin, DE 19707
(302) 998-1181
MO
Solid brass box locks — exterior reproduction of antique originals, interior a modern cylinder lock. Also cabinet and furniture hardware, door knockers, H and H-L hinges. Free catalog.

• See Advertisers' Index on page 22 for more details.

Mittermeir, Frank Inc.
3577 E. Tremont Ave., Box 2 Dept. OHJ
Bronx, NY 10465
(212) 828-3843
MO
Imported and domestic quality tools for woodcarvers, sculptors, engravers, ceramists, and potters. Of special interest are their tools for ornamental plasterwork. They also sell a number of books on sculpture, wood carving, and related arts. Free catalog.

Monarch Range Co. Consumer Prod. Div.
340 N. Water St. Dept. OHJ
Algoma, WI 54201
(414) 487-5236
MO RS/O
An old-time stove manufacturer, this company can still furnish some Monarch parts back to 1896. Also makes kitchen heater and combination ranges, fireplace inserts, add-a-furnaces, and room circulators. Free brochure.

Monroe Coldren and Sons
723 East Virginia Ave. Dept. OHJ
West Chester, PA 19380
(215) 692-5651
MO RS/O
18th and 19th century hardware, completely restored original in stock or custom reproduction. They also have original doors, shutters, mantels and a complete line of original accessories for the hearth and home. Call for more information or consultation.

• **Montclair Restoration Craftsmen**
21 Clover Hill Pl. Dept. OHJ
Montclair, NJ 07042
(201) 783-4519
RS/O
Restoration partnership specializing in: interior woodwork stripped and refinished on site, specialized carpentry, furniture repair and restoration. Also experienced in color mixing, design, historical research. New York metropolitan area. Also, (201) 783-1320.

J.H. Monteath Co. — Arch. Rep.
2500 Park Ave. Dept. OHJ
Bronx, NY 10451
(800) 522-6210
ID
A major supplier of foreign and domestic hardwoods — in matched plywood, architectural veneer, custom mouldings and lumber. Every specie from American ash thru African zebrawood. Calls welcome for consultation.

• **Moore, E.T., Jr. Co.**
3100 N. Hopkins Rd. Ste 101 Dept. OHJ
Richmond, VA 23224
(804) 231-1823
MO RS/O
This company salvages beams, joists, and other pieces of heart pine from buildings being demolished, and reworks them into custom and stock products: mantels, columns, flooring, mouldings, and panelling. Also hand-hewn beams, and custom furniture & cabinets. Free brochure.

Moravian Pottery & Tile Works
Swamp Road Dept. OHJ
Doylestown, PA 18901
(215) 345-6722
MO RS/O
A living history museum reproducing hand-made decorative tiles and mosaics as originally produced between 1898 and 1952. Tile catalog, $3.

Morgan Bockius Studios, Inc.
1412 York Road Dept. OHJ
Warminster, PA 18974
(215) 672-6547
RS/O MO
Stained, painted, and leaded glass, period and custom designs. Their artists design and craft Victorian and contemporary adaptations for any architectural situation. Coats of arms, and other decorative work available including mirrors, beveled glass, etched and carved panels on clear and tinted glass. Custom designed lamps; repairs to old fixtures including glass bending and painting, and metal work. Call for more information or driving directions. Free brochure.

Morgan Woodworking Supplies
1123 Bardstown Rd. Dept. OO3K1
Louisville, KY 40204
(502) 456-2545
MO RS/O
Numerous woodworking supplies including foreign and domestic veneer, patterns, books, domestic hardwoods, turning squares, basswood carving blocks, hand tools, toymaking parts, Shaker pegs, mug pegs, candle cups, dowels, buttons, spindles, inlays, chair cane and seating supplies. Also brass reproduction hardware. Catalog, $1.

Moriarty's Lamps
9 West Ortega Street Dept. OHJ
Santa Barbara, CA 93101
(805) 966-1124
RS/O
Sells old chandeliers, wall sconces, kerosene lamps, old electric and gas-electric fixtures, old shades. Also metal refinishing and old lamp parts. Also refinishes old doorknobs, window latches, plumbing fixtures, etc. Inquiries answered; no literature.

• **Mosca, Matthew**
2513 Queen Anne Rd. Dept. OHJ
Baltimore, MD 21223
(301) 566-9047
RS/O
Historic paint specialist. Microscopic techniques and chemical testing are used to determine the original composition and color of paints and other architectural finishes. Has done work on Mt. Vernon and National Trust properties. Can analyze samples taken by architect or homeowner. Complete interior design capability available utilizing research for restorations and historically compatible rehabilitations. Before taking samples, write describing your needs and objectives.

• **Moultrie Manufacturing Company**
PO Drawer 1179 Dept. OHJ
Moultrie, GA 31768
(800) 841-8674
MO RS/O
Ornamental columns, gates, and fences of cast aluminum. Old South Reproductions catalog shows selection of period-style fence panels and gates; also aluminum furniture, fountains, urns, plaques, etc. Catalog is $1.00. In Georgia, call (912) 985-1312.

• **Mountain Lumber Company, Inc.**
Rt. 2, Box 43-1 Dept. 12
Ruckersville, VA 22968
(804) 985-3646
MO DIST RS/O
Specializing in Longleaf heart pine flooring; also heart pine panelling, doors, rough sawn and hand-hewn beams, period mouldings, trim, rough sawn heart pine boards, and custom cabinetry. All lumber is kiln-dried to stabilize it against shrinkage and/or warp and precisely graded for grain, sap content, defects, and shake. Call or write for free color brochure and price list.

Mr. Slate - Smid Incorporated
Dept. OHJ
Sudbury, VT 05733
(802) 247-8809
RS/O
Quality salvaged roofing slate for repair work, restorations, and new construction. Inventory includes most colors and sizes. Antique/salvage slate tiles, 'Vermont Cobble Slate', for flooring, hearths, and countertops. Also new slate from the quarries of the East Coast. Color brochure and sample, $2.

• **David G. Mulder**
PO Box 1614 Dept. OHJ
Battle Creek, MI 49016
(616) 965-2676
RS/O
Constructs, by hand, custom-made handsome circular stairs in your choice of woods. They build it in their factory, then deliver and install it. Brochure, $1.

Munsell Color
2441 North Calvert St. Dept. OHJ
Baltimore, MD 21218
(301) 243-2171
MO RS/O
The Munsell color notation system is a professional reference resource. In restoring an old house to its original appearance, color samples would be collected and checked against the Munsell Book of Colors. The painter or decorator would then be given the appropriate color codes and could mix the paints accurately. There are two basic books — glossy finish $717., and matte finish, $500. Free full-color brochure.

• **Muralo Company**
148 E. Fifth St. Dept. OHJ
Bayonne, NJ 07002
(201) 437-0770
DIST
Besides being the inventor (and major manufacturer) of Spackle®, the only surfacing compound that can use the name, this old company may be the only remaining maker of old-fashioned calcimine paint. Also makes a full line of latex paints, wallpaper adhesives, texture and sand finish, Georgetown colors in latex house paint, 100 percent pure linseed oil house paint, and fire-retardant paint. No literature — please write for name of distributor.

Murphy Door Bed Co., Inc.
5300 New Horizons Blvd. Dept. OHJ
Amityville, NY 11701
(212) 682-8936
MO DIST RS/O
The original Murphy bed company. Beds available in standard twin, double, queen, and king sizes. Free catalog. They also sell compact kitchens, and built-in ironing centers by Iron-A-Way.

Museum of American Textile History — Cons. Center
800 Massachusetts Ave. Dept. OHJ
N. Andover, MA 01845
(617) 686-0191
MO RS/O
A center specializing in the preservation and conservation of textiles. Services include collections surveys, conservation treatment, and fabric analysis. Conservation workshops and lectures are arranged for groups. Free brochure.

Museum of the City of New York
1220 Fifth Avenue Dept. OHJ
New York, NY 10029
(212) 534-1672
MO RS/O
Large selection of reproduction Edwardian (1901-1910) Christmas decorations. Catalog, $1.

N

Nanik
7200 West Stewart Ave. Dept. OHJ
Wausau, WI 54401
(715) 842-4653
DIST
Manufactures traditional 2-inch wooden Venetian blinds, (custom sizes — 1-in., 1-3/8 in., & 2-3/8 in.) with or without tapes. Available in 34 colors, blinds are a long-lasting investment, but are historically authentic and provide some insulation value. Also a line of wood shutters and 3-1/2-in. wide vertical wood blinds. Write for free brochure/price list, and name of nearest distributor.

Nast, Vivian Glass and Design
49 Willow St., 3B Dept. OHJ
Brooklyn, NY 11201
(718) 596-5280
RS/O
Expert designer and colorist does commission work in stained and leaded glass. Also works in etched glass, both sandblasting and acid-etched. Will reproduce work from existing originals, or will create original designs in period styles. Makes etched patterns in flashed glass. Also fine art portraits of your historic building. Please call or write for further deatils.

National Guild of Professional Paperhangers, Inc.
PO Box 574 Dept. OHJ
Farmingdale, NY 11735
(516) 798-4339
RS/O
This nationwide non-profit organization will put you in contact with your local chapter of professional paperhangers. They also publish a bi-monthly newsletter. Free general information.

National Home Inspection Service of New England, Inc.
62 Theodore Rd. Dept. OHJ
Newton, MA 02159
(617) 923-2300
RS/O
Complete structural and mechanical pre-purchase home inspections anywhere in New England. After the inspection, a complete written report of the condition of the property is issued to you. Maintenance and restoration advice is also provided if desired. All inspectors are members of the American Society of Home Inspectors and subscribe to its Standards and Code of Ethical Conduct. No literature available.

National Screen Co.
P.O. Box 1608 Dept. OHJ
Suffolk, VA 23434
(804) 539-2378
DIST
Wholesale manufacturer of wooden screen doors and wooden combination storm/screen doors. Products include decorative doors with scrollwork and/or louvers. Sells through distributor only. Call or write for name of nearest dealer on Eastern Seaboard. No literature.

• **National SUPAFLU Systems, Inc.**
PO Box 89, South River Rd. Dept. OHJ
Walton, NY 13856
(607) 865-7636
RS/O DIST
A unique system of relining and rebuilding chimneys from the inside out with poured refactory material especially effective for chimneys with bends, offsets, or multi-flues. Supaflu lines, seals, insulates, strengthens a chimney, all in one process. 20-year history. Free literature.

Native American Hardwood Ltd.
RD 1, Box 6484 Dept. OHJ
West Valley, NY 14171
(716) 942-6631
RS/O MO
American hardwoods including walnut, butternut, cherry, and birdseye maple always in stock. Specializing in wide and thick stock, stock for flooring, panelling, and woodwork; both cabinet and economy grade. No minimum on orders — will ship. Listing $1.00.

Native Wood Products, Inc.
Drawer Box 469 Dept. OHJ
Brooklyn, CT 06234
(203) 774-7700
MO RS/O
Blueprint, material list, and instruction sheet for building a post and beam carriage shed, $15.00. Also, complete lumber package to customers in New England, NY, and PA. Many sizes and styles of post and beam buildings available, including post & beam houses with stresskin insulation. Information and prices available upon request. Also available, colonial reproduction wood products including beaded clapboard, wainscot paneling, and hand-forged hardware.

Natural Fiber Fabrics
Dept. OHJ
Putney, VT 05346
(802) 387-5875
RS/O MO
Country style floor rugs, woolen bedspreads and throws in colors and patterns. Cotton spreads. Loose wool net from Ireland for curtains. Wall hangings, including a Bayeux Tapestry panel. Irish tweeds, fine cottons, handkerchief linen, silks. Liberty, Khadi, many other natural fiber fabrics. Individual, personal attention. Brochure on receipt of a business-size self-addressed stamped envelope.

Navedo Woodcraft, Inc.
179 E. 119th St. Dept. OHJ
New York, NY 10035
(212) 722-4431
MO RS/O
An old line custom cabinetmaking shop. They fabricate furniture, doors, trims, and shutters as per drawings/ specifications. Millwork, including mouldings, custom duplicated in oak, poplar, and pine. No literature, call or write with specifics.

Nelson-Johnson Wood Products, Inc.
4326 Lyndale Ave., No. Dept. OHJ
Minneapolis, MN 55412
(612) 529-2771
MO RS/O
Custom wood turning: 10 ft. in length, 12 in. dia. maximum. One to 100 piece limit. Custom wood carvings — all done by hand (no machine or multiple parts done). Stock items include decorative wood ornaments, carved decorative mouldings, wood turnings including newels and balusters. Brochures, $1; free estimate for any inquiry.

• **Neri, C./Antiques**
313 South Street Dept. OHJ
Philadelphia, PA 19147
(215) 923-6669
RS/O
Fine antique furniture; the largest selections of American antique lighting fixtures in the country. Catalog, $5.

• **NET**
PO Box 30 Dept. OHJ
Chester, NY 10918
(914) 782-5332
MO RS/O
Fine metalwork, including finials, grilles, gates, garden ornaments, furniture. Free catalog.

Neuman Studios
Windmill Hill Road Dept. OH
Putney, VT 05346
(802) 387-4800
MO RS/O
Stained glass windows crafted with attention to architectural detail of church, home or commercial space. They specialize in glass painting and silver staining, and work from easels. They also do acid etching, sandblasting and slumping. They welcome restoration work from all eras. Illustrated brochure $1.

• **New England Firebacks**
PO Box 162 Dept. OHJ
Woodbury, CT 06798
(203) 263-4328
MO RS/O
Reproduction 18th- and 19th-century American firebacks taken from original designs. Placed in the rear of the fireplace, the fireback protects masonry and radiates heat. Send SASE for brochure.

New England Tool Co., Ltd.
PO Box 30 Dept. OHJ
Chester, NY 10918
(914) 782-5332
MO RS/O
Ornamental metal work: hand-forged wrought iron; brass, bronze, copper work. Stock and custom designs from Art Deco to Queen Anne; in-house design team. Everything from railings, grilles, gates, weathervanes, and roof finials to garden benches and planters, shelf brackets, table bases, and astrolabes. Free literature - specify interest. Shop phone: (914) 651-7550.

• **New England Woodturners**
PO Box 2151 Dept. OHJ
Short Beach, CT 06405
(203) 776-1880
MO RS/O
Hand-turned custom porch parts, and stairways. Call or write for more information.

The New Victorians, Inc. of Arizona
PO Box 32505 Dept. OHJ
Phoeniz, AZ 85064
(602) 956-0755
MO
12 Victorian house plans using today's energy saving materials and construction methods. Catalog, $6.

New York Carved Arts Co.
115 Grand Street Dept. OHJ
New York, NY 10013
(212) 966-5924
RS/O
Creates etched glass panels by the sand-blasting process. Will do custom work. Walk-in shop only.

KEY TO ABBREVIATIONS

MO	sells by Mail Order
RS/O	sells through Retail Store or Office
DIST	sells through Distributors
ID	sells only through Interior Designers or Archtects

New York Marble Works, Inc.
1399 Park Ave. Dept. OHJ
New York, NY 10029
(212) 534-2242
MO RS/O
Manufacturers of marble vanities, sinktops, fireplaces, hearthstones, pedestals, steps, saddles, table & furniture tops, and marble and granite floor/wall tiles. They also repair, restore, and repolish marble. Free literature.

• **Newe Daisterre Glas**
13431 Cedar Rd. Dept. OHJ
Cleveland Heights, OH 44118
(216) 371-7500
MO RS/O
Custom art glass studio works in stained and bevelled glass for commercial and residential markets. Will do etching, sandblasting, slumped glass, and painting on glass. Will do on-location restoration of leaded windows; restoration of stained & bevelled glass in studio. Custom framing, wood or metal. Free illustrated brochure.

• **Newstamp Lighting Co.**
227 Bay Rd. Dept. OH-87
North Easton, MA 02356
(617) 238-7071
RS/O MO
Large selection of Early American lanterns, sconces, and chandeliers. Catalog is $2. Also distributor of Hunter Olde Tyme Ceiling Fans.

Niece Lumber Co.
N. Union & Elm Sts., Box 68 Dept. OHJ
Lambertville, NJ 08530
(609) 397-1200
RS/O
Genuine Idaho white pine paneling with an edge bead, edge and center bead or vee. 200,000 board feet of white pine, cedar, and hardwoods in stock. Write for list of inventory.

• **Nixalite of America**
1025 16th Ave./Box 727 Dept. OHJ
East Moline, IL 61244
(309) 755-8771
MO
Solution to bird pollution through architectural bird control by NIXALITE. Can be used on historic sites. Ideal for Victorian and pre-1930s homes. Lasting stainless steel needle strips. Will not harm or kill. Inconspicuous. See OHJ June 1981 for details on this quality product. Brochure available, phone calls welcomed.

Nomaco Decorative Products, Inc.
Hershey Drive Dept. OHJ
Ansonia, CT 06401
(203) 736-9231
MO DIST
Nomaco sells and distributes moulding, crown moulding, and ceiling medallions. Made of polystyrene or polyurethane, these are easy to apply and light weight. Brochures, $2.

Norcross Galleries
5070 Peachtree Ind. Blvd. Dept. OHJ
Chamblee, GA 30341
(404) 448-1932
MO RS/O
Aluminum lamps, benches, tables, fountains, urns, and other accessories — many of which are cast from original turn-of-the-century molds. Street lamps a specialty. Catalog, $3.

• **Norman, W.F., Corporation**
P.O. Box 323 Dept. OHJ
Nevada, MO 64772
(800) 641-4038
MO DIST
This company is again producing an 81-year old line of metal ceiling, wainscotting, wall panels, cornices, mouldings and metal Spanish Tile roofing. Patterns come in many architectural styles: Greek, Gothic, Rococo, Colonial Revival. Unique patterns; made from original dies. Write for: Ceiling Catalog No. 350 — $3.00. In Missouri, (417) 667-5552.

• **North Pacific Joinery**
76 W. Fourth St. Dept. OHJ
Eureka, CA 95501
(707) 443-5788
MO RS/O
Custom fabrication of millwork, turnings, and trim: Newels, balusters, handrails, mantels, windows, doors, wainscot, scrollwork. Design service available. Catalog, $3, or call, or write with your specific request.

Nostalgia
307 Stiles Ave. Dept. OHJ
Savannah, GA 31401
(912) 232-2324
RS/O MO
Architectural antiques of all kinds. Demands for fireplace surrounds and certain items prompted them to develop a selection of reproductions: dolphin downspouts, brass hardware, summer fireplace covers, and balcony brackets. They carry salvaged English church pieces (pulpits, fonts, pews, lecterns, etc.) Also, Hodkin & Jones (Sheffield, England) 'Simply Elegant' decorative plasterwork. Brochures — Simply Elegant, $1.50; Antique stained & beveled glass Nostalgia catalog, $2.50.

• **Nowell's, Inc.**
PO Box 295 Dept. OHJ
Sausalito, CA 94966
(415) 332-4933
RS/O MO DIST
Victorian reproduction brass lighting fixtures, made by hand. Aladdin Lamps, parts and shades. Brass oil lamps both table and hanging. Complete line of Victorian glass shades and lamp parts. Fixture catalog $3.50, refundable with purchase.

Nutt, Craig, Fine Wood Works
2014 Fifth St. Dept. OHJ
Northport, AL 35476
(205) 752-6535
RS/O MO
Fine cabinet-making and joinery; wood carving. Museum-quality furniture: reproductions, adaptations, and custom designs. Southern American furniture is a specialty. Mostly custom work. Small showroom with ready-to-sell items. Send $.50 for brochure and current price list.

Nye's Foundry Ltd.
503 Powell St., E. Dept. OHJ
Vancouver, BC, Canada V6A1G8
(604) 254-4121
RS/O
A small foundry offering prompt service on specialty parts. They are cast in fine-grained Olivine molding sand, using the old part as a pattern, when possible. Gray & ductile iron, aluminum alloys. Cast-aluminum or cast-iron benches. Pattern making and machine shop service available. No literature.

O

• **Oak Crest Mfg., Inc.**
6732 E. Emory Rd. Dept. OHJ
Knoxville, TN 37938
(615) 922-1323
MO
Authentic hand-split oak shakes, from veneer-quality red oak, chestnut, and white oak logs, cut from Tennessee trees. Oak shakes can last up to 80 years. Will ship: $1.25 charge per loaded mile. Free flyer.

Oak Leaves Woodcarving Studio
RR 6, The Woods, No. 12-OH Dept. OHJ
Iowa City, IA 52240
(319) 351-0014
MO RS/O
Twelve years of professional wood carving experience enables Oak Leaves Wood Carving Studio to produce a wide variety of carvings: carved wildlife with stained glass doors, residential and commercial signage, and commissioned church pieces. They specialize in naturalistic themes carved from large panels or blocks of wood, including walnut, oak, cherry or redwood. Brochure, $1.

Oberndorfer & Assoc.
1979 Quarry Rd. Dept. OHJ
Yardley, PA 19067
(215) 968-6463
RS/O
A house inspection company serving the Princeton-Bucks County and Philadelphia areas with complete structural, mechanical and electrical inspection of property. Free brochure.

O'Brien Bros. Slate Co., Inc.
57 North St. Dept. OHJ
Granville, NY 12832
(518) 642-2105
MO RS/O
Suppliers of slate for roofing. Will ship. No literature.

• **Ocean View Lighting**
2743 Ninth St. Dept. OHJ
Berkeley, CA 94710
(415) 841-2937
RS/O MO
Retail sellers of fine antique and reproduction lighting fixtures, & table lamps including Art Deco. Specializing in Classic Illumination products. Brochures on Classic Illumination products and mail order price list available for $1. Complete catalogs are $3.

Oehrlein & Associates
1702 Connecticut Ave., NW Dept. OHJ
Washington, DC 20009
(202) 387-8040
RS/O
Architectural firm specializing in technical consulting and architectural design for restoration/rehabilitation including condition surveys, materials analysis and conservation, maintenance programming, preparation of historic structures reports, Tax Act certification application and preparation of construction documents and administration. No literature.

• See Advertisers' Index
on page 22
for more details.

Off The Wall, Architectural Antiques
950 Glenneyre St. Dept. OHJ
Laguna Beach, CA 92651
(714) 497-4000
RS/O
Architectural antiques gathered from California to Massachusetts, England and France. Specialties: bathroom fittings, mantels and fireplaces. Design service and installation available. Call for specific information.

• **Ohman, C.A.**
455 Court Street Dept. OHJ
Brooklyn, NY 11231
(718) 624-2772
RS/O MO
Supplies and installs metal ceilings. Shipping and literature available.

Ohmega Salvage
2407 San Pablo Ave./Box 2125 Dept. OHJ
Berkeley, CA 94702
(415) 843-7368
RS/O
Architectural details of all kinds: antique plumbing fixtures (rebuilt and guaranteed), tubs, sinks, hardware, old wrought iron. They also stock both antique and made-to-order bevelled glass and zinc entry doors, sidelights, and fanlights. No literature.

Old Abingdon Weavers
PO Box 786 Dept. OHJ
Abingdon, VA 24210
(703) 628-4233
MO
This company has been in the weaving business for six generations. Their traditional two- and three-color overshot coverlets feature natural fibers & hand-finishing. Hand-tied fishnet canopies are also available. Catalog plus two fabric swatches (state color preference), $3.

• **Old Carolina Brick Co.**
Rt. 9, Box 77 Majolica Rd. Dept. OHJ
Salisbury, NC 28144
(704) 636-8850
RS/O DIST
Company produces hand-moulded bricks, architectural brick shapes, and arches in 8 color ranges. A complete line of patio pavers is available including 8″ x 8″ Dutch pavers, 4″ x 8″ pavers, and hexagonal pavers. Also available are detailed 17th- & 18th-century fireplace veneers, raised relief brick, name brick, and cornerstones. Can match existing handmade bricks: Send sample and indicate desired quantity. Illustrated brochure — $1.

Old-Fashioned Milk Paint Co.
Box 222H Dept. OHJ
Groton, MA 01450
(617) 448-6336
RS/O MO DIST
This is genuine milk paint, homemade in the traditional way. It gives an authentic look to reproduction furniture, walls and woodwork in old and new houses, outdoor signs, and furniture and wall stenciling. In powdered form, it is available in 8 colors to make pints, quarts, or gallons. Used by preservationists, restorers, museums, antique dealers, etc. Brochure and color card, $.60. (Stamps okay.)

• See Advertisers' Index on page 22 for more details.

Old Home Building & Restoration
P.O. Box 384 Dept. OHJ
West Suffield, CT 06093
(203) 668-2445
MO DIST RS/O
Antique building materials including, but not limited to: chestnut & wide pine flooring, chestnut beams, planks & timbers, hand hewn beams, post & beam barn and house frames for re-assembly, weathered barn siding in silver, gold, brown & colors, roofing slate, hardware, and door. They also use these materials in restoration and true reproduction to your specifications. Design & drafting services available. No literature.

Old House Gardens
536 Third St. Dept. OHJ
Ann Arbor, MI 48103
(313) 995-1486
MO
Historic landscape design and consulting services ranging from total restoration plans to an hour's worth of "informed advice" on a modern adaptation. Landscapes for private homes as well as public, commercial, and museum projects. Also lively, researched slde-lectures, workshops, and tour guide training in American landscape history and restoration. Free brochure.

The Old-House Gold Leaf People
3 Cross St. Dept. OHJ
Suffern, NY 10901
(800) 772-1212
MO
Genuine, variegated, and imitation gold leaf; sheets, rolls, brushes, tools, and supplies, plus technical books. Free product lists. In NY, HI, and AK, (914) 368-1100.

• **Old House Inspection Co., Inc.**
140 Berkeley Place Dept. OHJ
Brooklyn, NY 11217
(718) 857-3647
RS/O
House inspection service by licensed registered architect. Specializes in brownstones, old houses and cooperative apts. in the New York City metropolitan area. Member of "American Society of Home Inspectors" and "American Institute of Architects". No literature.

• **Old-House Journal**
69-A Seventh Ave. Dept. OHJ
Brooklyn, NY 11217
(718) 636-4514
MO
Sells the Heavy-Duty Master Heat Gun. Ideal for stripping paint when large areas are involved. Saves mess and expense of chemical removers. Won't scorch wood or vaporize lead pigments as a propane torch will. Paint bubbles up — & can then be lifted with a scraper. Minor cleanup with chemical remover usually required. Price of $77.95 includes shipping via United Parcel Service. Free flyer.

Old House - New House Restorations
169 N. Victoria St. Dept. OHJ
St. Paul, MN 55104
(612) 227-7127
MO RS/O
Carpentry, general contracting, cabinetmaking, and fine woodworking. They specialize in restoration of Victorian houses and commercial structures. Design services for Victorian recreation and architecturally compatible remodeling. Produce stock and custom mouldings, spindle work, etc. Dealers for many restoration products. 36-page millwork catalog, $2.

Old Lamplighter Shop
At the Musical Museum Dept. OHJ
Deansboro, NY 13328
(315) 841-8774
RS/O MO
Specialist in the restoration and repair of Victorian and turn-of-the-century lamps and lighting fixtures. They also sell restored lamps and lighting fixtures of these periods. Also a small stock of restored melodeons dating from 1850 — 1860. The Musical Museum workshop repairs melodeons, grind and pump organs, etc. Free brochure.

Old'N Ornate
PO Box 10493 Dept. OHJ
Eugene, OR 97440
(503) 345-7636
MO RS/O
A small eight-year old company dedicated to handcrafting fine, ornate wooden screen and storm doors. Over 30 styles in Douglas fir with various options & hardware. Custom orders including over- and under-sized doors and arched doorways. Doors shipped finished and ready to be installed. Brochure, $1.

Old Smithy Shop
Box 336 Dept. OHJ
Milford, NH 03055
(603) 673-0132
MO
Colonial hardware, including latches and hinges, drawer pulls, hooks, and racks. Interior and exterior. Also, black pyramid head screws and flat-head wood screws, fireplace cranes. Catalog, $1; refund with order.

Old Stone Mill Factory Outlet
2A Grove St., Route 8 Dept. OHJ
Adams, MA 01220
(413) 743-1015
DIST RS/O
Hand-printed wallpaper manufacturer. Also, factory outlet store selling hand-printed and machine-printed wallcoverings, as well as fabric and drapery linings. All goods sold as seconds. Savings to 70%. No literature.

Old Sturbridge Village
Dept. OHJ
Sturbridge, MA 01566
(617) 347-3362
RS/O
During the course of the year workshops are given on traditional crafts. Included in the selection is blacksmithing and weaving. Annual Fair of Traditional Crafts on the first weekend of November offers a variety of unusual decorative accessories for the old home, and an opportunity to meet skilled craftspersons who custom fabricate items to your needs. Free information.

Old Time Stove Co.
28 W. Main St. Dept. OHJ
Georgetown, MA 01833
(617) 352-2706
MO RS/O
Complete restoration of New England made antique stoves. They do cast-iron welding, nickel plating, recasting of parts (some from original molds), sandblasting, and painting. All stoves are guaranteed for one year. Nickel plating a lifetime written guarantee. Free flyer and price list. (617) 352-2938, evenings.

• **The Old Wagon Factory**
103 Russell St./PO Box 1427 Dept. OHJ
Clarksville, VA 23927
(804) 374-5787
MO RS/O
This family owned and operated business hand-builds wood, combination storm and screen doors. They also make English-style garden furniture, turned lamp posts, and door and gate hardware. Catalog $2.

Old World Moulding & Finishing Co., Inc.
115 Allen Boulevard Dept. OHJ
Farmingdale, NY 11735
(516) 293-1789
RS/O MO
Hardwood embossed mouldings, cornices, baseboards, mantels and a modular system of panelling suitable for a variety of period styles. Custom work also. Color catalog and price list - $2.

Old World Restorations, Inc.
347 Stanley Avenue Dept. OHJ
Cincinnati, OH 45226
(513) 321-1911
MO DIST RS/O
A full service art conservation lab specializing in paintings, frames, porcelain, gold leaf, ivory, stained glass, china, glass, sculpture, pottery, wood, stone, and antiques. All forms of art restoration from the cleaning and lining of an oil painting to invisible porcelain restoration. Crystal chandelier restoration and metal repairs. Free estimate and literature. Nationwide service.

• **Olde Bostonian Architectural Antiques**
135 Buttonwood St. Dept. OHJ
Dorchester, MA 02125
(617) 282-9300
RS/O
Has a wide collection of old doors, fireplace mantels, columns, floor registers, stained glass, brackets, newel posts, wainscotting, balusters, electric lighting and brass work. They specialize in mouldings. No literature; call or visit.

Olde Theatre Architectural Salvage Co.
2045 Broadway Dept. OHJ
Kansas City, MO 64108
(816) 283-3740
RS/O
Large selection of antique and recycled house parts. Free brochure.

Olde Village Smithery
PO Box 1815, 61 Finlay Rd. Dept. OHJ
Orleans, MA 02653
(617) 255-4466
MO RS/O
Traditional crafted period lighting fixtures in brass, tin, and copper: primitive Colonial, 18th century, and Pennsylvania Dutch designs. They offer chandeliers, sconces, lanterns, postlights, candlesticks, and beeswax candles. Catalog available, $2.50.

Olde & Oak Antiques
7186 Hwy. 72W Dept. OHJ
Madison, AL 35758
(205) 837-6330
RS/O
Architectural antiques, fine furniture, collectibles. Large selection of antique stained glass, original and refinished antique mantels, brass light fixtures. Also antique furniture, reproduction cast-aluminum street lamps, embossed wall coverings, and custom-made curtains, bedspreads, and accessories. No literature.

Oliver, Bradley C.
112 Park Ave. Dept. OHJ
Stroudsburg, PA 18360
(717) 629-1828
RS/O MO
Dealer in antique iron fences, urns, furniture, lighting fixtures and complete line of antiques. Write with a description of what you require. No literature, but inquiries will be answered. They can ship anywhere.

Olympic Stain
2233 112th Ave. NE Dept. OHJ
Bellevue, WA 98004
(800) 426-6306
DIST RS/O
Fifty-year-old manufacturer of wood stains: weather screen, semi-transparent, solid, overcoat, latex, and Lucite interior & exterior products. Available at most hardware stores.

Omnia Industries, Inc.
49 Park St., PO Box 263 Dept. OHJ
Montclair, NJ 07042
(201) 746-4300
DIST
Offers a collection of solid brass door hardware, including knob and lever latchsets, mortise entry locks, house numbers, hinges, bolts, door knockers, coat hooks, pushplates, door pulls, and cremone bolts. Free brochure offered on written request. Full catalog available at a charge of $7.50, with payment to accompany written order.

Oregon Wooden Screen Door Co.
330 High Street Dept. OH
Eugene, OR 97401
(503) 485-0279
MO
A consort of Oregon craftspeople that generates a rich resource of wood and glass skills and experience to create or recreate quality wood/glass products or materials. Services range from designing, pattern making, stencilling, carving, routing and milling. Finished or unfinished, kickdown or assembled. Brochure, $3.

Original Woodworks
PO Box 10600 Dept. OHJ
White Bear Lake, MN 55110
(612) 429-2222
MO RS/O
Specialists in wood furniture restoration products and services: furniture restoration, tools and safety equipment, veneers, glues; parts for staircases, mantels, doors, and furniture; mouldings; wicker, cane, and related tools and materials. Brochure, $1.

Ornamental Design Studios
1715 President Street Dept. OHJ
Brooklyn, NY 11213
(718) 774-2695
RS/O
Restoration of plaster ornamentation including mouldings, medallions, and bas relief. Muddled ornaments restored, missing elements replaced. Installation of stock and custom ornamentation. Literature $.50 to cover postage and handling.

Orr, J.F., & Sons
215 Boston Post Rd. Dept. OHJ
Sudbury, MA 01776
(617) 443-3650
MO RS/O
New England country furniture, including Windsor chairs, cupboards, dry sinks and tables, whose originals are in the possession of collectors, museums, and early inns. Pieces are constructed of wide, hand-planed New England pine and cut nails, with an antique pine finish and painted interiors. Send $4 for 32-page color catalog with prices and dimensions.

Osborne, C. S. & Co.
125 Jersey St. Dept. OHJ
Harrison, NJ 07029
(201) 483-3232
DIST
Manufactures a complete line of upholstering hand tools, including certain do-it-yourself kits with instruction books. Free upholstery tool brochure and name of nearest distributor available on receipt of self-addressed, stamped envelope.

Ostrom & Co., Inc.
2170 N. Lewis Dept. OHJ
Portland, OR 97227
(503) 281-6469
RS/O
Designs and produces period acid-etched, sandblasted and gluechip glass, mirrors, and signs. Reproduction of broken panels. Many old-style patterns available. All work custom made, no pre-made panels in stock. No literature.

O'Sullivan Co.
156 S. Minges Road Dept. OHJ
Battle Creek, MI 49017
(616) 964-1226
MO DIST
Manufactures O'Sullivans Liquid Wax Furniture Polish - an 18th century formula that is designed for wood panelling, board floors, kitchen cabinets as well as furniture. Dries to a soft luster without buffing. Cleans and polishes. Erases light scratches and white rings. Free descriptive folder and mail order form.

H.C. Oswald Supply Co., Inc.
120 E. 124th St. Dept. OHJ
New York, NY 10035
(212) 722-7000
MO RS/O
A stock of patterns and parts for coal-burning boilers. Also, conversion kits: oil to coal or wood. Free literature.

P

• **PRG**
5619 Southampton Drive Dept. OHJ
Springfield, VA 22151
(703) 323-1407
MO
Specialized tools and instruments to home owners and professionals for the restoration and care of buildings. These conservator's tools include moisture meters, profile gauge, temperature and humidity gauges, microscopes, lights and more. Also, books for instruction and reference on all aspects of historic preservation, building science and maintenance. New Products bulletin, illustrated catalog and booklist available free.

• **Pagliacco Turning & Milling Architectural Wood Turning**
PO Box 225 Dept. OHJ
Woodacre, CA 94973
(415) 488-4333
MO RS/O
Produces a complete line of stock and custom turnings & millwork. Over 150 stock designs of balusters, newel posts, porch posts, railings, & columns (all classic orders with true entasis). All products based on authentic designs and available from decay-resistant all-heart redwood, oak & mahogany. $3 charge for 24-page book (no charge to design & construction firms when requested on company letterhead).

Michael Pangia
63 Wyckoff St. Dept. OHJ
Brooklyn, NY 11217
(718) 875-0800
RS/O
This company specializes in building and repairing wooden cornices and architectural castings in a variety of materials — stone, synthetics — and finishes. They can make moulds from originals in any condition or from old photos. Call for more information.

Park Place
2251 Wisconsin Ave. NW Dept. OHJ
Washington, DC 20007
(202) 342-6294
MO RS/O
Victorian garden benches and street lamps; English garden teak furniture; weatherend Estate teak and mahogany and Chippendale outdoor furniture, unique-design solid oak porch furniture; Victorian reproduction garden urns, hitching posts, mailboxes; custom and stock beveled, stained, and etched glass; authentic reproduction plaster ceiling medallions and crown mouldings including Focal Point; also stone statuary and fountains, Hunter and Casablanca ceiling fans. Beautiful garden landscaped showroom. Illustrated catalog, $1.

William H. Parsons & Associates
420 Salmon Brook Dept. OHJ
Granby, CT 06035
(203) 653-2281
RS/O
Consulting in historic preservation projects. Specialize in historic masonry-buildings. Preparation of National Register applications for 25% ITC. Historic buildings for moving. Paint and graffiti removal. Also, chimney relining (National Supaflu Systems) and brokerage of historic buildings. Free literature.

• **Past Patterns**
PO Box 7587 Dept. OHJ
Grand Rapids, MI 49510
(616) 245-9456
MO
Past Patterns has been selling historical patterns by mail since 1979. They are accurate copies of antique garments. Professional pattern drafting assures consistent fit. Each pattern contains adult sizes 10 through 20. Easy step-by-step instructions. Ready-made corsets also available in sizes 21 through 29 inches. Free literature.

Pasvalco
400 Demarest Ave. Dept. OHJ
Closter, NJ 07624
(800) 222-2133
MO RS/O
New Brownstone from Canada. All types of natural stone. No literature.

Patterson, Flynn & Martin, Inc.
950 Third Ave. Dept. OHJ
New York, NY 10022
(212) 751-6414
ID
Patterson, Flynn & Martin Inc. specializes in reproductions of period carpeting, also offers a wide selection of 27" broadlooms, needlepoints, braided and bordered rugs. Savonnerie rugs are woven in their own factory in Spain. Dhurrie rugs from India, antique and fine oriental reproductions are presented in their showroom. Showrooms in New York and Chicago with representation in major cities throughout the United States. No literature.

Paul J. Foster
Box 113 Dept. OHJ
Cambridge, NY 12816
(518) 677-3509
RS/O
Restoration of old houses, and new (reproduction) construction such as salt boxes and gambrels. They make trim, doors, cupboards, fireplace walls, and so on. Serving Washington and Saratoga Counties, and Western Vermont. No literature.

Pawley's Island Hammock Co.
PO Box 9 Dept. OHJ
Pawleys Island, SC 29585
(800) 845-0311
MO DIST
Manufacturers of traditional rope hammocks. All hand-made, three sizes available in both natural cotton rope for comfort and polyester rope for durability. Varnished oak spreader bars curved for maximum stability; complete with hanging hardware and instructions. Hammock stand & hammock pillows and swings also available. Free literature.

Paxton Hardware Ltd.
7818 Bradshaw Rd. Dept. OHJ
Upper Falls, MD 21156
(301) 592-8505
MO RS/O
Large selection of solid brass period, Victorian, and contemporary furniture hardware. Locks, mirror screws, hinges, supports, table slides, chair-caning supplies, porcelain knobs, and more. Also a wide variety of reproduction lamp fittings, chimneys, and hand-blown and decorated glass shades. Catalog, $3.50. Free mini-catalog.

Pease Industries
7100 Dixie Highway Dept. OHJ
Fairfield, OH 45014
(513) 870-3600
DIST
Pease offers awnings in custom widths, with a choice of hand crank or electric motor and 14 colors. Also, steel doors with period details; 70 designs available. Free color brochures. "First Impressions," an entry design idea book, $3.50 to OHJ readers. (800) 543-1180 for information about nearest distributor.

Peerless Rattan and Reed
222 Lake Ave. Dept. OHJ
Yonkers, NY 10701
(914) 968-4046
MO RS/O
Small mail-order company offering basketry goods and caning supplies. Also fibre rush, natural and scraped rattan, seagrass, reeds, ash splints, stains, tools, kits, and assorted literature. Catalog, $.50.

Peg Hall Studios
111 Clapp Road Dept. OHJ
Scituate, MA 02066
(617) 545-3605
MO
Patterns and design books for decorating period furniture and accessories. Catalog and price list, $.25.

Peiser Floors
21 W. 100th St. Dept. OHJ
New York, NY 10025
(212) 222-3424
RS/O
They install, repair, and refinish parquet, hardwood, and tile floors. No literature.

Pella Windows & Doors
100 Main St. Dept. OHJ
Pella, IA 50219
(515) 628-1000
DIST
This major window manufacturer has a line of double-hung wood windows. Window pane dividers snap out for easy cleaning. Free brochure.

Frank Pellitteri Inc.
201 E. 56th St. Dept. OHJ
New York, NY 10022
(212) 486-0545
RS/O
Architectural panelling, window treatments, refinishing, fine mouldings, cabinetry. No literature.

Pelnik Wrecking Co., Inc.
1749 Erie Blvd., E. Dept. OHJ
Syracuse, NY 13210
(315) 472-1031
RS/O
Wreckers with 50-years' experience in sensitive salvaging. Bevelled and stained glass a specialty. Mantels, newel posts, railings, entryways, corbels, tin ceilings, brass rails, cast iron elements, columns, marble sinks, old brick and timber, terra-cotta friezes. Further services for restaurant designers and architects. Photos on request.

Pemaquid Floorcloths
PO Box 77 Dept. OHJ
Round Pond, ME 04564
(207) 529-5633
MO RS/O
Canvas floorcloths stencilled in country and traditional 18th- and 19th-century designs. Custom sizes up to 9-1/2 feet wide — any length. Custom colors and patterns also available. Send $2 for color brochure.

Penn Big Bed Slate Co., Inc.
PO Box 184 Dept. OHJ
Slatington, PA 18080
(215) 767-4601
MO RS/O
Suppliers of slate for roofing, fireplaces, floors, garden walks. Also sink tops. Roofing is $220 per square, $10 punching charge. Clear and natural slate, sand-rubbed or honed face. Free price list with list of custom services available.

Pennsylvania Dutch Quilts
Box 430 Dept. OHJ
Norristown, PA 19404
(215) 539-3010
MO RS/O
Handmade quilts in traditional and custom designs. 96-page catalog and sketchbook, $5.95.

• **Pennsylvania Firebacks, Inc.**
1011 E. Washington Lane Dept. OH5
Philadelphia, PA 19138
(215) 843-6162
MO
Manufactures a collection of cast-iron firebacks for the rear of the fireplace. A fireback radiates heat from the fire and protects back wall from deterioration. Eleven original designs in Colonial & contemporary motifs. New extra large fireback can be personalized with name and/or special year. Complete illustrated catalog available for $2.

Period Furniture Hardware Co., Inc.
Box 314, Charles St. Station Dept. OHJ
Boston, MA 02114
(617) 227-0758
RS/O MO
A selection of high-quality reproduction period accessories with the emphasis on solid brass. Items include a wide selection of furniture hardware and builders hardware, hand-crafted weathervanes, lighting fixtures, fireplace accessories, and bathroom fittings. 120-page catalog is available for $3.50.

• **Period Lighting Fixtures**
1 West Main Street Dept. OJ-7
Chester, CT 06412
(203) 526-3690
MO RS/O
Handmade 17th & 18th century early American lighting fixtures, chandeliers, wall sconces and lanterns. Finishes vary from hand rubbed pewter, naturally aged tin, and old glazed colors for interior fixtures, to exterior post and wall-mounted lanterns in oxidized copper. Their catalog is also a reference source on the origin, selection and installation of early lighting. Catalog & price list, $3.

Perkasie Industries Corp.
50 East Spruce Street Dept. OHJ
Perkasie, PA 18944
(215) 257-6581
MO
Thermatrol storm window kit is designed for the do-it-yourselfer. Surface mounts to the window frame on the interior side. Provides a thermal barrier by using lightweight acrylic framing and glazing, coupled with gasketing. Thermatrol is applicable to most window designs and can be designed so that it stores within itself for summer ventilation. Free literature.

Perkowitz Window Fashions
135 Green Bay Rd. Dept. OHJ
Wilmette, IL 60091
(312) 251-7700
RS/O MO
A majör supplier of louvered shutters carries a full line of stock shutters and custom sizes. Shutters are pine and can be ordered unfinished or with standard colors and stains, or matched to your sample. Catalog & price list, $1.

• **Perma Ceram Enterprises, Inc.**
65 Smithtown Blvd. Dept. OHJ
Smithtown, NY 11787
(516) 724-1205
DIST
Largest in-home bathroom resurfacing company in the country. Exclusive formula to resurface bathtubs, sinks, and tile. Applied only by authorized factory trained technicians. Available in all decorator colors. Work done in your house. Fully guaranteed. For a local Perma Ceram dealer: (800) 645-5039. Free brochure.

KEY TO ABBREVIATIONS

MO sells by Mail Order

RS/O sells through Retail Store or Office

DIST sells through Distributors

ID sells only through Interior Designers or Archtects

• **Perma-Chink Systems, Inc.**
PO Box 2603 Dept. OHJ
Redmond, WA 98073
(206) 885-6050
MO DIST
Manufacturers and distributors of Perma-chink, a latex-based sealant for log homes. Easy to apply, bonds to logs so remains water-tight even if logs move. Can be applied over failed mortar. Free "homeowner's package" includes price list and application instructions. Also: 1605 Prosser Rd., Knoxville, TN 37914. (615) 524-7343.

Permagrain Products, Inc.
13 W. Third St. Dept. OHJ
Media, PA 19063
(215) 565-1575
DIST
This company manufactures flooring materials made of wood parquet, cork, or natural brick that have been specially treated for high durability. PermaGrain parquet and PermaBrick are acrylic impregnated; Genuwood and DesignerCork have a 20-mil vinyl sheeting covering the surface. Free brochure.

Perry, Edward K., Co.
322 Newbury St. Dept. OHJ
Boston, MA 02115
(617) 536-7873
MO RS/O
A 4th-generation family business specializing in fine interior and exterior painting of historic structures and homes. Responsible for original painting in many McKim, Mead, and White, and H.H. Richardson buildings. Also involved with color selection and painting at Colonial Williamsburg, Old Sturbridge Village, Tryon Palace and Winterthur. Special decorative techniques include gilding, graining, glazing, encaustics, marbleizing, trompe l'oeil, and stencilling. Free brochure.

H. Pfanstiel Hardware Co.
Route 52 Dept. OHJ
Jeffersonville, NY 12748
(914) 482-4445
MO DIST
Manufactures and imports an extensive line of decorative hardware, of all brass, plus bathroom accessories, door hardware, and furniture hardware. Styles are French, Renaissance Revival, Rococo, and Georgian. Among their unusual items are decorative finials and finial-tipped hinges. Handsome 96 page catalog — $7.50.

Philip M. White & Associates
Box 47 Dept. OHJ
Mecklenburg, NY 14863
(607) 387-6370
RS/O MO
Founded in 1934, this company specializes in design and restoration of 19th and early 20th century gardens. Also, appraisal and damage estimate work for tax & insurance purposes. Services by a licensed landscape architect. Please call; free literature.

• See Advertisers' Index on page 22 for more details.

Phoenix Studio, Inc.
235 Congress St. Dept. OHJ
Portland, ME 04101
(207) 774-4154
MO RS/O
A design and stained glass studio. Specialize in restoration of all leaded work, and can furnish excellent references. They are also a retail outlet for related supplies (glass tools, etc.) and maintain a gallery in Portland. Classes are offered. Custom designed pieces for any period home. Free information sheet.

• **Phoneco**
Rt. 2, Box 590 Dept. OHJ
Galesville, WI 54630
(608) 582-4124
MO RS/O
Licensed telephone refurbishers who sell and repair all types of phones — from antique to contemporary. Small catalog is free; larger catalog is $2.

Pierce & Stevens Chemical Corp.
710 Ohio St., Box 1092 Dept. OHJ
Buffalo, NY 14240
(716) 631-8991
DIST
The manufacturers of Fabulon wood finishing products have a useful booklet, "How To Finish Wood Floors, Old or New."

• **Pietra Dura, Inc.**
340 East 6th St. Dept. OHJ
New York, NY 10003
(212) 260-6187
RS/O
Architectural stonework: restoration, retooling, honing, mould-making, replacement of missing sculpted elements; patching, rebuilding profiles. Brochure, $1, shows examples of their work with "before" and "after" pictures.

Pike Stained Glass Studios, Inc.
180 St. Paul Street Dept. OHJ
Rochester, NY 14604
(716) 546-7570
RS/O
Founded in 1908 by William J. Pike, and continued by James J. O'Hara, his nephew, Pike Stained Glass Studio, Inc. is currently under the direction of Mr. O'Hara's daughter, Valerie. Original designs, fabrication, installation and repair of stained glass & etched windows for churches, businesses, and homes. Storm protection is also available. Call or write for estimates. Free brochure.

Pine & Palette Studio
20 Ventura Drive Dept. OHJ
Danielson, CT 06239
(203) 774-5058
MO RS/O
Fireplace bellows hand-crafted with authentic Early American designs, on hardwood. Genuine brass fittings and leather gussetts. Will also do bellow repair and custom design orders on request. Satisfaction guaranteed. Brochure, $.50.

Pioneer Service Shake Company
Rt. 4 Box 10A Dept. OHJ
Houston, MO 65483
(417) 967-4406
MO
They specialize in oak shakes, made to order. No literature.

Piscatagua Architectural Woodwork, Co.
53 Bagdad Rd. Dept. OHJ
Durham, NH 03824
(603) 868-2663
MO DIST RS/O
Ten stock hand-run 18th-century style mouldings for use in quality restorations, reconstructions, and reproductions. On a custom basis, they produce interior & exterior doors, panelling, shutters, sash, etc., as well as any 18th-century moulding. All of their work is hand done using 18th and 19th century hand planes. Send a large SASE for information.

Pittsburgh Corning
800 Presque Isle Dr. Dept. OHJ
Pittsburgh, PA 15239
(412) 327-6100
DIST RS/O
Pittsburgh Corning Corporation has been manufacturing PC GlassBlock® products in a variety of patterns since 1937 and today is the only domestic manufacturer. Free brochure.

Plain and Fancy
RD 2, Box 450 Dept. OHJ
Bristol, VT 05443
(802) 453-3315
MO
Handwoven homespun-style blankets and table linens in authentic colors of checks and plaids. Natural fibers: Vermont wool and cotton-lines blend yarns. Color sheet and price sheet send SASE and $1.

Plannja AB International Attn* Richard B. Velleu
1450 Energy Park Dr.—63 Dept. OHJ
St. Paul, MN 55108
(612) 645-4652
DIST
Plannja's Scanroof panels have the look of tile and are compatible with older homes. They're lightweight and ice does not form on them. They can be anchored directly to sound rafters even if the roof decking has deteriorated. Free brochures.

Plaskolite, Inc.
1770 Joyce Ave., P.O. Box 1497 Dept. OHJ
Columbus, OH 43216
(614) 294-3281
DIST
Custom-made interior insulating windows of vinyl and acrylic. Three models: Flex-Tite Winsulator has a magnetic seal, Sliding Winsulator works either horizontally or vertically, and Economy Winsulator has a flexible gasket seal. Free brochures.

KEY TO ABBREVIATIONS

MO	sells by Mail Order
RS/O	sells through Retail Store or Office
DIST	sells through Distributors
ID	sells only through Interior Designers or Archtects

Plexacraft Metals Co.
5406 San Fernando Rd. Dept. OHJ
Glendale, CA 91203
(818) 246-8201
MO DIST
Plexacraft manufactures lucite hardware & hand-cast solid brass knobs & pulls in traditional styles. Catalog $7.50. The company has two other divisions. Southeast Hardware manufactures hand-cast ornamental hardware in brass, bronze, & aluminum for use on doors, furniture & windows. Custom duplication from samples as well. Catalog $15. M&M Porcelain Hardware makes porcelain hardware for doors, shutters, & furniture. Catalog $3.50.

Point Five Windows
1314 Duff Dr. Dept. OHJ
Fort Collins, CO 80524
(303) 482-6971
MO RS/O
Custom replacement windows that look old but meet current commercial standards. Can be fitted within old frames and mouldings; all have class A air infiltration and structural load performance. Also stock distributor of bull's eye etched glue-chip, and authentic hand-blown cylinder glass. Free brochure on custom windows, "Classic 1901," and price list.

Pollitt, E., AIA
Vista Drive Dept. OHJ
Easton, CT 06612
(203) 268-5955
MO
A collection of Colonial period house plans, measured and drawn from originals. Exteriors are faithfully reproduced; interiors are updated. Specifications make use of stock building materials. Full plans are $80. each, 5 sets for $120. Two portfolios available: Old Colonial Houses, 32 reproduction houses; Old Cape Cod Houses, 24 reproductions and adaptations. Each $5.

Polytek Development Corp.
PO Box 384 Dept. OHJ
Lebanon, NJ 08833
(201) 236-2990
MO
Liquid rubbers for flexible moulds, including Polygel, a quick-drying material that makes see-through, lightweight moulds. It can be brushed directly on the overhead or wall surfaces to be reproduced. Bulletins explaining the process and price list are free.

Pompei Stained Glass, Inc.
455 High St. (Rt. 60) Dept. OHJ
Medford, MA 02155
(617) 395-8867
RS/O MO
Custom design & fabrication, as well as stock architectural art glass including leaded and stained window panels of all types, doors, fan lights, side lights, transoms, cabinet doors, mantel mirrors, signs & logos. Beveled, etched and sand-blasted glass, choice of oak, ash, mahogany, or cypress frames. Installation services. Door and Window catalog, $2.

Poor Richard's Service Co.
101-103 Walnut Street Dept. OHJ
Montclair, NJ 07042
(201) 783-5333
RS/O
Furniture and architectural stripping, also Rainbow Stripping, refinishing and repair, metal polishing and plating; reupholstery work; cane and rush work and supplies. Furniture, cabinets, and paneling touch-ups, cleaning, and polishing done in the home. Walk-in shop. No literature.

Porcelain Restoration and Brass
1007 W. Morehead St. Dept. OHJ
Charlotte, NC 28208
(704) 372-9039
RS/O
Porcelain resurfacing in the home. They stock original and reproduction pedestal sinks, footed tubs, and water closets, original plumbing fixtures and reproduction brass hardware for fixtures. Brass-polishing available and wood washstands with china lavatory bowls — as well as over john cabinets & brass-railing. Large selection of pedestal lavatories and pullchain china and oak highboys. Also, decorative fluted drop-in bowls. No catalog.

Portland Willamette, Division Thomas Industries
6800 N.E. 59th Pl. Dept. OHJ
Portland, OR 97218
(503) 288-7511
DIST
A major manufacturer of firescreens, glass for firescreens, and fireplace accessories. "Complete Fireplace Furnishings" booklet, $2.

Potlatch Corp. — Townsend Unit
P.O. Box 916 Dept. OHJ
Stuttgart, AR 72160
(501) 673-1606
DIST
Prefinished hardwoods in 18 wood finishes. Random widths and lengths. Free 8 pg. brochure.

Potomac Products
HCR 71, Box 110-D Dept. OHJ
Hustontown, PA 17229
(717) 987-3107
MO
Specialize in replacement hardware for windows, patio doors, closets doors, mobile homes, etc. Inventory of thousands of items that are obsolete and hard-to-find, many of which have been discontinued by the original manufacturers. Free catalog.

Poxywood, Inc.
PO Box 4241 Dept. OHJ
Martinsville, VA 24115
(703) 638-6284
MO
Two-part catalyzed non-shrinking system available in quarts in Pine, Oak, or Universal wood tones. Accepts sanding and staining like wood. It has a six-month shelf life, but you can buy small quantities at a reasonable cost. Free literature.

Prairiewind Traditionals
1245 N. Third No. C Dept. OHJ
Lawrence, KS 66044
(913) 842-4300
MO
The company represents a number of Kansas craftspeople; their products iclude house portraits, floorcloths, and Shaker wall sconces for candles. Brochure, $1.

• See Advertisers' Index on page 22 for more details.

• **Pratt & Lambert**
75 Tonawanda Street Dept. OHJ
Buffalo, NY 14207
(716) 873-6000
DIST
A manufacturer of paints, chemical coatings, and adhesives with its origin in 1849. Pratt & Lambert is recognized as a color leader and has been authorized by the Henry Ford Museum and Greenfield Village in Michigan to produce a special series of interior and exterior paints "Early American Colours from Greenfield Village." These paints duplicate shades of the 18th and 19th centuries. Color card, $.50.

Pratt's House of Wicker
1 West Main Street Dept. OHJ
Adamstown, PA 19501
(215) 484-2094
RS/O MO
This company has several antique pieces for sale, but they deal primarily in new wicker. The emphasis is on Victorian reproductions. Their speciality, wicker porch furniture, is displayed on the large wrap-around porch of their 1845 home.

• **Premier Communications**
Box 1513 Dept. OHJ
High Point, NC 27261
(919) 841-4355
MO
Their state-of-the-art fire and burglar alarm systems have no visible wires to mar your decor. Free brochure. Also, (919) 272-0440.

Preservation Associates, Inc.
207 S. Potomac St. Dept. OHJ
Hagerstown, MD 21740
(301) 791-7880
RS/O
Nationwide building restoration and rehab consultation for individuals, organizations, and agencies. Full consulting services. Preparation of state and National Register nominations; rehab project planning and analysis; historic structures reports and historic preservation certifications. Please call or write for additional information and brochure.

Preservation Partnership
345 Union St. Dept. OHJ
New Bedford, MA 02740
(617) 996-3383
RS/O
A preservation firm whose architectural and planning services include surveys, historic structures reports, and the inspection, conservation, rehabilitation, restoration, and adaptive reuse of existing buildings. Some 300 completed projects range from private homes and house museums to multi-million dollar conservation of institutional and public property. Certified Rehabilitation is a specialty. Free brochure.

Preservation Resource Center of New Orleans
604 Julia Street Dept. OHJ
New Orleans, LA 70130
(504) 581-7032
MO RS/O
Promotion of preservation through publications, projects, programs, historical research, consultation, facade servitude donations and architectural tours. Monthly meetings are held to discuss issues. "Preservation in Print", a 16-20 page newspaper, is published monthly. Membership in the PRC is $15 annually. A Warehouse District Planning Study is $17.50. "Six City Sites: Studies in Contextual Design" addresses the issue of contemporary architecture in historic districts and is $6. (both prices include postage).

Preservation Resource Group
5619 Southampton Dr. Dept. OHJ
Springfield, VA 22151
(703) 323-1407
RS/O
Assists agencies, organizations and individuals in development of their historic preservation programs and personnel. Lectures and workshops for owners of old houses are conducted for groups on request. No literature, but will provide sample programs.

Preway, Inc.
1430 2nd Street, North Dept. OHJ
Wisconsin Rapids, WI 54494
(715) 423-1100
DIST RS/O
Energy efficient, heat-circulating built-in and freestanding fireplaces. Built-in units include "Super Energy Mizer" model, "Custom PLUS" series, and Royal Brass unit with solid polished front. "Freestanding Provider" comes in three decorator colors with porcelain finish. "Top Brass Insight" is a polished brass masonry fireplace insert. "Alterna" gas-fired fireplace is vent free and heat-circulating. Free color pamphlet illustrates full product line and describes all available accessories.

Price & Visser Millwork
2536 Valencia St. Dept. OHJ
Bellingham, WA 98226
(206) 734-7700
ID
Victorian and traditional mouldings from your sample, or picture, or choose one of their stock patterns. Also interior and exterior door and entries, cabinets, windows, and miscellaneous millwork of all sorts custom made. Free brochure.

Priscilla Ceramic Tiles
32-35 210th Street Dept. OHJ
Bayside, NY 11361
(718) 631-4330
RS/O
Supplier of commercial tiles which are hand-painted and matched to wallpaper or fabrics. Also (718) 423-1919.

ProSoCo, Inc.
P.O. Box 1578 Dept. OHJ
Kansas City, KS 66117
(913) 281-2700
DIST RS/O
Manufacturers of Sure Klean masonry cleaning and weather- proofing materials. For restoring brick, stone and other masonry surfaces. Chemicals do not harm the masonry surface and are less costly than sandblasting. Sells to contractors only; will not deal with homeowners. Free brochures.

Puccio
661 Driggs Ave Dept. OHJ
Brooklyn, NY 11211
(718) 387-9778
Producers of onyx and marble interiors, floors, walls, moulding, fireplaces, sink tops, furniture tops and baths. Free flyer.

Puma Iron Works
326 Butler St. Dept. OHJ
Brooklyn, NY 11217
(212) 643-1338
MO RS/O
Company does a lot of standard ironwork for old-house owners in the New York area, including: window grilles, balconies, decks, spiral stairs, fences, cast iron fence repairs and complete cast-iron fence reproductions. No literature; call for appointment.

Purcell, Francis J., II
88 North Main Street Dept. OHJ
New Hope, PA 18938
(215) 862-9100
RS/O
Antique American fireplace mantels dating from 1750 to 1850. Large collection of formal and folk art mantels. 100 examples are cleaned of paint and have hand-rubbed finishes. Majority of mantels priced between two and three thousand dollars. No literature — collection seen by appointment only, please.

• **Putnam Rolling Ladder Co., Inc.**
32 Howard St. Dept. SA
New York, NY 10013
(212) 226-5147
RS/O MO
Of special interest is their oak rolling library ladder — made-to-order and finished to customer's specifications. Other woods available. Hardware for rolling ladder available in four finishes including chrome and brass plated and polished. They make an oak pulpit ladder, "office ladders", stools, oak garden furniture (benches, tables, and chairs) and library carts. Also full line of wood, aluminum, and fiberglass step, straight and extension ladders, and aluminum scaffolds, Catalog No. 660, $1.

Pyfer, E.W.
218 North Foley Ave. Dept. OHJ
Freeport, IL 61032
(815) 232-8968
MO DIST RS/O
Lamp repair and rewiring: chandeliers restored, oil and gas lamps converted, replacement of missing lamp parts. Brass plating service. Chair recaning (rush, reed, and splint). Also sells caning supplies and instruction books. Free description of services — please call for appointment before visiting.

Q

QRB Industries
3139 US 31 North Dept. OHJ
Niles, MI 49120
(616) 683-7908
MO
A restoration system that rapidly removes old finish and allows for immediate application of new finish. Q.R.B. Remover: non-caustic solvent; eliminates grain raising, bleaching, scraping, sanding, and burning of skin. Q.R.B. Instant Finish resists moisture; no sanding, will not mar while drying. Also, a staining kit that can match up to 16 million colors. Write for free restoration "mini-course." Send S.A.S.E.

• **Quaker City Manufacturing Co.**
701 Chester Pike Dept. OHJ
Sharon Hill, PA 19079
(215) 727-5144
DIST
WINDOW FIXER Replacement Window Channels can be used with standard wood sash to give snug fit and prevent heat loss. Available through most lumber yards, home centers and major hardware stores. Free literature.

Quaker Lace Co.
24 West 40th Street Dept. OHJ
New York, NY 10018
(212) 221-0480
DIST
Quaker Lace Company is a manufacturer of lace tablecloths & placemats, runners, napkins, curtains, and bed coverlets. Many of the patterns are made on the famed Nottingham Lace machines. Free brochures available with listing of major retail department stores carrying Quaker Lace products.

Quali-Craft Constructors
3259 Orange St. Dept. OHJ
Riverside, CA 92501
(714) 784-3600
RS/O
Contracting firm serving the Riverside, San Bernardino & Claremont area. Restoration and period-style additions, including custom-duplication of existing architectural details. No literature.

R

• **REM Associates**
Box 504 Dept. OHJ
Northboro, MA 01532
(617) 393-8424
MO
Manufactures custom shutters for interior and exterior use. Will make with movable or fixed louvers. Brass hardware for exterior shutters. Literature, $1.

RWL/Welsbach Lighting
240 Sargent Dr. Dept. OHJ
New Haven, CT 06511
(203) 789-1710
RS/O
This 100 year old company supplies street lighting fixtures, brackets, and posts. Originally designed for gas-lighting, these Victorian-styled fixtures & posts are now available with incandescent or high-intensity discharge light sources. They also make cast-aluminum landscape accessories such as bollards and gazebos. Call the factory for further information and the name of a local representative.

Raintree Designs, Inc.
979 Third Ave. Dept. OHJ
New York, NY 10022
(212) 477-8594
RS/O DIST
Distributors of Laura Ashley country prints (three collections) — wall paper, plus coordinating fabric and borders. Also "English Country Decoration" wallpaper, fabric, and borders. No literature.

• **Raleigh, Inc.**
1921 Genoa Road Dept. OHJ
Belvidere, IL 61008
(815) 544-4141
MO RS/O
Concrete tiles designed to resemble wood shakes, clay tiles, and slate shingles. Offered in eleven colors and three styles with a 50-year guarantee. Roof restoration/repair is available with their large selection of salvaged concrete, slate, and clay tiles. Free brochure.

Ramase
Route 47 Dept. OHJ
Woodbury, CT 06798
(203) 263-3332
RS/O
Architectural salvaged materials including hand-hewn beams, wide-board flooring, doors, mouldings, mantels, window glass, bricks, and early American hardware. Also custom cabinet work and raised panelling. No literature.

Rambusch
40 West 13th St. Dept. OHJ
New York, NY 10011
(212) 675-0400
ID
Company specializes in major restoration projects for museums, churches and public buildings. Has a large staff of skilled craftsmen in such areas as painting and decorating, lighting and stained glass, and they offer an extensive line of historic fixtures adapted to current lighting standards. Free brochure: "Restorations By Rambusch." Through interior designers and architects only.

• **Rastetter Woolen Mill**
5802 Star Rt. 39 Dept. OHJ
Millersburg, OH 44654
(216) 674-2103
MO DIST RS/O
5th generation manufacturers, wholesalers, and retailers of hand-woven rag rugs, including throw rugs, stair runners, and treads, area rugs, & wall-to-wall carpet. Available in 100% cotton; wool; cotton/rayon rug yarn; or various synthetics. Custom work and reasonable prices are their specialty. Brochure, $1.

• **Readybuilt Products, Co.**
Box 4425, 1723 McHenry St. Dept. OHJ
Baltimore, MD 21223
(301) 233-5833
MO DIST RS/O
More than 25 different styles of hand-crafted ready to install wood mantels for built-in masonry fireplaces or factory-built metal units. Most mantels have wood openings 50" wide x 30" high and can be modified at additional cost. A Booklet, 'Wood Mantel Pieces" shows styles and a diagram for taking measurements — $2.50.

Recommended Builders
1427 Elmwood Ave. Dept. OHJ
Evanston, IL 60201
(312) 328-6174
RS/O
This construction company handles all types of residential repairs and remodelling. They specialize in the restoration of Victorian and other vintage homes. They'll do large or small restoration jobs. Free flyer.

Red Devil, Inc.
2400 Vauxhall Rd. Dept. OHJ
Union, NJ 07083
(201) 688-6900
DIST
Wide line of home maintenance and decorating products, including wood & paint scrapers; putty & taping knives; glaziers tools; spackling compounds; and caulks & sealants. Available at most hardware, paint, and home center stores.

The Reggio Register Co.
20 Central Ave., PO Box 511 Dept. 105D
Ayer, MA 01432
(617) 772-3493
MO
Manufacturers of a complete line of quality, decorative, cast-iron and solid brass floor registers and grilles from the turn-of-the-century period. Suitable for use with either natural convection or forced-hot-air heating systems. A complete detailed catalog is available for $1.

• **Rejuvenation House Parts Co.**
901 N. Skidmore Dept. OHJ
Portland, OR 97217
(503) 249-0774
RS/O MO
Manufacturers of reasonably priced solid brass Victorian, turn-of-the century, and early Twentieth Century light fixtures. All are authentic and meticulous recreations of the originals. Their mail order catalog of light fixtures is available for $3. The retail store has 10,000 sq. ft. of antique plumbing and lighting fixtures, doors, millwork, hardware, etc. Free brochure of Mission light fixtures.

Reliance Industries, Inc.
PO Box 129 Dept. OHJ
Richland, IA 52585
(319) 456-6030
MO DIST
Reliance Industries is a manufacturer and distributor of four matched lines of traditional mouldings including corner bullets; also supplies custom moulding to match historical profiles. Can make profiles fit arched and round windows. Choice of poplar, red or white oak, ash, maple. Free flyer.

• **Remodelers & Renovators**
512 W. Idaho St. Dept. OHJ
Boise, ID 83702
(208) 344-8612
MO RS/O
Suppliers of quality building, finishing & decorating products for renovators. Old-style faucets, fittings, pedestal sinks in ceramic or wood, brass sinks, Victorian mouldings, fretwork & millwork, reproduction gas/electric lighting, brass hardware, tin ceilings, old-style entrance doors & screen doors. Large inventory hard-to-find items. Catalog, $2.

Renaissance Decorative Hardware Co.
PO Box 332 Dept. OHJ
Leonia, NJ 07605
(201) 568-1403
MO
Renaissance Decorative Hardware Co. is an importer of solid brass door, cabinet and furniture hardware. The door hardware includes pulls, knobs, and lever handles. The knobs and lever handles are intended for older homes utilizing mortise mechanisms. Catalog—$2.50.

Renaissance Marketing, Inc.
PO Box 360 Dept. OHJ
Lake Orion, MI 48035
(313) 693-1109
MO RS/O
A source for high-quality reproduction Tiffany table lamps, including the 12-stem table lily. Also art glass accessories and art glass shades; reproduction bronzes and sculptured bronze lighting in Art Nouveau and Art Deco styles. Full color catalot, $2.

KEY TO ABBREVIATIONS

MO	sells by Mail Order
RS/O	sells through Retail Store or Office
DIST	sells through Distributors
ID	sells only through Interior Designers or Archtects

Renaissance Woodcarving, Inc.
324 Ten Eyck St. Dept. OHJ
Brooklyn, NY 11206
(718) 417-0583
MO RS/O
Custom manufactures reproductions in carved wood. Specialize in English and French furniture, cabinets, mantels, tables, capitals, and hand-carved wooden decorative ornaments. Will design to your specs. No literature.

• **Renovation Concepts, Inc.**
213 Washington Ave., North Dept. OHJ
Minneapolis, MN 55401
(612) 333-5766
RS/O MO
A unique showroom with decorative products for home and commercial renovation; 'theme' bars and restaurants and condominimums. Materials available include: mouldings & fretwork, tin ceilings, brass rail & fittings, plumbing hardware, hardwood panelled doors, lighting fixtures, door locksets and trim, wood columns, and many more products. Catalog for the trade only, $12. Free brochure.

Renovation Source, Inc., The
3512 N. Southport Ave. Dept. OHJ
Chicago, IL 60657
(312) 327-1250
RS/O
Firm provides both architectural consulting/design services, and restoration/renovation products. Architectural services from site consultation to a complete set of construction drawings. Supplier of salvaged architectural trim, newly reproduced decorative materials, and restoration aids. Also represent a great number of old-house products manufacturers. Write for information.

• **The Renovator's Supply**
Renovators Old Mill 6119 Dept. OHJ
Millers Falls, MA 01349
(413) 659-2211
MO RS/O
Factory-direct items of brass, wrought iron, solid oak, porcelain, and glass including lighting and plumbing fixtures, home hardware, and decor representative of Colonial and Victorian times. Illustrated catalog, $2.

Reproduction Distributors, Inc.
Box 638 Dept. OHJ
Joliet, IL 60434
MO
Colonial reproduction brass rim locks, hinges, and hardware. Authorized replicas of those used at Williamsburg, VA. Some internal adaptations have been made to meet modern security requirements. A Colonial Williamsburg ™ registered certificate is enclosed with each lock. Send $.40 in stamps for brochure.

Restech Industries
Box 2747 Dept. OHJ
Eugene, OR 97402
(503) 345-1142
MO DIST
Restore-X Exterior Paint Remover can be brushed on with standard brushes or rollers, and then swept or hosed off. Safe, bio-degradable, water-based. Also, Restore-X Weathered Wood Renewer removes cloudy stains and restores grey, weathered wood to a "like new" appearance. Water-based, safe. A "Helpful Hints" brochure is included with each purchase. Plus the company offers a free Historical Preservation Manual upon request, a guide to stripping paint from older homes. Also, (800) 345-1144.

Restoration A Specialty
6127 N.E. Rodney Dept. OHJ
Portland, OR 97211
(503) 285-5250
RS/O MO
Restoration contracting/interior design services for authentic individual home restoration. Individualized custom design for period homes. Serving Pacific NW. Work-ups available for individualized work.

Restoration Fraternity
PO Box 234 Dept. OHJ
Lima, PA 19037
(215) 565-6885
RS/O
Contractors specializing in authentic restoration, repairs, and replacements, including new work. Custom doors, sash, breakfronts, mantels, panelled walls, and wainscot for early period work. Send specifications for consultation or free estimates on millwork. Additions and alterations designed and constructed to duplicate existing structures. No literature.

• **Restoration Millworks**
PO Box 28, 325 Mill St. Dept. OHJ
Bayfield, CO 81122
RS/O
Period windows duplicated with thermal glazing, modern weatherstripping, moulding line. Does installations.

Restoration Treasures
Box 724 Dept. OHJ
Cooperstown, NY 13326
(315) 858-0315
MO
Architectural antiques salvaged from unrestorable buildings or buildings in imminent and irreversible danger of demolition. All items offered in unrestored condition to keep prices low. Inventory includes mantels, wainscotting, roof/porch brackets, antique plumbing. Firm will locate hard-to-find architectural elements. Illustrated brochure, $1 with SASE.

Restoration Works, Inc.
PO Box 486/810 Main St. Dept. OHJ
Buffalo, NY 14205
(716) 856-8000
MO RS/O
Importers, manufacturers, and distributors of high-quality hardware and plumbing, ceiling medallions and trims. Wide range of brass and porcelain. Selected lighting. Catalog, $2.

Restoration Workshop Nat Trust For Historic Preservation
635 South Broadway Dept. OHJ
Tarrytown, NY 10591
(914) 631-6696
RS/O
Preservation/restoration construction and maintenance services provided on a contractual basis, contact the Director, Restoration Workshop. If travel and living expenses are reimbursed they can serve nationwide. Also: paid apprenticeships available to those committed to a career in the preservation trade. Brochure available on request.

• See Advertisers' Index on page 22 for more details.

Restorations, Inc.
382 Eleventh Street Dept. OHJ
Brooklyn, NY 11215
(718) 788-7909
RS/O MO
Quality restoration of antique needlepoint, tapestry, lace curtains, hooked rugs, quilts, samplers and household textiles. Pillows made from your antique fabrics. Consulting services and lectures available on textile conservation, and American rugs and carpets from the 17th century to present. Floor covering consultant. Textile restoration supplies available. Free price list on request.

• **Restorations Unlimited, Inc.**
24 West Main St. Dept. OHJ
Elizabethville, PA 17023
(717) 362-3477
RS/O
Full restoration contracting and interior period design services, including: Analysis of remodeled old houses for reconstruction of original layout; Design and execution of period and creative interiors; Custom cabinets, furnishings, and woodwork; Period and modern kitchen and bath design and installation services. Consulting services for do-it-yourselfers. Seminars in all aspects of restoration. Will work in mid-Atlantic states and southern New England. Also authorized dealer of Rich Craft Custom Cabinets. Literature available.

• **Restore-A-Tub and Brass, Inc.**
1991 Brownsboro Road Dept. OHJ
Louisville, KY 40206
(502) 895-2912
MO RS/O
Specialists in early 1900 bathrooms, restoring bathtubs including antique clawfoot tubs, pedestal sinks. They carry solid brass and chrome plumbing fixtures for all types of sinks and tubs, marble tubwalls, as well as custom-made shower doors, pull chain toilets, and handmade oak medicine cabinets. Also whirlpools & Hydro spas for existing bathtubs — installed while in place — including clawfoot tubs. Free information.

Retinning & Copper Repair
525 West 26th St. Dept. OHJ
New York, NY 10001
(212) 244-4896
MO RS/O
Specializes in hot-dip tinning and finishing of copper cookware, bakery equipment and refrigerator racks. Repairs on all copper, brass and tin items. Cleaning and buffing included in services. Goods accepted at shop in person or via UPS. Estimates available by phone or mail. A selection of copperware available on sale at shop. No literature.

• **Rich Craft Custom Kitchens, Inc.**
141 West Penn Avenue Dept. OHJ
Robesonia, PA 19551
(215) 693-5871
DIST
Manufacturers of a variety of kitchen cabinet work. A few are period-inspired. There are 100 door styles, available in 8 different woods. Cabinets produced to buyer's specifications, so you may want to purchase them through Rich Craft distributors (designers, architects) who will help plan your kitchen. Send $1.00 for catalog.

Richards, R.E., Inc.
P.O. Box 285 Dept. OHJ
West Simsbury, CT 06092
(203) 658-4347
RS/O
Home design and restoration firm serving Connecticut. This small firm works closely with homeowners to solve the particular problems of individual houses. Please call for an appt — No literature.

• **Richmond Doors**
P.O. Box 65 Dept. OHJ
Manchester, NH 03105
(603) 487-3347
MO DIST
Manufacturers of quality custom built, odd size and reproduction solid panel doors in sugar pine, oak, mahogany and a variety of other hardwoods. Interior/exterior. All mortise and tenon. Specialize in early New England designs developed from existing 18th century doors. Will quote from blue prints, sketch or clear photo. Commercial restoration work welcomed. Literature, $1.

• **Rinder's New York Flooring**
979 3rd Ave., Rm. 201 Dept. OHJ
New York, NY 10022
(212) 427-6262
RS/O
Since 1911, this company has been offering quality wood floor refinishing and restoration. Also, new installations and custom stencilling. Free literature.

Ring, J. Stained Glass, Inc.
2724 University Ave. SE Dept. OHJ
Minneapolis, MN 55401
(612) 379-0920
MO RS/O
Fine art-glass studio specializing in restoration/ reproduction for major commissions (architects, government, etc.) Hand-bevelling, etching, & engraving, stained glass work, glass painting and bending; reproduction of quality antique pieces; mirror restoration. Also stock bevels, retail and wholesale stained glass supplies. Some literature available: Please specify interest.

Timothy G. Riordan
423 W. 55th St. Dept. OHJ
New York, NY 10019
(212) 581-3033
RS/O
Antique furniture restoration, conservation, architectural woodwork restorations, French polishing on site. No literature.

Rising & Nelson Slate Co.
Dept. OHJ
West Pawlet, VT 05775
(802) 645-0150
MO
Vermont Colored Roofing Slate available in all colors, sizes, thicknesses, designs to match and restore old roofs. Also slate flagstone. Brochure with descriptive and technical information available free.

Ritter & Son Hardware
PO Box 578, (38401 Hwy 1) Dept. OHJ
Gualala, CA 95445
(707) 884-3363
DIST
Full line of late-19th-century furniture trim: pulls, knobs, hinges, oak, gingerbread, bed parts, etc. Firm does not sell direct to retail customers. Write for nearest dealer.

River City Restorations
623 Collier, PO Box 1065 Dept. OHJ
Hannibal, MO 63401
(314) 248-0733
RS/O
Serves northeastern Missouri, west central Illinois, and southern Iowa. Specializing in non-abrasive cleaning, paint stripping, repointing. Other services include exterior /interior restoration and rehabilitation of private residences and commercial properties. Contracting business helps clients with design, estimates, and priorities. Answers to all inquiries. Free brochure available.

Riverbend Timber Framing, Inc.
PO Box 26 Dept. OHJ
Blissfield, MI 49228
(517) 486-4566
MO DIST RS/O
Using traditional heavy timber framing, this company can design and create a traditional or contemporary house with large open space and passive solar design. Sponsors annual classes on the craft of timber framing. Offers wide range of services to owner/builders. Suppliers of stress-skin panels and doors and windows. Free brochure.

Riverton Corporation
Dept. OHJ
Riverton, VA 22651
(703) 635-4131
DIST
A major manufacturer of lime-based masonry cement. Will match any mortar color from stock selection or create a custom color (and composition). Technical assistance is offered. Free literature. Can phone toll free (800) 336-2490, in VA (800) 572-2480.

• **Dana Robes Wood Craftsmen, Inc.**
Box 707, Lower Shaker Village Dept. OHJ
Enfield, NH 03748
(603) 632-5385
MO RS/O
Woodworking shop specializing in Shaker furniture and wooden doors — both standard four-and six-panel as well as with hand-blown bull's-eye glass. Showroom. Custom orders welcome. Brochures: doors, free; furniture, $2.

Robinson Iron Corporation
PO Drawer 1235 Dept. OHJ
Alexander City, AL 35010
(205) 329-8486
RS/O
Authentic 19th century cast iron for the home and garden including: flowing fountains, urns and vases, planters, statuary, fence posts, hitching posts, street lamp standards, garden furniture, and traditional railroad benches. Historic restoration and custom casting services also available. Send $3 to receive complete brochure. Also, (800) 824-2157.

Robinson Lumber Company
Suite 202, 512 S. Peters St. Dept. OHJ
New Orleans, LA 70130
(504) 523-6377
MO RS/O
Family owned lumber company started in 1893, offering long leaf heart pine flooring, beaded ceiling, wainscotting and timbers. Can custom cut to customer's specifications. Free brochure with price list. Samples available at cost.

Robson Worldwide Graining
4308 Argonne Dr. Dept. OHJ
Fairfax, VA 22032
(703) 978-5331
RS/O
Fifth-generation international grainer and marbler apprenticed for 15 years in England. Has worked throughout Europe, the Middle East, and America. Simulation of any wood, marble, or glazed finish. Has worked in Buckingham Palace, Mount Vernon, and the Philadelphia Athenaeum, as well as private residences worldwide. Please call for prices and a personal viewing of styles and colors available.

Rocco V. De Angelo
RD 1, Box 187R Dept. OHJ
Cherry Valley, NY 13320
(607) 264-3607
RS/O
Cast-iron restoration; custom fabrication; sandblasting, priming, finishing services. No literature.

Rocker Shop of Marietta, GA
1421 White Circle NW, Box 12 Dept. OHJ
Marietta, GA 30061
(404) 427-2618
RS/O MO
The Brumby and Melson rockers made of solid red oak with cane seat and back. A smaller, armless rocker is part of the line, as are a child's rocker and an oak slat porch swing (4, 5, and 6 feet lengths available). Also 2 country-style dining chairs, 2 stools, a lap desk, and small round and oval tables (coordinating). Many other types of rockers, too. Free catalog and price list.

Rockland Industries, Inc. Thermal Products Division
1601 Edison Highway Dept. OHJ
Baltimore, MD 21213
(800) 638-6390
DIST
Energy-efficient window shades that will fit almost any size and shape window. Sold in a variety of forms: Do-it- yourself Kit with your choice of fabric, the Insul-Trac alone, or made to measure and custom. Write or call for a free brochure and a dealer in your area. Ask for The Intelligent Window.

Mario Rodriguez Cabinetmaker
419 Manhattan Ave. Dept. OHJ
Brooklyn, NY 11222
(718) 387-6685
MO RS/O
Handcrafted 18th-century furniture made faithfully following the techniques of that period. Restoration services available. No literature.

Roger A. Reed Inc.
165 Pleasant St., Box 508 Dept. OHJ
Reading, MA 01867
(617) 944-4640
MO DIST RS/O
Mail-order source of Beaute Satin Creme furniture polish. It glides on easily, is made of all-natural ingredients, and resists both alcohol and water. Free flyer.

Rohlf's Stained & Leaded Glass Studio
783 South 3rd Ave. Dept. OHJ
Mount Vernon, NY 10550
(212) 823-4545
RS/O MO
Since 1920 this company has been designing and making stained (i.e. painted not merely colored) and leaded glass windows for the religious community. They also provide an extensive leaded glass selection to the furniture industry. Not for the budget-minded home owner. A repair and restoration service for glass and windows. Free literature.

Rollerwall, Inc.
PO Box 757 Dept. OHJ
Silver Spring, MD 20901
(301) 589-5516
MO
Sells the design paint roller. A wallpaper effect can be obtained by the use of a 6-in. rubber roller with a design embossed on its surface. Can also be used on fabric and furniture. Over 100 patterns including wood grain. Illustrated brochure — free.

• Roman Marble Co.
120 W. Kinzie Dept. OHJ
Chicago, IL 60610
(312) 337-2217
RS/O MO
Company sells very large selection of imported and domestic antique marble mantels. Restoration and installation of marble mantels. Also — custom marble pieces, pedestals and statuary of marble, from Italy and France. Shipment can be arranged. Literature available — please come in or telephone.

Rose, Barry
1450 Logan St. Dept. OHJ
Denver, CO 80203
(303) 832-3250
RS/O
Barry Rose has been a professional artist for 10 years. He's completed over 30 architectural/ceramic murals, both interior and exterior. He now does historic restoration work including research, design, sculpting and casting of terra cotta, stone work cladding, glaze research, and duplication of destroyed historic tile work. Free brochure.

Rosenau, Marion, Sculptor
1516 Naudain St. Dept. OHJ
Philadelphia, PA 19146
(215) 735-3252
MO RS/O
Custom restoration of ornamental plaster. Specialize in residential cornices, models, casts, moulds, and sculpture. Homeowner or contractor responsible for installation. Diverse materials available. Will design to your needs. No literature.

Ross, Douglas — Woodworker
P.O. Box 480 Dept. OHJ
Brooklyn, NY 11215
(718) 499-5152
RS/O
Custom cabinetwork and furniture; restoration and finish carpentry. Free estimate; portfolio and references available, no literature.

Roth Painting, Co., Inc.
866 United Nations Plaza Dept. OHJ
New York, NY 10017
(212) 758-2170
RS/O
Full-service, insured decorating contractor. Decorative painting, gilding, glazing, marbleizing, and wood graining specialists in complete interior restorations, including incidental carpentry and cabinetry. Projects from private residences to major hotels. Clients include the Cooper-Hewitt Museum and Bronx Zoo. Services available 24 hours a day, 7 days a week. Free flyer and estimates.

Round Oak Metal Specialties
PO Box 108 Dept. OHJ
Hudson, MA 01749
(617) 568-0597
MO RS/O
Their bronze-headed snow guards can be installed without removing any roof shingles. They also make copper roofing (standing seam), gutters, flashing, custom cornices, nails, and hooks. Free brochures.

• See Advertisers' Index on page 22 for more details.

• Roy Electric Co., Inc.
1054 Coney Island Avenue Dept. OHJ
Brooklyn, NY 11230
(718) 339-6311
RS/O MO
Large selection of original and reproduction interior and exterior lighting fixtures. Victorian to Art Deco gas, electric and oil fixtures, sconces, pendants, brackets, pole lights, desk lamps, emeralites, parts, glass shades, bathroom fixtures, brass and chrome shower units, faucets, soap dishes, towel accessories, porcelain handles, brass and iron beds, and hard to find parts. They restore, replace, repair, cast, bend, plate, polish, and lacquer. Lighting catalog photos, $3; plumbing color photos, $5.

Rue de France
78 Thames St. Dept. OH5
Newport, RI 02840
(401) 846-2084
MO RS/O
A mail-order source of fine, French lace in traditional patterns. Can be purchased by the yard or made up into cafe curtains, tiebacks, flat panels, tablerunners, bed linens. Send $2 for a 24-page color catalog.

Rumford Fireplaces
110 West Spruce St. Dept. OHJ
Columbus, OH 43215
(614) 221-6918
MO RS/O
A small company that manufactures modular, all-masonry Rumford fireplaces. Also specializes in the restoration of fireplaces and chimneys in old and historic houses as well as the conversion of coal and gas fireplaces to wood-burning. (See article in OHJ, Jan./Feb. 1985, p. 8.) Write for more detailed inforation.

Rumplestiltskin Designs
8967 David Ave. Dept. OHJ
Los Angeles, CA 90034
(213) 839-4747
MO
A source for hard-to-find, beaded lampshade fringe. Different patterns and colors are available. Also, replacement panels with embroidered designs for recovering an old shade. Send request on letterhead for wholesale price list. Send $1 and SASE for photos and current price list.

Russell & Company Victorian Bathrooms
PO Box 6018 Dept. OHJ
Anaheim, CA 92806
(818) 965-6083
MO
This company's oak bathroom accessories are available at a reasonable cost. They also stock vanities and 3 styles of high-tank toilets with and without carving, toilet seats, and will make custom vanities. Brochure, $1.

Russell Restoration of Suffolk
5550 Bergen Ave. Dept. OHJ
Mattituck, NY 11952
(516) 765-2481
RS/O
Quality restoration of ornamental plaster and lath plaster (flat work): cornice mouldings, ceilings, medallions, and brackets. Also custom niches, columns, light domes and other architectural details. From one foot of moulding to an entire room reconstructed. Any period or style from Colonial to Rocco to Art Deco. Will travel. Brochure.

W.N. Russell and Co.
34-60 Albertson Ave. Dept. OHJ
Westmont, NJ 08108
(609) 858-1057
DIST RS/O
Specialize in cast stone, including capitals (Doric & Composite), mouldings, gargoyles, arches, and cornices. Product can simulate any natural cut building stone. Custom work and some stock items. Free brochure.

"Rustic Barn" Wood Products
Rt. 1, Box 205 Dept. OHJ
Stephens City, VA 22655
(703) 869-4654
MO RS/O
"Rustic Barn" specializes in random-width flooring, wainscotting, casing, crown mould, base mould, chair rail, timber in cherry, maple, walnut, oak, poplar.

Rutland Products
P.O. Box 340 Dept. OHJ
Rutland, VT 05701
(802) 775-5519
DIST RS/O
Home repair products — glazing compounds, caulks, sealants, adhesives, putty, grout, spackle, metal roofpaint, clearwood finish, roof cement, coating and patching compounds, furnace cement, stove lining compound. Free catalogs.

Ryther — Purdy Lumber Co., Inc.
69 Elm St., PO Box 622 Dept. OHJ
Old Saybrook, CT 06475
(203) 388-4405
DIST RS/O
Builds decorative lighting standards, guard railings, signs, benches etc. Mostly from Western red cedar, primarily for commercial use. Also makes a turned redwood lamp post and a cedar flag pole. Free brochures.

S

S.P.N.E.A. Conservation Center
185 Lyman Street Dept. OHJ
Waltham, MA 02154
(617) 891-1985
RS/O
A consulting group of the Society for the Preservation of New England Antiquities offering expert advice to owners of older properties concerned with the restoration, preservation and conservation of their structures. Specialized advice on historic paints, masonry and wood conservation, and plaster repair. Physical and documentary research into the history, development and condition of historic properties. Also furniture conservation and surveys of furniture collections for museums, historical organizations, and individuals. Free brochure.

S & W Framing Supplies, Inc.
120 Broadway Dept. OHJ
Garden City Park, NY 11040
(516) 746-1000
MO RS/O
Major distributor of framing supplies and machinery, serving the picture framing trade and art galleries. Their picture rail hangers, sold in gold with gold buttons and rope, were recommended by an OHJ subscriber. Free illustrated catalog.

Saco Manufacturing & Woodworking
39 Lincoln St., PO Box 149 Dept. OHJ
Saco, ME 04072
(207) 284-6613
MO RS/O
Founded in 1872 as manufacturers of wooden water pumps, this company now manufactures laminated wood columns, lamp posts, and hitching posts. Can do custom turnings from samples, drawings, or photographs. Free literature.

Sadowski, Robert
1038 W. 9th St. Dept. OHJ
Erie, PA 16502
(814) 454-8019
MO
Restoration of pianos, 1900 to present: Refinishing and total rebuilding. Call for information.

• **St. Louis Antique Lighting Co., Inc.**
801 N. Skinker Dept. OHJ
St. Louis, MO 63130
(314) 863-1414
MO RS/O DIST
Antique and authentic handcrafted brass reproduction ceiling fixtures, sconces and lamps. Gas, electric and combination fixtures from 1880 to 1930. "Mission Oak" ceiling fixture now available. Will also manufacture to your design specifications. New line of Deco wall sconces & Holophane shades. Catalog, $3.

St. Luke's Studio
Belcourt Castle, Ledge Rd. Dept. OHJ
Newport, RI 02840
(401) 846-0669
RS/O
St. Luke's Studio, founded in 1895 by Josiah Gilbert Dudley, a Victoria prize-winning artist, was purchased in 1961 by the Tinney Family of Belcourt Castle, Newport, RI. The chief designer, Donald Tinney, is at home in many media from stained glass and woodcarving to oil painting & murals, etc. Restoration work is a speciality. The emphasis in this Studio is in Gothic & Early Resaissance styles, but other styles are also utilized.

Salamandra Glass
133-143 Market St. Dept. OHJ
Portsmouth, NH 03801
(603) 431-4511
MO DIST RS/O
Custom Bullseye windows are a specialty of this company, in operation for more than 10 years. They also do limited-edition art glass, both functional and decorative pieces. Also custom lighting, Salamandra Art Glass Block, and tiles. Send SASE for information.

• **Saltbox**
3004 Columbia Ave. Dept. OHJ
Lancaster, PA 17603
(717) 392-5649
RS/O MO DIST
American period lighting fixtures: Extensive collection of lanterns, post lights, and chandeliers handcrafted of tin, copper, brass and pewter. The Period Collection is designed for traditional, Early American and Colonial homes in primitive, country or formal styles. Reproduction lamp posts and Early American hardware also available. Store also in Saumico, WI. Illustrated brochure showing 25 of over 250 pieces — $1.

Salvage One
1524 S. Sangamon St. Dept. OHJ
Chicago, IL 60608
(312) 733-0098
MO RS/O
Enormous selection of architectural artifacts, housed in multi-storey 360,000 sq. ft. warehouse. Can supply complete room interiors for restorations, or period decor in restaurants, etc. In-stock items available for prop rentals. Also, zinc for bevelled windows. Walk-in store only, open to the public. Free literature.

Sammamish Woodworks
2450 W. Lake Sammamish Rd. NE Dept. OHJ
Redmond, WA 98052
(206) 883-0558
MO RS/O
Gable vents in eight shapes and custom sizes, including arched, round, and octagonal. Kiln-dried wood. Can be custom ordered. Also porch trim and gingerbread. Free flyer and price sheet.

Samuel B. Sadtler, Importers
340 S. 4th St. Dept. OHJ
Philadelphia, PA 19106
(215) 923-3714
MO RS/O
Importers of box locks similar to those used in the 18th and 19th centuries. Steel model, $42. Polished cast brass, $152. Call or write for more information.

San Do Designs/Spanish Tile Factoria
2201 E. 7th Ave. Dept. OHJ
Tampa, FL 33605
(813) 254-2015
MO RS/O
Custom hand-painted tile. Will match color and design samples or paint on your tiles. Custom painted bath accessories including sinks, lavatories, bidets, toothbrush holders, etc. Free flyer.

San Francisco Color Service
855 Alvarado Dept. OHJ
San Francisco, CA 94114
(415) 285-4544
RS/O
Specializes in exterior and interior architectural colors and available as a consultant. Will do mail-order coloring from photos. No literature.

San Francisco Victoriana
2245 Palou Avenue Dept. OHJ
San Francisco, CA 94124
(415) 648-0313
RS/O MO
Manufactures and supplies stock reproduction Victorian and traditional wood mouldings, ceiling cornices, and fireplace surrounds; also reproductions of fibrous plaster ceiling centerpieces, cornices, and brackets. Supplies embossed anaglypta wallcoverings and embossed wall and frieze border papers. Also, custom duplications from plaster or wood samples. 70-page product catalog, $3.

• See Advertisers' Index on page 22 for more details.

Sandy Springs Galleries
233 Hilderbrand Dr., N.E. Dept. OHJ
Atlanta, GA 30328
(404) 252-3244
RS/O
Specializes in old lighting fixtures and sconces, many of which were originally gas or kerosene, in brass, wood, and wrought iron, all rewired to meet the National Code. They also have 5000 square feet of European and American furniture & mirrors. No literature.

Sawdust Room
P.O. Box 327, 1856 S. Sierra Dept. OHJ
Stevensville, MI 49127
(616) 429-5338
MO RS/O
Early American wood products made and repaired: canopy beds, spinning wheels, custom wood products. Cylindrical lathe duplications. Will replace missing wooden parts: chair rungs, rockers, spokes, Shaker clothes racks, etc. No literature.

Scalamandre, Inc.
950 Third Ave. Dept. OHJ
New York, NY 10022
(212) 980-3888
ID
For over 50 years this company has been making superb period fabrics. The authenticity of their fabrics, wallpapers, carpets and trimmings is acknowledged by museums. Scalamandre has been involved in restorations throughout the U.S.A., including Monticello, Kenmore, Viscaya, and San Simeon. A research library and consulting services are available to those persons involved in the restoration of public buildings. No literature.

• **Schlitz Studios**
245 N. Water St. Dept. OHJ
Milwaukee, WI 53202
(414) 277-0742
MO RS/O
This studio designs original lamps, windows, mosaics, and small decorative pieces as well as making Tiffany reproductions. Catalog, $2.

F. Schumacher & Co.
79 Madison Ave. Dept. OHJ
New York, NY 10016
(212) 213-7900
DIST RS/O
Schumacher has a large line of period and traditional fabrics and wallcoverings available at decorating shops and department stores. The documentary patterns have the historical information printed on back of the samples. They also have a fine line of damasks and brocades and Victorian prints, but these are decorator only. No literature.

Bess Schuyler Ceramics
246 W. 16th St. Dept. OHJ
New York, NY 10011
(212) 255-4611
MO RS/O
All works are glazed ceramic plaques sculpted by Bess Schuyler in her NYC and Truro, MA studios. House and door portraits are done from photographs to scale. Plaques are done in relief and are finished with backing and ready to be hung. Personal details, pets, etc. can be included. Work takes 4-6 weeks. In addition to accepting commissions, she is constantly adding to a varied collection of facades that are of historical and visual interest. Studio visits by appointment are most welcome. Now doing ceramic portraits of interiors.

Schwartz's Forge & Metalworks, Inc.
P.O. Box 205 Dept. OHJ
Deansboro, NY 13328
(315) 841-4477
RS/O MO
Designs and executes architectural ironwork in a variety of styles, for use as gates, railings, grilles, furnishings etc. Traditional blacksmithing techniques used on all work. Custom design work. Will work with architect. Representative portfolio available for $3.50.

• **A.F. Schwerd Manufacturing Co.**
3215 McClure Avenue Dept. OHJ
Pittsburgh, PA 15212
(412) 766-6322
MO RS/O
Aesthetically pleasing, mathematically correct wooden columns. Available in Tuscan, Greek, and Roman orders, fluted or plain; round, square, or octagon shapes. Can manufacture columns to stock designs, or to your specifications. Ornamental caps: Scamozzi, Ionic, Doric, Temple of the Winds, Erechtheum, Roman Corinthian. Also — wooden lamp posts and lanterns. Specify interest for free brochure.

Sculpture Associates, Ltd.
40 East 19th Street Dept. OHJ
New York, NY 10003
(212) 777-2400
MO RS/O
Fine imported tools including rasps and carving tools. Also large selection of wood, clay, and stone. Moulding materials include latex, alginate, and R.T.V. rubbers. Casting materials include plaster, hydrocals, and resins. MASTER heat guns and small dental-type tools for paint removal. Carries complete line of METABO power tools. Also has AKEMI glue for marble and marble cleaners, polishes and buffing compounds. Catalog, $2.

Sculpture House
38 East 30th St. Dept. OHJ
New York, NY 10016
(212) 679-7474
MO DIST RS/O
Manufacturers of handmade tools, and suppliers of material for all forms of three dimensional art. Tools are available for working in plaster, ceramics, wood, and stone. Complete catalogue with prices available for $2.00.

Seaport Village Associates
PO Box 277 Dept. OHJ
Barnstable, MA 02630
(617) 778-4600
RS/O
Supplier of English conservatories, sunrooms, and glass gazebos. Options include French doors, stained glass windows, and insulated panels. Color portfolio, $5.

Second Chance
230 7th St. Dept. OHJ
Macon, GA 31202
(912) 742-7874
RS/O MO
Specializes in hard-to-find restoration items. Inventory includes brass hardware, plumbing fixtures, fireplace tile, and old stained and beveled glass. A large collection of corbels, gingerbread, columns, entrance frames, heavily carved doors, mantels and antique staircase parts. Serves the middle Georgia area. No literature, but photographs can be supplied on request with a stamped, self-addressed envelope.

• **Security Home Inspection, Inc.**
5906 Avenue T Dept. OHJ
Brooklyn, NY 11234
(718) 763-5589
RS/O
Pre-purchase inspection of Brownstones, Townhouses, Co-ops, 1-2 family homes and commercial buildings. Provides oral and full written report. Free brochure.

Sedgwick House
15231 Harriman Blvd. Dept. OHJ
Noblesville, IN 46060
(317) 773-7372
MO
A wonderful selection of period inspired frames for photographs and paintings/drawings. Finishes include: antique gold, walnut, oak, gold, and silver. Free literature.

Sedgwick Lifts, Inc.
PO Box 630 Dept. OHJ
Poughkeepsie, NY 12602
(914) 454-5400
DIST
Sedgwick Lifts has been manufacturing dumbwaiters and residence elevators for 90 years. Products available are electric dumbwaiters, hand-powered dumbwaiters, residential elevators, cart lifts, material lifts, automatic transfer devices, dumbwaiter doors and residential swing hoistway doors. Free catalog.

Julius Seidel & Co.
3514 Gratiot St. Dept. OHJ
St. Louis, MO 63103
(314) 772-4000
MO RS/O
Major mid-west distributor of Shakertown's machine-cut shingles of cedar, some in fancy shapes. Free color brochures.

Seitz, Robert/Fine Woodworking
88 Farwell Rd., Box 203 Dept. OHJ
Tyngsboro, MA 01879
(617) 649-7707
RS/O
Custom cabinetry, casework and architectural detailing in Boston and southern New Hampshire area. Well-equipped shop. Send $1. for brochure; or send sketch, photo, for consultation and estimate.

Select Interior Door, Ltd.
2074 Perry Rd., PO Box 178 Dept. OHJ
North Java, NY 14113
(716) 535-9900
RS/O
Interior and exterior solid hard wood raised panel doors, some with leaded and insulated glass and hand carvings. Pre-hanging, pre-finishing and design services available. Free literature.

KEY TO ABBREVIATIONS

MO	sells by Mail Order
RS/O	sells through Retail Store or Office
DIST	sells through Distributors
ID	sells only through Interior Designers or Archtects

• **Sellrite Millwork Corp.**
581 Rahway Ave. Dept. OHJ
Union, NJ 07083
(800) 672-1036
MO RS/O
In business for over 35 years, Sellrite Millwork builds custom architectural windows and doors. Authorized dealer for CARADCO windows. Showroom hours: 8-5 daily; 9-12 Saturday or by appointment. Free literature.

Selva — Borel
PO Box 796-A Dept. OHJ
Oakland, CA 94604
(415) 832-0356
MO RS/O
Supplier of clocks, clock kits, tools, parts and materials — including cases, hands, and movement. Quartz, battery-operated clock movements available. German Clock Catalog, $2.00, refundable on purchase.

Sentry Electric Corp.
185 Buffalo Ave. Dept. OHJ
Freeport, NY 11520
(516) 379-4660
DIST
They make a number of vintage-looking lampposts, including the "Bishop's Crook," available with mercury, HPS, or metal halide lamps. Free flyer.

Sepp Leaf Products
381 Park Ave. South Dept. OHJ
New York, NY 10016
(212) 683-2840
MO
Distributors of German and Italian gold leaf and related products including brushes, knives, and instruction guides. Free price list of all products.

Seraph, The
P.O. Box 500, Route 20 Dept. OHJ
Sturbridge, MA 01566
(617) 347-2241
RS/O MO
Reproduction country sofas and wing chairs from $695. Frames are handcrafted and upholstery fabric is by Waverly, Greeff, Schumacher, and others. Color catalog and fabric samples — $3.

Shades of Victoriana
31420-14 Highway 550 N. Dept. OHJ
Durango, CO 81301
(303) 259-0146
MO DIST
Fabric lampshades handmade with laces, velvets, and satins. Custom work a specialty. Beaded fringe available. They also offer coodinated drapes, curtains, and comforters. Brochure, $3.

Shades of the Past
PO Box 502 Dept. OH
Corte Madera, CA 94925
(415) 459-6999
MO
A collection of Victorian, Deco, & Traditional silk lampshades & fine quality bases. Each shade is original, hand sewn & custom designed. Only the finest quality materials are used. Color brochure, $3.

Shadovitz Bros. Distributors, Inc.
1565 Bergen Street Dept. OHJ
Brooklyn, NY 11213
(718) 774-9100
DIST MO
Patterned picture frame mouldings available in lengths, cut and mitred, or finished. Mat boards, tools, and other supplies for framers are available. They also have a glazing division that can provide curved, colored, or insulated glass. Free flyer.

Shady Lady
418 E. 2nd St. Dept. OHJ
Loveland, CO 80537
(303) 669-1080
MO RS/O
Carries a wide variety of lampshade styles. Can recover old frames and do custom work. Catalog includes drawings of the basic shapes; shades can look Victorian, Art Deco, Oriental, or contemporary depending upon fabric, trim, and use of fringe. Prices range from $30 for simple, small model to $475 for the most complex. $2.50 for 14-page catalog and price list.

Shaker Carpenter Shop
8267 Oswego Rd. Dept. OHJ
Liverpool, NY 13088
(315) 652-7778
MO
Shaker and country furniture, plus accessories. Hand-cut dovetails, custom orders quoted free. Brochure, $1, refundable.

Shaker Workshops
PO Box 1028OHJ Dept. OHJ
Concord, MA 01742
(617) 646-8985
MO RS/O
Reproduction Shaker furniture kits, needlework kits, oval boxes, baskets, pegs & pegrail, & lighting fixtures. Of special interest are the Shawl-Back and Tape-Back Rockers, in child and adult sizes, identical to those made by the Mt. Lebanon, NY Shakers. Replacement chair tape also available in authentic Shaker colors. Showroom is at Old Schwamb Mill, Mill Lane, Arlington, Mass. Mail-order source of Stulb Old Village period paints. Patterns for Shaker cloaks. Catalog and tape samples, $1.

Shakertown Corporation
P.O. Box 400 Dept. OH
Winlock, WA 98596
(206) 785-3501
MO RS/O DIST
A major manufacturer of shakes and shingles has red cedar shingles in 9 specialty patterns appropriate for Queen Anne and shingle-style houses. Fancy-butt shingles are 18 in. long and 5 in. wide, and are available for prompt shipment. Shakertown also manufactures 8′ and 4′ lengths of wood shingle & shakes panels. Free illustrated brochure, catalog $4.

• **Shanker Steel Ceiling Co., Inc.**
2400 Bedle Pl. Dept. OHJ
Linden, NJ 07036
(201) 925-7700
MO RS/O
Company is a major manufacturer of pressed steel ceilings. Catalog, price list and brochure on how to put material up are available free. In the east, call toll free (800) SHANKER.

Gerry Sharp Trunk Doctor
HCR 1, Box 762 Dept. OHJ
Bandera, TX 78003
(512) 796-8462
MO
Sharp has 22 years experience in the restoration of trunks. He also decorates trunks with hand painting. Will also give classes and seminars on trunk restoration. Restoration Manual — $5 ppd.

R.W. Shattuck Co.
444 Mass. Ave. Dept. OHJ
Arlington, MA 02174
(617) 643-0114
MO RS/O
Early style brass picture moulding hooks. Assorted styles of wall picture hangers, frame hangers and ring hangers. No literature.

Shaw Marble Works Mid-America Marble & Granite
5012 S. 38th St. Dept. OHJ
St. Louis, MO 63116
(314) 481-5860
RS/O
Supply and/or install all types of marble. Custom cut to individual needs, from small bases to fireplaces, bathrooms, office lobbies, etc. No literature.

Shelley Signs
Box 94 Dept. OHJ
West Danby, NY 14896
(607) 564-3527
MO
Signs (carved/painted) designed & executed in a traditional American vein. Custom carving work, including door panels, shells, scrolls. Handcarved wooden placques. Please send SASE with specific requests. Slides of work are available with $5. deposit, refunded when slides are returned.

Shenandoah Manufacturing Co.
P.O. Box 839 Dept. OHJ
Harrisonburg, VA 22801
(703) 434-3838
DIST
Wood stoves, a coal model stove, and furnaces; thermostatically regulated, utilitarian in design. Fireplace insert that will increase the efficiency of a fireplace. Also a new hearth heater with applications for either hearth or free-standing; add-on furnaces, to be used alone or added to an existing forced-air heating system. Free literature.

Sheppard Millwork, Inc.
21020 70th Ave. W. Dept. OHJ
Edmonds, WA 98020
(206) 771-4645
MO RS/O
A custom woodworking shop. They make custom & stock entry and interior doors, bifolds, mouldings, stair parts, sashes, mantels, turnings, etc. Can also supply stock doors and stair parts. Can do a wide variety of mouldings as they grind their own knives. Turnings are done by hand to match drawings or the existing work in a house. Brochure available upon request.

Sherman Hill Antiques
707 19th St. Dept. OHJ
Des Moines, IA 50314
(515) 282-0885
RS/O
Restoration supply store specializing in antique lighting (gas lamps, electric/gas combinations, pre-World-War-II electric lighting fixtures). Will also restore lamps: rewire, polish, lacquer, rebuild, and convert gas to electricity. Also carries brass hardware for doors and windows, architectural salvage, and brass reproductions of bathroom hardware. Call or write for more information.

KEY TO ABBREVIATIONS

MO	sells by Mail Order
RS/O	sells through Retail Store or Office
DIST	sells through Distributors
ID	sells only through Interior Designers or Archtects

• **Shingle Mill, Inc.**
Box 134, 6 Cote Ave. Dept. OHJ
South Ashburnham, MA 01466
(617) 827-4889
MO DIST RS/O
Manufactures wooden shingles used in restoration work for roofing and exterior siding. Also, a wide variety of special architectural shapes. Where it is within their range of capability, they'll cut to order any special size or shape you may desire. If unable to meet your needs exactly, they'll send a sample of the closest possible alternative. Free catalog.

Ship 'n Out
8 Charles St. Dept. OHJ
Pawling, NY 12564
(800) 431-8242
MO
Manufactures solid brass rails and fittings. Also has a large selection of door hardware and some stained glass panels. Glass racks, wine racks, pot racks, and coat racks, too. Also sells Brasswax. Catalog $1.

• **Shuttercraft**
282 Stepstone Hill Rd. Dept. OHJ
Guilford, CT 06437
(203) 453-1973
MO RS/O
Authentic exterior wood shutters with moveable louvers. Over 100 sizes. Also, two- and three-panel styles, plus standard fixed-louver models. Priming painting in your color choice, $12 per panel. Trimming, rabbeting, and hardware also available. Free brochure.

Sierra Lamp Company
15941 Hwy. 49 Dept. OHJ
Drytown, CA 95699
(209) 245-3106
MO RS/O
Manufacturers of turn-of-the-century style lamps. Mostly desk lamps with brass, emeralite-style, or Tiffany-style shades. Also parts available to repair old lamps. Catalog $1.

Sign of the Crab
3756 Omec Circle Dept. 132
Rancho Cordova, CA 95670
(916) 638-2722
RS/O DIST
Manufacturer of brass hardware, plumbing fixtures, lamps, clocks, antique re-creations and nauticals. Wholesale catalog and price list to dealers. Call or write for name of distributor nearest you.

Silk Surplus Inc.
37-24 24th St. Dept. OHJ
Long Island City, NY 11101
(718) 361-3500
MO
A wide range of discounted textiles (silk, damask, velvet, linen, cotton, tapestry, crewel), drapery and upholstery trimmings, and wallpaper. Exclusive distributor of Scalamandre's discontinued lines (limited quantities). Other brands available in unlimited quantities. No literature.

• **Silver Dollar Trading Co.**
1591 Main St., PO Box 394 Dept. OHJ
San Elizario, TX 79849
(915) 851-3458
MO DIST RS/O
This company carries Victorian reproduction spiral staircases, street lights, mailboxes, light fixtures, fountains, and benches. Free catalog.

• **Silver Tree Farms**
51579 Gates Bridge E. Box 222 Dept. OHJ
Gates, OR 97346
(503) 897-3132
MO RS/O
Manufacturers of cedar shingles appropriate for old houses. Write for information.

• **Silverton Victorian Millworks**
PO Box 850 Dept. OHJ
Silverton, CO 81433
(303) 387-5716
MO
Offer a variety of custom Victorian and Colonial mouldings, as well as the standard patterns. They also have window and door rosettes available in many combinations. The millwork is available in pine or oak. They welcome any inquiries concerning custom milling. For custom mouldings, send a detailed drawing or sample for prompt quotation. Catalog — $3.50.

Simms & Thayer Cabinetmakers
PO Box 35 OH Dept. OHJ
North Marshfield, MA 02059
(617) 826-7221
MO DIST
Signed authentic reproductions of fine American country furniture recreated exactly as the originals — tables, hutches, cupboards, beds and chairs. 24-page color catalog includes showroom location. Catalog, $3.

• **The Sink Factory**
2140 San Pablo Ave. Dept. OHJ
Berkeley, CA 94702
(415) 548-3967
MO RS/O
Manufacturers of hand-crafted porcelain, specializing in pedestal sinks and floral vanity basins. Victorian design fluted base pedestal sink, and 1920s smooth pedestal sink. Bathroom accessories. Custom orders welcomed. Catalog, $3. (Formerly Stringer's Environmental Restoration & Design.) Also (415) 540-8193.

Sky Lodge Farm
Box 62 Dept. OHJ
Shutesbury, MA 01072
(413) 259-1271
MO
Producers of Early American clapboards with quartersawn squared edges. Also, 18th & 19th century building materials, and bricks. Send $1. for brochure.

• **Skyline Engineers of Maryland, Inc.**
Heritage Hills, 2329 Dixon Rd. Dept. OHJ
Frederick, MD 21701
(301) 831-8800
MO RS/O
Specialists in steeple restoration, gold-leafing, and the preservation of historic buildings. Nationwide services include: sandblasting, chemical restoration, repointing, carpentry, painting, roofing (slate and copper), masonry, bird-proofing, lightning protection, and waterproofing. Projects include: four state capitol buildings, Georgetown University, St. James, Brooklyn, NY, the "clustered spires of Frederick, Md."; Faneuil Hall; Old State House, Boston, Mass, and SS. Philip & James, Baltimore, MD. Call collect.

Skyline Windows
625 W. 130th St. Dept. OHJ
New York, NY 10027
(212) 491-3000
MO RS/O
Skyline distributes Hope steel casement windows, the ubiquitous apartment window beginning in the 1920s. Its classic look, a narrow frame with window hinged to open in, remains the same, though the materials and technology have been updated. Call or write for more information; direct inquiries to Kenneth Kraus.

Smith-Cornell, Inc.
P.O. Box 686 Dept. OHJC
Auburn, IN 46706
(800) 325-0248
MO
Manufactures plaques for National Register of Historic Places, Historic American Buildings Survey, or other custom specifications. Plaques are made of sandcast bronze, sandcast aluminum, and GraphicsPlus©. Markers are made of anodized aluminum with image permanently embedded in bronze or pewter finish. No extra charges for letters, lines, logos, or design. Free brochure or quotation. Also, in IN (219) 925-1172.

Smith, F.E., Castings, Inc.
PO Box 2126 Dept. OHJ
Kingsford, MI 49801
(906) 774-4956
RS/O
Smith specializes in small orders from loose patterns. They have made some parts for antique stoves and want to do more. Will make new patterns for deteriorated parts. Also, decorative figures for iron fencing. No literature, write with specific needs.

Smith, Whitcomb & Cook Co.
PO Box 480 Dept. OHJ
Barre, VT 05641
(802) 476-4161
MO RS/O
Stove replacement parts from fine quality drawings, patterns, and original pieces. Can also manufacture or duplicate fences, railings, lamp posts, and the like. Good thin-wall capability. Orders normally completed 4 to 6 weeks. Call or write for more information.

Smithy, The
Box 2180 Dept. OHJ
Wolcott, VT 05680
(802) 472-6508
MO RS/O
Hand-forged iron executed in the centuries-old manner, with forge, hammer, and anvil. Diversified work includes hardware necessary in restoration of old houses and construction of new reproductions: hinges, door latches, fireplace equipment, kitchen items, lighting fixtures, weathervanes, etc. Write with SASE for free brochure.

Smithy Hearth Products
174 Cedar St., PO Box 840 Dept. OHJ
Branford, CT 06405
(203) 488-7225
MO DIST
Custom-built fireplace screens, using black enamel wire mesh cloth, hand-clinched to a steel frame, furnished with two brass support handles. Smith also manufactures wrought iron log holders, child guards and mitten dryers. Free brochure.

• **The Smoot Lumber Company**
PO Box 88, 1201 N. Royal St. Dept. OHJ
Alexandria, VA 22313
(703) 549-0960
MO RS/O
This firm has been in business since 1858. They carry an extensive selection of mouldings, including 75 patterns of solid red oak in stock and Focal Point's line of synthetic moulding. They will custom run any moulding in soft or hardwoods. Custom doors, especially panelled doors, are also available. Free mouldings brochure. 80-page full-scale tracing file for architects, $10.

Somerset Door & Column Co.
P.O. Box 328 Dept. OHJ
Somerset, PA 15501
(800) 242-7916
MO DIST RS/O
Company has been manufacturing wood columns since 1906. Composition capitals also available. Column sizes from 6-in. bottom diameter to 40-in. diameter by 40 ft. long. They can also provide custom millwork such as stair parts, sash, moulding, panelling, and doors to customer's specifications. Columns brochure is free. In PA, phone (800) 242-7915.

Sound Beginnings
Gristmill Rd. Dept. OHJ
Tillson, NY 12486
(914) 658-3270
RS/O
Custom and reproduction turnings of all types. Also custom and reproduction mouldings. Wood of any type. Custom furniture, reproduction and period. No literature.

South Bound Millworks
PO Box 349 Dept. OHJ
Sandwich, MA 02563
MO
Their unfinished birch brackets and rods are pre-drilled, with hardware included, and sell for $6 per set ($4 for brackets alone). Various mount types (open, closed, single, double); also wrought iron poles and finials, as well as curtain tiebacks. Some Early American style fireplace tools and lamps. Free catalog.

• **South Coast Shingle Co.**
2220 E. South Street Dept. OHJ
Long Beach, CA 90805
(213) 634-7100
RS/O MO
Manufactures fancy butt red cedar shingles. Also distributes cedar shakes and shingles for roofing and siding. Free flyer — please specify.

Southern Accents Architectural Antiques
312 Second Ave., SE Dept. OHJ
Cullman, AL 35055
(205) 734-4799
RS/O MO
Architectural furnishings, including wood mantels, brass & crystal light fixtures, staircases, antique ceiling fans, urns, light posts, entire porches with gingerbread trim. Specialists in bath fixtures & fittings, dealing in completely restored tubs, commodes, & pedestal sinks. Complementary line of brass bath accessories & medicine chests. Photos available on specific inquiry; shipment arranged.

• See Advertisers' Index on page 22 for more details.

• Southington Specialty Wood Co.
100 West Main St. Dept. OHJ
Plantsville, CT 06479
(203) 621-6787
RS/O
Deal strictly with wood products, expertly milled to pattern for random width floor planning in oak, ash, cherry, maple, and whatever else suits your fancy. Specialize in wide (8-in. to 14-in.) kiln-dried oak, cherry, & pine. Delivery available based on quantity and distance. Free brochure.

Spanish Pueblo Doors
PO Box 2517 Dept. OHJ
Santa Fe, NM 87504
(505) 473-0464
MO RS/O
Exterior and interior doors of select hardwoods, Ponderosa pine, Phillipine mahogany, red alder, red oak, or other woods. All custom milled to your size specifications in standard or custom designs. Custom furniture. Free literature.

Spencer, William, Inc.
Creek Road Dept. OHJ
Rancocas Woods, NJ 08060
(609) 235-1830
RS/O MO
Manufacturers of solid brass chandeliers and sconces made according to blueprints dating from 1897. Fine materials and workmanship. Custom work and refinishing of metals an added service. Also manufactures the Philadelphia Busybody. Lighting fixture catalog available for $2.

Tomas Spiers & Associates
PO Box 3742 Dept. OHJ
Harrisburg, PA 17105
(717) 763-7396
RS/O
Architectural/Engineering firm specializing in preservation consultation and professional services including restoration rehabilitation and adaptive use, preparation of historic structure reports, condition surveys, research, state and national register nominations and grant-in-aid applications, in Pennsylvania and surrounding states. No literature.

Spiess Antique Building Materials
228-230 E. Washington Dept. OHJ
Joliet, IL 60433
(815) 722-5639
RS/O
Antique architectural ornamentation. Interior and exterior ornamental wood, mantels a specialty. Stained, leaded and bevelled glass; antique and custom fabrication. Custom bevelling. Also handles antique tavern back bars. Good general architectural selection. No literature.

Spiral Manufacturing, Inc.
17251 Jefferson Hwy. Dept. OHJ
Baton Rouge, LA 70817
(504) 293-8336
MO RS/O
Wood, steel, aluminum and cast aluminum spiral stairs in diameters from 48 in. up to 96 in. Available in kit form for do-it-yourselfers or contractors. Call Toll free (800) 535-9956 (outside Louisiana) for additional information and a free catalog.

• See Advertisers' Index
on page 22
for more details.

Splendor in Brass
123 Market St. Dept. OHJ
Havre de Grace, MD 21078
(301) 939-1312
DIST RS/O MO
Manufacturers of solid brass beds and accessories. Authentic reproductions of turn-of-the-century brass beds. Wholesale to the trade and factory retail outlet. Also a large inventory of antique stained glass windows, doors, landing windows. Catalog for brass and brass and iron beds available, $6.

Spring City Electrical Mfg. Co
Drawer A, Hall & Main Sts. Dept. OHJ
Spring City, PA 19475
(215) 948-4000
MO RS/O
Manufactures cast-iron ornamental lamp posts and bollards. Lamp posts are suitable for street use. Color brochure — $3.

Squaw Alley, Inc.
401 S. Main Street Dept. OHJ
Naperville, IL 60540
(312) 357-0200
RS/O
A restoration supply source, specializing in sale and restoration of oil lamps (including Aladdins), gas and early electric fixtures. Also lamp repair parts, lampshades, reproduction hardware (very large stock), and caning supplies. Serves mainly Chicago area.

Stair-Pak Products Co., Inc.
24 County Line Rd. Dept. OHJ
Somerville, NJ 08876
(201) 231-1111
MO DIST RS/O
Manufactures all-wood spiral stairways for both interior and exterior use. Interior units come in oak or a poplar/particle board combination; exterior units come in Philippine mahogany with brass hardware. Standard interior styles are Colonial, Mediterranean, and Contemporary; other styles as special orders. Also conventional wooden stairways to customer specifications and pre-assembled stair rail systems. Free brochures.

Standard Trimming Co.
1114 First Ave. (61st St.) Dept. OHJ
New York, NY 10021
(212) 755-3034
ID
Manufacturers of trimmings and crystal drapery hardware. Antique tassels, fringes and tiebacks. Special cords and ropes. No literature.

Stanfield Shutter Co.
3214 S. 300 W. Dept. OHJ
Salt Lake City, UT 84115
(801) 467-8823
RS/O
The company has created custom-designed shutters for many historic homes in Utah, including the Governor's mansion. No literature.

• Stanley Galleries
2118 N. Clark Street Dept. OHJ
Chicago, IL 60614
(312) 281-1614
MO RS/O
They specialize in restoring and selling American antique lighting from 1850 to 1925. All fixtures are thoroughly researched so that antique shades can be matched with them. Only old glass is used, not reproductions. All fixtures are taken apart, stripped, rewired, and relacquered. Walk-in store has large selection; mail orders also taken. Call or write about specific fixtures; a Polaroid photo will be sent on request.

• Staples, H. F. & Co., Inc.
Webb Drive, Box 956 Dept. OHJ
Merrimack, NH 03054
(603) 889-8600
MO DIST
Founded in 1897 as the manufacturer of carnauba paste waxes for wood floors and furniture, Staples now manufactures several products for the do-it- yourselfer and professional. These products include "Dry Strip" powdered paint remover, paste waxes, "Miracle Wood", "Decto-Stick", Wood Tone Putty, Ladder Mitts, William's Stove Polish, and Patina Rub. Free literature.

Star Metal
974 Grand St. Dept. OHJ
Brooklyn, NY 11211
(718) 384-2766
RS/O
Will do custom original and restoration work in metal: balconies, gates, railings, utensils, and decorative pieces. Free flyer.

• Starbuck Goldner
315 W. 4th St. Dept. OHJ
Bethlehem, PA 18015
(215) 866-6321
MO RS/O
Handmade ceramic tile, including glazed, embossed, hand-painted, and roof. Stock and custom work; will do research for period reproductions. Call or write for more information.

Stark Carpet Corp.
979 Third Ave. Dept. OHJ
New York, NY 10022
(212) 752-9000
ID
Documented carpets for historical restorations. Also a stock line of historical Wilton carpets; machine-made and handmade rugs from over 20 countries, including Portuguese needlepoints, Romanian kilims, and orientals. Also custom designs and colors of hardwood flooring. Please inquire on your letterhead.

States Industries
PO Box 7037 Dept. OHJ
Eugene, OR 97401
(800) 547-8928
DIST
Beaded, veneered panelling for wainscotting and ceilings that comes in easily applied 48 in. x 96 in. panels; finished or unfinished, four solid colors, and matching chair-rail moulding trim. Free flyer.

Stencil School
Box 94 Dept. OHJ
Shrewsbury, MA 01545
MO
Hand-stenciled country accessories and stencils printed on mylar. Country gifts including: towels, placemats, aprons, woodenware and more. Stencil designs including country village, schoolhouse, apple tree farm, etc. Brochure, $1.

Stencilsmith
71 Main St. Dept. OHJ
ColdSpring on Hudson, NY 10516
(914) 265-9561
RS/O
Small company specializing in fine painted finishes and decoration: services include stencilling on walls, furniture, fabric, window and lampshades; custom historical and contemporary motifs. Also murals, trompe l'oeil, glazing, gilding, faux finishes, and house portraits. Free flyer and press clippings.

• **W. P. Stephens Lumber Co.**
145 Church St., PO Box 1267 Dept. OHJ
Marietta, GA 30061
(404) 428-1531
MO RS/O
Since 1925, this company's architectural millwork includes custom mouldings, sidings, flooring, panelling, doors, shutters, mantels, and cabinet work. Stock lumber includes oak, honduras mahogany, cherry, birch, black walnut, poplar, clear yellow pine, and virgin long leaf heart pine. Stock moulding catalog, $1. Can match customer profiles.

• **Steptoe and Wife Antiques Ltd.**
322 Geary Ave. Dept. OHJ
Toronto, ON, Canada M6H2C7
(416) 530-4200
MO RS/O DIST
Reproduction Victorian style cast-iron spiral & straight staircases. Knock-down for shipping and on-site assembly — modular units for any elevation. They also distribute W.F. Norman sheet metal ceiling panels, plaster cornices & medallions, brass & steel railing systems and "Converto"™ showers. Canadian distributor of Lawler rail/fence castings and Crown's® Anaglypta and Lincrusta wallcoverings. Product catalog, $2.

Steptoe's Old House Store, Ltd.
322 Geary Avenue Dept. OHJ
Toronto, ON, Canada M6H2C7
(416) 537-5772
MO RS/O
Wide range of reproduction renovation products. Brass hardware accessories, and decorative items. Full range of plumbing and bath fixtures suited for old style bathrooms. W.F. Norman steel ceilings, Steptoe cast iron staircases, and Barclay plumbing accessories. Catalog $2.

Sterline Manufacturing Corp.
410 N. Oakley Blvd. Dept. OHJ
Chicago, IL 60612
(312) 226-1555
DIST
"CONVERTO" Shower systems for adding a shower to old bathtubs. Includes tub and shower faucet, rectangular, corner, and straight shower rods. Available in chrome-plated brass and polished brass. A free brochure is available.

Arthur Stern Studios Arch. Glass
1221 8th Ave. Dept. OHJ
Oakland, CA 94606
(415) 835-5162
MO RS/O
Their leaded glass windows are available in a variety of hardwood frames; custom sizes and finishes can be ordered. Free color brochure.

Sternberg Lanterns, Inc.
5801 N. Tripp Dept. OHJ
Chicago, IL 60646
(312) 252-8200
DIST ID
Manufacturer of traditional street lighting in Victorian and turn-of-the-century styles since 1923. Heavy cast-aluminum lighting poles and bollards. Literature, $1.

Donald C. Stetson, Sr., Enterprises
Rt. 112, PO Box 146 Dept. OHJ
Colrain, MA 01340
(413) 625-2614
MO RS/O
Hand-crafted, wrought-iron items ranging from candle holders to fireplace accessories, etc. Various types of hooks, handmade nails, hardware for kitchen cabinets, and other decorative items. Free literature.

Stevens, John R., Associates
1 Sinclair Drive Dept. OHJ
Greenlawn, NY 11740
(516) 249-9385
RS/O
Specializing in the restoration of buildings from the 17th century to the mid 19th century and restoration of antique street railway rolling stock. New York metropolitan region and New Haven, Connecticut area. Free flyer.

• **Stewart Manufacturing Company**
511 Enterprise Drive Dept. OHJ
Covington, KY 41017
(606) 331-9000
MO DIST RS/O
They manufacture ornamental iron fence and gates. Each design is custom made, with the ability to match various old designs manufactured after 1886. No cost or obligation for an estimate. A complete, illustrated catalog is available upon request.

Stone Ledge Co.
170 Washington St. Dept. OHJ
Marblehead, MA 01945
DIST
This company imports, from France, coal- and wood-burning stoves, as well as cast-iron tables, chairs, and park benches. Free catalogs on both stoves and furniture, with price list.

• **Stortz, John & Son, Inc.**
210 Vine Street Dept. OHJ
Philadelphia, PA 19106
(215) 627-3855
MO DIST
A supplier for 132 years, this company manufactures a line of hand tools for the building trade, used in old and new construction. These high-quality tools are for the professional or the serious-minded user who appreciates long-lasting tools. Included are slater's hammers, rippers, stakes, cutters, specialty chisels, star drills for concrete, etc. Catalog $5. Slater's tools available through slate dealers.

Thomas Strahan Co.
Corp. Pl. 128 Bldg. 3 Dept. OHJ
Wakefield, MA 01880
(617) 246-5130
DIST RS/O
Thomas Strahan Co. is a major manufacturer of traditional wallcoverings and matching fabrics. Available through most wallpaper stores.

William H. Straus
1435 Lexington Ave. Dept. OHJ
New York, NY 10128
(212) 410-5682
MO RS/O
Antique brass lighting fixtures — candlesticks, chandeliers and sconces — from the 15th through 18th centuries, some from the 19th and 20th centuries. Viewing by appointment only. Telephone inquiries welcome.

KEY TO ABBREVIATIONS

MO	sells by Mail Order
RS/O	sells through Retail Store or Office
DIST	sells through Distributors
ID	sells only through Interior Designers or Archtects

Strobel Millwork
P.O. Box 26, Route 7 Dept. OHJ
Cornwall Bridge, CT 06754
(203) 672-6727
RS/O MO
Stock and custom architectural millwork. Company specializes in the exact duplication of all styles of wood windows, doors, and entrance frames, particularly Italianate or Renaissance styles. Also stock size fanlight windows with etched glass accents. Brochure, $2.

Stroheim & Romann
155 E. 56th St. Dept. OHJ
New York, NY 10022
(212) 691-0700
ID
Fabric, documentary reproductions, including horsehair and a line for Winterthur museum. Call or write for more information.

• **Structural Slate Company**
222 E. Main St. Dept. OHJ
Pen Argyl, PA 18072
(215) 863-4141
RS/O DIST
A primary source of structural slate products for flooring, stair treads, and accent trim; slate tile for slate roofs. Free brochure.

Studio Design, Inc., t/a Rainbow Art Glass
49 Shark River Rd. Dept. OHJ
Neptune, NJ 07753
(201) 922-1090
MO RS/O
One of the largest dealers of stained glass kits and supplies. Kits come with pre-cut glass pieces, mold, pattern, and all supplies necessary. Large selection of lamps, clocks, mirrors, wall & window decor, terrariums, and suncatchers. Also available: mold and patterns only for those who enjoy cutting their own glass. Catalog, $3.

Studio Workshop, Ltd.
22 Bushy Hill Rd. Dept. OHJ
Simsbury, CT 06070
(203) 658-6374
MO RS/O
Studio Workshop does restoration work on both antique furniture and stained glass. They will do extensive repair & refinishing using either hand rubbed oil, or lacquer finishes. They do custom designs in stained, etched & glue chip glass, specializing in turn-of-the- century and Victorian windows, as well as repair of antique windows. No literature.

• **The Stulb Co.**
618 W. Washington St., POB 297 Dept. OHJ
Norristown, PA 19404
(215) 272-6660
MO DIST
Manufacturers of authentic 18th and 19th century paint colors for furniture, walls, woodwork — interior and exterior. Oil-based, lead-free, water-based buttermilk reproduction colors. Also, polyurethane paste stain and clear paste varnish, for use inside or outside. Exclusive maker of Old Sturbridge Village colors. Send $1 for color cards and literature.

Sturbridge Yankee Workshop
Blueberry Road Dept. OHJ
Westbrook, ME 04096
(800) 343-1144
MO RS/O
For over 33 years, a source of traditional American home furnishings, gifts and decorative accessories. Catalog features over 1,000 items including Traditional, Country, Colonial, and Victorian decorating styles. Cast-aluminum house plaques also available. All price ranges. Send $2. for catalog.

• **Sun Designs**
PO Box 206 Dept. OHJ
Delafield, WI 53018
(414) 567-4255
MO DIST RS/O
Design books for a variety of structures. Includes Gazebos & other garden structures — 55 gazebo designs, 13 strombellas, 7 arbors, & 18 bird feeders. Outhouse: 25 designs (can be converted to sauna, playhouse, garden shed, etc.) — $7.95. Bridges and Cupolas, $7.95. Construction plans available for all designs. All PPD. Backyard structures has 65 designs for all kinds of storage. Full color, $8.95. Free literature.

Sunburst Stained Glass Co.
20 W. Jennings Dept. OHJ
Newburgh, IN 47630
(812) 853-0460
MO RS/O
Design, construction, restoration, and repair of stained, etched, and bevelled glass windows. Also dimensional sandblasting. Will travel for on-site work when appropriate. Services range from complete releading to minor repair to creating a new-old window. Cabinet doors, custom wood doors, and entries with bevelled, etched, or stained glass. Brochure, $2.50.

Sundance Studios
418 Walnut St. Dept. OHJ
Waterloo, IA 50703
(319) 232-0801
MO
Sundance Studios is an art gallery and frame shop housed in a turn-of-the-century Queen Anne, specializing in fine art reproductions suitable for historically decorated rooms. Our "Masterpiece Collection" includes 1,000 masterpieces from the world's great Galleries reproduced on canvas and overpainted to duplicate the look and feel of originals. Framed in antique style mouldings. Canvas alone, or catalog, $3.

Sunflake/Restoration Millwork
17 Mill Street Dept. OHJ
Bayfield, CO 81122
(303) 884-9546
MO
Sunflake is the sole manufacturer of the R-18 window with built-in sliding shutters. In addition to this, Sunflake produces copies of periods window using the latest in insulated glass and window hardware. Free catalog.

Sunflower Glass Studio
PO Box 99 Dept. OHJ
Sergeantsville, NJ 08557
(609) 397-8188
MO RS/O
This studio makes leaded and stained glass and other decorative interior supplies. Call for more information.

• **Sunrise Specialty Co., Inc.**
2204 San Pablo Ave. Dept. COHJ
Berkeley, CA 94702
(415) 845-4751
MO DIST RS/O
Supplier of complete selection of bath fixtures and faucets for the older house. Specializes in brass and china shower systems for claw foot tubs. Also oak and brass toilet-tanks, both pull chain and low-tank types, china pedestal sinks, claw foot tub, oak toilet seats. Color catalog and price list, $3.

Sunshine Architectural Woodworks
Rt. 2, Box 434 Dept. O
Fayetteville, AR 72703
(501) 521-4329
MO
Solid-hardwood, raised-panel, fireplace mantels, interior shutters, wainscotting, wall panels, trim mouldings. Stock sizes and custom-made. Detailed color catalog, $4.

• **Superior Clay Corporation**
P.O. Box 352 Dept. OHJ
Uhrichsville, OH 44683
(800) 848-6166
MO RS/O DIST
Manufacturers of clay flue linings and clay chimney tops. The clay chimney tops come in various sizes & styles. In Ohio, phone (800) 282-6103. Free brochure.

• **Supradur Mfg. Corp.**
PO Box 908 Dept. OHJ
Rye, NY 10580
(800) 223-1948
DIST
Manufacturer of mineral-fiber (asbestos-cement) roofing shingles: an acceptable substitute for slate when replacement becomes necessary. Supra-Slate line closely approximates color and size of real quarry slate. Also available — Dutch Lap, Twin Lap, American Traditional, Western Shake and Hexagonal shingles appropriate for early 20th century houses. Also offers Tegusol, an "S" style clay tile which is economical, double-interlocking, and freeze-thaw resistant. Free literature.

Sutherland Welles Ltd.
302 E. Pettigrew Dept. OHJ
Durham, NC 27702
(919) 967-1972
RS/O MO DIST
Tung Oil finishing, restoring and maintenance products for wood, concrete, and masonry. Easy-to-use for both exterior and interior surfaces including walls, floors, paneling, cabinets, fine furniture. Custom stain, paint, finish, varnish and maintenance products. Consultation for custom finishing. Send for Tung Oil catalog, $3.

Swan Brass Beds
1955 East 16th Street Dept. OHJ
Los Angeles, CA 90021
(800) 421-0141
DIST
Solid brass beds, etageres, wrought iron baker racks, solid brass desks, planters, coat trees. Many other reproductions including 19th century wood carousel horses. Through retail outlets only. No literature but to find nearest distributor, call toll-free number.

• **Swan Wood**
1513 Golden Gate Ave. Dept. OHJ
San Francisco, CA 94115
(415) 567-3263
MO
Manufacturers of a hand-crafted, solid oak Victorian medicine cabinet with a mirrored door, adjustable glass shelves, and gingerbread-style decoration. 26-1/2 x 17-1/2 x 7-1/2. $185, 6% tax added in Calif. Corner cabinets available, as are custom orders.

Sweet William House
P. O. Box 230 Dept. OHJ
Lake Forest, IL 60045
(312) 234-8767
MO
Manufacturers of bronze historic markers indicating the name and date of your house. They also manufacture a bronze plaque with a poem about old houses. Free flyer with SASE.

• **M. Swift & Sons, Inc.**
10 Love Lane, PO Box 150 Dept. OHJ
Hartford, CT 06141
(203) 522-1181
MO RS/O DIST
A primary supplier of gold leaf, roll gold, silver and palladium leaf. Also composition and aluminum leaf. How-to booklet, free.

Swiss Foundry, Inc.
518 S. Gilmor St. Dept. OHJ
Baltimore, MD 21223
(301) 233-2001
MO RS/O
Custom ornamental and decorative castings. Replication of original antique castings for restoration of historic buildings including gates, porches, fences, railings, statues. Also custom-made newly designed castings.

T

TAG Architect & Laurence Carpentry
226 88th St. Dept. OHJ
Brooklyn, NY 11209
(718) 748-4934
RS/O
Architectural and interior design and construction. Specializing in all phases of restoration and adaptive re-use, from design to construction. Serves New York metropolitan area, including northern New Jersey and southern Connecticut. No literature.

TALAS
213 West 35th Street Dept. OHJ
New York, NY 10001
(212) 736-7744
MO RS/O
Company sells supplies to art restorers. Several products are of special interest to those restoring old houses: textile cleaner; Wishab and Absorene wallpaper cleaners; Vulpex liquid soap for cleaning stone and marble. Catalog, $5.00 — please call or write for specifics and prices.

Tennessee Fabricating Co.
1822 Latham Dept. OHJ
Memphis, TN 38106
(901) 948-3354
DIST
Supplier of full line of aluminum and iron ornamental castings. Reproductions of lawn furniture, fountains, urns, planters. Will reproduce customer's designs or create new designs. Booklet of patio furniture and ornamental accessories $1.00. Full catalog of architectural ornamental metal-work $3.

Tennessee Tub Inc. & Tubliner Co.
6682 Charlotte Pk. Dept. OHJ
Nashville, TN 37209
(615) 352-1939
MO RS/O
Antique claw foot tubs and pedestal wash basins dating from 1880s sold and completely restored. Reproduction pull-chain toilets and a Victorian china basin are also available. Brochure $.50. Complimentary brass fittings and accessories to complete bath. 40-page color catalog $2.50. Broadway Collection $1.50. Will ship.

Terra Cotta Productions, Inc.
PO Box 99781 · Dept. OHJ
Pittsburgh, PA 15233
(412) 321-2109
DIST RS/O
Manufacturers and supplier of architectural terra cotta, chimney tops, wall coping, flue liners, and various custom clay products such as tile fireplace fronts, house numbers, signage, and decorative tile inserts. Free color flyer.

Terra Designs, Inc.
19 Market St. Dept. OHJ
Morristown, NJ 07960
(201) 267-2200
DIST RS/O
Hand-moulded, hand-painted ceramic tiles with country charm. Designs include reproductions of antique buttermolds, garden flowers, gamebirds, seashells & custom work. Old-world tiles available in pastels, earthtones, delft blue and traditional colors. These tiles can be used for kitchen backsplashes and counters and fireplace treatments. Catalog, $2.

George J. Thaler, Inc.
1300 E. Madison Street Dept. OHJ
Baltimore, MD 21205
(301) 276-4659
MO RS/O
This company primarily offers replacement parts for stoves from Maryland and Pennsylvania manufacturers since 1860. Write or call for details.

Thermocrete Chimney Systems, Inc.
7111 Ohms Lane Dept. OHJ
Minneapolis, MN 55432
(800) 328-6347
DIST
Thermocrete installs cast-in-place chimney lining through franchised dealers. Seamless one-piece masonry liner can reline old and damaged chimneys with no major construction required. Seals and insulates flues. Reduces risk of chimney fire. Contact for free brochure, nearest dealer, and free estimate.

Thompson & Anderson, Inc.
53 Seavey Street Dept. OHJ
Westbrook, ME 04092
(207) 854-2905
RS/O MO DIST
Complete line of stove pipe, including insulated chimney adapters. Spot-welded seam construction, heat-proof finish. Supplies insulated pipe and fittings. General sheetmetal work. Illustrated literature and price list, free.

Tiffany Design Lamps
2375 E. Tropicana Ave., Ste 43 Dept. OHJ
Las Vegas, NV 89119
(702) 369-0179
DIST RS/O
They'll custom design a Tiffany-style lamp in any color combination you request. More than 90 different basic patterns. Catalog, $2.

• See Advertisers' Index on page 22 for more details.

Timberpeg, East Inc.
Box 1500 Dept. OHJ
Claremont, NH 03603
(603) 542-7762
RS/O DIST
Post-and-beam homes with traditional designs and contemporary open spaces, cathedral ceilings, and greenhouses. The mortise-and-tenon pegged frame is accented with natural wood finishes. Fully insulated. Solar series models also. They also make a Victorian house kit — $36,409 shipped to your site, with all ports and plans needed. Plans only $105 plus $4 postage. Portfolio — $10.

The Tin Bin
20 Valley Rd. Dept. OHJ
Neffsville, PA 17601
(717) 569-6210
MO RS/O
Various stock Early American lighting fixtures in tin, copper, and brass. Various finishes but no custom work available. Chandeliers, lanterns, sconces (electrified and non-electrified). Also electrified brass candlesticks, snuffers, other accessories. 14-page catalog, $1.

Tioga Mill Outlet
200 S. Hartman St. Dept. OHJ
York, PA 17403
(717) 843-5139
RS/O MO
Drapery and upholstery fabrics including imported Lizere, damasks, tapestry, crewel, linen and cotton. Send $2. with color preferences for swatches and approximate yardage needed.

• Tiresias, Inc.
PO Box 1864 Dept. OHJ
Orangeburg, SC 29116
(803) 534-8478
MO RS/O
This company specializes in remilling old heart pine timbers (from 250-400 years old) into heart pine flooring, v-groove panelling, stair treads, risers, beams, and other assorted heart pine products. Free literature.

Tomahawk Foundry
Rt. 4 Dept. OHJ
Rice Lake, WI 54868
(715) 234-4498
RS/O
This company has 17 years' experience in custom-casting parts for old stoves. Pattern making available. They now do custom casting of architectural features. No literature.

Tomblinson Harburn Assoc. Arch., Eng., & Planners, Inc.
705 Kelso St. Dept. OHJ
Flint, MI 48506
(313) 767-5600
RS/O
An architectural firm involved in restoration and preservation. Among the services offered are: historical research, exterior stabilization, photographic documentation, and measured drawings. Free brochure.

Town & Country Decorative and Functional Metalcraft
Main St. Dept. OHJ
E. Conway, NH 04037
(603) 939-2698
MO DIST RS/O
Decorative and functional period metalcraft in hand-wrought iron and various cast metals. Cookware, iron toys cast from originals, early American style hardware, signs, sundials, 300 different weathervanes. Call or write for free brochure.

Traditional American Concepts
1843 Seminole Tr. Dept. OHJ
Charlottesville, VA 22901
(804) 973-3155
MO
Architectural firm specializing in restoration, adapative renovation, compatible new design, and maintenance -consulting. Reconstruction or new design of period buildings, both residential and commercial. Planning surveys and inventories. References and full written proposals available. Catalog of mail-order house plans available, $20.

• Traditional Line Ltd.
35 Hillside Ave. Dept. OHJ
Monsey, NY 10952
(914) 425-6400
MO RS/O
These craftsmen have a commitment to historic preservation and architectural conservation. They specialize in period restorations, architectural conservation, consulting, and furniture restoration. Museum-quality craftsmanship throughout. Offices in Manhattan and Montclair, N.J. More information on request.

• Transylvania Mountain Forge
Graystone Manor 2270 Cross St. Dept. OH-1
La Canada, CA 91011
(818) 248-7878
MO RS/O
A wide variety of hardware including iron and brass window stays, window casement stays and fasteners, door and furniture hardware, and coat hooks. Imported from Europe. Catalog, $1.

• Travis Tuck, Inc. — Metal Sculptor
Box 1832J Dept. OHJ
Martha's Vineyard, MA 02568
(617) 693-3914
RS/O MO
Specializes in full-bodied hollow copper weathervanes, including weathercock, osprey with fish, cod, humpback whale, ram, goose, and styled gold arrow. Gold leaf available. Also copper lantern styled after New York City post-civil war street lantern. Custom work invited. Color brochure, $1.

• Tremont Nail Company
P.O. Box 111 Dept. OHJC7
Wareham, MA 02571
(617) 295-0038
RS/O MO DIST
In business since 1819, this company manufactures old-fashioned cut nails that are useful for restoration work. These decorative antique nails include Wrought Head, Hinge, Rose Head Clinch and Common; also the DECOR-NAIL® and many others. A sample card with 20 patterns of actual cut nails attached, history and complete ordering information is available for $3.75 ppd. Free brochure and price list.

KEY TO ABBREVIATIONS

MO	sells by Mail Order
RS/O	sells through Retail Store or Office
DIST	sells through Distributors
ID	sells only through Interior Designers or Archtects

TrimbleHouse Corporation
4658 Old Peachtree Rd. Dept. OHJ
Norcross, GA 30071
(800) 241-4317
DIST
Manufacturer of high quality, cast-aluminum ornamental posts for use with TrimbleHouse traditional, Colonial, Victorian, and Contemporary luminaires. These authentically-styled lights are available in a wide choice of light sources, from natural gas to incandescent to high intensity discharge (H.I.D.), the most energy efficient.

Tromploy Inc.
400 Lafayette St. Dept. OHJ
New York, NY 10003
(212) 420-1639
RS/O
Trompe l'oeil, murals, faux bois and faux marbre, all types of decorative painting. Will do work on canvas that can be removed from walls if necessary. $5 for press kit with photos; free information sheet.

Trow & Holden Co.
P.O. Box 475 Dept. OHJ
Barre, VT 05641
(800) 451-4349
MO DIST RS/O
Manufacturers of a complete line of stoneworking and masonry tools including pneumatic carving hammers, pneumatic drills, carbide tipped hand tools, and stone splitting tools. Also specialty tools for repointing/ restoring old masonry. Free catalog and price list available upon request.

Troyer, Le Roy and Associates
415 Lincolnway East Dept. OHJ
Mishawaka, IN 46544
(219) 259-9976
RS/O
Serves Indiana, Illinois, Ohio, and southern Michigan area with architectural restoration services. National register applications. Information on previous restoration projects available on request.

Turn-of-the-Century Lighting
118 Sherbourne St. Dept. OHJ
Toronto, Canada M5A2R2
(416) 362-6203
RS/O
Specialize in quality vintage lighting, circa 1850—1920, suitable for both residential and commercial application. Will also restore. No literature.

Turnbull's Lumber Company
1379 Klees Rd., NW Dept. OHJ
Stanton, MI 48888
(517) 831-4876
MO RS/O
Specialize in quality, kiln-dried hardwoods at wholesale prices. Also supply Shaker pegs, spindles, candle cups, etc. Brochure and hardwood price list, $.50.

Turtle Lake Telephone Co.
Dept. OHJ
Turtle Lake, WI 54889
(715) 986-2233
MO RS/O
This company sells antique telephones including hand-crank phones and iron phones, as well as rare telephone parts. Catalog $1.

U

USG Corporation
101 South Wacker Drive Dept. OHJ
Chicago, IL 60606
(312) 321-3863
DIST
Products produced by this major construction products company include plaster and plaster patching materials, textured paints, gypsum, dry wall, waterproofing paints, ceiling tiles and panels and thermal entry doors in classical styles. Also shower & bathtub doors, ceramic tile cement backer board, wood stove backer board. Free literature.

Union Metal Corp.
1022-9th St. SW Dept. OHJ
Canton, OH 44707
(216) 456-7653
MO DIST RS/O
Period lighting poles and luminaires; the company has been making lampposts and fixtures since 1906, and uses the same designs as it introduced in the '10s and '20s. Color brochure, "Nostalgia Lighting Series," free.

United Ceramic Tile Arch. Design Div.
156 Fifth Ave., Ste. 1002 Dept. OHJ
New York, NY 10003
(212) 691-3600
DIST RS/O
Various tiles in ceramic, slate, and granite; marble in easily applied tile form. Also, (516) 582-3300. Free literature; specify interest.

United Gilsonite Laboratories
Box 70 Dept. OHJ
Scranton, PA 18501
(717) 344-1202
DIST
UGL manufactures a complete line of products for home repair and maintenance, including ZAR "Rain Stain" for exterior surfaces, ZAR Clear Finishes and Stains, DRYLOK masonry treatment products, Temproof Stove & Fireplace maintenance and repair products, caulks and sealants, paint and varnish removers, among others. Free descriptive literature. Three booklets SASE for each — "The Finishing Touch", a beginners guide to wood finishing. "How to Waterproof Masonry Walls," and "Tips on Texturing."

• **United House Wrecking Corp.**
328 Selleck Street Dept. OHJ
Stamford, CT 06902
(203) 348-5371
RS/O
Six acres of antique, salvage and reproduction architectural artifacts and treasures. Stained and bevelled glass, fancy doors and windows, marble and wood mantels, French doors, panelling, ironwork, Victorian gingerbread, plumbing fixtures, fencing, lighting fixtures. Also butcher block, baker's racks, marine and subway salvage, farm items. Plus capitals, gargoyles, keystones, friezes, and ornaments from old buildings. Free illustrated brochure.

United Stairs Corp.
Highway 35 Dept. OHJ
Keyport, NJ 07735
(201) 583-1100
MO RS/O
A complete line of wood staircases, straight, circular & spiral. Available assembled or knocked down. Prefabricated and prefinished wood railing systems. Free brochure.

United States Ceramic Tile Company
10233 Sandyville Rd., S.E. Dept. OHJ
East Sparta, OH 44626
(216) 866-5531
DIST
Glazed and unglazed ceramic tiles for residential or commercial installations in a variety of shapes and colors. Floor and wall tiles. Free literature.

U.S. General Supply Corp.
100 Commercial Street Dept. OHJ
Plainview, NY 11803
(516) 349-7275
MO RS/O
A first-rate mail order source for name-brand tools and hardware at lower prices. Catalog offers traditional tools — everything from drawknives and spokeshaves to mitre boxes and handsaws. Plus modern power tools for saving time. Catalog has over 4,000 items in 179 pages. Fully illustrated — $1. Also (800) 645-7077 for orders.

Universal Clamp Corp.
6905 Cedros Ave. Dept. OHJ
Van Nuys, CA 91405
(818) 780-1015
MO DIST
Manufactures a variety of clamps for repairing and restoring antiques, cabinetmaking and fine woodwork. Produces the popular "805" Porta-Press frame jig for assembly of mitered frames and doors. Also, a salvage pry bar, an electric doweling machine, and a drum sander and lathe duplicator for the shopsmith Mark V. Brochures and prices upon request.

Urban Archaeology
137 Spring St. Dept. OHJ
New York, NY 10012
(212) 431-6969
RS/O
Architectural ornaments and antiques 1880 — 1930. Complete interiors, selected furnishings and fixtures. Carved and cast stonework, stained glass, doors, plumbing, hardware. Bars, soda fountains, barbershops. Also stock reproduction iron spiral staircase. Literature on bars and paneling available. Please come in.

V

Van Cort Instruments, Inc.
PO Box 5049 Dept. OHJ
Holyoke, MA 01041
(413) 533-5995
MO DIST RS/O
This company manufactures reproduction 18th and 19th century telescopes, sundials, compasses, cameras, microscopes, orreries, planespheres, and kaleidoscopes in limited editions for institutions, museums, and private companies. They will also repair and refabricate damaged or lost parts from old instruments, as well as optical work. Catalog, $5.

Vande Hey Raleigh
1665 Bohm Drive Dept. OHJ
Little Chute, WI 54140
(414) 766-1181
MO DIST
Major supplier of traditional architectural rock tile. Four styles available: Rough Shake, Early American Slate, Rivera Style, and Spanish Mission. Will custom color tile for new construction and hard to match restoration projects. Call for details and nearest distributor.

Verine Products & Co.
Goldhanger Dept. OHJ
Maldon, Essex, UK
(0621) 88611
DIST
From U.K. authentic reproductions in fiberglass of original 18th century lead garden tubs and planters, and Georgian mantelpieces, overdoors, Ionic and Doric columns, and porticos. Over 25 years experience. Name & address of U.S. distributor supplied. Specify product interest. Literature — $1 each, $3 for all.

Vermont Castings, Inc.
Prince Street Dept. OHJ
Randolph, VT 05060
(802) 728-3111
RS/O MO
Vermont Castings manufactures quality cast iron wood-burning heaters. Beautiful, classic design, airtight efficiency. Doors that open for fire viewing, convenient top loading, thermostatic control, and a polished griddle for stovetop cooking are standard. Options include a selection of lustrous enamel finishes, a water heater, coal burning models, and a full line of accessories. A size for every heating need: Defiant, Vigilant, Resolute, Intrepid, and Fireplace Insert. Also a cast-iron and wooden wood rack. Illustrated literature and price list, $1.

Vermont Country Store
531 Main St. Dept. OHJ
Weston, VT 05161
(802) 362-2400
MO RS/O
The Vermont Country Store, in the mail order business since 1946, publishes three catalogs a year full of common-sense and useful merchandise, such as natural fiber clothing, bedding and sleepwear, Vermont food products, personal care items, and many old fashioned household products not generally found elsewhere.

Vermont Industries, Inc.
Box 301, Rt. 103 Dept. OHJ
Cuttingsville, VT 05738
(802) 492-3451
MO RS/O
Manufacturers of hand-forged products in the tradition of the country blacksmith. Offering a complete line of fireplace and woodstove tools and accessories. Also, various reproduction kitchen accessories, lighting fixtures, and custom fabrication of functional and ornamental iron products. Catalog is $1.

Vermont Iron
611 Prince St. Dept. OHJ
Waterbury, VT 05676
(802) 244-5254
MO RS/O
Manufacturer of a cast iron and wood bench line. The "Catamount" bench line consists of hardwood slats, class 30 grey cast iron, stainless steel hardware, solid bronze medallions, urethane paint on castings, and clear wood finish on slats. Benches are weather resistant for use indoors or outdoors, for both commercial and residential use. Also available are planters, trash receptacles, and woodstoves. Free literature.

Vermont Marble Co.
61 Main St. Dept. OHJ
Proctor, VT 05765
(802) 459-3311
MO RS/O
Manufacturer of 12-in. x 12-in. marble floor tiles, fireplaces, building veneers, and window sills. Factory direct pricing. Free literature.

Vermont Soapstone Co.
RR 1, Box 514 Dept. OHJ
Perkinsville, VT 05151
(802) 263-5404
MO DIST RS/O
Custom-cut soapstone available for sinks, countertops, stovetops, fireplaces. Also handcrafted griddles, bedwarmers, etc. Brochure and price list — $.50.

• Vermont Structural Slate Co.
P.O. Box 98 Dept. OHJ
Fair Haven, VT 05743
(800) 343-1900
RS/O MO DIST
"Slate Roofs" — a handbook of data on the construction and laying of all types of slate roofs. A 1926 reprint. Send $7.95. Besides roofing, company also fabricates slate flooring, sink tops, etc. Also has brownstone — typically used for replacement balustrades, cap, dentil course and lintels. Non-laminated stone with sufficient range of colors to match in restoration. Fact sheet, available: please specify. In VT, phone (802) 265-4933.

Victorian Accents
661 West Seventh St. Dept. OHJ
Plainfield, NJ 07060
(201) 757-8507
MO
Books of every kind for old-house lovers — architectural details, style guides, scaled drawings, furnishings & interiors, period photos (interiors & fashions), needlework & fancywork, signpainting & gilding, gardening & landscaping. Reproduction Christmas ornaments, decorations & cards. Also (800) 524-2577 outside NJ. Also, a book with some 90 gazebo plans. Free catalog.

• Victorian Collectibles Ltd.
845 E. Glenbrook Rd. Dept. OHJ
Milwaukee, WI 53217
(414) 352-6910
MO DIST
This company sells a large selection of Victorian reproduction wallpaper, c. 1860-1902, called the "Brillion Collection." Also matching Victorian fabrics, ceiling and border papers, plaster mouldings, canvas panels, ceramic tiles, lighting fixtures (Arts & Crafts). 100% wool rugs. Art Nouveau, early Art Deco, Arts & Crafts, and other early 20th-century papers are available. They own over 2,500 antique designs and have a curator and designer on staff. Write for further information. Brochures, $2.

• Victorian Construction Co.
25 E. Church St. Dept. OHJ
Frederick, MD 21701
MO RS/O
Complete Victorian and colonial house plans based on original designs. $12 per portfolio. Also, will research, design, and build Victorian Revival homes to suit in the central Maryland/northern Virginia area. New construction only.

Victorian Glass Works
476 Main Street Dept. OHJ
Ferndale, CA 95536
(707) 786-4237
RS/O
Restorers of antique furniture, complete rebuilding of wood components and all types of caning and rattan work. They also specialize in repairing and restoring most types of antique picture frames. Can frame old photos and prints, reproducing old mat designs. No literature.

• Victorian Glassworks
904 Westminster St., NW Dept. OHJ
Washington, DC 20001
(202) 462-4433
RS/O
A small company specializing in leaded art glass: contemporary, Victorian, Art Deco, and Art Nouveau. Specialists in small commercial jobs, and any size residential. Also restoration of glass panels and lamp shades, custom etching, and gold leaf. Antique windows available. Knowledgeable about specific 19th century styles, such as Aesthetic, Renaissance Revival, Classical Revival. Brochure & photos available; $3.50, refundable; please specify interests.

Victorian Homes
500 Union St, 1047 Logan Bld Dept. OHJ
Seattle, WA 98101
(206) 329-8002
MO DIST
They sell pen and ink prints of West Coast Victorian homes. Prints are 12 in. x 16 in., mat included. They come framed or unframed. Also custom drawings or watercolors from photographs, $75 and up. Distributor, wholesale inquiries welcome. Free literature.

• Victorian Interior Restoration
POB 42311, 1713 E. Carson St. Dept. OHJ
Pittsburgh, PA 15203
(412) 381-1870
MO RS/O
A competitively priced design/contracting firm for historic homes, and small commercial structures. Retail mail-order showroom of decorative amenities for the do-it-yourselfer. Serving the north eastern U.S. Catalog and information on request.

• Victorian Lightcrafters, Ltd.
PO Box 350 Dept. OHJ/86
Slate Hill, NY 10973
(914) 355-1300
MO RS/O
Manufacturers of authentic design, solid brass Victorian and turn-of-the-century lighting fixtures. They are available with a variety of appropriate glass shades. The fixtures are custom made in electric, gas, or combination, and are polished and lacquered. They also sell carbon filament light bulbs. Illustrated catalog, $3, refundable with first order.

• See Advertisers' Index on page 22 for more details.

KEY TO ABBREVIATIONS

MO	sells by Mail Order
RS/O	sells through Retail Store or Office
DIST	sells through Distributors
ID	sells only through Interior Designers or Archtects

• **Victorian Lighting Co.**
PO Box 579 Dept. OHJ
Minneapolis, MN 55440
(612) 338-3636
MO DIST RS/O
Manufacturers of quality solid brass period lighting, reproduced using 19th-century techniques and original manufacturers' designs. Styles are from late 1880s to 1920s. Many of the designs offered are unique; all have excellent visual continuity and design balance. This company has supplied fixtures nationwide to many historic restorations, commercial and residential. Fixtures are U.L. listed. Catalog No. 3, $4. Foldout lighting poster, $1.50. Office hours Mon. - Fri. 10 am to 3 pm.

• **Victorian Lighting Works, Inc.**
Box 469, 251 S Pennsyl. Ave. Dept. OHJ
Centre Hall, PA 16828
(814) 364-9577
MO DIST RS/O
Authentic, handcrafted reproductions of Victorian and turn-of-the-century electric and gas-style chandeliers and wall brackets. Fixtures are crafted in solid brass and available with a variety of shades. UL listed—send $3 for complete catalog. Will also restore antique fixtures.

Victorian Reproductions Enterprises, Inc.
1601 Park Ave., South Dept. OHJ
Minneapolis, MN 55404
(612) 338-3636
MO RS/O
Suppliers of reproduction products for residential, commercial, restaurant projects. Glass or cloth lamp shades, foiled Tiffany-style shades & lighting parts. Hand-carved solid mahogany furniture, marble top tables, solid brass hardware, brass bathroom accessories, & custom duplication of original hardware. Lightning rods/weathervanes, stamped metal ceilings, chimney pots. Catalog, edit. 3: Lighting, $4; Catalog, edit. 2: Furniture, etc., $3. Lighting brochure, $1.50.

• **Victorian Warehouse**
190 Grace St. Dept. OHJ
Auburn, CA 95603
(916) 823-0374
MO
Their mail-order catalog contains some 150 items for restoring a mid-to-late 19th-century house: screen doors, parlor stoves, lighting, doors, stained glass millwork, tin ceilings, bath fixtures and fittings, moulding, custom window shades. 24-page illustrated catalog with price list: $2.50.

Village Antique Lighting Co.
847 Ionia NW Dept. OHJ
Grand Rapids, MI 49503
MO RS/O
Stock and custom fixtures in solid brass; also restoration of antique fixtures. Free literature.

• **Vintage Lumber Co.**
9507 Woodsboro Rd. Dept. OHJ
Frederick, MD 21701
(301) 898-7859
RS/O MO
Specialists in antique lumber reclaimed from vintage structures. They re-mill southern longleaf heart pine, American chestnut, oak, poplar, fir, and white pine from old boards and beams, and mill new random-width and wide board oak, white pine, poplar, cherry, and walnut into flooring, paneling, and mouldings. They also handle hand-hewn, old sawn, or re-sawn antique beams for structural or decorative applications. Free brochure.

• **Vintage Plumbing Specialties**
17800 Minnehaha St. Dept. OHJ
Granada Hills, CA 91344
(818) 368-1040
MO RS/O
Firm has been dealing in fancy circa 1900 bathroom fixtures, i.e., toilets, showers, pedestal lavs, unusual claw foot tubs, foot and sitz baths for ten years. Also accessories. Most items restored, but some in original condition. Faucets & handles not sold separately. Lots of free advice and reference info. Will restore old fixtures. Free flyer.

Vintage Storm Window Co.
6755 8th NW Dept. OHJ
Seattle, WA 98117
(206) 782-5656
RS/O
Storm windows, made with 1-3/8 in. clearfir, custom fitted, sealed, & installed creating a double window system. Traditionally handcrafted with careful attention to the architectural detail and scale of the original window treatment. Double hung, fixed and casement replacement sash also available. They can also repair or replace zinc casement windows; will cut window glass to size. Phone or write for details.

• **Vintage Tub & Sink Restoration Service**
701 Center St. Dept. OHJ
Ludlow, MA 01056
(413) 589-0769
MO RS/O
They restore old tubs and pedestal sinks and sell restored bathroom fixtures. Brochure, $2.

Vintage Valances
Box 635J Dept. OHJ
Whitmore Lake, MI 48189
(313) 878-6670
MO
Custom-made Greek Revival, Victorian, and early 20th-century soft drapery valances designed and cut historically correct. Custom by-mail service, with catalog and fabric swatches, $12.

• **Vintage Wood Works**
513 S. Adams Dept. OHJ/645
Fredericksburg, TX 78624
(512) 997-9513
MO RS/O
Produces a line of authentic Victorian gingerbread for interior and exterior use. Brackets, running trims, fret work, fans, gable treatments, porch posts, spindles, & railings, signs, and gazebos are stocked in inventory for prompt shipment. Quotes are given for variations on standard designs, as well as for custom designs. All work is shop sanded, ready for paint or stain. Illustrated catalog, $2.

Virginia Metalcrafters
1010 East Main St. Dept. OHJ
Waynesboro, VA 22980
(703) 949-8205
DIST
Cast brass rimlock and hinge reproductions approved and licensed by the Colonial Williamsburg Foundation. These are authentic replicas of locks, hinges, and trim found in the original Colonial buildings at Williamsburg, VA. Modern lock cylinders available for exterior doors. Brochure, $3.

• See Advertisers' Index on page 22 for more details.

Visible Glass
2303 Kennedy St., NE Dept. OHJ
Minneapolis, MN 55413
(612) 378-1162
MO
Visible Glass offers a complete line of custom glass services, including high-fired glass enameled works, bent glass, high-detail sandblasted etched glass, along with duplication services for most glass processes and pieces. Free information sheet with prices.

Vixen Hill Manufacturing
R D 2 Dept. OHJ
Phoenixville, PA 19460
(215) 286-0909
MO RS/O
Prefabricated Victorian-style gazebos in Western red cedar. Free brochure. 16-page catalog, $2.

Vulpiani
8 Bridge St. Dept. OHJ
Florida, NY 10921
(914) 651-7331
MO
Designers and builders of early 20th-century-style furniture, (Stickley, Wright, Hoffman, Mackintosh, and Greene and Greene), this company's services include furniture replication, metal and glass inlay work, custom hardware, fine finishing, and colored lacquer. They also provide consultation, renderings, and original design motifs for walls, rugs, floors, and glass. Color brochure, $2.

W

WSI Distributors/ The Brass Tree
PO Box 1235 Dept. OHJ
St. Charles, MO 63302
(314) 946-5811
MO RS/O
Brass hardware including door, furniture, Hoosier, ice box, desk, and trunk hardware. Wood & porcelain casters, furniture locks, fiber and wood chair seats, caning and weaving supplies, wood veneer, and wood ornaments. Catalog — $2. They sell retail through The Brass Tree, 308 N. Main St., St. Charles, MO 63301. (314) 723-1041.

R. Wagner Co. Painted Finishes
714 NW 24th Dept. OHJ
Portland, OR 97210
(503) 626-4360
RS/O
Wallglazing, marbleizing, trompe l'oeil, graining, stencilling, painted finish design, and consulting. Also custom floorcloths. No literature.

• **Wagner, Albert J., & Son**
3762 N. Clark Street Dept. OHJ
Chicago, IL 60613
(312) 935-1414
RS/O
Established in 1894. Architectural sheet metal contractor working in ferrous and copper metals: cornice mold; inlaid cornice mold gutter; facade; and hip and ridge cap. Fabrication and installation of metal and glass gable end and hip style skylights. Specialty roofing (slate, tile). Will travel. Call for appointment. No literature.

Walbrook Mill & Lumber Co., Inc.
2636 W. North Ave. Dept. OHJ
Baltimore, MD 21216
(301) 462-2200
RS/O
A 65 year old family owned company. A complete mill — will reproduce anything made of wood — sashes, doors, mouldings, curved wood members, carved items, lathe turned items. Active in the restoration & renovation of homes and old commercial buildings. No literature.

• **Walker Mercantile Company**
P.O. Box 129 Dept. OHJ
Bellevue, TN 37221
(615) 646-5084
MO
Full line of old-style bathroom fixtures, includes 7 styles of pull-chain toilets (19th century railroad-station lettered type to carved throne). Solid brass & copper vanity bowls and kitchen sinks. Solid copper bathtubs with brass clawfeet and wooden rims. All-china fluted Victorian pedestal sink with oval basin & brass faucets. Color catalog $5.80 includes postage. Also, (800) 645- 3213 USA Watts; (800) 325-5037 Tenn. instate Watts.

Walker's
PO Box 309 Dept. OHJ
Tallmadge, OH 44278
(216) 633-1081
MO RS/O
Dismantled barns, log cabins, and homes; hand-hewn beams, weathered barn siding, old flooring, doors. Beams, approx. $4 per foot; barn siding begins at $1 per foot. Buildings come with drawings; will replace missing parts and assist in rebuilding. Free brochure.

• **Wallace & Hinz**
1065 K St. Dept. OHJ
Arcata, CA 95521
(707) 826-1729
MO RS/O
Makers of bar components: raised panels in various shapes, rails, columns (classical, rococo, Victorian), corbels; free illustrated brochure includes building instructions.

Wallin Forge
Route 1, Box 65 Dept. OHJ
Sparta, KY 41086
(606) 567-7201
RS/O MO
Makes a wide range of custom handforged iron door hardware, boot scrapers, fireplace equipment, lighting fixtures, kitchen utensils, etc. Custom only. No literature.

• **Jack Wallis' Doors**
Rt. 1, Box 22A Dept. OHJ
Murray, KY 42071
(502) 489-2613
MO DIST RS/O
A large selection of handcrafted wood doors, with stained, etched, or bevelled glass inserts. Will also custom build any type door or glass. Also offer carved components and will custom make carvings in quantities. Color catalog, $3. Dealer inquiries welcome.

Walpole Woodworkers
767 East St. Dept. OHJ
Walpole, MA 02081
(800) 343-6948
MO
They manufacture cedar rustic furniture, sold in easy-to-assemble kits. Some wicker pieces also. Color catalog, $1. In MA, HI, or AK phone (617) 668-2800.

Walsh Screen Products
24 East Third St. Dept. OHJ
Mount Vernon, NY 10550
(914) 668-7811
MO RS/O
Interior, rolled screens custom-made to fit almost any window. Ideal for casement windows. Free information.

Walton Stained Glass
209 Railway Dept. OHJ
Campbell, CA 95008
(408) 866-0533
RS/O
Stained glass artisans; specialists in traditional, bevelled windows. No literature.

Warwick Refinishers
PO Box 35 Dept. OHJ
Warwick, NY 10990
(914) 342-1200
RS/O
Architectural woodwork refinishing; 14-year-old company with staff of 20. Works primarily on churches, museums, offices, and brownstones with advanced equipment. Operates on East Coast and as far west as Chicago. Free brochures.

Washburne, E.G. & Co., Inc.
88 Andover St., Rte. 114 Dept. OHJ
Danvers, MA 01923
(617) 774-3645
MO RS/O
Founded in 1853, they still make copper weathervanes, lanterns, and flag pole balls and ornaments on the original moulds. Large flag and fireplace shop. Free brochure.

• **Washington Copper Works**
South St. Dept. OHJ
Washington, CT 06793
(203) 868-7527
RS/O MO
Hand-fabricated lighting fixtures in styles compatible with the 18th and 19th centuries. Copper post lights, wall lanterns for indoors, outdoors, and entryways. Chandeliers, candelabras, weatherproof kerosene lanterns, and an unusual selection of candle lanterns. Each original piece is hand-wrought, initialed and dated. U-L approved. 52-page illustrated catalog, price list, and area map included. $3, refundable with an order.

Washington House Reproductions
PO Box 246 Dept. OHJ
Washington, VA 22747
(703) 675-3385
MO DIST RS/O
Manufacturers of Eldred Reproduction Lighting (many very reasonbly priced), particularly gas, in solid brass. Will also restore old fixtures — rebuild, clean, strip nickel plating, convert to electricity, and replace missing parts. Custom fixtures a specialty. Residential, commercial, & museum work. Personalized attention given to customers' individual needs.

Washington Stove Works
P.O. Box 687 Dept. OHJ
Everett, WA 98206
(206) 252-2148
DIST RS/O
Manufacturers of heaters and stoves since 1875: cast-iron heaters, wood and coal cook ranges, fireplace inserts, and freestanding pedestal models. Various doors available: hand-etched glass, solid brass, or basic black with glass. Free literature.

• **Watercolors, Inc.**
Dept. OHJ
Garrison on Hudson, NY 10524
(914) 424-3327
MO DIST
Exclusive importer of authentic English and French Edwardian bathroom fixtures and other traditional faucet and accessory designs. Complete fittings for U.S. specifications. Washbasin sets, bathtub/shower sets, and bidet sets in chrome, brass, gold and enamel finishes. Complete catalog available through the trade or to public for $1.

Wayne Towle Inc.
3 Parker Hill Terr. Dept. OHJ
Boston, MA 02120
(617) 738-9121
RS/O
Architectural wood stripping and refinishing services, including fine period detailing. Historic finishes a specialty. Free flyer.

Weathervanes
Box 132J Dept. OHJ
Norwell, MA 02061
(617) 659-4646
MO
Handmade copper weathervanes using traditional methods. Each weathervane is silver soldered together for strength. Steel weathervanes are two dimensional and painted with durable enamel. Both types are designed for outdoor use or interior decorating. Custom designs are a specialty. Brochure and price list, $.50.

J.P. Weaver Co.
2301 W. Victory Blvd. Dept. OHJ
Burbank, CA 91506
(818) 841-5700
RS/O MO
Manufacturers of composition ornaments since 1914. Over 6,500 ornaments for architectural interiors, woodwork, furniture, frames, etc., made from the original European formula. Flexible (will fit a radius or OG moulding) and self-bonding, these ornaments are historically authentic. Completed jobs include Sacramento State Capitol restoration in California. Custom designing and installation services, also seminars in installation. Literature and catalog information, $3.

• **Weaver, W. T. & Sons, Inc.**
1208 Wisconsin Ave., N.W. Dept. OHJ
Washington, DC 20007
(202) 333-4200
RS/O MO
Firm has been selling decorative hardware and building supplies since 1889. Stock includes porcelain and brass furniture hardware, knobs, rim locks, front door hardware, shutter hardware, full line of solid brass switchplates, lavatory bowls, sconces, hooks, and decorative ornaments and ceiling medallions (styrene). Literature on ceiling pieces is free.

KEY TO ABBREVIATIONS

MO	sells by Mail Order
RS/O	sells through Retail Store or Office
DIST	sells through Distributors
ID	sells only through Interior Designers or Archtects

Weavers Unlimited
PO Box 99 Dept. OHJ
Mount Vernon, WA 98273
(206) 757-0064
MO DIST RS/O
Country handwoven rag rugs and placemats give warmth and color to your home or office. All cotton or wool, machine washable. Choice of predominant colors or shades of blue, brown, red, pink, orange, green, or gray. Custom weaving available. Will match wallpaper abd paint samples. Satisfaction guaranteed. Send for brochure: $.75.

Weird Wood
Box 190-OH Dept. OHJ
Chester, VT 05143
(802) 875-3535
RS/O MO
Company specializes in rare and unusual woods. Twenty or so varieties on hand, including butternut, rosewood. Also thick slabs, burls, carving pieces. They sell clock movements and wood finishing products too. Catalog $.50.

Welles Fireplace Company
287 East Houston St. Dept. OHJ
New York, NY 10002
(212) 777-5440
RS/O
They service fireplaces in the metropolitan New York area. Mantels installed; chimneys repaired, cleaned and relined; gas and coal fireplaces converted to woodburning; diagnosis of fireplace smoking problems; fireplace and chimney design; and construction of new fireplaces and chimneys. On-site consultation, $50.00. Flyer on request.

Wendall's Wood Stoves
19964 Inks Dr. Dept. OHJ
Tuolumne, CA 95379
(209) 928-4508
MO RS/O
Restored kitchen ranges and parlor stoves, 1880-1930, in a variety of sizes and styles. Also restoration. Shipping available. Flyer on request.

• **Otto Wendt & Co.**
217 Main Dept. OHJ
Spring, TX 77373
(713) 288-8295
MO RS/O
Cast-aluminum products for commercial and residential projects: Street lights, park benches, fountains, mail boxes, patio sets, urns, and plant stands. Period designs from Federal to Victorian are available.

• **Wes-Pine Wood Windows**
PO Box 1157 Dept. OHJ
West Hanover, MA 02339
(617) 878-2102
MO DIST
"Self-storing" storm windows made of Ponderosa pine and replacement sash — for double-hung windows. True divided lights or insulating glass. Their "Yankee Spirit" window features low-e glass and colonial-style divided lights. Custom and stock sizes. Free brochure.

Westal Contracting
20 Madison Avenue Dept. OHJ
Valhalla, NY 10595
(914) 948-3450
RS/O
Excellent roofing company specializing in architectural copper work, slate roofs, etc. — everything but asphalt shingles. Westchester, Rockland, and NYC area. No literature.

Western Reserve Antique Furniture Kit
Box 206A Dept. OHJ
Bath, OH 44210
MO DIST
Reproductions of Shaker, New England, and Pennsylvania Dutch furniture and house accessories are available in either kit or assembled and finished form. A newly expanded line is pictured and fully described in the brochure about Western Reserve New 'Connecti-Kit". Special order items can be built for customers needing something not in regular catalog. Cost of the brochure is $1.

Westlake Architectural Antiques
3315 Westlake Drive Dept. OHJ
Austin, TX 78746
(512) 327-1110
RS/O MO
Architectural antiques, American, and European stained glass panels. Also bevelled, leaded, glass doors, sidelights, wood doors, wood & marble mantels. Returnable 200-page Xerox color brochure — $5, postage charge.

Whit Hanks at Treaty Oak
1009 W. 6th St. Dept. OHJ
Austin, TX 78703
(512) 478-2101
RS/O
Architectural antiques: Doors, entryways, fireplaces, bevelled, etched, and stained glass, ironwork, panelling and panelled rooms, flooring, and garden furnishings. European architectural and decorative items. No literature.

• **Whitco — Vincent Whitney Co.**
PO Box 335 Dept. OHJ
Sausalito, CA 94966
(415) 332-3260
MO DIST
Firm specializes in residential and commercial hand-operated dumbwaiters with lifting capacities from 65-500 lbs. Firm also manufacturers hardware for wood sash windows. Clerestory operators for awning and casement windows available in hand-operated and electric models. Product literature and price lists can be provided at no charge. Staff on hand for consultation to builders, distributors, designers, architects and homeowners.

Whittemore-Durgin Glass Co.
Box 20650H Dept. OHJ
Hanover, MA 02339
(617) 871-1790
RS/O MO
Everything for the stained glass craftsman presented in an illustrated catalog that is unusually helpful, and amusing. Also "Baroques" — pieces of stained glass onto which designs in black ceramic paint are fused. Can be used to create panels, or as replacements in windows. Antique-type window glass. Two retail stores: Rockland, MA; E. Lyme CT. Catalog, $1.

Whitten Enterprises, Inc.
PO Box 1121 Dept. OHJ
Bennington, VT 05201
(802) 442-8344
MO
Manufacturers of iron spiral staircases and ships' ladders. Also available as kits. Iron or wood treads; interior & exterior applications. Design is elegant, simple and contemporary. Staircase planning guide, $1.

The Wicker Garden
1318 Madison Ave. Dept. OHJ
New York, NY 10128
(212) 410-7000
RS/O
Sell elaborate Victorian and 20th-century wicker furniture and original (old) brass and iron beds. Catalog with in-stock, one-of-a-kind items illustrated, $5.

Wiebold Art Conservation Lab.
413 Terrace Place Dept. OHJ
Terrace Park, OH 45174
(513) 831-2541
MO RS/O
An art and antique restoration laboratory with 40 years experience and 12 technicians. Specialize in invisible restorations of oil painting, miniatures on ivory, porcelain, pottery, china, glass assembly and chip grinding, all types of metals. World wide service. Inquiries welcome. Free literature.

Wigen Restorations
R.D. No. 1, Box 281 Dept. OHJ
Cobleskill, NY 12043
(518) 234-7946
MO RS/O
Will dismantle and move any house or barn. Dutch and New England barn frames available - will move to your location. Also small house frames, floor boards, old pine boards, weathered siding, mantels, hand-hewn beams, etc. Free flyer.

Wiggins Brothers
Hale Road, Box 420 Dept. OHJ
Tilton, NH 03276
(603) 286-3046
RS/O
Itinerant artists. Period interiors, painted and stencilled; murals and marbleizing — anything to do with paint. 15 years experience, second generation in antique business. Specialize in traditional interior folk painting. Also quality restorations of existing designs. They prefer to be contacted by telephone or in person.

Wikco Industries
Rt. 2, Box 154 Dept. OHJ
Broken Bow, NE 68822
(308) 872-5327
MO
Manufacturers of a wrought-iron park bench, an exact copy of a turn-of-the-century model. Various lengths and colors are available. Shipped fully assembled; can be ordered on approval. Free brochure.

Wikkmann House
18728-3 Bryant Dept. OHJ
Northridge, CA 91324
(818) 780-1015
MO
Home renovator and wood craftsman tools. Also a line of woodworking clamps, frame and door jigs. Of special interest is their pry bar — a tool to aid in structural dismantling without destroying timbers. Evenings — (818) 349-5148. Pry bar info free. Catalog package, $1.

Frederick Wilbur, Carver
PO Box 425 Dept. OHJ
Lovingston, VA 22949
(804) 263-4827
MO RS/O
Specialize in architectural hand carving and shaping. Most work is commissioned by architects, interior decorators, and designers, but will consider any carving from individuals. Also carved signs. Free brochure.

Lt. Moses Willard, Inc.
1156 U.S. 50 Dept. OHJ
Milford, OH 45150
(513) 831-8956
MO DIST RS/O
An array of folk art creations, plus Early American, 18th century and Colonial lighting. Chandeliers, lanterns, sconces, candleholders and lamps. 40-page catalog available: $2.

Willet Stained Glass Studio, Inc.
10 East Moreland Avenue Dept. OHJ
Philadelphia, PA 19118
(215) 247-5721
MO RS/O
One of the oldest glass studios in America. Stained and leaded glass pieces designed and executed to order. Also has extensive facilities for restoration of antique leaded glass. No literature; call for more information.

Williams & Hussey Machine Co.
Elm Street Dept. OHJ
Milford, NH 03055
(603) 673-3446
MO DIST RS/O
Manufacturer of a small Molder Planer that is capable of planing up to fourteen inches wide (by reversing). Ideal for renovating old homes as any molding can be reproduced exactly from any sketch or sample sent to us. Planes thicknesses up to 8′. Made of heavy cast iron with ground surfaces. Also wood lathe. Send for free brochure and price sheet.

• **Williams Art Glass Studio, Inc./Sunset Antiques, Inc.**
22 N. Washington (M-24) Dept. OHJ
Oxford, MI 48051
(313) 628-1111
RS/O
Antique stained and bevelled glass windows, doors, sidelights. Architectural salvage including mantels. Also known as Williams Art Glass Studios, Inc.: Restoration and custom designing of stained, bevelled, etched, or glue chip glass. Personalized sandblasted designs in mirror or glass. Brochure, $1.

Helen Williams—Delft Tiles
12643 Hortense Street Dept. OHJ
North Hollywood, CA 91604
(818) 761-2756
MO
17th and 18th century antique Dutch Delft tiles, in colors of blue, manganese, tortoise shell, white and polychrome. Also: English Liverpool tiles, 17th century Dutch firebacks and fire grates, Spanish and Portugese tiles. Free literature and price list with stamped, self-addressed envelope.

• **Williamsburg Blacksmiths, Inc.**
1 Buttonshop Road Dept. OHJ
Williamsburg, MA 01096
(413) 268-7341
RS/O MO DIST
Manufactures authentic reproductions of Early American wrought iron hardware. This hardware is suitable for use throughout period homes. Door latches now include both Suffolk and Norfolk styles. Other products include cabinet and furniture hardware. All items are hand-finished and treated with a rust inhibitor. 24-page reference catalog and price list $3. Free introductory brochure.

Willis Lumber Co.
PO Box 84, 545 Millikan Ave. Dept. OHJ
Washington C.H., OH 43160
(614) 335-2601
RS/O
A supplier of kiln-dried hardwood lumber, in several different grades. Free delivery to Ohio customers; will ship nationwide. Free catalog.

The Willow Place
374 S. Atlanta St. Dept. OHJ
Roswell, GA 30075
(404) 587-5541
MO RS/O
Rustic willow or twig furniture, including custom work. Brochure and price list, $2.

Wilson, H. Weber, Antiquarian
9701 Liberty Road Dept. OHJ
Frederick, MD 21701
(301) 898-9565
MO RS/O
Fine decorative components recycled from antique buildings. Stained and leaded glass a specialty: repairs, creations, windows and lamps bought, sold & traded. Also serves as consultant on projects involving new & antique decorative windows; available for lectures and seminars. Please write or call for free information and list of stained-glass publications.

Winans Construction
2004 Woolsey St. Dept. OHJ
Berkeley, CA 94703
(415) 843-4796
RS/O
Design & construction services in the San Francisco Bay Area. Specializing in renovation & restoration of old residential and commercial structures. Initial design plan through project completion. Stock and custom millwork available through this firm. Portfolio & references available during client's first consultation. No literature by mail.

Window Components Mfg. A Harrow Co.
3443 N.W. 107th St. Dept. OHJ
Miami, FL 33167
(305) 688-2521
MO RS/O
Specialize in difficult to obtain obsolete hardware for all types of windows and doors. Many parts can be adapted if original cannot be duplicated. Selection includes casement operators and transom latches. Free catalog.

Window Grille Specialists
790HJ Cromwell Dept. OH3
St. Paul, MN 55114
(800) 328-5187
MO
Supplier of hardwood grilles designed to give the appearance of traditional muntins. In rectangular or diamond patterns, they are easy to install and remove quickly for window cleaning. Custom made to fit your windows. Free catalog.

• **Windy Hill Forge**
3824 Schroeder Ave. Dept. OHJ
Perry Hall, MD 21128
(301) 256-5890
MO
This forge makes a variety of hand-forged items, from turnbuckle stars to porch furniture. Shutter holdbacks, wall washers, snow guards. Will do custom manufacturing and restoration; can repair colonial box locks and latches. Send description of needs for free brochures.

KEY TO ABBREVIATIONS

MO	sells by Mail Order
RS/O	sells through Retail Store or Office
DIST	sells through Distributors
ID	sells only through Interior Designers or Archtects

Windy Lane Fluorescents, Inc.
35972 Highway 6 Dept. OHJC-86
Hillrose, CO 80733
(303) 847-3351
MO
Manufacturers of Victorian Era parlour or library lamp reproductions, updated with energy saving and color enhancing fluorescent bulbs. The collection includes both decorated and undecorated lamps in one basic style to complement its versatile use. Color brochure, $1.50.

Winters Textile Mill
PO Box 614 Dept. OHJ
Winters, CA 95694
(916) 795-2141
MO DIST
On 19th-century looms they weave coverlets in early period patterns, (such as whig rose,) out of virgin wool or cotton. Choice of five colors and several sizes. Prices up to $270 (king size). Brochure, with samples, $1.

Winterthur Museum and Gardens
Dept. OHJ
Winterthur, DE 19735
(302) 656-8591
MO RS/O
The Winterthur Collection of Reproductions is available to the public in galleries on the museum grounds and in over 60 cities throughout the United States. Furniture, textiles, and decorative accessories representing the "Golden Age" of American design (1740-1815) are among the objects reproduced. Three mail-order catalogs are available: The Gift and Garden Sampler and Winterthur Gift Catalogue, $2; Winterthur Reproductions, $10. Also offered: various decorative arts seminars.

Wise Company, The
PO Box 118J Dept. OHJ
Arabi, LA 70032
(504) 277-7551
MO RS/O
Authentic solid-brass reproduction hardware for antique furniture and house parts. Furniture hardware 1700-1900. Also, cast brass card frames for file drawers; iron key blanks; claw-foot casters; brass knobs; coat hooks; metal bed parts; hinges; desk accessories; English, American & imported hardware from around the world. Complete foundry & machine shop. Caning supplies, too. Two volume catalog set, $4.

Wolchonok, M. and Son, Inc.
155 E. 52 St. Dept. OHJ
New York, NY 10022
(212) 755-2168
RS/O MO
Two sister companies: Decorators Wholesale Hardware carries an extensive line of reproduction hardware by quality manufacturers like Baldwin, Shepherd, Artistic Brass. Locksets, faucets, and casters available as well as most furniture hardware. Of particular interest is the second company, Legs-Legs-Legs, selling an extensive line of furniture legs and table pedestals: iron, brass, wood. Also, decorative carpet rods; many wood, iron and brass shelf brackets. Free descriptive literature available when SASE enclosed — specify interest and wholesale/retail.

• See Advertisers' Index on page 22 for more details.

• **Wolf Paints And Wallpapers**
771 Ninth Ave. (At 52nd St.) Dept. OHJ
New York, NY 10019
(212) 245-7777
RS/O MO
An incredibly stocked paint store, with a large supply of hard-to-find finishes and supplies. Among the exotic items carried are: graining brushes, specialty waxes like beeswax, crystalline shellac, Behlen wood finishes, casein paints, gold leaf and gilder's supplies, wall canvas, and plaster patching materials. Will also handle mail orders (prompt shipment). Call or write for color cards and information.

Wollon, James Thomas, Jr., A.I.A.
600 Craigs Corner Road Dept. OHJ
Havre de Grace, MD 21078
(301) 879-6748
RS/O
Architect, specializing in historic preservation, restoration, adaptation and additions to historic structures. Services range from consultation to full professional services, Historic Structures Reports, National Register nominations. Building types include residential, exhibit, commercial, religious. Resume and references on request.

Wood and Stone, Inc.
10115 Residency Road Dept. OHJ
Manassas, VA 22110
(703) 369-1236
MO DIST RS/O
Distributes a stone adhesive, AKEMI, for bonding together two pieces of stone, filling natural faults, or mending accidental breaks. AKEMI accepts iron oxide colors, so restoration can be matched to any color stone. Can also be polished to high gloss. Also supplies marble, granite, limestone, red sandstone, quartz, slate, and other natural stone. Specialty items, including custom sizes. Information sheet and price list free.

Wood Classics, Inc.
R 1, Box 455-E Dept. OHJ
High Falls, NY 12440
(914) 687-7288
MO
Their line of solid teak and mahogany outdoor furniture includes the popular Adirondack chair, classic English garden benches, porch swings, picnic tables, planters. Kits or assembled. Color catalog, $1.

Wood Designs
100 Jupiter St., PO Box 282 Dept. OHJ
Washington C.H., OH 43160
(614) 335-6367
RS/O
Custom-made quality hardwood furniture. Reproduction of hardwood paneling, flooring, millwork, mouldings, and panel doors for restoration. Specialize in all hardwoods, including walnut, Honduras mahogany, cherry, and quarter- sawn oak. No literature. Call or write for free quotations.

Wood Finishing Supply Co., Inc.
1267 Mary Dr. Dept. OH-1
Macedon, NY 14502
(315) 986-4517
MO
A company supplying finishing items to both individuals and the wood finishing trades: Glue, removers, coloring mediums, brushes, lacquers, varnishes, gold leaf, stains, analine dyes, and touch up materials to fine brushes, tack rags, abrasives and more. 35-page Catalog includes an 11-page section of helpful finishing information.

Wood Masters, Inc.
87 Augusta Street Dept. OHJ
South Amboy, NJ 08879
(201) 721-9111
MO RS/O
Manufacturers of architectural woodwork: Specialists in custom hardwood mouldings and butcher block tops in hard maple or red oak — in any size or thickness. For a prompt quote, mail sample or sketch of moulding & quantity needed. No literature.

Wood Moulding & Millwork Producers Association
PO Box 25278 Dept. OHJ
Portland, OR 97225
(503) 292-9288
DIST
Wood mouldings available in retail stores throughout the U.S. A brochure and order form describing wood moulding literature is free.

Woodbridge Manufacturing, Inc.
375 Gundersen Drive Dept. OHJ
Carol Stream, IL 60188
(312) 682-9300
MO
Steel stair manufacturer specializing in spiral and curved stairways. Contemporary and traditional styling with a variety of tread frame designs and tread surface materials. Stairs are custom fabricated to meet your dimensional specifications. Bolt-together installation requires only common hand tools. Consulting service for custom-design, and cost-free estimates available from Chicago office. Call or write for free brochure.

Woodbury Blacksmith & Forge Co.
P.O. Box 268, 181 Main St. Dept. OHJ
Woodbury, CT 06798
(203) 263-5737
RS/O MO
Custom-made recreations of Colonial hardware, lighting devices, kitchen utensils, and fireplace equipment. Catalogue of hardware available for $2. Custom orders by mail, shipment can be arranged.

• **Woodcare Corporation Metal & Wood Restoration Prod.**
P.O. Box 92 H Dept. OHJ
Butler, NJ 07405
(201) 838-9536
MO DIST RS/O
Products for refinishing, restoring, or reconditioning woodwork, floors, furniture, aged wood, or metals. Follow- ups to heat gun removal of heavy paint finishes. Beeswax finish reviver (in 4 shades), a product designed to dissolve old wax polish and restore original finish. Also: metal polish, rust & tarnish remover, penetrating oil finishes, and varnish & paint removers. Send SASE for free brochures on all products.

Woodcraft Supply Corp.
41 Atlantic Ave., Box 4000 Dept. OHJ
Woburn, MA 01888
(617) 935-5860
RS/O MO
Woodworking hand tools, finishing supplies, hardware, and books on woodworking. Many high quality tools and supplies necessary for restoration — including cabinet scrapers. Also, carving tools and equipment, wooden and metal planes, wood-turning equipment, and supplies. Illustrated comprehensive color catalog — free.

Woodmart
PO Box 45 Dept. OHJ
Janesville, WI 53547
(608) 752-2816
MO
Chimney & flue brushes available made of steel or polypropyl 4-3/4" to 14" diameter round or 6 x 6" to 14 x 14" square. Information sent free with a stamped, self-addressed envelope only.

Woodpecker Products Inc.
1010 N. Cascade Dept. OHJ
Montrose, CO 81401
(303) 249-2616
MO RS/O
Moderately priced solid hardwood, raised four-panel doors; six panels and custom designs and sizes available. Also wain-scotting, bar backs, cabinet doors. Three free brochures: doors, cabinets/drawers, bar backs/ wainscotting.

• **Woods American Co.**
123 S. Main St. Dept. OHJ
Brownsville, MD 21715
(301) 432-8419
MO RS/O
Supplier of flooring, moulding, and millwork made of both new hardwoods and recycled antique heart pine, oak, and chestnut. Can match any moulding profile. Staircase-building and woodworking services available. Free literature.

Woodstock Soapstone Co., Inc.
Airpark Road, Box 37H/395 Dept. OHJ
W. Lebanon, NH 03784
(603) 298-5955
MO
Manufactures classic 1867-design wood-burning parlour stoves made of soapstone. Fine-textured soapstone panels with cast-iron mouldings. A pretty, formal stove, but also functional: 10-12 hour burning time, even heat. Available with porcelain-enamel finish, catalytic combusters. Literature package, free.

• **Woodstone Co.**
P.O. Box 223 Patch Road Dept. OHJC-87
Westminster, VT 05158
(802) 722-4784
RS/O
Manufactures reproductions of period entrances, mortise and tenon doors, wainscotting, along with custom mouldings and wood turnings. Insulated foam-core wooden panel doors in traditional styles, multi-lite sidelites, straight & fanned transoms, and Palladian windows available with double & triple glazing. Brochure, $1.

Woodworker's Supply of New Mexico
5604 Alameda N.E. Dept. OHJ
Albuquerque, NM 87113
(800) 645-9292
MO RS/O
A mail-order source for hardware, finishes, tools, machinery, etc. Many items are new. 2-year catalog subscription — $2.

• **Worthington Group Ltd.**
PO Box 53101 Dept. OHJ
Atlanta, GA 30355
(404) 872-1608
MO
They offer many stock styles, from Doric to Corinthians, of classical columns sculpted in Ponderosa pine. Custom shapes and widths available. Also, pedestals, table bases, and architectural elements in pine. Two free brochures, "Columns" and "Classics."

Worthington Trading Company
222 N. Main St. Dept. OHJ
St. Charles, MO 63301
(314) 723-5862
MO RS/O
Retailers of woodburning stoves, Aladdin oil lamps, Hunter Ceiling Fans. High quality merchandise in traditional styles. Stoves: Esse Dragon, Petit Godin, Webster Oak, Cawley, Hearthstone Soapstone, & Elmira Cookstoves. Serving St. Louis metro area. Will ship many items in continental U.S. Literature includes booklet "Installing and Using Woodburning Stoves" $5.

Wrecking Bar of Atlanta
292 Moreland Ave., NE Dept. OHJ
Atlanta, GA 30307
(404) 525-0468
RS/O
One of the nation's largest collections (18,000 sq. ft., 3 million dollar inventory) of authentic architectural antiques. Items include doors, mantels, statuary, columns, capitals, wrought iron, bevelled and stained glass, and lighting fixtures. Restoration design, and installation services available. Customers providing details of decorating/restoration projects will be sent photos of in-stock items for approval. Free literature.

J.A. Wright & Co.
60 Dunbar St. Dept. OHJ
Keene, NH 03431
(603) 352-2625
MO DIST
In 1873, after a cow mired in a bog prompted the chance discovery of a natural buffing agent, J.A. Wright & Co. began the namufacture of their silver polish. Today, Wright's Silver Cream® is one of America's leading silver polishes. In addition, J.A. Wright & Co. manufactures a brass polish, a copper polish, and a liquid anti-tarnish silver polish. Meticulous attention is paid to product formulation and to quality control. Free booklet.

Wrisley, Robert T.
417 Childers Street Dept. OHJ
Pulaski, TN 38478
MO RS/O
A one-man workshop in an old former church building. Will repair antiques (no stripping, refinishing, or chair-seat caning), especially those items requiring replacement carving. Also designs and builds custom furniture, mostly in reproduction styles.Stair handrail volutes and curved parts designed and carved. All inquiries answered.

X

Xenia Foundry & Machine Co. Specialty Castings Dept.
PO Box 397 Dept. OHJ
Xenia, OH 45385
(513) 372-4481
MO RS/O
Founded in 1920, this family-owned business primarily makes industrial iron castings from 1 to 500 pounds. Specialty castings or one-of-a-kind pieces are a sideline. Skilled molders are capable of making stove parts, lawn or house ornamental pieces. If original object is unable to be used as a pattern, custom pattern making is available. Castings priced at time and material. Literature available.

Y

Yankee Craftsman
357 Commonwealth Rd. Rt. 30 Dept. OHJ
Wayland, MA 01778
(617) 653-0031
MO RS/O
Yankee Craftsman deals primarily in the restoration and sale of authentic antique lighting fixtures. Tiffany, Handel and other leaded-glass repairs. Custom lighting designed and executed using old lamp parts. Fine quality custom-leaded shades. Restoration and sale of antique furniture. No catalog; specific information and photo furnished free in response to serious inquiries.

Yankee Pride
29 Parkside Circle Dept. OHJ
Braintree, MA 02184
(617) 848-7610
MO
Selection of wool braided and hooked rugs, Berbers, rag rugs, and quilts. Color catalog, 23 pages, $3.

Yankee Shutter & Sash Co.
480 Bedford Rd. Dept. OHJ
New Boston, NH 03070
(603) 487-3347
MO
Specialize 1n double hung and stationary sash for historical renovation. Products include: Sash — double hung (single glazed or insulating with fixed muntin bars); awning, quarter round, Palladian, fanlight; raised panel shutters; louvered doors; window blinds; cabinet doors; raised panel doors (interior/exterior). Custom or standard sizes. One item or 1,000. No literature. Call or write with specific request for price quote. Residential or commercial welcomed.

• **Yestershades**
3534 S.E. Hawthorne Dept. OHJ
Portland, OR 97214
(503) 238-5755
MO RS/O
Handcrafted shades: Victorian styling in silks, satins, lace, and georgette. Trimmed with beads and silk fringes. Bases for sale separately. Custom work. They are also experimenting with 1930s-style parchment shades, "glace" or "sugar" shades, and antique style dressing screens or room dividers. Please inquire. Catalog, $3.50, refundable.

Yield House, Inc.
Rt. 16 Dept. OHJ
North Conway, NH 03860
(800) 258-4720
MO RS/O
Quality solid pine & solid oak furniture direct from factory, fully-finished or easy-to-assemble kits. Range of designs includes traditional, Early American, and classic Queen Anne. Furniture for every room in the home. Unique gifts & accessories. Free color catalog. In NH (800) 552-0320.

York Spiral Stair
Route 32 Dept. OHJ
North Vassalboro, ME 04962
(207) 872-5558
MO
Spiral staircases crafted in oak or other fine hardwoods. A unique design has provided for inner and outer handrails for safety. This feature allows the stair to be uninterrupted by a centerpost. Staircases are available in diameters of 5'-0", 6'-0", 8'-6", finished or unfinished. Free brochure and price list available.

Wick York
PO Box 334 Dept. OHJ
Stonington, CT 06378
(203) 535-1409
RS/O
Consultant in historic building preservation providing services to owners of historic houses and commercial buildings, museums, preservation organizations, architects, and developers. Services include: building inspections and maintenance programs, architectural and historical research, house dating, materials analysis and conservation, on site supervision of restoration work, National Register nominations, Tax Act Certification, and grant writing. Available for lectures on restoration and maintenance of historic houses. Free literature.

You Name It, Inc.
Box 1013 Dept. OHJ
Middletown, OH 45044
(513) 932-1383
MO RS/O
Brokerage/consignment sales of antique, salvage & recycled building materials, houseparts, fixtures & hardware, furniture & accessories, period clothing, prints & original art, tools, etc. Search service — call or send requests. Free information.

Z

Zappone Manufacturing
N. 2928 Pittsburg Dept. OHJ
Spokane, WA 99207
(509) 483-6408
MO RS/O
Manufactures solid copper and aluminum interlocking shingles with matching accessories. Free literature.

Zetlin, Lorenz — Muralist
248 East 21st St. Dept. OHJ
New York, NY 10010
(212) 473-3291
RS/O
Handpainted, custom murals, trompe l'oeil rendering. Also marbleizing — mantels, baseboards. Will do store fronts, exteriors, decorations, screens and window shades. Free illustrated flyer.

Zina Studios, Inc.
85 Purdy Avenue Dept. OHJ
Port Chester, NY 10573
(914) 937-5661
MO DIST
Design and art studio, manufacturing wallcoverings and matching fabrics in custom colors, on a very high level. Reproductions are done for the restoration projects themselves, and Zina Studios has permission to use them thereafter. Besides Camron- Stanford House, Zina Studios made several wallpapers for Chateau-sur Mer, Newport, RI, other mansions in Newport, as well as other restoration projects nationwide. Free price list of museum reproduction papers.

• See Advertisers' Index on page 22 for more details.

Indexes for this Catalog begin on page 13.

ORDER FORM

The Old-House Journal

Our magazine — published ten times per year — is the only how-to-do-it periodical in America for old-house people. Filled with money-saving, mistake-saving ideas and techniques, *The Old-House Journal* will help you restore, maintain, and decorate your pre-1939 house. Every issue is packed with practical advice, and generously illustrated with drawings, photos, and step-by-step diagrams.

☐ New Subscription ☐ Renewal (Enclose Current Mailing Label)

☐ 1 Year — $18 ☐ 2 Years — $32 ☐ 3 Years — $42

Bound Back Issues
The OHJ Yearbooks

We keep back issues in print, bound in sturdy, softcover books. Our set of 'Yearbooks' is like a Restoration Encyclopedia: the biggest, most complete, most authoritative reference on old-house restoration available anywhere. Over 2,000 pages in all!

700 ☐ The 1970s Set — $39.00
1976-1979 at 77% the price. You save $17!

801 ☐ The 1980s Set — $69.00
1980-1985 at 64% the price. You save $39!

700-805 INDEX ☐ The Full Set — $108.00
All 10 Yearbooks at 66% the price — plus a FREE Cumulative Index. You save $56!

Individual Yearbooks are also available:

76 ☐ 1976 — $14
77 ☐ 1977 — $14
78 ☐ 1978 — $14
79 ☐ 1979 — $14
80 ☐ 1980 — $18
81 ☐ 1981 — $18
82 ☐ 1982 — $18
83 ☐ 1983 — $18
84 ☐ 1984 — $18
85 ☐ 1985 — $18

The OHJ Cumulative Index

INDEX ☐ Complete Index to all articles published in The Old-House Journal from Oct. 1973 (Vol. 1, No. 1) through Dec. 1984. 48 pages. Softcover. $9.95. *(FREE if you order the Full Set of OHJ Yearbooks!)*

Paint-Stripping Tools

OHJ's staff has tried just about every paint-stripping method known, and these tools are the best at their respective tasks. *The Master Heavy-Duty Heat Gun* is the finest tool around for stripping paint from interior woodwork — mouldings, corners, recesses, turned wood. *The HYDElectric Heat Plate* is the best tool for large jobs such as exterior clapboards, shingles, and flush doors. Both are backed with the OHJ Guarantee: If the tool fails for any reason within 60 days, we'll take it back and replace it.

11 ☐ Master Heavy-Duty Heat Gun — $77.95

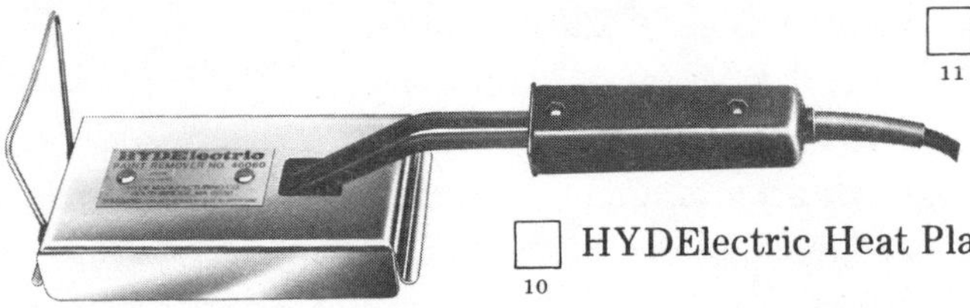

10 ☐ HYDElectric Heat Plate — $41.95

All prices postpaid, and include fast UPS shipping.

Send My Order To:

Name ______________________

Address ______________________

City ______________ State ________ Zip ________

Amount enclosed: $ ______________________

BGC87

NY State residents please add applicable sales tax.

The OHJ Catalog

12 ☐ Please send me ______ more copies of the *OHJ Buyer's Guide Catalog*. (The book is $11.95 ppd. for current OHJ subscribers; $14.95 for non-subscribers.)

NOTE: If your order includes books or merchandise, you must give us a STREET ADDRESS — not a P.O. Box number. We ship via United Parcel Service (UPS), and they will not deliver to a P.O. Box.

Prices valid until Sept. 1, 1987

Please clip this page and mail together with check payable to The Old-House Journal to THE OLD-HOUSE JOURNAL, 69A Seventh Avenue, Brooklyn, NY 11217.